AI-Enhanced Teaching Methods

Zeinab E. Ahmed
Department of Computer Engineering, University of Gezira, Sudan & Department of Electrical and Computer Engineering, International Islamic University Malaysia, Malaysia

Aisha A. Hassan
International Islamic University of Malaysia, Malaysia

Rashid A. Saeed
Taif University, Saudi Arabia

A volume in the Advances in Educational
Technologies and Instructional Design (AETID)
Book Series

Published in the United States of America by
    IGI Global
    Information Science Reference (an imprint of IGI Global)
    701 E. Chocolate Avenue
    Hershey PA, USA 17033
    Tel: 717-533-8845
    Fax: 717-533-8661
    E-mail: cust@igi-global.com
    Web site: http://www.igi-global.com

Library of Congress Cataloging-in-Publication Data

CIP DATA PROCESSING

AI-Enhanced Teaching Methods
  Zeinab E. Ahmed, Aisha A. Hassan, Rashid A. Saeed
  2024 Information Science Reference
ISBN: 9798369327289(h/c) I ISBN: 9798369344873(s/c) I eISBN: 9798369327296

This book is published in the IGI Global book series Advances in Educational Technologies and Instructional Design (AE-TID) (ISSN: 2326-8905; eISSN: 2326-8913)

British Cataloguing in Publication Data
A Cataloguing in Publication record for this book is available from the British Library.

All work contributed to this book is new, previously-unpublished material. The views expressed in this book are those of the authors, but not necessarily of the publisher.

For electronic access to this publication, please contact: eresources@igi-global.com.

Advances in Educational Technologies and Instructional Design (AETID) Book Series

Lawrence A. Tomei
Robert Morris University, USA

ISSN:2326-8905
EISSN:2326-8913

MISSION

Education has undergone, and continues to undergo, immense changes in the way it is enacted and distributed to both child and adult learners. In modern education, the traditional classroom learning experience has evolved to include technological resources and to provide online classroom opportunities to students of all ages regardless of their geographical locations. From distance education, Massive-Open-Online-Courses (MOOCs), and electronic tablets in the classroom, technology is now an integral part of learning and is also affecting the way educators communicate information to students.

The **Advances in Educational Technologies & Instructional Design (AETID) Book Series** explores new research and theories for facilitating learning and improving educational performance utilizing technological processes and resources. The series examines technologies that can be integrated into K-12 classrooms to improve skills and learning abilities in all subjects including STEM education and language learning. Additionally, it studies the emergence of fully online classrooms for young and adult learners alike, and the communication and accountability challenges that can arise. Trending topics that are covered include adaptive learning, game-based learning, virtual school environments, and social media effects. School administrators, educators, academicians, researchers, and students will find this series to be an excellent resource for the effective design and implementation of learning technologies in their classes.

COVERAGE

- Virtual School Environments
- Collaboration Tools
- Hybrid Learning
- Curriculum Development
- Social Media Effects on Education
- Instructional Design
- Adaptive Learning
- Educational Telecommunications
- Game-Based Learning
- Digital Divide in Education

IGI Global is currently accepting manuscripts for publication within this series. To submit a proposal for a volume in this series, please contact our Acquisition Editors at Acquisitions@igi-global.com or visit: http://www.igi-global.com/publish/.

Titles in this Series

For a list of additional titles in this series, please visit:
www.igi-global.com/book-series/advances-educational-technologies-instructional-design/73678

Effective and Meaningful Student Engagement Through Service Learning
Sharon Valarmathi (Christ University, India) Jacqueline Kareem (Christ University, India) Veerta Tantia (Christ University, India) Kishore Selva Babu (Christ University, India) and Patrick Jude Lucas (Christ University, ndia)
Information Science Reference • © 2024 • 293pp • H/C (ISBN: 9798369322567) • US $275.00

Integrating Cutting-Edge Technology Into the Classroom
Ken Nee Chee (Universiti Pendidikan Sultan Idris, Malaysia) and Mageswaran Sanmugam (Universiti Sains Malaysia, Malaysia)
Information Science Reference • © 2024 • 425pp • H/C (ISBN: 9798369331248) • US $300.00

Embracing Technological Advancements for Lifelong Learning
Mahmoud M. Kh. Hawamdeh (Al-Quds Open University, Palestine) and Faiz Abdelhafid (Al-Istiqlal University, Palestine)
Information Science Reference • © 2024 • 365pp • H/C (ISBN: 9798369314104) • US $230.00

Unlocking Learning Potential With Universal Design in Online Learning Environments
Michelle Bartlett (Old Dominion University, USA) and Suzanne M. Ehrlich (University of North Florida, USA)
Information Science Reference • © 2024 • 286pp • H/C (ISBN: 9798369312698) • US $240.00

Navigating Innovative Technologies and Intelligent Systems in Modern Education
Madhulika Bhatia (Amity University, India) and Muhammad Tahir Mushtaq (Cardiff Metropolitan Univesity, UK)
Information Science Reference • © 2024 • 307pp • H/C (ISBN: 9798369353707) • US $245.00

Transforming Education for Personalized Learning
Afzal Sayed Munna (University of Sunderland in London, UK) Husam Alharahsheh (University of Wales Trinity Saint David, UK) Alessandro Ferrazza (University of Sunderland in London, UK) and Abraham Pius (York St. John University, UK & Arden University, UK)
Information Science Reference • © 2024 • 312pp • H/C (ISBN: 9798369308684) • US $225.00

Teacher and Student Perspectives on Bilingual and Multilingual Education
Hung Phu Bui (University of Economics Ho Chi Minh City, Vietnam) Truong Cong Bang (University of Economics and Law, Ho Chi Minh City, Vietnam & Vietnam National University, Ho Chi Minh City, Vietnam) and Cuong Huy Nguyen (International University, Vietnam National University, Ho Chi Minh City, Vietnam)
Information Science Reference • © 2024 • 296pp • H/C (ISBN: 9798369353653) • US $245.00

701 East Chocolate Avenue, Hershey, PA 17033, USA
Tel: 717-533-8845 x100 • Fax: 717-533-8661
E-Mail: cust@igi-global.com • www.igi-global.com

Table of Contents

Preface...xv

Chapter 1
AI as a Teacher: A New Educational Dynamic for Modern Classrooms for Personalized Learning
Support..1
    Robertas Damasevicius, Vytautas Magnus University, Lithuania
    Tatjana Sidekerskiene, Kaunas University of Technology, Lithuania

Chapter 2
AI in Educational Design and Technological Development..25
    Salaheldin M. I. Edam, Sudan University of Science and Technology, Sudan

Chapter 3
AI Technologies in Engineering Education..61
    Mamoon M. A. Saeed, Department of Communications and Electronics Engineering, Faculty
        of Engineering, University of Modern Sciences, Yemen
    Rashid A. Saeed, College of Computers and Information Technology, Taif University, Saudi
        Arabia
    Zeinab E. Ahmed, Department of Computer Engineering, University of Gezira, Sudan &
        Department of Electrical and Computer Engineering, International Islamic University
        Malaysia, Malaysia
    AbdulGuddoos S. A. Gaid, Faculty of Engineering and Information Technology Taiz
        University, Yemen
    Rania A. Mokhtar, College of Computers and Information Technology, Taif University, Saudi
        Arabia

Chapter 4
AI-Enhanced Education: Bridging Educational Disparities...88
    Zeinab E. Ahmed, Department of Computer Engineering, University of Gezira, Sudan &
        Department of Electrical and Computer Engineering, International Islamic University
        Malaysia, Malaysia
    Aisha Hassan Abdalla Hashim, International Islamic University Malaysia, Malaysia
    Rashid A. Saeed, Taif University, Saudi Arabia
    Mamoon M. A. Saeed, Department of Communications and Electronics Engineering, Faculty
        of Engineering, University of Modern Sciences, Yemen

Chapter 5

AI-Enhanced Engineering Education: Customization, Adaptive Learning, and Real-Time Data Analysis...108
    Mohammed Balfaqih, University of Jeddah, Saudi Arabia
    Zain Balfagih, Effat University, Saudi Arabia

Chapter 6

An Overview of Artificial Intelligence-Enhanced Teaching Methods..132
    Wasswa Shafik, School of Digital Science, Universiti Brunei Darussalam, Brunei & Dig
        Connectivity Research Laboratory (DCRLab), Kampala, Uganda

Chapter 7

Artificial Intelligence's Role and Future Implementation in Education 160
    Komal Bhardwaj, Maharishi Markandeshwar Institute of Management, Maharishi
        Markandeswar University (Deemed), Mullana, India
    Garima, Maharishi Markandeshwar Institute of Management, Maharishi Markandeswar
        University (Deemed), Mullana, India
    Sachin Sudan, RIMT University, Mandi Gobindgarh, India

Chapter 8

Comprehensive Survey of Adaptive and Intelligent Education System Using Reinforcement Learning 176
    Mehdy Roayaei, Tarbiat Modares University, Iran

Chapter 9

Enhancing Literacy Education in Higher Institutions With AI Opportunities and Challenges..........198
    Tarun Kumar Vashishth, IIMT University, India
    Vikas Sharma, IIMT University, India
    Kewal Krishan Sharma, IIMT University, India
    Bhupendra Kumar, IIMT University, India

Chapter 10

Evaluating the Potential of Artificial Intelligence in Islamic Religious Education: A SWOT Analysis Overview 216
    Mussa Saidi Abubakari, Sultan Hassanal Bolkiah Institute of Education, Universiti Brunei
        Darussalam, Brunei
    Wasswa Shafik, School of Digital Science, Universiti Brunei Darussalam, Brunei & Dig
        Connectivity Research Laboratory (DCRLab), Kampala, Uganda
    Ahmad Fathan Hidayatullah, Department of Informatics, Universitas Islam Indonesia,
        Indonesia

Chapter 11

Navigating AI Integration: Case Studies and Best Practices in Educational Transformation 240
    Shahinaz Abdelrahman Osman, City University Ajman, UAE
    Zeinab E. Ahmed, Department of Computer Engineering, University of Gezira, Sudan &
        Department of Electrical and Computer Engineering, International Islamic University
        Malaysia, Malaysia

Chapter 12
Navigating the AI Landscape: Student and Teacher Perceptions of AI in Assessments in High
School and College Settings 268
    Leesha Nicole Roberts, The University of Trinidad and Tobago, Trinidad and Tobago
    Fanta N. Solomon, Bishop's Centenary College, Trinidad and Tobago
    Reccia Cummings, The University of Trinidad and Tobago, Trinidad and Tobago

Chapter 13
Preparing Students for an AI-Enhanced Future 286
    Rawya Elmahi Gobara Elmahi Gobara, Sudan University of Science and Technology, Sudan
    Zeinab E. Ahmed, Department of Computer Engineering, University of Gezira, Sudan &
        Department of Electrical and Computer Engineering, International Islamic University
        Malaysia, Malaysia

Chapter 14
The Impact and Future of AI-Enhanced Teaching Methods in the Use of Business Simulations 305
    Hélder Fanha Martins, Polytechnic University of Lisbon, Portugal

Chapter 15
Transforming Classroom Dynamics: The Social Impact of AI in Teaching and Learning 322
    Tarun Kumar Vashishth, IIMT University, India
    Vikas Sharma, IIMT University, India
    Kewal Krishan Sharma, IIMT University, India
    Bhupendra Kumar, IIMT University, India
    Sachin Chaudhary, IIMT University, India
    Rajneesh Panwar, IIMT University, India

Compilation of References 347

About the Contributors 396

Index 403

Detailed Table of Contents

Preface xv

Chapter 1

AI as a Teacher: A New Educational Dynamic for Modern Classrooms for Personalized Learning
Support 1

Robertas Damasevicius, Vytautas Magnus University, Lithuania
Tatjana Sidekerskiene, Kaunas University of Technology, Lithuania

This chapter discusses the impact and integration of artificial intelligence (AI) in education, with a focus on AI chatbots like ChatGPT. The study synthesizes findings from scholarly articles, offering a holistic view of how AI is transforming educational methodologies, classroom dynamics, and the roles of educators. Key areas of investigation include the transformation of classroom dynamics through AI-enabled smart classrooms, innovative AI-driven teaching methods, and the specific applications and implications of ChatGPT and generative AI in education. The study also focuses on the dynamics of teacher-AI collaboration, discussing the potential benefits and ethical considerations that arise from the integration of AI technologies in teaching and learning processes. Furthermore, it examines AI's role in educational assessment and learning analytics, highlighting both the capabilities and limitations of AI tools in these domains. The example of using ChatGPT for AI-driven student assessment and personalized learning recommendation generation is presented.

Chapter 2

AI in Educational Design and Technological Development 25

Salaheldin M. I. Edam, Sudan University of Science and Technology, Sudan

Artificial intelligence (AI) has both benefits and challenges in education. AI can customize learning experiences, enhance teaching methods, and foster equal opportunities in education. However, ethical implications and potential biases linked to AI-generated data are concerns. AI-driven tools like adaptive learning systems and intelligent tutoring systems have the potential to revolutionize education. The chapter explores a range of AI-driven tools and systems, including natural language processing. The ethical implications and potential biases linked to AI-generated data are thoroughly analyzed. Suggestions on how to responsibly incorporate AI into the field of education are offered. The utilization of AI has been discovered to enhance learning experiences and address the disparity in educational opportunities, ultimately resulting in a more inclusive and equitable education system. The development of AI curricula for various educational levels is also a key area of focus to ensure that the potential of AI in education is realized in an inclusive and responsible manner.

Chapter 3
AI Technologies in Engineering Education 61
Mamoon M. A. Saeed, Department of Communications and Electronics Engineering, Faculty of Engineering, University of Modern Sciences, Yemen
Rashid A. Saeed, College of Computers and Information Technology, Taif University, Saudi Arabia
Zeinab E. Ahmed, Department of Computer Engineering, University of Gezira, Sudan & Department of Electrical and Computer Engineering, International Islamic University Malaysia, Malaysia
AbdulGuddoos S. A. Gaid, Faculty of Engineering and Information Technology Taiz University, Yemen
Rania A. Mokhtar, College of Computers and Information Technology, Taif University, Saudi Arabia

The chapter investigates how artificial intelligence (AI) technologies are incorporated into engineering education and looks at how they affect methods of instruction and learning. An overview of the many uses of AI in engineering education is given, including data analytics, intelligent tutoring systems, adaptive learning platforms, virtual laboratories, and robotics training made possible by AI. The chapter explores how AI may improve the engineering curriculum by addressing market demands and future skills, integrating AI tools and software, and introducing AI concepts into coursework. It also discusses performance monitoring, intelligent feedback, automated grading, competency assessment in engineering education, and AI-assisted assessment and feedback systems. The chapter also looks at how AI affects engineering education, including using augmented and virtual reality, flipped classrooms, personalized learning, and collaborative learning.

Chapter 4
AI-Enhanced Education: Bridging Educational Disparities 88
Zeinab E. Ahmed, Department of Computer Engineering, University of Gezira, Sudan & Department of Electrical and Computer Engineering, International Islamic University Malaysia, Malaysia
Aisha Hassan Abdalla Hashim, International Islamic University Malaysia, Malaysia
Rashid A. Saeed, Taif University, Saudi Arabia
Mamoon M. A. Saeed, Department of Communications and Electronics Engineering, Faculty of Engineering, University of Modern Sciences, Yemen

This chapter explores the symbiotic relationship between AI and education, highlighting its transformative impact and potential to bridge educational disparities. It provides insights into using AI to create engaging and efficient learning environments, covering various topics such as AI-driven teaching techniques, ethical considerations, and case studies. AI tools enhance learning experiences and help address disparities among students. The integration of AI in education can optimize resources, personalize learning, and improve academic performance. However, challenges such as lack of familiarity and technical difficulties need to be addressed through training and support for teachers. By embracing AI, educators can revolutionize teaching methods and promote equity and inclusivity in education.

Chapter 5

AI-Enhanced Engineering Education: Customization, Adaptive Learning, and Real-Time Data Analysis.. 108

Mohammed Balfaqih, University of Jeddah, Saudi Arabia
Zain Balfagih, Effat University, Saudi Arabia

The chapter explores AI integration in engineering education, emphasizing customization, adaptive learning, and real-time data analysis. It discusses AI's role in enhancing student efficacy through personalized learning and early identification of learning difficulties. Innovative elements like wearables for self-monitoring are examined. Pedagogical frameworks and case studies of successful AI implementations are presented. Ethical and societal considerations including privacy and inclusiveness are addressed. It provides a comprehensive understanding of AI in engineering education, concluding with key insights and implications for proactive engagement with AI technologies to enhance student learning.

Chapter 6

An Overview of Artificial Intelligence-Enhanced Teaching Methods... 132

Wasswa Shafik, School of Digital Science, Universiti Brunei Darussalam, Brunei & Dig
Connectivity Research Laboratory (DCRLab), Kampala, Uganda

This study dichotomizes AI's profound impact on traditional teaching, defines its role, and explores AI-enhanced methods. It critiques lecture-based and textbook learning for lacking personalization and prompt feedback. It details AI integration, emphasizing personalized learning, immersive tech like virtual and augmented reality, and key components: machine learning and natural language processing. Use cases demonstrate personalized learning paths and real-time feedback. The study further dives into AI-enhanced teaching: adaptive learning, intelligent tutoring, gamification, chatbots, and assessment automation, highlighting their transformative potential. It finally addresses challenges and ethics and projects AI's future contributions in research and curriculum development, urging adoption for future learners' benefit.

Chapter 7

Artificial Intelligence's Role and Future Implementation in Education 160

Komal Bhardwaj, Maharishi Markandeshwar Institute of Management, Maharishi
Markandeswar University (Deemed), Mullana, India
Garima, Maharishi Markandeshwar Institute of Management, Maharishi Markandeswar
University (Deemed), Mullana, India
Sachin Sudan, RIMT University, Mandi Gobindgarh, India

Artificial intelligence (AI) has become a disruptive force that has greatly benefited education, which is a vital aspect for both society evolution and personal growth. The purpose of this study is to analyze the multifaceted impact of AI in education and on the application and impact of AI learning, instruction, and administration. AI is the study and creation of computers, machines, and other artifacts with human like cognitive capacities, learning, and adaptability and decision-making capabilities. The objectives of this chapter are to present a comprehensive outline in addition to a more in-depth analysis of three main elements: roles, consequences, and future implications. The study also states the emergence of AI-enabled individualized learning, offers universal access to high-quality education at all levels by offering exciting new opportunities and applications. AI systems can successfully identify and rectify skill gaps, allowing individuals to adapt to shifting jobs and advancements in technology.

Chapter 8
Comprehensive Survey of Adaptive and Intelligent Education System Using Reinforcement
Learning 176
Mehdy Roayaei, Tarbiat Modares University, Iran

Adaptive and intelligent educational systems (AIES) have the potential to revolutionize learning by personalizing the educational experience for each student. This chapter presents a comprehensive survey of the application of reinforcement learning in AIES. The authors discuss the use of reinforcement learning to formulate personalized learning plans and pedagogical policies. The chapter also explores the integration of reinforcement learning to build intelligent environments that provide personalized learning recommendations based on students' cognitive attributes and learning styles. By reviewing contemporary work and historical contexts, this survey aims to provide a thorough understanding of the role of reinforcement learning in shaping the future of AIES.

Chapter 9
Enhancing Literacy Education in Higher Institutions With AI Opportunities and Challenges 198
Tarun Kumar Vashishth, IIMT University, India
Vikas Sharma, IIMT University, India
Kewal Krishan Sharma, IIMT University, India
Bhupendra Kumar, IIMT University, India

Enhancing literacy education in higher institutions through the integration of artificial intelligence (AI) presents significant opportunities and challenges. This chapter explores the role of AI in literacy education, showcasing its potential to revolutionize teaching methodologies, personalized learning, and student outcomes. AI-powered tools, such as natural language processing (NLP), chatbots, and adaptive learning platforms, offer unique opportunities to engage students, improve language proficiency, and address individual learning needs effectively. The chapter delves into the various opportunities AI presents in higher education literacy, emphasizing the benefits of AI-driven content recommendation systems, personalized feedback, and early intervention for struggling students. However, along with the opportunities come several challenges, including ethical considerations surrounding data privacy, faculty readiness, and the potential displacement of traditional teaching approaches.

Chapter 10
Evaluating the Potential of Artificial Intelligence in Islamic Religious Education: A SWOT
Analysis Overview 216
Mussa Saidi Abubakari, Sultan Hassanal Bolkiah Institute of Education, Universiti Brunei
Darussalam, Brunei
Wasswa Shafik, School of Digital Science, Universiti Brunei Darussalam, Brunei & Dig
Connectivity Research Laboratory (DCRLab), Kampala, Uganda
Ahmad Fathan Hidayatullah, Department of Informatics, Universitas Islam Indonesia,
Indonesia

Artificial intelligence (AI) has become enormously prominent in various industries in recent years, completely changing the way humans accomplish their daily activities, especially the educational process. While integrating AI technologies in educational settings might present new potential, there are drawbacks and challenges as well, particularly in the Islamic religious educational context. Therefore, the purpose of this chapter is to assess the viability of incorporating AI into Islamic religious educational settings by doing a thorough SWOT (strengths, weaknesses, opportunities, and threats) analysis. The chapter explores the benefits, drawbacks, opportunities, and risks of implementing AI in the context of Islamic education. Thus, the factors, both internal and external, that may have an impact on the effective integration of AI in Islamic educational environments are evaluated. Policymakers, educators, and other educational stakeholders may make well-informed judgments on the utilization of AI technologies in Islamic religious education by recognizing these analytical aspects.

Chapter 11
Navigating AI Integration: Case Studies and Best Practices in Educational Transformation 240
    Shahinaz Abdelrahman Osman, City University Ajman, UAE
    Zeinab E. Ahmed, Department of Computer Engineering, University of Gezira, Sudan &
        Department of Electrical and Computer Engineering, International Islamic University
        Malaysia, Malaysia

This chapter explores the practical applications and effective methods of integrating artificial intelligence (AI) into various educational settings. It examines how educational institutions, ranging from K-12 to higher education, have successfully utilized AI to enhance teaching methods, strategies, and learning outcomes through the presentation of compelling case studies. In addition to theoretical frameworks, the chapter offers practical insights into the challenges faced, strategies employed, and lessons learned during the implementation of AI-enhanced teaching approaches. The adoption of AI in education can facilitate personalized learning journeys by tailoring instruction, materials, pacing, and resources to individual learners' needs and preferences. It also enables adaptive assessments and feedback systems that provide real-time feedback, identify areas for improvement, and contribute to more nuanced grading systems. The chapter highlights examples of AI-powered platforms, such as adaptive learning platforms, intelligent tutoring systems, smart content recommendation systems, and gamified learning paths, illustrating their effectiveness in meeting the unique requirements of students and promoting engagement and mastery. Furthermore, it discusses the importance of immediate and targeted feedback and individualized content structuring in adaptive learning environments. The chapter also explores AI-assessment tools, real-time feedback systems, learning analytics dashboards, and peer learning facilitation platforms as valuable resources for educators. By leveraging AI technologies, educational institutions can transform teaching and learning practices, promote personalized and adaptive learning, and ensure the alignment of AI-based systems with human values.

Chapter 12
Navigating the AI Landscape: Student and Teacher Perceptions of AI in Assessments in High
School and College Settings 268
    Leesha Nicole Roberts, The University of Trinidad and Tobago, Trinidad and Tobago
    Fanta N. Solomon, Bishop's Centenary College, Trinidad and Tobago
    Reccia Cummings, The University of Trinidad and Tobago, Trinidad and Tobago

This chapter examines AI's role in Caribbean high school and college assessments, analyzing teacher and student perspectives. A quantitative study surveyed 160 students and 102 teachers via Google Forms in September 2023, investigating AI tool usage, its effects on grading and feedback, fairness, and ethical concerns. Key findings include students' prevalent use of Grammarly and ChatGPT and plagiarism software by teachers, with significant AI encounters at the high school level. Positive correlations emerged between teachers' views on AI's grading efficiency, optimism for its future, and students' appreciation for AI's timely feedback. Concerns about AI-induced discrimination showed no significant differences across countries or educational levels, highlighting ethics and transparency as crucial. The need for targeted AI integration training is emphasized, suggesting future research should address AI biases and explore new tools for enhancing Caribbean educational outcomes.

Chapter 13
Preparing Students for an AI-Enhanced Future 286
Rawya Elmahi Gobara Elmahi Gobara, Sudan University of Science and Technology, Sudan
Zeinab E. Ahmed, Department of Computer Engineering, University of Gezira, Sudan &
Department of Electrical and Computer Engineering, International Islamic University
Malaysia, Malaysia

In this regard, the purpose of this study is to examine artificial intelligence and its impact on technology, the future of students, and education. It can be said that education is one of the most important areas that will be affected sooner or later by the development of technology, especially artificial intelligence techniques. This impact naturally has both positive and negative aspects, so how can we benefit from it? This chapter discusses the most important potential applications of artificial intelligence that can be used in the educational process. It explains to them the positive and negative impact of technology on education, clarifies the strengths and weaknesses, and shows how to benefit from these points. It also helps them develop critical thinking skills, enhances creativity and development, and encourages them to experiment with tools.

Chapter 14
The Impact and Future of AI-Enhanced Teaching Methods in the Use of Business Simulations 305
Hélder Fanha Martins, Polytechnic University of Lisbon, Portugal

This chapter examines the transformative role of AI-enhanced teaching methods in business simulation studies. With a focus on the integration of AI in education, it highlights a paradigm shift towards more dynamic, personalized, and effective learning environments. The chapter delves into the implications of AI in enhancing decision-making knowledge, student engagement, and learning outcomes, aligning educational practices with future business leadership and management needs. It underscores AI's role in fostering a practice-oriented approach, enhancing teaching processes and creating personalized learning experiences. Furthermore, the chapter explores the impact of AI on teaching and learning in business education, emphasizing the need for educators to adapt and leverage AI tools to augment pedagogical approaches and improve student outcomes. As AI reshapes the educational landscape, the chapter calls for a collaborative approach among technology developers, educators, and policymakers to integrate AI tools effectively and ethically into educational frameworks.

Chapter 15
Transforming Classroom Dynamics: The Social Impact of AI in Teaching and Learning 322
Tarun Kumar Vashishth, IIMT University, India
Vikas Sharma, IIMT University, India
Kewal Krishan Sharma, IIMT University, India
Bhupendra Kumar, IIMT University, India
Sachin Chaudhary, IIMT University, India
Rajneesh Panwar, IIMT University, India

The integration of artificial intelligence (AI) in education is reshaping classroom dynamics and fostering a social impact on teaching and learning. This chapter explores the historical evolution of classroom dynamics, from traditional settings to 21st-century learning environments, highlighting the pivotal role of AI in this transformative journey. Understanding AI in education involves delving into its historical overview and current landscape. The research investigates AI's influence on teacher support and development, encompassing AI-assisted lesson planning, teacher training, and enhanced classroom management. The conclusion reflects on the future directions and trends, emphasizing the global potential of AI to democratize education, address language barriers, and provide inclusive learning experiences. The study envisions a future where AI optimally contributes to creating a more equitable, interconnected, and culturally sensitive educational landscape globally.

Compilation of References 347

About the Contributors 396

Index 403

Preface

Welcome to *AI-Enhanced Teaching Methods*, a dynamic compilation that explores the intersection of artificial intelligence (AI) and education. In an era defined by rapid technological advancement, the integration of AI into teaching methodologies represents a groundbreaking paradigm shift with far-reaching implications for educators, learners, and educational systems worldwide.

As editors, we are thrilled to present this comprehensive volume, which examines the transformative potential of AI in revolutionizing traditional teaching approaches and enriching the learning journey for students of all ages and backgrounds. Through a collaborative effort, we have curated a diverse array of perspectives, insights, and practical applications from esteemed contributors across the globe.

In this book, readers will embark on a journey through the multifaceted landscape of AI-enhanced education, exploring key topics such as personalized learning, classroom management, and the ethical considerations inherent in AI integration. Each chapter offers invaluable resources, including case studies, best practices, and actionable strategies, designed to empower educators, administrators, researchers, and policymakers in leveraging AI to its fullest potential.

Moreover, this volume transcends disciplinary boundaries, catering to a diverse audience ranging from educators and technology developers to students, parents, and general readers interested in the future of education. By engaging with the foundational principles of AI in education and exploring cutting-edge advancements in AI technologies, readers will gain a holistic understanding of how AI can shape the educational landscape and prepare learners for an increasingly AI-integrated world.

The thematic breadth of this book reflects our commitment to fostering dialogue and collaboration among stakeholders invested in harnessing the power of AI to unlock new possibilities in education. From examining AI-powered learning platforms to navigating ethical and societal considerations, each chapter serves as a beacon guiding readers towards innovative approaches to teaching and learning.

We extend our sincere gratitude to our esteemed contributors for their invaluable insights and scholarly contributions, without which this endeavor would not have been possible. We also express our gratitude to the readers whose curiosity and dedication to advancing education continue to inspire our collective efforts.

In conclusion, *AI-Enhanced Teaching Methods* serves as a testament to the transformative potential of AI in education and as a catalyst for shaping the future of learning. As editors, we invite you to embark on this intellectual journey, engage with the diverse perspectives presented herein, and join us in envisioning an AI-enhanced educational landscape that empowers learners and fosters lifelong curiosity and growth.

Chapter 1: AI as a Teacher: A New Educational Dynamic for Modern Classrooms for Personalized Learning Support

Authored by Robertas Damasevicius and Tatjana Sidekerskiene from Vytautas Magnus University and Kaunas University of Technology respectively, this chapter provides a comprehensive exploration of the integration of Artificial Intelligence (AI) in education, with a particular focus on AI chatbots such as ChatGPT. Drawing from a synthesis of scholarly articles, the chapter offers a nuanced understanding of how AI is reshaping educational methodologies and classroom dynamics. Key topics covered include the transformation of classroom dynamics through AI-enabled smart classrooms, innovative teaching methods driven by AI, and the specific applications and implications of AI chatbots in education. Moreover, the chapter delves into the dynamics of collaboration between teachers and AI, discussing both the potential benefits and ethical considerations that arise from this integration. Additionally, it examines AI's role in educational assessment and learning analytics, showcasing examples such as the utilization of ChatGPT for AI-driven student assessment and personalized learning recommendation generation.

Chapter 2: AI in Educational Design and Technological Development

Written by Salaheldin Edam from Sudan University of Science and Technology, this chapter explores the benefits and challenges of Artificial Intelligence (AI) in education. It discusses how AI can customize learning experiences, enhance teaching methods, and promote equal opportunities in education, while also addressing ethical implications and potential biases associated with AI-generated data. The chapter provides insights into various AI-driven tools and systems, including adaptive learning systems and intelligent tutoring systems, and examines their potential to revolutionize education. Through a thorough analysis of ethical considerations, the chapter offers suggestions on responsibly incorporating AI into educational practices to ensure inclusivity and effectiveness.

Chapter 3: AI Technologies in Engineering Education

Authored by Mamoon Saeed, Rashid Saeed, Zeinab Ahmed, AbdulGuddoos Gaid, and Rania Mokhtar, this chapter investigates the integration of Artificial Intelligence (AI) technologies into engineering education. It offers an overview of the diverse applications of AI in engineering education, ranging from data analytics to robotics training, made possible by AI. The chapter explores how AI can enhance the engineering curriculum by addressing market demands, integrating AI tools and software, and introducing AI concepts into coursework. Additionally, it examines AI's impact on engineering education, including the use of augmented and virtual reality, personalized learning, and collaborative learning, providing valuable insights into the transformative potential of AI in this field.

Chapter 4: AI-Enhanced Education: Bridging Educational Disparities

In this chapter, Zeinab Ahmed, Aisha Hashim, Rashid Saeed, and Mamoon Saeed explore the symbiotic relationship between Artificial Intelligence (AI) and education, emphasizing its transformative impact and potential to bridge educational disparities. The authors provide insights into leveraging AI to create engaging and efficient learning environments, covering various topics such as AI-driven teaching techniques, ethical considerations, and case studies. They highlight how AI tools enhance learning experiences and help address disparities among students, optimizing resources, personalizing learning, and improving academic performance. Furthermore, the chapter addresses challenges such as lack of familiarity and technical difficulties, proposing solutions through training and support for teachers, thus enabling educators to revolutionize teaching methods and promote equity and inclusivity in education.

Chapter 5: AI-Enhanced Engineering Education: Customization, Adaptive Learning, and Real-Time Data Analysis

Authored by Mohammed Balfaqih and Zain Balfagih, this chapter explores the integration of Artificial Intelligence (AI) in engineering education, emphasizing customization, adaptive learning, and real-time data analysis. The authors discuss AI's role in enhancing student efficacy through personalized learning and early identification of learning difficulties, examining innovative elements such as wearables for self-monitoring. Pedagogical frameworks and case studies of successful AI implementations are presented, alongside discussions of ethical and societal considerations, including privacy and inclusiveness. The chapter concludes with key insights and implications for proactive engagement with AI technologies to enhance student learning in engineering education.

Chapter 6: An Overview of Artificial Intelligence-Enhanced Teaching Methods

Written by Wasswa Shafik, this chapter provides a comprehensive overview of Artificial Intelligence's profound impact on traditional teaching methods and explores AI-enhanced methods. Critiquing lecture-based and textbook learning for lacking personalization and prompt feedback, the chapter details AI integration, emphasizing personalized learning and immersive technologies like virtual and augmented reality. Case studies demonstrate personalized learning paths and real-time feedback, diving into AI-enhanced teaching methods such as adaptive learning, intelligent tutoring, gamification, chatbots, and assessment automation. The chapter addresses challenges and ethics while projecting AI's future contributions in research and curriculum development, advocating for adoption for future learners' benefit.

Chapter 7: Artificial Intelligence Role and Future Implementation in Education

Authored by Komal Bhardwaj, Garima, and Sachin Sudan, this chapter delves into the disruptive force of Artificial Intelligence (AI) in education, crucial for societal evolution and personal growth. The authors present a comprehensive outline of AI's multifaceted impact in education, examining its application and consequences in learning, instruction, and administration. Through a thorough analysis, the chapter explores the emergence of AI-enabled individualized learning, offering universal access to high-quality education and exciting new opportunities. Moreover, the study discusses how AI systems can identify and rectify skill gaps, enabling individuals to adapt to shifting job landscapes and technological advancements, emphasizing the importance of preparing students for an AI-enhanced future.

Chapter 8: Comprehensive Survey of Adaptive and Intelligent Education System Using Reinforcement Learning: Adaptive and Intelligent Education System

Authored by Mehdy Roayaei, this chapter presents a comprehensive survey of the application of reinforcement learning in adaptive and intelligent educational systems (AIES). The chapter explores how reinforcement learning can personalize learning plans and pedagogical policies, integrating into intelligent environments to provide personalized learning recommendations based on students' cognitive attributes and learning styles. Through contemporary work and historical contexts, the survey aims to provide a thorough understanding of reinforcement learning's role in shaping the future of AIES, offering insights into personalized learning experiences and enhancing student efficacy.

Chapter 9: Enhancing Literacy Education in Higher Institutions With AI Opportunities and Challenges

Authored by Tarun Vashishth, Vikas Sharma, Kewal Sharma, and Bhupendra Kumar, this chapter explores the significant opportunities and challenges of integrating Artificial Intelligence (AI) into literacy education in higher institutions. The authors examine AI's potential to revolutionize teaching methodologies, personalized learning, and student outcomes, showcasing tools such as Natural Language Processing (NLP) and adaptive learning platforms. While highlighting the benefits of AI-driven content recommendation systems and personalized feedback, the chapter also addresses ethical considerations surrounding data privacy and faculty readiness, emphasizing the need for responsible integration of AI into education.

Chapter 10: Evaluating the Potential of Artificial Intelligence in Islamic Religious Education: A SWOT Analysis Overview

Authored by Mussa Abubakari, Wasswa Shafik, and Ahmad Hidayatullah, this chapter assesses the viability of incorporating Artificial Intelligence (AI) into Islamic religious educational settings through a thorough SWOT (Strengths, Weaknesses, Opportunities, and Threats) analysis. By exploring the benefits, drawbacks, opportunities, and risks of implementing AI in the context of Islamic education, the authors provide insights into the factors influencing the effective integration of AI in Islamic educational environments. Policymakers, educators, and other stakeholders can make well-informed judgments on the utilization of AI technologies in Islamic religious education by recognizing these analytical aspects.

Chapter 11: Navigating AI Integration: Case Studies and Best Practices in Educational Transformation

Authored by Shahinaz Osman and Zeinab Ahmed, this chapter explores the practical applications and effective methods of integrating Artificial Intelligence (AI) into various educational settings. The authors present compelling case studies showcasing how educational institutions, from K-12 to higher education, have successfully utilized AI to enhance teaching methods, strategies, and learning outcomes. The chapter highlights examples of AI-powered platforms, such as adaptive learning platforms and intelligent tutoring systems, illustrating their effectiveness in meeting the unique requirements of students and promoting engagement and mastery. Furthermore, the chapter discusses the importance of immediate and targeted feedback and individualized content structuring in adaptive learning environments, providing educators with valuable insights and strategies for AI integration.

Chapter 12: Navigating the AI Landscape: Student and Teacher Perceptions of AI in Assessments in High School and College Settings

Authored by Leesha Roberts, Fanta Solomon, and Reccia Cummings, this chapter delves into the role of Artificial Intelligence (AI) in Caribbean high school and college assessments, analyzing both teacher and student perspectives. Through a quantitative study surveying students and teachers, the chapter investigates AI tool usage, its effects on grading and feedback, fairness, and ethical concerns. Key findings highlight prevalent AI tool usage among students and teachers, with significant encounters at the high school level. Positive correlations emerge between teachers' views on AI's grading efficiency and students' appreciation for AI's timely feedback. The chapter emphasizes concerns about AI-induced discrimination and the need for targeted AI integration training, suggesting future research directions to address biases and enhance educational outcomes in the Caribbean context.

Chapter 13: Preparing Students for an AI-Enhanced Future

Authored by Rawya Elmahi Gobara and Zeinab Ahmed, this chapter provides a brief overview of Artificial Intelligence (AI) and its impact on technology, students' future, and education. The authors offer insights into AI developments over the years, including key drivers and topics of interest to students, preparing them for an AI-enhanced future. Students are taught the basics of AI and its workings, as well as the potential applications of AI in education. The chapter emphasizes the positive impact of technology on education, promoting critical thinking skills, creativity, and development, while encouraging students to explore AI tools and inspiring them with stories of individuals using AI for positive purposes, thereby motivating them to contribute innovative ideas and useful information.

Chapter 14: The Impact and Future of AI-Enhanced Teaching Methods in the Use of Business Simulations

Authored by Hélder Martins, this chapter examines the transformative role of AI-enhanced teaching methods in business simulation studies. Focusing on the integration of AI in education, the chapter highlights a paradigm shift towards more dynamic, personalized, and effective learning environments. It explores the implications of AI in enhancing decision-making knowledge, student engagement, and learning outcomes, aligning educational practices with future business leadership and management needs. Furthermore, the chapter explores the impact of AI on teaching and learning in business education, emphasizing the need for educators to adapt and leverage AI tools to augment pedagogical approaches and improve student outcomes. As AI reshapes the educational landscape, the chapter calls for a collaborative approach among technology developers, educators, and policymakers to integrate AI tools effectively and ethically into educational frameworks.

Chapter 15: Transforming Classroom Dynamics: The Social Impact of AI in Teaching and Learning

Authored by Tarun Vashishth, Vikas Sharma, Kewal Sharma, Bhupendra Kumar, Sachin Chaudhary, and Rajneesh Panwar, this chapter explores the integration of Artificial Intelligence (AI) in education, reshaping classroom dynamics and fostering a social impact on teaching and learning. The chapter examines the historical evolution of classroom dynamics, highlighting AI's pivotal role in this transformative journey. It investigates AI's influence on teacher support and development, encompassing AI-assisted lesson planning, teacher training, and enhanced classroom management. The conclusion reflects on future directions and trends, emphasizing AI's potential to democratize education, address language barriers, and provide inclusive learning experiences globally.

These chapters collectively provide a comprehensive overview of the multifaceted impact of Artificial Intelligence (AI) on education, offering insights into its transformative potential, challenges, and ethical considerations. Each chapter delves into specific aspects of AI integration in education, ranging from personalized learning to ethical implications, providing valuable resources for educators, policymakers, researchers, and other stakeholders invested in shaping the future of education in an AI-enhanced world.

As editors of *AI-Enhanced Teaching Methods*, we are delighted to conclude this groundbreaking volume, which has brought together diverse perspectives and insights into the transformative potential of AI in education. Throughout these chapters, we have embarked on a journey through the multifaceted landscape of AI-enhanced education, exploring topics such as personalized learning, classroom management, and ethical considerations.

One of the key takeaways from this compilation is the profound impact that AI has on traditional teaching methodologies and the learning journey of students. From personalized learning paths to real-time feedback mechanisms, AI offers innovative solutions to longstanding challenges in education. Moreover, the exploration of AI's role in addressing educational disparities underscores its potential as a tool for promoting equity and inclusivity in learning environments.

Ethical considerations surrounding AI integration have also been thoroughly examined, emphasizing the importance of responsible AI deployment and the preservation of human educators' roles in holistic education. By addressing privacy concerns, biases in algorithms, and the need for transparency and oversight, educators and policymakers can ensure that AI is leveraged ethically and responsibly in educational settings.

Furthermore, the chapters in this volume transcend disciplinary boundaries, catering to a diverse audience ranging from educators and technology developers to students, parents, and general readers interested in the future of education. By engaging with the foundational principles of AI in education and exploring cutting-edge advancements in AI technologies, readers have gained a holistic understanding of how AI can shape the educational landscape and prepare learners for an increasingly AI-integrated world.

We extend our sincere gratitude to our esteemed contributors for their invaluable insights and scholarly contributions, which have enriched this volume immeasurably. Their dedication to advancing education through AI is truly commendable and has laid the groundwork for future research and innovation in this field.

In conclusion, "Artificial Intelligence Enhanced Teaching Methods" serves as a testament to the transformative potential of AI in education and as a catalyst for shaping the future of learning. As editors, we invite you to embark on this intellectual journey, engage with the diverse perspectives presented herein, and join us in envisioning an AI-enhanced educational landscape that empowers learners and fosters lifelong curiosity and growth.

Zeinab E. Ahmed
Department of Computer Engineering, University of Gezira, Sudan & Department of Electrical and
Computer Engineering, International Islamic University Malaysia, Malaysia

Aisha A. Hassan
International Islamic University of Malaysia, Malaysia

RashidA. Saeed
Taif University, Saudi Arabia

Chapter 1
AI as a Teacher:
A New Educational Dynamic for Modern Classrooms for Personalized Learning Support

Robertas Damasevicius
Vytautas Magnus University, Lithuania

Tatjana Sidekerskiene
Kaunas University of Technology, Lithuania

ABSTRACT

This chapter discusses the impact and integration of artificial intelligence (AI) in education, with a focus on AI chatbots like ChatGPT. The study synthesizes findings from scholarly articles, offering a holistic view of how AI is transforming educational methodologies, classroom dynamics, and the roles of educators. Key areas of investigation include the transformation of classroom dynamics through AI-enabled smart classrooms, innovative AI-driven teaching methods, and the specific applications and implications of ChatGPT and generative AI in education. The study also focuses on the dynamics of teacher-AI collaboration, discussing the potential benefits and ethical considerations that arise from the integration of AI technologies in teaching and learning processes. Furthermore, it examines AI's role in educational assessment and learning analytics, highlighting both the capabilities and limitations of AI tools in these domains. The example of using ChatGPT for AI-driven student assessment and personalized learning recommendation generation is presented.

INTRODUCTION

The integration of Artificial Intelligence (AI) into educational paradigms marks a significant milestone in the evolution of teaching and learning processes. The genesis of AI in education can be traced back to the advent of computer-assisted learning, where rudimentary AI was used to deliver basic educational content. Over the decades, advancements in AI technology have dramatically transformed its capabilities

DOI: 10.4018/979-8-3693-2728-9.ch001

and applications in the educational sector (Chiu, 2024). Initially seen as a tool for automating simple tasks, AI has evolved to become a sophisticated partner in the educational process, capable of providing personalized learning experiences, data-driven insights, and interactive learning environments. The development of AI in education has been driven by both technological progress and an evolving understanding of learning processes. Early applications of AI in education focused primarily on addressing logistical and administrative challenges, such as grading and scheduling (Kay, 2012). This early work laid the groundwork for the more sophisticated applications we see today. Today, AI is utilized not only for administrative tasks but also for enhancing learning experiences, personalizing educational content, and providing insights into student performance and learning needs. The transition to these advanced applications is supported by developments in personalized learning through AI (Jian, 2023), the role of AI in education (Harry, 2023), and the potential for AI-powered learning to revolutionize education (Kataria, 2023).

The incorporation of AI into educational practices is closely intertwined with modern educational theories that emphasize personalized, adaptive, and student-centered learning. AI technologies align well with constructivist theories, which advocate for learning as an active, contextualized process of constructing and transferring knowledge (Damasevicius, 2014) rather than acquiring it passively. AI-powered tools can create personalized learning paths, adapt to individual student needs, and provide interactive, experiential learning experiences. Furthermore, AI has a significant role in the implementation of contemporary pedagogical approaches such as differentiated instruction and inquiry-based learning. By leveraging AI's data processing capabilities, educators can better understand and respond to the diverse learning styles, abilities, and interests of their students. AI's ability to analyze images and datasets enables educators to make informed decisions about curriculum design, instructional strategies, and student support. AI's capabilities extend to the realm of educational assessment (Zirar, 2023), aligning with modern theories that advocate for continuous, formative assessment strategies over traditional summative approaches. AI tools can provide ongoing feedback to students, enabling them to understand their learning progress and areas for improvement in real-time.

The primary purpose of this chapter is to explore the multifaceted role of AI in enhancing and transforming educational practices. It aims to provide a comprehensive analysis of how AI technologies are being integrated into various aspects of education, from elementary to higher education, and their impact on teaching methodologies, student learning experiences, and educational outcomes. The scope of this chapter encompasses an examination of AI's applications in automating routine tasks, personalizing learning experiences, supporting educators, and developing innovative teaching methods. Additionally, it focuses on the ethical implications and challenges associated with the deployment of AI in educational settings.

The chapter seeks to bridge the gap between theoretical understanding of AI in education and its practical implementation, offering insights into effective strategies for integrating AI into the classroom. It also aims to provide a critical analysis of the potential and limitations of AI in education, helping educators, policymakers, and stakeholders make informed decisions about incorporating AI technologies into educational systems.

This chapter contributes to the research field as follows:

- Provides an up-to-date and nuanced perspective on the role of AI in education.
- Utilizes a comprehensive and multidimensional approach to examine AI's impact on various stakeholders in the educational ecosystem, including students, teachers, administrators, and policymakers.
- Offers a holistic view that considers both the technological advancements in AI and their pedagogical implications, moving beyond the scope of previous studies that focused on isolated aspects of AI in education.
- Introduces new insights into the integration of AI within modern educational theories, demonstrating how AI can be aligned with and enhance contemporary pedagogical approaches.
- Presents a perspective on the ethical and practical challenges of implementing AI in education, addressing concerns such as data privacy, equity, and the balance between human and AI in the teaching and learning processes.

RELATED WORKS

We provide a comprehensive overview of the role and impact of AI, specifically AI chatbots and language models (chatbots) (EL Azhari et al., 2023) like ChatGPT, in various educational settings follows:

Okewu et al. (2021) and Pacheco-Mendoza et al. (2023) focus on the use of AI, particularly Artificial Neural Networks, for educational data mining in higher education. They highlight AI's potential in harnessing student data for in-formed academic advisory, predicting student performance, and enhancing adaptive learning. These studies indicate the growing significance of AI in optimizing educational processes and outcomes through data-driven insights. Wogu et al. (2019) and Kamalov et al. (2023) discuss the transformation brought about by AI in the education sector. They explore the implications of AI in smart class-rooms and online education, highlighting both the opportunities for enhanced learning experiences and concerns about the diminishing role of human teachers. These papers emphasize the need for a balanced integration of AI in educational systems. Sidekerskiene and Damasevicius (2023) and Grassini (2023) investigate innovative AI-driven teaching methods like digital escape rooms and ChatGPT's applications. They underscore AI's ability to create immersive learning environments that promote critical thinking and problem-solving skills, particularly in STEM education. The studies point to AI's role in breaking down barriers in traditional education and fostering active learning. The articles by Ali et al. (2023), Ansari et al. (2023), Bahroun et al. (2023), and Boubker (2024) delve into the specific use of ChatGPT and generative AI in educational contexts. They discuss how these tools assist in self-directed learning, personalized tutoring, and resource generation. Concerns regarding accuracy, reliability, and the impact on cognitive and social development are also addressed, highlighting the need for responsible use and further research. Chan and Lee (2023) and Chen et al. (2023) explore the dynamics of teacher-AI collaboration, emphasizing the importance of combining technology with traditional teaching methods. They highlight the potential benefits of AI in education but also raise ethical concerns about overreliance and the need for proper guidelines to ensure responsible use of AI technologies. AI's Role in Assessment and Learning Analytics: Clark (2023) and Chiu et al. (2023) assess the use of AI chatbots like ChatGPT in educational assessments and learning analytics. They investigate AI's efficacy in answering exam questions and supporting student motivation to learn, revealing its limitations and areas for improvement. Glaser (2023) and Yang et al. (2023) discuss the potential of ChatGPT as an educational technology, focusing on its relevance for learning, instruction, and assessment. They also consider the ethical implications and limitations of using ChatGPT in education, suggesting the need for further exploration of its integration into educational settings. Hutchins and Biswas (2023) and Limna et al. (2023) offer insights into generational perspectives on AI in education, examining the experiences and perceptions of different age groups towards AI tools like ChatGPT. They underscore the varying levels of optimism and concern among students and educators regarding the integration of AI in teaching and learning.

These studies collectively highlight the transformative potential of AI and tools like ChatGPT in education (Kim, 2023; Kim and Adlof, 2023; Rahman and Watanobe, 2023; Labadze et al., 2023), while also acknowledging the challenges, ethical considerations, and the need for balanced and responsible integration of these technologies in educational settings. They provide valuable insights into the current state and future directions of AI in education, emphasizing its role in enhancing learning experiences, supporting educators, and shaping educational practices. However, the literature review reveals a significant gap in the current understanding of the potential role of AI as a teacher in educational settings. Despite considerable research into the integration and impact of AI on various aspects of education, including student learning experiences, pedagogical methodologies, and administrative efficiency, there remains a paucity of comprehensive analysis regarding AI's ability to act as a teacher rather than a tool.

AI'S ROLE IN SUPPORTING EDUCATORS IN THE CLASSROOM

In the contemporary educational landscape, the advent of AI has heralded a transformative shift in pedagogical methodologies challenging the existing consensus (S´anchez-Ruiz et al., 2023; Damasevicius, 2023). The utility of AI extends beyond mere augmentation of the learning process, positioning itself as an in-dispensable ally to educators (de Winter et al., 2023). This section elucidates the multifaceted role of AI in buttressing educators, particularly focusing on automating routine tasks, providing analytical insights for personalized teaching (Van Schoors et al., 2023), fostering the development of innovative teaching methods, and outlining effective integration strategies for AI technologies (also see Figure 1).

Automating Routine Educational Tasks

The automation of routine tasks by AI marks a pivotal development in educational settings. Such tasks, often administrative and time-consuming, include grading, attendance tracking, and the organization of educational material. By delegating these tasks to AI systems, educators can reallocate their time and focus towards more nuanced pedagogical endeavours, such as curriculum development (Davis and Lee, 2024) and direct student engagement. The automation provided by AI not only enhances operational efficiency but also reduces the propensity for human error, ensuring a more streamlined educational process.

Providing Analytical Insights for Personalized Teaching

AI's capability to analyze vast datasets is leveraged to glean critical insights into student learning patterns, preferences, and challenges. These insights enable educators to tailor their teaching methodologies to the individual needs of students, thus embracing the ethos of personalized education. AI-driven analytics can identify areas where students struggle, allowing for the timely and targeted intervention by educators. This personalized approach is not merely reactive but also proactive, as AI can predict potential learning obstacles and suggest remedial measures, thereby fostering a more inclusive and effective learning environment.

Figure 1. Integration of AI in education

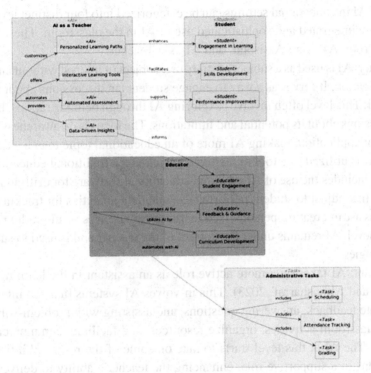

Development of Innovative Teaching Methods

The integration of AI in education also serves as a catalyst for the development of innovative teaching methods. AI can simulate complex real-world scenarios, facilitate game-based learning, and create immersive educational experiences through technologies such as augmented and virtual reality. These methods, underpinned by AI, make learning more engaging and relatable to students, thereby enhancing their cognitive and experiential learning. Furthermore, AI's ability to provide instant feedback and adapt to the learning pace of each student encourages a more dynamic and interactive classroom atmosphere, fostering deeper understanding and retention of knowledge.

Integration Strategies for AI Technologies

The effective integration of AI technologies in educational settings necessitates a strategic approach. This involves ensuring that the technology is aligned with the educational goals and curriculum, training educators to proficiently use AI tools, and maintaining a balance between AI-driven and traditional teaching methods. It is imperative that the integration of AI is seen as a complementary relationship (Jeon and Lee, 2023) rather than a replacement of the educator's role. Furthermore, ethical considerations, such as data privacy and the digital divide, must be addressed to ensure an equitable and responsible adoption of AI in education.

AI Deployment in Classroom

The deployment of AI in educational settings can be categorized into four distinct levels, each reflecting a progressively more integrated and sophisticated use of AI in the classroom. These levels are AI-as-a-Curiosity, AI-as-a-Tool, AI-as-an-Assistant, and AI-as-a-Teacher.

AI-as-a-Curiosity: AI is used as a subject of study or an object of interest without any specific rigorous framework of application. It serves as a way to engage students in discussions about technology, ethics, and the future of AI. This level often involves exploring AI through demonstrations, basic programming exercises, or discussions about its potential and limitations. The focus is on awareness and understanding rather than practical application, making AI more of an educational topic than a teaching tool.

AI-as-a-Tool: AI is utilized as a tool to facilitate and enhance traditional educational practices (Ansari et al., 2023). It includes the use of AI-powered educational software for drill-and-practice, adaptive learning platforms that adjust to student performance, and data analytics for tracking student progress. AI tools can also assist in creating personalized learning experiences or in grading and assessing student work. At this level, AI remains under the control of the teacher and is used to supplement standard teaching methodologies.

AI-as-an-Assistant: AI takes on a more active role as an assistant in the learning process (Hashem et al., 2024; Imran and Almusharraf, 2023). This in-volves AI systems that can interact with students, providing immediate feedback, answering questions, and assisting with problem-solving. AI assistants can help manage classroom activities, organize resources, and facilitate communication between students and teachers. The AI at this level starts to take on some of the responsibilities of a teacher, but it primarily functions in a supportive role, enhancing the teacher's ability to deliver personalized and efficient education.

AI-as-a-Teacher: The most advanced level, where AI acts as a teacher or tutor, taking a central role in delivering education. AI systems at this level are capable of designing lesson plans, delivering instructional content, assessing stu-dent performance, and adapting teaching strategies to meet the individual needs of each student. AI-as-a-Teacher involves a significant degree of autonomy, with AI being responsible for much of the direct educational interaction with students. This level requires sophisticated AI capable of understanding complex student responses, engaging in dialogue, and making pedagogical decisions, effectively mimicking the roles traditionally played by human teachers.

In all these levels, it's important to maintain a balance between technological advancement and the human aspects of education, ensuring that the deployment of AI supports and enhances the learning experience without overshadowing the essential human elements of teaching and learning. Each level offers different benefits and challenges, and the choice of level should be aligned with educational goals, the needs of students, and the capacity of the educational institution to integrate AI effectively.

AI-AS-A-TEACHER: CORE COMPONENTS

The concept of AI-as-a-Teacher embodies a revolutionary approach in educational methodology, characterized by the integration of advanced AI technologies into the learning environment. This section focuses on the core components that define AI's role as a teacher, emphasizing the facets of interactive and personal-ized learning. These components underscore the transformative potential of AI in education and highlight how AI can be leveraged to create more dynamic, responsive, and individualized educational experiences.

Interactive and Personalized Learning

The cornerstone of AI-as-a-Teacher is its ability to foster an interactive and personalized learning environment. This is achieved through dynamic interaction with students, personalization of learning content, adaptive learning pathways, and feedback mechanisms. Each of these subcomponents plays a crucial role in enhancing the learning experience, making it more engaging, relevant, and effective for each student.

Table 1. Comparison of requirements and capabilities of AI at different levels of classroom deployment

Level of AI Deployment	AI-as-a- Curiosity	AI-as-a-Tool	AI-as-an- Assistant	AI-as-a- Teacher
Technological Requirements	Basic programming and AI demonstration tools	AI-powered educational software, data analytics tools	Interactive AI systems, communication platforms	Advanced AI systems with adaptive learning capabilities, sophisticated data processing
AI Capabilities	Basic demonstrations and discussions about AI	Personalized learning experiences, grading and assessment automation	Interaction with students, feedback provision, classroom management	Lesson planning, content delivery, student performance assessment, pedagogical decision making
Role of AI	Educational topic for awareness and understanding	Supplement to traditional teaching methodologies	Supportive role in assisting both teaching, with a student	Central role in high degree of autonomy

AI technologies enable a level of interaction that goes beyond traditional educational tools. Through natural language processing and machine learning, AI can engage in meaningful dialogues with students, responding to their queries, and providing explanations. This dynamic interaction facilitates a more engaging and responsive learning environment, where students feel heard and supported in their educational journey. AI's ability to simulate human-like interactions contributes to a more immersive and interactive learning experience, fostering greater student engagement and motivation.

One of the most significant advantages of AI-as-a-Teacher is its ability to tailor learning content to the individual needs and preferences of each student. By analyzing data on student performance, learning styles, and preferences, AI can customize educational materials and resources to suit each learner's unique requirements. This personalization ensures that each student encounters learning content that is most relevant and conducive to their educational growth, thereby maximizing the efficacy of the learning process.

AI technologies are adept at creating adaptive learning pathways for students. These pathways are dynamic and evolve based on continuous assessment of a student's progress, strengths, and areas for improvement. By adjusting the difficulty level and pace of the learning content, AI ensures that each student is challenged appropriately, thereby facilitating optimal learning outcomes. This adaptability not only caters to the diverse learning needs within a classroom but also ensures that each student's educational journey is as efficient and effective as possible.

Feedback is a critical component of the learning process, and AI-as-a-Teacher excels in providing automated assessment (Gao et al., 2024) as well as timely and adaptive feedback. Utilizing real-time data and analytics, AI systems can offer instant, personalized feedback to students on their performance. This feed-back is not just corrective but also predictive, offering guidance on how students can improve and what areas they should focus on. The immediacy and relevance of this feedback enable students to quickly adjust their learning strategies and understand concepts more deeply, thereby enhancing the overall learning experience.

Curriculum Planning and Delivery

The implementation of AI in the realm of curriculum planning and delivery signifies a paradigm shift in educational methodologies. AI-as-a-Teacher not only automates and streamlines the process of curriculum design but also ensures that the educational content is highly relevant and adaptive to diverse learning environments. This section explores the capabilities of AI in automating lesson planning, tailoring content, and seamlessly integrating with existing curricula.

AI systems excel in the domain of automated lesson planning by leveraging data analytics and machine learning algorithms (van den Berg and du Plessis, 2023). This process involves the AI analyzing a vast array of educational re-sources and curricular standards to develop comprehensive lesson plans. These plans are not static; AI continuously refines them based on the evolving educational objectives and student performance data. This automation saves educators significant time and effort, allowing them to focus more on the qualitative aspects of teaching, such as student engagement and mentorship.

The strength of AI in education lies in its ability to tailor and adapt content to meet the diverse needs of students. By processing data on individual learning styles, pace, and comprehension levels, AI can customize educational materials to suit each learner. This adaptability ensures that the content is not only aligned with the learners' academic needs but also resonates with their interests and preferences. Such a tailored approach facilitates a deeper and more meaningful learning experience, catering to the unique educational journey of every student.

Integrating AI into the existing curriculum is a critical aspect of its implementation in the educational process. AI systems are designed to complement and enhance traditional curricular frameworks, ensuring that the transition to AI-assisted teaching is seamless and efficient. This integration involves aligning AI-generated content and methodologies with existing educational standards and teaching practices. AI's role is to augment and enrich the curriculum, not to re-place the fundamental pedagogical principles that underpin it. By doing so, AI bridges the gap between traditional educational paradigms and the innovative possibilities offered by modern technology, creating a harmonious and effective educational ecosystem.

Student Performance Assessment and Analytics

In the contemporary educational context, AI-as-a-Teacher plays a pivotal role in the assessment and analysis of student performance. This involves leveraging AI capabilities to continuously monitor student progress, derive data-driven insights for performance enhancement, and generate customized reports. This approach not only facilitates a more nuanced understanding of student learning trajectories but also enables educators to make informed decisions to optimize teaching strategies.

AI systems are uniquely equipped to offer continuous monitoring of student progress. Utilizing sophisticated algorithms, these systems track a wide range of metrics, such as assignment completion rates, quiz scores, and interactive session responses. This continuous monitoring allows for real-time assessment of student learning, providing an ongoing snapshot of their academic journey. The advantage of such a system lies in its ability to detect learning patterns, identify areas of struggle, and signal the need for intervention at the earliest possible stage, thus preventing students from falling behind.

The core strength of AI in educational settings is its capacity to analyze complex datasets to extract meaningful insights. By processing data collected from various educational interactions and assessments, AI can uncover trends and correlations that may not be immediately apparent. These insights can inform educators about the effectiveness of teaching methods, the impact of different learning materials, and the overall educational environment. Armed with this information, educators can tailor their instruction to better suit the needs of their students, thereby enhancing overall academic performance.

Another significant capability of AI in the realm of education is the generation of customized reports. AI systems can collate and analyze student data to produce detailed reports on individual and class-wide performance. These re-ports can include various metrics, such as progress over time, mastery of specific skills, and comparative analyses. Customized reports serve as valuable tools for educators, students, and parents alike, offering clear and actionable insights into the learning process. They also facilitate transparent communication between all stakeholders, ensuring that everyone is aligned in the pursuit of educational goals. By automating the report generation process, AI allows educators to focus more on interpreting the data and less on the administrative aspects of report compilation.

Supporting Diverse Learning Needs

In the realm of AI-as-a-Teacher, one of the most critical aspects is the capacity to support the diverse learning needs of students. This inclusivity is essential in modern education, as it acknowledges and addresses the wide range of learning styles, abilities, and backgrounds present in any educational setting. AI's capabilities in this area are explored through its adaptability to different learning styles, assistance to students with special needs, and accommodation of various language and cultural backgrounds.

AI systems are adept at catering to the multitude of learning styles that students exhibit. By leveraging AI's data processing and machine learning capabilities, educational content can be tailored to suit visual, auditory, kinesthetic, or reading/writing preferences. AI can present information in multiple formats, such as interactive simulations for kinesthetic learners, visual aids for visual learners, or narrated content for auditory learners. This ability to adapt teaching materials to different learning styles not only enhances the educational experience for each student but also promotes better understanding and retention of information.

AI technologies have a profound impact on the education of students with special needs. These systems can provide customized learning experiences that accommodate various disabilities, such as text-to-speech for visually impaired students or speech recognition for those with motor skill challenges. AI can also adjust the pace of learning and provide additional resources or support as needed, ensuring that these students receive an equitable and effective education. The adaptability and responsiveness of AI systems make them an invaluable tool in creating an inclusive learning environment where all students have the opportunity to succeed.

One of the standout features of AI in education is its ability to transcend language and cultural barriers. AI systems can offer content in multiple languages, making education accessible to students who are non-native speakers of the language of instruction. These systems can incorporate culturally relevant examples and materials, enhancing the relatability and engagement of the content for students from diverse backgrounds. This adaptability not only aids in better comprehension but also fosters a more inclusive and respectful learning environment. By recognizing and addressing the cultural and linguistic diversity of the student body, AI-as-a-Teacher plays a crucial role in preparing students for a globalized world.

Enhancing Student Engagement and Motivation

A key attribute of AI-as-a-Teacher is its capability to significantly enhance student engagement and motivation. This is achieved through innovative methods such as gamification, real-world problem-solving, and fostering curiosity and in-dependent learning. Each of these approaches plays a vital role in making the learning process more interactive, relevant, and enjoyable for students, thereby increasing their enthusiasm and commitment to learning.

Gamification, the incorporation of game design elements in non-game contexts, is an effective strategy employed by AI to boost student engagement (Bachiri et al., 2023; Swacha et al., 2021). By integrating elements such as points, badges, and leaderboards into educational activities, AI makes learning more ex-citing and competitive. Additionally, AI-powered interactive learning tools such as simulations, virtual labs, and interactive quizzes provide hands-on learning experiences that are both engaging and informative. These tools not only make learning fun but also cater to different learning styles, ensuring a more inclusive educational experience.

AI facilitates the integration of real-world problem-solving into the curriculum, thereby bridging the gap between theoretical knowledge and practical ap-plication. Through project-based learning and case studies, AI enables students to work on complex, real-life problems, encouraging them to apply their learning in meaningful ways. This approach enhances understanding and retention of aca-demic concepts and develops critical thinking, creativity, and collaborative skills. AI's ability to provide relevant data, simulations, and resources supports these project-based learning initiatives, making them more impactful and reflective of real-world scenarios.

A significant contribution of AI in education is its ability to foster curiosity and promote independent learning. AI systems can offer personalized learning paths, allowing students to explore topics at their own pace and according to their interests. By providing resources and activities that challenge students and spark their curiosity, AI encourages them to delve deeper into subjects and discover new areas of interest. This autonomy in learning not only motivates students but also instills in them a sense of responsibility for their own educational journey. The role of AI in facilitating a self-directed learning environment is paramount in preparing students for lifelong learning and adaptability in a rapidly changing world.

CASE STUDY: AI-DRIVEN PERSONALIZED LEARNING

Course Description

The primary objective of the Mathematics 2 course (delivered at Faculty of Natural Sciences and Mathematics, Kaunas University of Technology) is to provide university students with a comprehensive understanding of advanced mathematical concepts. The course focuses on topics such as indefinite, definite, multiple, and linear integrals, as well as differential equations and series. Throughout the duration of the course, university students will not only grasp the fundamental principles but also develop practical skills in applying these mathematical concepts to real-world problems. Course prerequisites and requirements are summarized in Table 2.

The course content is structured to cover a range of topics. Complex numbers and their operations are explored, along with the implementation of polar coordinate systems. The significance of indefinite integrals is underscored, and university students delve into the realm of definite integrals and their practical applications. The use of software in solving real tasks becomes a crucial skill set, as university students navigate through the complexities of improper integrals. The course tackles first and second-order differential equations, providing university students with a profound understanding of their derivation and classification.

Table 2. Course prerequisites and requirements

Intended Learning Outcomes	Applied Study Methods	Assessment Methods
Demonstrate the ability to apply theorems, calculus, differential equations, and infinite series covered in the course to solve both theoretical and practical problems.	Assignments, Experiential learning, Lecture	Individual work, Mid-term examination, Written examination
Apply integral calculus and infinite series methods to analyze the relationships between various parameters of objects under investigation	Assignments, Experiential learning, Lecture	Written examination
Apply relevant mathematical models and algorithms to solve practical problems related to the concept of integral	Assignments, Experiential learning, Lecture	Mid-term examination, Written examination
Utilize Matlab/Octave software to solve tasks involving integral calculus, differential equations, and infinite series.	Assignments, Experiential learning, Lecture	Mid-term examination, Written examination
Demonstrate the ability to study independently in selected fields of applied integral calculus and differential equations, infinite series, and plan the study process	Assignments	Mid-term examination, Oral presentation
Effectively present the results of problem-solving achieved through individual or team efforts.	Assignments, Collaborative learning, Group work	Individual work, Oral presentation

The practical aspect is once again emphasized through the application of soft-ware tools in solving real tasks. Infinite series and line integrals are also explored, exposing university students to the broader applications of these mathematical concepts. The course goes further to equip university students with the necessary tools to master methods for finding indefinite integrals, compute definite, double, and linear integrals, and derive as well as classify differential equations. The application of these mathematical concepts to real-world problem-solving is emphasized, and university students are introduced to the use of software tools for efficient and accurate computations. This integration of software applications not only enhances the learning experience but also prepares university students for the practical demands of applying mathematical knowledge in diverse fields. The Mathematics 2 course aims not only to impart theoretical knowledge but also to cultivate a strong foundation for practical problem-solving. By the end of the course, university students are expected to have a well-rounded under-standing of these advanced mathematical concepts and the proficiency to apply them effectively in various real-world scenarios.

The assessment methods of this course include Mid-term examination and Written examination delivered in writing form on chapter. The examples of tasks are given in Table 3.

Table 3. Examples of tasks

Questions	Answers
Calculate the area between the curves $y = 2 - 2x^2$, $y = 1 - x^2$, $x \in [-1; 1]$. Draw a graph. Which answer is correct?	(a) 0 (b) $\frac{8}{3}$ (c) 2 (d) $\frac{4}{3}$ (e) $-\frac{8}{3}$
Calculate the integral $\int_{AB} (x - y) ds$, where AB is the line segment defined by $y = 2x - 1$ between the points $A(1; 1)$ and $B(2; 3)$. Which answer is correct?	(a) $-\frac{\sqrt{5}}{2}$ (b) $\frac{\sqrt{5}}{2}$ (c) 2 (d) -2 (e) $-\frac{2}{\sqrt{5}}$
Calculate the mass of the plate when its density $\gamma(x, y) = x^2 + y^2$, and its shape is defined by the equation $x^2 - 4x + y^2 = 0, y \geq 0$. Which answer is correct?	(a) 12π (b) 24 (c) π (d) 0 (e) 24π

Analysis of Exemplar AI Generated Assessment

The AI-based methodology for assessing student work follows these steps out-lined in Table 4. We used the paid version of ChatGPT (ChatGPT 4), based on the GPT-4 architecture OpenAI and et al. (2024).

The students' responses to tasks were thoroughly analyzed using the advanced capabilities of Chat-GPT. As an example, the student responses to the first task are visually represented in Figure 2, offering a detailed insight into their solutions.

The following prompt was given to ChatGPT - Evaluate the solution of the mathematical problem contained in this image. Is the answer correct? - and the image given in Figure 2 was attached. The result, as illustrated in Fig. 3, the Chat-GPT demonstrates a commendable understanding of both the assigned task and the data encapsulated within the accompanying image. It is evident that the ChatGPT success-fully parses the complexities of the task, showcasing a high level of proficiency in data interpretation. Regrettably, in contrast, the student's response contains an error, leading to an inaccurately formulated answer. De-spite the student's misstep, ChatGPT emerges as a valuable resource, adeptly rectifying the issue and providing a precise and correct solution to the task at hand. This discrepancy highlights the robust capabilities of ChatGPT in not only comprehending intricate tasks but also in rectifying errors and offering accurate solutions. The contrast between the student's response and the Chat-GPT's correction underscores the potential of advanced AI models in enhancing task accuracy and knowledge application.

Table 4. AI-based methodology for student work assessment

No.	Action	Description
1	Collection and Preparation	Students complete their work on chapter, which is then collected and scanned to create digital images.
2	Uploading	The scanned images are uploaded to a computer system.
3	Image Processing	Optical Character Recognition (OCR) technology is applied to the scanned images to extract text, if necessary. This action can be performed by ChatGPT 4 version.
4	AI Assessment	ChatGPT analyzes the content against the learning objectives and marking scheme.
5	Error Identification	ChatGPT identifies errors or omissions in the student's work and assesses the methods used.
6	Feedback Generation	ChatGPT generates specific feedback for each student's work, providing suggestions for improvement.
7	Feedback Review (if necessary)	An educator may review the AI-generated feedback to ensure its appropriateness.
8	Delivery of Feedback	Feedback is delivered to students digitally or in printed form
9	Action by Students	Students review the feedback and are advised on course materials to revisit for improvement.
10	Data Analysis for Course Improvement	Aggregate data from the AI-generated assessment is used to identify common difficulties for course enhancement.

Figure 2. Student's solution to the first task

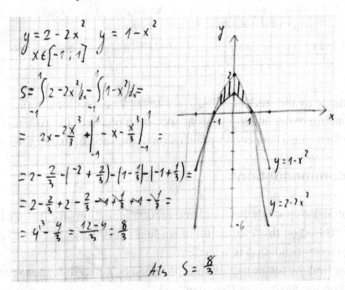

Next, ChatGPT was asked to find an exact location in the solution where an error was based using the following prompt: "Show a specific line in the provided solution in which the error was made". The capabilities of ChatGPT are noted as it precisely pinpoints the exact location in the solution, where the student made a mistake. The AI not only identifies errors but also offers valuable insights into the nature of the mistake, showcasing its capacity to provide detailed and instructive feedback. This nuanced analysis by the AI not only aids in correcting

Figure 3. ChatGPT checked step-by-step the student's solution of the task

The problem involves finding the area S between the curves $y = 2 - 2x^2$ and $y = 1 - x^2$ over the interval $x \in [-1, 1]$.

The solution given in the image is as follows:

$$S = \int_{-1}^{1} (2 - 2x^2)dx - \int_{-1}^{1} (1 - x^2)dx$$

Carrying out the integration, the solution continues with:

$$= \left[2x - \frac{2}{3}x^3\right]_{-1}^{1} - \left[x - \frac{1}{3}x^3\right]_{-1}^{1}$$

Plugging in the limits of integration, the solution shows:

$$= \left(2 - \frac{2}{3}\right) - \left(-2 + \frac{2}{3}\right) - \left(1 - \frac{1}{3}\right) - \left(-1 + \frac{1}{3}\right)$$

This simplifies to:

$$= \frac{4}{3} + \frac{4}{3} - \frac{2}{3} - \frac{2}{3}$$

Which then simplifies further to:

$$= \frac{4}{3} + \frac{4}{3} - \frac{2}{3} - \frac{2}{3} = \frac{8}{3}$$

The final answer given is $S = \frac{8}{3}$.

To verify the correctness of this solution, I will calculate the integrals independently. [-]

The evaluated area S between the curves $y = 2 - 2x^2$ and $y = 1 - x^2$ over the interval $x \in [-1, 1]$ is $\frac{4}{3}$ or approximately 1.333, not $\frac{8}{3}$ as given in the image.

Therefore, the answer provided in the image is incorrect. The correct value for the area S is $\frac{4}{3}$. [-]

the specific error made by the student but also serves as an educational tool, guiding the student toward a better understanding of the underlying concepts. It emphasizes the AI's role not just in providing correct answers but in fostering a deeper comprehension of the subject matter through targeted feedback.

Personalized Recommendations

Finally, we asked ChatGPT to provide personalized recommendations for further learning. The following prompt was used: "Based on this evaluation of student's mistakes, provide a real-world example of personalized learning recommendation to a student".

In Figure 5, you can find the recommendations provided by ChatGPT, show-casing the AI's insights and suggestions based on the analysis of the given tasks.

Based on the evaluation of the student's work provided in Figure 4, where the student incorrectly added terms that should have cancelled out due to symmetry, a personalized learning recommendation would focus on reinforcing the concepts of symmetry in integration and the properties of definite integrals, especially when integrating over symmetric limits.

Figure 4. ChatGPT found the mistake in the student's solution

ChatGPT

Upon reviewing the image of the solution, the error occurs in the final step where the individual integrals are combined:

$$= \left(2 - \frac{2}{3}\right) - \left(-2 + \frac{2}{3}\right) - \left(1 - \frac{1}{3}\right) - \left(-1 + \frac{1}{3}\right)$$

The terms -2 and $+2$ from the first integral and -1 and $+1$ from the second integral should cancel each other out because of symmetry, but instead, they have been incorrectly added. This mistake has led to the incorrect doubling of the area. The correct evaluation should have been:

$$= \left(2 - \frac{2}{3}\right) + \left(2 - \frac{2}{3}\right) - \left(1 - \frac{1}{3}\right) - \left(1 - \frac{1}{3}\right)$$

This simplifies to:

$$= \left(\frac{4}{3} + \frac{4}{3}\right) - \left(\frac{2}{3} + \frac{2}{3}\right) = \frac{8}{3} - \frac{4}{3} = \frac{4}{3}$$

The incorrect step in the provided solution is the addition of the values that should have cancelled each other out.

DISCUSSION: FUTURE OF AI IN EDUCATION

Emerging Trends and Technologies

The horizon of AI in education is marked by several emerging trends and technologies that promise to further revolutionize the field. One such trend is the increasing use of AI for personalized learning experiences, where algorithms be-come more refined in tailoring education to individual student needs and learning styles. Another trend is the integration of AI with immersive technologies like virtual reality (VR) and augmented reality (AR), which can create highly engaging and interactive learning environments. Advancements in natural language processing (NLP) and machine learning are making AI systems more sophisticated in understanding and responding to human language, thereby enhancing their capabilities in areas like tutoring, student assessment and support (Rasul et al., 2023; Ramandanis and Xinogalos, 2023; Lin et al., 2023). The development of AI-driven predictive analytics is another trend, which can provide educators and policymakers with valuable insights for decision-making in curriculum de-sign and educational policies. These emerging technologies not only enhance the learning experience but also open new avenues for research and innovation in smart education (Stuikys and Burbaite, 2018).

Potential Impact on Global Education Systems

The integration of AI into education holds the potential to profoundly impact global education systems acting as a disruptor (Pǎvǎloaia and Necula, 2023). One significant area of impact is the democratization of education, as AI-driven platforms can provide high-quality educational resources to remote and under-served regions, thereby reducing educational disparities. AI also has the potential to reshape the role of teachers, transitioning them from information providers to facilitators of learning, mentors, and guides while supporting their creativity.

Figure 5. Example of personalized learning recommendation generated by ChatGPT

Personalized Learning Recommendation for Understanding Symmetry in Integration

Dear [Student's Name],

After reviewing your recent exam on definite integrals, it's clear that you have a good grasp of finding antiderivatives. However, there seems to be a bit of confusion when it comes to the properties of definite integrals, particularly regarding the concept of symmetry.

Recommendations:

1. **Review Symmetric Intervals:**
   * Take some time to review the theory behind integrating functions over symmetric intervals. This is crucial when the limits of integration are equal and opposite in sign, such as from -a to a.
2. **Practice with Odd and Even Functions:**
   * Work through practice problems that involve odd and even functions. Remember that the integral of an odd function over symmetric limits is zero, while the integral of an even function will double from 0 to a.
3. **Visual Learning:**
   * Use graphing tools to visualize the functions you are integrating. Seeing the symmetry can help you understand why certain terms cancel out.
4. **Worked Examples:**
   * Go through worked examples that specifically deal with the properties of definite integrals and symmetry. Pay close attention to how the terms are combined and canceled.
5. **Interactive Simulations:**
   * Engage with interactive simulations that allow you to manipulate the limits of integration and the types of functions. This hands-on approach can solidify your understanding.
6. **Tutoring Session:**
   * Consider scheduling a one-on-one tutoring session to go over the concepts. A tutor can provide immediate feedback and help you through the process.
7. **Group Study:**
   * Join a study group where you can discuss and solve integral problems with peers. Explaining the concepts to others can also improve your understanding.
8. **Feedback Loop:**
   * After you've reviewed and practiced, attempt the problem again and send it for feedback. This will help gauge your improvement.

By focusing on these areas, you'll be able to strengthen your understanding of definite integrals and avoid similar mistakes in the future. Remember, mastery comes with practice, and every mistake is an opportunity to learn and grow.

(Liu et al., 2023). The adoption of AI in education can lead to more efficient education systems, where resources are optimized, and education is more aligned with labor market demands and societal needs. However, this also raises chal-lenges such as ensuring equitable access to AI technologies and addressing ethical concerns related to data privacy and algorithmic bias. The successful integration of AI in global education systems will require careful planning, policy-making, and collaboration among educators, technologists, and policymakers.

Limitations of AI in Education

AI in education is positioned as a transformative force, aimed at addressing a multitude of challenges that span pedagogical methodologies, administrative efficiency, and the inclusivity of diverse learning needs. At its core, AI endeavors to deliver a personalized learning experience, tailoring educational content to the individual preferences, needs, and pace of each student (Jian, 2023; Montebello, 2021; Maghsudi et al., 2021). This approach not only enhances engagement but also optimizes learning outcomes by aligning educational materials with varied learning styles. Beyond education, AI extends its utility to automating routine administrative tasks such as grading, attendance tracking, and scheduling (Ahmad et al., 2022; Chen et al., 2020), thus liberating educators to devote more time to pedagogical activities. Another significant aim of AI in education is to enhance accessibility for students with disabilities through technologies like speech-to-text and text-to-speech functionalities, thereby promoting a more inclusive learning environment (Jian, 2023). Moreover, AI facilitates real-time feedback and assessment, offering students immediate insights into their performance and areas for improvement (Maghsudi et al., 2021). Additionally, AI-powered tools are designed to foster interactive and engaging learning experiences, potentially increasing student motivation and participation (Montebello, 2021). However, the effectiveness of AI in education is nuanced by inherent limitations and trade-offs. While AI-driven personalization has shown promise in boosting student engagement and learning outcomes, the technology's potential to perpetuate existing biases presents a considerable challenge (Maghsudi et al., 2021; Ntoutsi et al., 2020). These biases, embedded within the training data, can lead to unequal treatment of certain student groups, undermining the fairness and inclusivity of educational opportunities. Furthermore, the implementation of AI risks depersonalizing the educational experience. The reliance on data-driven personalization may diminish the human touch, empathy, and the valuable interpersonal relationships between teachers and students (Harry, 2023). Concerns about data privacy and security also emerge with AI's integration into education, necessitating robust protection measures against data breaches and misuse (Huang, 2023; Wang, 2020). Additionally, there's apprehension that dependency on AI for educational and administrative tasks could erode critical thinking and problem-solving skills among students and educators. Another significant trade-off involves accessibility and equity; although AI seeks to make education more accessible, disparities in access to AI-powered tools could exacerbate educational inequities among students from different socio-economic backgrounds (Harry, 2023).

Ethical Considerations

The integration of AI in education presents a complex interplay of benefits and ethical challenges. The use of AI in education necessitates the collection and analysis of vast amounts of personal data from students to tailor learning experiences and improve educational outcomes. This raises privacy concerns regarding the handling, storage, and potential misuse of such data. Ensuring data security be-comes paramount, requiring robust encryption methods, strict access controls, and transparent data usage policies to protect sensitive information from unauthorized access and breaches (Huang, 2023; Elliott and Soifer, 2022). AI systems are only as unbiased as the data they are trained on. There is a risk that AI in education could perpetuate existing societal biases, leading to unfair treatment or discrimination against certain groups of students. To address this, it is crucial to develop AI systems with diverse and inclusive training datasets and implement ongoing monitoring and adjustment processes to identify and mitigate bias (Srinivasan and Chander, 2021; Baker and Hawn, 2021). The integration of AI in education also poses challenges to employment within the sector, particularly concerning the roles of teachers and administrative staff. While AI can automate routine tasks and provide analytical support, it is essential to emphasize the ir-replaceable value of human interaction, empathy, and professional judgment in education. Training programs and policy measures should be implemented to up-skill educators, enabling them to work effectively alongside AI technologies and secure their roles in an AI-enhanced educational landscape (Mandhala et al., 2022).

To address the ethical challenges associated with AI in education, stakeholders should consider implementing the following strategies:

- Develop and enforce strict privacy regulations and data security measures to protect student information.
- Invest in the creation of diverse and inclusive AI training datasets and establish processes for ongoing bias monitoring and mitigation.
- Support professional development and training programs for educators to ensure they remain integral to the educational process in an AI-enhanced landscape.
- Foster collaboration between AI developers, educators, and policymakers to design AI tools that complement traditional teaching methods and address the specific needs of diverse student populations.

The impact of AI on Educational Equity and Accessibility

A critical and perhaps underexplored aspect of AI integration in education is its impact on educational equity and accessibility. The capacity of AI to either widen or bridge gaps in education for underserved or disadvantaged communities is a matter of significant concern that warrants a more nuanced discussion (Wiburg, 2003; Shaheen and Watulak, 2019). AI holds the promise of making education more accessible and personalized, offering students with diverse learning needs tailored educational experiences that can cater to their specific requirements. For instance, AI-powered tools can provide adaptive learning environments that adjust to the pace and style of each learner, potentially levelling the playing field for students who might not thrive in traditional learning settings (Okello, 2023). However, the deployment of AI in education also raises concerns about exacerbating existing inequalities. The digital divide—a gap between those with easy access to digital technology and those without—poses a significant challenge in leveraging AI to enhance educational equity. Students from underserved communities might lack the necessary technological infrastructure, including re-liable internet access and digital devices, to benefit from AI-powered educational tools. This disparity risks widening the educational gap between students with readily available access to technology and those without, undermining the efforts to use AI as a means to bridge educational inequities (Chen et al., 2020). The development and implementation of AI systems often require substantial financial investments, which may not be feasible for underfunded schools that predominantly serve disadvantaged communities. As a result, the benefits of AI in education could become disproportionately available to students from well-resourced schools, further entrenching socio-economic disparities in educational outcomes (Dignum, 2021).

Preparing for a Digitally Enhanced Educational Future

Preparing for a future where education is significantly enhanced by digital technologies, particularly AI, involves several key considerations. Firstly, there is a need for comprehensive digital literacy and AI education for both students and educators, ensuring that all parties are equipped to use and interact with AI technologies effectively. This also involves continuous professional development for educators to keep pace with technological advancements.

Infrastructure development is crucial, particularly in ensuring that schools and educational institutions have the necessary technological resources and connectivity. Policymakers and educational leaders must also consider the ethical implications of AI in education, developing guidelines and policies that safeguard student data privacy and promote fair and unbiased use of AI.

Fostering a culture of innovation within the educational sector is essential, encouraging experimentation and adoption of new technologies in teaching and learning. By preparing adequately for this digitally enhanced future, the education sector can leverage AI to its full potential, creating more effective, inclusive, and dynamic learning environments.

CONCLUSION AND FUTURE RESEARCH

Our findings underscore the multifaceted role of AI in education, highlighting its transformative impact in various domains. AI has demonstrated significant potential in personalizing learning experiences, enhancing student engagement, and supporting educators in curriculum planning and delivery. Its role in automating routine tasks and providing analytical insights is invaluable in optimizing educational processes and outcomes. AI's ability to cater to diverse learning needs and its application in innovative teaching methods have emerged as key factors in enhancing the quality of education. However, alongside these advancements, the chapter also acknowledges the challenges and ethical considerations that ac-company the integration of AI in education, including concerns regarding data privacy, equity, and the preservation of human elements in teaching.

Educators are encouraged to embrace AI as a complementary tool that can augment teaching and learning processes. It is important for educators to acquire digital literacy skills and stay abreast of technological advancements to effectively integrate AI into their teaching practices. Collaboration between educators and AI developers is essential to ensure that AI tools are designed and implemented in ways that meet educational needs and ethical standards. Educators should also strive to maintain a balance between AI-driven and traditional teaching methods, ensuring that the human aspects of teaching, such as empathy and moral guidance, are preserved.

Looking ahead, there are several promising directions for future research in the field of AI in education. One area involves exploring the long-term impacts of AI on learning outcomes and student development. Research can also be directed towards developing more sophisticated AI technologies that are capable of understanding and adapting to complex human emotions and behaviors. An-other significant area of research is the exploration of strategies to mitigate the ethical and equity challenges posed by AI, ensuring that its benefits are accessible to all students, regardless of their socio-economic background. Additionally, investigating the implications of AI on the role of educators and the structure of education systems can provide deeper insights into how education might evolve in an AI-enhanced future.

REFERENCES

Ahmad, S., Alam, M. M., Rahmat, M. K., Mubarik, M., & Hyder, S. (2022). Academic and administrative role of artificial intelligence in education. *Sustainability (Basel)*, *14*(3), 1101. doi:10.3390/su14031101

Ali, F., Choy, D., Divaharan, S., Tay, H., & Chen, W. (2023). Supporting self-directed learning and self-assessment using teachergaia, a generative ai chatbot appli-cation: Learning approaches and prompt engineering. Learning. *Research and Practice*, *9*(2), 135–147.

Ansari, A., Ahmad, S., & Bhutta, S. (2023). Mapping the global evidence around the use of chatgpt in higher education: A systematic scoping review. *Education and Information Technologies*. Advance online publication. doi:10.1007/s10639-023-12223-4

Azhari, E. L. (2023). K., Hilal, I., Daoudi, N., Ajhoun, R.: Smart chatbots in the e-learning domain: A systematic literature review. *International Journal of Interactive Mobile Technologies*, *17*(15), 4–37. doi:10.3991/ijim.v17i15.40315

Bachiri, Y. A., Mouncif, H., & Bouikhalene, B. (2023). Artificial intelligence empowers gamification: Optimizing student engagement and learning outcomes in e-learning and moocs. *International Journal of Engineering Pedagogy*, *13*(8), 4–19. doi:10.3991/ijep.v13i8.40853

Bahroun, Z., Anane, C., Ahmed, V., & Zacca, A. (2023). Transforming education: A com-prehensive review of generative artificial intelligence in educational settings through bibliometric and content analysis. *Sustainability (Basel)*, *15*(17), 12983. doi:10.3390/su151712983

Baker, R., & Hawn, A. (2021). Algorithmic bias in education. *International Journal of Artificial Intelligence in Education*, *32*(4), 1052–1092. doi:10.1007/s40593-021-00285-9

Boubker, O. (2024). From chatting to self-educating: Can ai tools boost student learning outcomes? *Expert Systems with Applications*, *238*, 238. doi:10.1016/j.eswa.2023.121820

Chan, C., & Lee, K. (2023). The ai generation gap: Are gen z students more interested in adopting generative ai such as chatgpt in teaching and learning than their gen x and millennial generation teachers? *Smart Learning Environments, 10*(1).

Chen, L., Chen, P., & Lin, Z. (2020). Artificial intelligence in education: A review. *IEEE Access : Practical Innovations, Open Solutions*, *8*, 75264–75278. doi:10.1109/ACCESS.2020.2988510

Chen, Y., Jensen, S., Albert, L., Gupta, S., & Lee, T. (2023). Artificial intelligence (ai) student assistants in the classroom: Designing chatbots to support student success. *Information Systems Frontiers*, *25*(1), 161–182. doi:10.1007/s10796-022-10291-4

Chiu, T. (2024). Future research recommendations for transforming higher education with generative ai. *Computers and Education: Artificial Intelligence, 6.*

Chiu, T., Moorhouse, B., Chai, C., & Ismailov, M. (2023). Teacher support and student motivation to learn with artificial intelligence (ai) based chatbot. *Interactive Learning Environments*, 1–17. doi:10.1080/10494820.2023.2172044

Clark, T. (2023). Investigating the use of an artificial intelligence chatbot with general chemistry exam questions. *Journal of Chemical Education*, *100*(5), 1905–1916. doi:10.1021/acs.jchemed.3c00027

Damasevicius, R. (2014). Towards empirical modelling of knowledge transfer in teach-ing/learning process. *Communications in Computer and Information Science*, *465*, 359–372. doi:10.1007/978-3-319-11958-8_29

Damasevicius, R. (2023). *The rise of chatgpt and the demise of bloom's taxonomy of learning stages.* Creative AI Tools and Ethical Implications in Teaching and Learning.

Davis, R. O., & Lee, Y. J. (2024). Prompt: Chatgpt, create my course, please! *Education Sciences, 14*(1), 24. doi:10.3390/educsci14010024

de Winter, J. C. F., Dodou, D., & Stienen, A. H. A. (2023). Chatgpt in education: Empow-ering educators through methods for recognition and assessment. *Informatics (MDPI), 10*(4), 87. doi:10.3390/informatics10040087

Dignum, V. (2021). The role and challenges of education for responsible ai. *London Review of Education, 19*(1). Advance online publication. doi:10.14324/LRE.19.1.01

Elliott, D., & Soifer, E. (2022). Ai technologies, privacy, and security. *Frontiers in Artificial Intelligence,* 5. PMID:35493613

Gao, R., Merzdorf, H. E., Anwar, S., Hipwell, M. C., & Srinivasa, A. R. (2024). Automatic assessment of text-based responses in post-secondary education: A systematic review. *Computers and Education: Artificial Intelligence, 6,* 24. doi:10.1016/j.caeai.2024.100206

Glaser, N. (2023). Exploring the potential of chatgpt as an educational technology: An emerging technology report. Technology. *Knowledge and Learning, 28*(4), 1945–1952. doi:10.1007/s10758-023-09684-4

Grassini, S. (2023). Shaping the future of education: Exploring the potential and con-sequences of ai and chatgpt in educational settings. *Education Sciences, 13*(7), 692. doi:10.3390/educsci13070692

Harry, A. (2023). *Role of ai in education. Interdisciplinary Journal and Humanity.*

Hashem, R., Ali, N., Zein, F., Fidalgo, P., & Khurma, O. (2024). Ai to the rescue: Explor-ing the potential of chatgpt as a teacher ally for workload relief and burnout prevention. *Research and Practice in Technology Enhanced Learning,* 19.

Huang, L. (2023). *Ethics of artificial intelligence in education: Student privacy and data protection.* Science Insights Education Frontiers.

Hutchins, N., & Biswas, G. (2023). Co-designing teacher support technology for problem-based learning in middle school science. *British Journal of Educational Technology.*

Imran, M., & Almusharraf, N. (2023). Analyzing the role of chatgpt as a writing assistant at higher education level: A systematic review of the literature. *Contemporary Educational Technology, 15*(4), ep464. doi:10.30935/cedtech/13605

Jeon, J., & Lee, S. (2023). Large language models in education: A focus on the comple-mentary relationship between human teachers and chatgpt. *Education and Information Technologies, 28*(12), 15873–15892. doi:10.1007/s10639-023-11834-1

Jian, M. J. K. O. (2023). *Personalized learning through ai.* Advances in Engineering In-novation. doi:10.54254/2977-3903/5/2023039

Kamalov, F., Santandreu Calonge, D., & Gurrib, I. (2023). New era of artificial intelligence in education: Towards a sustainable multifaceted revolution. *Sustainability (Basel)*, *15*(16), 12451. doi:10.3390/su151612451

Kataria, K. (2023). Ai-powered learning: The future of education. *International Journal of Advanced Research*, *11*(9), 199–203. doi:10.21474/IJAR01/17520

Kay, J. (2012). Ai and education: Grand challenges. *IEEE Intelligent Systems*, *27*(5), 66–69. doi:10.1109/MIS.2012.92

Kim, J. (2023). Leading teachers' perspective on teacher-ai collaboration in education. *Education and Information Technologies*. Advance online publication. doi:10.1007/s10639-023-12109-5

Kim, M., & Adlof, L. (2023). Adapting to the future: Chatgpt as a means for supporting constructivist learning environments. *TechTrends*.

Labadze, L., Grigolia, M., & Machaidze, L. (2023). Role of ai chatbots in education: Sys-tematic literature review. *International Journal of Educational Technology in Higher Education*, *20*(1), 56. doi:10.1186/s41239-023-00426-1

Limna, P., Kraiwanit, T., Jangjarat, K., Klayklung, P., & Chocksathaporn, P. (2023). The use of chatgpt in the digital era: Perspectives on chatbot implementation. *Journal of Applied Learning and Teaching*, *6*(1), 64–74.

Lin, C.C., Huang, A., & Lu, O. (2023). Artificial intelligence in intelligent tutoring systems toward sustainable education: a systematic review. *Smart Learning Environments, 10*(1).

Liu, Z., Vobolevich, A., & Oparin, A. (2023). The influence of ai chatgpt on improving teachers' creative thinking. International Journal of Learning. *Teaching and Educational Research*, *22*(12), 124–139.

Maghsudi, S., Lan, A.S., Xu, J., & Schaar, M. (2021). *Personalized education in the ai era: What to expect next?* ArXiv abs/2101.10074.

Mandhala, V. N., Bhattacharyya, D., & Midhunchakkaravarthy, D. (2022). Need of miti-gating bias in the datasets using machine learning algorithms. *2022 International Conference on Advances in Computing, Communication and Applied Informatics (ACCAI)*. 10.1109/ACCAI53970.2022.9752643

Montebello, M. (2021). *Personalized learning environments. 2021 International Sympo-sium on Educational Technology*. ISET.

Ntoutsi, E., Fafalios, P., Gadiraju, U., Iosifidis, V., Nejdl, W., Vidal, M. E., Ruggieri, S., Turini, F., Papadopoulos, S., Krasanakis, E., Kompatsiaris, I., Kinder-Kurlanda, K., Wagner, C., Karimi, F., Fern'andez, M., Alani, H., Berendt, B., Kruegel, T., Heinze, C., … Staab, S. (2020). Bias in data-driven artificial intelligence systems—An introduc-tory survey. *Wiley Interdisciplinary Reviews. Data Mining and Knowledge Discovery*, 10.

Okello, H. T. I. (2023). *Analyzing the impacts of artificial intelligence on education.* IAA Journal of Education. doi:10.59298/IAAJE/2023/2.10.1000

Okewu, E., Adewole, P., Misra, S., Maskeliunas, R., & Damasevicius, R. (2021). Artificial neural networks for educational data mining in higher education: A systematic literature review. *Applied Artificial Intelligence*, *35*(13), 983–1021. doi:10.1080/08839514.2021.1922847

Pacheco-Mendoza, S., Guevara, C., Mayorga-Alb'an, A., & Fern'andez-Escobar, J. (2023). Artificial intelligence in higher education: A predictive model for academic performance. *Education Sciences*, *13*(10), 990. doi:10.3390/educsci13100990

Pˇavˇaloaia, V. D., & Necula, S. C. (2023). Artificial intelligence as a disruptive technol-ogy—A systematic literature review. *Electronics (Basel)*, *12*(5), 1102. doi:10.3390/electronics12051102

Rahman, M., & Watanobe, Y. (2023). Chatgpt for education and research: Opportunities, threats, and strategies. *Applied Sciences (Basel, Switzerland)*, *13*(9), 5783. doi:10.3390/app13095783

Ramandanis, D., & Xinogalos, S. (2023). Investigating the support provided by chatbots to educational institutions and their students: A systematic literature review. *Multimodal Technologies and Interaction*, *7*(11), 103. doi:10.3390/mti7110103

Rasul, T., Nair, S., Kalendra, D., Robin, M., Santini, F., Ladeira, W., Sun, M., Day, I., Rather, R., & Heathcote, L. (2023). The role of chatgpt in higher education: Benefits, challenges, and future research directions. *Journal of Applied Learn-ing and Teaching*, *6*(1), 41–56.

S'anchez-Ruiz, L. M., Moll-L'opez, S., Nu˜nez-P'erez, A., Mora˜no-Fern'andez, J. A., & Vega-Fleitas, E. (2023). Chatgpt challenges blended learning methodologies in en-gineering education: A case study in mathematics. *Applied Sciences (Basel, Switzerland)*, *13*(10).

Shaheen, N. L., & Watulak, S. L. (2019). Bringing disability into the discussion: Examining technology accessibility as an equity concern in the field of instructional technology. *Journal of Research on Technology in Education*, *51*(2), 187–201. doi:10.1080/15391523.2019.1566037

Sidekerskiene, T., & Damasevicius, R. (2023). Out-of-the-box learning: Digital escape rooms as a metaphor for breaking down barriers in stem education. *Sustainability (Basel)*, *15*(9), 7393. doi:10.3390/su15097393

Stuikys, V., & Burbaite, R. (2018). *Smart STEM-Driven Computer Science Education: Theory*. Methodology and Robot-based Practices. doi:10.1007/978-3-319-78485-4

van den Berg, G., & du Plessis, E. (2023). Chatgpt and generative ai: Possibilities for its contribution to lesson planning, critical thinking and openness in teacher education. *Education Sciences*, *13*(10), 998. doi:10.3390/educsci13100998

Van Schoors, R., Elen, J., Raes, A., & Depaepe, F. (2023). Tinkering the teacher–technology nexus: The case of teacher- and technology-driven per-sonalisation. *Education Sciences*, *13*(4), 349. doi:10.3390/educsci13040349

Wang, Y. (2020). When artificial intelligence meets educational leaders' data-informed decision-making: A cautionary tale. *Studies in Educational Evaluation*.

Wiburg, K. (2003). Technology and the new meaning of educational equity. *Computers in the Schools*, *20*(1-2), 113–128. doi:10.1300/J025v20n01_09

Wogu, I., Misra, S., Assibong, P., Olu-Owolabi, E. F., Maskeliunas, R., & Dama-sevicius, R. (2019). Artificial intelligence, smart classrooms and online education in the 21st century: Implications for human development. *Journal of Cases on Information Technology, 21*(3), 66–79. doi:10.4018/JCIT.2019070105

Yang, X., Wang, Q., & Lyu, J. (2023). *Assessing chatgpt's educational capabilities and application potential.* ECNU Review of Education.

Zirar, A. (2023). Exploring the impact of language models, such as chatgpt, on student learning and assessment. *Review of Education, 11*(3), e3433. doi:10.1002/rev3.3433

Chapter 2
AI in Educational Design and Technological Development

Salaheldin M. I. Edam

https://orcid.org/0000-0002-8280-8745

Sudan University of Science and Technology, Sudan

ABSTRACT

Artificial intelligence (AI) has both benefits and challenges in education. AI can customize learning experiences, enhance teaching methods, and foster equal opportunities in education. However, ethical implications and potential biases linked to AI-generated data are concerns. AI-driven tools like adaptive learning systems and intelligent tutoring systems have the potential to revolutionize education. The chapter explores a range of AI-driven tools and systems, including natural language processing. The ethical implications and potential biases linked to AI-generated data are thoroughly analyzed. Suggestions on how to responsibly incorporate AI into the field of education are offered. The utilization of AI has been discovered to enhance learning experiences and address the disparity in educational opportunities, ultimately resulting in a more inclusive and equitable education system. The development of AI curricula for various educational levels is also a key area of focus to ensure that the potential of AI in education is realized in an inclusive and responsible manner.

INTRODUCTION

The emergence of Artificial Intelligence (AI) has brought about a new era of progress and change in various industries, particularly in the field of education. With the advent of AI technologies, there are now novel tools and applications that can revolutionize the conventional methods of teaching and learning. The potential uses of AI in education (AIEd) are vast and varied, ranging from enhancing productivity and learning outcomes to providing personalized instruction, immediate feedback, and increased student engagement (Adiguzel, Kaya, & Cansu, 2023). Technology such as artificial intelligence (AI) has been gaining popularity in education. For almost thirty years since its introduction in education, AI has been recognized as a valuable resource for creating innovative approaches to instructional design, technological advancement, and educational research, which would not have been possible in the con-

DOI: 10.4018/979-8-3693-2728-9.ch002

ventional education model (Ouyang & Jiao, 2021; K. Zhang & Aslan, 2021). AI innovation in the field of education has progressed from theoretical laboratory settings to practical learning environments that are more intricate. Within the educational technology (EdTech) sector, companies have created various systems to enhance the learning experience. These include the Individual Adaptive Learning System, which enables personalized learning, the Aided Teaching System, which assists in managing classroom dynamics, grading, evaluation, and addressing second-language difficulties, and the Institute Administration System, which aids in student enrollment and handling inquiries, among other functions (Guan, Mou, & Jiang, 2020). Over the years, it has been proven through numerous studies that utilizing artificial intelligence (AI) techniques in a manner that aligns with human learning methods results in better performance compared to conventional computer-assisted instructional systems (Lane & D'Mello, 2019). An AI-assisted learning environment for precision education is anticipated to offer teachers and students more responsive and consistent feedback on their learning progress, thereby enhancing the quality of problem-based learning (PBL) classrooms. One such application of AI is the automatic recording of student behavior and identification of individual learners (Hu, 2022).

The implementation of AI in schools heavily relies on the teachers who act as the intermediaries between the school's AI policies and the student's requirements. Therefore, teachers play a crucial role in the successful deployment of AI in educational institutions. Despite being aware of the potential benefits of AI in education, many teachers may not be fully prepared for AI-enhanced teaching. This lack of readiness may be one of the reasons for the slow and unsatisfactory adoption of AI technologies in education, which lags behind the rapid advancements in AI (X. Wang, Li, Tan, Yang, & Lei, 2023). The authors (George & Wooden, 2023) stated that AI-driven data management systems can collect and analyze student performance data, enabling the identification of areas where students might encounter difficulties. By examining grades and test scores, these systems can precisely determine the courses in which students require additional support. Consequently, the university can offer personalized assistance to these students, addressing their specific needs and enhancing their chances of success.

Bridging the knowledge gap in utilizing AI technologies for students with special needs is crucial in advancing inclusive education. By addressing the digital divide and guaranteeing equal access to AI resources, educators can maximize the benefits of cutting-edge technologies to improve the educational journey of special needs learners. To accomplish this, it is crucial to prioritize comprehensive training for educators, enhance the accessibility and affordability of AI resources, and adapt these technologies to meet the unique requirements of students in special education. By closing the gap in knowledge and access to technology, we can empower special needs learners with the necessary assistance and opportunities to flourish in the era driven by artificial intelligence (Mpu, 2023). To further the discussion on the most effective method of incorporating AI education, this chapter delves into exploring its potential across various domains as shown in Figure 1.

Motivation

Artificial intelligence possesses numerous capabilities, such as catering to diverse educational requirements of students irrespective of their abilities and individual skills, thereby leading to improved educational outcomes. Additionally, AI can revolutionize the educational landscape by offering intelligent teaching systems. I am driven to write a chapter on the utilization of artificial intelligence in education to elucidate the benefits and present remedies for the drawbacks. This will enable education authorities to effectively implement AI solutions.

Figure 1. AI in education

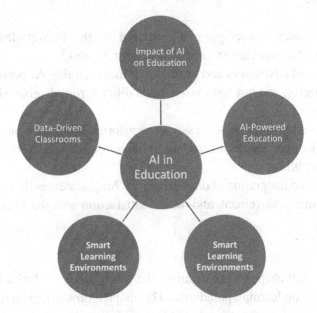

Significance

The integrating AI into education offers numerous advantages, such as enhancing the learning experience for students by tailoring it to their individual needs and promoting efficiency (Zaman, 2023). It expedites and offers a more convenient avenue for teachers to receive feedback, allowing them to offer timely assistance and direction. As AI progresses, its incorporation into educational environments can revolutionize conventional learning approaches, dismantling obstacles, and enriching the overall learning journey (Su & Yang, 2023). A rapidly evolving digital landscape necessitates a better understanding and utilization of AI in education. The research aims to provide valuable insights for educators, policymakers, and researchers by analyzing important factors like smart learning environments, inclusive education strategies, and data-driven classrooms.

Research Problem

AI is presently advancing inventive educational solutions that are presently undergoing testing in diverse environments. The challenge lies in how educators can proficiently utilize AI-generated insights from student data to customize teaching approaches and enhance learning outcomes in a wide range of classroom settings. Data-driven insights can be used for enhanced personalized and effective instruction in this research problem, which addresses leveraging AI in education. Researchers could examine the practical application of AI in educational settings, analyzing its effects on student engagement and academic performance. Additionally, they could focus on devising strategies to promote inclusivity and adaptability in different educational environments.

Research Questions

- How are educators presently leveraging AI-generated insights from student data to shape and adjust their instructional approaches in varied classroom settings?
- What are the perceived advantages and obstacles of incorporating AI-powered data analytics into teaching methodologies, and how do these factors differ across diverse educational contexts and student demographics?
- How can AI-generated insights be successfully transformed into actionable strategies to improve personalized learning experiences for students, taking into account individual learning styles and academic requirements?
- To what extent does the integration of data-driven teaching strategies through AI influence student engagement, academic achievement, and overall satisfaction with the learning process?

Aim and Objectives

The purpose of this research chapter is to examine the significance of Artificial Intelligence (AI) in education and its influence on learning paradigms. The chapter aims to offer a futuristic outlook on the possibilities of AI in education, assisting stakeholders in effectively incorporating AI into educational practices while addressing the intricacies involved. The chapter endeavors to achieve the following objectives:

- Discovering the Influence of AI on Education
- Investigate the potential of AI-powered education to overcome obstacles and improve learning experiences
- Recognize and assess AI approaches that foster inclusive and personalized education
- Analyze the impact of AI in redefining teaching methodologies and fostering data-driven classrooms.
- Formulate a strategic framework for maximizing the effectiveness of AI in educational environments through optimized implementation.

Methodology

The study employs a hybrid methodology, incorporating both qualitative and quantitative methodologies to thoroughly examine the influence of AI on education. Qualitative techniques entail a thorough examination of the integration of AI in education, and its impact on educators, students, and AI experts, to gather nuanced insights into the challenges and opportunities brought about by the integration of AI. Moreover, a thorough examination of scholarly literature and educational policies will furnish a conceptual framework for comprehending the digital transformation in the field of education. In terms of quantitative analysis, data analytics will be utilized to evaluate the efficacy of AI strategies in various educational environments. The research will additionally utilize case studies of educational institutions or schools that have effectively integrated AI into their systems, providing valuable practical knowledge on how to strategically implement AI. This integrated approach seeks to offer a comprehensive comprehension of the present condition of AI in education, enabling a forward-thinking investigation into its potential future paths.

Sections Layout

Section two examines the pertinent literature regarding the historical aspect of technology's development in education, as well as the significant milestones in the incorporation of AI within educational environments. A discussion of AI's impact on education is explored in section three, including examples of AI-enhanced learning. Section four provides a comprehensive examination of the progress and influence of intelligent learning environments. Additionally, it assesses the role of AI technologies in enhancing educational outcomes. Section five delves into the investigation of AI strategies that foster inclusivity and personalization in teaching, alongside the presentation of successful case studies. Section six explores the impact of AI on the development of data-driven classrooms, as well as its implications for teaching approaches and educational approaches. Figure 2 shows connection of the different sections.

Figure 2. Section layout

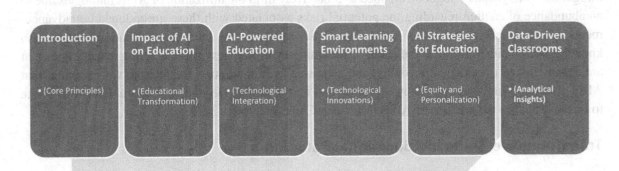

Introduction	Impact of AI on Education	AI-Powered Education	Smart Learning Environments	AI Strategies for Education	Data-Driven Classrooms
• (Core Principles)	• (Educational Transformation)	• (Technological Integration)	• (Technological Innovations)	• (Equity and Personalization)	• (Analytical Insights)

IMPACT OF AI ON EDUCATION

AI possesses immense power and holds the potential to profoundly influence and revolutionize various sectors of society, particularly the education sector (Chen, Chen, & Lin, 2020). The identification of AI's impact on education necessitates a thorough examination of how AI influences the educational landscape. To effectively identify the impact of AI on education, it is crucial to explore the implementation of artificial intelligence in education (AIED) through an educational AI system (Paek & Kim, 2021). Those researchers employed a blended research methodology to examine the influence of Artificial Intelligence (AI) on language acquisition and skill enhancement. This methodology integrated both quantitative and qualitative techniques to offer a comprehensive comprehension of the topic. Surveys were utilized to collect quantitative data from learners and educators engaged in AI-driven language learning and skill development initiatives.

Unveiling the Technological Revolution in Learning

The emergence of artificial intelligence (AI) in the academic domain, specifically in ChatGPT, has triggered a variety of responses. These responses are similar to the reactions that were seen previously in response to technological developments such as the internet and calculators (Tarisayi, 2023). The emergence of the new industrial revolution is still ongoing, and it is primarily driven by advancements in science and technology. The latest AI technology has brought about new features such as deep learning through which significant advancements in computer vision have been accomplished. However, Augmented intelligence (AuI) leverages the strengths of both human intelligence (HI) and artificial intelligence (AI) to maximize the advantages offered by each, while compensating for their respective limitations. These features have opened up new avenues for human thinking, enabling us to comprehend complex systems and technologies. With the ability to reconstruct both nature and society, the new generation of AI is providing humankind with innovative ways of approaching various challenges (Yau et al., 2021; Zhou et al., 2018). The implementation of novel AI technologies necessitates meticulous strategizing and risk mitigation. Policymakers might be inclined to proactively limit the utilization of AI technologies due to an abundance of caution regarding the potential risks associated with these groundbreaking advancements (Dixit, Quaglietta, & Gaulton, 2021; Thierer & Castillo, 2016). Intelligent education systems, also known as AIEd, aim to improve the quality of learning by utilizing machine learning technologies that are closely linked to statistical modeling and cognitive learning theory. Despite the vast potential that AIEd offers, it is crucial to persist in exploring and investigating effective ways to implement its usage to further enhance the practice of AIEd (Martínez-Comesaña et al., 2023).

Transformative Shifts in Educational Paradigms

In the era of the Information Age, the integration of learning systems will take place. The fundamental principles governing these systems will revolve around "knowledge-based" accompanied by "demonstrated mastery." Throughout a learner's educational journey, various learning tools and resources will be employed, and they will be revisited in updated formats to ensure continuous learning, refreshing, and acquiring new skills (Dolence & Norris, 1995). The implementation of the Independent Curriculum for Learning represents a significant change in higher education, emphasizing the importance of learner autonomy and adaptability. By incorporating AI applications into this curriculum, we gain valuable insights into how technology can enhance student-centered approaches. Understanding the practical implications and challenges associated with integrating AI into the independent curriculum is crucial for universities to design effective language learning programs that cater to the unique needs of each student. These findings are consistent with research conducted by esteemed educators (Hasibuan, Parta, Sholihah, Damayanto, & Farihatun, 2023). The researcher explores various paradigm shifts in educational technology through the application of two analytical approaches. Firstly, he examines the evolution of educational technology within the Association for Educational Communication and Technology (AECT), a well-established organization with a significant impact on the field. Secondly, then investigates a distinct educational technology movement that operates outside the purview of AECT (Subkhan, 2012). In the realm of educational technology, particularly in practical applications, the utilization of various learning media and methods is contingent upon adherence to several systematic learning and educational paradigms (Subkhan, 2012). The following contains several AI educational paradigms as shown in Figure 3:

Figure 3. AI education paradigms

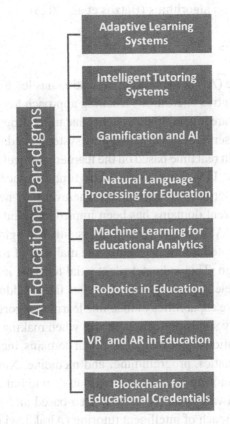

Adaptive Learning Systems

Teachers, students, and school administrators can all benefit from adaptive learning as an educational technology (Aleven, McLaren, Sewall, & Koedinger, 2009; Ni & Cheung, 2023). Adaptive learning technology is a valuable tool for educators as it not only saves them time but also provides them with insightful data on each student's progress and learning potential. By utilizing this assistive platform, teachers can create personalized teaching experiences for each student, tailored to their unique learning needs. This includes developing customized resources and activities that cater to individual strengths and weaknesses, ultimately leading to a more effective and engaging learning environment (Aleven et al., 2009). By automating feedback cycles within these systems, students can track their learning journeys independently from their instructors and keep track of their progress. Learning analytics, AI-enabled tutoring, and educational data mining techniques have been investigated to develop AI-enabled learning systems (Ni & Cheung, 2023). The objectives of each system and the desired outcome are linked to the source of adaptation, which can be the learner, environment, or device. When the focus is on the learner, their characteristics become more significant. These relevant characteristics are incorporated into the learner model, which is a crucial element for any adaptive e-learning system (Lin, Huang, & Lu, 2023). There are various types of learning algorithms used in adaptive learning systems, including artificial intelligence and machine learning (Alrakhawi, Jamiat, & Abu-Naser, 2023), (Alrakhawi et al., 2023), personalization algorithms (Nguwi, 2023), data-driven educational algorithms (Saleem, Noori, & Ozdamli, 2022), and adaptation algorithms (Batzos et al., 2023).

Intelligent Tutoring Systems

The rise of artificial intelligence (AI) in the field of education has led to a resurgence of Intelligent Tutoring Systems (ITSs) as an effective one-on-one teaching approach to cater to the growing demand for personalized learning. The ITSs are instructional systems that utilize cognitive principles and algorithms to provide personalized tutoring services to learners. These systems are data-based and adaptive, meaning they can adjust their instruction in real time based on the learner's subject knowledge, abilities, emotions, and learning styles. Importantly, ITSs are not limited by time or space constraints, allowing learners to access personalized tutoring services whenever and wherever they need them(Ni & Cheung, 2023). Students learning in many different domains has been improved by intelligent tutoring systems (ITS) using a diversity of approaches (Aleven et al., 2009). AI is either integrated into the tutoring system or it is not. In the case of AI-integrated tutoring systems, the majority of results suggest that the accuracy of performance prediction is high. This indicates a potential to assist individuals who are predicted to have low performance. Nevertheless, the majority of studies fail to address the underlying reasons and mechanisms behind the predictive capabilities of machine learning algorithms. Consequently, educators are left with no choice but to rely solely on their expertise when making informed decisions (Lin et al., 2023). The ITS has found applications in various educational domains, including information technology, engineering, languages, mathematics, programming, and medicine. Numerous tools exist to facilitate the development of intelligent tutoring systems for individuals without programming expertise. These tools enable the creation of software systems, such as web-based and mobile-based systems, thereby expanding the accessibility and reach of intelligent tutoring (Alrakhawi et al., 2023).

Gamification and AI

In recent years, gamification has emerged as a prominent constructivist approach to learning, garnering considerable interest across various fields such as commerce, health, and more notably, education (Dahalan, Alias, & Shaharom, 2023). Gamification enhances learner engagement by creating learning activities that guide learners through a sequence of narratives, establishing game rules, and implementing reward systems. Gamification is a versatile strategy aimed at augmenting learners' involvement through the use of dynamic visual hues and auditory stimuli to enhance cognitive reasoning. Gamification systems employ various game components to captivate learners, such as online activity, badges, challenges, levels, points, and leaderboards (Nguwi, 2023). The utilization of gamification in the realm of e-learning is experiencing a surge in growth and garnering increasing popularity (Saleem et al., 2022). Gamification is employed as a means to enhance students' engagement and enthusiasm towards their academic pursuits (Batzos et al., 2023). Gamification is commonly employed within university environments, where students have the autonomy to select their desired courses and address any concerns they may encounter. A primary goal for students is to acquire knowledge in the most convenient manner possible. Hence, gamification leverages information and communication technology (ICT) to enhance student learning and enable learning opportunities at any time and in any place. Gamification aids educators in conducting formative assessments to ascertain the subjects in which students are encountering difficulties (Cavus, Ibrahim, Okonkwo, Ayansina, & Modupeola, 2023).

Natural Language Processing for Education

Machines are capable of understanding the way human language is spoken through Natural Language Processing (NLP). The NLP refers to the capability of computer programs to comprehend human language in its natural form. It aids in the understanding, manipulation, and interpretation of human language by computers (Khensous, Labed, & Labed, 2023). A fusion of robots and NLP is transforming the educational landscape. Using NLP algorithms, robots can provide customized tutoring for each student, adapting to the student's needs. In addition, they foster communication, critical thinking, and collaborative learning (Younis, Ruhaiyem, Ghaban, Gazem, & Nasser, 2023). NLP holds the potential to revolutionize educational technology in various ways. Firstly, it plays a crucial role in automating the assessment of student texts by evaluating linguistic aspects such as grammar and organizational structure. Secondly, dialogue technologies leverage NLP to replicate the benefits of one-on-one human tutoring, particularly in Science, Technology, Engineering, and Mathematics (STEM) fields, offering a cost-effective and scalable solution. The third role involves utilizing NLP to process web-based text, enabling the personalization of instructional materials based on individual student interests. Additionally, it facilitates the automated generation of test questions for educators and contributes to (semi-) automating the creation of educational technology systems (Litman, 2016).

Machine Learning for Educational Analytics

The use of Machine Learning (ML) algorithms in education is increasing as well, as several other disciplines have used it in recent years to improve efficiency and outcomes (L. T. Liu, Wang, Britton, & Abebe, 2023). In recent years, there has been a significant surge in the volume of data gathered from E-learning platforms. This wealth of information can be effectively harnessed through the application of machine learning and data analytics in the realm of online education. Emerging fields like educational data mining and learning analytics are focused on leveraging these technologies to enhance the teaching and learning experience, employing machine learning and visualization techniques for improved educational outcomes (Badal & Sungkur, 2023). With predictive analytics, it becomes feasible to generate future forecasts by analyzing historical trends in learning experiences. In the last decade, the advancement of machine and deep learning has led to the creation of efficient and sophisticated predictive models, enabling the discovery of intricate hidden characteristics within data (Sghir, Adadi, & Lahmer, 2023). Educational scientists, corporate partners, and stakeholders have the opportunity to leverage machine learning techniques in crafting sophisticated and scalable educational processes. These processes can be tailored to address individual learner needs, offering valuable support to existing learning infrastructure. The adept application of machine learning methods holds the potential to introduce crucial innovations to educational sciences, including (semi-)automated assessments, algorithmic grading, and personalized feedback (Hilbert et al., 2021). The incorporation of machine learning education at the K-12 level is a relatively recent area of research interest that necessitates further study to ensure its seamless integration into the school system and effectiveness in educational settings (Sanusi, Oyelere, Vartiainen, Suhonen, & Tukiainen, 2023).

Robotics in Education

Educational Robotics (ER) has become a popular optional subject in primary and preschool practices in numerous countries in recent times (Mangina, Psyrra, Screpanti, & Scaradozzi, 2023). Educational Robotics serves as a valuable asset that can effectively address educational challenges by enhancing opportunities and elevating students' learning capabilities (Kerimbayev, Nurym, Akramova, & Abdykarimova, 2023). In (Darmawansah, Hwang, Chen, & Liang, 2023) the authors stated that a methodological and innovative approach to learning has been encouraged with robotics in STEM education. Studies have also revealed that robots can enhance students' creativity and logic in school settings. It is possible to promote STEM disciplines such as engineering concepts and interdisciplinary practices through robots and educational robotics when they are a core part of STEM education. The authors (Madaev, Turluev, & Batchaeva, 2023) stated that by using robotics, students can gain hands-on experience with problem-solving that facilitates learning. Learning this way is not just fun, but it also develops essential skills such as critical thinking, which can be applied to many different areas of life. Educational robots, categorized under educational technology, serve multiple purposes, including enhancing academic performance and promoting effective learning. Within this category, there exists a specific type of robot known as humanoid robots, which possess human-like characteristics. These humanoid robots have been utilized in the field of education for a considerable period. Specific personal names are commonly given to educational robots, and in certain cases, robotics kits are employed for educational purposes (Chaka, 2023).

Virtual Reality and Augmented Reality in Education

Virtual reality (VR) and augmented reality (AR) have emerged as two distinct technological advancements that are revolutionizing the entertainment industry. Nevertheless, these cutting-edge technologies are not limited to entertainment alone; they are also being harnessed in the field of education to provide students with a fresh outlook and facilitate the acquisition of new skills (X. Zhao, Ren, & Cheah, 2023). AR and VR provide students with immersive digital understandings that go beyond the limitations of traditional teaching methods. These technologies allow students to engage more effectively with complex material, moving beyond conventional lectures and textbooks (Al-Ansi, Jaboob, Garad, & Al-Ansi, 2023). The study expands the existing knowledge on the significance of AR and VR in online education and their potential for the future. AR and VR have proven to be highly beneficial in enhancing teaching methods across various disciplines (Tiwari, Bhaskar, & Pal, 2023).

Blockchain for Educational Credentials

The utilization of blockchain technology in different sectors, such as medical services, finance, and education, can bring about a significant transformation. Incorporating blockchain technology into the educational system holds the promise of enhancing the effectiveness, protection, and trustworthiness of the educational procedure (El Koshiry, Eliwa, Abd El-Hafeez, & Shams, 2023). Blockchain technology is a distributed database that securely records and keeps track of transactions in sealed blocks. Blockchain technology has the potential to completely transform the education industry in several ways, including providing the tools for decentralizing online learning and assisting students in keeping track of the micro-credentials they have earned throughout their lives, which serve as certificates of achievement (Alsobhi, Alakhtar, Ubaid, Hussain, & Hussain, 2023). Blockchain and blockchain-upheld ideas, like self-sovereign personality frameworks, irrefutable accreditations, and decentralized identifiers, are slowly changing data the board frameworks in different public area spaces. Schooling is a conspicuous public area space where blockchain arrangements are effectively being created and tried (Tan, Lerouge, Du Caju, & Du Seuil, 2023).

AI-POWERED EDUCATION

Simulated intelligence-fueled AI-powered Educational Technology (EdTech) centers around PC frameworks equipped for achieving errands and exercises that have generally depended on human insight, for example, normal language handling and thinking. Past examination demonstrates that the previously mentioned "Artificial intelligence nature" of innovation assumes a critical part in shaping specialists' discernments and perspectives towards taking on computer-based intelligence-based EdTech (Nazaretsky, Ariely, Cukurova, & Alexandron, 2022). The utilization of artificial intelligence-fueled coaches, for instance, may prompt understudies to depend intensely on innovation and not foster the decisive reasoning and critical thinking abilities that accompany collaborating with a human instructor (Skrabut, 2023). Simulated intelligence-fueled apparatuses have a place in the present arising fields in instructive innovation and many creators see tremendous advantages they might bring both to understudies and educators. Computer-based intelligence-fueled schooling offers the chance to discover what is more customized, adaptable, comprehensive, and locking in (Pokrivcakova, 2019).

Classroom Dynamics With AI

Seismic movements have as of late happened in the customary study hall educating educational experience, which utilizes board strategies. Innovation has altogether worked on this cycle over the most recent couple of years, with educators, understudies, robots, digital books, workstations, and books becoming players in the cutting-edge homeroom. The instructing educational experience can now rise above geological lines with the assistance of e-talks and instructional exercises, and a tremendous measure of data is effectively accessible (El Koshiry et al., 2023). On the off chance that educators have a fitting preparation for utilizing simulated intelligence advancements and positive computer-based intelligence-related insight, they will be bound to carry out smart PC-helped language learning (ICALL) in their homerooms. An essential state of progress is to assist them with feeling good ready and certain to act in artificial intelligence innovation-upgraded conditions (Pokrivcakova, 2019). One of the purposes of IoT in learning is E.Learning which can be utilized as a virtual study hall and might meet up close and personal with educators/mentors basically through gadgets associated with cameras (Fitria, 2023). The student response systems (SRS) gamification is achieved by briefly transforming the classroom into a television game show, with the instructor taking on the role of a gameshow host and the students participating as contestants (A. I. Wang & Lieberoth, 2016).

AI Tools for Teaching Excellence

Online education, or the utilization of web-based learning platforms, enables individuals to access educational materials from any corner of the globe. Additionally, it incorporates various facets of artificial intelligence, including translation tools, to enhance the learning experience (Shvetsova, 2023). The combination of generative artificial intelligence (AI) tools and instructional design matrices has completely transformed the approach to conceptualizing and implementing learning activities. AI tools were utilized by educators to enhance the efficiency and effectiveness of evaluating student performance. By employing these tools, teachers were able to analyze responses generated by students, evaluate their understanding, and deliver personalized feedback in real time (Ruiz-Rojas, Acosta-Vargas, De-Moreta-Llovet, & Gonzalez-Rodriguez, 2023). Based on the findings of authors (Abu Owda, Abu Mousa, Shakfa, & Al-Hidabi, 2023), the study suggests that it would be beneficial to educate gifted students on the principles of artificial intelligence and its associated tools, while also exploring the educational effects it may have on other factors. On the other hand, the authors (Baidoo-Anu & Ansah, 2023) stated that it's crucial to remember that ChatGPT and other generative AI models are powerful tools, but they cannot substitute human teachers and tutors. Responsible usage involves employing these tools in tandem with human instruction and support, recognizing the complementary roles they play.

Elevating Student Engagement With AI-Driven Learning

Throughout the evolution of technology, universities have continuously embraced digital advancements to improve the quality of education. Starting from the early days of utilizing computers and the internet to streamline administrative tasks, we have now entered an era of AI-driven personalized learning. This progressive approach has not only made education more accessible but also more cost-effective for students (George & Wooden, 2023). Adaptive assessments powered by AI can dynamically adapt to students' performance levels, offering tailored assessments and feedback. This capability enhances the effectiveness and efficiency of the assessment process. Future studies should give priority to conducting thorough investigations into the impact of AI on student learning outcomes, the professional growth of faculty and staff, and the overall effectiveness of AI-driven changes in higher education (Saaida). AI-powered evaluation tools effectively assess assignments and exams, delivering prompt feedback and enabling educators to dedicate more time to teaching and guiding students (Saxena, Sethi, & Singh, 2023). AI-powered technology and resources enhance the educational experience for students by offering personalized assistance and prompt feedback. This plays a crucial role in harnessing their motivation and involvement(Altememy et al., 2023).

The Impact of AI on Educational Equity

While the terms equity and equality are frequently used interchangeably, they possess distinct meanings from a philosophical perspective. Equity pertains to the notions of justice and fairness, embodying a value and principle. On the other hand, equality refers to the extent or condition of being equal, particularly in terms of one's status, rights, and opportunities (Metsämuuronen & Lehikko, 2023). Despite the promising vision of technology-based education in promoting educational equity and enhancing educational quality, there is a potential for it to intensify pre-existing educational disparities. Achieving equalization of educational resources and ensuring equality in education can be challenging if the digital infrastructure is not flawless (Tanga & Chen, 2023). One commonly accepted concept of educational fairness revolves around educational results, affirming that fairness involves students from diverse backgrounds attaining equal outcomes, such as academic achievement (Dumont & Ready, 2023). Also, the results (Dakakni & Safa, 2023) indicated that students' interactions with AI were characterized by a complex "love/hate" dynamic, whereby they utilized AI while harboring reservations about privacy and fairness.

Ethical AI in Education

The responsible and ethical application of artificial intelligence in education extends beyond technical precision to encompass the social and ethical consequences of its integration, including issues related to privacy, bias, and the impact of AI on shaping the future of education (Mhlanga, D. (2023). To ensure a delicate equilibrium between the rapid growth of technology and the ethical implications of AI, governments and international organizations are actively involved in formulating AI regulations and ethical guidelines (Chen, H. (2024). Safeguarding the confidentiality of individuals within the realm of artificial intelligence necessitates a blend of technical strategies like data anonymization and differential privacy, alongside strong governance and regulatory structures (Alam, A. (2023). Implicit biases can arise in AI as a result of data or algorithmic flaws, leading to discriminatory outcomes and a decline in trust towards AI. To tackle the problem of AI implicit biases, it is essential to regularly monitor and evaluate their performance, and train them using unbiased data and algorithms (Roshanaei, M. (2024).

SMART LEARNING ENVIRONMENTS

The self-regulated intelligent learning environment is a smart learning environment that utilizes artificial intelligence in the pedagogical process (Gambo & Shakir, 2023). Smart learning environments aim to enhance and accelerate training that supports technology through physical environments enhanced with digital devices (Mutizwa, Ozdamli, & Karagozlu, 2023). Students can benefit from the advancement of personalized and adaptive learning through smart devices and intelligent technologies within smart learning environments. In terms of promoting the development of personalized learning and adaptive learning, the smart learning environment has enormous potential (Cheung, Kwok, Phusavat, & Yang, 2021).

Intelligent Spaces

Some scholars argue that the integration of embedded network sensors and intelligent devices within the smart space is crucial for offering users a wide range of beneficial services. Among these services, the primary function of the smart space is considered to be the ability to track and identify users. Several other authors have highlighted the objective of intelligent learning environments, which is to facilitate autonomous learning, self-motivation, and personalized services for learners. The primary emphasis of intelligent learning lies in catering to the needs of learners and the learning content, rather than focusing on the equipment involved (Z. Liu, 2023). Active, digital, networked, and secure smart spaces are comprised of a variety of technologies. The environment in smart spaces is detected and controlled through the use of sensors, actuators, and computers (Meepung, Kannikar, Chaiyarak, & Meepueng, 2023). Smart classrooms can allow students to create real memories by creating virtual spaces that mimic real places (Dimitriadou & Lanitis, 2023). There are a variety of learning spaces available in modern higher education, including a traditional classroom, an online platform, and a virtual reality environment. These spaces facilitate a range of teaching and learning methodologies, encompassing collaboration, project-based learning, and experiential learning (Papaioannou, Volakaki, Kokolakis, & Vouyioukas, 2023).

Enhancing Educational Quality Through Smart Technologies

To address the significant obstacle in the professional growth of teachers, novel technologies are employed to generate continuous automatic feedback that is both of superior quality and meaningful for educators (Dimitriadou & Lanitis, 2023). In the context of an inventive learning environment paradigm, intelligent classrooms serve as a tangible setting enhanced with digital, adaptable, and environment-sensitive devices. The functional aspects of smart classrooms encompass technologies, the learning environment, and the processes involved (Omirzak, Alzhanov, Kartashova, & Ananishnev, 2022). Smart classrooms provide students with a tangible reason to utilize technology for educational purposes. The primary objective of a smart classroom is to enhance the process of teaching and learning. Typically, these classrooms are equipped with a variety of multimedia components (Kuppusamy, 2020). Smart classrooms provide teachers and students with the opportunity to tailor their teaching and learning experiences according to their preferences. Innovative technologies, such as pervasive computing, artificial intelligence, electronic chalkboards, distributed registering designs, and the design of quick spaces, are among the parameters of smart classrooms (AlFarsi et al., 2021; Palanivel, 2020).

Optimizing Learning Experiences With AI Integration

The utilization of AI in personalizing learning experiences for students is a significant advancement in education. The implementation of generative AI enables the creation of content that is specifically tailored to meet the unique needs and learning styles of individual students (Rane, 2023). It is evident that the application of AI in education has been evaluated and it has been shown that AI has the potential to enhance access to learning by removing obstacles, streamlining administrative tasks in educational institutions, and optimizing both instruction and learning processes. Additionally, AI can also facilitate evidence-based decision-making and initiatives in the field of education (Chen et al., 2020). The advent of AI in education has played a pivotal role in fostering the development of novel features within the field of education. These include the ability to predict learning performance, recommend personalized learning paths, and optimize teaching strategies (Ouyang, Wu, Zheng, Zhang, & Jiao, 2023). AI has the potential to enhance access to education by removing obstacles to learning, streamlining administrative tasks in educational institutions, optimizing instructional methods and learning processes, and promoting evidence-based decision-making and initiatives in the field of education(Chen et al., 2020; Ouyang et al., 2023).

The Role of AI in Smart Education

Undoubtedly, every individual holds a perspective regarding AI and its prospective contributions to the forthcoming education, lifetime learning, and society. While determining whether it has fully realized its potential and revolutionized any aspect of education remains subjective, the author contends that AI's track record thus far has been unsatisfactory, particularly in terms of providing learning support through technology-mediated means (Montebello, 2018). According to the author (Shah, 2023), it is crucial to underscore the human aspect of education and emphasize how AI can augment, rather than supplant, the role of educators. The author (N. D. Nguyen, 2023) stated that grouping the applications of artificial intelligence (AI) in the field of education enables us to make generalizations about various AI approaches. For instance, AI approaches focused on "Student" and "Teaching" are directly related to education. Therefore, any AI approach aimed at enhancing student learning or empowering teachers should be based on principles derived from cognitive science or educational research. However, in (No), the utilization of AI and Analytics plays a pivotal role in transforming decision-making procedures, enabling institutions to effectively navigate intricate obstacles, improve student achievements, and maintain adaptability and competitiveness in the constantly evolving realm of higher education. AI has revolutionized the field of education by introducing innovative and tailored learning approaches that have the potential to greatly enhance students' educational journeys. Through the implementation of AI technology, students now have access to personalized and comprehensive feedback, allowing them to receive individualized guidance and support. This groundbreaking development in smart education showcases the various ways in which AI is being utilized and advanced to optimize the learning experience for students (Palanivel, 2020). AI's role in education is diverse and constantly developing. The potential of AI technologies to revolutionize different facets of education is immense as follows:

Innovative Solutions for Educational Advancement Through AI

AI innovation in the field of education has progressed from idealized laboratory scenarios to practical learning environments that are more intricate (Guan et al., 2020). An important advancement in this field involves the integration of AI-based learning systems, which combine the functionalities of AI technology with pedagogical methods (Soelistiono, 2023). The company, known as the AI lab, elucidates the utilization of visual, voice, and natural language processing, besides machine learning techniques to aid students in their education. This is achieved through the implementation of an Intelligent Teaching System, an Intelligent Practice System, and a Personalized Learning System. These systems aim to enhance classroom engagement, foster student interest, and facilitate intelligent interactions (Knox, 2020). Below are a few pioneering approaches to enhance education through the utilization of artificial intelligence (AI):

Personalized Learning Platforms

AI technology has paved the way for a shift from traditional, uniform teaching methods to personalized learning experiences, thereby gradually replacing the one-size-fits-all approach (Pratama, Sampelolo, & Lura, 2023). Personalized education is an instructional strategy that strives to tailor the learning experience to the unique strengths, requirements, abilities, and interests of individual students. Every student is provided with a customized learning plan that takes into account their existing knowledge and optimal learning methods (Somasundaram, Junaid, & Mangadu, 2020). Personal Learning Environments (PLEs) have garnered growing attention in recent times. The prominent personalized learning platforms position themselves as complementary to instruction, offering guidance to educators without any intention of displacing the role of the teacher (Bulger, 2016; ES, RODRIGUES, & de la TORRE, 2011). Authors (ES et al., 2011) stated that PLEBOX expands the notion of a Personal Learning Environment (PLE) by incorporating the concept of Remote Desktop, thereby facilitating the installation of learning tools, monitoring, and communication.

Intelligent Tutoring Systems

Intelligent tutoring systems (ITSs) refer to computer-based learning systems that leverage artificial intelligence (AI) to deliver tailored and adaptable instruction to students (Lin et al., 2023). Intelligent tutoring robots possess a diverse set of abilities, encompassing the provision of guidance across various subjects. The support they offer in teaching, aiding in learning, administering educational activities through robotics, and more, can all be categorized into five primary classifications (Alam, 2022). AI-powered evaluation tools effectively assess assignments and exams, delivering prompt feedback and enabling educators to dedicate greater attention to teaching and guiding students.

Automated Grading and Feedback

Artificial intelligence (AI) serves as an immensely potent tool, enabling the automatic provision of regular feedback to students. Moreover, when teachers are faced with a substantial number of students, AI can assist them in this endeavor. Furthermore, numerous research studies have demonstrated that the automatic assessment of students is one of the key objectives sought after by AI tools, in addition to the valuable feedback they can offer (González-Calatayud, Prendes-Espinosa, & Roig-Vila, 2021). Automatic grading tools are now widely used in enormous undergraduate programming courses to cater to the growing number of students in both classical computer science programs and online courses (Leite & Blanco, 2020).

AI STRATEGIES FOR INCLUSIVE AND PERSONALIZED EDUCATION

Balancing innovation and confidentiality in the AI era necessitates the implementation of effective strategies. Robust data anonymization techniques and prioritizing data minimization in AI algorithms are two crucial strategies that can help achieve this delicate balance. By adopting these strategies, organizations can foster innovation while respecting and protecting the privacy of individuals (Rayhan & Rayhan, 2023). Adaptive learning schemes refer to personalized learning platforms that adjust themselves according to the learning policies, task capabilities' sequence and difficulty, feedback timing, and students' preferences (Kabudi, Pappas, & Olsen, 2021). Inclusive education encompasses the arrangement of schools, classrooms, instructional materials, teaching methods, and activities in a manner that caters to the needs of all students, ensuring equal opportunities for learning and participation (Garg & Sharma, 2020).

Closing Educational Disparities Through AI

The advancement of the internet and the proliferation of mobile technology have significantly amplified the potential to address educational disparities. The access gap, denoting variations in the accessibility of educational opportunities and resources, remains a crucial challenge within the realm of education (Ali, 2023). The motivation behind the creation of Artificial Intelligence in Education (AIEd) systems frequently stems from their capacity to enhance educational fairness and diminish disparities in achievement among various learner groups. One such example is the ability to extend the advantages of personalized human tutoring to a wider audience, thereby scaling up its benefits. Additionally, AIEd systems aim to address any existing gaps in educational services, ensuring a more comprehensive and inclusive learning experience for all (Holstein & Doroudi, 2021).

Personalization in Education: A Path to Inclusivity

The concept of personalized learning may appear to be a promising approach to education, but in reality, there is a lack of consensus regarding its true definition and a limited grasp on the practical aspects of creating and implementing a personalized learning environment that caters to the needs of every learner (Basham, Hall, Carter Jr, & Stahl, 2016). Inclusive education aims to cater to the needs of all students, providing tailored teaching methods that facilitate academic as well as social and emotional growth in the company of their classmates (AuCoin, Porter, & Baker-Korotkov, 2020). To encompass a wide range of learners, personalized learning must steer clear of culturally or epistemologically biased explanations. With this objective in mind, personalized learning can be defined as the customization of education on a large scale, achieved by blending automated and student-centered teaching methodologies (Lokey-Vega & Stephens, 2019).

AI Approaches to Individualized Learning Journeys

Adaptive learning refers to a teaching methodology that employs sophisticated technologies, specifically machine learning algorithms, to customize educational materials, teaching techniques, and evaluation methods according to the unique needs of each learner (Gligorea et al., 2023). It is imperative to comprehend the potential advantages and obstacles linked to the integration of AI to successfully execute AI-driven methodologies (Tahir & Tahir, 2023). Here are several essential AI techniques and strategies utilized in personalized learning journeys:

Recommendation Systems

In the domain of electronic learning, the incorporation of artificial intelligence and machine learning, specifically adaptive learning algorithms, serves as a fundamental element that significantly impacts various sectors ranging from customized learning experiences to sophisticated recommendation systems (Gligorea et al., 2023). By analyzing a student's interests and past interactions, AI-driven recommendation systems offer valuable educational resources, such as articles, videos, and books that are specifically tailored to their individual needs and preferences (T. Zhao, 2023). The realm of e-learning has experienced an increasing fascination with recommendation systems, supervised learning algorithms, machine learning, and the potential they hold for applications in the field of education (Otero-Cano & Pedraza-Alarcón, 2021).

Predictive Analytics

Student exam performance prediction is a widely recognized and valuable application of learning analytics. Its primary objective is to offer an estimation of forthcoming student accomplishments in particular exams or assessments (Tomasevic, Gvozdenovic, & Vranes, 2020). Developing a system that can consistently monitor students' academic progress and make accurate predictions about their future performance, including graduation timelines and estimated final GPAs, is a crucial aspect of effective intervention (Xu, Moon, & Van Der Schaar, 2017). The utilization of machine learning methods in forecasting the academic achievements of students, considering their background and in-term performance, has demonstrated its efficacy as a valuable instrument for anticipating both subpar and exceptional performances across different educational stages (Ofori, Maina, & Gitonga, 2020). The literature has extensively examined the prediction of student performance, with a primary focus on Intelligent Tutoring Systems (ITSs), classroom settings, and Massive Open Online Courses (MOOC) platforms (Prasad, Padala, & Kishore; Xu et al., 2017).

Learning Analytics

In recent years, there has been a growing fascination with the automated examination of educational data to improve the learning process. This field of research, known as learning analytics, has gained significant attention (Chatti et al., 2014). In recent times, the emergence of multimodal learning analytics has presented new prospects for investigating the regulation of learning as a time-based phenomenon in collaborative learning (A. Nguyen, Järvelä, Rosé, Järvenoja, & Malmberg, 2023). The fascination with learning analytics arises from the field's association with the utilization of educational technologies, coupled with its perceived advantages in tackling the frequently encountered difficulties in modern teaching methods. Learning analytics has the potential to offer personalized and timely evaluation and feedback on a large scale to classes with a significant number of students (Joksimović, Kovanović, & Dawson, 2019). Recent studies on the adoption and implementation of learning analytics (LA) in Australasia have emphasized the crucial role of teachers as the main implementers of such tools. These reports underscore the importance of involving teachers in the design of learning analytics approaches that are tailored to their specific educational contexts. These approaches need to be sensitive to the unique environments in which teachers operate, while also addressing their pedagogical needs and allowing for flexibility. By actively involving teachers in the design process, learning analytics can be effectively integrated into the educational landscape, ultimately enhancing teaching and learning outcomes (Arthars et al., 2019).

Gamification and Personalized Challenges

Gamification is gaining recognition as a compelling form of technology that holds immense promise and can be applied across various domains (Bezzina & Dingli, 2023; Khoshkangini, Valetto, Marconi, & Pistore, 2021). Adaptive gamification in e-learning is becoming increasingly important due to the need for personalized and user-centered approaches. Integrating artificial intelligence (AI) can play a crucial role in enhancing the adaptability and personalization of gamified e-learning experiences. By leveraging AI technologies, educators can create intelligent systems that analyze learner data and provide real-time feedback and recommendations, thereby enhancing the effectiveness and engagement of adaptive gamification in e-learning (Bennani, Maalel, & Ben Ghezala, 2022). The author stated that research reveals that gamification is frequently employed as a fusion within adaptive environments, such as intelligent tutoring systems (ITS) or learning environments. In this context, the adaptive component aims to cater to the individual needs of students, while the gamification aspect plays a supportive role in enhancing engagement within the adaptive environment (Böckle, Novak, & Bick, 2017).

Adaptive Learning Systems

Intelligent tutoring schemes, adaptive learning systems, and recommender systems are all notable instances of AI-enabled learning surroundings (Kabudi et al., 2021). Artificial Intelligence (AI) supported techniques for evaluating knowledge have transitioned from research laboratories to practical implementation in real-world classrooms, facilitating adaptive learning environments (Minn, 2022). Adaptive learning systems are commonly regarded as synchronous as they not only provide students with the necessary material and comprehension, but also collect developmental and behavioral data for further analysis and additional suggestions (Kakish, Robertson, & Pollacia, 2022). Adaptive learning systems employ artificial intelligence algorithms to consistently evaluate the progress of students and adapt the level of difficulty and the nature of exercises accordingly (Aggarwal, 2023).

Feedback and Assessment Automation

At present, the realm of online learning has placed significant emphasis on the investigation of automated feedback as a burgeoning area of research (Hooda, Rana, Dahiya, Rizwan, & Hossain, 2022). The field of education has witnessed significant adoption of diverse technologies due to recent technological advancements. For instance, Intelligent Tutoring Systems (ITS) have gained popularity as they aim to provide automated personalized feedback (Deeva, Bogdanova, Serral, Snoeck, & De Weerdt, 2021). The authors highlight the efficacy of artificial intelligence (IA) in feedback, assessment, and formative evaluation through the utilization of machine learning and checklists. Their study revealed that automated responses proved to be effective in monitoring students' advancement and pinpointing areas for enhancing clinical practices (González-Calatayud et al., 2021).

Natural Language Processing

AI and Natural Language Processing (NLP) facilitate the cultivation of metacognitive abilities by providing prompt feedback and guidance. This, in turn, encourages learners to contemplate their strategies for improvement while simultaneously training them to acquire time management skills and adopt effective learning methods. Consequently, these technological advancements contribute to enhancing the overall educational process (Alqahtani et al., 2023), (Abu-Ghuwaleh & Saffaf, 2023). AI incorporates NLP techniques to actively engage with student feedback, analyze it, and generate anticipatory observations regarding their perspectives on the educational framework (Shaik et al., 2022). Moreover, the potential of NLPs and Large Language Models (LLMs) to enhance the quality of education and research is substantial (Alqahtani et al., 2023).

Using AI for Educational Equity

AI and AIED experts are placing a growing emphasis on matters of diversity, inclusion, equity, ethics, belonging, and justice as transformative change in their field (Roscoe et al., 2022). Examining educational equity from the lens of technology-enabled education is a crucial research direction in the era of AI (Tanga & Chen, 2023). The fundamental principle of fairness in education lies in offering personalized learning opportunities, resources, and settings that address the distinct requirements and capabilities of each student. This approach aims to reduce inequalities and promote inclusivity by acknowledging and accommodating the diverse needs and potential of every learner (Roshanaei, Olivares, & Lopez, 2023). The concept of educational equity can be categorized into three fundamental dimensions, namely starting point equity, process equity, besides outcome equity (L. Zhang & Zhou, 2021). Online courses and remote service schemes, which utilize artificial intelligence technologies like the Internet, and cloud computing, besides big data, have a significant impact on enhancing the distribution of educational resources worldwide and fostering educational fairness (Tanga & Chen, 2023).

DATA-DRIVEN CLASSROOMS

The utilization of data-driven artificial intelligence (AI) in the field of education has brought about a significant shift, completely transforming conventional teaching approaches. This paradigm shift encompasses various applications such as tailored learning trajectories for individual students, adaptive evaluation and feedback systems, and predictive analytics aimed at identifying students who may be at risk (Ahmad et al., 2023). Both time and commitment are essential to effectively implement data-driven improvement processes. (Farran, Meador, Christopher, Nesbitt, & Bilbrey, 2017). Data-driven decision-making involves the methodical gathering, examination, and utilization of diverse data from various sources to improve student performance and cater to their learning requirements within the classroom setting (Schifter, Natarajan, Ketelhut, & Kirchgessner, 2014). Various research communities have adopted diverse strategies when it comes to utilizing data-driven methods to tackle educational issues across various levels. For example, the data mining research community employs a big data approach to address educational research problems, whereas AI communities concentrate on algorithms and methodologies as they strive to create interactive and adaptive learning environments (Ahmad et al., 2023). The discipline of Educational Data Mining (EDM) is dedicated to devising approaches for examining vast amounts of educational data to comprehend and cater to the needs of students more effectively (Singer, 2023). EDM is often regarded as the sibling discipline of Learning Analytics (LA). Its primary focus lies in the application of machine learning, and statistics, besides data mining techniques to educational characteristics (Sghir et al., 2023). The improvement of teaching quality in the educational big data environment necessitates the use of data mining to identify genuine teaching problems and enhance teachers' decision-making processes (Cui et al., 2023). A summary of the available data-driven classrooms and assessment tools and platforms is presented in Table 1.

Table 1. Summary of data-driven classrooms

Name	Key topics	Focus	Aim	Methods	format	Audience	Outcomes
(Chalong & Sripicharn, 2023)	Application of data-driven learning in CLIL	Investigates the impact of a data-driven learning approach in a Content and Language Integration Learning (CLIL) classroom	Aims to contribute insights into the effectiveness of data-driven learning within a CLIL framework	Discusses the study's methodology, including data collection methods and analysis techniques.	Offering detailed insights into the study's methodology, findings, and implications of the integration of data-driven approaches in content and language education.	Intended for educators, language instructors, researchers, and policymakers interested in the intersection of data-driven learning and CLIL methodologies	The results providing evidence of the impact of data-driven learning in a CLIL environment
(Chang, 2023)	Use of Massive Open Online Courses (MOOCs) in language education	The research examines the effectiveness of integrating MOOCs with data-driven learning activities to improve English as a Foreign Language (EFL) university students' preparedness for studying academic content in English.	Aims to contribute insights into the potential benefits of integrating MOOCs and data-driven learning activities in EFL instruction, offering implications for language classrooms	Discusses the study's methodology, including the design of MOOC integration, data-driven activities, and assessment methods	The paper providing detailed insights into the study's methodology, findings, and implications for the integration of MOOCs and data-driven activities in EFL instruction.	Intended for language educators, researchers, and policymakers interested in innovative approaches to EFL instruction	The findings from the surveys indicated that the incorporation of MOOCs, data-driven learning, and collaborative discussion activities could potentially enhance learners' acquisition of additional skills required in English as a Medium of Instruction (EMI) settings
(Zare, Karimpour, & Aqajani Delavar, 2023)	Application of data-driven learning in language education	Explores the implication of data-driven learning through the use of classroom concordance in the context of English academic lecture comprehension	The research aimed to investigate the effectiveness of implementing data-driven learning (DDL) to enhance learners' comprehension of discourse organizers in English academic lectures using concordance.	Discusses the study's methodology, including the design of concordance activities and data collection methods	The paper offering detailed insights into the study's methodology, findings, and implications for the integration of data-driven learning in language education	Intended for language educators, researchers, and practitioners interested in incorporating data-driven learning techniques in language instruction	The findings from the assessment on English academic lecture comprehension indicated that the implementation of a DDL approach, specifically through concordance, enhances the students' understanding of English academic content.
(Dunn, Airola, Lo, & Garrison, 2013)	Teachers' sense of efficacy	Investigates the process of becoming data-driven in education, with a focus on the influence of teachers' sense of efficacy on concerns related to data-driven decision-making	Aims to offer implications for fostering a data-driven culture in schools, considering the dynamics between teachers' confidence and concerns	Discusses the study's methodology, including data collection methods and analysis techniques	The research providing detailed insights into the study's methodology, findings, and implications for supporting teachers in the adoption of data-driven decision-making in education.	Targeted towards educators, administrators, and researchers interested in understanding the psychological and practical factors influencing the integration of data-driven decision-making in education.	The research present findings on how teachers' sense of efficacy influences their comfort and concerns regarding data-driven decision-making.
(Šarić, Grubišić, Šerić, & Robinson, 2019)	Data-driven analysis of online learning behavior	Explores the use of data-driven techniques to identify student clusters based on online learning behavior in a flipped classroom with an Intelligent Tutoring System.	Aims to discuss implications for instructional design and student support, considering the personalized learning needs identified through clustering.	Discusses the methodology used for clustering students based on online learning behavior, including data collection and analysis techniques.	The research paper, providing insights into the application of data-driven techniques in tailoring instruction within a flipped classroom with an Intelligent Tutoring System.	Targeted towards educators, researchers, and technologists interested in leveraging data-driven approaches for personalized learning in a flipped classroom context	Expected to present findings on identified student clusters and insights gained from the data-driven analysis

Insights From AI-Infused Classrooms

The integration of artificial intelligence (AI) in the field of education offers a significant chance to completely transform various facets of the educational system (Chen et al., 2020). The integration of game-based learning and problem-based learning shows considerable potential in developing learning experiences infused with artificial intelligence (Lee et al., 2020). The examination of students' learning outcomes about traditional ELT approaches and AI-infused methodologies demonstrated encouraging findings. Individuals who participated in AI-infused ELT exhibited heightened levels of involvement and enhanced understanding (Eslit, 2023). Recent studies have indicated that incorporating AI-infused teaching methods has demonstrated significant promise in improving language learning results. These methods offer personalized and adaptable learning experiences, while also encouraging students to become more independent and self-directed in their learning journey (Abrenilla, Redido, Abendan, & Kilag, 2023). Students must acquire the essential skills required for AI-driven problem-solving in STEM fields to better meet the requirements of the present job market (Akram et al., 2022). Research studies that have reviewed papers on AI-infused classrooms are recorded in Table 2. The themes covered in these reviews include AI application areas, integration of AI in education, tools used, approaches, and types of assessment. As can be seen from the table, the majority of AI integration in current applications is in elementary schools, middle-grade classrooms, and English Language Teaching, which is quite common. However, there are a few applications in various disciplines in some universities. Most of the authors aim listed in the table is to integrate AI in education to enhance learning experiences.

Table 2. AI- infused classrooms

Name	Application Area	AI Integration	AI Tools Used	Approach	Assessment
(Lee et al., 2021)	Upper Elementary School	Incorporation of AI tools to enhance learning experiences	Specify the AI tools and technologies utilized in the approach	Game-Based Learning with AI infusion	Methods for evaluating individual and collaborative learning
(Akram et al., 2022)	Middle-Grade Classrooms (Specify the grade range)	Specify the AI concepts integrated into the curriculum	List resources, tools, and materials essential for implementation	Curriculum Design Integrating AI concepts across multiple disciplines	Evaluation criteria for assessing student understanding and skills
(Abrenilla et al., 2023)	English Language Teaching (ELT)	Inclusion of AI technologies to enhance language learning	Specify learning and assessment tools	Emphasis on student engagement and personalized learning	Adoption of innovative assessment methods
(Lee et al., 2020)	Elementary School (Specify the grade range)	Integration of gaming elements - Gamification to enhance learning experience	Specify AI tools used (e.g., chatbots, virtual assistants)	Describe the iterative design process - Incorporation of feedback from teachers and students	Continuous assessment of individual and collaborative tasks - Gamified assessment elements

Case Studies and Examples AI innovations in Educational

- **MATHia** by Carnegie Learning utilizes GPT-4 to efficiently rephrase math questions, resulting in clearer content, enhancing student comprehension, and streamlining the process of generating customized math queries (Miao, X., Brooker, R., & Monroe, S. (2024).

- The **ASSISTments** program offers students feedback while they work on their homework problems and generates reports for teachers regarding student performance on a daily basis (Feng, M., Huang, C., & Collins, K. (2023, June).

- The **'Study Buddy Club'** demonstrates the efficacy of cloud-based programs and video conferencing technology in addressing the difficulties encountered by working parents who are homeschooling their children, university students seeking work experience, and the negative consequences of children's absence from school. This university-wide project was implemented promptly to tackle these challenges (Pinnell, J., Sabine, A., & Caroll-Meehan, C. (2021).

- **PeerWise** enables students to generate and respond to multiple-choice queries while also offering feedback to question creators regarding question quality, fostering additional opportunities for students to participate in dialogues with their classmates regarding the questions (Kay, A. E., Hardy, J., & Galloway, R. K. (2020).

- Kahoot! has gained immense popularity in Spain as a digital learning tool focused on entertainment. It is widely appreciated for its user-friendly interface, cost-free accessibility, and ability to enhance classroom dynamics effectively (Aibar-Almazán, et al., A. M. (2024).

Shaping the Future of Learning

The advancements in educational environments will be immense due to the vast capabilities of emerging AI technology and its potential future applications. Presently, we have two types of learners - humans and machines - both capable of acquiring knowledge and making intelligent decisions, metaphorically referred to as deep learners. Human learning emphasizes the creation of meaningful knowledge, in contrast to superficial learning, while machine deep learning involves intricate programming with multiple layers of diverse networks. The possibilities for leveraging AI to enhance learning are extensive; however, it is crucial to integrate AI with pedagogy and cater to the requirements of human learning (Niemi, 2021). In the future, advancements in technology might enable a greater understanding and appreciation of the essence of human learning. Similarly, when it comes to educators, the design concept recognizes the inadequacy of technology in effectively facilitating the dynamic nature of classroom instruction and the authentic expression of students' evolving comprehension (Roschelle, Lester, & Fusco, 2020). To effectively collaborate in shaping the future of education in an AI-driven world, educators and learners must have a secure environment. This environment would allow educators to contribute their professional knowledge and learners to share their distinct experiences and aspirations. Together, they can seamlessly merge ideas, establish common goals, and determine the desired values, as well as the outcomes of teaching and learning (Carvalho, Martinez-Maldonado, Tsai, Markauskaite, & De Laat, 2022). Based on the findings of the research participants, higher education (HE) students must cultivate a deep understanding of their current level of competence to meet future demands. In addition to possessing the skills to guide their competence growth with a focus on goals and the future, they must also possess attributes such as accountability, effective time management, and an entrepreneurial mindset. These qualities are collectively referred to as self-management in this study (Kleimola & Leppisaari, 2022). The search for new methods to support future capability orientation has led to a significant increase in interest regarding the potential of learning analytics. Specifically, learning analytics is seen as a promising tool for assessing future competencies due to its ability to utilize extensive datasets (Kleimola & Leppisaari, 2022). By utilizing learning analytics, a smart learning environment can observe the learning progress of students, identify potential academic setbacks, implement timely and efficient interventions to address learning difficulties, and offer personalized support services to students (Cheung et al., 2021). In the forthcoming years, the field of education will witness a surge in personalized learning, predictive analytics, and adaptive learning, thanks to the valuable insights derived from education big data and learning analytics. This will pave the way for data-driven decision-making, further solidifying the importance of education big data and learning analytics in the realm of education (Samsul, Yahaya, & Abuhassna, 2023).

CONCLUSION

The incorporation of artificial intelligence (AI) in the field of education holds immense potential to transform the methods of teaching and learning. The utilization of AI-based tools and systems can amplify the effectiveness of personalized learning, foster fairness in education, and elevate the standards of teaching. The careful addressing of ethical considerations and potential biases is essential for the responsible integration of AI-generated data. To shape the future of education, educators must be willing to adapt to the technological revolution in learning and embrace data-driven classrooms. Through harnessing the capabilities of AI, learning experiences can be enhanced and bridged the gap in educational opportunities, leading to a more inclusive and equitable education system

REFERENCES

Abrenilla, E. M., Redido, C., Abendan, C. F., & Kilag, O. K. (2023). The Next Chapter of ELT: Embracing AI-Infused Pedagogies and Evolving Educational Strategies in the Post-Pandemic Landscape. *Excellencia: International Multi-disciplinary Journal of Education, 1*(5), 124-135.

Abu-Ghuwaleh, M., & Saffaf, R. (2023). *Integrating AI and NLP with Project-Based Learning in STREAM Education*. Academic Press.

Abu Owda, M. F., Abu Mousa, A. H., Shakfa, M. D., & Al-Hidabi, D. A. (2023). *The Impact of Teaching Artificial Intelligence Concepts and Tools in Improving Creative Thinking Skills Among Talented Students Technological Sustainability and Business Competitive Advantage*. Springer.

Adiguzel, T., Kaya, M. H., & Cansu, F. K. (2023). Revolutionizing education with AI: Exploring the transformative potential of ChatGPT. *Contemporary Educational Technology, 15*(3), ep429. doi:10.30935/cedtech/13152

Aggarwal, D. (2023). Integration of innovative technological developments and AI with education for an adaptive learning pedagogy. *China Petroleum Processing and Petrochemical Technology, 23*(2).

Ahmad, K., Iqbal, W., El-Hassan, A., Qadir, J., Benhaddou, D., Ayyash, M., & Al-Fuqaha, A. (2023). Data-driven artificial intelligence in education: A comprehensive review. *IEEE Transactions on Learning Technologies*.

Aibar-Almazán, A., Castellote-Caballero, Y., Carcelén-Fraile, M. D. C., Rivas-Campo, Y., & González-Martín, A. M. (2024). Gamification in the classroom: Kahoot! As a tool for university teaching innovation. *Frontiers in Psychology*, *15*, 1370084. doi:10.3389/fpsyg.2024.1370084

Akram, B., Yoder, S., Tatar, C., Boorugu, S., Aderemi, I., & Jiang, S. (2022). Towards an AI-Infused Interdisciplinary Curriculum for Middle-Grade Classrooms. *Proceedings of the AAAI Conference on Artificial Intelligence*. 10.1609/aaai.v36i11.21544

Al-Ansi, A. M., Jaboob, M., Garad, A., & Al-Ansi, A. (2023). Analyzing augmented reality (AR) and virtual reality (VR) recent development in education. *Social Sciences & Humanities Open*, *8*(1), 100532. doi:10.1016/j.ssaho.2023.100532

Alam, A. (2022). Employing adaptive learning and intelligent tutoring robots for virtual classrooms and smart campuses: Reforming education in the age of artificial intelligence. *Advanced Computing and Intelligent Technologies Proceedings of ICACIT*, *2022*, 395–406.

Alam, A. (2023). Developing a Curriculum for Ethical and Responsible AI: A University Course on Safety, Fairness, Privacy, and Ethics to Prepare Next Generation of AI Professionals. In *Intelligent Communication Technologies and Virtual Mobile Networks* (pp. 879–894). Springer Nature Singapore. doi:10.1007/978-981-99-1767-9_64

Aleven, V., McLaren, B., Sewall, J., & Koedinger, K. R. (2009). *Example-tracing tutors: A new paradigm for intelligent tutoring systems*. Academic Press.

AlFarsi, G., Tawafak, R. M., ElDow, A., Malik, S. I., Jabbar, J., & Al Sideiri, A. (2021). *Smart classroom technology in artificial intelligence: A review paper*. Paper presented at the International Conference on Culture Heritage, Education, Sustainable Tourism, and Innovation Technologies.

Ali, A. (2023). Exploring the Transformative Potential of Technology in Overcoming Educational Disparities. *International Journal of Multidisciplinary Sciences and Arts*, *2*(1). Advance online publication. doi:10.47709/ijmdsa.v2i1.2559

Alqahtani, T., Badreldin, H. A., Alrashed, M., Alshaya, A. I., Alghamdi, S. S., bin Saleh, K., Alowais, S. A., Alshaya, O. A., Rahman, I., Al Yami, M. S., & Albekairy, A. M. (2023). The emergent role of artificial intelligence, natural learning processing, and large language models in higher education and research. *Research in Social & Administrative Pharmacy*, *19*(8), 1236–1242. doi:10.1016/j.sapharm.2023.05.016 PMID:37321925

Alrakhawi, H. A., Jamiat, N., & Abu-Naser, S. S. (2023). Intelligent Tutoring Systems in Education: A Systematic Review of Usage, Tools, Effects and Evaluation. *Journal of Theoretical and Applied Information Technology*, *101*(4), 1205–1226.

Alsobhi, H. A., Alakhtar, R. A., Ubaid, A., Hussain, O. K., & Hussain, F. K. (2023). Blockchain-based micro-credentialing system in higher education institutions: Systematic literature review. *Knowledge-Based Systems*, *265*, 110238. doi:10.1016/j.knosys.2022.110238

Altememy, H. A., Neamah, N. R., Mazhair, R., Naser, N. S., & Fahad, A. A., Abdulghffar Al-Sammarraie, N., . . . Al-Muttar, M. Y. O. (2023). AI Tools' Impact on Student Performance: Focusing on Student Motivation & Engagement in Iraq. *Social Space*, *23*(2), 143–165.

Arthars, N., Dollinger, M., Vigentini, L., Liu, D. Y.-T., Kondo, E., & King, D. M. (2019). Empowering Teachers to Personalize Learning Support: Case Studies of Teachers' Experiences Adopting a Student- and Teacher-Centered Learning Analytics Platform at Three Australian Universities. *Utilizing learning analytics to support study success*, 223-248.

AuCoin, A., Porter, G. L., & Baker-Korotkov, K. (2020). New Brunswick's journey to inclusive education. *Prospects*, *49*(3-4), 313–328. doi:10.1007/s11125-020-09508-8

Badal, Y. T., & Sungkur, R. K. (2023). Predictive modelling and analytics of students' grades using machine learning algorithms. *Education and Information Technologies*, *28*(3), 3027–3057. doi:10.1007/s10639-022-11299-8 PMID:36097545

Baidoo-Anu, D., & Ansah, L. O. (2023). Education in the era of generative artificial intelligence (AI): Understanding the potential benefits of ChatGPT in promoting teaching and learning. *Journal of AI*, *7*(1), 52–62. doi:10.61969/jai.1337500

Basham, J. D., Hall, T. E., Carter, R. A. Jr, & Stahl, W. M. (2016). An operationalized understanding of personalized learning. *Journal of Special Education Technology*, *31*(3), 126–136. doi:10.1177/0162643416660835

Batzos, Z., Saoulidis, T., Margounakis, D., Fountoukidis, E., Grigoriou, E., Moukoulis, A., . . . Bibi, S. (2023). *Gamification and Serious Games for Cybersecurity Awareness and First Responders Training: An overview*. Academic Press.

Bennani, S., Maalel, A., & Ben Ghezala, H. (2022). Adaptive gamification in E-learning: A literature review and future challenges. *Computer Applications in Engineering Education*, *30*(2), 628–642. doi:10.1002/cae.22477

Bezzina, S., & Dingli, A. (2023). *Rethinking gamification through artificial intelligence*. Paper presented at the International Conference on Human-Computer Interaction.

Böckle, M., Novak, J., & Bick, M. (2017). *Towards adaptive gamification: a synthesis of current developments*. Academic Press.

Bulger, M. (2016). Personalized learning: The conversations we're not having. *Data and Society*, *22*(1), 1–29.

Carvalho, L., Martinez-Maldonado, R., Tsai, Y.-S., Markauskaite, L., & De Laat, M. (2022). How can we design for learning in an AI world? *Computers and Education: Artificial Intelligence*, *3*, 100053. doi:10.1016/j.caeai.2022.100053

Cavus, N., Ibrahim, I., Okonkwo, M. O., Ayansina, N. B., & Modupeola, T. (2023). The Effects of Gamification in Education: A Systematic Literature Review. BRAIN. *Broad Research in Artificial Intelligence and Neuroscience*, *14*(2), 211–241. doi:10.18662/brain/14.2/452

Chaka, C. (2023). Fourth industrial revolution—A review of applications, prospects, and challenges for artificial intelligence, robotics and blockchain in higher education. *Research and Practice in Technology Enhanced Learning, 18*.

Chalong, P., & Sripicharn, P. (2023). The Effects of Data-Driven Learning Approach in a Content and Language Integration Learning Classroom: A Study of Economics Subject in a Thai High School. *English Language Teaching, 16*(7), 1–59. doi:10.5539/elt.v16n7p59

Chang, C.-c. (2023). Enhancing EFL University Students' Readiness for Learning Academic Content in English: The Effectiveness of Combining MOOCs with Data-Driven Learning Activities in an English Language Classroom. *English Teaching & Learning*, 1-26.

Chatti, M. A., Lukarov, V., Thüs, H., Muslim, A., Yousef, A. M. F., Wahid, U., . . . Schroeder, U. (2014). Learning analytics: Challenges and future research directions. *eleed, 10*(1).

Chen, H. (2024). The ethical challenges of educational artificial intelligence and coping measures: A discussion in the context of the 2024 World Digital Education Conference. *Science Insights Education Frontiers, 20*(2), 3263-3281.

Chen, L., Chen, P., & Lin, Z. (2020). Artificial intelligence in education: A review. *IEEE Access : Practical Innovations, Open Solutions, 8*, 75264–75278. doi:10.1109/ACCESS.2020.2988510

Cheung, S. K., Kwok, L. F., Phusavat, K., & Yang, H. H. (2021). Shaping the future learning environments with smart elements: Challenges and opportunities. *International Journal of Educational Technology in Higher Education, 18*(1), 1–9. doi:10.1186/s41239-021-00254-1 PMID:34778521

Cui, Y., Ma, Z., Wang, L., Yang, A., Liu, Q., Kong, S., & Wang, H. (2023). A survey on big data-enabled innovative online education systems during the COVID-19 pandemic. *Journal of Innovation & Knowledge, 8*(1), 100295. doi:10.1016/j.jik.2022.100295

Dahalan, F., Alias, N., & Shaharom, M. S. N. (2023). Gamification and game based learning for vocational education and training: A systematic literature review. *Education and Information Technologies*, 1–39. PMID:36688221

Dakakni, D., & Safa, N. (2023). Artificial intelligence in the L2 classroom: Implications and challenges on ethics and equity in higher education: A 21st century Pandora's box. *Computers and Education: Artificial Intelligence*, 100179.

Darmawansah, D., Hwang, G.-J., Chen, M.-R. A., & Liang, J.-C. (2023). Trends and research foci of robotics-based STEM education: A systematic review from diverse angles based on the technology-based learning model. *International Journal of STEM Education, 10*(1), 1–24. doi:10.1186/s40594-023-00400-3

Deeva, G., Bogdanova, D., Serral, E., Snoeck, M., & De Weerdt, J. (2021). A review of automated feedback systems for learners: Classification framework, challenges and opportunities. *Computers & Education, 162*, 104094. doi:10.1016/j.compedu.2020.104094

Dimitriadou, E., & Lanitis, A. (2023). A critical evaluation, challenges, and future perspectives of using artificial intelligence and emerging technologies in smart classrooms. *Smart Learning Environments, 10*(1), 1–26. doi:10.1186/s40561-023-00231-3

Dixit, A., Quaglietta, J., & Gaulton, C. (2021). *Preparing for the future: How organizations can prepare boards, leaders, and risk managers for artificial intelligence.* Paper presented at the Healthcare Management Forum. 10.1177/08404704211037995

Dolence, M. G., & Norris, D. M. (1995). *Transforming higher education.* Society for College and University Planning.

Dumont, H., & Ready, D. D. (2023). On the promise of personalized learning for educational equity. *NPJ Science of Learning*, *8*(1), 26. doi:10.1038/s41539-023-00174-x PMID:37542046

Dunn, K. E., Airola, D. T., Lo, W.-J., & Garrison, M. (2013). Becoming data driven: The influence of teachers' sense of efficacy on concerns related to data-driven decision making. *Journal of Experimental Education*, *81*(2), 222–241. doi:10.1080/00220973.2012.699899

El Koshiry, A., Eliwa, E., Abd El-Hafeez, T., & Shams, M. Y. (2023). Unlocking the power of blockchain in education: An overview of innovations and outcomes. Blockchain: Research and Applications, 100165.

Es, T. M. S., Rodrigues, J. J., & de la Torre, I. (2011). Personal Learning Environment Box (PLEBOX): A New Approach to E-Learning Platforms. *Education, 5*, 6.

Eslit, E. R. (2023). *Revitalizing English Language Teaching (ELT).* Unveiling Evolving Pedagogies and AI-Driven Dynamics in the Post-Pandemic Era.

Farran, D. C., Meador, D., Christopher, C., Nesbitt, K. T., & Bilbrey, L. E. (2017). Data-driven improvement in prekindergarten classrooms: Report from a partnership in an urban district. *Child Development*, *88*(5), 1466–1479. doi:10.1111/cdev.12906 PMID:28752921

Feng, M., Huang, C., & Collins, K. (2023, June). Promising Long Term Effects of ASSISTments Online Math Homework Support. In *International Conference on Artificial Intelligence in Education* (pp. 212-217). Cham: Springer Nature Switzerland. 10.1007/978-3-031-36336-8_32

Fitria, T. N. (2023). Augmented Reality (AR) and Virtual Reality (VR) Technology in Education: Media of Teaching and Learning: A Review. *International Journal of Computer and Information System*, *4*(1), 14–25.

Gambo, Y., & Shakir, M. Z. (2023). Evaluating students' experiences in self-regulated smart learning environment. *Education and Information Technologies*, *28*(1), 547–580. doi:10.1007/s10639-022-11126-0 PMID:35814807

Garg, S., & Sharma, S. (2020). Impact of artificial intelligence in special need education to promote inclusive pedagogy. *International Journal of Information and Education Technology (IJIET)*, *10*(7), 523–527. doi:10.18178/ijiet.2020.10.7.1418

George, B., & Wooden, O. (2023). Managing the strategic transformation of higher education through artificial intelligence. *Administrative Sciences*, *13*(9), 196. doi:10.3390/admsci13090196

Gligorea, I., Cioca, M., Oancea, R., Gorski, A.-T., Gorski, H., & Tudorache, P. (2023). Adaptive Learning Using Artificial Intelligence in e-Learning: A Literature Review. *Education Sciences*, *13*(12), 1216. doi:10.3390/educsci13121216

González-Calatayud, V., Prendes-Espinosa, P., & Roig-Vila, R. (2021). Artificial intelligence for student assessment: A systematic review. *Applied Sciences (Basel, Switzerland)*, *11*(12), 5467. doi:10.3390/app11125467

Guan, C., Mou, J., & Jiang, Z. (2020). Artificial intelligence innovation in education: A twenty-year data-driven historical analysis. *International Journal of Innovation Studies*, *4*(4), 134–147. doi:10.1016/j.ijis.2020.09.001

Hasibuan, R., Parta, I. B. M. W., Sholihah, H. I. a., Damayanto, A., & Farihatun, F. (2023). Transformation of Indonesian language learning with artificial intelligence applications: The era of the independent curriculum for learning in universities in Indonesia. *Indonesian Journal of Education*, *3*(2), 341–363.

Hilbert, S., Coors, S., Kraus, E., Bischl, B., Lindl, A., Frei, M., Wild, J., Krauss, S., Goretzko, D., & Stachl, C. (2021). Machine learning for the educational sciences. *Review of Education*, *9*(3), e3310. doi:10.1002/rev3.3310

Holstein, K., & Doroudi, S. (2021). Equity and Artificial Intelligence in Education: Will "AIEd" Amplify or Alleviate Inequities in Education? *arXiv preprint arXiv:2104.12920*.

Hooda, M., Rana, C., Dahiya, O., Rizwan, A., & Hossain, M. S. (2022). Artificial intelligence for assessment and feedback to enhance student success in higher education. *Mathematical Problems in Engineering*, *2022*, 2022. doi:10.1155/2022/5215722

Hu, Y.-H. (2022). Effects and acceptance of precision education in an AI-supported smart learning environment. *Education and Information Technologies*, *27*(2), 2013–2037. doi:10.1007/s10639-021-10664-3

Joksimović, S., Kovanović, V., & Dawson, S. (2019). The journey of learning analytics. *HERDSA Review of Higher Education*, *6*, 27–63.

Kabudi, T., Pappas, I., & Olsen, D. H. (2021). AI-enabled adaptive learning systems: A systematic mapping of the literature. *Computers and Education: Artificial Intelligence*, *2*, 100017. doi:10.1016/j.caeai.2021.100017

Kakish, K., Robertson, C., & Pollacia, L. (2022). Advancing Adaptive Learning via Artificial Intelligence. *Intelligent Systems and Applications: Proceedings of the 2021 Intelligent Systems Conference (IntelliSys)*, 3.

Kay, A. E., Hardy, J., & Galloway, R. K. (2020). Student use of PeerWise: A multi-institutional, multidisciplinary evaluation. *British Journal of Educational Technology*, *51*(1), 23–35. doi:10.1111/bjet.12754

Kerimbayev, N., Nurym, N., Akramova, A., & Abdykarimova, S. (2023). Educational Robotics: Development of computational thinking in collaborative online learning. *Education and Information Technologies*, *28*(11), 1–23. doi:10.1007/s10639-023-11806-5 PMID:37361771

Khensous, G., Labed, K., & Labed, Z. (2023). Exploring the evolution and applications of natural language processing in education. *Romanian Journal of Information Technology and Automatic Control*, *33*(2), 61–74.

Khoshkangini, R., Valetto, G., Marconi, A., & Pistore, M. (2021). Automatic generation and recommendation of personalized challenges for gamification. *User Modeling and User-Adapted Interaction, 31*(1), 1–34. doi:10.1007/s11257-019-09255-2

Kleimola, R., & Leppisaari, I. (2022). Learning analytics to develop future competences in higher education: A case study. *International Journal of Educational Technology in Higher Education, 19*(1), 1–25. doi:10.1186/s41239-022-00318-w PMID:35013716

Knox, J. (2020). Artificial intelligence and education in China. *Learning, Media and Technology, 45*(3), 298–311. doi:10.1080/17439884.2020.1754236

Kuppusamy, P. (2020). Emerging technologies to smart education. *International Journal of Computer Trends and Technology, 68*(2), 5–16. doi:10.14445/22312803/IJCTT-V68I2P102

Lane, H. C., & D'Mello, S. K. (2019). Uses of physiological monitoring in intelligent learning environments: A review of research, evidence, and technologies. *Mind, Brain and Technology: Learning in the Age of Emerging Technologies*, 67-86.

Lee, S., Mott, B., Ottenbreit-Leftwich, A., Scribner, A., Taylor, S., Park, K., ... Lester, J. (2021). AI-infused collaborative inquiry in upper elementary school: A game-based learning approach. *Proceedings of the AAAI conference on artificial intelligence.* 10.1609/aaai.v35i17.17836

Lee, S., Mott, B., Ottenbriet-Leftwich, A., Scribner, A., Taylor, S., Glazewski, K., ... Lester, J. (2020). Designing a collaborative game-based learning environment for AI-infused inquiry learning in elementary school classrooms. *Proceedings of the 2020 ACM conference on innovation and technology in computer science education.* 10.1145/3341525.3393981

Leite, A., & Blanco, S. A. (2020). Effects of human vs. automatic feedback on students' understanding of AI concepts and programming style. *Proceedings of the 51st ACM Technical Symposium on Computer Science Education.* 10.1145/3328778.3366921

Lin, C.-C., Huang, A. Y., & Lu, O. H. (2023). Artificial intelligence in intelligent tutoring systems toward sustainable education: A systematic review. *Smart Learning Environments, 10*(1), 41. doi:10.1186/s40561-023-00260-y

Litman, D. (2016). Natural language processing for enhancing teaching and learning. *Proceedings of the AAAI conference on artificial intelligence.* 10.1609/aaai.v30i1.9879

Liu, L. T., Wang, S., Britton, T., & Abebe, R. (2023). Reimagining the machine learning life cycle to improve educational outcomes of students. *Proceedings of the National Academy of Sciences of the United States of America, 120*(9), e2204781120. doi:10.1073/pnas.2204781120 PMID:36827260

Liu, Z. (2023). Construction and Application of Smart Learning Space in Local Universities in China. *International Journal of Education and Humanities, 7*(1), 70–73. doi:10.54097/ijeh.v7i1.5064

Lokey-Vega, A., & Stephens, S. (2019). A batch of one: A conceptual framework for the personalized learning movement. *Journal of Online Learning Research, 5*(3), 311–330.

Madaev, S., Turluev, R., & Batchaeva, Z. (2023). *Robotics and Automation in Education.* Paper presented at the SHS Web of Conferences.

Mangina, E., Psyrra, G., Screpanti, L., & Scaradozzi, D. (2023). Robotics in the Context of Primary and Pre-School Education: A Scoping Review. *IEEE Transactions on Learning Technologies.*

Martínez-Comesaña, M., Rigueira-Díaz, X., Larrañaga-Janeiro, A., Martínez-Torres, J., Ocarranza-Prado, I., & Kreibel, D. (2023). Impact of artificial intelligence on assessment methods in primary and secondary education: systematic literature review. Revista de Psicodidáctica (English ed.). doi:10.1016/j.psicoe.2023.06.002

Meepung, T., Kannikar, P., Chaiyarak, S., & Meepueng, S. (2023). Digital Learning on Smart Space to Promote High Performance Digital University. *International Journal of Educational Communications and Technology, 3*(2), 64–73.

Metsämuuronen, J., & Lehikko, A. (2023). Challenges and possibilities of educational equity and equality in the post-COVID-19 realm in the Nordic countries. *Scandinavian Journal of Educational Research, 67*(7), 1100–1121. doi:10.1080/00313831.2022.2115549

Mhlanga, D. (2023). Open AI in education, the responsible and ethical use of ChatGPT towards lifelong learning. In *FinTech and Artificial Intelligence for Sustainable Development: The Role of Smart Technologies in Achieving Development Goals* (pp. 387–409). Springer Nature Switzerland. doi:10.1007/978-3-031-37776-1_17

Miao, X., Brooker, R., & Monroe, S. (2024). Where Generative AI Fits Within and in Addition to Existing AI K12 Education Interactions: Industry and Research Perspectives. *Machine Learning in Educational Sciences: Approaches, Applications and Advances*, 359-384.

Minn, S. (2022). AI-assisted knowledge assessment techniques for adaptive learning environments. *Computers and Education: Artificial Intelligence, 3*, 100050.

Montebello, M. (2018). *AI injected e-learning*. Cham: Springer International Publishing.

Mpu, Y. (2023). *Bridging the Knowledge Gap on Special Needs Learner Support: The Use of Artificial Intelligence (AI) to Combat Digital Divide Post-COVID-19 Pandemic and beyond–A Comprehensive Literature Review*. Academic Press.

Mutizwa, M. R., Ozdamli, F., & Karagozlu, D. (2023). Smart Learning Environments during Pandemic. *Trends in Higher Education, 2*(1), 16–28. doi:10.3390/higheredu2010002

Nazaretsky, T., Ariely, M., Cukurova, M., & Alexandron, G. (2022). Teachers' trust in AI-powered educational technology and a professional development program to improve it. *British Journal of Educational Technology, 53*(4), 914–931. doi:10.1111/bjet.13232

Nguwi, Y. Y. (2023). Technologies for Education: From Gamification to AI-enabled Learning. *International Journal of Multidisciplinary Perspectives in Higher Education, 8*(1).

Nguyen, A., Järvelä, S., Rosé, C., Järvenoja, H., & Malmberg, J. (2023). Examining socially shared regulation and shared physiological arousal events with multimodal learning analytics. *British Journal of Educational Technology, 54*(1), 293–312. doi:10.1111/bjet.13280

Nguyen, N. D. (2023). Exploring the role of AI in education. *London Journal of Social Sciences*, (6), 84–95. doi:10.31039/ljss.2023.6.108

Ni, A., & Cheung, A. (2023). Understanding secondary students' continuance intention to adopt AI-powered intelligent tutoring system for English learning. *Education and Information Technologies, 28*(3), 3191–3216. doi:10.1007/s10639-022-11305-z PMID:36119127

Niemi, H. (2021). AI in learning: Preparing grounds for future learning. *Journal of Pacific Rim Psychology, 15*, 18344909211038105. doi:10.1177/18344909211038105

Ofori, F., Maina, E., & Gitonga, R. (2020). Using machine learning algorithms to predict students' performance and improve learning outcome: A literature based review. *Journal of Information Technology, 4*(1), 33–55.

Omirzak, I., Alzhanov, A., Kartashova, O., & Ananishnev, V. (2022). Integrating Mobile Technologies in a Smart Classroom to Improve the Quality of the Educational Process: Synergy of Technological and Pedagogical Tools. *World Journal on Educational Technology: Current Issues, 14*(3), 560–578. doi:10.18844/wjet.v14i3.7194

Otero-Cano, P. A., & Pedraza-Alarcón, E. C. (2021). Recommendation systems in education: A review of recommendation mechanisms in e-learning environments. *Revista Ingenierías Universidad De Medellín, 20*(38), 147–158. doi:10.22395/rium.v20n38a9

Ouyang, F., & Jiao, P. (2021). Artificial intelligence in education: The three paradigms. *Computers and Education: Artificial Intelligence, 2*, 100020. doi:10.1016/j.caeai.2021.100020

Ouyang, F., Wu, M., Zheng, L., Zhang, L., & Jiao, P. (2023). Integration of artificial intelligence performance prediction and learning analytics to improve student learning in online engineering course. *International Journal of Educational Technology in Higher Education, 20*(1), 1–23. doi:10.1186/s41239-022-00372-4 PMID:36683653

Paek, S., & Kim, N. (2021). Analysis of worldwide research trends on the impact of artificial intelligence in education. *Sustainability (Basel), 13*(14), 7941. doi:10.3390/su13147941

Palanivel, K. (2020). Emerging technologies to smart education. *International Journal of Computer Trends and Technology, 68*(2), 5–16. doi:10.14445/22312803/IJCTT-V68I2P102

Papaioannou, G., Volakaki, M.-G., Kokolakis, S., & Vouyioukas, D. (2023). Learning Spaces in Higher Education: A State-of-the-Art Review. *Trends in Higher Education, 2*(3), 526–545. doi:10.3390/higheredu2030032

Pinnell, J., Sabine, A., & Caroll-Meehan, C. (2021). *Engaging Children Online at The Study Buddy Club: A Novel Case Study*. Academic Press.

Pokrivcakova, S. (2019). Preparing teachers for the application of AI-powered technologies in foreign language education. *Journal of Language and Cultural Education, 7*(3), 135–153. doi:10.2478/jolace-2019-0025

Prasad, V. S., Padala, V. K., & Kishore, C. (n.d.). *A Novel Machine Learning Approach for Tracking and Predicting Student Performance in Degree Programs*. Academic Press.

Pratama, M. P., Sampelolo, R., & Lura, H. (2023). Revolutionizing education: Harnessing the power of artificial intelligence for personalized learning. *Klasikal: Journal of Education, Language Teaching And Science, 5*(2), 350–357. doi:10.52208/klasikal.v5i2.877

Rane, N. (2023). ChatGPT and Similar Generative Artificial Intelligence (AI) for Smart Industry: Role, Challenges and Opportunities for Industry 4.0, Industry 5.0 and Society 5.0. *Challenges and Opportunities for Industry, 4.*

Rayhan, R., & Rayhan, S. (2023). *AI and Human Rights: Balancing Innovation and Privacy in the Digital Age.* Academic Press.

Roschelle, J., Lester, J., & Fusco, J. (2020). *AI and the Future of Learning: Expert Panel Report.* Digital Promise. doi:10.51388/20.500.12265/106

Roscoe, R. D., Salehi, S., Nixon, N., Worsley, M., Piech, C., & Luckin, R. (2022). *Inclusion and equity as a paradigm shift for artificial intelligence in education Artificial intelligence in STEM education: The paradigmatic shifts in research, education, and technology.* CRC Press.

Roshanaei, M. (2024). Towards best practices for mitigating artificial intelligence implicit bias in shaping diversity, inclusion and equity in higher education. *Education and Information Technologies*, 1–26. doi:10.1007/s10639-024-12605-2

Roshanaei, M., Olivares, H., & Lopez, R. R. (2023). Harnessing AI to Foster Equity in Education: Opportunities, Challenges, and Emerging Strategies. *Journal of Intelligent Learning Systems and Applications, 15*(04), 123–143. doi:10.4236/jilsa.2023.154009

Ruiz-Rojas, L. I., Acosta-Vargas, P., De-Moreta-Llovet, J., & Gonzalez-Rodriguez, M. (2023). Empowering Education with Generative Artificial Intelligence Tools: Approach with an Instructional Design Matrix. *Sustainability (Basel), 15*(15), 11524. doi:10.3390/su151511524

Saaida, M. B. (n.d.). *AI-Driven transformations in higher education: Opportunities and challenges.* Academic Press.

Saleem, A. N., Noori, N. M., & Ozdamli, F. (2022). Gamification applications in E-learning: A literature review. Technology. *Knowledge and Learning, 27*(1), 139–159. doi:10.1007/s10758-020-09487-x

Samsul, S. A., Yahaya, N., & Abuhassna, H. (2023). Education big data and learning analytics: A bibliometric analysis. *Humanities & Social Sciences Communications, 10*(1), 1–11. doi:10.1057/s41599-023-02176-x

Sanusi, I. T., Oyelere, S. S., Vartiainen, H., Suhonen, J., & Tukiainen, M. (2023). A systematic review of teaching and learning machine learning in K-12 education. *Education and Information Technologies, 28*(5), 5967–5997. doi:10.1007/s10639-022-11416-7

Šarić, I., Grubišić, A., Šerić, L., & Robinson, T. J. (2019). *Data-driven student clusters based on online learning behavior in a flipped classroom with an intelligent tutoring system.* Paper presented at the Intelligent Tutoring Systems: 15th International Conference, ITS 2019, Kingston, Jamaica.

Saxena, S., Sethi, S., & Singh, M. (2023). Transforming Decision Making in Higher Education: The Impact of Artificial Intelligence Interventions. *Themes/Subthemes for the Special Issues of University News, 61*, 12.

Schifter, C., Natarajan, U., Ketelhut, D. J., & Kirchgessner, A. (2014). Data-driven decision-making: Facilitating teacher use of student data to inform classroom instruction. *Contemporary Issues in Technology & Teacher Education, 14*(4), 419–432.

Sghir, N., Adadi, A., & Lahmer, M. (2023). Recent advances in Predictive Learning Analytics: A decade systematic review (2012–2022). *Education and Information Technologies, 28*(7), 8299–8333. doi:10.1007/s10639-022-11536-0 PMID:36571084

Shah, P. (2023). *AI and the Future of Education: Teaching in the Age of Artificial Intelligence*. Jossey-Bass, An Imprint of Wiley.

Shaik, T., Tao, X., Li, Y., Dann, C., McDonald, J., Redmond, P., & Galligan, L. (2022). A review of the trends and challenges in adopting natural language processing methods for education feedback analysis. *IEEE Access : Practical Innovations, Open Solutions, 10*, 56720–56739. doi:10.1109/ACCESS.2022.3177752

Shvetsova, I. (2023). *The Use of Artificial intelligence in education as an effective tool for developing foreign language communicative competency*. Academy of Silesi.

Singer, C. G. (2023). *Educational Data Mining: An Application of a Predictive Model of Online Student Enrollment Decisions*. Arizona State University.

Skrabut, S. (2023). *80 Ways to Use ChatGPT in the Classroom: Using AI to Enhance Teaching and Learning*. Academic Press.

Soelistiono, S., & Wahidin. (2023). Educational Technology Innovation: AI-Integrated Learning System Design in AILS-Based Education. *Influence: International Journal of Science Review, 5*(2), 470–480. doi:10.54783/influencejournal.v5i2.175

Somasundaram, M., Junaid, K. M., & Mangadu, S. (2020). Artificial intelligence (AI) enabled intelligent quality management system (IQMS) for personalized learning path. *Procedia Computer Science, 172*, 438–442. doi:10.1016/j.procs.2020.05.096

Su, J., & Yang, W. (2023). Unlocking the power of ChatGPT: A framework for applying generative AI in education. *ECNU Review of Education*.

Subkhan, E. (2012). *Paradigm shifts on educational technology and its possibilities for transformative action*. Paper presented at the First International Conference on Current Issues in Education (ICCIE) held by Yogyakarta State University and National University of Malaysia, Yogyakarta.

Tahir, A., & Tahir, A. (2023). *AI-driven Advancements in ESL Learner Autonomy: Investigating Student Attitudes Towards Virtual Assistant Usability*. Paper presented at the Linguistic Forum-A Journal of Linguistics.

Tan, E., Lerouge, E., Du Caju, J., & Du Seuil, D. (2023). Verification of Education Credentials on European Blockchain Services Infrastructure (EBSI): Action Research in a Cross-Border Use Case between Belgium and Italy. *Big Data and Cognitive Computing, 7*(2), 79. doi:10.3390/bdcc7020079

Tanga, H., & Chen, Q. (2023). *The Opportunities, Challenges and Realization Path of Educational Equity in the age of Artificial Intelligence.* Academic Press.

Tarisayi, K. S. (2023). Lustre and shadows: Unveiling the gaps in South African University plagiarism policies amidst the emergence of AI-generated content. *AI and Ethics,* 1–7. doi:10.1007/s43681-023-00333-1

Thierer, A., & Castillo, A. (2016). *Preparing for the future of artificial intelligence.* Public Interest Comment.

Tiwari, C. K., Bhaskar, P., & Pal, A. (2023). Prospects of augmented reality and virtual reality for online education: A scientometric view. *International Journal of Educational Management, 37*(5), 1042–1066. doi:10.1108/IJEM-10-2022-0407

Tomasevic, N., Gvozdenovic, N., & Vranes, S. (2020). An overview and comparison of supervised data mining techniques for student exam performance prediction. *Computers & Education, 143,* 103676. doi:10.1016/j.compedu.2019.103676

Wang, A. I., & Lieberoth, A. (2016). *The effect of points and audio on concentration, engagement, enjoyment, learning, motivation, and classroom dynamics using Kahoot.* Paper presented at the European conference on games based learning.

Wang, X., Li, L., Tan, S. C., Yang, L., & Lei, J. (2023). Preparing for AI-enhanced education: Conceptualizing and empirically examining teachers' AI readiness. *Computers in Human Behavior, 146,* 107798. doi:10.1016/j.chb.2023.107798

Xu, J., Moon, K. H., & Van Der Schaar, M. (2017). A machine learning approach for tracking and predicting student performance in degree programs. *IEEE Journal of Selected Topics in Signal Processing, 11*(5), 742–753. doi:10.1109/JSTSP.2017.2692560

Yau, K.-L. A., Lee, H. J., Chong, Y.-W., Ling, M. H., Syed, A. R., Wu, C., & Goh, H. G. (2021). Augmented intelligence: Surveys of literature and expert opinion to understand relations between human intelligence and artificial intelligence. *IEEE Access : Practical Innovations, Open Solutions, 9,* 136744–136761. doi:10.1109/ACCESS.2021.3115494

Younis, H. A., Ruhaiyem, N. I. R., Ghaban, W., Gazem, N. A., & Nasser, M. (2023). A Systematic Literature Review on the Applications of Robots and Natural Language Processing in Education. *Electronics (Basel), 12*(13), 2864. doi:10.3390/electronics12132864

Zaman, B. U. (2023). *Transforming Education Through AI.* Benefits, Risks, and Ethical Considerations.

Zare, J., Karimpour, S., & Aqajani Delavar, K. (2023). Classroom concordancing and English academic lecture comprehension: An implication of data-driven learning. *Computer Assisted Language Learning, 36*(5-6), 885–905. doi:10.1080/09588221.2021.1953081

Zhang, K., & Aslan, A. B. (2021). AI technologies for education: Recent research & future directions. *Computers and Education: Artificial Intelligence*, *2*, 100025. doi:10.1016/j.caeai.2021.100025

Zhang, L., & Zhou, Y. (2021). *Education Informatization: An Effective Way to Promote Educational Equity.* Paper presented at the 2020 International Conference on Data Processing Techniques and Applications for Cyber-Physical Systems: DPTA 2020. 10.1007/978-981-16-1726-3_103

Zhao, T. (2023). *AI in Educational Technology.* Academic Press.

Zhao, X., Ren, Y., & Cheah, K. S. (2023). Leading Virtual Reality (VR) and Augmented Reality (AR) in Education: Bibliometric and Content Analysis From the Web of Science (2018–2022). *SAGE Open*, *13*(3). doi:10.1177/21582440231190821

Zhou, J., Li, P., Zhou, Y., Wang, B., Zang, J., & Meng, L. (2018). Toward new-generation intelligent manufacturing. *Engineering (Beijing)*, *4*(1), 11–20. doi:10.1016/j.eng.2018.01.002

Chapter 3
AI Technologies in Engineering Education

Mamoon M. A. Saeed
 https://orcid.org/ 0000-0002-6081-2559
Department of Communications and Electronics Engineering, Faculty of Engineering, University of Modern Sciences, Yemen

Zeinab E. Ahmed
 https://orcid.org/0000-0002-6144-8533
Department of Computer Engineering, University of Gezira, Sudan & Department of Electrical and Computer Engineering, International Islamic University Malaysia, Malaysia

Rashid A. Saeed
 https://orcid.org/0000-0002-9872-081X
College of Computers and Information Technology, Taif University, Saudi Arabia

AbdulGuddoos S. A. Gaid
 https://orcid.org/0009-0009-3055-1659
Faculty of Engineering and Information Technology Taiz University, Yemen

Rania A. Mokhtar
 https://orcid.org/0000-0001-9221-4214
College of Computers and Information Technology, Taif University, Saudi Arabia

ABSTRACT

The chapter investigates how artificial intelligence (AI) technologies are incorporated into engineering education and looks at how they affect methods of instruction and learning. An overview of the many uses of AI in engineering education is given, including data analytics, intelligent tutoring systems, adaptive learning platforms, virtual laboratories, and robotics training made possible by AI. The chapter explores how AI may improve the engineering curriculum by addressing market demands and future skills, integrating AI tools and software, and introducing AI concepts into coursework. It also discusses performance monitoring, intelligent feedback, automated grading, competency assessment in engineering education, and AI-assisted assessment and feedback systems. The chapter also looks at how AI affects engineering education, including using augmented and virtual reality, flipped classrooms, personalized learning, and collaborative learning.

DOI: 10.4018/979-8-3693-2728-9.ch003

1. INTRODUCTION

Industry after industry, AI is quickly becoming a game-changer, and engineering education is no exception. The way study of students, practice, and apply engineering principles could be completely changed by incorporating AI technologies into engineering education. This chapter will examine the various uses of AI technology in engineering education as well as the advantages and difficulties of putting them into practice. We'll look at how AI can improve conventional teaching strategies and open up new possibilities for individualized, interactive learning. Adaptive learning systems are one of the main areas where AI technologies have had a big impact (Pedro, Subosa, Rivas, & Valverde, 2019). By analyzing student performance data and customizing instructional content to meet each student's needs and learning preferences, these systems make use of machine learning techniques. AI-powered systems can streamline the learning process and help students better understand complicated engineering ideas by intelligently adjusting the curriculum and offering customized feedback (Adiguzel, Kaya, & Cansu, 2023; M. M. Saeed, Mohammed, et al., 2023).

Machine Learning (ML) has various applications in the field of education in engineering. Here are some types of ML used in education in engineering such as personalized learning, intelligent tutoring systems, recommender systems, automated grading and feedback, predictive analytics, Natural Language Processing (NLP) for text analysis, virtual laboratories and simulations, and adaptive assessments:

Furthermore, by offering immersive and interactive learning environments, AI technologies like virtual reality (VR) and augmented reality (AR) have completely changed engineering education. Previously unavailable, students can now participate in realistic simulations and hands-on learning opportunities. Engineering topics can be verified, replicated, and represented using VR and AR, allowing students to improve their problem-solving skills and acquire useful talents.

Nevertheless, there are certain difficulties in integrating AI technologies into engineering education. To guarantee the responsible application of AI, ethical issues, data privacy, and algorithmic biases must be properly addressed. To successfully incorporate AI into teaching techniques, faculty professional development is necessary and may also encounter opposition to change (Alam, 2021a; M. M. Saeed, R. A. Saeed, R. A. Mokhtar, et al., 2022; M. M. Saeed, Saeed, & Saeid, 2021).

We will examine these subjects and talk about the practical applications of AI in engineering education in this chapter. We'll also look at the prospects and possible developments in this area going forward, emphasizing how AI can completely change engineering students' education and equip them for the demands of the contemporary world.

Educators and institutions can make well-informed judgments regarding incorporating AI technologies into their curricula by having a thorough awareness of the applications, advantages, difficulties, and prospects of these technologies in engineering education. The objective is to establish a stimulating, welcoming, and productive learning environment that gives engineering students the information and abilities they need to prosper in a world driven by technology (Lijia Chen, Chen, & Lin, 2020).

Come along as we explore the amazing possibilities that AI technologies hold for influencing engineering practice and learning as we set out to explore its use in engineering education. Figure 1 shows the design for Artificial Intelligent education.

The chapter provides insight into how AI technology might transform engineering education and learning, making several noteworthy contributions:

Figure 1. AI education conceptual design and structure

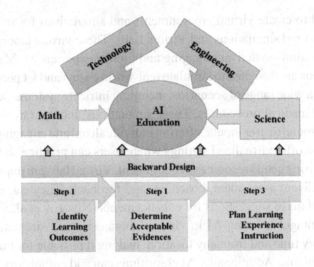

- The chapter focuses on how AI technologies, like adaptive learning platforms and intelligent tutoring systems, can tailor engineering students' educational experiences.
- Critical engineering abilities are fostered by AI technology, as discussed in this chapter.
- The chapter highlights the value of AI and data analytics in engineering education.
- The chapter examines how AI tools might help engineering students collaborate and communicate with one another.
- The ethical implications of AI technologies in engineering education are discussed in the chapter.
- The chapter focuses on how AI technologies help get engineering students ready for the workforce of the future.

The remainder of this chapter is organized as follows: in sections one and two Artificial Intelligence applications in engineering education and engineering curriculum are discussed. Section three presents an AI-assisted evaluation and comment on technical education, then in section four AI's influences on engineering education are discussed finally the lessons learned and conclusion for the chapter are presented.

2. ARTIFICIAL INTELLIGENCE APPLICATIONS IN ENGINEERING EDUCATION

The use of AI tools and methods to improve and revolutionize the engineering classroom experience is referred to as AI applications in engineering education. These apps use AI techniques such as machine learning, natural language processing, data analytics, and algorithms to enhance several facets of engineering education (Lijia Chen et al., 2020; Malik, Srivastava, Sood, & Ahmad, 2018; M. M. Saeed et al., 2022). The following are some significant uses of AI in engineering education.

2.1 AI-Powered Simulations and Virtual Labs

AI technologies are used to create virtual environments and simulations for training and education, a practice known as AI-powered simulations and Virtual Labs. These virtual laboratories and simulations use AI methods and algorithms to deliver engaging and lifelike experiences (Malik et al., 2018).

AI-powered simulations are designed to simulate real-world events and let people engage with virtual worlds. They may mimic a wide range of scenarios, including intricate systems, scientific investigations, engineering designs, and medical procedures. These simulations' incorporation of AI enables them to dynamically adapt and respond to user inputs, offering individualized and engaging learning experiences.

In contrast, virtual labs offer virtualized settings where users can practice skills or conduct practical experiments without requiring actual resources or equipment. Virtual labs are improved by AI technology since they allow for intelligent assessment, coaching, and feedback. They can evaluate user behavior, give instant feedback, and make suggestions for enhancements (Niyozov et al., 2023).

There are many advantages to using AI in virtual laboratories and simulations. Users can access virtual environments at any time and from any location, making it possible for training and education to be both affordable and scalable. Additionally, AI algorithms can add complexity and realism to simulations, increasing their educational value and effectiveness. Furthermore, data gathering and analysis are made possible by AI-powered simulations and virtual labs, which can offer insightful information about user performance and learning objectives (Niyozov et al., 2023; M. M. Saeed et al., 2023). Artificial Intelligence (AI) has numerous applications in the field of engineering. Here are some examples of how AI is used in engineering as shown in Figure 2:

Figure 2. Examples of how AI is used in engineering

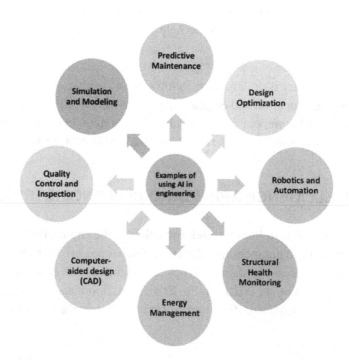

- **Predictive Maintenance**

AI-powered predictive maintenance has a lot to offer the engineering sector. It lowers unscheduled downtime, increases operating efficiency, prolongs the life of equipment, and optimizes maintenance expenses. Through proactive maintenance scheduling, firms can boost output, guarantee security, and enhance engineering operations performance.

- **Design Optimization**

In engineering design optimization, artificial intelligence (AI) is used to manage multi-objective optimization, automate design exploration, simulate and evaluate designs, enable generative design, optimize design parameters, take manufacturing restrictions into account, exploit large data, and promote human-AI collaboration. These AI-driven methods boost performance, increase design efficiency, and assist engineers in coming up with creative, well-thought-out solutions.

- **Robotics and Automation**

In engineering, artificial intelligence is widely applied to robotics and automation applications. Enhancements to perception and sensing capacities, autonomous navigation, support for robot learning and adaptation, collaboration between humans and robots, assistance with fault detection and diagnostics, control and trajectory planning optimization, quality control and inspection improvement, predictive maintenance, and human-machine interface enhancements are all made possible by it. More intelligent, effective, and adaptable systems across a range of sectors and domains are produced by combining AI with robotics and automation.

- **Structural Health Monitoring**

Engineers can improve the efficiency, safety, and dependability of infrastructure systems by utilizing artificial intelligence (AI) in structural health monitoring. Artificial Intelligence facilitates the timely discovery of structural problems, precise assessment of damage, estimation of remaining usable life, continuous monitoring, and well-informed decision-making. This helps to optimize resource allocation, prevent failures, and minimize downtime in the management and maintenance of structures.

- **Energy Management**

Engineers can maximize the integration of renewable energy sources, lower costs, increase energy efficiency, and increase the sustainability of energy systems by utilizing AI in energy management. Predictive analytics, load optimization, defect detection, and the integration of renewable energy sources are all made possible by artificial intelligence. This results in lower environmental impact, more profitable operations across a range of industries, and more efficient use of energy.

- **Computer-Aided Design (CAD)**

Engineers can improve the effectiveness, originality, and caliber of the design process by introducing artificial intelligence into computer-aided design. Design optimization, parametric design, generative design, intelligent CAD modeling, design verification, and simulation are all made possible by AI. In addition, it helps with design, facilitates teamwork, automates tedious work, and manages design uncertainty. AI integration with CAD systems enables engineers to investigate novel concepts, maximize efficiency, and shorten the time it takes to build a new product.

- **Quality Control and Inspection**

Quality control and inspection procedures can benefit from artificial intelligence (AI) to improve quality management's precision, efficacy, and efficiency. Artificial Intelligence facilitates real-time monitoring, statistical process control, anomaly identification, automated fault detection, and predictive maintenance. It enables quality data analysis, quality prediction, automated visual inspection, and data-driven decision-making. In many industries, consistent, dependable, high-quality output is ensured by integrating AI with quality control and inspection systems.

- **Simulation and Modeling**

The accuracy, efficiency, and capacities of engineering processes can be improved by integrating AI into simulation and modeling. Virtual prototyping, digital twins, CFD simulations, uncertainty analysis, optimization, physics-based modeling, data-driven modeling, structural analysis, and multi-physics modeling are all made possible by AI. Engineers can evaluate, forecast, and optimize complex systems through the integration of AI with simulation and modeling, which improves designs, lowers costs, and boosts performance.

2.2 Intelligent Engineering Concepts Tutoring Systems

Concepts of Intelligent Engineering Teaching Systems (IECTS) are learning environments that use AI technologies to deliver individualized, interactive engineering concept teaching as shown in Figure 3. These systems use intelligent feedback and adaptive learning to help students grasp and master difficult engineering subjects (Sriram, 2012).

IECTS analyzes student performance using AI algorithms to pinpoint areas of weakness and customize the learning process for each learner. Depending on the student's success and preferred method of learning, these systems can modify the material, speed, and level of difficulty of the tutoring sessions. IECTS seeks to improve student engagement, comprehension, and recall of engineering ideas by offering individualized education.

The intelligent feedback that IECTS can offer is one of its main characteristics. After analyzing student responses, AI algorithms give prompt feedback by highlighting mistakes, recommending different strategies, and providing justifications. Students' comprehension of engineering principles is strengthened by this real-time feedback, which assists them in recognizing and fixing their faults (Xue & Wu, 2019).

Figure 3. Artificial intelligence engineering concerns

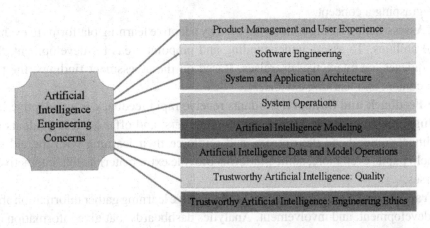

To give students practical experience and visual aids for understanding engineering ideas, IECTS frequently integrates interactive components such as virtual labs, multimedia content, and simulations. These interactive elements foster a deeper comprehension of the material by enabling students to apply theoretical knowledge in real-world situations. IECTS is also capable of tracking and monitoring the progress of students, gathering information about their abilities, shortcomings, and performance. Teachers can evaluate student learning outcomes and pinpoint areas that might need more support by using this data to create comprehensive reports and analytics.

Intelligent Engineering Concepts Tutoring Systems provide quick feedback, interactive experiences, tailored training, adaptive learning, and data-driven insights. These tools can help students gain a strong foundation in engineering principles and problem-solving techniques, which can improve the efficacy and efficiency of engineering education (Burton, 2013; Xue & Wu, 2019).

2.3 Engineering Courses Using Adaptive Learning Platforms

Engineering courses that use adaptive learning platforms are defined as online courses or educational programs that use adaptive learning strategies to deliver engineering content and customize the learning process for each student. Personalized learning experiences for students are achieved through the use of AI algorithms, data analytics, and technology by adaptive learning systems (Liu, Gao, & Jiao, 2021; Mora-Salinas, Perez-Rojas, & De La Trinidad-Rendon, 2022).

Adaptive learning platforms provide numerous important characteristics for engineering courses:

Personalized Learning Paths: To provide individualized learning paths, adaptive learning systems evaluate students' prior knowledge, abilities, and learning preferences. Students receive focused education and practice by having the platform recommend subjects, modules, or tasks based on their strengths and shortcomings.

Adaptive Content Delivery: These platforms adapt the content distribution dynamically in response to the development and performance of the students. When a learner shows proficiency in a given subject, the platform could provide more difficult content or graduate to more complex subjects. On the other hand, the platform can provide more clarifications, illustrations, or remediation materials if a learner is having trouble grasping a concept.

Intelligent Assessments: AI algorithms are used by adaptive learning platforms to evaluate students' knowledge and abilities. To assess understanding and pinpoint areas for development, they can give examinations, quizzes, or interactive exercises. Based on the assessment findings, the platform then modifies more content and learning exercises.

Real-Time Feedback and Support: Students receive rapid feedback from adaptive learning technologies that highlight right answers, clarify wrong answers, and offer advice. Students may clear up misunderstandings, comprehend their errors, and reinforce their learning with the aid of immediate feedback. To help pupils even more, some platforms provide extra materials like interactive simulations and video courses.

Progress Tracking and Analytics: Platforms for adaptive learning gather information about students' performance, development, and involvement. Analytics dashboards that give information on individual and group performance are available to teachers and students, enabling focused interventions and individualized support. These analytics support teachers in tracking student progress, identifying difficult pupils, and making data-driven decisions about their instruction.

Teachers can give students a more tailored and efficient learning experience in engineering courses by utilizing adaptive learning technologies. In addition to receiving individualized coaching and having access to interactive content that improves learning, students can learn at their own pace. Furthermore, instructors may monitor student progress, spot knowledge gaps, and take appropriate action when needed thanks to adaptive learning platforms, which eventually improve engineering education's learning outcomes.

Adaptive learning platforms that utilize AI in the field of education engineering can provide personalized and customized learning experiences for students. Figure 4 gives some examples of that.

Figure 4. Platforms that utilize AI in the field of education engineering

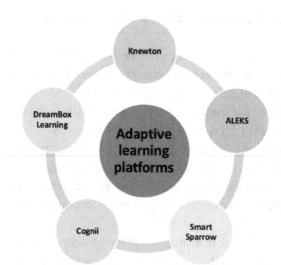

2.4 Engineering Teaching Data Analytics

The use of data analysis tools and techniques to improve teaching and learning outcomes in the field of engineering education is known as "data analytics in the teaching of engineering." It entails gathering, processing, and analyzing data about curriculum design, instructional strategies, student performance, and other pertinent factors (Ifenthaler & Gibson, 2020; Raj et al., 2019). Some important components of data analytics in the teaching of engineering include the following:

A. **Student Performance Analysis:** Data analytics allows educators to examine student performance data, such as grades, assessments, and project outcomes. By analyzing this data, instructors can identify patterns, trends, and areas where students may be struggling. This information helps educators understand individual and collective student progress, identify knowledge gaps, and tailor their teaching strategies accordingly.

B. **Assessment and Feedback:** Data analytics can be used to analyze assessment results and provide meaningful feedback to students. By analyzing assessment data, educators can identify common misconceptions, areas of weakness, and strengths among students. This information can guide instructors in providing targeted feedback and designing interventions to address specific learning needs.

C. **Curriculum Evaluation and Improvement:** Data analytics can inform the evaluation and improvement of engineering curricula. By analyzing student performance data and feedback, educators can identify areas of the curriculum that may need revision or enhancement. Data analytics can provide insights into the effectiveness of specific instructional materials, activities, or approaches, enabling educators to make data-driven decisions for curriculum development and improvement.

D. **Predictive Analytics:** Predictive analytics techniques can be applied to anticipate student performance and identify students who may require additional support. By analyzing historical data, educators can identify patterns and factors that contribute to student success or challenges. Predictive analytics can help identify students at risk of falling behind or dropping out, allowing for early intervention and targeted support.

E. **Learning Analytics:** Learning analytics involves the collection and analysis of data generated by digital learning platforms and tools. In engineering education, learning analytics can provide insights into student engagement, usage patterns, and learning behaviors. Educators can use this data to understand how students interact with online resources, identify areas of improvement, and optimize the design of digital learning materials.

By leveraging data analytics in the teaching of engineering, educators can make evidence-based decisions, personalize instruction, identify areas for improvement, and enhance student outcomes. It enables educators to gain insights into student performance, instructional effectiveness, and curriculum design, ultimately leading to more effective and engaging learning experiences for engineering students.

3. AI FOR ENGINEERING CURRICULUM

Enhancing engineering curriculum with AI entails utilizing AI tools and methods to improve student engagement, improve learning outcomes, and match academic programs with industrial needs (Chiu et al., 2021).

3.1 AI Concepts in Coursework

Including AI concepts in engineering courses entails incorporating AI's theories, applications, and guiding principles into the curriculum. Through this integration, students are better able to comprehend AI technologies, their underlying theories, and how applicable they are to other engineering fields (Alter, 2022; Liuqing Chen et al., 2019). The following are some crucial elements of teaching AI topics in the classroom:

Introduction to AI: An introduction to AI can start a course and cover basic ideas including computer vision, machine learning, neural networks, and natural language processing. Students can study the background of AI, its uses, and the moral issues raised by these applications (M. M. Saeed, Saeed, Gaid, et al., 2023).

Algorithms and Techniques: Specific AI algorithms and methods, including deep learning, reinforcement learning, clustering, regression, and classification, can be covered in depth in courses. The methods' implementation, algorithms, and mathematical underpinnings can all be taught to students. To provide students with practical experience applying AI algorithms to real-world engineering challenges, practical exercises and projects can be incorporated (M. M. Saeed, Saeed, Mokhtar, et al., 2023).

Tools and Frameworks: Popular AI frameworks and tools like scikit-learn, PyTorch, and TensorFlow can be introduced to students. They can get knowledge on how to create and implement AI models, do data analysis, and resolve technical issues using these technologies. These frameworks can be used to create AI algorithms for practical tasks and projects.

Applications in Engineering: The use of AI in a variety of engineering fields, including robots, autonomous systems, manufacturing, energy, healthcare, and transportation, can be covered in courses. In these disciplines, students can learn how AI is used to create predictions, automate operations, optimize processes, and enhance decision-making. AI in engineering can be demonstrated practically through case studies and real-world examples.

Ethical and Social Implications: The ethical and social ramifications of AI can be covered in courses. Bias, justice, accountability, and transparency in AI systems are topics that students might study. The appropriate application of AI, privacy issues, and the effects of AI on society can all be topics of discussion. Students can investigate moral standards and rules for the creation and application of AI (M. Saeed et al., 2022; R. A. Saeed, Saeed, Mokhtar, Alhumyani, & Abdel-Khalek, 2021).

Project Work: Project work in courses may require students to tackle engineering problems using AI principles and methodologies. This could entail creating models, optimizing processes, analyzing data, or creating AI-based solutions. Students can work in groups, obtain real-world experience, and apply their knowledge to situations in the real world through project work.

Students receive a strong foundation in AI concepts and methodologies through coursework, which equips them for the growing integration of AI in engineering domains. They gain the ability to create AI models, evaluate data, and use AI methods to resolve challenging engineering issues. With this understanding, they will be prepared to contribute in their future employment to the development and application of AI technology.

3.2 AI Software and Tools in Engineering Programs

Integrating industry-standard software and tools that support the creation, use, and deployment of AI technologies is necessary to include AI software and tools in engineering programs. Engineering students are given practical experience with the technologies typically utilized in AI development by integrating these tools into the curriculum (Choi, Lee, & Kim, 2021; Krishnamoorthy & Rajeev, 2018). The following are a few instances of AI tools and software that can be used in engineering programs:

1. **Machine Learning Libraries and Frameworks:** Popular machine learning frameworks and libraries including TensorFlow, PyTorch, sci-kit-learn, and Keras are available for students to learn. These tools facilitate the development and training of machine learning models by offering a large selection of pre-built algorithms and models. With these libraries, students can practice applying and optimizing models (M. M. Saeed, Saeed, Abdelhaq, et al., 2023; M. M. A. Saeed, Ahmed, Saeed, & Azim).

2. **Data Visualization Tools:** Insights from AI models must be understood and communicated, which requires data visualization. Students can be introduced to tools like Tableau, Power BI, or Python's Matplotlib to assist them in visualizing and analyzing data. To help with the interpretation and presentation of AI-driven data, students can learn how to construct relevant visualizations.

3. **Natural Language Processing (NLP) Libraries:** To help students deal with text data, NLP libraries such as spaCy and NLTK (Natural Language Toolkit) can be added. Text categorization, named entity identification, sentiment analysis, and text preprocessing are just a few of the functions that these libraries can do. Using NLP technologies, students can learn how to process and evaluate textual data.

4. **Deep Learning Frameworks:** Deep neural networks are commonly developed and trained using deep learning frameworks such as TensorFlow and PyTorch. A high-level interface for creating intricate neural network designs is offered by these frameworks. Deep learning models can be designed and trained by students, giving them practical experience in areas like speech recognition, image recognition, and natural language processing.

5. **AI Development Platforms:** AI development and deployment platforms such as Google Cloud AI, Microsoft Azure AI, and Amazon Web Services (AWS) AI services offer an extensive range of tools and services. These platforms provide infrastructure for scalable AI solutions, pre-built AI models, and APIs for diverse AI tasks. The development and implementation of AI applications can be taught to students by utilizing these platforms.

6. **Robotics and Simulation Tools:** In robotics-focused engineering curricula, ROS (Robot Operating System) and other similar tools can be useful. A framework for creating robotic systems and incorporating AI algorithms is offered by ROS. With the use of tools like Gazebo, students may study how to program robots, apply AI algorithms for perception and control, and model robot behavior.

Engineering programs that incorporate AI software and tools give students hands-on exposure to the tools that are frequently used in AI development. They gain knowledge on how to use these tools to create AI-driven solutions, analyze data, and put AI algorithms into practice. Through practical experience, they get the skills necessary to contribute to the advancement and use of AI technologies in engineering domains, as well as to meet industrial demands. Figure 5 shows the areas and industries that use AI-driven solutions.

Figure 5. Areas and industries that use AI-driven solutions

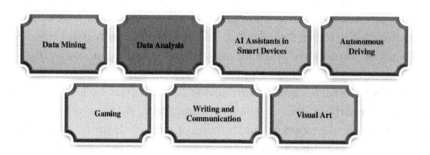

3.3 Projects and Capstone Experiences Driven by AI

Engineering students can apply their knowledge and abilities in real-world circumstances and receive practical experience with AI technology through projects and capstone experiences powered by AI. Through these projects, students can take on challenging issues, create AI-driven solutions, and showcase their skills to prospective employers (Gonzalez, Neyem, Contreras-McKay, & Molina, 2022; Martonosi & Williams, 2016). The following are some essential elements of AI-driven projects and capstone experiences:

Problem Identification: Students can recognize technical issues that AI solutions can help with. These issues may involve robotics applications, anomaly detection, image recognition, natural language processing, optimization difficulties, predictive modeling, or anomaly detection. The projects must be in line with the interests of the students as well as the particular technical field they are studying.

Data Preparation and Collection: For their AI projects, students must compile pertinent data. This may entail gathering information from a variety of sources, including databases, sensors, and publicly accessible datasets. To make sure the data is suitable for AI algorithms and of high quality, they must also preprocess and clean it.

AI Model Development: To solve the noted issue, students can create AI models. This can entail putting machine learning concepts into practice, creating neural network designs, or choosing the right algorithms. Using the gathered data, they must train and evaluate their models while modifying parameters and maximizing efficiency.

Deployment and Implementation: Students ought to incorporate their AI models into useful programs or systems. This may entail creating user interfaces, delivering the models on cloud platforms, or integrating the models into software platforms. They must guarantee the scalability, effectiveness, and user-friendliness of the AI-driven solutions.

Evaluation and Performance Analysis: Students should analyze how well their AI models work and how well they address the given issue. Metrics like recall, accuracy, precision, and F1-score can be used to gauge performance. Along with analyzing these shortcomings and potential biases, they should suggest solutions for their models.

Presentation and Documentation: Students should record all aspects of their project work, such as the problem description, data gathering procedure, creation of the AI model, implementation specifics, and assessment outcomes. To demonstrate their work, they can produce technical papers, presentations, or demos. To prove their comprehension and abilities to prospective employers or academic audiences, students must effectively communicate the results of their projects.

Collaboration and Interdisciplinary Approach: Students from many disciplines must frequently work together on AI-driven projects. Pupils with domain-specific knowledge, computer science, engineering, and data analysis skills can collaborate to establish interdisciplinary teams. This cooperative method promotes communication, cooperation, and the blending of many viewpoints.

Students gain a hands-on understanding of AI technologies and their applications in engineering through projects and capstone experiences that are driven by AI. Students can hone their critical thinking, problem-solving, and project management skills through these activities. They also assist students in creating a portfolio of AI projects that might improve their resumes and show potential employers what they are capable of. Additionally, by tackling practical issues and encouraging creativity, these programs enhance AI in engineering domains.

4. AI-ASSISTED EVALUATION AND COMMENTING IN TECHNICAL EDUCATION

Engineering students can apply their knowledge and abilities in real-world circumstances and receive practical experience with AI technology through projects and capstone experiences powered by AI. Through these projects, students can take on challenging issues, create AI-driven solutions, and showcase their skills to prospective employers.

Figure 6. AI technologies in education

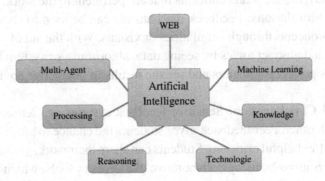

Students gain a hands-on understanding of AI technologies and their applications in engineering through projects and capstone experiences that are driven by AI as shown in Figure 6. Students can hone their critical thinking, problem-solving, and project management skills through these activities. They also assist students in creating a portfolio of AI projects that might improve their resumes and show potential employers what they are capable of. Additionally, by tackling practical issues and encouraging creativity, these programs enhance AI in engineering domains (Ngoc et al., 2023; Vinutha, Kavyashree, Vijay, Raju, & Paradigm, 2022).

4.1 Perceptive Feedback Mechanisms for Technical Projects

Using AI and other technologies, perceptive feedback methods for technical projects offer input that goes beyond conventional evaluation and grading. These tools are designed to give students incisive and informative feedback so they may better their technical projects and learn more (Chapman & Ward, 2003; Chu et al., 2021; Saunders, Gale, & Sherry, 2015). The following are some essential elements of technical project perceptive feedback mechanisms:

Multimodal Feedback: Several modalities can be combined via perceptive feedback mechanisms to offer a thorough grasp of the project. This can involve written remarks, voice comments, graphic annotations, or even instructional videos. Students can obtain feedback that is more interesting, educational, and understandable by utilizing a variety of modalities.

Contextual Feedback: The particular context of the technical project might be taken into consideration by feedback methods. This entails taking into account the goals of the project, as well as the limitations and prerequisite knowledge of the students. Students are better able to comprehend how their work fits with the intended aims and expectations when they receive feedback that is specific to the project context.

Diagnostic Feedback: Beyond just highlighting flaws or errors, perceptive feedback techniques can also offer diagnostic feedback. This entails pinpointing the root causes of problems or project flaws and making recommendations for enhancements. Students who receive diagnostic feedback are better able to identify the underlying reasons for their problems and are directed toward more efficient problem-solving techniques.

Explanatory Feedback: Perceptive feedback mechanisms can do more than just point out mistakes—they can also justify and explain the input. This aids students in comprehending the reasons behind defective or needlessly improved project elements. Explaining feedback helps students learn more deeply by illuminating the underlying ideas and concepts that are pertinent to the work.

Visualizations and Simulations: Feedback mechanisms can be used to show different techniques or to illustrate complex concepts through simulations or visuals. With the aid of visualizations, students can more easily understand abstract topics by seeing data, algorithms, or system behavior. Students can experiment with various project parameters and see the results in interactive environments provided by simulations.

Peer Feedback and Collaboration: Sensitive feedback systems can let students collaborate and provide feedback to each other. Peer feedback gives students the chance to share knowledge, see things from other angles, and offer helpful criticism. Students can share their work, give and receive comments, and participate in conversations by using collaborative platforms or tools, which promotes a collaborative learning environment.

Continuous Feedback and Iteration: Technical initiatives that are developed iteratively and continuously benefit from perceptive feedback mechanisms. At various points during the project, students can get feedback, which enables them to make changes and improvements as they go. Constant feedback fosters contemplation, an iterative mentality, and the growth of resilient problem-solving abilities.

Students receive feedback on technical projects that goes beyond superficial evaluation when perceptive feedback mechanisms are included. They receive opportunities for introspection and growth, acquire a greater understanding of their work, and comprehend the rationale behind criticism. These strategies improve the entire learning process in technical fields, promote critical thinking, and cultivate a growth mentality.

4.2 Predictive Analytics and Performance Monitoring

Predictive analytics and performance monitoring entail the use of tools and techniques for data analysis to forecast future events and track the effectiveness of processes, systems, or people. Numerous industries, including business, banking, healthcare, and engineering, heavily rely on these techniques (Asiah et al., 2019; Masood, Hashmi, Masood, Hashmi, & TensorFlow, 2019). Predictive analytics and performance monitoring are summarized as follows:

Predictive Analytics: In predictive analytics, past data is analyzed to find trends, correlations, and patterns that can be utilized to forecast upcoming occurrences or results. To find patterns and make predictions, it makes use of data mining methods, machine learning algorithms, and statistical modeling. Any quantifiable event, including sales, consumer behavior, equipment failure, resource demand, and so on, can be predicted with predictive analytics.

Performance Monitoring: Monitoring performance is keeping tabs on and assessing how well people, systems, or processes are doing either in real-time or over a predetermined amount of time. Its objective is to measure key performance indicators (KPIs) and evaluate if they are in line with predetermined benchmarks or targets. Efficiency, efficacy, quality, and other performance measures can all be learned through performance monitoring. It aids in locating inefficiencies, bottlenecks, or potential improvement locations.

Data Collection and Integration: Performance monitoring and predictive analytics depend on gathering pertinent data from multiple sources. Both structured (like databases and spreadsheets) and unstructured (like text, photos, and sensor data) data can be included in this data. Consolidating and merging data from several sources to produce a sizable dataset for analysis is known as data integration.

Data Preprocessing and Cleaning: Preprocessing and cleansing data are crucial tasks before implementing predictive analytics or performance monitoring. To guarantee data quality and consistency, this entails managing missing data, eliminating outliers, normalizing data, and changing variables. Preprocessing improves the quality and dependability of the outcomes while preparing the data for analysis.

Statistical Modeling and Machine Learning: Regression analysis, time series analysis, and classification algorithms are examples of statistical modeling approaches used in predictive analytics. By using past data, these models are taught to identify trends and correlations and forecast future results. Predictive models can also be created using machine learning methods like neural networks, decision trees, and random forests.

Performance Metrics and Dashboards: Determining pertinent performance indicators and building dashboards or visualizations to track and show this information in real time are both components of performance monitoring. Dashboards give performance indicators a visual representation that enables stakeholders to track developments, spot trends, and make informed decisions. Productivity, efficiency, customer happiness, and any other pertinent performance measure might be considered key metrics.

Alerting and Anomaly Detection: Alerting mechanisms are a feature of predictive analytics and performance monitoring that can be used to notify stakeholders when specific thresholds or circumstances are fulfilled. This facilitates the real-time detection of anomalies, performance variations from expectations, or other problems. Alerting allows for proactive measures to reduce harmful effects and solve issues quickly.

Continuous Improvement and Optimization: Both performance monitoring and predictive analytics are iterative processes. Organizations can find opportunities for optimization, update their models and plans, and continuously improve their operations by reviewing historical data, forecasting, tracking performance, and gathering new data.

Organizations may enhance outcomes, streamline processes, and make data-driven decisions with the help of predictive analytics and performance monitoring. Through the utilization of past data and current monitoring, establishments can acquire significant knowledge, spot patterns, predict upcoming occurrences, and adopt preemptive measures to accomplish their objectives. These procedures are essential in many domains, supporting firms in increasing productivity, lowering risks, and promoting ongoing development.

4.3 AI to Evaluate Engineering Competencies

Leveraging AI technology to appraise and quantify engineers' abilities, skills, and knowledge is known as using AI to evaluate engineering competencies. AI can improve and automate the assessment process, producing standardized and impartial evaluations (Cruz, Saunders-Smits, & Groen, 2020; Khan, Blessing, & Ndiaye, 2023). AI can be applied in the following ways to assess engineering competencies:

Automated Coding Assessments: AI systems are capable of analyzing engineer-written code to determine its accuracy, effectiveness, and conformity to coding standards. Programming languages like Python, C++, and MATLAB which are often used in engineering can be evaluated using automated coding tests. Software development best practices, problem-solving abilities, and coding expertise can all be measured with these tests.

Technical Knowledge Testing: Technical knowledge assessments can be conducted using AI-powered platforms to gauge engineers' comprehension of basic ideas, theories, and engineering principles. The subjects covered in these exams may include electrical circuits, control systems, mechanics, thermodynamics, and structural analysis. AI systems are capable of scoring the exams and giving the developers quick feedback.

Simulation-Based Assessments: AI can help with simulation-based tests to gauge engineers' aptitude for system design, analysis, and optimization. Through the creation of virtual simulations that resemble real-world situations, engineers can demonstrate their aptitude for problem-solving and making decisions. AI systems can evaluate how engineers performed in the simulations and offer suggestions for improvement in terms of methodology and results.

Natural Language Processing (NLP) for Documentation Evaluation: Engineers' technical reports, paperwork, and design requirements can all be assessed using natural language processing techniques. AI algorithms possess the ability to evaluate written communication quality, explanation clarity, and conformity to industry norms. Additionally, NLP can point out frequent mistakes, recommend grammatical and stylistic changes, and offer input on how the documentation is structured and organized.

Peer Review and Collaboration Analysis: AI can help with cooperation analysis and peer review to evaluate engineers' teamwork skills. AI algorithms can assess engineers' leadership abilities, abilities to operate in a team, and communication patterns, contributions, and interactions inside collaborative platforms.

Performance Analytics and Feedback: Engineers' performance can be tracked and analyzed over time by AI-powered systems, which can reveal their strengths, shortcomings, and opportunities for development. Metrics like project completion time, accuracy, efficiency, or innovation can be included in performance analytics. Engineers can improve their competencies by using tailored feedback and recommendations generated by AI systems.

Adaptive Assessments: AI can modify tests according to the performance and learning requirements of individual engineers. AI algorithms can create customized assessments that challenge engineers at the right level by examining data from prior evaluations and taking into account each engineer's unique strengths and shortcomings. Engineers are assessed according to their unique abilities thanks to adaptive tests, which also offer focused learning opportunities.

An advantage of using AI to assess engineering competencies is efficiency, scalability, objectivity, and customized feedback. It makes standardized assessments possible, lessens prejudice, and gives businesses and engineers fast insights. Engineering evaluations can be made more thorough, precise, and in line with industry standards by utilizing AI technology, which will ultimately aid in the development and advancement of skilled engineers.

4.4 The Pedagogical Theories Underpinning AI Applications in Education

Depending on the particular setting and objectives of the application, many pedagogical theories support AI applications in education. Some common educational conceptions that guide the creation and application of AI in education are depicted in Figure 7.

Figure 7. The pedagogical theories that support AI uses in education

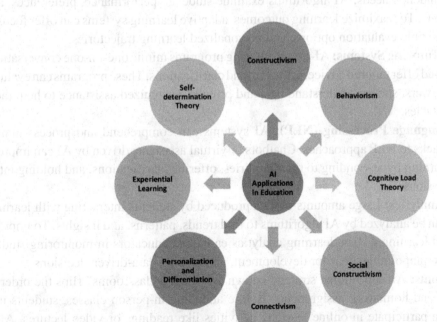

5. AI'S INFLUENCES ON ENGINEERING EDUCATION

AI has revolutionized engineering education, changing how study of students, work together and apply engineering concepts.

Even though AI has greatly benefited engineering education, there are still some potential drawbacks and ethical issues to take into account. These include concerns about algorithmic bias, data privacy, and the necessity of human supervision and direction during the learning process. Engineering education can harness AI's potential to improve learning outcomes, foster innovation, and get students ready for the changing needs of the engineering profession by judiciously and properly utilizing it (Alam, 2021b; M. M. Saeed, M. K. Hasan, et al., 2022; M. M. Saeed, Saeed, & Saeid, 2019; Shen, Yu, Lu, Zhang, & Zeng, 2021).

5.1 AI-Enhanced Learning Methodologies and Flipped Classrooms

The term AI-enhanced learning methodologies describes the use of AI tools and strategies in teaching methods to improve student learning and outcomes. One such technique is the flipped classroom approach, which flips the sequence in which homework assignments and information are typically assigned (Huang et al., 2023; Lin, Mubarok, & Society, 2021). The flipped classroom and AI-enhanced learning approaches are explained as follows:

1. **AI-Enhanced Learning Methodologies:** AI has the potential to improve several facets of education, including feedback, personalization, evaluation, and content delivery. Among the AI-enhanced learning techniques are:
    A. **Adaptive Learning:** To offer individualized information and modify the learning process to meet each student's needs, AI algorithms examine students' performance, preferences, and learning habits. To maximize learning outcomes, adaptive learning systems can offer focused resources, flexible evaluation options, and personalized learning trajectories.
    B. **Intelligent Tutoring Systems:** AI-driven tutoring programs mimic one-on-one conversations with pupils and offer tailored advice, criticism, and clarifications. These programs can evaluate students' answers, spot misunderstandings, and provide customized assistance to help them get over obstacles.
    C. **Natural Language Processing (NLP):** AI systems can comprehend and process human language thanks to NLP approaches. Chatbots or virtual assistants driven by AI can improve students' learning by responding to their inquiries, offering clarifications, and holding interactive discussions.
    D. **Learning Analytics:** Large amounts of data produced by students interacting with learning platforms can be analyzed by AI algorithms to find trends, patterns, and insights. To improve teaching and learning tactics, learning analytics can assist educators in monitoring student achievement, pinpointing areas for development, and making data-driven decisions.
2. **Flipped Classrooms:** An educational strategy known as "flipped classrooms" flips the order of standard lectures and homework assignments. Before attending in-person classes, students in a flipped classroom participate in online learning activities like readings or video lectures. After that, class time is devoted to discussions, problem-solving techniques, and participatory activities.

AI has the potential to enhance the flipped classroom approach by offering customized learning experiences and extra resources. As an illustration:

A. *Pre-Class Content Delivery:* AI-driven systems can provide students with online readings, interactive tutorials, or pre-recorded video lectures before class. Based on performance statistics and the learning preferences of students, AI algorithms might suggest pertinent resources.

B. *Assessment and Feedback:* AI can automate the assessment of pre-class assignments, quizzes, or practice exercises. AI algorithms can provide immediate feedback, identify areas of weakness, and suggest personalized remedial activities.

C. *In-Class Activities:* Class time is devoted to group projects, debates, and problem-solving in a flipped classroom. AI tools can help with group projects, give instant feedback on student work, and assist teachers in directing and tracking their students' progress.

D. *Personalized Support:* During the flipped classroom sessions, students can receive individualized guidance from AI-powered tutoring systems or virtual assistants. They can help students apply the lessons they've learned outside of the classroom, respond to inquiries, and offer clarifications.

A more dynamic, personalized, and engaging learning environment can be produced by combining the flipped classroom strategy with AI-enhanced learning approaches. It encourages active learning, lets students access the material at their speed, and frees up teachers to concentrate on helping students develop higher-order thinking abilities and deeper knowledge during in-class sessions.

5.2 Tailored Educational Opportunities in Engineering

Customized learning experiences and programs created to match the unique needs, interests, and objectives of individual engineering students are referred to as tailored educational opportunities in the area. With the help of these changes, students will be able to follow their intended professional paths and acquire knowledge and skills on individualized tracks (Crosthwaite, 2021; López-Fernández, Ezquerro, Rodríguez, Porter, & Lapuerta, 2019; Oliveira & Bittencourt, 2019). Here are a few instances of customized engineering education programs:

Specialization Tracks: Within their chosen engineering subject, students might concentrate on certain areas of interest through specialized tracks or emphases offered by engineering programs. For instance, there can be tracks available in environmental, transportation, or structural engineering within a civil engineering curriculum. These tracks offer specialized projects, research opportunities, and coursework that are in line with the career goals of the students.

Research Opportunities: Research opportunities are a common feature of engineering education that is tailored to the student. Under the supervision of faculty mentors, students can work on research projects that explore issues of interest and enhance their field. Research opportunities give students the chance to learn more about particular subjects, hone their critical thinking abilities, and get practical experience carrying out scientific experiments.

Internships and Co-op Programs: Cooperative education (co-op) programs and internships are two ways that engineering education can include industrial experience and expose students to real-world engineering techniques. Through these programs, students can use their knowledge and abilities in real-world settings by working in government agencies, engineering firms, and research facilities. Co-ops and internships provide customized chances to close the knowledge gap between academics and business, improving students' employability and professional growth.

Project-Based Learning: Project-based learning techniques are frequently used in engineering education that are customized for each student. Students utilize their skills to tackle real-world challenges as they work on engineering projects that match their interests and career ambitions. Through project-based learning, students can investigate particular areas of engineering that are in line with their passions while also developing their cooperation, creativity, and problem-solving abilities.

Continuing Education and Professional Development: Customized learning experiences go beyond typical undergraduate or graduate courses. Professionals in engineering can improve their abilities, stay current on new developments, and work toward advanced degrees or specialized certifications by enrolling in continuing education and professional development programs. These programs offer customized learning experiences that address the unique requirements and professional objectives of engineers in practice.

Mentorship Programs: Engineering students can engage with seasoned practitioners in their area through mentoring programs. Mentors assist students in navigating their academic journeys, making wise career decisions, and building professional networks by offering direction, support, and counsel. Mentorship programs help students grow both personally and professionally by providing them with individualized advice and insights.

Online Learning Platforms: Massive Open Online Courses (MOOCs) and online learning platforms offer a variety of courses and resources to create customized training opportunities in engineering. Students can tailor their learning path by selecting courses according to their areas of interest and skill gaps. Self-paced learning is a feature of many online learning environments that lets students customize their study plans to meet their requirements.

Engineering programs that are specifically designed take into account each student's interests, strengths, and desired career path. Academic institutions and programs can better fulfill the unique requirements of engineering students and professionals by offering specialized tracks, customized pathways, research opportunities, internships, and other tailored approaches that support their growth and success in the field.

5.3 Virtual and Augmented Reality in Engineering Education

Through the provision of immersive and interactive learning experiences, virtual and augmented reality (VR/AR) technologies have completely transformed the engineering education landscape as shown in Figure 8 (Criollo-C et al., 2021; Hu, Goh, & Lin, 2021). Using them in engineering education is summarized as follows:

Visualization of Complex Concepts: Students who struggle to learn challenging engineering concepts using traditional techniques can benefit from the visualization and comprehension provided by VR/AR. For instance, students can study three-dimensional (3D) models of complex engineering structures to learn more about the layout, operation, and spatial linkages of machines or buildings.

Virtual Laboratories and Simulations: Through the use of virtual reality and augmented reality, educators may design virtual labs and simulations where students can practice engineering skills and conduct experiments in a secure setting. With the use of this technology, students may test theories, replicate real-life situations, examine data, and see how their actions affect the world around them. This encourages critical thinking and hands-on learning.

Figure 8. Augmented realty vs. virtual realty vs. mixed realty

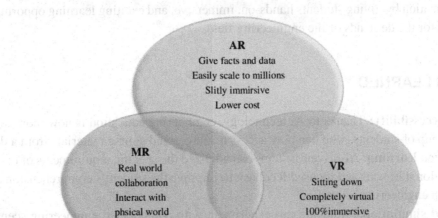

AR
Give facts and data
Easily scale to millions
Slitly immirsive
Lower cost

MR
Real world
collaboration
Interact with
phsical world
Expensive headers

VR
Sitting down
Completely virtual
100%immersive

Design and Prototyping: Students can create and prototype engineering projects in a virtual environment thanks to VR/AR tools. They can test various design iterations, visualize the effects of design decisions, and generate and manipulate 3D models. Participating in this immersive creative process improves teamwork, creativity, and problem-solving abilities.

Field Trips and Site Visits: Construction sites, factories, and engineering landmarks are just a few examples of the inaccessible or far-off places that VR/AR may take students to. Students get the opportunity to investigate these settings, see procedures, and learn about practical engineering methods without having to worry about safety or physical constraints thanks to virtual field visits.

Collaborative Learning: In engineering education, collaborative learning experiences are made easier by VR/AR technologies. Students can work together on projects, engage with virtual worlds and objects, and communicate in real-time. This encourages collaboration across disciplines, teamwork, and communication skills, reflecting the collaborative nature of engineering practice.

Augmented Work Instructions: AR can give real-time direction for engineering jobs by superimposing digital data, instructions, or notes in the real world. While working on engineering projects or repairs, students can use AR-enabled smartphones to view measurements, get step-by-step directions, and access pertinent information (Ahmed, Hashim, Saeed, & Saeed, 2023).

Accessibility and Inclusivity: VR/AR technologies have the potential to improve diversity and accessibility in engineering education. For pupils who have varied learning preferences or physical constraints, they can offer substitute learning opportunities. Geographical obstacles can also be overcome via VR/AR, giving distant students access to excellent technical resources and instruction.

Soft Skills Development: Essential soft skills in engineering, such as leadership, teamwork, and communication, can be developed with VR/AR. Students can practice these abilities in realistic circumstances through interactive experiences and simulated scenarios, which can help them get ready for professional engineering environments.

Even if VR and AR technologies have many advantages, there are drawbacks as well, such as expense, the necessity for suitable content creation, and the requirements for technological infrastructure. But as these technologies develop and become more widely available, they have the power to revolutionize engineering education by giving students hands-on, immersive, and exciting learning opportunities that will equip them for the demands of the engineering field.

6. LESSONS LEARNED

- **Greater accessibility:** Thanks to AI technology, engineering education is now more available to a larger group of students, who can now access resources and course materials from a distance.
- **Personalized learning:** AI-driven systems can adjust to the specific requirements of each learner, offering tailored lessons and focused feedback to improve the student's comprehension and proficiency with engineering principles.
- **Real-world simulations:** Students can experiment with complicated engineering scenarios in a secure and regulated setting while gaining practical experience using AI-based simulations and virtual laboratories.
- **Improved problem-solving abilities:** AI platforms and tools can give students the chance to approach engineering challenges using computational thinking and AI methods, enhancing their critical thinking and problem-solving abilities.
- **Collaborative learning:** With the use of AI technology, students can work together on engineering projects, exchange ideas, and participate in peer-to-peer learning.
- **Continuous evaluation and feedback:** Students can monitor their progress, pinpoint areas for growth, and modify their learning tactics by using AI systems to offer continuous assessment and real-time feedback.
- **Bridging the gap between academia and industry:** By exposing students to tools, methods, and difficulties pertinent to the industry, artificial intelligence (AI) technology in engineering education can aid in bridging the gap between academic learning and practical industrial practices.
- **Lifelong learning and upskilling:** By offering individualized learning pathways and materials catered to their specific professional demands, AI-powered platforms, and adaptive learning systems allow engineers to participate in lifelong learning and upskilling.
- **Ethical issues:** Talks and considerations regarding ethical consequences, such as privacy, bias, and responsible use of AI in engineering practice, are necessary when integrating AI technologies into engineering education.

7. CONCLUSION

AI technology integration in engineering education can completely transform the educational process and better equip students for the always-changing demands of their field. Learning analytics, intelligent tutoring systems, and adaptive learning are a few examples of AI-enhanced learning approaches that provide individualized and customized learning experiences that maximize student learning results while meeting the needs of each student. With the aid of AI, the flipped classroom model encourages active learning and interactive participation by letting students access material at their speed and make the most of class time for group projects and problem-solving. Additionally, the immersive and interactive experiences offered by using virtual and augmented reality (VR/AR) in engineering education allow students to create and prototype engineering projects, conduct experiments in virtual laboratories, and visualize complicated ideas. In addition, virtual reality and augmented reality (VR/AR) enable virtual field trips, collaborative learning, and the development of critical soft skills, improving accessibility and diversity and equipping students for engineering settings in the real world. Even if there are still obstacles to overcome in the form of money, technological infrastructure, and content creation, the continued development of AI technologies and the growing accessibility of VR/AR tools are making these methods more workable and viable for incorporation into engineering curricula. All things considered, AI technologies in engineering education have the potential to improve learning outcomes, increase student engagement, and close the knowledge gap between theory and practice. By utilizing AI, instructors may design specialized learning experiences, develop students' critical thinking and problem-solving abilities, and get the next generation of engineers ready to take on challenging projects and lead innovation in their industry.

REFERENCES

Adiguzel, T., Kaya, M. H., & Cansu, F. K. (2023). Revolutionizing education with AI: Exploring the transformative potential of ChatGPT. *Contemporary Educational Technology, 15*(3), ep429. doi:10.30935/cedtech/13152

Ahmed, Z. E., Hashim, A. A., Saeed, R. A., & Saeed, M. M. (2023). Mobility management enhancement in smart cities using software-defined networks. *Scientific African, 22,* e01932. doi:10.1016/j.sciaf.2023.e01932

Alam, A. (2021a, November). Possibilities and apprehensions in the landscape of artificial intelligence in education. In *2021 International Conference on Computational Intelligence and Computing Applications (ICCICA)* (pp. 1-8). IEEE. 10.1109/ICCICA52458.2021.9697272

Alam, A. (2021b, December). Should robots replace teachers? Mobilisation of AI and learning analytics in education. In *2021 International Conference on Advances in Computing, Communication, and Control (ICAC3)* (pp. 1-12). IEEE. 10.1109/ICAC353642.2021.9697300

Alter, S. (2022). Understanding artificial intelligence in the context of usage: Contributions and smartness of algorithmic capabilities in work systems. *International Journal of Information Management, 67,* 102392. doi:10.1016/j.ijinfomgt.2021.102392

Asiah, M., Zulkarnaen, K. N., Safaai, D., Hafzan, M. Y. N. N., Saberi, M. M., & Syuhaida, S. S. (2019). A review on predictive modeling technique for student academic performance monitoring. In *MATEC Web of Conferences* (Vol. 255, p. 03004). EDP Sciences. 10.1051/matecconf/201925503004

Burton, R. R. (2013). The environment module of intelligent tutoring systems. In *Foundations of intelligent tutoring systems* (pp. 109–142). Psychology Press.

Chapman, C., & Ward, S. (2003). *Project risk management processes, techniques, and insights.* John Wiley & Sons Ltd.

Chen, L., Chen, P., & Lin, Z. (2020). Artificial intelligence in education: A review. *IEEE Access : Practical Innovations, Open Solutions, 8,* 75264–75278. doi:10.1109/ACCESS.2020.2988510

Chen, L., Wang, P., Dong, H., Shi, F., Han, J., Guo, Y., Childs, P. R. N., Xiao, J., & Wu, C. (2019). An artificial intelligence based data-driven approach for design ideation. *Journal of Visual Communication and Image Representation, 61*, 10–22. doi:10.1016/j.jvcir.2019.02.009

Chiu, T. K., Meng, H., Chai, C. S., King, I., Wong, S., & Yam, Y. (2021). Creation and evaluation of a pretertiary artificial intelligence (AI) curriculum. *IEEE Transactions on Education, 65*(1), 30–39. doi:10.1109/TE.2021.3085878

Choi, S. W., Lee, E. B., & Kim, J. H. (2021). The engineering machine-learning automation platform (emap): A big-data-driven ai tool for contractors' sustainable management solutions for plant projects. *Sustainability (Basel), 13*(18), 10384. doi:10.3390/su131810384

Chu, W., Wuniri, Q., Du, X., Xiong, Q., Huang, T., & Li, K. (2021). Cloud control system architectures, technologies and applications on intelligent and connected vehicles: A review. *Chinese Journal of Mechanical Engineering, 34*(1), 1–23. doi:10.1186/s10033-021-00638-4

Criollo-C, S., Abad-Vásquez, D., Martic-Nieto, M., Velásquez-G, F. A., Pérez-Medina, J. L., & Luján-Mora, S. (2021). Towards a new learning experience through a mobile application with augmented reality in engineering education. *Applied Sciences (Basel, Switzerland), 11*(11), 4921. doi:10.3390/app11114921

Crosthwaite, C. (2021). Engineering futures 2035 engineering education programs, priorities & pedagogies. *Australian Council of Engineering Deans, Report.*

Cruz, M. L., Saunders-Smits, G. N., & Groen, P. (2020). Evaluation of competency methods in engineering education: A systematic review. *European Journal of Engineering Education, 45*(5), 729–757. doi:10.1080/03043797.2019.1671810

Gonzalez, L. A., Neyem, A., Contreras-McKay, I., & Molina, D. (2022). Improving learning experiences in software engineering capstone courses using artificial intelligence virtual assistants. *Computer Applications in Engineering Education, 30*(5), 1370–1389. doi:10.1002/cae.22526

Hu, X., Goh, Y. M., & Lin, A. (2021). Educational impact of an Augmented Reality (AR) application for teaching structural systems to non-engineering students. *Advanced Engineering Informatics, 50*, 101436. doi:10.1016/j.aei.2021.101436

Huang, X., Zou, D., Cheng, G., Chen, X., & Xie, H. (2023). Trends, research issues and applications of artificial intelligence in language education. *Journal of Educational Technology & Society, 26*(1), 112–131.

Ifenthaler, D., & Gibson, D. (Eds.). (2020). *Adoption of data analytics in higher education learning and teaching.* Springer. doi:10.1007/978-3-030-47392-1

Khan, S., Blessing, L., & Ndiaye, Y. (2023, January). Artificial intelligence for competency assessment in design education: a review of literature. In *International Conference on Research into Design* (pp. 1047-1058). Singapore: Springer Nature Singapore. 10.1007/978-981-99-0428-0_85

Krishnamoorthy, C. S., & Rajeev, S. (2018). *Artificial intelligence and expert systems for engineers.* CRC press.

Lin, C. J., & Mubarok, H. (2021). Learning analytics for investigating the mind map-guided AI chatbot approach in an EFL flipped speaking classroom. *Journal of Educational Technology & Society, 24*(4), 16–35.

Liu, X., Gao, F., & Jiao, Q. (2021). Massive open online course fast adaptable computer engineering education model. *Complexity, 2021*, 1–11. doi:10.1155/2021/7428927

López-Fernández, D., Ezquerro, J. M., Rodríguez, J., Porter, J., & Lapuerta, V. (2019). Motivational impact of active learning methods in aerospace engineering students. *Acta Astronautica, 165*, 344–354. doi:10.1016/j.actaastro.2019.09.026

Malik, H., Srivastava, S., Sood, Y. R., & Ahmad, A. (2018). Applications of artificial intelligence techniques in engineering. *Sigma, 1*.

Martonosi, S. E., & Williams, T. D. (2016). A survey of statistical capstone projects. *Journal of Statistics Education : An International Journal on the Teaching and Learning of Statistics, 24*(3), 127–135. doi: 10.1080/10691898.2016.1257927

Masood, A., Hashmi, A., Masood, A., & Hashmi, A. (2019). AIOps: predictive analytics & machine learning in operations. *Cognitive Computing Recipes: Artificial Intelligence Solutions Using Microsoft Cognitive Services and TensorFlow*, 359-382.

Mora-Salinas, R. J., Perez-Rojas, D., & De La Trinidad-Rendon, J. S. (2022, September). Real-Time Sensory Adaptive Learning for Engineering Students. In *International Conference on Interactive Collaborative Learning* (pp. 820-831). Cham: Springer International Publishing.

Ngoc, T. N., Tran, Q. N., Tang, A., Nguyen, B., Nguyen, T., & Pham, T. (2023). AI-assisted Learning for Electronic Engineering Courses in High Education. *arXiv preprint arXiv:2311.01048*.

Niyozov, N., Saburov, S., Ganiyev, S., & Olimov, S. (2023). AI-powered learning: revolutionizing technical higher education institutions through advanced power supply fundamentals. In *E3S Web of Conferences* (Vol. 461, p. 01092). EDP Sciences. doi:10.1051/e3sconf/202346101092

Oliveira, W., & Bittencourt, I. I. (2019). *Tailored gamification to educational technologies* (Vol. 10). Springer Singapore. doi:10.1007/978-981-32-9812-5

Pedro, F., Subosa, M., Rivas, A., & Valverde, P. (2019). *Artificial intelligence in education: Challenges and opportunities for sustainable development*. Academic Press.

Raj, R. K., Parrish, A., Impagliazzo, J., Romanowski, C. J., Aly, S. G., Bennett, C. C., ... Sundin, L. (2019). An empirical approach to understanding data science and engineering education. In *Proceedings of the working group reports on innovation and technology in computer science education* (pp. 73-87). 10.1145/3344429.3372503

Saeed, M. M., Ali, E. S., & Saeed, R. A. (2023). Data-Driven Techniques and Security Issues in Wireless Networks. *Data-Driven Intelligence in Wireless Networks: Concepts, Solutions, and Applications*, 107.

Saeed, M. M., Hasan, M. K., Obaid, A. J., Saeed, R. A., Mokhtar, R. A., Ali, E. S., Akhtaruzzaman, M., Amanlou, S., & Hossain, A. Z. (2022). A comprehensive review on the users' identity privacy for 5G networks. *IET Communications, 16*(5), 384–399. doi:10.1049/cmu2.12327

Saeed, M. M., Kamrul Hasan, M., Hassan, R., Mokhtar, R., Saeed, R. A., Saeid, E., & Gupta, M. (2022). Preserving Privacy of User Identity Based on Pseudonym Variable in 5G. *Computers, Materials & Continua, 70*(3). Advance online publication. doi:10.32604/cmc.2022.017338

Saeed, M. M., Mohammed, H. N. R., Gazem, O. A. H., Saeed, R. A., Morei, H. M. A., Eidah, A. E. T., . . . Al-Madhagi, M. G. Q. (2023, October). Machine Learning Techniques for Detecting DDOS Attacks. In *2023 3rd International Conference on Emerging Smart Technologies and Applications (eSmarTA)* (pp. 1-6). IEEE. 10.1109/eSmarTA59349.2023.10293366

Saeed, M. M., Saeed, R. A., Abdelhaq, M., Alsaqour, R., Hasan, M. K., & Mokhtar, R. A. (2023). Anomaly Detection in 6G Networks Using Machine Learning Methods. *Electronics (Basel), 12*(15), 3300. doi:10.3390/electronics12153300

Saeed, M. M., Saeed, R. A., Azim, M. A., Ali, E. S., Mokhtar, R. A., & Khalifa, O. (2022, May). Green Machine Learning Approach for QoS Improvement in Cellular Communications. In *2022 IEEE 2nd International Maghreb Meeting of the Conference on Sciences and Techniques of Automatic Control and Computer Engineering (MI-STA)* (pp. 523-528). IEEE. 10.1109/MI-STA54861.2022.9837585

Saeed, M. M., Saeed, R. A., Gaid, A. S., Mokhtar, R. A., Khalifa, O. O., & Ahmed, Z. E. (2023, August). Attacks Detection in 6G Wireless Networks using Machine Learning. In *2023 9th International Conference on Computer and Communication Engineering (ICCCE)* (pp. 6-11). IEEE.

Saeed, M. M., Saeed, R. A., Mokhtar, R. A., Alhumyani, H., & Ali, E. S. (2022). A novel variable pseudonym scheme for preserving privacy user location in 5G networks. *Security and Communication Networks, 2022,* 2022. doi:10.1155/2022/7487600

Saeed, M. M., Saeed, R. A., Mokhtar, R. A., Khalifa, O. O., Ahmed, Z. E., Barakat, M., & Elnaim, A. A. (2023, August). Task Reverse Offloading with Deep Reinforcement Learning in Multi-Access Edge Computing. In *2023 9th International Conference on Computer and Communication Engineering (ICCCE)* (pp. 322-327). IEEE. 10.1109/ICCCE58854.2023.10246081

Saeed, M. M., Saeed, R. A., & Saeid, E. (2019, December). Preserving privacy of paging procedure in 5 th G using identity-division multiplexing. In *2019 First International Conference of Intelligent Computing and Engineering (ICOICE)* (pp. 1-6). IEEE.

Saeed, M. M., Saeed, R. A., & Saeid, E. (2021, March). Identity division multiplexing based location preserve in 5G. In *2021 International Conference of Technology, Science and Administration (ICTSA)* (pp. 1-6). IEEE. 10.1109/ICTSA52017.2021.9406554

Saeed, M. M. A., Ahmed, E. S. A., Saeed, R. A., & Azim, M. A. Green machine learning protocols for cellular communication. In *Green Machine Learning Protocols for Future Communication Networks* (pp. 15–62). CRC Press.

Saeed, R. A., Saeed, M. M., Mokhtar, R. A., Alhumyani, H., & Abdel-Khalek, S. (2021). Pseudonym Mutable Based Privacy for 5G User Identity. *Computer Systems Science and Engineering, 39*(1). Advance online publication. doi:10.32604/csse.2021.015593

Saunders, F. C., Gale, A. W., & Sherry, A. H. (2015). Conceptualising uncertainty in safety-critical projects: A practitioner perspective. *International Journal of Project Management, 33*(2), 467–478. doi:10.1016/j.ijproman.2014.09.002

Shen, Y., Yu, P., Lu, H., Zhang, X., & Zeng, H. (2021). An AI-based virtual simulation experimental teaching system in space engineering education. *Computer Applications in Engineering Education, 29*(2), 329–338. doi:10.1002/cae.22221

Sriram, R. D. (2012). *Intelligent systems for engineering: a knowledge-based approach.* Springer Science & Business Media.

Vinutha, D. C., Kavyashree, S., Vijay, C. P., & Raju, G. T. (2022). Innovative Practices in Education Systems Using Artificial Intelligence for Advanced Society. *The New Advanced Society: Artificial Intelligence and Industrial Internet of Things Paradigm*, 351-372.

Xue, R., & Wu, Z. (2019). A survey of application and classification on teaching-learning-based optimization algorithm. *IEEE Access : Practical Innovations, Open Solutions, 8*, 1062–1079. doi:10.1109/ACCESS.2019.2960388

Chapter 4
AI–Enhanced Education:
Bridging Educational Disparities

Zeinab E. Ahmed

ⓘ https://orcid.org/0000-0002-6144-8533

Department of Computer Engineering, University of Gezira, Sudan & Department of Electrical and Computer Engineering, International Islamic University Malaysia, Malaysia

Aisha Hassan Abdalla Hashim

International Islamic University Malaysia, Malaysia

Rashid A. Saeed

ⓘ https://orcid.org/0000-0002-9872-081X

Taif University, Saudi Arabia

Mamoon M. A. Saeed

ⓘ https://orcid.org/0000-0002-6081-2559

Department of Communications and Electronics Engineering, Faculty of Engineering, University of Modern Sciences, Yemen

ABSTRACT

This chapter explores the symbiotic relationship between AI and education, highlighting its transformative impact and potential to bridge educational disparities. It provides insights into using AI to create engaging and efficient learning environments, covering various topics such as AI-driven teaching techniques, ethical considerations, and case studies. AI tools enhance learning experiences and help address disparities among students. The integration of AI in education can optimize resources, personalize learning, and improve academic performance. However, challenges such as lack of familiarity and technical difficulties need to be addressed through training and support for teachers. By embracing AI, educators can revolutionize teaching methods and promote equity and inclusivity in education.

DOI: 10.4018/979-8-3693-2728-9.ch004

1. INTRODUCTION

Artificial intelligence (AI) technologies are fundamentally changing how digital machines accomplish tasks, completely altering communication, learning, and work processes. Recent researchers are exploring the integration of AI in Education (AI-Edu), from K-12 to higher education levels. AI tools like intelligent tutoring systems, chatbots, and robotics aid kindergarten teachers and enhance student learning (Su et al., 2023). It offers personalized learning, enhances teaching, and administration by providing immediate feedback and machine-supported queries. The impact of AI-Edu extends to transforming teaching methods and program development, rendering it a pivotal focus in educational research which can be supported by adaptive learning systems personalize experiences, data-driven insights improve strategies, and task automation frees time for innovation; enhanced collaboration among educators fosters continuous improvement, while personalized feedback and predictive analytics support student success and program refinement (Liang et al., 2023). It contributes to enhancing teachers' insights into students' learning processes. However, there is a need for additional endeavors to seamlessly integrate advanced AI and deep learning technologies into educational environments. The various roles of AI applications encompass intelligent tutor, tutee, learning tool/partner, and policy-making advisor.

Artificial intelligence (AI) has promise for addressing some of the most pressing issues facing education today, innovating in methods of instruction and learning, and accelerating the achievement of SDG 41. AI can help educators identify and address disparities among students individually, develop balanced and meaningful curriculum plans, and optimize learning resources. AI tutoring systems can adapt to students' learning progression in real-time, while machine learning programs could tailor college recruiting efforts to reach more students from underrepresented groups. In order to achieve the Education 2030 Agenda, UNESCO is dedicated to supporting Member States in utilizing AI technology, while making sure that the basic principles of equity and inclusivity serve as a guide for its application in educational settings. Global initiatives and policy changes highlight the importance of AI-Edu. Countries like China and the US are promoting AI integration in education, focusing on teacher development (Chiu et al., 2023). Funding in the US supports AI-based personalized learning platforms to improve academic performance and reduce inequalities. Figure 1 shows the challenges in conventional educations and the needs for new types of education.

AI can play a significant role in identifying and addressing learning gaps in students. Intelligent tutoring systems and AI-driven learning platforms can collect and analyze data on students' behavior and interactions. This data can provide insights into individual students' strengths, weaknesses, and learning progress. AI algorithms can then generate personalized recommendations, tasks, and resources tailored to each student's specific needs. By leveraging AI, educators can identify learning gaps more efficiently and provide targeted interventions to address them, ultimately enhancing students' learning outcomes.

The need for AI in education arises from its potential to bring about significant benefits at both personal and societal levels. Although AI is often underutilized due to resistance to change, it has great potential to improve educational systems. AI should not be seen as a replacement for human teachers but as a tool to assist and empower them. By automating administrative tasks such as grading and data analysis, AI frees up teachers' time, allowing them to focus on more productive work (Srinivasa et al., 2022). It can also help struggling students by providing personalized study plans tailored to their individual needs. AI's ability to understand and adapt to students' responses to different teaching methods can assist teachers in delivering more effective instruction. Therefore, recognizing the need for AI in education and embracing its benefits can lead to enhanced educational experiences and better outcomes for students. The utilization of AI-Edu presents multifaceted opportunities, for example of how AI-Edu will be applied for Sustainable Development Goals (SDGs) i.e., Personalized Learning (SDG 4 - Quality Education), Augmented Teaching (SDG 4 - Quality Education), Enhanced Content Creation (SDG 4 - Quality Education), Data-driven Decision Making (SDG 4 - Quality Education), Accessibility and Inclusivity (SDG 4 - Quality Education), Lifelong Learning and Skills Development (SDG 4 - Quality Education and SDG 8 - Decent Work and Economic Growth), Automated Administrative Tasks (SDG 9 - Industry, Innovation, and Infrastructure and SDG 16 - Peace, Justice, and Strong Institutions)

Figure 1. Challenges in conventional education systems

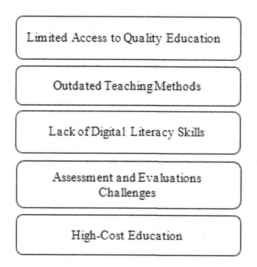

AI-driven technologies enhance the learning experience by providing intelligent tutoring, personalized learning, and recommendation systems, allowing for tailored learning profiles based on individual needs, abilities, and preferences. The increased accessibility of AI-equipped learning management tools fosters widespread availability in online education. AI facilitates improved instructional design, enabling the generation of personalized support, automatic communication, and interactive learning environments (Owoc et al., 2021). Simulated and authentic learning experiences, powered by AI, offer realistic scenarios and virtual agents, enhancing learners' understanding.

AI contributes to personalized feedback, automated grading, and early identification of at-risk students, fostering better academic performance. Data-driven decision-making empowers teachers to adapt strategies based on real-time insights, while AI technologies streamline administrative tasks, freeing up time for instructional activities. Moreover, the adoption of AI-Edu provides professional development opportunities for educators to enhance their AI digital competencies, ultimately enriching students' learning experiences in online and blended learning environments. It is imperative for educators to seize this opportunity and cultivate their AI proficiency for the benefit of teaching and student engagement. While there are numerous opportunities associated with the integration of AI in education (AI-Edu), it is crucial to acknowledge that there are also substantial challenges. These challenges can be summarized as follows:

- Lack of familiarity with novel technologies: Teachers may not be familiar with the technical aspects of AI and other broader skills required for effective implementation, such as communication, collaboration, and multidisciplinary skills. This lack of familiarity can hinder their ability to effectively use AI applications in their teaching.

- Technical difficulties: Designing an AI-driven learning environment can pose technical challenges for teachers. They may face difficulties in enabling students to use AI applications and compile algorithms. This requires technical expertise and support, which may not be readily available.

- Insufficient funding and resources: The implementation of AI in education may require additional funding and resources. Teachers may face challenges in accessing the necessary tools, curricula, and evaluation methods for effective integration of AI technologies.

- Adaptation to digital transformation: AI-driven platforms offer new ways of creating and delivering instructional content. However, teachers may find it challenging to adapt to these new requirements, especially if they have not received training or support in utilizing AI technologies. The rapid shift to online learning and the incorporation of AI education present additional complexities and demands for teachers.

- Technical problems affecting instructional quality: Technical difficulties can have a negative impact on the quality of content delivery, instructional design, and assessments. Teachers may struggle to overcome these technical challenges, leading to limitations in their ability to effectively use AI and deliver high-quality instruction.

- Need for technological knowledge and skills: Teachers need to acquire AI-related technological skills to enhance student learning. This includes skills in facilitating knowledge acquisition and expression, as well as interacting with learners using AI technologies such as chatbots and automatic feedback systems.

To ensure well-qualified teachers in AI-enhanced classrooms, it is important for teachers to receive training and support to develop the necessary technological skills and overcome the challenges associated with AI integration in online teaching. Figure 2 shows the role of AI in bridging educational disparities.

The reminder of this chapter is structured as follows: in section Two the Role of AI in Modern Education and Personalized Learning is discussed. Section Three Addressing the Disparities in Education with AI. The Emerging Trends and Future Prospects were presented in section Four. Finally, the chapter is concluded in Section Five.

2. THE ROLE OF AI IN MODERN EDUCATION AND PERSONALIZED LEARNING

The significance of Artificial Intelligence (AI) in contemporary education and the realm of personalized learning is a subject of considerable interest. AI-driven personalized learning represents a student-centric methodology designed to counteract issues of student disengagement in the educational landscape. Through tailoring learning experiences to individual requirements, interests, and pace, AI introduces adaptive content, interactive elements, and data analysis to enhance learning outcomes. The incorporation of AI into education dates back to the 1970s, covering applications related to personalized learning, assessment tools, and administrative systems. Leveraging AI technologies, educational institutions can analyze extensive datasets, including students' performance metrics, learning tendencies, and preferences, to customize instruction according to individual needs. AI-infused learning platforms have the capability to adjust the content and pacing of instruction based on each student's learning style, capabilities, and interests, offering personalized learning trajectories. This personalized approach fosters more effective student engagement, allows progression at individualized paces, and contributes to improved learning achievements. Furthermore, AI facilitates the automation of administrative tasks like grading, scheduling, and course planning, enabling educators to allocate more time to providing personalized guidance and support to students. The following outlines key facets of AI's role in contemporary education and personalized learning:

Figure 2. The role of AI in learning

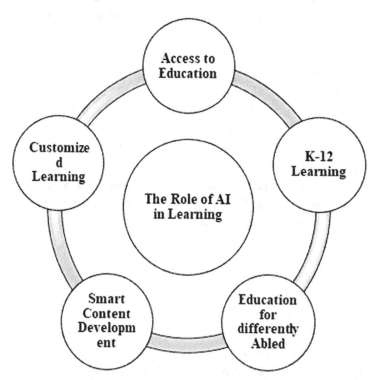

Personalized Learning: According to (Einarsson et al., 2024), personalized learning is a successful strategy that aims to improve each learner's educational experience. All learners, regardless of their unique requirements and preferences, get access to the same information with traditional e-learning platforms. But now that AI-based personalized e-learning systems have been developed, it is possible to give every learner with tests and learning content that are tailored to their needs. These personalized systems utilize artificial intelligence techniques to determine the learner's level of comprehension and preferred modes of learning (Murtaza et al., 2022). By analyzing factors such as the learner's strengths and weaknesses, personalized e-learning systems can deliver targeted content, repeat challenging topics, and provide advanced materials to promote individual progress. Adaptive learning and adaptable learning are two widely employed methods for delivering personalized content, where recommendations and content delivery modes are customized based on the learner's comprehension level and preferred learning style (Ingavelez-Guerra et al., 2022).

The integration of knowledge tracing, learning mode adaptation, and recommender systems within a comprehensive framework further strengthens the efficacy of personalized e-learning systems. Such systems not only address the challenges of delivering effective online education but also provide cost-effective methods to educate the masses (Ouyang et al., 2022). To implement personalized e-learning successfully, there is a need for robust mechanisms for continuous learner assessment, appropriate content matching using machine learning and deep learning models, and efficient recommendation systems. The field of personalized e-learning offers immense potential for future research and development, paving the way for innovative approaches to education (Teh & Baskaran, 2022).

Intelligent Tutoring Systems (ITS): ITS have emerged as influential tools for delivering personalized and adaptive learning experiences, representing a prominent area of research and development within Artificial Intelligence in Education (Heck & Meurers, 2023). These systems are designed to enhance the learning journey by offering individualized and adaptive instruction. Recent literature extensively explores the transformative potential of AI in shaping education and advancing the realm of interactive learning systems. AI, particularly in the form of ITS, utilizes machine learning algorithms to discern students' individual strengths, weaknesses, and learning behaviors. Through this analysis, these systems can provide instantaneous feedback, furnish personalized guidance, and tailor learning materials to align with the unique needs of each student, thereby fostering more effective and efficient learning outcomes (Baş et al., 2023).

Data Analysis and Insights: Learning analytics, situated at the crossroads of education, AI, and data science, seeks to elevate learning experiences by gathering, scrutinizing, and presenting students' learning data (L. Chen et al., 2020). The Society for Learning Analytics Research (SoLAR) defines it as the process of measuring, collecting, analyzing, and reporting data about learners and their contexts. The fundamental components encompass data collection, the application of analytics, and the formulation of an action plan that aligns insights with learning objectives (Santamaría-Bonfil et al., 2020). The study introduces a hierarchical structure for learning analytics, categorizing it into four levels: descriptive, diagnostic, predictive, and prescriptive analytics. Descriptive analytics delves into historical data, diagnostic identifies patterns, predictive anticipates future possibilities, and prescriptive foresees outcomes for intervention strategies.

Widely applied examples include Purdue University's Course Signal system, which predicts and intervenes early with at-risk students (Viberg et al., 2020). While learning analytics facilitates accurate predictions and interventions, challenges emerge in addressing course-specific and institute-specific contexts, necessitating tailored analytics models. Applications span student behavior modeling, learning performance prediction, AI-assisted self-reflection, and administrative management for student retention and dropout issues. AI possesses the capability to analyze extensive educational data, including student performance, engagement, and behavior, extracting valuable insights. These insights aid educators in recognizing trends, patterns, and areas for improvement. AI-driven analytics also contribute to predicting student outcomes, identifying students at risk, and informing instructional decision-making (Ifenthaler et al., 2019).

Virtual Assistants and Chatbots: As learning aids, chatbots and virtual assistants have grown in popularity. These AI-driven chatbots employ natural language processing techniques to explore their knowledge bases for pertinent information in response to user queries or questions (Han et al., 2023). These knowledge bases can be customized to specific domains of knowledge, whether open or closed. Diverging from traditional chatbots that rely on pre-written scripts and offer limited responses, recent advancements in large pre-trained language models have facilitated the creation of more adaptable conversational AI. These AI-driven virtual assistants and chatbots provide immediate support to students, addressing questions, aiding with homework, offering explanations, and engaging in interactive conversations. Additionally, they offer the benefit of being accessible 24/7, alleviating educators by handling routine administrative tasks and addressing common inquiries (Qian et al., 2023).

Automating Administrative Tasks: One of the key benefits of AI in education is its potential to automate administrative tasks, streamlining processes and enhancing efficiency. Through the utilization of AI technologies like machine learning, natural language processing, and big data analytics, tasks such as student enrollment, record-keeping, scheduling, and data management can be automated. AI systems possess the capability to swiftly and accurately process vast amounts of data, minimizing the manual effort required from administrators (Chiu et al., 2023). Furthermore, AI-driven chatbots or virtual assistants can offer immediate and personalized assistance to students, staff, and parents, addressing queries and delivering pertinent information.

By automating administrative tasks, AI contributes to the liberation of valuable time and resources, enabling administrators to concentrate on more strategic and value-added endeavors that enhance the overall functioning of educational institutions. AI also facilitates the automation of tasks like grading assignments, generating reports, and managing schedules, thereby reducing the administrative workload on educators and allowing them to dedicate more time and energy to instructional activities and student support. Figure 3 shows the AI in Modern Education and Personalized Learning.

Figure 3. Personalized learning based on AI

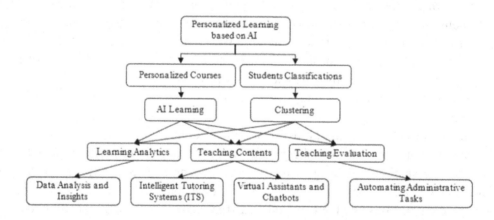

AI has revolutionized education by enabling personalized learning, a student-centric approach that addresses disengagement by tailoring educational experiences to individual needs and preferences. AI-based systems, such as Intelligent Tutoring Systems (ITS), use machine learning algorithms to understand students' strengths, weaknesses, and learning patterns, providing real-time feedback and adaptive learning materials. Learning analytics, a combination of education, AI, and data science, uses data collection, analytics applications, and action plans to enhance learning experiences. AI-powered virtual assistants and chatbots offer immediate support and engage in interactive conversations, allowing educators to focus on strategic activities.

AI also automates administrative tasks, streamlining processes and enhancing efficiency. This allows for tasks like student enrollment, record-keeping, and scheduling to be automated, reducing manual effort and allowing educators to focus on instructional activities and student support. In summary, AI's multifaceted role in contemporary education encompasses personalized learning, intelligent tutoring systems, learning analytics, virtual assistants, chatbots, and the automation of administrative tasks. These advancements underscore the transformative potential of AI in shaping the future of education, fostering more engaging, efficient, and customized learning experiences for students. The evolving landscape of AI in education offers a promising avenue for continued research, development, and innovation in the field.

3. DISPARITIES IN EDUCATION WITH AI

Disparities in education encompass inequalities in access to quality education and educational outcomes among different groups. These inequities manifest in socioeconomic challenges, where students from low-income backgrounds may struggle to access resources and support services. Racial and ethnic minorities often experience unequal treatment, resulting in lower academic achievement and limited opportunities. Geographic disparities impact those in rural or underserved areas, limiting access to quality schools and resources. Gender disparities persist in some societies, with girls facing barriers to education. Students with disabilities encounter challenges due to inadequate accommodations and limited access to specialized services. Addressing these disparities necessitates targeted interventions, including ensuring access to quality schools, well-trained teachers, and support services. Efforts to reduce disparities are vital for fostering a more just and equitable society. Figure 4 shows bridging educational disparities using AI.

Figure 4. Bridging education using AI

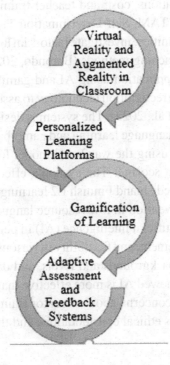

AI holds promise in addressing educational disparities through various avenues. Personalized learning powered by AI analyzes individual students' data, tailoring instructional content and pace to bridge knowledge gaps. AI facilitates access to education by delivering resources to underserved areas through online platforms. Intelligent tutoring systems act as virtual tutors, offering personalized guidance and support, thereby addressing disparities in understanding. Language translation and accessibility features enable diverse linguistic backgrounds to access educational content, promoting inclusivity. AI's early intervention and predictive analytics identify at-risk students, allowing for timely support and preventing disparities from widening. Additionally, AI contributes to bias mitigation by ensuring fair algorithmic design and ongoing ethical considerations. However, thoughtful implementation, collaboration among stakeholders, and human expertise are essential to harness AI's potential for promoting educational equity and inclusivity (Albacete et al., 2019).

AI in education addresses disparities over personalized learning, enhancing accessibility with tools like text-to-speech and adaptive platforms. It enables remote learning, reducing geographical barriers and providing equal access to education. Data-driven visions identify gaps in learning outcomes and inform targeted interferences to support at-risk students. AI supports teachers with personalized insights and resources, enlightening teaching quality and addressing individual student needs efficiently. Moreover, AI-generated contents like virtual simulations improves the learning experiences, catering to diverse learning preferences and bridging disparities in rendezvous and learning outcomes. Overall, AI plays a essential role in endorsing equitable access to quality education for all students.

- Personalized Learning:

Berondo's research paper examines the use of augmented reality (AR) technology in classrooms, revealing its positive impact on student engagement and learning outcomes. The study, based on data from students at Guimaras State College, suggests that AR can improve learning outcomes and motivation. However, barriers like technical limitations, cost, and teacher training hinder its implementation. The research, grounded in constructivism, TAM, Self-Determination Theory, and Social Learning Theory, aims to identify challenges and opportunities, investigate factors influencing AR acceptance, and explore its potential to transform traditional teaching methods (Berondo, 2023c).

Getman et al presented a mobile application using AI and gamification to aid children in learning spoken languages. The app uses speech recognition technology to assess pronunciation and provide feedback to non-native children (Getman et al., 2023). The system is designed to enhance language learning outcomes, utilizing computer-assisted language learning and game-based spoken language learning. The authors propose a multitask approach using the wav2vec2 model for simultaneous Automatic Speech Recognition (ASR) and pronunciation scoring. The system's effectiveness is evaluated on Swedish Speech Sound Disorder (SSD) and Swedish and Finnish L2 learning datasets. The research contributes to language teaching and clinical intervention in low-resource languages.

The study investigated the use of artificial intelligence (AI) in personalized learning, focusing on its effectiveness, impact on student engagement, and feasibility in various educational settings. The research involved 100 students from different backgrounds and levels, and data was collected through surveys, interviews, and assessments. Results showed AI is more effective than traditional methods in improving student learning outcomes. However, concerns about educator training, data privacy, and algorithmic bias were raised. The study emphasizes ethical considerations and the potential future impact of AI on remote education (Berondo, 2023b).

Murtaza et al. discussed personalized e-learning systems, highlighting their effectiveness in delivering personalized learning experiences (Murtaza et al., 2022). It advocates for AI techniques to provide tailored learning materials based on individual comprehension levels and preferences. The authors propose a comprehensive framework with five modules, emphasizing learning models and theories. Challenges include continuous learner assessment, content matching using machine and deep learning, and adaptable learning preferences. The paper provides a comprehensive analysis of requirements, challenges, and AI-driven solutions in personalized e-learning, catering to academics and researchers interested in the field's methodologies and complexities. This study investigates the impact of holograms and virtual classrooms on student learning outcomes and engagement in remote education (Berondo, 2023a).

Using a quasi-experimental research design, it found that these technologies can enhance learning experiences. However, it stressed the need for student-centered approaches, clear instructions, interactive activities, and accessibility. The study recommends best practices for augmented reality technology use in classrooms and evaluates remote education programs' effectiveness. It explores theories like holographic telepresence, virtual classrooms, adaptive learning, flipped classrooms, and microlearning. The research aims to assess the effectiveness of these technologies.

Einarsson et al. used ChatGPT to reframe problems from probability theory and statistics, making them accessible to students from various academic fields (Einarsson et al., 2024). A pilot study showed significant potential in reshaping problems across 17 disciplines, preserving theoretical meaning in 77.1% of cases and requiring minor revisions in 74%. Domain experts evaluated the reframed problems, highlighting the importance of considering student preferences and learning styles in educational content design. The study provides insights into the practicality and effectiveness of using large language models to improve interdisciplinary education and student engagement.

The authors discussed the use of ChatGPT, a generative artificial intelligence language model, in the learning process of students (Niedbał et al., 2023). It highlights the potential of ChatGPT to revolutionize various fields, including education. The study evaluates the application of ChatGPT for full-time and part-time students and assesses their familiarity with intelligent chat functionality and ability to construct queries. The results show that ChatGPT is more beneficial for full-time students, but there is no significant difference in the knowledge and query construction ability between full-time and part-time students.

- Intelligent Tutoring Systems (ITS)

The article explores the creation and evaluation of a novel AI curriculum designed for secondary schools in Hong Kong, part of the AI for the Future (AI4Future) initiative. The objective was to assess the curriculum's efficacy in enhancing students' perceived competence, attitude, and motivation in AI learning. The study involved 335 students and eight teachers across various schools, employing a mixed-method approach that included both quantitative and qualitative data collection. Results indicated that students experienced an increased sense of competence and developed a more favorable attitude toward AI learning. The collaborative creation process also enriched teachers' understanding of AI, enabling them to seamlessly incorporate the subject matter into their classrooms.

The authors investigated the application of deep auto encoders (DEA) to improve adaptive e-learning systems (Gomede et al., 2021). It assesses three types of DEA: Collaborative Denoising Auto Encoders (CDAE), Deep Auto Encoders for Collaborative Filtering (DAE-CF), and Deep Auto Encoders for Collaborative Filtering using Content Information (DAE-CI). The research underscores the significance of adaptive e-learning systems in enhancing student results and underscores the goals of relevance, novelty, serendipity, and diversity in generating appropriate recommendations. The evaluation of recommendation systems is carried out through the utilization of performance metrics. RoboboITS is a tutoring system designed to educate pre-university students about artificial intelligence (AI) using robotics (Guerreiro-Santalla et al., 2023).

The system, based on the Robobo educational robot, aims to address challenges in high school AI teaching due to students' diverse programming backgrounds and teachers' confidence. It consists of four modules: Domain, Tutor, Student, and Interface, providing personalized AI training through autonomous robotics challenges. A prototype version was tested, showing promising results for future development.

- Data Analysis and Insights

This research investigated the application of artificial intelligence (AI) tools within higher education, with a specific focus on a private university in Latin America (Grájeda et al., 2024). Employing a validated instrument, the study evaluates five crucial aspects: the efficacy of AI tool utilization, the effectiveness of ChatGPT use, student proficiency, teacher proficiency, and advanced student skills. The outcomes reveal a favorable influence of AI tools on students' academic encounters, leading to improved understanding, creativity, and productivity.

The study underscores the significance of both educators' and students' proficiency in AI and promotes its incorporation as a pedagogical advancement. Shafique et al. examines the impact of artificial intelligence (AI), specifically machine learning (ML) and deep learning (DL), on online education. It highlights the benefits of AI, such as personalized learning, progress tracking, and increased productivity (Shafique et al., 2023). The study addresses challenges in delivering quality education and assessing student performance. It uses a systematic mapping methodology to investigate the evolution of ML and DL techniques in online education. The research questions focus on their application in education analysis, development, classifiers, feature engineering, and data sources.

In this study discusses the growth and development of the field of learning analytics. It emphasizes the importance of collaboration and convergence with related fields in order to advance the field and address open challenges (Baker et al., 2021). The paper proposes a framework for analyzing how different methodological paradigms in related fields (such as educational data mining, quantitative ethnography, and learning at scale) influence learning analytics. The goal is to identify gaps in the literature and highlight areas for future research. The document also mentions the establishment of the field of learning analytics, its impact on education policy and practice, and the growth of its community through conferences, journals, and networking initiatives.

The need of incorporating cultural competency and ethics into AI education for K–12 children is emphasized in the study (Sanusi & Olaleye, 2022). Cultural competency and ethics have a considerable impact on AI content, with ethics having the highest predictive value, according to surveys given to high school students in Nigeria. The survey also discovered that compared to rural pupils, urban students had a higher favorable perception of AI material. The authors demand that while designing AI curricula, cultural components, humanistic ideas, and ethical issues be given top priority.

Alwarthan et al. explored the use of educational data mining techniques to predict and identify students at risk of failing the preparatory year (Alwarthan et al., 2022). It uses classification models like Random Forest, Support Vector Machine, and Artificial Neural Network, and examines feature selection methods. The study uses imbalanced datasets and sampling approaches, with RF outperforming other techniques. Explainable AI techniques like Local Interpretable Modelagnostic Explanations method

(LIME), SHapley Additive exPlanations (SHAP), and global surrogate model are also used to explain prediction models and identify reasons for student failure.

The importance of self-regulated learning (SRL) in predicting academic performance, particularly in online learning settings, is well-acknowledged. Learning analytics (LA) has been identified as a tool that can enhance SRL by reshaping learning practices (Viberg et al., 2020). Utilizing Zimmerman's model (2002) to explore the different phases of SRL, the study investigated the relationship between LA and four propositions: the potential of LA to enhance learning outcomes, improve learning support and teaching, its widespread deployment, and ethical considerations. The results revealed that the majority of studies focused on SRL aspects during the forethought and performance phases, with limited evidence supporting improvements in learning outcomes (20%), enhancements in learning support and teaching (22%), and widespread deployment. Furthermore, ethical considerations were scarcely addressed in the studies. These findings imply that LA research tends to measure rather than actively support SRL, emphasizing the need to leverage LA support mechanisms to foster SRL effectively in online learning environments (Viberg et al., 2020).

The study investigates Live-line maintenance, a high-risk activity requiring effective training for lineworkers. Virtual Reality Training Systems (VRTS) offer a cost-effective alternative, but their effectiveness relies on meaningful learning activities and detecting untrained students (Santamaría-Bonfil et al., 2020). A student model using Learning Analytics (LA) was built using data from 1399 students in 329 courses from 2008 to 2016. The model distinguishes between trained and untrained students in different maneuvers, with Random Forest being the best classifier. The model also reveals non-observable behavioral variables related to errors. LA enhances evaluation by identifying error patterns in VRTS data. The authors introduced an interactive test dashboard called ITD-DFM, which offers high-quality, visual feedback on students' test performance (C. M. Chen et al., 2021). A quasi-experimental study with Grade 8 students showed that the ITD-DFM group demonstrated better learning performance, physics self-efficacy, and technology acceptance compared to the control group. The study emphasizes the importance of feedback in learning assessment and the role of digital dashboards for learning in providing visual feedback. The ITD-DFM is a novel tool that combines summative assessment and self-assessment, offering potential benefits in physics courses.

- Virtual Assistants and Chatbots

In this study explored the use of an adaptive virtual learning assistant to enhance learners' self-regulatory skills in online learning environments (Pogorskiy & Beckmann, 2023). The research involved 157 online learners and used behavioral trace data and self-reporting measures. The study suggests that self-regulation is crucial for success in online learning and can be acquired. Various intervention options, such as personalized feedback systems, mobile apps, virtual companions, and adaptive assistance tools, have been proposed to support learners' self-regulatory skills.

The findings suggest that adaptive assistance can compensate for deficits in self-regulatory skills, highlighting the potential of adaptive virtual learning assistants in enhancing learners' engagement with online educational content. Another article explored the use of an AI model in an online learning portal for Indonesian primary school students, focusing on personalized learning (Pardamean et al., 2022). The model uses a collaborative filtering-based approach to predict students' learning styles, resulting in improved learning performance. The study emphasizes the importance of active learning and the role of technology in creating interactive learning environments. The benefits of personalized learning and AI's application in predicting students' learning styles are also highlighted.

- Automating Administrative Task

Bajaj & Sharma 's paper emphasizes the need for adaptability in educational systems and the importance of customizing content and learning paths for individual students. It suggests a framework for a software tool that uses multiple learning models and artificial intelligence techniques to determine students' learning styles (Bajaj & Sharma, 2018). The tool compares different models and selects the most suitable one for a specific environment. The authors suggest deploying this tool in a cloud environment for a scalable solution. They emphasize the need for a standardized approach and a software tool to facilitate learning styles based on student behavior data. The article investigates the use of generative artificial intelligence (AI) in English as a foreign language (EFL) writing processes (Liu et al., 2024). It examines two groups of EFL writers who use PowerPoint projects and traditional argumentative essay projects. The study reveals that the PPT group constructs bridge texts, borrows search results from Bing Chat, and uses AI-generated descriptions for image generation. The study highlights the pedagogical implications of AI in multimodal writing and suggests further research. It also discusses the growing trend of digital multimodal composing.

- Ethics in AI Education

The research by Akgun & Greenhow (2022) explores the ethical implications of integrating artificial intelligence (AI) in K-12 education. It highlights the potential benefits of AI, such as personalized learning and automated assessment systems, but also highlights ethical challenges like bias, discrimination, and injustice. The study recommends addressing these issues and providing instructional materials for teaching AI and ethics in K-12 classrooms. It also suggests creating educational opportunities and curricula to educate teachers and students about AI's ethical implications. Albacete et al. examines a pilot study on Rimac, a natural-language tutoring system that uses a student model to guide discussions and support students solving physics problems.

The experimental version, which updated the model based on students' responses, was compared to a control version (Albacete et al., 2019). Although no significant difference was found, the experimental group completed the study more efficiently. The study also discusses instructional scaffolding and Rimac's adaptive nature, highlighting its dynamic model updates during dialogues. The study concludes with a discussion on the student model's implementation and potential impact on student learning. A study by Sanusi et al. (2022) reveals that cognitive abilities, human-tool collaboration, self-learning, skill competence, and ethics significantly influence AI content for K-12 students in Nigeria. The findings suggest that these competencies can guide educators in developing AI content and enabling students to navigate the realm effectively. The study also highlights the global landscape of AI education in K-12 settings and the importance of fostering AI literacy among younger generations (Sanusi et al., 2022).

In conclusion, this section of research papers provides an overview of various studies and initiatives related to personalized learning, intelligent tutoring systems, data analysis, virtual assistants, chatbots, and administrative task automation in education. The papers highlight the potential of emerging technologies like augmented reality, artificial intelligence, and adaptive learning systems to improve student engagement and learning outcomes. They emphasize the need to consider technical limitations, cost, teacher training, and ethical considerations when integrating these technologies into educational settings.

The studies also highlight the positive impact of AI and machine learning techniques in predicting student performance, identifying at-risk students, and providing personalized recommendations. The articles emphasize the importance of collaboration, convergence, and interdisciplinary approaches in learning analytics and AI education. They contribute to the ongoing discourse on improving teaching methodologies, enhancing learning experiences, and shaping the future of education through innovative technologies.

4. AI ABILITY TO IMPROVE THE EDUCATIONAL SYSTEMS

AI tools have the extraordinary ability to improve educational systems in several key ways. One important impact is through personalized learning, where AI algorithms analyze individual student data to create custom-made learning paths. This customization safeguards those students receive content at a pace and in a format that aligns with their exclusive learning styles, ultimately improving engagement and knowledge retention.

Moreover, AI's data-driven competences provide educators and policy-makers with valuable insights. By processing large volumes of educational data, AI can classify learning trends, assess the efficiency of teaching strategies, and even forecast student performance. This information enables informed decision-making, permitting for targeted adjustments and interventions to educational programs to better meet student requirements and improve overall outcomes. Moreover, AI mechanizes routine administrative tasks such as scheduling and grading, freeing up educators' time to emphasis more on teaching and individual student support. This mechanization not only increases competence but also diminishes the load on teachers, enabling them to deliver higher-quality education.

Additionally, AI-powered assessment tools provide improved feedback mechanisms, offering students with immediate and detailed feedback on their performance and progress. This feedback loop is invaluable for guiding students' learning voyages, assisting them identify areas for improvement and amend their study plans accordingly. Inventively, AI technologies can generate engaging and interactive learning materials, such as virtual simulations and multimedia presentations, inspiring the educational experience to varied learning preferences. Furthermore, AI's accessibility features, such as text-to-speech and adaptive learning platforms, endorse inclusivity by confirming that disabilities students have equal access to educational opportunities and resources.

Overall, the ability of AI tools to improve educational systems lies in their capacity to personalize learning, provide data-driven insights, automate tasks, enhance feedback mechanisms, foster innovation, and promote inclusivity, ultimately contributing to a more effective and equitable education landscape.

5. EMERGING TRENDS AND FUTURE PROSPECTS

Artificial intelligence (AI) stands poised to transform the field of education, ushering in innovative teaching approaches and personalized learning encounters. The ongoing evolution of AI technologies holds the potential to revolutionize conventional educational models, introducing a more engaging, personalized, and effective learning paradigm. Nevertheless, it is imperative to confront challenges such as ethical considerations, data privacy, and equitable access to ensure that AI serves the best interests of all learners (Zhang & Aslan, 2021). The collaborative efforts of educators, researchers, policymakers, and AI experts are crucial in shaping the future trajectory of AI in education and fully realizing its capabilities.

As AI technologies continue to progress, several emerging trends and future prospects are influencing the landscape of AI-driven teaching methods and education. The evolving terrain of AI-based teaching methods signifies a shift in the role of educators towards facilitation and coaching, utilizing digital technologies and AI to facilitate personalized learning experiences. The emergence of AI-EDU as a prominent trend impacts various stakeholders, emphasizing intelligent tutoring systems, real-time responses, and adaptive learning (Srinivasan, 2022). Recognition of the importance of equity in education is prominent, with AI offering scalable and affordable solutions to customize instruction and bridge gaps between privileged and underserved students. The digital age, social learning, and the impact of the COVID-19 pandemic have accelerated the adoption of remote and hybrid learning, presenting both advantages and challenges.

The optimistic future outlook for AI-based teaching methods envisions more sophisticated and personalized learning experiences, real-time feedback, adaptive assessments, and automated administrative tasks. As AI advances, educators have the opportunity to establish inclusive and effective learning environments, addressing equity concerns and empowering learners in the digital age. AI's future in education holds promise for bridging disparities. Personalized learning tailors education to individual needs, while accessibility features ensure inclusivity. Data-driven decisions target gaps, and remote learning expands access. AI aids teachers and offers adaptive assessments, enhancing support and accuracy. These prospects aim to create equitable and inclusive learning environments for all students (Niemi et al., 2022).

6. CONCLUSION

This chapter extensively delves into the transformative influence of AI technologies on educational methodologies, learning experiences, and the transformation of conventional teaching paradigms. It underscores the wide-ranging applications of AI in education, spanning from intelligent tutoring systems to personalized learning platforms and adaptive learning environments. The incorporation of AI has the capacity to revolutionize both how students learn and how educators deliver instruction. Through the utilization of AI tools, educators can construct learning environments that are not only more engaging and efficient but also tailored to the individual needs, capacities, and preferences of each student. AI-driven technologies support personalized learning experiences, intelligent tutoring, and recommendation systems, enabling the targeted delivery of content and support. Furthermore, AI streamlines administrative tasks, allowing teachers to redirect their time towards instructional activities and providing personalized guidance to students. However, the successful integration of AI in education is not devoid of challenges. Educators may encounter difficulties in acclimating to AI technologies, accessing necessary resources and funding, and adapting to the digital transformation of educational practices. Therefore, it is imperative for educators to receive training and support, equipping them with the technological skills needed to overcome these challenges. In essence, the incorporation of AI in education unfolds numerous opportunities to enhance the learning experience, refine instructional design, and empower educators. By embracing the capabilities of AI, educators, administrators, and educational researchers can bridge the gap between traditional education and the innovative possibilities introduced by AI. It is essential to approach AI in education with a keen focus on inclusion, equity, and ethical considerations, ensuring its application aligns with the fundamental principles of education. With careful implementation and ongoing support, AI has the potential to significantly improve educational outcomes and equip students with the necessary skills for the challenges of the modern era.

REFERENCES

Abdalla, R. S., Mahbub, S. A., Mokhtar, R. A., Ali, E. S., & Saeed, R. A. (2020). IoE Design Principles and Architecture; Book: Internet of Energy for Smart Cities: Machine Learning Models and Techniques. *Internet of Energy for Smart Cities: Machine Learning Models and Techniques.*

Albacete, P., Jordan, P., Katz, S., Chounta, I.-A., & Mclaren, B. M. (2019). *The impact of student model updates on contingent scaffolding in a natural-language tutoring system.* Academic Press.

Ali, E. S., Hasan, M. K., Hassan, R., Saeed, R. A., Hassan, M. B., Islam, S., Nafi, N. S., & Bevinakoppa, S. (2021). Machine learning technologies for secure vehicular communication in internet of vehicles: Recent advances and applications. *Security and Communication Networks, 2021,* 1–23. doi:10.1155/2021/8868355

Alqurashi, F. A., Alsolami, F., Abdel-Khalek, S., Sayed Ali, E., & Saeed, R. A. (2022). Machine learning techniques in internet of UAVs for smart cities applications. *Journal of Intelligent & Fuzzy Systems, 42*(4), 3203–3226. doi:10.3233/JIFS-211009

Alwarthan, S., Aslam, N., & Khan, I. U. (2022). An Explainable Model for Identifying At-Risk Student at Higher Education. *IEEE Access : Practical Innovations, Open Solutions, 10,* 107649–107668. doi:10.1109/ACCESS.2022.3211070

Aswathy, R. H., Suresh, P., Sikkandar, M. Y., Abdel-Khalek, S., Alhumyani, H., Saeed, R. A., & Mansour, R. F. (2022). Optimized tuned deep learning model for chronic kidney disease classification. *Computers, Materials & Continua, 70,* 2097–2111. doi:10.32604/cmc.2022.019790

Bajaj, R., & Sharma, V. (2018). Smart Education with artificial intelligence based determination of learning styles. *Procedia Computer Science, 132,* 834–842. doi:10.1016/j.procs.2018.05.095

Baker, R. S., Gašević, D., & Karumbaiah, S. (2021). Four paradigms in learning analytics: Why paradigm convergence matters. *Computers and Education: Artificial Intelligence, 2,* 100021. Advance online publication. doi:10.1016/j.caeai.2021.100021

Baş, İ., Alp, D., Ergenç, L. C., Koçak, A. E., & Yalçın, S. (2023). DancÆR: Efficient and Accurate Dance Choreography Learning by Feedback Through Pose Classification. doi:10.1007/978-3-031-36336-8_115

Berondo, R. (2023a). *From holograms to virtual classrooms: An investigation into the future of remote education.* https://doi.org/ doi:10.48047/ecb/2023.12.10.0882023.30/06/2023

Berondo, R. (2023b). *Harnessing the power of artificial intelligence for personalized learning in education.* https://doi.org/ doi:10.48047/ecb/2023.12.10.0892023.30/06/2023

Berondo, R. (2023c). Revolutionizing education: Exploring the impact of augmented reality in the classroom. *European Chemical Bulletin, 12*(10), 1221–1228. doi:10.48047/ecb/2023.12.10.0872023. 30/06/2023

Chan, C. K. Y. (2023). A comprehensive AI policy education framework for university teaching and learning. *International Journal of Educational Technology in Higher Education, 20*(1), 38. Advance online publication. doi:10.1186/s41239-023-00408-3

Chen, C. M., Wang, J. Y., & Hsu, L. C. (2021). An interactive test dashboard with diagnosis and feedback mechanisms to facilitate learning performance. *Computers and Education: Artificial Intelligence, 2*, 100015. Advance online publication. doi:10.1016/j.caeai.2021.100015

Chen, L., Chen, P., & Lin, Z. (2020). Artificial Intelligence in Education: A Review. *IEEE Access : Practical Innovations, Open Solutions, 8*, 75264–75278. doi:10.1109/ACCESS.2020.2988510

Chiu, T. K. F., Xia, Q., Zhou, X., Chai, C. S., & Cheng, M. (2023). Systematic literature review on opportunities, challenges, and future research recommendations of artificial intelligence in education. In Computers and Education: Artificial Intelligence (Vol. 4). Elsevier B.V. doi:10.1016/j.caeai.2022.100118

Dirar, R. O., Saeed, R. A., Hasan, M. K., & Mahmud, M. (2017). Persistent overload control for backlogged machine to machine communications in long term evolution advanced networks. *Journal of Telecommunication, Electronic and Computer Engineering, 9*(3-10), 109-113.

Einarsson, H., Lund, S. H., & Jónsdóttir, A. H. (2024). Application of ChatGPT for automated problem reframing across academic domains. *Computers and Education: Artificial Intelligence, 6*, 100194. Advance online publication. doi:10.1016/j.caeai.2023.100194

Elfatih, N. M., Hasan, M. K., Kamal, Z., Gupta, D., Saeed, R. A., Ali, E. S., & Hosain, M. S. (2022). Internet of vehicle's resource management in 5G networks using AI technologies: Current status and trends. *IET Communications, 16*(5), 400–420. doi:10.1049/cmu2.12315

Elmoiz Alatabani, L., Sayed Ali, E., Mokhtar, R. A., Saeed, R. A., Alhumyani, H., & Kamrul Hasan, M. (2022). Deep and reinforcement learning technologies on internet of vehicle (IoV) applications: Current issues and future trends. *Journal of Advanced Transportation, 2022*, 2022. doi:10.1155/2022/1947886

Getman, Y., Phan, N., Al-Ghezi, R., Voskoboinik, E., Singh, M., Grosz, T., Kurimo, M., Salvi, G., Svendsen, T., Strombergsson, S., Smolander, A., & Ylinen, S. (2023). Developing an AI-Assisted Low-Resource Spoken Language Learning App for Children. *IEEE Access : Practical Innovations, Open Solutions, 11*, 86025–86037. doi:10.1109/ACCESS.2023.3304274

Gomede, E., de Barros, R. M., & Mendes, L. de S. (2021). Deep auto encoders to adaptive E-learning recommender system. *Computers and Education: Artificial Intelligence, 2*, 100009. Advance online publication. doi:10.1016/j.caeai.2021.100009

Grájeda, A., Burgos, J., Córdova, P., & Sanjinés, A. (2024). Assessing student-perceived impact of using artificial intelligence tools: Construction of a synthetic index of application in higher education. *Cogent Education, 11*(1), 2287917. Advance online publication. doi:10.1080/2331186X.2023.2287917

Guerreiro-Santalla, S., Crompton, H., & Bellas, F. (2023). *RoboboITS: A Simulation-Based Tutoring System to Support AI Education Through Robotics*. doi:10.1007/978-3-031-36336-8_62

Han, S., Jung, J., Ji, H., Lee, U., & Liu, M. (2023). *The Role of Social Presence in MOOC Students' Behavioral Intentions and Sentiments Toward the Usage of a Learning Assistant Chatbot: A Diversity*. Equity, and Inclusion Perspective Examination. doi:10.1007/978-3-031-36336-8_36

Hassan, M. B., Ali, E. S., Nurelmadina, N., & Saeed, R. A. (2021). Artificial intelligence in IoT and its applications. In Intelligent Wireless Communications (pp. 33-58). Institution of Engineering and Technology. doi:10.1049/PBTE094E_ch2

Heck, T., & Meurers, D. (2023). *Exercise Generation Supporting Adaptivity in Intelligent Tutoring Systems*. doi:10.1007/978-3-031-36336-8_102

Ifenthaler, D., Mah, D.-K., & Yau, J. Y.-K. (2019). Utilising Learning Analytics for Study Success: Reflections on Current Empirical Findings. In Utilizing Learning Analytics to Support Study Success (pp. 27–36). Springer International Publishing. doi:10.1007/978-3-319-64792-0_2

Ingavelez-Guerra, P., Robles-Bykbaev, V. E., Perez-Munoz, A., Hilera-Gonzalez, J., & Oton-Tortosa, S. (2022). Automatic Adaptation of Open Educational Resources: An Approach From a Multilevel Methodology Based on Students' Preferences, Educational Special Needs, Artificial Intelligence and Accessibility Metadata. *IEEE Access : Practical Innovations, Open Solutions*, 10, 9703–9716. doi:10.1109/ACCESS.2021.3139537

Khan, A., Li, J. P., Hasan, M. K., Varish, N., Mansor, Z., Islam, S., Saeed, R. A., Alshammari, M., & Alhumyani, H. (2022). PackerRobo: Model-based robot vision self supervised learning in CART. *Alexandria Engineering Journal*, 61(12), 12549–12566. doi:10.1016/j.aej.2022.05.043

Liang, J.-C., Hwang, G.-J., Chen, M.-R. A., & Darmawansah, D. (2023). Roles and research foci of artificial intelligence in language education: An integrated bibliographic analysis and systematic review approach. *Interactive Learning Environments*, 31(7), 4270–4296. doi:10.1080/10494820.2021.1958348

Liu, M., Zhang, L. J., & Biebricher, C. (2024). Investigating students' cognitive processes in generative AI-assisted digital multimodal composing and traditional writing. *Computers & Education*, 211, 104977. doi:10.1016/j.compedu.2023.104977

Murtaza, M., Ahmed, Y., Shamsi, J. A., Sherwani, F., & Usman, M. (2022). AI-Based Personalized E-Learning Systems: Issues, Challenges, and Solutions. In IEEE Access (Vol. 10, pp. 81323–81342). Institute of Electrical and Electronics Engineers Inc. doi:10.1109/ACCESS.2022.3193938

Niedbał, R., Sokołowski, A., & Wrzalik, A. (2023). Students' Use of the Artificial Intelligence Language Model in their Learning Process. *Procedia Computer Science*, 225, 3059–3066. doi:10.1016/j.procs.2023.10.299

Niemi, H., Pea, R. D., & Lu, Y. (2022). AI in Learning: Designing the Future. In *AI in Learning: Designing the Future*. Springer International Publishing. doi:10.1007/978-3-031-09687-7

Ouyang, F., Zheng, L., & Jiao, P. (2022). Artificial intelligence in online higher education: A systematic review of empirical research from 2011 to 2020. *Education and Information Technologies*, *27*(6), 7893–7925. doi:10.1007/s10639-022-10925-9

Owoc, M. L., Sawicka, A., & Weichbroth, P. (2021). *Artificial Intelligence Technologies in Education: Benefits*. Challenges and Strategies of Implementation. doi:10.1007/978-3-030-85001-2_4

Pardamean, B., Suparyanto, T., Cenggoro, T. W., Sudigyo, D., & Anugrahana, A. (2022). AI-Based Learning Style Prediction in Online Learning for Primary Education. *IEEE Access : Practical Innovations, Open Solutions*, *10*, 35725–35735. doi:10.1109/ACCESS.2022.3160177

Pogorskiy, E., & Beckmann, J. F. (2023). From procrastination to engagement? An experimental exploration of the effects of an adaptive virtual assistant on self-regulation in online learning. *Computers and Education: Artificial Intelligence*, *4*, 100111. Advance online publication. doi:10.1016/j.caeai.2022.100111

Qian, K., Shea, R., Li, Y., Fryer, L. K., & Yu, Z. (2023). *User Adaptive Language Learning Chatbots with a Curriculum*. doi:10.1007/978-3-031-36336-8_48

Saeed, R. A., Omri, M., Abdel-Khalek, S., Ali, E. S., & Alotaibi, M. F. (2022). Optimal path planning for drones based on swarm intelligence algorithm. *Neural Computing & Applications*, *34*(12), 10133–10155. doi:10.1007/s00521-022-06998-9

Santamaría-Bonfil, G., Ibáñez, M. B., Pérez-Ramírez, M., Arroyo-Figueroa, G., & Martínez-Álvarez, F. (2020). Learning analytics for student modeling in virtual reality training systems: Lineworkers case. *Computers & Education*, *151*, 103871. doi:10.1016/j.compedu.2020.103871

Sanusi, I. T., & Olaleye, S. A. (2022). An Insight into Cultural Competence and Ethics in K-12 Artificial Intelligence Education. *IEEE Global Engineering Education Conference, EDUCON, 2022-March*, 790–794. 10.1109/EDUCON52537.2022.9766818

Sanusi, I. T., Olaleye, S. A., Oyelere, S. S., & Dixon, R. A. (2022). Investigating learners' competencies for artificial intelligence education in an African K-12 setting. *Computers and Education Open*, *3*, 100083. doi:10.1016/j.caeo.2022.100083

Shafique, R., Aljedaani, W., Rustam, F., Lee, E., Mehmood, A., & Choi, G. S. (2023). Role of Artificial Intelligence in Online Education: A Systematic Mapping Study. *IEEE Access : Practical Innovations, Open Solutions*, *11*, 52570–52584. doi:10.1109/ACCESS.2023.3278590

Srinivasa, K. G., Kurni, M., & Saritha, K. (2022). *Harnessing the Power of AI to Education*. doi:10.1007/978-981-19-6734-4_13

Srinivasan, V. (2022). AI & learning: A preferred future. *Computers and Education: Artificial Intelligence*, *3*, 100062. Advance online publication. doi:10.1016/j.caeai.2022.100062

Su, J., Ng, D. T. K., & Chu, S. K. W. (2023). Artificial Intelligence (AI) Literacy in Early Childhood Education: The Challenges and Opportunities. In Computers and Education: Artificial Intelligence (Vol. 4). Elsevier B.V. doi:10.1016/j.caeai.2023.100124

Teh, Y. Y., & Baskaran, V. (2022). The Effectiveness of eAssessments to Encourage Learning Among Gen Z Students. In *Alternative Assessments in Malaysian Higher Education* (pp. 259–267). Springer Singapore. doi:10.1007/978-981-16-7228-6_26

Viberg, O., Khalil, M., & Baars, M. (2020). Self-regulated learning and learning analytics in online learning environments. *Proceedings of the Tenth International Conference on Learning Analytics & Knowledge*, 524–533. 10.1145/3375462.3375483

Chapter 5
AI–Enhanced Engineering Education:
Customization, Adaptive Learning, and Real–Time Data Analysis

Mohammed Balfaqih

https://orcid.org/0000-0002-6498-2408

University of Jeddah, Saudi Arabia

Zain Balfagih

Effat University, Saudi Arabia

ABSTRACT

The chapter explores AI integration in engineering education, emphasizing customization, adaptive learning, and real-time data analysis. It discusses AI's role in enhancing student efficacy through personalized learning and early identification of learning difficulties. Innovative elements like wearables for self-monitoring are examined. Pedagogical frameworks and case studies of successful AI implementations are presented. Ethical and societal considerations including privacy and inclusiveness are addressed. It provides a comprehensive understanding of AI in engineering education, concluding with key insights and implications for proactive engagement with AI technologies to enhance student learning.

1. INTRODUCTION

The term Artificial Intelligence (AI) encompasses a wide range of methodologies, algorithms, and systems designed to learn from data (including data science, statistical learning, machine learning, and deep learning), as well as those aimed at developing machine intelligence capable of tasks such as perception, reasoning, and inference (including expert systems, probabilistic graphical models, and Bayesian networks). In contemporary usage, these terms are often employed interchangeably (Mitchell, M. 2019).

The education is undergoing a significant transformation through the integration of AI, presenting opportunities to gain insights into student learning processes, personalize educational experiences, enhance

DOI: 10.4018/979-8-3693-2728-9.ch005

decision-making capabilities, and model intricate interactions between students, knowledge domains, and learning tools. Education 4.0, born out of the demands of Industry 4.0, necessitates a transformation in skills, competencies, instructional methodologies, and assessment practices to adapt to the evolving landscape (Ciolacu, M., et al. 2017a). AI emerges as a pivotal component driving this revolution in the education sector, with its proactive involvement crucial for achieving enhanced performance. Education 4.0 is characterized by blended learning and incorporates seven AI-driven features, including personalized learning processes, game-based learning leveraging virtual reality/augmented reality (VR/AR), communities of practice, adaptive technologies, learning analytics, intelligent chatbots, and e-assessment.

AI's role spans the entire educational continuum, contributing to improved outcomes from inception to culmination. Research predominantly focuses on enhancing student efficacy through personalized learning and early identification of learning difficulties with automated responses. Studies primarily rely on the analysis of Learning Management System (LMS) logs, although some studies integrate innovative elements such as wearables and smart sensors for self-monitoring of students' cognitive states within the learning environment (Ciolacu, M., et al. 2017b). Future applications may involve wearable gadgets and smart sensing devices to model student behavior by monitoring various health indicators including movement patterns, hydration levels, breaks, ambient temperature, and even emotional states (Bienkowski, M. et al. 2012).

However, technology often challenges established practices, necessitating adaptation and careful consideration of its benefits and drawbacks (Mander, J. 1978). Previous inquiries have scrutinized the impact of Google on education, pondering whether it enriches knowledge or fosters superficiality, and even questioning the necessity of teachers in contemporary times (Carr, N. 2010, Gilbert, I. 2014). The rise of Massive Open Online Courses (MOOCs) in the early 2010s garnered considerable attention but fell short of expectations, leading to shifts in focus and business models (Pappano, L. 2012, Kent, M., & Bennett, R. 2017). Echoes of caution regarding technology's effects can be traced back to Plato, who warned of the potential for memory atrophy with the advent of the written word, fearing it would impart only a semblance of truth (Thunstrom, A. O. 2022). Similar concerns extend to modern technologies like ChatGPT, which, while holding significant promise, also pose risks such as job displacement, particularly for low-skilled workers (Brynjolfsson, E., & McAfee, A. 2014). The engineering education community must proactively address these issues, developing clear guidelines to maximize the benefits of such tools while mitigating potential downsides.

The chapter is structured to provide a comprehensive understanding of AI Technologies in Engineering Education. The primary objectives of this research are to:

- Examine the current landscape of AI integration in engineering education and its impact on teaching and learning processes.
- Investigate how AI-driven tools and platforms are being utilized to mitigate knowledge disparities among students.
- Assess the effectiveness of AI technologies in enhancing student engagement, academic performance, and reducing teacher workload.

The chapter begins with an introduction highlighting the significance of this integration, followed by exploration of key components such as customization, adaptive learning systems, and real-time data analysis. Pedagogical frameworks including constructivism, social constructivism, and behaviorism are discussed, alongside case studies showcasing successful AI implementations and best practices. Ethical and societal considerations, encompassing privacy, transparency, inclusiveness, and educational equity, are addressed. The chapter concludes by summarizing key insights and implications for the field.

2. MAIN ROLES OF AI INTEGRATION

AI integration in education includes three main roles. Firstly, Customization and Personalization in Learning involve tailoring teaching methods to individual learner requirements, resulting in the development of Intelligent Tutoring Systems (ITS) that rival human tutors in effectiveness (Sajja, R., et al. 2023). Secondly, Managing Learning Systems at the Class Level entails AI support for teachers in overseeing entire classrooms, encompassing tasks such as tutoring, grading, and implementing Virtual Reality (VR) based learning to enrich the classroom experience (Holstein, K. 2018). Lastly, Real-time Data Analysis for Personalized Feedback involves AI-driven analysis of learner interactions to fine-tune learning systems based on their successes and failures. This role includes identifying at-risk learners, understanding interests, behaviors, performance, and predicting potential dropouts (Wang, D., Tao, Y., & Chen, G. 2024).

2.1 Customization and Personalization in Learning

A significant contributor to knowledge disparities resulting in learning gaps among both undergraduate and graduate students is the challenge instructors face in aligning their communication methods with students' individual learning schedules and styles (Williamson, B., et al. 2020). Scholarly research consistently underscores the effectiveness of teaching methodologies that facilitate the development of conceptual understanding in students often necessitating opportunities for independent reflection (Konicek-Moran, R., & Keeley, P. 2015, Rahem, A. A. T., et al. 2017, Lin, F., & Chan, C. K. 2018). Allowing students, the flexibility to progress at their own pace has been demonstrated to markedly enhance learning motivation and foster the cultivation of creative thinking abilities (Ciampa, K. 2014). Figure 1 shows the learning platform-student model for customize and personalize learning.

Given that a majority of students engage in studying outside of traditional hours, there arises a demand for support during unconventional times (Mounsey, R., et al. 2013). The absence of immediate assistance can lead to feelings of frustration and stagnation, despite the fact that many queries could be addressed with readily available resources rather than specialized expertise (Seeroo, O., & Bekaroo, G. 2021). While teaching assistants may offer support, their availability may be limited due to their own commitments, such as classes, research, and grading, particularly during critical periods like exam weeks when student assistance is paramount (Howitz, W. J., et al. 2020).

An automated system designed in Sajja, R., et al. (2023) for answering logistical questions in online course platforms and educational applications. The system sought to enhance course content quality and individualized student advising by delegating instructors' repetitive duties to virtual assistants, thereby mitigating inequality among students in accessing knowledge and narrowing retention and graduation gaps. Moreover, by providing support for students navigating complex trajectories, such as changes in degree programs, the virtual assistant facilitated better decision-making and smoother transitions between academic paths. While conducted under controlled circumstances rather than in actual classrooms, the research provided significant insights into VirtualTA's capabilities for bolstering student learning and engagement. The architecture enables integration with various third-party applications, simplifying access for users through familiar communication channels. While chatbots cannot entirely replace human support, with proper development and implementation, they can enhance the learning experience by reducing instructors' and teaching assistants' workload. However, educators and developers should address potential errors, leveraging natural language processing algorithms to identify and mitigate ambiguities in questions posed to chatbots.

Another example is NLP models hold promise in offering virtual intelligent tutoring services, allowing students to seek personalized responses and feedback (Qadir, J. 2023). This feedback-driven iterative

Figure 1. Interactions between an administrator, a learning platform, and a student

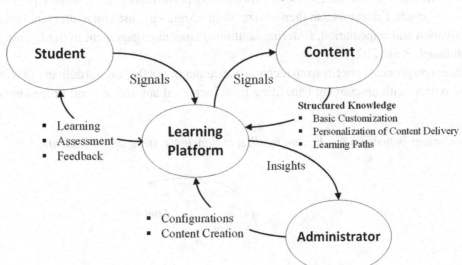

learning approach, supported by the "Two Sigma Effect," demonstrates significant performance gains compared to traditional instruction, attributed to the rapid and frequent feedback provided by intelligent tutoring systems. This methodology aligns with mastery learning, enabling students to progress at their own pace and solidify foundational knowledge before tackling advanced material. Virtual tutors prove particularly valuable in scenarios where access to human instructors is limited. NLP models' conversational style enhances student engagement, mimicking the feedback and social interaction of human tutors. However, it's essential to recognize that while virtual intelligent tutoring systems offer assistance, they cannot replace human instructors and may lack the same level of personalized support.

2.2 Managing Learning Systems at Class Level

AI techniques have been systematically leveraged to create reactive and adaptive tutorials, contributing to the establishment of tailored learning environments. Intelligent tutoring systems (ITS) have emerged as a solution to address teacher shortages, offering personalized educational support (Du Boulay, B. 2016). Ikedinachi, A. P., et al. (2019) advocate for this method as a preferable approach to education, suggesting that it can mitigate the risks associated with contemporary AI-driven methods while still fulfilling educational objectives and aspirations. The ITS represents a paradigm where computing systems autonomously deliver personalized feedback to learners, a concept envisioned since the inception of AI (Kokku, R., et al. 2018, Balfaqih, M., & Alharbi, S. A. 2022). ITSs serve as supplementary learning tools, both within and beyond traditional classroom settings. In classrooms, they augment multi-student environments, automating various teaching and learning tasks, thereby enabling educators to focus on tasks requiring human qualities such as empathy and creativity. Recent AI advancements foster stronger collaboration between humans and machines in the learning process, allowing ITSs to scale up to accommodate larger student populations.

As shown in Figure 2, the conventional instructor-student model could be incorporated to an ITS, configured by educators with specific learning objectives. The ITS tailors personalized learning and assessment activities for each student, while also monitoring performance and behavior, providing valuable insights to teachers. Educators can then utilize these insights to customize interventions and offer informed motivation and remediation, fostering continued student engagement in the learning journey (Okewu, Emmanuel, et al., 2021).

This collaborative process benefits from recent advancements, notably digital delivery of learning and assessment activities, with assessment benefiting from increased automation and processing capabili-

Figure 2. Interactions between a teacher, an intelligent tutoring system, and a student

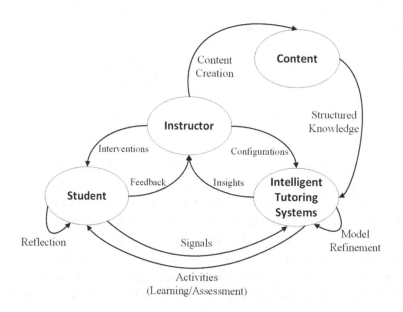

ties. Moreover, students' widespread access to smart devices equipped with sensors offers valuable data for understanding context and usage patterns. These advancements yield vast amounts of data, which, when mined using AI algorithms, provide crucial insights into learning behavioral processes. However, leveraging this data for optimal learning outcomes necessitates the synthesis of actionable intelligence from the vast data pool and abstract decision-making capabilities, underscoring the symbiotic relationship between educators and digital assistants in enriching the learning experience for students.

Integrating LMS and intelligent tutoring systems into classroom management has demonstrated a notable reduction in teacher workload. These systems automate numerous administrative tasks such as attendance tracking, grade recording, and the distribution of course materials, allowing teachers to devote more time to instructional activities and personalized student interaction. According to Palomino, et al. (2014), the integration of Intelligent Tutoring System and Moodle LMS approaches have greatly benefited learning and reduced the teacher's workload notably. The personalized learning experiences offered by class-level learning systems have significantly enhanced student engagement. Adaptive learning platforms, for example, tailor content and assessments to individual student needs, ensuring that learning activities are optimally challenging and engaging. For example, Using Wordtune AI application in L2 education significantly increased students' writing engagement, feedback literacy, and outcomes, showcasing the positive impact of integrating AI for student engagement.

2.3 Real-Time Data Analysis for Personalized Feedback

Personalized learning has undergone significant transformations driven by diverse factors such as student needs, state requirements, globalization, and advancements in education management and technology. These shifts are reshaping traditional learning paradigms, moving away from static, one-size-fits-all approaches toward interactive, student-centered models. The emergence of methodologies like the flipped classroom has further accelerated this trend, fostering better engagement, interaction, and comprehension among learners. Concurrently, developments like Competency-Based Learning, particularly in fields like health and medicine education, contribute to the evolution of personalized learning.

Leveraging technology, including Deep and Reinforcement Learning, enables the customization of learning experiences to individual learner needs. The use of Reinforcement Learning (RL) as a cognitive computing catalyst has been discussed to provide adaptive learning materials and paths tailored to learners' requirements (Shawky, D., & Badawi, A. 2019). By analyzing various factors influencing the learning experience, RL-based systems adapt to learners' changing needs, recommending suitable learning materials in real-time. While the flipped classroom model, wherein students engage with course content prior to class and use class time for collaborative activities, isn't explicitly designed for personalized learning, it aligns with adaptive learning principles. Recent advances in educational technology and instructional design have been highlighted in Sein-Echaluce, M. L., et al. (2019), emphasizing tailored learning experiences for students. They demonstrate the positive impact of personalized learning approaches on academic outcomes and student retention rates. Digital technology, coupled with pedagogical innovations, facilitates the development of AI-driven personalized learning tools and platforms, supporting instruction based on individual student knowledge and understanding levels.

3. PEDAGOGICAL FRAMEWORKS

Teaching pedagogies enables educators to understand how people process information. The relevant literature is both extensive as much as it is diverse with many proposed pedagogies (Psoinos, D. I. 2021). While the terminology and emphasis may vary, the underlying principles of these teaching pedagogies share similarities with the common pedagogies that we outline in this section. We aim to open the window of inquiry by providing an overview of the main teaching pedagogies and relate them directly to AI . Such awareness and insight is essential for practitioners of all disciplines as teacher and learner roles, identity, as well as AI based practices are decidedly affected by one's perceptions of how people learn or acquire knowledge. Table 1 summarizes the integration of AI in pedagogical frameworks

3.1 Constructivism Pedagogy

Table 1. A summary of AI integration in pedagogical frameworks

Pedagogical Framework	AI Integration
Constructivism	Learners actively construct understanding through experiences and interactions. Methods include problem-based learning and inquiry-based learning. AI enhances personalization and interactivity through adaptive learning systems and immersive simulations, empowering students as active constructors of knowledge.
Social Constructivism	Emphasizes collaborative learning through interactions with peers and teachers. Techniques include group work and peer tutoring. AI enriches collaborative experiences with real-time collaboration platforms, adaptive grouping, and sentiment analysis, fostering collective knowledge construction and inclusive learning environments.
Behaviorism	Focuses on observable behaviors and external stimuli to explain learning. Methods include direct instruction and reinforcement. AI modernizes instructional methods with Intelligent Tutoring Systems (ITS), personalized feedback, and automated grading, optimizing learning outcomes and promoting mastery of objectives within a behaviorist framework.

Constructivism is a teaching pedagogy that posits that learners actively construct their understanding and knowledge through their experiences and interactions with the world (Piaget, J. 2005, Chomsky, N. 1980). Rather than passively receiving information from teachers, students engage in hands-on activities, discussions, and reflection to build their own understanding of concepts. Techniques commonly used in constructivist pedagogy include problem-based learning, where students solve real-world problems to apply their knowledge, and inquiry-based learning, where students ask questions, investigate topics, and draw conclusions through guided exploration. Additionally, collaborative learning activities, such as group projects and peer discussions, are often employed to promote social interaction and shared learning experiences.

Incorporating AI into Constructivist teaching pedagogy can enhance the personalized and interactive nature of learning experiences, further empowering students as active constructors of their knowledge. For instance, AI-powered adaptive learning systems can analyze students' learning preferences, strengths, and weaknesses to tailor learning materials and activities accordingly. Students can engage with content at their own pace and receive customized feedback, allowing for a more personalized learning experience that aligns with the constructivist principle of individualized knowledge construction. Additionally, AI technologies can facilitate immersive learning experiences through interactive simulations and virtual laboratories. Students can explore complex concepts and phenomena in a hands-on manner, conducting experiments, making observations, and analyzing data in a virtual environment. These simulations provide opportunities for active experimentation and discovery, aligning with the constructivist emphasis on learning through experience (Xu, W., & Ouyang, F. 2022). By integrating AI technologies into Constructivist pedagogy, educators can foster a dynamic and adaptive learning environment that empowers students to actively engage in the construction of their knowledge while receiving personalized support and feedback tailored to their individual needs and preferences.

Incorporating AI into Constructivist pedagogy doesn't replace the role of the instructor but rather enhances it (Baskara, F. R. 2023). With AI-powered tools providing personalized learning paths and facilitating immersive learning experiences, instructors can shift their focus from content delivery to guiding and supporting students' inquiry and exploration (DSouza, K., et al. 2023). Instructors become facilitators of learning, leveraging AI-generated insights to better understand students' learning needs and providing targeted interventions when necessary. By leveraging AI technologies, instructors can create a more dynamic and adaptive learning environment that promotes student agency and fosters deeper engagement with the learning process.

3.2 Social Constructivism Pedagogy

Social constructivism expands upon constructivist principles by emphasizing the collaborative nature of learning (Vigotsky, L. S. 1939). It asserts that learning is a social process that occurs through interactions with others, including peers and teachers (Guterman, J. T. 2014). In social constructivist pedagogy, techniques such as collaborative group work, peer tutoring, and cooperative learning activities are utilized to foster a sense of community and shared knowledge construction. Teachers facilitate learning by providing scaffolding and guidance, encouraging dialogue and collaboration among students. Peer teaching and reciprocal teaching techniques are also common, where students take turns teaching and learning from one another, reinforcing understanding through shared experiences.

Integrating AI into Social Constructivism pedagogy enhances collaborative learning by providing AI-driven platforms for group work and problem-solving, such as real-time editing and shared whiteboards. These tools enable students and teachers to collaborate remotely, building a sense of community and shared knowledge. AI-powered adaptive learning systems personalize group formation based on diverse skills and preferences, promoting collaborative experiences that leverage collective intelligence. Additionally, AI-driven sentiment analysis monitors online learning communities' emotional tone, helping instructors create a supportive and inclusive environment. By incorporating AI into Social Constructivism, educators can create dynamic, interactive learning spaces that encourage collaboration, dialogue, and collective knowledge construction (Psoinos, D. I. 2021). AI-driven sentiment analysis tools can assess the emotional tone and engagement in online learning communities, offering insights into student attitudes and perceptions (Ouyang, F. et al. 2023). Instructors can use this information to proactively address challenges and foster a supportive, inclusive environment for collaborative learning. Integrating AI into Social Constructivism teaching pedagogy enables educators to create dynamic, interactive learning spaces that encourage collaboration and collective knowledge construction among students and teachers.

AI integration in Social Constructivism pedagogy transforms the role of the instructor into that of a facilitator and moderator. With AI-powered collaborative tools and personalized learning platforms, instructors can create an environment that fosters meaningful interactions and collective knowledge construction among students (Balaji, K. 2022). Instructors guide discussions, provide scaffolding, and offer feedback while AI tools monitor group dynamics and sentiment, allowing instructors to intervene proactively when needed. By leveraging AI-driven insights, instructors can cultivate a supportive and inclusive learning community that encourages collaboration, critical thinking, and active participation.

3.3 Behaviorism Pedagogy

Behaviorism is a teaching pedagogy that focuses on observable behaviors and external stimuli to explain learning (Michael, J. 1984). It emphasizes the role of the teacher as the central authority figure who directs the learning process through structured instruction and reinforcement. In behaviorist pedagogy, techniques such as direct instruction, lectures, and drills are commonly employed to convey information and shape student behavior. Repetition and practice are emphasized to reinforce desired behaviors and skills. Additionally, behaviorist approaches often utilize rewards and consequences to motivate learning and encourage desired outcomes. While behaviorism traditionally places less emphasis on student autonomy and critical thinking, modern iterations may incorporate elements of active learning and technology-enhanced instruction to enhance engagement and promote deeper learning.

Integrating AI into Behaviorism pedagogy updates teaching methods, improves learning outcomes, and increases knowledge transmission efficiency. AI-powered Intelligent Tutoring Systems (ITS) provide interactive support, simulating a human tutor's role (Saputra, I. et al. 2023). These platforms deliver instant feedback and personalized learning experiences, aligning with Behaviorism's focus on observable behaviors. AI analytics tools help instructors analyze student performance data to inform instructional decisions, improving teaching effectiveness and promoting skill acquisition in line with Behaviorism's principles (McCardle, J. R. 2002).

Additionally, AI-enabled grading systems can automate the assessment process, providing instant feedback on assignments, quizzes, and exams. By employing natural language processing (NLP) and machine learning algorithms, these systems can evaluate written responses, detect errors, and provide constructive feedback to students. Automated grading streamlines the assessment workflow for instructors, enabling more timely and comprehensive feedback to students, while also reinforcing behaviorist principles of immediate reinforcement and corrective feedback.

In Behaviorism pedagogy, AI augments the role of the instructor by providing valuable insights and support for personalized instruction and assessment (Eager, B., & Brunton, R. 2023). Instructors leverage AI-driven Intelligent Tutoring Systems (ITS) to deliver targeted feedback and adaptive instruction, enabling students to progress at their own pace and receive immediate reinforcement. With AI analytics tools, instructors can analyze student performance data to identify areas for improvement and tailor instruction accordingly. The role of the instructor evolves into that of a data-informed facilitator, using AI-generated insights to optimize instructional strategies and enhance learning outcomes (Rismanchian, S., & Doroudi, S. 2023). Additionally, AI-enabled grading systems streamline the assessment process, allowing instructors to focus more on providing personalized feedback and support for student growth. Through the integration of AI technologies, instructors can create a more efficient and effective learning environment that promotes student mastery and success.

The integration of AI in education is transforming both the delivery of content and its compatibility with pedagogical frameworks. AI aligns with constructivist frameworks by enabling personalized learning, yet it may simplify complex human learning processes. In contrast, AI disrupts behaviorist models by automating grading and shifting focus from summative to formative feedback, potentially weakening the educator-student relationship.

4. CASE STUDIES AND BEST PRACTICES

The section firstly explores notable instances of AI integration in educational settings, showcasing advancements across various platforms and disciplines. Then, best practices for optimizing AI-enhanced educational experiences are discussed.

4.1 Successful Implementations of AI in Education

Several successful implementations of AI in education across various platforms and disciplines are discussed including ElectronixTutor (Graesser, A. C., 2018), Sketchtivity (Linsey, J. et al. 2022), and Augmented Reality-based Learning (Tuli, N. et al. 2022).

- **ElectronixTutor:** An integrated educational platform has been developed, incorporating various intelligent learning resources such as AutoTutor, Dragoon, LearnForm, ASSISTments, and BEETLE-II, alongside textual and video materials (Graesser, A. C., 2018). Its architecture features a student model comprising a standardized knowledge base on electronic circuits, enriched by contributions from individual learning resources, alongside a comprehensive record of student performance and attributes. The system employs a recommender system to provide personalized guidance to students based on their progress.

    The ElectronixTutor platform adopts a systematic approach to recommend learning resources tailored to students' current needs and abilities. Initially, recommendations are aligned with the curriculum calendar, focusing on the designated topic of the day. Additionally, a set of suggested topics is provided based on the student's historical performance data and other relevant attributes. Each topic is organized into bundles, with learning resources dynamically allocated based on real-time performance. While all topics and resources are accessible to self-regulated learners, data collection informs iterative adjustments to this structure. Benefits vary with student proficiency: advanced students benefit from AutoTutor's questioning and Dragoon's mental model construction, novices from foundational materials in ASSISTments and BEETLE-II, and intermediate students from AutoTutor's knowledge checks and LearnForm's problem-solving tasks. These allocations are based on personalized learning principles, with empirical validation through ongoing assessment and feedback processes.

    The system is currently undergoing testing and revision processes. Pilot testing has been initiated with engineering students to gather user feedback, while extensive input has been received from both lay and professional electrical engineering educators. Future plans include conducting tests on engineering students at the University of Memphis and Florida Institute of Technology to evaluate the system's impact on learning outcomes, using a comprehensive test covering approximately 80 knowledge components. ElectronixTutor is intended to serve as a supplementary tool in university courses and may potentially be incorporated into the curriculum.

- **Sketchtivity:** The project aimed to enhance engineers' freehand sketching skills through Sketchtivity, an intelligent tutoring software (Linsey, J. et al. 2022). Implemented across diverse universities, Sketchtivity provided lessons and feedback on two-point perspective sketching. The research explored the impact of the software on skill development, with initial findings indicating no negative effects on students' abilities. Further experiments delved into how students utilized the feedback provided by the software. Additionally, the project sought to expand Sketchtivity's functionality to cover more complex sketching tasks and offer more precise feedback. Understanding the implications of improved sketching skills, the research investigated measurement strategies, self-efficacy, and the relationship between sketching and creativity in engineering design. Overall, the project endeavored to improve sketching skills while exploring their broader implications in engineering education and practice.

Currently, the project team is conducting further analysis to explore the software's influence on the advancement of sketching skills. Preliminary findings suggest a likely disconnect between proficiency in sketching and the ability to generate ideas, indicating that designers, regardless of their skill level, can produce a multitude of concepts. Improved understanding of sketch evaluation techniques will facilitate more deliberate and insightful inquiries into the role of sketching in engineering education. Taken together, these components contribute to a broader comprehension of the underlying principles and methodologies for refining sketching techniques in engineering pedagogy.

- **Augmented Reality-Based Learning:** Tuli, N. et al. (2022) developed an augmented reality (AR)-based learning platform for teaching electronics engineering concepts and evaluated its impact on students' academic performance, learning attitudes, and attitudes toward AR technology. A quasi-experimental design was used, involving 107 first-year engineering students divided into control and experimental groups. The control group (n=53) used traditional teaching methods, while the experimental group (n=54) used an AR-based Lab Manual. The results showed that the experimental group had better post-test performance and higher academic scores. The study also found a positive impact of AR on students' attitudes toward learning, a significant correlation between attitudes toward electronics courses and academic achievement, and a positive relationship between academic performance and attitudes toward AR technology, indicating that exposure to AR technology improved students' outlook on the electronics course and AR technology.

Utilizing augmented reality (AR) in education presents several challenges and opportunities. While smartphones and tablets with built-in cameras facilitate AR application usage, there's a need for basic training to familiarize educators and students with the technology. Developing unique and content-valid AR experiences requires expertise in game development and design, necessitating financial support for professional software tools. Despite these hurdles, AR has significant potential to enhance online learning experiences, especially amid the COVID-19 pandemic. It's crucial for academic institutions to support educators and researchers in creating and deploying AR-based learning experiences on a broader scale.

Presently, the team is expanding the range of topics within the AR-based Learning Manual for electronics engineering. Subsequent research endeavors could investigate the influence of AR technology on students' memory retention, assessing the durability of knowledge acquired through AR over time. Furthermore, AR holds potential for application across various educational domains beyond electronics engineering.

4.2 Best Practices for Optimizing AI-Enhanced Educational Experiences

This sub-section delves into best practices for optimizing AI-enhanced educational experiences. It provides insights into navigating the complexities of AI-enhanced educational experiences and maximizing their benefits for learners and educators alike. The practices are summarized in Table 2.

Table 2. A summary of best practices for optimizing AI-enhanced educational experiences

Practice	Strategy
Policy Frameworks and Open-Source Adoption	- Develop robust public policies to guide AI's role in fostering sustainable development. - Focus on inclusivity and equity in AI implementation. - Equip educators with AI literacy and foster mutual understanding between AI and educational principles. - Establish quality and inclusive data frameworks. - Enhance the significance of AI in education research. - Uphold ethics and transparency in data utilization. - Advocate for open-source methodologies in software and hardware endeavors.
Leveraging Educator Input and Data Networks	- Acknowledge the necessity of input from educators in AI-based systems. - Update educational models and curricula to align with changing contexts and technological advancements. - Aggregate data through educational networks to develop robust algorithms trained on diverse student populations. - Minimize errors and facilitate adaptation to evolving trends.
Ethical Considerations in AI Integration	- Collaborate with ethics experts to address concerns such as overreliance on AI tools and biases within AI systems. - Conduct thorough evaluations to prevent negative outcomes like cheating and misinformation. - Discuss the incorporation of ethics courses into engineering curricula. - Address privacy and data management issues. - Adhere to principles of "FAIR" data management to promote educational equity.
Enhancing Professional Development for Educators	- Provide continuous professional development opportunities for engineering educators. - Offer ongoing education and training, including courses on AI principles and their application to teaching. - Integrate other technological topics relevant to Industry 4.0. - Stay abreast of advancements in the field.

- **Policy Frameworks and Open-Source Adoption:** The imperative of developing robust public policies to guide AI's role in fostering sustainable development has been underscored in (Pedro, F. et al. 2019), with a focus on ensuring inclusivity and equity in AI implementation. Equipping educators with AI literacy and fostering mutual understanding between AI and educational principles are deemed essential, alongside the establishment of quality and inclusive data frameworks. Furthermore, enhancing the significance of AI in education research and upholding ethics and transparency in data utilization and knowledge dissemination are paramount. Dynamic policy frameworks are recognized as vital catalysts for enhancing AI's educational efficacy, particularly in higher education and engineering disciplines

In the pursuit of educational and technological equity, the adoption of open-source methodologies in software and hardware endeavors is advocated, mirroring transformative practices in global product development. Notably, prominent entities in the AI domain are increasingly embracing open-source paradigms, as evidenced by initiatives such as Google's TensorFlow, IBM's open solutions, and the Acumos AI platform, thereby fostering sustainable growth within the AI industry. Looking ahead, the future landscape of engineering education, whether AI-enabled or not, is poised to thrive on collaborative efforts and the dissemination of engineering solutions, pedagogical resources, and project outcomes, as supported by recent research findings.

Leveraging Educator Input and Data Networks

AI-based systems primarily rely on vast datasets derived from past observations, which inherently limits their ability to anticipate future scenarios and catalyze radical innovations. However, such transformative breakthroughs are imperative, particularly in higher education, notably within engineering disciplines, to align with the relentless pace of technological advancement. Hence, despite the assistance of AI tools, input from educators remains indispensable. The evolving landscape of student demographics, influenced by changing contexts and generational shifts, necessitates ongoing updates to educational models. Moreover, engineering curricula undergo regular revisions to incorporate emerging technologies, techniques, and discoveries. Consequently, a singular professor's data may not suffice for effective AI applications. Data aggregation through educational networks enables the development of more robust algorithms trained on diverse student populations. This comprehensive dataset minimizes errors and facilitates swift adaptation to evolving social, technological, and educational trends.

- **Ethical Considerations in AI Integration for Education:** Significant attention has been dedicated to ethical considerations surrounding artificial intelligence, leading key stakeholders in the AI domain to collaborate with ethics experts in software and hardware development efforts. AI, pivotal in digital transformation and machine-generated media content, presents vast potential, as evidenced by ChatGPT's utilization of machine learning to generate text responses from user-input prompts, drawing from extensive internet-based knowledge (Pavlik, J. V. 2023). However, concerns arise regarding students' potential overreliance on this technology, prompting scrutiny of its impact on education to ensure it does not impede writing skills or foster dependency on AI tools. Cautionary notes from experts emphasize the need for thorough evaluation to prevent negative outcomes like cheating and misinformation (Tlili, A. et al. 2023).

The integration of AI in higher education, particularly in engineering curricula, raises ethical considerations that extend beyond course content to include privacy and data management. As AI relies on extensive datasets, including personal information, addressing issues like data accessibility and interoperability is crucial for expanding AI solutions and promoting educational equity (Wilkinson, M. D. et al. 2016). Additionally, the presence of biases in AI tools highlights the need for diverse development teams to ensure equitable education outcomes. Ignoring these ethical concerns risks perpetuating past errors and hindering progress towards fairness in education.

- **Enhancing Professional Development for Engineering Educators:** It is crucial for leveraging AI in engineering education, as the current cohort of professors often lacks formal AI training in their disciplines. Continuous professional development is essential, with universities offering ongoing education and training, including specialized courses by departments of educational innovation and pedagogical sciences centers. Lifelong learning, vital for career advancement, should be emphasized, with programs typically focusing on pedagogical resources, software, e-learning tools, programming, and research statistical methods (Redondo, A. C. et al. 2018). To improve these programs, integrating "AI principles" and "AI applied to teaching" courses is recommended, along with other Industry 4.0 technologies like big data, cloud computing, augmented reality, cybersecurity, and advanced simulation. These topics are crucial for keeping up with technological advancements in the field.

5. ETHICAL AND SOCIETAL CONSIDERATIONS

Rapid advances in AI technology in education have raised ethical concerns regarding student data privacy and AI ethics (Huang, L. 2023). The use of AI systems in education can have both positive and negative impacts, depending on how they are used (Gartner, S., & Krašna, M. 2023, Balfaqih M. 2023). Students' perceptions and attitudes towards AI tools in academia vary, with students from technology and science-focused schools displaying higher levels of concern about data privacy (Irfan, M., et al. 2023). In the field of biomedical and engineering education, integrating AI applications raises unique ethical challenges that need to be addressed (Busch, F. et al. 2023). Biased algorithms, displacement of human educators, and transparency and accountability in decision-making processes are key ethical concerns in higher education AI use (Slimi, Z., & Carballido, B. V. 2023). Stakeholders must work together to address these challenges and ensure responsible AI deployment in education, while maximizing its benefits and minimizing risks .

The Challenges of AI in education can be classified as critical societal issues such as systemic bias, discrimination, inequality for marginalized groups of students, and xenophobia, or as ethical issues related to privacy and safety in data collection and processing (Holmes, W., et al. 2021, Hwang, G. J., et al. 2020). In this section, we will discuss the source of both ethical and societal considerations with some of the measures that should be taken to mitigate their risk.

5.1 Ethical Issues

The ethical challenges and risks posed by AI systems seemingly run counter to marketing efforts that present algorithms to the public as if they are objective and value-neutral tools (Akgun, S., & Greenhow, C. 2022). Considering the different forms of bias and ethical challenges of AI applications, we will focus on privacy, transparency, accountability, security and safety, sustainability, and proportionality.

5.1.1 Privacy

AI in education often involves the collection and analysis of vast amounts of personal data from learners and educators. This data may include sensitive information such as academic performance, learning preferences, and behavioral patterns. As AI systems become more integrated into educational settings, there is a growing concern about the potential for privacy breaches, unauthorized access to personal data, and misuse of sensitive information. Protecting privacy in education is essential for maintaining trust between educational institutions, learners, and educators. Breaches of privacy can lead to violations of individuals' rights, loss of trust in educational systems, and potential harm to learners' academic and personal development (Rahman, M. M., et al. 2023). Moreover, privacy breaches can have legal and ethical ramifications, resulting in financial penalties and reputational damage to institutions. To address privacy concerns in AI education, institutions should implement robust data protection policies and practices. This includes obtaining informed consent from individuals before collecting their data, implementing secure data storage and transmission protocols, and providing transparency about how data will be used. Additionally, educational stakeholders should prioritize data minimization, ensuring that only necessary data is collected and retained (Laato, S., et al. 2020). Regular audits and assessments of data practices can help identify and mitigate potential privacy risks, while ongoing education and training can raise awareness among learners and educators about their rights and responsibilities regarding data privacy.

5.1.2 Transparency and Accountability

AI algorithms used in education often operate as "black boxes," making it difficult for stakeholders to understand how decisions are made. Lack of transparency in data usage and algorithmic decision-making can lead to distrust, uncertainty, and potential biases in educational outcomes (Richter, F. 2021). Transparency and accountability are essential for fostering trust and confidence in AI systems used in education. Without transparency, stakeholders may question the fairness and reliability of AI-driven decisions, leading to skepticism and resistance to adoption. Moreover, accountability ensures that individuals and organizations are held responsible for the consequences of their actions, promoting ethical behavior and adherence to best practices.

To promote transparency and accountability in AI education, institutions should prioritize explainable AI (XAI) techniques that provide insight into how AI systems make decisions (Rachha, A., & Seyam, M. 2023). This includes documenting and communicating the data sources, algorithms, and decision-making processes used in AI-driven educational tools. Additionally, institutions should establish clear policies and procedures for data governance, risk management, and compliance with relevant regulations. Regular audits and assessments of AI systems can help ensure compliance with ethical standards and identify areas for improvement (Raj, A., et al. 2023) Finally, fostering a culture of transparency and accountability among educational stakeholders through education and training can promote responsible use of AI in education.

5.1.3 Security and Safety

The integration of AI in education introduces new security risks, including cybercrimes, data breaches, and threats to personal safety. AI systems may be vulnerable to hacking, unauthorized access, and manipulation, posing risks to the privacy and security of learners' personal information (Yu, H., et al. 2023). Ensuring the security and safety of AI systems in education is paramount to protect learners, educators, and institutions from potential harm. Data breaches and cyberattacks can result in identity theft, financial loss, and reputational damage, undermining trust in educational institutions and hindering the learning process. Moreover, ensuring the safety of AI systems is essential to prevent physical harm or accidents resulting from malfunctioning or maliciously manipulated AI algorithms. To address security and safety concerns in AI education, institutions should implement robust cybersecurity measures, including encryption, authentication, and access controls to protect sensitive data (Rahman, M. M., et al. 2023).

Regular security audits and vulnerability assessments can help identify and mitigate potential security risks. Additionally, institutions should prioritize safety-critical considerations in the design and development of AI systems, including fail-safe mechanisms, error handling procedures, and emergency shutdown protocols. Educating and training learners and educators about cybersecurity best practices and safe use of AI technologies can also help raise awareness and mitigate security risks in educational settings. Finally, collaborating with cybersecurity experts and regulatory authorities to stay informed about emerging threats and compliance requirements can help institutions stay ahead of security challenges and ensure the ongoing safety of AI systems in education.

5.1.4 Sustainability and Proportionality

The widespread adoption of AI in education can have significant environmental, economic, and societal impacts. AI systems may consume large amounts of energy and resources, contributing to environmental degradation and climate change. Moreover, AI-driven educational technologies may exacerbate existing inequalities and disrupt social and economic systems, leading to unintended consequences and disproportionate outcomes (Chen, Z., et al. 2023). Addressing sustainability and proportionality in AI education is essential to minimize the negative environmental and societal impacts associated with AI adoption. Sustainable AI practices can help reduce energy consumption, minimize ecological footprint, and promote responsible resource management. Additionally, ensuring proportionality in AI deployment can help mitigate the risk of exacerbating inequalities and social injustices, promoting fair and equitable access to educational opportunities for all learners.

To promote sustainability and proportionality in AI education, institutions should prioritize the development and adoption of energy-efficient AI technologies and practices. This includes optimizing AI algorithms for resource efficiency, minimizing data storage and processing requirements, and leveraging renewable energy sources where possible (Schiff, D. 2022). Additionally, institutions should conduct thorough impact assessments to evaluate the potential environmental, economic, and societal implications of AI adoption and identify strategies to mitigate negative effects. Collaborating with policymakers, industry partners, and community stakeholders can help develop regulatory frameworks and best practices to promote sustainable and equitable AI deployment in education.

5.2 Societal Issues

The societal challenges raised by AI systems comes mainly from the lack of ethical principals that govern AI systems development (Akgun, S., & Greenhow, C. 2022). Considering the different forms of societal challenges of AI applications, we will focus on inclusiveness, Human-Centered AI in Education, education Equity, and educational outcomes.

5.2.1 Inclusiveness

The adoption of AI in education has the potential to either exacerbate or mitigate existing inequalities in access to educational opportunities. AI-driven educational technologies may inadvertently exclude certain groups of learners, such as those with disabilities or from marginalized communities, if they are not designed with inclusivity in mind. Moreover, biased algorithms and data sources may perpetuate discrimination and reinforce societal inequities (Chan, C. K. Y. 2023). Promoting inclusiveness in AI education is essential to ensure that all learners have equitable access to educational opportunities and resources. Addressing barriers to inclusivity can help reduce disparities in educational outcomes and promote social justice and equality. Moreover, fostering a culture of inclusivity can enrich the learning experience for all learners, fostering diversity, creativity, and innovation. To promote inclusiveness in AI education, institutions should prioritize diversity and inclusion in the design, development, and implementation of AI-driven educational technologies. This includes ensuring that AI systems are accessible to learners with disabilities, culturally sensitive, and responsive to the needs of diverse learners. Additionally, institutions should address bias and discrimination in AI algorithms and data sources through comprehensive data collection, validation, and validation processes (Holmes, W., et al. 2021). Collaborating with diverse stakeholders, including learners, educators, community organizations, and policymakers, can help identify and address barriers to inclusivity and promote a more inclusive and equitable learning environment.

5.2.2 Human-Centered AIED

The integration of AI in education has the potential to transform teaching and learning practices, but it also raises concerns about the impact on human autonomy, agency, and well-being. AI-driven educational technologies may influence learners' decision-making processes, limit their autonomy, and shape their behavior in ways that may not align with their best interests (Mittal, A., et al. 2023). Promoting human-centered AI in education is essential to ensure that AI technologies enhance, rather than diminish, human autonomy, agency, and well-being. By prioritizing human values and interests in the design, development, and implementation of AI-driven educational technologies, institutions can empower learners, educators, and communities to make informed decisions and pursue their educational goals in alignment with their values and preferences. To promote human-centered AI in education, institutions should prioritize ethical considerations, such as transparency, accountability, fairness, and user empowerment, in the design, development, and deployment of AI-driven educational technologies. This includes incorporating principles of human rights, social justice, and ethical decision-making into AI design and development processes. Additionally, institutions should prioritize user-centered design practices that involve learners, educators, and other stakeholders in the co-design and evaluation of AI-driven educational technologies. Finally, institutions should prioritize education and training programs to raise awareness about the ethical implications of AI in education and empower learners and educators to make informed decisions about the use of AI technologies in their learning environments (Brusilovsky, P. 2023).

5.2.3 Impact on Education Equity

The integration of AI in education has the potential to either exacerbate or mitigate existing disparities in educational equity. AI-driven educational technologies may perpetuate inequalities by reinforcing existing biases and discriminating against marginalized groups. For example, biased algorithms and data sources may result in unequal access to educational opportunities and resources for learners from underserved communities. On the other hand, AI technologies have the potential to enhance educational equity by providing personalized learning experiences, adaptive support, and targeted interventions to address individual learners' needs and strengths. Addressing the impact of AI on education equity is crucial to promote fairness, inclusivity, and social justice in education. Ensuring equitable access to high-quality education for all learners is essential for promoting equal opportunities, social mobility, and economic prosperity. By addressing disparities in educational equity, institutions can help close the achievement gap and empower learners from diverse backgrounds to reach their full potential. To address the impact of AI on education equity, institutions should prioritize equity considerations in the design, development, and implementation of AI-driven educational technologies. This includes ensuring that AI systems are designed to promote fairness, inclusivity, and accessibility for all learners, regardless of their background or circumstances. Additionally, institutions should prioritize targeted interventions and support services to address the specific needs of underserved learners and communities. Collaborating with diverse stakeholders, including educators, policymakers, community organizations, and learners themselves, can help identify and address barriers to educational equity and promote more equitable outcomes for all learners.

5.2.4 Educational Outcomes and Learning Experiences

The integration of AI in education has the potential to influence educational outcomes and learning experiences in various ways. AI-driven educational technologies can personalize learning experiences, provide real-time feedback, and adapt instructional content to meet individual learners' needs and preferences. However, there are concerns about the impact of AI on educational outcomes, such as academic achievement, critical thinking skills, and social-emotional development (Raj, A., et al. 2023). Additionally, there is a need to ensure that AI technologies complement, rather than replace, human teaching and support services to promote holistic learning experiences. Addressing the impact of AI on educational outcomes and learning experiences is essential to ensure that AI technologies enhance, rather than detract from, the quality and effectiveness of education. By prioritizing evidence-based practices and pedagogical approaches, institutions can leverage AI to improve student engagement, motivation, and learning outcomes. Additionally, institutions should prioritize research and evaluation efforts to assess the effectiveness of AI-driven educational technologies and identify areas for improvement. To address the impact of AI on educational outcomes and learning experiences, institutions should prioritize research-informed practices and pedagogical approaches that leverage AI to enhance teaching and learning. This includes designing AI-driven educational technologies that promote active learning, critical thinking, and collaboration among learners. Additionally, institutions should prioritize professional development and training programs to support educators in effectively integrating AI technologies into their teaching practices and fostering positive learning experiences for all students Hong, Y., et al. 2022). Finally, institutions should prioritize ongoing evaluation and refinement of AI-driven educational technologies to ensure that they align with educational goals and promote positive outcomes for all learners.

6. CONCLUSION

This chapter has examined the significant role of Artificial Intelligence (AI) in transforming various aspects of education. Through a comprehensive review of literature and case studies, we have explored how AI technologies are revolutionizing teaching and learning practices, enhancing personalization, adaptability, and effectiveness in educational settings. From the integration of AI-driven adaptive learning systems to the utilization of real-time data analysis for personalized feedback, it is evident that AI holds immense potential to cater to diverse learner needs and foster better learning outcomes. Moreover, the ethical and societal considerations surrounding the adoption of AI in education have been highlighted, emphasizing the importance of ensuring privacy, transparency, inclusiveness, and educational equity. As AI continues to evolve and permeate educational landscapes, it is crucial for educators, policymakers, and stakeholders to embrace proactive engagement with AI technologies, leveraging their capabilities to create dynamic, interactive, and inclusive learning environments. By harnessing the power of AI, we can pave the way for a more equitable, accessible, and effective education system that empowers learners to thrive in the digital age.

REFERENCES

Akgun, S., & Greenhow, C. (2022). Artificial intelligence in education: Addressing ethical challenges in K-12 settings. *AI and Ethics*, *2*(3), 431–440. doi:10.1007/s43681-021-00096-7 PMID:34790956

Balaji, K., Selvam, M., & Rajeswari, R. (2022). Impact of Artificial Intelligence (AI), Internet of Things (IoT) & STEM Social Enterprise Learning Based Applications in the Teaching and Learning Process of Engineering Education. In *ICDSMLA 2020: Proceedings of the 2nd International Conference on Data Science, Machine Learning and Applications* (pp. 1217-1226). Springer Singapore. 10.1007/978-981-16-3690-5_116

Balfaqih, M. (2023). A Hybrid Movies Recommendation System Based on Demographics and Facial Expression Analysis using Machine Learning. *International Journal of Advanced Computer Science and Applications*, *14*(11). Advance online publication. doi:10.14569/IJACSA.2023.0141177

Balfaqih, M., & Alharbi, S. A. (2022). Associated Information and Communication Technologies Challenges of Smart City Development. *Sustainability (Basel)*, *14*(23), 16240. doi:10.3390/su142316240

Baskara, F. R. (2023). Personalised learning with ai: implications for Ignatian pedagogy. *International Journal of Educational Best Practices*, *7*(1), 1–16. doi:10.31258/ijebp.v7n1.p1-16

Bienkowski, M., Feng, M., & Means, B. (2012). *Enhancing Teaching and Learning through Educational Data Mining and Learning Analytics: An Issue Brief*. Office of Educational Technology, US Department of Education.

Brusilovsky, P. (2023). AI in Education, Learner Control, and Human-AI Collaboration. *International Journal of Artificial Intelligence in Education*, 1–14.

Brynjolfsson, E., & McAfee, A. (2014). *The second machine age: Work, progress, and prosperity in a time of brilliant technologies*. WW Norton & Company.

Busch, F., Adams, L. C., & Bressem, K. K. (2023). Biomedical Ethical Aspects Towards the Implementation of Artificial Intelligence in Medical Education. *Medical Science Educator*, *33*(4), 1–6. doi:10.1007/s40670-023-01815-x PMID:37546190

Carr, N. (2010). *The shallows: How the internet is changing the way we think, read and remember*. Atlantic Books Ltd.

Chan, C. K. Y. (2023). A comprehensive AI policy education framework for university teaching and learning. *International Journal of Educational Technology in Higher Education*, *20*(1), 38. doi:10.1186/s41239-023-00408-3

Chen, Z., Wu, M., Chan, A., Li, X., & Ong, Y. S. (2023). Survey on AI Sustainability: Emerging Trends on Learning Algorithms and Research Challenges. *IEEE Computational Intelligence Magazine*, *18*(2), 60–77. doi:10.1109/MCI.2023.3245733

Chomsky, N. (1980). Rules and representations. *Behavioral and Brain Sciences*, *3*(1), 1–15. doi:10.1017/S0140525X00001515

Ciampa, K. (2014). Learning in a mobile age: An investigation of student motivation. *Journal of Computer Assisted Learning*, *30*(1), 82–96. doi:10.1111/jcal.12036

Ciolacu, M., Svasta, P. M., Berg, W., & Popp, H. (2017a). Education 4.0 for tall thin engineer in a data driven society. In *2017 IEEE 23rd International Symposium for Design and Technology in Electronic Packaging (SIITME)* (pp. 432-437). IEEE.

Ciolacu, M., Tehrani, A. F., Beer, R., & Popp, H. (2017b). Education 4.0—Fostering student's performance with machine learning methods. In *2017 IEEE 23rd international symposium for design and technology in electronic packaging (SIITME)* (pp. 438-443). IEEE.

Dsouza, K., Zhu, L., Varma-Nelson, P., Fang, S., & Mukhopadhyay, S. (2023, May). AI-Augmented Peer Led Team Learning for STEM Education. In *2023 IEEE 17th International Symposium on Applied Computational Intelligence and Informatics (SACI)* (pp. 000581-000586). IEEE.

Du Boulay, B. (2016). Artificial intelligence as an effective classroom assistant. *IEEE Intelligent Systems*, *31*(6), 76–81. doi:10.1109/MIS.2016.93

Eager, B., & Brunton, R. (2023). Prompting higher education towards AI-augmented teaching and learning practice. *Journal of University Teaching & Learning Practice, 20*(5), 02.

Gartner, S., & Krašna, M. (2023, June). Artificial intelligence in education-ethical framework. In *2023 12th Mediterranean Conference on Embedded Computing (MECO)* (pp. 1-7). IEEE. 10.1109/MECO58584.2023.10155012

Gilbert, I. (2014). *Why do I need a teacher when I've got google?: The Essential Guide to the big issues for every teacher*. Routledge. doi:10.4324/9781315767628

Giuffra Palomino, C. E., Azambuja Silveira, R., & Nakayama, M. K. (2014). An intelligent LMS model based on intelligent tutoring systems. *Intelligent Tutoring Systems: 12th International Conference, ITS 2014, Honolulu, HI, USA, June 5-9, 2014 Proceedings*, *12*, 567–574.

Graesser, A. C., Hu, X., Nye, B. D., VanLehn, K., Kumar, R., Heffernan, C., Heffernan, N., Woolf, B., Olney, A. M., Rus, V., Andrasik, F., Pavlik, P., Cai, Z., Wetzel, J., Morgan, B., Hampton, A. J., Lippert, A. M., Wang, L., Cheng, Q., ... Baer, W. (2018). ElectronixTutor: An intelligent tutoring system with multiple learning resources for electronics. *International Journal of STEM Education*, *5*(1), 1–21. doi:10.1186/s40594-018-0110-y PMID:30631705

Guterman, J. T. (2014). *Mastering the art of solution-focused counseling*. John Wiley & Sons.

Holmes, W., Porayska-Pomsta, K., Holstein, K., Sutherland, E., Baker, T., Shum, S. B., ... Koedinger, K. R. (2021). Ethics of AI in education: Towards a community-wide framework. *International Journal of Artificial Intelligence in Education*, 1–23.

Holstein, K. (2018). Towards teacher-ai hybrid systems. *Companion Proceedings of the Eighth International Conference on Learning Analytics & Knowledge.*

Hong, Y., Nguyen, A., Dang, B., & Nguyen, B. P. T. (2022, July). Data Ethics Framework for Artificial Intelligence in Education (AIED). In *2022 International Conference on Advanced Learning Technologies (ICALT)* (pp. 297-301). IEEE. 10.1109/ICALT55010.2022.00095

Howitz, W. J., Thane, T. A., Frey, T. L., Wang, X. S., Gonzales, J. C., Tretbar, C. A., Seith, D. D., Saluga, S. J., Lam, S., Nguyen, M. M., Tieu, P., Link, R. D., & Edwards, K. D. (2020). Online in no time: Design and implementation of a remote learning first quarter general chemistry laboratory and second quarter organic chemistry laboratory. *Journal of Chemical Education*, 97(9), 2624–2634. doi:10.1021/acs.jchemed.0c00895

Huang, L. (2023). Ethics of artificial intelligence in education: Student privacy and data protection. *Science Insights Education Frontiers*, 16(2), 2577–2587. doi:10.15354/sief.23.re202

Hwang, G. J., Xie, H., Wah, B. W., & Gašević, D. (2020). Vision, challenges, roles and research issues of Artificial Intelligence in Education. *Computers and Education: Artificial Intelligence*, 1, 100001. doi:10.1016/j.caeai.2020.100001

Ikedinachi, A. P., Misra, S., Assibong, P. A., Olu-Owolabi, E. F., Maskeliūnas, R., & Damasevicius, R. (2019). Artificial intelligence, smart classrooms and online education in the 21st century: Implications for human development. *Journal of Cases on Information Technology*, 21(3), 66–79. doi:10.4018/JCIT.2019070105

Irfan, M., Aldulaylan, F., & Alqahtani, Y. (2023). Ethics and Privacy in Irish Higher Education: A Comprehensive Study of Artificial Intelligence (AI) Tools Implementation at University of Limerick. *Global Social Sciences Review*, 8(2), 201–210. doi:10.31703/gssr.2023(VIII-II).19

Kent, M., & Bennett, R. (2017). What was all that about? Peak MOOC hype and post-MOOC legacies. *Massive open online courses and higher education: What went right, what went wrong and where to next*, 1-8.

Kokku, R., Sundararajan, S., Dey, P., Sindhgatta, R., Nitta, S., & Sengupta, B. (2018, April). Augmenting classrooms with AI for personalized education. In 2018 IEEE international conference on acoustics, speech and signal processing (ICASSP) (pp. 6976-6980). IEEE. doi:10.1109/ICASSP.2018.8461812

Laato, S., Farooq, A., Tenhunen, H., Pitkamaki, T., Hakkala, A., & Airola, A. (2020, July). Ai in cybersecurity education-a systematic literature review of studies on cybersecurity moocs. In *2020 IEEE 20th International Conference on Advanced Learning Technologies (ICALT)* (pp. 6-10). IEEE. 10.1109/ICALT49669.2020.00009

Lin, F., & Chan, C. K. (2018). Examining the role of computer-supported knowledge-building discourse in epistemic and conceptual understanding. *Journal of Computer Assisted Learning*, 34(5), 567–579. doi:10.1111/jcal.12261

Linsey, J., Hammond, T., Douglas, K., Viswanathan, V., Krishnamurthy, V., Merzdorf, H., Jaison, D., Ray, S., Weaver, M., & Li, W. (2022, August), *Sketchtivity, an Intelligent Tutoring Software: Broadening Applications and Impact* Paper presented at 2022 ASEE Annual Conference & Exposition, Minneapolis, MN. 10.18260/1-2--42014

Mander, J. (1978). *Four arguments for the elimination of television.* Quill.

McCardle, J. R. (2002). The challenge of integrating ai & smart technology in design education. *International Journal of Technology and Design Education, 12*(1), 59–76. doi:10.1023/A:1013089404168

Michael, J. (1984). Verbal behavior. *Journal of the Experimental Analysis of Behavior, 42*(3), 363–376. doi:10.1901/jeab.1984.42-363 PMID:16812395

Mitchell, M. (2019). Artificial intelligence: A guide for thinking humans. Academic Press.

Mittal, A., Ramachandran, K. K., Lakshmi, K. K., Hasbullah, N. N., Ravichand, M., & Lourens, M. (2023, May). Human-cantered Artificial Intelligence in Education, present and future opportunities. In *2023 3rd International Conference on Advance Computing and Innovative Technologies in Engineering (ICACITE)* (pp. 1003-1008). IEEE. 10.1109/ICACITE57410.2023.10182647

Mounsey, R., Vandehey, M., & Diekhoff, G. (2013). Working and non-working university students: Anxiety, depression, and grade point average. *College Student Journal, 47*(2), 379–389.

Okewu, E., Adewole, P., Misra, S., Maskeliunas, R., & Damasevicius, R. (2021). Artificial neural networks for educational data mining in higher education: A systematic literature review. *Applied Artificial Intelligence, 35*(13), 983–1021. doi:10.1080/08839514.2021.1922847

Ouyang, F., Dinh, T. A., & Xu, W. (2023). A systematic review of AI-driven educational assessment in STEM education. *Journal for STEM Education Research, 6*(3), 408–426. doi:10.1007/s41979-023-00112-x

Pappano, L. (2012). The Year of the MOOC. *The New York Times, 2*(12).

Pavlik, J. V. (2023). Collaborating with ChatGPT: Considering the implications of generative artificial intelligence for journalism and media education. *Journalism & Mass Communication Educator, 78*(1), 84–93. doi:10.1177/10776958221149577

Pedro, F., Subosa, M., Rivas, A., & Valverde, P. (2019). *Artificial intelligence in education: Challenges and opportunities for sustainable development.* Academic Press.

Piaget, J. (2005). *The psychology of intelligence.* Routledge. doi:10.4324/9780203981528

Psoinos, D. I. (2021). *Adapting Approaches and Methods to Teaching English Online: Theory and Practice.* Springer Nature. doi:10.1007/978-3-030-79919-9

Qadir, J. (2023, May). Engineering education in the era of ChatGPT: Promise and pitfalls of generative AI for education. In *2023 IEEE Global Engineering Education Conference (EDUCON)* (pp. 1-9). IEEE. 10.1109/EDUCON54358.2023.10125121

Rachha, A., & Seyam, M. (2023). Explainable AI In Education: Current Trends, Challenges, And Opportunities. *SoutheastCon,* 232–239. doi:10.1109/SoutheastCon51012.2023.10115140

Rahem, A. A. T., Ismail, M., Najm, I. A., & Balfaqih, M. (2017). Topology sense and graph-based TSG: Efficient wireless ad hoc routing protocol for WANET. *Telecommunication Systems*, *65*(4), 739–754. doi:10.1007/s11235-016-0242-7

Rahman, M. M., Arshi, A. S., Hasan, M. M., Mishu, S. F., Shahriar, H., & Wu, F. (2023, June). Security Risk and Attacks in AI: A Survey of Security and Privacy. In *2023 IEEE 47th Annual Computers, Software, and Applications Conference (COMPSAC)* (pp. 1834-1839). IEEE. 10.1109/COMPSAC57700.2023.00284

Raj, A., Sharma, V., Rani, S., Balusamy, B., Shanu, A. K., & Alkhayyat, A. (2023, February). Revealing AI-Based Ed-Tech Tools Using Big Data. In *2023 3rd International Conference on Innovative Practices in Technology and Management (ICIPTM)* (pp. 1-6). IEEE. 10.1109/ICIPTM57143.2023.10118162

Redondo, A. C., de Pablo Lerchundi, I., Martí-Blanc, G., Martín, J. L., & Núñez, J. A. S. (2018). Training profile of faculty in applied sciences. *International Journal of Engineering Education*, *34*(5), 1504–1515.

Richter, F. (2021, October). Ethics of AI as practical ethics. In *2021 IEEE International Symposium on Technology and Society (ISTAS)* (pp. 1-1). IEEE.

Rismanchian, S., & Doroudi, S. (2023). *Four Interactions Between AI and Education: Broadening Our Perspective on What AI Can Offer Education*. Academic Press.

Sajja, R., Sermet, Y., Cwiertny, D., & Demir, I. (2023). Platform-independent and curriculum-oriented intelligent assistant for higher education. *International Journal of Educational Technology in Higher Education*, *20*(1), 42. doi:10.1186/s41239-023-00412-7

Saputra, I., Astuti, M., Sayuti, M., & Kusumastuti, D. (2023). Integration of Artificial Intelligence in Education: Opportunities, Challenges, Threats and Obstacles. A Literature Review. *Indonesian Journal of Computer Science*, *12*(4). Advance online publication. doi:10.33022/ijcs.v12i4.3266

Schiff, D. (2022). Education for AI, not AI for education: The role of education and ethics in national AI policy strategies. *International Journal of Artificial Intelligence in Education*, *32*(3), 527–563. doi:10.1007/s40593-021-00270-2

Seeroo, O., & Bekaroo, G. (2021, December). Enhancing Student Support via the Application of a Voice User Interface System: Insights on User Experience. In *Proceedings of the International Conference on Artificial Intelligence and its Applications* (pp. 1-6). 10.1145/3487923.3487936

Sein-Echaluce, M. L., Fidalgo-Blanco, A., & García-Peñalvo, F. J. (Eds.). (2019). *Innovative trends in flipped teaching and adaptive learning*. IGI Global. doi:10.4018/978-1-5225-8142-0

Shawky, D., & Badawi, A. (2019). Towards a personalized learning experience using reinforcement learning. *Machine learning paradigms: Theory and application*, 169-187.

Slimi, Z., & Carballido, B. V. (2023). Navigating the Ethical Challenges of Artificial Intelligence in Higher Education: An Analysis of Seven Global AI Ethics Policies. *TEM Journal*, *12*(2).

Thunstrom, A. O. (2022). We asked GPT-3 to write an academic paper about itself: Then we tried to get it published. *Scientific American*, 30.

Tlili, A., Shehata, B., Adarkwah, M. A., Bozkurt, A., Hickey, D. T., Huang, R., & Agyemang, B. (2023). What if the devil is my guardian angel: ChatGPT as a case study of using chatbots in education. *Smart Learning Environments, 10*(1), 15. doi:10.1186/s40561-023-00237-x

Tuli, N., Singh, G., Mantri, A., & Sharma, S. (2022). Augmented reality learning environment to aid engineering students in performing practical laboratory experiments in electronics engineering. *Smart Learning Environments, 9*(1), 1–20. doi:10.1186/s40561-022-00207-9

Vigotsky, L. S. (1939). Thought and speech. *Psychiatry, 2*(1), 29–54. doi:10.1080/00332747.1939.11022225

Wang, D., Tao, Y., & Chen, G. (2024). Artificial intelligence in classroom discourse: A systematic review of the past decade. *International Journal of Educational Research, 123*, 102275. doi:10.1016/j.ijer.2023.102275

Wilkinson, M. D., Dumontier, M., Aalbersberg, I. J., Appleton, G., Axton, M., Baak, A., Blomberg, N., Boiten, J.-W., da Silva Santos, L. B., Bourne, P. E., Bouwman, J., Brookes, A. J., Clark, T., Crosas, M., Dillo, I., Dumon, O., Edmunds, S., Evelo, C. T., Finkers, R., ... Mons, B. (2016). The FAIR Guiding Principles for scientific data management and stewardship. *Scientific Data, 3*(1), 1–9. doi:10.1038/sdata.2016.18 PMID:26978244

Williamson, B., Eynon, R., & Potter, J. (2020). Pandemic politics, pedagogies and practices: Digital technologies and distance education during the coronavirus emergency. *Learning, Media and Technology, 45*(2), 107–114. doi:10.1080/17439884.2020.1761641

Xu, W., & Ouyang, F. (2022). The application of AI technologies in STEM education: A systematic review from 2011 to 2021. *International Journal of STEM Education, 9*(1), 1–20. doi:10.1186/s40594-022-00377-5

Yu, H., Liu, Z., & Guo, Y. (2023, April). application Status, Problems and Future Prospects of Generative ai in education. In *2023 5th International Conference on Computer Science and Technologies in Education (CSTE)* (pp. 1-7). IEEE.

Chapter 6
An Overview of Artificial Intelligence–Enhanced Teaching Methods

Wasswa Shafik

https://orcid.org/0000-0002-9320-3186

School of Digital Science, Universiti Brunei Darussalam, Brunei & Dig Connectivity Research Laboratory (DCRLab), Kampala, Uganda

ABSTRACT

This study dichotomizes AI's profound impact on traditional teaching, defines its role, and explores AI-enhanced methods. It critiques lecture-based and textbook learning for lacking personalization and prompt feedback. It details AI integration, emphasizing personalized learning, immersive tech like virtual and augmented reality, and key components: machine learning and natural language processing. Use cases demonstrate personalized learning paths and real-time feedback. The study further dives into AI-enhanced teaching: adaptive learning, intelligent tutoring, gamification, chatbots, and assessment automation, highlighting their transformative potential. It finally addresses challenges and ethics and projects AI's future contributions in research and curriculum development, urging adoption for future learners' benefit.

INTRODUCTION

Artificial intelligence[1] (AI) pertains to the emulation of human intellect within computer systems or the creation of algorithms enabling robots to do tasks that conventionally necessitate human intelligence and academic approaches such as data science (Shafik, 2024a). These tasks involve a diverse array of activities, which include but are not limited to problem-solving, decision-making, audio and picture recognition, natural language understanding, and learning from data (Pheng et al., 2022). AI systems are specifically engineered to do comprehensive analyses of extensive datasets, discern recurring patterns, generate predictions, and dynamically adjust their behavior in response to the information they have

DOI: 10.4018/979-8-3693-2728-9.ch006

processed (Yachen, 2022). The overarching objective of AI is to develop computers or software capable of demonstrating cognitive abilities comparable to human intelligence.

AI can be classified into two primary categories: narrow or weak AI and general or strong AI[2]. Narrow AI[3] refers to a type of AI that is specifically built to perform well-defined tasks, such as those involving virtual personal assistants, recommendation systems, and self-driving automobiles (Fan & Zhong, 2022). These systems demonstrate a high level of specialization and proficiency within their respective fields. However, they do not possess the broader cognitive capabilities that humans possess, and some AI challenges differ according to current technological acceptance and trust (Shafik, 2024b). On the other hand, the objective of generated AI[4] is to develop robots that possess intellect comparable to that of humans, enabling them to comprehend and execute a diverse array of activities with the same level of adaptability as people (Wei et al., 2022; Shafik, 2024c). The concept of AI, although a prominent objective, is predominantly theoretical and has yet to be fully actualized.

More still, AI systems are constructed based on a variety of foundational technologies, which encompass machine learning, neural networks, natural language processing, and expert systems. Machine learning, which falls under the umbrella of AI, enables systems to acquire knowledge from data and enhance their performance through iterative processes without the need for explicit programming (Russell et al., 2023). Neural networks[5], which draw inspiration from the structure and functioning of the human brain, serve as the fundamental framework for deep learning, a specialized branch of machine learning that has gained significant acclaim for its remarkable achievements in several domains, such as image and speech recognition. Natural language processing[6] (NLP) enables robots to understand and produce human language, a crucial capability for applications such as chatbots[7], virtual assistants, and language translation (Shafik, 2023; Abdalgane & Othman, 2023). Expert systems employ rule-based logic in order to replicate the decision-making procedures of human experts within particular fields.

AI exhibits extensive applicability across diverse sectors, encompassing education, healthcare, banking, autonomous vehicles, and manufacturing. The phenomenon possesses the capacity to bring about significant changes in our contemporary society, which is increasingly reliant on data. This completely transforms various aspects of our lives, professional endeavors, and interactions with technological advancements (Bilgic et al., 2022). The rapid expansion of AI capabilities necessitates thoughtful examination and regulation of ethical concerns, including algorithmic prejudice and its implications for employment, in order to safeguard the overall societal benefits of AI. With the ongoing progression of AI, the potential for addressing intricate challenges and enhancing human capacities arises, thereby envisioning a future characterized by the coexistence of people and intelligent machines in a mutually beneficial and interdependent manner (An, 2022).

AI functions by using the principles of pattern recognition and data analysis, employing algorithms to detect connections and generate predictions from extensive datasets. The rapid advancement of AI can be attributed, in part, to the abundant availability of extensive datasets and the corresponding computer capabilities necessary for their processing (Lindegger et al., 2022). Machine learning algorithms exhibit enhanced performance when exposed to a significant volume of data, enabling them to iteratively improve their models and produce more precise and reliable insights. The utilization of data-driven methodologies has brought about significant transformations in various domains, including healthcare and finance. In the healthcare sector, AI has demonstrated its capability to examine patient records and diagnostic imaging, thereby aiding in the identification and planning of treatment for diseases (Hsieh et al., 2020). Similarly, in the realm of finance, AI-powered algorithms have proven effective in forecasting market trends and effectively managing investment portfolios.

Neural networks, which draw inspiration from the structural and functional characteristics of the human brain, constitute another essential element within the field of AI. Neural networks are comprised of interconnected nodes, also known as neurons, which undertake the processing and transmission of information (Chassignol et al., 2018). Deep learning, which is a specialized branch of machine learning, largely relies on neural networks to autonomously identify patterns within data. This characteristic renders deep learning very proficient in tasks such as picture recognition, speech synthesis, and natural language comprehension (Hogg et al., 2023). The ability of deep learning to effectively handle unstructured data, such as photos, audio, and text, has resulted in notable progress in various domains, including autonomous vehicles, facial recognition, and virtual assistants. Figure 1 demonstrates the AI generation from the year 1642 through the present and above.

Figure 1. Artificial intelligence generation history

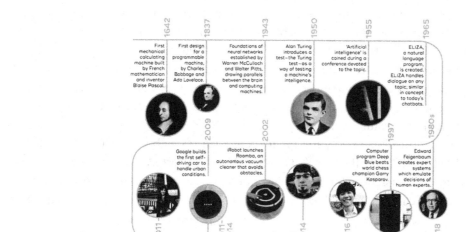

NLP is a crucial component of AI that facilitates the comprehension and production of human language by machines. NLP enables the advancement of conversational chatbots, voice-activated virtual assistants, and real-time language translation such as ChatGPT-4[8]. The fundamental effect of NLP lies in its ability to enable humans to engage in more natural and intuitive communication with machines (Kao et al., 2023). This capability opens up possibilities for enhancing human-computer interaction and improving user experiences. AI, despite its vast potential, gives rise to ethical concerns. As AI systems become increasingly interwoven into our daily lives, it is imperative to address critical concerns such as algorithmic bias, privacy implications, and potential job displacement (Mnguni, 2023).

One example of a potential consequence is the perpetuation of current biases in decision-making processes through algorithmic bias. Additionally, the utilization of AI in surveillance and data collection has the potential to infringe on individuals' privacy. Furthermore, the automation of specific tasks by AI raises worries regarding its impact on employment, necessitating societal adjustments to facilitate possibilities for the reskilling and upskilling of the workforce (Weng et al., 2023). The ongoing advancement of AI necessitates the establishment of a harmonious equilibrium between technological development and the ethical and societal consequences it encompasses. This equilibrium is crucial to ensure that AI is utilized for the betterment of society while simultaneously upholding the principles of individual rights and values (Grubaugh et al., 2023).

Motivation of Artificial Intelligence-Enhanced Teaching Methods

The rationale behind the use of AI-enhanced instructional approaches is based on the aspiration to revolutionize the field of education via the effective utilization of AI. This is done with the aim of leveraging the profound capabilities of AI to cater to the varied and ever-changing requirements of the learners' workforce (Weng et al., 2023). AI has the potential to revolutionize education by enabling personalized learning experiences that adapt to individual learning styles and paces. This technology enhances student engagement and provides targeted real-time feedback, ultimately leading to improved learning outcomes (Bilgic et al., 2022). Through the automation of administrative chores such as grading and evaluation, AI enables instructors to allocate their attention toward student-centered activities that hold significant educational value. The utilization of AI-powered technology possesses the potential to enhance the availability of high-quality education and address disparities in educational fairness (Tambuskar, 2022). This would guarantee that individuals across the globe, irrespective of their geographical location or socio-economic status, are afforded equal prospects to avail themselves of new and efficient pedagogical approaches. The convergence of these elements highlights the impetus to utilize AI in the field of education, establishing a flexible and responsive educational setting that equips students with the necessary skills to thrive in a society increasingly influenced by AI (Russell et al., 2023).

The Contribution of the Chapter

This study presents the following summarized contributions:

- The study opens with a discussion on how AI is transforming teaching methods.
- Examines the traditional lecture-based approach, exploring traditional learning from textbooks and identifying the shortcomings of traditional methods.
- It seeks to understand AI application in education and explore its impact in the educational context, highlighting the advantages of integrating AI in education.
- Illumination of core AI technologies used in the education sector and providing examples of how AI is used in education.
- Explains how AI enables personalized learning paths, demonstrates how AI supports self-paced learning, and discusses the use of AI in making learning more engaging.
- Unfolding the role of AI-powered chatbots and virtual assistants by showing how AI streamlines the assessment and grading process.
- Challenges and Concerns of AI in education are demonstrated by addressing issues related to accessibility and fairness, analyzing the impact of AI on the teacher-student dynamic, and examining ethical and social concerns associated with AI in education.
- Finally, it presents the future directions and trends, discussing how AI in education will continue to evolve recognizing the potential for improved collaboration in education, among others.

The Organization of the Chapter

The rest of this research is structured as follows. Section 2 presents the role of AI in education, then illustrates the traditional teaching methods, including lecture-based instruction and textbook-based learning, and explains some challenges and limitations in section 3. Section 4 demonstrates AI in education, mainly in understanding AI in education, the benefits of AI-enhanced teaching, Crucial AI technologies in education, and use cases in educational AI. Section 5 presents AI-enhanced teaching Methods, including adaptive learning systems, intelligent tutoring systems, gamification and AI, chatbots and virtual assistants, and assessment and grading automation. Section 6 depicts the Challenges and Concerns, including Privacy and Data Security, Equity and Accessibility, teacher-student relationships, ethical considerations, and societal factors, among others. Section 7 presents the future directions and trends, like Continued AI Advancements, Enhanced Collaboration, AI-driven research, and curriculum development. Section 8 presents the conclusion of the chapter.

THE ROLE OF ARTIFICIAL INTELLIGENCE IN EDUCATION

This section opens by discussing the role of AI in transforming teaching methods and checking the technology's benefits to create a foundation for dissecting traditional teaching approaches.

Personalized Learning

The function of AI in education is characterized by its notable capacity to provide tailored learning experiences. Through the examination of individual student data, AI systems possess the capability to customize educational content and instructional approaches in accordance with the unique requirements and learning preferences of each student (Hu, 2023). For instance, educational platforms such as Khan Academy[9] and Duolingo[10] employ AI to deliver personalized courses tailored to individual students' progress and abilities. The implementation of personalized learning strategies has been found to have a positive impact on student engagement and comprehension. This is due to the ability of learners to advance through the material at their speed while also receiving tailored support when needed (An, 2022).

Improved Instruction

AI enables educators by equipping them with tools and insights that enhance their instructional approaches. The system provides feedback based on data analysis of student performance, allowing teachers to pinpoint areas that require more assistance. An example of educational software, such as DreamBox Learning[11], provides teachers with real-time analytics, enabling them to identify pupils who are encountering difficulties and customize treatments accordingly (Lindegger et al., 2022). The utilization of data-driven strategies boosts the efficacy of pedagogical practices and contributes to the establishment of a more individualized educational milieu.

Automation of Administrative Tasks

This AI technology enhances efficiency in educational settings by automating administrative duties, including grading and assessment processes. The implementation of automation in the grading process not only offers significant time-saving benefits for instructors but also mitigates the potential for human error (Wei et al., 2022). An example that has gained significant recognition is Gradescope[12]. This platform uses AI to enhance the grading of assignments and examinations, thereby increasing efficiency and precision in the evaluation process (Russell et al., 2023). By implementing automation for these administrative tasks, AI enables educators to allocate their focus toward more effective and student-oriented endeavors.

Inclusivity and Accessibility

AI plays a key role in enhancing the accessibility and inclusivity of education. Technological advancements such as text-to-speech and voice recognition systems play a pivotal role in facilitating inclusive education by providing learners with disabilities the necessary tools to access educational information (Wei et al., 2022). For instance, assistive technologies such as screen reading software such as JAWS and speech recognition software like Dragon NaturallySpeaking[13] offer assistance to students who have visual or aural impairments, thereby guaranteeing equal accessibility to education for anyone, irrespective of their physical capabilities (Russell et al., 2023).

Continuous and Accelerated Learning

Without a doubt, AI facilitates lifelong learning by providing learners with extensive access to a wide range of information and resources. AI-powered recommendation systems enable students to access educational materials, courses, and resources that are specifically curated to align with their individual interests and professional aspirations (Abdalgane & Othman, 2023). Online learning platforms such as Coursera[14] and edX[15] use AI algorithms to provide personalized course recommendations and learning trajectories that are tailored to a student's previous academic experiences and professional goals (Bilgic et al., 2022). The implementation of this ongoing learning strategy facilitates the cultivation of self-directed education and enables individuals to remain up-to-date in their respective professions, as demonstrated in Figure 2.

Figure 2. Artificial intelligence application aspects in education

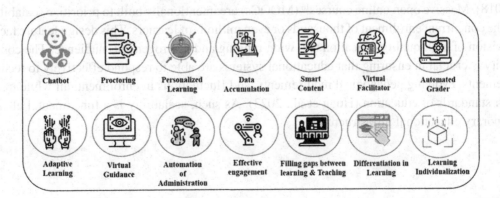

Data-Driven Decision Making

Through a systematic process of collecting and evaluating diverse educational data, such as student performance, attendance, and demographic information, educators and institutions are able to derive significant insights and identify recurring patterns. These insights provide valuable guidance for making informed decisions at both the classroom and institutional levels, enabling the implementation of customized instruction, allocation of resources, and implementation of focused interventions (An, 2022). Furthermore, the use of data-driven decision-making plays a crucial role in the endeavor to achieve educational equity as it enables the identification of discrepancies and disparities in academic performance, thus guaranteeing that every student has fair and impartial access to educational possibilities (Lindegger et al., 2022). Establishing explicit educational objectives and milestones and evaluating advancement through evidence-based analysis are fundamental components of this approach, eventually fostering the ongoing enhancement of education.

Instantaneous Feedback

Alternatively referred to as real-time feedback, it is a crucial pedagogical approach that offers learners prompt and precise information regarding their performance or comprehension during the educational endeavor. The provision of timely feedback to students facilitates their understanding and proficiency in the subject matter by providing them with information about their actions or replies in a timely manner (Hsieh et al., 2020). By utilizing technological advancements, such as online assessment platforms and interactive learning tools, educators provide students with prompt feedback on their tests. This enables students to have a comprehensive understanding of the subject matter and promptly address any errors or areas for growth (Hsieh et al., 2020). This methodology promotes active learning, adaptability, and motivation, as it allows students to swiftly confront their misconceptions and alter their learning tactics in real-time, hence enhancing the effectiveness and efficiency of their learning results.

Scalability

The notion holds significant importance in contemporary education, particularly within the context of the digital era, wherein the demand for online courses, virtual classrooms, and educational resources has experienced a tremendous surge. The concept of scalability allows educational institutions and online learning platforms to effectively cater to a broad and varied audience, irrespective of their geographic location. This ensures that education stays accessible and impactful on a worldwide level (Chassignol et al., 2018). Massive open online courses[16] (MOOCs) are intentionally built to prioritize scalability, enabling the concurrent enrollment of thousands or even millions of learners. This design feature facilitates the provision of high-quality education to a wide-ranging and heterogeneous audience. The concept of scalability is crucial in ensuring that educational systems are able to respond effectively to technology improvements, evolving pedagogical requirements, and fluctuations in enrollment, all while maintaining high standards of education (Hogg et al., 2023). As such, scalability is a fundamental element of contemporary educational infrastructure.

Adaptation to Technological Advances

The concept refers to the capacity of educational institutions and educators to effectively utilize emerging technologies and innovations in order to address evolving pedagogical demands and adapt to the dynamic technology environment. The ability to adapt ensures the ongoing relevance and alignment of education with contemporary breakthroughs, helping students acquire important skills and knowledge in the digital era (Kao et al., 2023). An instance of this may be observed in the integration of virtual reality[17] (VR) and augmented reality[18] (AR) technologies into the educational context, which enables students to participate actively in immersive learning encounters. Through these technologies, students are afforded the opportunity to engage in activities such as exploring historical landmarks[19,20], conducting virtual scientific experiments, or simulating intricate scenarios (Mnguni, 2023). In addition, the expeditious integration of online learning management systems[21] (LMS) and collaborative tools has facilitated the smooth shift of educational establishments towards remote and blended learning, effectively meeting the requirements of an interconnected digital society.

Innovation and Advanced Research

AI plays a significant role in driving research and fostering innovation within the field of education. It accomplishes this by facilitating the examination of extensive educational datasets, conducting educational experiments, and offering valuable insights to support evidence-based educational methods (Weng et al., 2023). Researchers and institutions utilize AI to analyze patterns in student performance, forecast learning outcomes, and devise novel pedagogical approaches. This facilitates the advancement of teaching and learning methodologies, hence promoting enhancements in educational practices and the creation of more efficient educational technologies (Grubaugh et al., 2023). Based on the explained benefits obtained from AI, we now present in detail traditional and AI-assisted approaches to education.

TRADITIONAL TEACHING METHODS

This section demonstrates the four main traditional teaching approaches. Traditional teaching methods have been widely utilized in the field of education, although they have been subject to criticism due to their inherent limits. Some of the obstacles associated with online learning are a lack of flexibility in accommodating different learning styles, decreased levels of involvement, restricted availability of immediate feedback, and difficulties in meeting the varying needs and skills of students (Pheng et al., 2022). The introduction of digital technologies and the rise of novel pedagogical methods, such as personalized learning, project-based learning, and active learning strategies, have instigated a transition towards more dynamic and student-centered instructional approaches in contemporary education.

Lecture-Based Instruction

A conventional pedagogical approach wherein instructors disseminate course material through oral presentations, commonly conducted within a physical classroom environment. The predominant type of communication in the educational setting is characterized by a unidirectional flow, wherein the instructor imparts knowledge, and the pupils assume a passive role of receiving information and documenting it through note-taking (Yachen, 2022). Lectures frequently adhere to a well-organized framework and address particular subjects or concepts, offering a systematic approach to pedagogy. Although lectures have the potential to provide valuable information, they frequently face criticism due to their lack of interactivity, which can result in decreased student engagement and limited chances for active participation (Wei et al., 2022). Nevertheless, the utilization of interactive components, conversations, or multimedia materials in conjunction with these methods can augment the efficacy of their application and enrich the overall educational encounter.

Textbook-Based Learning

The approach of Textbook-Based Learning centers around the utilization of textbooks as the principal educational tool for students to acquire knowledge and information. The textbooks, regardless of their medium of presentation, function as extensive resources that encompass a wide range of subject matter, providing detailed explanations, illustrative examples, and practical exercises (Abdalgane & Othman, 2023). Students actively participate in self-directed learning through the process of reading, studying, and fulfilling assignments derived from these materials. Textbooks are frequently subject to criticism due to their passive nature and potential lack of accommodation for varied learning styles despite their provision of structured and meticulously organized knowledge (Bilgic et al., 2022). To overcome these constraints, contemporary education frequently integrates traditional textbook-based instruction with interactive and immersive methodologies, thereby fostering a more dynamic and student-centric learning environment.

Classroom-Based Instruction

This is also a conventional method in which students convene in a physical classroom or educational institution to partake in face-to-face instruction facilitated by a teacher. This educational approach encompasses in-person encounters, dialogues, and active involvement with the instructor and fellow students (An, 2022). Classroom-based instruction provides a well-organized and formal educational setting, which has proven to be extremely productive for specific academic disciplines and particular age cohorts. Nonetheless, this approach may exhibit inflexibility and encounter difficulties in adapting to personalized pace or the requirements of distant or online learning, which have gained significance in the present multifaceted educational environment (Lindegger et al., 2022). Thus, contemporary education is undergoing a transformation whereby traditional classroom-based teaching is being integrated with online elements to offer a learning experience that is characterized by enhanced flexibility and accessibility.

Teacher-Centered Approach

The educational style known as teacher-centered places the instructor at the focal point of the teaching and learning process, wherein the teacher assumes a central and authoritative position inside the classroom. Within the confines of this conventional pedagogical framework, the instructor assumes the duty of imparting knowledge, determining the tempo of instruction, and exercising authority over matters pertaining to curriculum, methodologies, and evaluations (Hsieh et al., 2020). The major emphasis lies on the teacher as the principal purveyor of knowledge and the central facilitator of the educational process. At the same time, students assume a more passive position as consumers of information. This pedagogical approach exhibits a higher degree of authoritarianism, wherein the instructor assumes the primary responsibility for determining the content and methods of student learning (Chassignol et al., 2018). Although teacher-centered techniques have traditionally been a prominent feature of formal education, they have been subject to criticism due to their inherent inflexibility, diminished student involvement, and inadequate attention to individual learning requirements. In light of these constraints, contemporary education is transforming pedagogical methods that prioritize student engagement and interactivity (Wei et al., 2022). These techniques aim to enable learners to assume a proactive stance in their educational journey, thereby cultivating essential cognitive abilities such as critical thinking, problem-solving, and self-directed learning proficiencies.

Challenges and Limitations of Traditional Teaching Methods

Conventional pedagogical approaches, although having served as the fundamental framework of education across successive generations, are not without inherent difficulties and constraints. Several significant limitations are associated with traditional teaching approaches, which warrant careful consideration, as explained.

Limited Engagement and Interactivity

Conventional pedagogical approaches, such as didactic lectures and reliance on textbooks, frequently exhibit limitations in effectively fostering active student engagement within the learning environment. The implementation of passive methods may result in a decrease in learners' motivation and attentiveness. Instead of cultivating critical thinking and problem-solving skills, students run the risk of assuming a passive role as just users of information, overlooking valuable chances for active engagement and intellectual inquiry (Pheng et al., 2022). This constraint holds particular significance at a time when there is a growing emphasis on the need for collaborative and interactive learning experiences that provide students with the necessary skills to tackle real-world difficulties and seize opportunities.

One-Size-Fits-All Approach

Conventional pedagogical approaches sometimes prioritize standardized curricula and uniform pacing, thereby potentially neglecting the unique learning styles, abilities, and requirements of individual pupils. Consequently, certain students may encounter difficulties in comprehending the information due to its advanced nature, resulting in feelings of irritation and disinterest (Yachen, 2022). Conversely, other students may perceive the material as lacking in complexity, which could lead to feelings of boredom and a diminished drive to interact with the subject matter. By customizing education to accommodate the unique needs of each student and offering flexibility in the pace of learning, these challenges can be effectively addressed, ensuring an equal opportunity for all students to acquire knowledge and succeed (Fan & Zhong, 2022).

Limited Real-Time Feedback

Prompt feedback is a crucial element of successful learning since it allows students to clarify any misconceptions and make timely adjustments swiftly. Conventional pedagogical approaches, which often involve didactic instruction and standardized evaluations, frequently fail to incorporate this essential component (Truong et al., 2022). The lack of immediate feedback can impede a student's capacity to comprehend and utilize topics with efficacy. Contemporary education is progressively integrating technological advancements that offer immediate feedback, augmenting student learning and fostering a more profound comprehension of the subject matter.

Inflexibility and Adaptability

Conventional pedagogical approaches may encounter difficulties in adapting to the swiftly changing educational environment and improvements in technology. These approaches may exhibit a slower rate of adaptation to changes in curriculum, teaching practices, or growing skills required by the labor market (Iacucci et al., 2022). The lack of adaptability exhibited by students might lead to a failure to gain the essential skills and information required for success in a rapidly evolving global environment. To tackle this issue, modern education places a high value on adaptability, integrating developing technology and pedagogical methods to ensure that students are sufficiently equipped to meet the requirements of a society that is driven by digital advancements and knowledge (Liu et al., 2022).

Overreliance on Memorization

Certain conventional pedagogical approaches place a strong emphasis on the memorizing of facts and information through repetitive learning, often neglecting the cultivation of critical thinking abilities and problem-solving aptitude (Bucea-Manea-ṭoniş et al., 2022). Merely relying on rote memory does not adequately prepare pupils to apply their acquired knowledge in practical situations effectively or to engage in critical and creative thinking. In contemporary society, there is a high value placed on persons who possess the ability to critically assess, integrate, and utilize information in order to tackle intricate problems and confrontations effectively (Tambuskar, 2022). Consequently, there is a discernible movement in the field of education towards instructional approaches that foster the development of higher-order cognitive abilities and the pragmatic utilization of acquired knowledge.

Homogeneous Assessment

Conventional pedagogical approaches frequently include standardized examinations and consistent assessments, which may not effectively capture the broad range of abilities and comprehension levels exhibited by individual pupils. This methodology may fail to consider the distinct capabilities and limitations of individual learners, resulting in an inadequate evaluation of their overall advancement (Tew et al., 2022). In modern education, there is a growing acknowledgment of the significance of employing a range of assessment methods that encompass project-based assessments, portfolio evaluations, and performance-based assessments. These approaches offer a more thorough and nuanced understanding of students' abilities.

Limited Student Autonomy

Conventional pedagogical approaches often relegate students to a passive position, wherein educators assume primary responsibility for determining the content, methodology, and timing of students' learning experiences. The presence of limited autonomy can impede the cultivation of self-directed learning skills, which are crucial in the contemporary context of abundant knowledge and swift transformations (Demertzi & Demertzis, 2023). Modern education places significant emphasis on cultivating autonomous and self-regulated learning, empowering students to assume responsibility for their educational endeavors and develop into individuals committed to continuous learning, capable of adapting to dynamic circumstances and prospects.

Teacher Workload

Traditional teaching methods, characterized by a teacher-centered approach, can place a substantial burden on educators, particularly in areas such as grading and administrative duties. The allocation of this task may impede the teacher's ability to offer individualized assistance and prompt feedback to students, potentially compromising the educational standard (Qi et al., 2022). As a result, the integration of technology and automation technologies is being employed to mitigate administrative constraints, enabling educators to prioritize meaningful contact with pupils and the formulation of inventive teaching methodologies.

Ineffectiveness of Diverse Learning Styles

Traditional teaching methods, characterized by a teacher-centered approach, can place a substantial burden on educators, particularly in areas such as grading and administrative duties. The allocation of this task may impede the teacher's ability to offer individualized assistance and prompt feedback to students, potentially compromising the educational standard (Fei, 2022). As a result, the integration of technology and automation technologies is being employed to mitigate administrative constraints, enabling educators to prioritize meaningful contact with pupils and the formulation of inventive teaching methodologies.

Lack of Real-World Application

Conventional pedagogical approaches frequently place a strong emphasis on rote memorizing of factual information and conceptual understanding, occasionally neglecting the practical utilization of knowledge within real-life scenarios. Many students memorize material proficiently yet encounter difficulties when attempting to apply this knowledge effectively in real-world situations. To address this disparity, contemporary education places significant emphasis on the incorporation of pragmatic and applied learning encounters (Saranya et al., 2023). This approach enables students to cultivate their ability to solve problems and effectively apply their knowledge in practical scenarios, thus enhancing their readiness for the demands of both professional pursuits and everyday life in the 21st century.

CRUCIAL ARTIFICIAL INTELLIGENCE TECHNOLOGIES IN EDUCATION

The integration of AI into the field of education signifies a significant shift in the way sophisticated technologies are utilized to improve the methods and outcomes of teaching and learning aided by critical technologies, as explained below, transforming the manner in which students attain knowledge and educators enable its dissemination.

Machine Learning

Machine learning[22] (ML) algorithms are utilized in the field of education for the purpose of analyzing extensive datasets, hence facilitating the customization of learning experiences. ML models detect and analyze patterns in various aspects of student behavior, academic achievement, and individual learning preferences (Ng et al., 2023). ML enhances engagement and comprehension by effectively accommodating individual learning styles through the adaptation of content. The implementation of personalized learning strategies cultivates a conducive atmosphere that enables pupils to advance at individualized rates, hence augmenting their overall educational journey. Moreover, ML has the potential to support educators in the identification of pupils who are facing difficulties and require supplementary assistance, as well as in the implementation of early intervention approaches (Li, 2023). The utilization of machine learning in predictive analytics also plays a role in enhancing resource allocation efficiency, hence enhancing the whole educational process.

Natural Language Processing

This technology facilitates efficient interaction between students and various educational technologies, such as chatbots, virtual assistants, and language translation systems. An illustration of this may be seen in the use of chatbots, which replicate conversations, thereby offering language learners advantageous opportunities for practice and prompt evaluation (Tiwari, 2023). Language translation systems play a vital role in overcoming language barriers, hence facilitating students' access to educational content in their preferred language. NLP is also utilized in sentiment analysis, a technique that enables instructors to assess the emotional state of students and identify individuals who may be experiencing difficulties or disinterest (Furube et al., 2023). This technological advancement facilitates the increased availability of educational resources and promotes the cultivation of multilingual and inclusive educational settings.

Immersive Technologies

These technologies facilitate student interaction with educational material within dynamic and immersive settings. For example, AR superimpose digital content onto physical items, generating interactive and educational encounters. VR technology immerse students in simulated worlds, enabling them to engage in hands-on learning experiences. This immersive approach has the potential to enhance the understanding of abstract concepts by making them more concrete and accessible (Fang & Tse, 2023). These technologies increase interest and facilitate comprehension, hence rendering intricate subjects more easily comprehensible. The institution provides students with practical training opportunities in various disciplines, including medicine, architecture, and engineering. These opportunities aim to provide students with authentic experiences that effectively prepare them to tackle real-world difficulties (Hu, 2023). The versatility of AR and VR facilitates adaptable learning opportunities, whether in a conventional classroom setting or through online platforms, hence introducing novel prospects for educational practices.

Recommendation Systems

AI-enabled recommendation systems play a crucial role in facilitating learners' exploration of instructional materials that are both pertinent and captivating. These systems utilize an analysis of a student's learning history, preferences, and behavior in order to provide recommendations for suitable courses, resources, and materials (Wei et al., 2022). The implementation of personalization in the educational process serves to optimize the learning experience by directing students toward materials that align with their interests and objectives. Not only does it enhance the efficiency of the learning process, but it also fosters student engagement and motivation (Russell et al., 2023). Recommendation systems play a significant role in facilitating self-directed learning, empowering students to assume responsibility for their educational trajectory through the exploration of materials that correspond with their specific aims.

Intelligent Tutoring Systems (ITS)

ITS[23] utilizes AI to deliver personalized training and assistance to students. The educational platform provides prompt and tailored feedback, adjusting the instructional trajectory in response to a student's academic progress and individual requirements (Bilgic et al., 2022). ITS emulates the functions of a human tutor, offering round-the-clock availability to provide students with prompt and continuous support as needed. These technologies enhance the educational experience by providing prompt and tailored guidance, ultimately leading to improved student outcomes (An, 2022). Self-paced online learning environments can greatly benefit from the use of these tools, particularly in situations where students do not have consistent access to educators. ITS provides students with the necessary assistance to comprehend complex subjects effectively, hence fostering a more profound comprehension of the content and encouraging self-directed learning as developed within the milestone deployment in Figure 3.

Figure 3. Artificial intelligence milestone deployment from 1985 to 2015

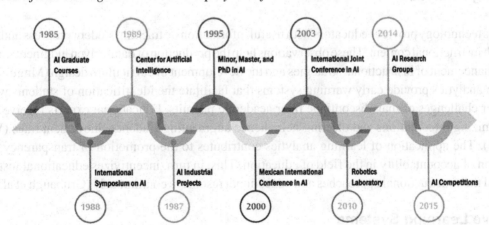

Gamification

Through the acquisition of incentives, engagement in competition with peers, and the accomplishment of in-game objectives, students are incentivized to engage and retain knowledge actively. The implementation of gamification in educational settings has been found to promote the development of collaboration and problem-solving skills (Lindegger et al., 2022). This is due to the fact that numerous games necessitate students to engage in cooperative efforts to accomplish objectives. The provision of rapid feedback within gaming settings catalyzes pupils to enhance their performance consistently (Hsieh et al., 2020). Gamified educational systems accommodate a wide range of learning styles and preferences, hence enhancing inclusivity and fostering a more enjoyable learning experience for a varied student body. They facilitate the transformation of education into an interactive and dynamic experience, thus fostering student motivation to engage actively in the exploration and mastery of diverse disciplines (Chassignol et al., 2018).

Assessment Automation

This technological advancement improves the effectiveness and precision of grading, resulting in time-saving benefits for educators. One illustration of the application of AI is the utilization of AI-powered tools for the assessment of assignments, essays, and multiple-choice examinations. This implementation serves to establish a standardized and unbiased approach to evaluation (Hogg et al., 2023). Automation enables instructors to allocate their time and energy to instructional activities and deliver tailored feedback, enhancing the educational experience with greater significance. This practice alleviates the workload associated with grading for educators, allowing them to dedicate a greater amount of time to educational endeavors (Kao et al., 2023). The increased efficacy of educational processes yields advantages for both instructors and learners, ultimately leading to an enhancement in the overall educational standard.

Learning Analytics

Analytics technology provides educators with useful information by tracking student progress and interactions with instructional content. These observations help the production of data-driven judgments, assisting in the enhancement of instructional strategies and the development of curriculum design (Mnguni, 2023). Learning analytics provide early warning systems that facilitate the identification of students who may encounter challenges or may discontinue their academic pursuits. Educational experts receive support in customizing interventions and offering help, hence augmenting student achievement rates (Weng et al., 2023). The application of learning analytics contributes to the promotion of transparency and the cultivation of accountability in the field of education. This, in turn, incentivizes educational institutions to expand their instructional approaches and educational resources continuously (Grubaugh et al., 2023).

Adaptive Learning Systems

These systems are designed to continuously assess the performance of students and make adjustments to the difficulty level and pace of sessions based on their individual needs. The educational institution provides focused assistance and deliberate practice opportunities, ensuring that pupils comprehend and retain the subject matter (Hu, 2023). Adaptive learning systems play a crucial role in effectively addressing the varied learning requirements of students, facilitating individualized instruction, and allowing learners to progress at their speed. Continuous feedback and adaptive curriculum are employed to optimize the educational process, hence enhancing the overall learning experience (Fang & Tse, 2023). These educational systems facilitate the acquisition of comprehensive knowledge in a particular field, hence cultivating achievement and self-assurance among students.

Artificial Intelligence Impact in the Educational Context

The influence of AI in the educational sphere is extensive and significant. AI is revolutionizing the methods of instruction, acquisition of knowledge, and management of educational systems, presenting a multitude of advantages and prospects for students and educators alike. The following are a few prominent avenues via which AI is exerting a substantial influence:

Privacy Concerns

The integration of AI in the field of education necessitates the acquisition and examination of a substantial volume of personal data, encompassing aspects such as student academic achievements, conduct, and physiological measurements. If adequate safeguards are not implemented, this data may be vulnerable to unauthorized access and exploitation (Furube et al., 2023). Privacy concerns are particularly pertinent when contemplating the delicate nature of student information. The implementation of robust security measures, data encryption, and tight access controls is necessary for educational institutions in order to protect the integrity and confidentiality of their data (Tiwari, 2023). Furthermore, it is imperative to establish comprehensive policies and regulations that effectively safeguard data privacy and effectively tackle the ethical concerns that may arise from the implementation of AI in the field of education.

Overreliance on Technology

Although the integration of AI in education can significantly increase the overall learning experience, excessive dependence on technology may lead to unforeseen repercussions. The overreliance on AI as a means of acquiring knowledge might result in a decline in one's ability to engage in critical thinking and problem-solving (Li, 2023). There is a potential decline in students' ability to actively participate in self-directed learning, engage in critical analysis, and exhibit creative thinking skills. In order to address this issue, educational institutions must find a harmonious equilibrium between harnessing the potential of AI to enhance efficiency and safeguarding the continued relevance and prominence of conventional pedagogical approaches (Ng et al., 2023). Promoting a combination of AI-enhanced learning and regular classroom interactions is crucial in cultivating learners who possess a comprehensive skill set and the ability to adapt.

Inequality and Accessibility Issues

The integration of AI in education is hindered by a notable obstacle known as the digital divide. Educational disparities arise due to unequal access to technology and the Internet among students. Lack of consistent access to digital resources among students can pose challenges in effectively utilizing AI-driven educational technologies, hence amplifying existing discrepancies in academic performance

(Saranya et al., 2023). To tackle this matter, educational institutions must prioritize the consideration of accessibility and inclusivity for all students in their AI implementations. This could entail the provision of technological resources, the reduction of the digital gap, or the provision of alternative solutions for students who do not have access to AI-driven tools (Fei, 2022).

Bias and Discrimination

AI systems have a vulnerability to acquiring biases that exist within their training data, resulting in the potential for discriminatory consequences within the educational domain. One potential issue with automated grading systems is their accidental tendency to exhibit bias towards or against specific groups of pupils, influenced by their demographic attributes (Qi et al., 2022). Educational institutions must demonstrate a proactive approach to detecting and mitigating prejudice within AI systems. This can be achieved through the use of various methodologies, including fairness audits and continuous monitoring (Demertzi & Demertzis, 2023). Establishing clear criteria for ethical AI use and investing in AI development that stresses justice and inclusion are of utmost importance.

Loss of Jobs for Educators

AI has the potential to augment pedagogical practices and optimize administrative operations in the field of education. However, it is important to acknowledge that the implementation of AI may lead to a decrease in the need for specific positions within the education sector. The transition at hand presents difficulties for educators who may be required to adjust to novel responsibilities or gain supplementary competencies to sustain their competitiveness in the labor market (Tew et al., 2022). In order to address this impact, educational institutions must prioritize the emphasis on educators' roles as facilitators, mentors, and guides within the learning process. The utilization of AI should be seen as a means to enhance the role of educators rather than supplant them, enabling educators to concentrate on more advanced responsibilities that necessitate human attributes like empathy and inventiveness (Tambuskar, 2022).

Use Cases in Educational Artificial Intelligence

We briefly present five examples of how AI is used in education.

Personalized Learning

AI-powered personalized learning platforms utilize AI algorithms to dynamically adjust learning materials and instructional pace in order to meet the unique needs of individual students (Bucea-Manea-ţoniş et al., 2022). These systems employ data analytics techniques to ascertain a student's areas of proficiency and deficiency, preferred learning modality, and academic advancement. Adaptive learning systems offer tailored exercises, practice quizzes, and feedback to enhance students' comprehension of subjects more efficiently (Liu et al., 2022). An illustration of this can be seen in the utilization of Knewton's adaptive learning platform, which employs AI to tailor learning trajectories and enhance student achievements.

Intelligent Tutoring Systems

ITS utilizes AI to deliver individualized tutoring to students in real-time. These educational systems give personalized training, track the progress of students, and deliver prompt feedback. They assist students in achieving mastery of subjects through the provision of customized lectures and practice assignments (Iacucci et al., 2022). Carnegie Learning's MATHia serves as an exemplar of an ITS that effectively facilitates mathematics education through its provision of tailored feedback and instructional guidance.

Language Learning and Translation

Language learning applications that utilize AI technology provide users with interactive language training, as well as features such as voice recognition and speech synthesis. Various language learning applications, like Duolingo, Rosetta Stone, and Babbel, employ AI technology to replicate authentic conversations, assess pronunciation accuracy, and offer a range of exercises aimed at enhancing language proficiency (Truong et al., 2022). AI-powered translation technologies, such as Google Translate, facilitate the dismantling of linguistic obstacles, enabling students to gain access to educational materials in their mother tongue and enhance their understanding of languages.

Virtual and Augmented Reality for Education

VR and AR provide learners with immersive educational experiences. AR is a technology that superimposes digital information onto the physical environment, enabling users to engage in interactive and informative experiences. VR technology enables students to be immersed in simulated surroundings, so providing them with interactive and experiential learning experiences (Fan & Zhong, 2022). Emerging technologies, shown by apps such as Google[24] Expeditions for VR and AR, have the potential to animate history, science, and geography classes, thereby augmenting comprehension of intricate topics.

Automated Grading and Assessment

The utilization of AI-based assessment and grading technologies facilitates the efficient and systematic evaluation of student assignments and tests. These systems possess the capability to effectively evaluate and assign grades to essays, mathematical problems, and multiple-choice questions with a high level of accuracy (Yachen, 2022). One example of an AI-powered tool is Turnitin, which uses AI to assess written material for originality and offer comments to students. This technology effectively lessens the burden of grading for educators while also maintaining uniformity in the evaluation process (Pheng et al., 2022).

ARTIFICIAL INTELLIGENCE-ENHANCED TEACHING METHODS

This section presents an overview of AI-assisted teaching methods.

Educational Recommendation Systems

AI-powered recommendation systems are employed within the field of education to provide students with personalized suggestions for learning resources, courses, and materials that are pertinent to their needs. These systems utilize an analysis of a student's learning history, preferences, and behavior to offer personalized content recommendations (Yachen, 2022). Recommendation systems play a crucial role in augmenting the learning process and fostering self-directed learning by assisting students in identifying resources that are congruent with their interests and objectives.

Language Learning and Translation Tools

AI-driven language learning and translation systems play a crucial role in facilitating the process of acquiring and comprehending languages. These tools employ NLP techniques to assist those learning a language through interactive activities, evaluation of pronunciation, and recognition of speech (Fan & Zhong, 2022). AI-powered translation systems overcome linguistic barriers, enabling students to engage with educational materials in their mother tongue or enhance their language proficiency by utilizing translation and language assistance. Figure 4 illustrates the five instruction skills used in education (Truong et al., 2022).

Data-Driven Decision Making

AI-powered data analytics tools are utilized to gather and evaluate data pertaining to various aspects of student performance, engagement, and behavior. Educational institutions employ these insights to make well-informed decisions pertaining to curriculum design, resource allocation, and instructional methodologies (Iacucci et al., 2022). Learning analytics solutions, such as Tableau[25] and Power BI[26], provide universities with vital information that enables them to improve the quality of education and the overall student experience.

Chatbots and Virtual Assistants

Chatbots and virtual assistants are conversational interfaces that utilize AI technology to deliver prompt responses to student inquiries and provide assistance in a way that resembles natural English. Digital companions enhance the learning experience through the facilitation of access to course-related material, provision of answers to inquiries on assignments, timetables, and resources, reduction of time allocated to administrative activities, and promotion of efficiency and engagement throughout the educational journey (Iacucci et al., 2022). In addition, these platforms facilitate inclusivity and accessibility through the provision of text-to-speech and speech-to-text functionalities, ensuring that educational materials can be accessed and comprehended by students with impairments. The utilization of AI tools in the education sector holds significant promise for transformative impact (Yachen, 2022). These tools possess the capacity to change the field by delivering tailored support, facilitating language acquisition, and offering round-the-clock assistance. Consequently, education stands to become more malleable, engaging, and responsive to the varied requirements of students.

Figure 4. Instruction skills and associated entities

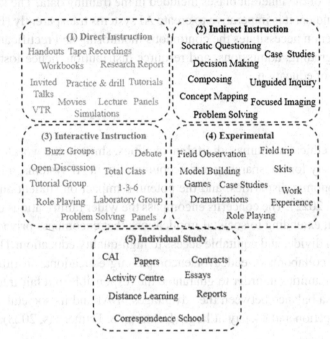

ARTIFICIAL INTELLIGENCE CHALLENGES AND CONCERNS

The resolution of these issues and concerns necessitates a collective endeavor involving educators, institutions, policymakers, and AI developers. The ethical and societal development of AI, together with the implementation of transparent standards, ensuring data security, and promoting fair access, are essential factors in effectively utilizing AI in the field of education while minimizing any adverse consequences.

Data Privacy and Security

In the realm of education, safeguarding data privacy assumes utmost significance due to the sensitive nature of student information. An illustrative example would be a learning analytics platform that gathers data on student behavior in order to tailor learning experiences to individual needs. Insufficient management of this data may result in privacy breaches and the disclosure of personal information (Fan & Zhong, 2022). The observation made is that the preservation of robust data security is of utmost importance. To safeguard student data and maintain compliance with data protection requirements, institutions are required to allocate resources toward the implementation of encryption, secure storage, and access controls (Iacucci et al., 2022). This measure is essential for establishing trust and assuring the security of sensitive information.

Ethical Considerations

The presence of bias inside AI systems can provide significant and wide-ranging ramifications. An AI-powered admissions process may unintentionally exhibit prejudice towards candidates from specific demographics as a result of the inherent biases included in the training data. The key observation is that in order to mitigate prejudice, it is imperative to create AI systems transparently (Bucea-Manea-țoniș et al., 2022). The phenomenon necessitates the continuous monitoring and rectification of biases in order to guarantee equitable grading, admissions, and resource distribution, hence fostering inclusivity and equity within the realm of education.

Societal Concerns

These concerns include ethical dilemmas, digital inequalities, shifts in the workforce, an evolving education divide, the necessity for transparency and accountability in AI systems, alignment with cultural and societal values, economic disparities, and the potential impact on student engagement and social development (Tew et al., 2022). The concerns encompass the wider ramifications of AI implementation in the field of education, extending to societal implications that encompass privacy, bias, employment displacement, the digital divide, and equitable access to high-quality education. The resolution of these concerns necessitates a collaborative endeavor encompassing educational institutions, policymakers, AI developers, and communities in order to guarantee the responsible and fair integration of AI, foster transparency, and strike a balance between the advantages of AI and its societal consequences, all for the advancement of education and society at large (Demertzi & Demertzis, 2023).

Accessibility

The utilization of AI-enhanced learning technologies may inadvertently result in the exclusion of students who lack consistent access to technology or internet connectivity. An instance might be observed wherein a virtual classroom that extensively depends on AI might pose a disadvantage to students residing in regions with restricted access to internet connectivity (Qi et al., 2022). The observation is that there is a need to address digital inequities. The impact of AI-powered education necessitates educational institutions to either grant access to technology or create other means to ensure equitable opportunities for all students, thereby addressing the digital gap.

Overreliance on Technology

The excessive dependence on AI has the potential to undermine the development and application of critical thinking skills. For example, if students only depend on problem-solving tools driven by AI, they could potentially forego the opportunity to cultivate autonomous analytical abilities (Saranya et al., 2023). The key observation is that achieving equilibrium is of utmost importance. The impact necessitates the adoption of a comprehensive approach that incorporates AI as a supplementary tool to conventional pedagogical techniques, hence promoting flexibility and comprehensive learning (Li, 2023).

Job Displacement

The implementation of AI in automating administrative activities has prompted apprehensions regarding the potential displacement of educators from their jobs. One potential benefit of automated grading is the potential reduction in the necessity for teachers to perform manual grading (Tiwari, 2023). The observation made is that AI serves as a supplementary tool to educators rather than functioning as a complete replacement for them. The impact of AI integration in education necessitates educators to acquire supplementary skills and transfer into jobs that emphasize human values, such as empathy and creativity, to maintain their significance as contributors to the educational process (Fang & Tse, 2023).

Inadequate Training and Support

The effectiveness of AI integration is contingent upon the instructors' ability to utilize AI tools proficiently. For example, the implementation of a sophisticated AI-driven educational platform without adequate training can result in suboptimal use (Hu, 2023). The observation that emerges from this analysis is that instructors necessitate comprehensive training and ongoing assistance. The impact of this situation necessitates that educational institutions allocate resources toward the implementation of comprehensive training programs and continuous support mechanisms (Grubaugh et al., 2023). These initiatives aim to equip educators with the necessary skills and knowledge to properly utilize AI technology, hence optimizing the advantages derived from their integration.

Cost and Resource Allocation

The integration of AI in the field of education can incur significant financial expenses. To illustrate, the implementation of AI-powered virtual reality classrooms necessitates financial allocations toward hardware, software, and ongoing maintenance (Mnguni, 2023). The key observation is that the meticulous allocation of resources is of utmost importance. The impact of AI technologies necessitates prudent budget management by institutions to ensure their sustainable utilization while concurrently addressing other financial obligations in the realm of education (Mnguni, 2023).

Lack of Personalization and Human Interaction

Although AI has the potential to facilitate tailored learning, there exists a legitimate concern regarding the potential diminishment of meaningful human interactions. An instance of concern is the potential consequence of over-dependence on AI tutors, which could lead to the deprivation of significant teacher-student connections (Kao et al., 2023). The underlying understanding is that achieving equilibrium is of utmost importance. The impact of incorporating AI into educational settings is that instructors are encouraged to utilize AI as a means of augmenting personalization, all the while upholding the significance of human interaction and fostering social growth (Hogg et al., 2023). This approach aims to cultivate comprehensive learning experiences.

FUTURE RESEARCH DIRECTIONS AND TRENDS

This section highlights the possible future research trends.

AI is poised to further augment the efficacy of personalized learning through the analysis of individual students' learning styles, progress, and preferences. Adaptive learning platforms possess the capability to adjust both the content and pace of instruction, hence facilitating students' more efficient comprehension of topics (Chassignol et al., 2018). This emerging phenomenon has the potential to democratize the provision of tailored education, yielding advantages for both individuals engaged in traditional forms of learning as well as those pursuing online educational opportunities. The COVID-19 epidemic expedited the transition towards a blended approach to education, including both in-person and virtual learning modalities (Hsieh et al., 2020; Alaziz et al., 2023). AI has the potential to facilitate smooth transitions between traditional face-to-face education and online learning, providing a flexible and adaptable approach to material delivery. This technology empowers students to acquire knowledge and skills in a manner that aligns with their individual preferences and availability.

Instead of displacing educators, AI will provide them with resources to enhance their teaching practices. AI systems designed to support educators will provide valuable insights into student performance, streamline administrative work through automation, and offer personalized recommendations for instructional strategies (Lindegger et al., 2022). These advancements have the potential to greatly enhance the teacher's position as a facilitator of learning. AI is poised to assume a pivotal role in facilitating data-driven decision-making within the field of education. Learning analytics is a valuable tool that can offer educators and institutions comprehensive information regarding student performance, behavior, and engagement (Bilgic et al., 2022). This data enables them to make well-informed decisions regarding curriculum design, resource allocation, and intervention tactics.

The education sector will prioritize the ethical utilization and equitable implementation of AI. Efforts will be made by developers and institutions to mitigate bias within AI systems, with the aim of fostering equity in grading, admissions, and resource allocation while concurrently advancing openness in decision-making processes facilitated by AI (Abdalgane & Othman, 2023). The advancement of AI-driven evaluation systems will lead to the provision of extensive feedback and valuable insights regarding student performance. These tools possess the capability to not only streamline the grading process but also offer valuable data to educators, enabling them to assess learning results and customize training accordingly and effectively (Russell et al., 2023).

The advancement of AI-driven evaluation technologies will lead to the provision of extensive feedback and in-depth analysis regarding student performance. These solutions possess the capability to not only streamline the grading process but also furnish educators with valuable data, enabling them to assess learning outcomes more effectively and customize instruction accordingly (Wei et al., 2022). The AI-powered educational technology (EdTech[27]) industry is expected to persist in its pursuit of innovation through the integration of AI, hence providing adaptive learning platforms, interactive language learning aids, and virtual classrooms. EdTech solutions will effectively address a wide range of learning requirements and individual preferences, providing valuable assistance to both students and educators (Pheng et al., 2022).

AI has the potential to transform the process of skills assessment and certification significantly. The recognition of digital badges and micro-credentials, which are validated through assessments helped by AI, is expected to increase. This recognition will offer learners more flexible opportunities to showcase their skills and expertise within the professional sphere (Fan & Zhong, 2022). AI has the potential to enhance lifelong learning through the provision of tailored recommendations for those seeking to enhance their skills or acquire new ones. AI has the potential to monitor and assess individuals' development, curate educational resources, and assist in maintaining competitiveness within a dynamic and swiftly evolving labor market (Liu et al., 2022).

AI also has the potential to facilitate the development of highly interactive and collaborative online learning environments. The educational program will incorporate collaborative assignments, interactive conversations, and AI-enabled peer assessments, thereby cultivating students' abilities in teamwork and communication (Tambuskar, 2022). The development of language translation and language learning technologies driven by AI is expected to progress, facilitating instantaneous communication and overcoming the obstacles posed by language differences. AI has the potential to enhance language learning by offering immersive experiences, hence increasing both engagement and effectiveness in the process of acquiring a new language (Demertzi & Demertzis, 2023).

The integration of AI technology, along with the expansion of internet connectivity, holds the potential to facilitate the provision of high-quality education to geographically isolated and marginalized communities (Fei, 2022). This initiative aims to mitigate educational inequalities at a worldwide level and enhance the accessibility of learning to a wider demographic. AI is expected to have a significant impact on bolstering the security of online assessments. To maintain the authenticity of assessments in online educational settings, sophisticated proctoring and anti-plagiarism measures will be implemented (Ng et al., 2023). As the field of quantum computing continues to advance, it is anticipated that it will provide unparalleled opportunities for enhancing educational practices. This encompasses the resolution of intricate problems within disciplines such as physics, chemistry, and cryptography, facilitating the execution of sophisticated simulations and data analysis for educational research purposes (Furube et al., 2023).

CONCLUSION

AI holds the potential to change the field of education by transforming several aspects, such as personalized learning, intelligent tutoring, gamification, and assessment automation. This technology provides instructors with significant insights into student performance, enhances efficiency in administrative activities, and fosters a learning environment that is more accessible and adaptable. The future of education, propelled by AI, holds the potential for a paradigm shift wherein personalized instruction becomes the prevailing approach, the disparity in access to digital resources is diminished, and the process of learning evolves into an ongoing, adaptable voyage throughout one's lifetime. As we contemplate the future of education, the effect of AI will certainly continue to expand. These factors will contribute to the formation of hybrid learning environments, facilitate the ethical utilization of AI, and foster the worldwide availability of educational opportunities. The current task at hand involves wholeheartedly adopting these advancements. The purpose of our call to action is to urge educators and institutions to utilize the capabilities of AI-enhanced teaching approaches effectively. By using AI, educational institutions can access a multitude of opportunities for students, guaranteeing that education stays pertinent, motivating, and life-altering. The guidance of this transformation is a shared responsibility, necessitating the careful management of the advantages of AI while also safeguarding crucial human connections. This endeavor aims to shape a future wherein all individuals have the opportunity to thrive and develop as learners.

REFERENCES

Abdalgane, M., & Othman, K. A. J. (2023). Utilizing Artificial Intelligence Technologies in Saudi EFL Tertiary Level Classrooms. *Journal of Intercultural Communication*, 23(1), 92–99. Advance online publication. doi:10.36923/jicc.v23i1.124

Alaziz, S. N., Albayati, B., El-Bagoury, A. A., & Shafik, W. (2023). Clustering of COVID-19 Multi-Time Series-Based K-Means and PCA With Forecasting. *International Journal of Data Warehousing and Mining*, *19*(3), 1–25. doi:10.4018/IJDWM.317374

An, K. (2022). Exploration of Intelligent Teaching Methods for Ideological and Political Education in Colleges and Universities under the Background of "Mass Entrepreneurship and Innovation." In International Journal of Antennas and Propagation (Vol. 2022). doi:10.1155/2022/2294908

Bilgic, E., Gorgy, A., Yang, A., Cwintal, M., Ranjbar, H., Kahla, K., Reddy, D., Li, K., Ozturk, H., Zimmermann, E., Quaiattini, A., Abbasgholizadeh-Rahimi, S., Poenaru, D., & Harley, J. M. (2022). Exploring the roles of artificial intelligence in surgical education: A scoping review. In American Journal of Surgery (Vol. 224, Issue 1). doi:10.1016/j.amjsurg.2021.11.023

Bucea-Manea-țoniș, R., Kuleto, V., Gudei, S. C. D., Lianu, C., Lianu, C., Ilić, M. P., & Păun, D. (2022). Artificial Intelligence Potential in Higher Education Institutions Enhanced Learning Environment in Romania and Serbia. *Sustainability (Basel)*, *14*(10), 5842. Advance online publication. doi:10.3390/su14105842

Chassignol, M., Khoroshavin, A., Klimova, A., & Bilyatdinova, A. (2018). Artificial Intelligence trends in education: A narrative overview. *Procedia Computer Science*, *136*, 16–24. Advance online publication. doi:10.1016/j.procs.2018.08.233

Demertzi, V., & Demertzis, K. (2023). A Hybrid Ontology Matching Mechanism for Adaptive Educational eLearning Environments. *International Journal of Information Technology & Decision Making*, *22*(6), 1813–1841. Advance online publication. doi:10.1142/S0219622022500936

Fan, X., & Zhong, X. (2022). Artificial intelligence-based creative thinking skill analysis model using human–computer interaction in art design teaching. *Computers & Electrical Engineering*, *100*, 107957. Advance online publication. doi:10.1016/j.compeleceng.2022.107957

Fang, C., & Tse, A. W. C. (2023). Case Study: Postgraduate Students' Class Engagement in Various Online Learning Contexts When Taking Privacy Issues to Incorporate with Artificial Intelligence Applications. *International Journal of Learning and Teaching*, *9*(2). Advance online publication. doi:10.18178/ijlt.9.2.90-95

Fei, Q. (2022). Innovative Research on Ideological and Political Education in Colleges and Universities Based on Intelligent Wireless Network Environment. *Wireless Communications and Mobile Computing*, *2022*, 1–10. Advance online publication. doi:10.1155/2022/1960520

Furube, T., Takeuchi, M., Kawakubo, H., Matsuda, S., Fukuda, K., Nakamura, R., & Kitagawa, Y. (2023). Automated phase recognition for esophageal endoscopic submucosal dissection using artificial intelligence. *Gastrointestinal Endoscopy*, *97*(6), AB763. Advance online publication. doi:10.1016/j.gie.2023.04.1248 PMID:38185182

Grubaugh, S., Levitt, G., & Deever, D. (2023). Harnessing AI to Power Constructivist Learning: An Evolution in Educational Methodologies. *EIKI Journal of Effective Teaching Methods*, *1*(3). Advance online publication. doi:10.59652/jetm.v1i3.43

Hogg, H. D. J., Brittain, K., Teare, D., Talks, J., Balaskas, K., Keane, P., & Maniatopoulos, G. (2023). Safety and efficacy of an artificial intelligence-enabled decision tool for treatment decisions in neovascular age-related macular degeneration and an exploration of clinical pathway integration and implementation: Protocol for a multi-methods validation study. *BMJ Open*, *13*(2), e069443. Advance online publication. doi:10.1136/bmjopen-2022-069443 PMID:36725098

Hsieh, Y. Z., Lin, S. S., Luo, Y. C., Jeng, Y. L., Tan, S. W., Chen, C. R., & Chiang, P. Y. (2020). ARCS-assisted teaching robots based on anticipatory computing and emotional Big Data for improving sustainable learning efficiency and motivation. *Sustainability (Basel)*, *12*(14), 5605. Advance online publication. doi:10.3390/su12145605

Hu, W. (2023). The Application of Artificial Intelligence and Big Data Technology in Basketball Sports Training. *EAI Endorsed Transactions on Scalable Information Systems*, *10*(4), e2. Advance online publication. doi:10.4108/eetsis.v10i3.3046

Iacucci, M., Cannatelli, R., Parigi, T. L., Buda, A., Labarile, N., Nardone, O. M., Tontini, G. E., Rimondi, A., Bazarova, A., Bhandari, P., Bisschops, R., De Hertogh, G., Del Amor, R., Ferraz, J. G., Goetz, M., Gui, S. X., Hayee, B., Kiesslich, R., Lazarev, M., ... Grisan, E. (2022). A virtual chromoendoscopy artificial intelligence system to detect endoscopic and histologic remission in ulcerative colitis. *Gastrointestinal Endoscopy*, *95*(6), AB229–AB230. Advance online publication. doi:10.1016/j.gie.2022.04.585 PMID:36228649

Kao, C. L., Chien, L. C., Wang, M. C., Tang, J. S., Huang, P. C., Chuang, C. C., & Shih, C. L. (2023). The development of new remote technologies in disaster medicine education: A scoping review. In Frontiers in Public Health (Vol. 11). doi:10.3389/fpubh.2023.1029558

Li, Z. (2023). Application of artificial intelligence and internet of things in medical imaging teaching. *Journal of Biotech Research*, 15.

Lindegger, D. J., Wawrzynski, J., & Saleh, G. M. (2022). Evolution and Applications of Artificial Intelligence to Cataract Surgery. *Ophthalmology Science*, *2*(3), 100164. Advance online publication. doi:10.1016/j.xops.2022.100164 PMID:36245750

Liu, X., Han, X., Lin, X., & Yang, J. H. (2022). National Ballad Creation Education Under Artificial Intelligence and Big Data. *Frontiers in Psychology*, *13*, 883096. Advance online publication. doi:10.3389/fpsyg.2022.883096 PMID:35800943

Mnguni, L. (2023). A critical reflection on the affordances of web 3.0 and artificial intelligence in life sciences education. *Journal of Pedagogical Sociology and Psychology*. doi:10.33902/jpsp.202322298

Ng, P. K., Koo, V. C., Ng, Y. J., & Yeow, J. A. (2023). Blending a sweet pill to swallow with TRIZ and industry talks for enhanced learning during the COVID-19 pandemic. *Human Systems Management*, *42*(2), 163–178. Advance online publication. doi:10.3233/HSM-220080

Pheng, H. S., Chin, T. A., Lai, L. Y., & Choon, T. L. (2022). E-Learning as a Supplementary Tool for Enhanced Students' Satisfaction. *AIP Conference Proceedings*, *2433*, 030005. Advance online publication. doi:10.1063/5.0072901

Qi, S., Liu, L., Kumar, B. S., & Prathik, A. (2022). An English teaching quality evaluation model based on Gaussian process machine learning. *Expert Systems: International Journal of Knowledge Engineering and Neural Networks*, *39*(6), e12861. Advance online publication. doi:10.1111/exsy.12861

Russell, R. G., Lovett Novak, L., Patel, M., Garvey, K. V., Craig, K. J. T., Jackson, G. P., Moore, D., & Miller, B. M. (2023). Competencies for the Use of Artificial Intelligence-Based Tools by Health Care Professionals. *Academic Medicine*, *98*(3), 348–356. Advance online publication. doi:10.1097/ACM.0000000000004963 PMID:36731054

Saranya, V., Devi, T., & Deepa, N. (2023). Text Normalization by Bi-LSTM Model with Enhanced Features to Improve Tribal English Knowledge. *Proceedings of the 7th International Conference on Intelligent Computing and Control Systems, ICICCS 2023*. 10.1109/ICICCS56967.2023.10142508

Shafik, W. (2023). *Artificial intelligence and Blockchain technology enabling cybersecurity in telehealth systems. In Artificial Intelligence and Blockchain Technology in Modern Telehealth Systems*. IET. doi:10.1049/PBHE061E_ch11

Shafik, W. (2024a). *Navigating Emerging Challenges in Robotics and Artificial Intelligence in Africa. Examining the Rapid Advance of Digital Technology in Africa* (Vol. 1). IGI Global. doi:10.4018/978-1-6684-9962-7.ch007

Shafik, W. (2024b). *Toward a More Ethical Future of Artificial Intelligence and Data Science. In The Ethical Frontier of AI and Data Analysis*. IGI Global. doi:10.4018/979-8-3693-2964-1.ch022

Shafik, W. (2024c). *Introduction to ChatGPT. Advanced Applications of Generative AI and Natural Language Processing Models* (Vol. 1). IGI Global. doi:10.4018/979-8-3693-0502-7.ch001

Tambuskar, S. (2022). Challenges and Benefits of 7 Ways Artificial Intelligence in Education Sector. *Review of Artificial Intelligence in Education*, *3*(00), e03. Advance online publication. doi:10.37497/rev.artif.intell.education.v3i00.3

Tew, Y., Lim, K. Y., & Joan, H. (2022). An Evaluation of Virtual Classroom Performance with Artificial Intelligence Components. *The Journal of The Institution of Engineers, Malaysia*, *82*(3). Advance online publication. doi:10.54552/v82i3.116

Tiwari, H. P. (2023). An optimization-based artificial intelligence framework for teaching English at the college level. *LLT Journal: A Journal on Language and Language Teaching, 26*(1). doi:10.24071/llt.v26i1.5954

Truong, H., Qi, D., Ryason, A., Sullivan, A. M., Cudmore, J., Alfred, S., Jones, S. B., Parra, J. M., De, S., & Jones, D. B. (2022). Does your team know how to respond safely to an operating room fire? Outcomes of a virtual reality, AI-enhanced simulation training. *Surgical Endoscopy, 36*(5), 3059–3067. Advance online publication. doi:10.1007/s00464-021-08602-y PMID:34264400

Wei, J., Marimuthu, K., & Prathik, A. (2022). College music education and teaching based on AI techniques. *Computers & Electrical Engineering, 100*, 107851. Advance online publication. doi:10.1016/j.compeleceng.2022.107851

Weng, C., Chen, C., & Ai, X. (2023). A pedagogical study on promoting students' deep learning through design-based learning. *International Journal of Technology and Design Education, 33*(4), 1653–1674. Advance online publication. doi:10.1007/s10798-022-09789-4 PMID:36466720

Yachen, W. (2022). Application of AI-Enhanced Analytic Hierarchy Process in the Online PHP System. *6th International Conference on I-SMAC (IoT in Social, Mobile, Analytics and Cloud), I-SMAC 2022 - Proceedings*.

ENDNOTES

1. https://en.wikipedia.org/wiki/Artificial_intelligence
2. https://www.ibm.com/topics/strong-ai
3. https://www.datacamp.com/blog/what-is-narrow-ai
4. https://en.wikipedia.org/wiki/Generative_artificial_intelligence
5. https://www.ibm.com/topics/neural-networks
6. https://en.wikipedia.org/wiki/Natural_language_processing
7. https://www.chatbot.com/
8. https://en.wikipedia.org/wiki/GPT-4
9. https://www.khanacademy.org/
10. https://www.duolingo.com/
11. https://www.dreambox.com/
12. https://www.gradescope.com/
13. https://www.nuance.com/dragon.html
14. https://www.coursera.org/
15. https://www.edx.org/
16. https://www.mooc.org/
17. https://en.wikipedia.org/wiki/Virtual_reality
18. https://en.wikipedia.org/wiki/Augmented_reality
19. https://www.headout.com/blog/historical-landmarks-world/
20. https://travel.usnews.com/gallery/17-historical-landmarks-to-see-around-the-world
21. https://www.anthology.com/discover/apac-theres-more-to-learn/
22. https://en.wikipedia.org/wiki/Machine_learning
23. https://en.wikipedia.org/wiki/Intelligent_tutoring_system
24. https://www.google.com/
25. https://www.tableau.com/
26. https://www.microsoft.com/en-us/power-platform/products/power-bi
27. https://edtechhub.org/

Chapter 7
Artificial Intelligence's Role and Future Implementation in Education

Komal Bhardwaj

(iD) https://orcid.org/0000-0002-9378-5542

Maharishi Markandeshwar Institute of Management, Maharishi Markandeswar University (Deemed), Mullana, India

Garima

(iD) https://orcid.org/0000-0002-1793-8084

Maharishi Markandeshwar Institute of Management, Maharishi Markandeswar University (Deemed), Mullana, India

Sachin Sudan

(iD) https://orcid.org/0000-0003-2186-4476

RIMT University, Mandi Gobindgarh, India

ABSTRACT

Artificial intelligence (AI) has become a disruptive force that has greatly benefited education, which is a vital aspect for both society evolution and personal growth. The purpose of this study is to analyze the multifaceted impact of AI in education and on the application and impact of AI learning, instruction, and administration. AI is the study and creation of computers, machines, and other artifacts with human like cognitive capacities, learning, and adaptability and decision-making capabilities. The objectives of this chapter are to present a comprehensive outline in addition to a more in-depth analysis of three main elements: roles, consequences, and future implications. The study also states the emergence of AI-enabled individualized learning, offers universal access to high-quality education at all levels by offering exciting new opportunities and applications. AI systems can successfully identify and rectify skill gaps, allowing individuals to adapt to shifting jobs and advancements in technology.

DOI: 10.4018/979-8-3693-2728-9.ch007

1. INTRODUCTION

Nowadays artificial intelligence (AI) has been widely adopted and employed in different industries, including education and hold a promise to facilitate meaningful interactions in online, mobile, and blended learning experiences for providing personalised learning and dynamic evaluation which is safe, effective, and scalable. The introduction and adoption of Artificial Intelligence (AI) in learning and teaching has rapidly evolved over the past twenty years. Artificial intelligence (AI) has developed into a creative, inventive, and resourceful teaching instrument in the international academic setting.

Initially, artificial intelligence (AI) took the form of computers and computer-related technologies and involved embedded computer systems and other technologies, along with web-based catboats and humanoid robots, to carry out teaching tasks either independently or in conjunction with instructors. Furthermore Artificial intelligence (AI) has become a disruptive force that has greatly benefited education, which is a vital aspect for both society evolution and personal growth. The integration of AI in educational systems has completely changed the ways that teachers teach, students learn, and institutions operate. AI will play a gigantic role in higher education since it gives students the opportunity to tackle learning problems in a way that is tailored to their individual preferences and experiences.

To maximise learning outcomes, AI-based digital learning solutions can adjust to each student's knowledge base, pace of learning, and intended learning objectives. Moreover, it can examine past academic records of students to pinpoint areas of weakness and recommend courses that will enhance their individualised learning experience highlight a dual-teacher model with artificial intelligence in terms of individualised education: teachers spend a lot of time on administrative and routine tasks, like repeating things over and over again and answering questions about a variety of topics. Moreover, by having artificial intelligence-supported assistants in the classroom, teachers will be able to spend less time on these routine procedures and more time guiding students and communicating one-on-one.

Nevertheless, the term "artificial intelligence" was first used by John McCarthy in 1956, and since then, it has become widely used in the fields of physics, technology, computer science, engineering, and mathematics, though less known in the education pedagogy. Since then, though, researchers have come to comprehend the cutting edge of artificial intelligence (AI) and have been using it extensively in computer modelling, machine learning, and probability statistics to develop useful applications of these scientific techniques in academic contexts, mostly in the fields of education. However the impact of artificial intelligence in education is already visible in the world economy and has captured the attention of many analysts in recent times. Since this study is conducted for two main prospective. Firstly, the purpose of this study is to examine the role of AI artificial intelligence (AI) in management and promotion of education which describe the effect of AI in education Sector. Secondly, to examine the consequences of artificial intelligence (AI): positive and negative aspects and challenges of AI implementation in education.

This study is expected to determine the overall instructional and learning effectiveness of AI in education. This articles also intended to support the broader AIEd community, which includes educators, educational researchers, AI technology creators, and other stakeholders, in developing a deeper understanding of AIEd, including its current state, potentials, challenges, and future directions, in an effort to further advance AI technologies for education.

2. LITERATURE REVIEW

Global interest in AI research has increased after 2016 when AlphaGo upset world Go champion Lee Sedol (Borowiec, 2016) with a high score of 4:1 in the game. An increasing amount of research on artificial intelligence (AI) in education focuses on using AI to support instruction, create smart campuses, and achieve intelligent teaching, learning, and administration. The use of AI technologies such as face recognition, image recognition, adaptive learning, and others to the area of education has sparked a number of improvements and also improved learning outcomes of student, teacher (Cui, Xue, & Thai, 2019) and work efficiency of educators (Kuo, 2020). Additionally, big data and AI technologies are integrated thoroughly to examine and analyse instructional data; this may also support educational reform and raise the standard of instruction (Williamson, 2018).

Moreover, Artificial Intelligence (AI) has become a ubiquitous technology in various fields, including education. It can mimic human listening (Delić et al., 2019), speaking (speech synthesis, human-computer dialogue) (Chiba, Nose, Kase, Yamanaka, & Ito, 2019), watching (computer vision, image recognition, text recognition) (Paglen, 2019), thinking (Theorem Proving) (Sarma & Hay, 2017), learning (machine learning, intelligent adaptive learning) (Colchester et al., 2017), and action (robot) (Khandelwal et al., 2017). In particular, AI technologies like computer vision, natural language processing, and intelligent adaptive learning have transformed traditional education and teaching (Yufei, Saleh, Jiahui, & Abdullah, 2020), and AI in education plays most important role in promoting personalized teaching and learning. AI has altered how educators impart knowledge and how learners absorb it. It may create a customized learning plan based on the requirements and learning environment of the students (Dishon, 2017), offer an immersive learning environment (Ip et al., 2019), and use intelligent learning tracking to assist students become more proficient and capable learners. It also has the potential to lessen teachers' workloads and increase their attention to humanistic care, which is another benefit for education. These days, teachers spend a lot of time editing homework and assessment papers. The time instructors spend teaching, researching, and interacting with students is taken up by these monotonous chores. Teachers can solve many mechanically repeated daily tasks, like correcting homework and test papers, with the aid of intelligent tutor systems (Holstein, McLaren, & Aleven, 2017), intelligent assessment systems (CUI & LI, 2019), educational robots (Chevalier, Riedo, & Mondada, 2016), and other AIs. Teachers can also be relieved of some of their workloads and freed from heavy knowledge transfer. Moreover, educational robots are specifically designed with the goal of developing students' critical thinking, creativity, and practical skills in the classroom. It possesses the qualities of openness, scalability, interaction, and use in education (Miller, Nourbakhsh, & Siegwart, 2008). A wide range of artificial intelligence (AI) technologies are available for tutoring robots, including voice recognition, emotion recognition that interprets facial expressions and tones, and bionic technology that can mimic human speech, hearing, seeing, and thinking (Yang & Zhang, 2019). Scientific study on tutoring robots is multidisciplinary and cross-field, encompassing education, computer science, automated control, and materials science.

Adaptive Learning

AI facilitates the growth of adaptive learning, which applies real-time analysis, learning analytics, data mining, and intelligent teaching systems. In order to support students' learning, adaptive learning aims to integrate all facets of practice, instruction, assessment, and learning into the system (Van Der Vorst & Jelicic, 2019). According to Cui et al. (2019), the adaptive learning system may gather data on student learning behaviour, determine the best possible learning path for each student based on an analysis of their skills, and then push online instructional videos as the last step in the closed-loop learning process. When faced with issues that cannot be resolved through in-class instruction, teachers can receive help from artificial intelligence (AI) in the form of online question and answer services (Goel & Polepeddi, 2016). These days, a lot of businesses offer adaptive learning systems. Some of the more established ones are DreamBox Learning (Grammes, 2018), BYJU'S (Tripathy & Devarapalli, 2020), and IBM Watson Education (Russo-Spena, Mele, & Marzullo, 2019). Teachers use these systems in the classroom to enhance the educational outcomes.

Teaching Evaluation

AI-based teaching and assessment tools like computer vision, picture recognition, and prediction systems are convenient. One of the most important aspects of teaching is to evaluate students. Teachers must devote a significant amount of time in completing assessment duties in conventional education, including question preparation, scoring, performance rating, and test paper analysis. AI increases the variety of instructional assessment techniques, the scientific nature of the evaluation process, and the accuracy of the evaluation outcomes. AI technology may automatically correct test papers and assignments in addition to creating exam questions (Rahim, Aziz, Rauf, & Shamsudin, 2018). (Li et al., 2018).

Teachers often have to correct exam papers and assignments. Correcting homework and exam papers takes a lot of time, and teachers might get tired quickly. As a result, after a while, there will be some mistakes while revising exam papers. With a low mistake rate, image recognition technology relieves teachers of the laborious task of marking assignments and correcting homework (Li, Cao, & Lu, 2017). In addition to correcting test papers, artificial intelligence (AI) technology may identify blank and potentially similar papers, saving instructors' time in the classroom.

Virtual Classroom

The advancement of hearing, sensing, augmented reality, and virtual reality technology is helpful for changing the classroom experience. Create virtual labs and classrooms by integrating physical and virtual spaces via the use of ubiquitous computing technology (Encalada & Sequera, 2017; Krumm, 2018).

Natural phenomena or changes in things that are difficult or impossible to observe in real life can be presented in a smart classroom to give students a contextual learning environment. Virtual classrooms use technology to simulate teaching scenarios that are challenging to explain. Presenting information in multiple dimensions increases students' interest in learning and enhances teaching effects.

It also allows students to participate with their vision, hearing, kinesthetic, and other senses, giving them a strong sense of reality and making abstract concepts and theories more comprehensible and visual. Regarding flexibility in course attendance, the hybrid virtual classroom is particularly promising (Lakhal, Bateman, & Bédard, 2017) since it allows students to attend lectures from home or on campus.

Smart Campus

The campus serves as a vital hub for talent development, and the use of AI technology to create smart campuses is emerging as a new trend in the field of education (Dong, Zhang, Yip, Swift, & Beswick,

2020). AI is crucial to campus services and administration. The building of a smart campus makes use of technology for sensing, hearing, and face recognition (Zhou 2020, An & Xi 2020).

Intelligent management techniques are developed by gathering and examination of large amounts of data (Villegas- Ch, Molina-Enriquez, Chicaiza-Tamayo, Ortiz-Garcés, & Luján-Mora, 2019). A collaborative human-machine decision-making model between managers and AI is formed (Liu, Ma, & Jin, 2018). This model can identify issues with the education system's functioning early on, achieve more effective resource allocation, and successfully enhance campus safety.

Intelligent Tutoring Robots

Scientific research in education, computer science, automated control, materials science, psychology, optics, and other domains is being done on tutoring robots. According to the perspective of the robot development process, industrial robots served as the primary basis for early robotics technology research and development (Grau, Indri, Lo Bello, & Sauter, 2017).

The educational potential of robots has garnered growing attention along with the popularity of robotics technology. The first instructional robot was developed at the Massachusetts Institute of Technology's AI lab, which was started in the 1960s by Professor Papert (Catlin & Blamires, 2019).

Over the time, the robots gained intelligence. Educational robots are specifically designed with the goal of developing students' critical thinking, creativity, and practical skills in the classroom. It possesses the qualities of openness, scalability, interaction, and use in education (Miller, Nourbakhsh, & Siegwart, 2008).

A wide range of artificial intelligence (AI) technologies are available for tutoring robots, including voice recognition, emotion recognition that interprets facial expressions and tones, and bionic technology that can mimic human speech, hearing, seeing, and thinking (Yang & Zhang, 2019).Scientific study on tutoring robots is multidisciplinary and cross-field, encompassing education, computer science, automated control, and materials science.

3. RESEARCH METHODOLOGY

A qualitative descriptive research approach has been used in the present study's design. Qualitative research is preferred when it is desired to examine a problem or subject in depth.

Data sources are acquired through library research methods that make use of offline and online resources like news articles, books, and scientific journals published by reliable sources. Data is analyzed and then conclusions are drawn on the basis of study objectives.

Table 1. Objectives and tools of the study

Sr. No.	Objectives	Tools
1	To examine the role of artificial intelligence (AI) in management and promotion of education.	Descriptive and Exploratory analysis
2	To examine the potential consequences and challenges of artificial intelligence in education	Descriptive and Exploratory analysis

4. OBJECTIVES

The objectives of the research paper are as under:

1.   To examine the role of artificial intelligence (AI) in management and promotion of education.
2.   To examine the potential consequences and challenges of artificial intelligence in education.

5. ROLE OF AI IN EDUCATION SYSTEM

Over the years, Artificial intelligence (AI) and computer science have made rapid technological advancements as a challenge for all businesses, including education. AI in education has produced strong engaging interactive learning environments and increased efficiency in assessment and evaluation. This section represent the role of AI in education system in relation to three aspects better learning, increase efficiency and access to high quality education.

Figure 1. Role of AI in education

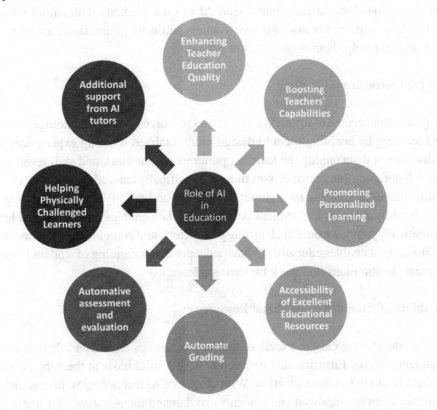

The Figure 1 gives a view that what role does AI plays in the education sector and how it can evolve the complete education sector and it is very much easy to understand that if education sector will evolve then all the sectors will get effected.

1.   Enhancing Teacher Education Quality:

Artificial Intelligence has the potential to significantly enhance teacher education. In India, intelligent ICT-based apps intended for digital learning are increasingly incorporating artificial intelligence. One of the major problem in teaching education is a solid basis in the subjects they teaching. AI can give educators access to excellent learning resources and materials that are customized to meet each student's needs. AI can also assist educators in identifying knowledge gaps and offering feedback on their areas of vulnerability. Educators can use AI to help them become better teachers.

2.   Boosting Teachers' Capabilities:

AI-powered assessment tools can provide teachers real-time feedback on student performance, enabling them to modify their teaching strategies to better meet the needs of their students. AI can also help teachers personalize learning, creating lessons that are tailored to each student's individual needs. Educational institutions have already introduced AI to their students. Humanoid robots are assisting teachers in the classroom. AI can also improve teachers' skills by giving them access to a range of tools and resources that can help them become better educators.

3.   Promoting Personalized Learning:

By giving educators access to a variety of tools and resources, artificial intelligence (AI) can support personalized learning by enabling them to design individualized learning experiences for students. AI can assist educators in determining the learning preferences, passions, and skill levels of their students. With this knowledge, they can create classes that are specifically catered to the needs of each student. AI can assist educators in monitoring their student's progress and modifying their pedagogical approaches accordingly. "Real-time analysis of student performance data enables a personalized learning environment to automatically provide feedback, learning parameters, and content that is tailored to the individual learner. Additionally, it enables educators to have a deeper understanding of student performance, which helps them create lesson plans that work for their students.

4.   Accessibility of Excellent Educational Resources:

AI can give educators access to excellent learning resources and materials that are customized to meet each student's needs. Ensuring that instructors have a solid basis in the subjects they teach is one of the biggest problems in teacher education. With the use of AI technologies, instructors can find places where their lessons can be improved and students can demand the assistance for material.

5.   Automate Grading:

Even though AI may never be prepared to completely replace human grading, it is getting close. Academics presently have the ability to change the way that almost all multiple-choice, fill-in-the-blank tests are graded, and automatic student essay grading may not be too far after.

6.   Additional support from AI tutors:

Some programs will teach students the fundamentals, but they aren't yet designed to help them learn higher-order and creative thinking—things that real-world lecturers are still needed to support. However, that shouldn't completely rule out the possibility in the future, AI instructors may be able to attempt these tasks.

7.   Helping Physically Challenged Learners:

All varieties of physically challenged learners, such as those who are hearing impaired, visually impaired, have low vision, or have a locomotors disability, can benefit from artificial intelligence (AI). Artificial intelligence (AI) apps can read texts in several languages for those who are blind or visually impaired. They can also expand and describe images to improve comprehension. With the use of this technology, students who are hard of hearing can read books in sign language and comprehend them better.

8.   Automotive assessment and evaluation:

A technology-based evaluation system based on artificial intelligence (AI) can be used to evaluate students' knowledge, comprehension, abilities (such perseverance and teamwork), and traits (like confidence and drive). An artificial intelligence (AI) evaluation system gathers data and analyzes it to assess each student's progress over time. Information on the curriculum, subjects, and learning activities, as well as the specifics of the actions that students took, by the AI assessment system.

6. AI AND LIFELONG LEARNING WITH POSITIVE RESULTS OF ARTIFICIAL INTELLIGENCE IN EDUCATION:

Nowadays, a number of educational institutions, including several universities, are gradually doing away with the outdated traditional methods of instruction. The positive results of AI in education have been studied on the basis of three aspects:

The Figure 2 gives a clear representation that how much positive results will be seen in the education sector with the introduction of AI and for the same the details are explained as follows.

1.   **Better Learning Outcomes:**

With personalised learning, students may go through the curriculum at their own speed and make sure they grasp a subject completely before moving on to the next. This tailored strategy may result in improved learning outcomes. Moreover, AI offers a variety of resources to those with hearing or vision impairments, multilingualism, or both. Presentation Translator is an AI-powered system application that offers subtitles in real-time.

Figure 2. Positive consequences of AI in education sector

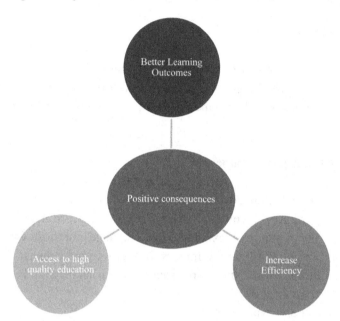

2.   **Increase Efficiency:**

Grading and assessing assessments takes time and work that can be greatly decreased with automation. Academics can save a significant amount of time by using computer-based grading systems, which can swiftly score multiple-choice, fill-in-the-blank, and even some types of open-ended questions. Furthermore AI can lower the expense of one-on-one tutoring by automating some parts of assistance and training.

3.   Access to high quality education:

AI-powered platforms are capable of providing a vast array of instructional resources, such as interactive simulations, multimedia materials, and e-books. With the help of these tools, teachers may quickly share resources with students and give students access to a wide variety of learning materials, extending the reach of education beyond traditional classroom barriers.

7. ETHICAL CONSIDERATIONS AND NEGATIVE CONSEQUENCES OF ARTIFICIAL INTELLIGENCE IN EDUCATION

Although artificial intelligence (AI) presents enormous opportunities, there may also be significant risks involved. AI is probably going to turn out to be the best or the worst thing that has ever happened to humans. The negative consequences of AI in education have been studied on the basis of three aspects:

Figure 3. Negative consequences of AI in education sector

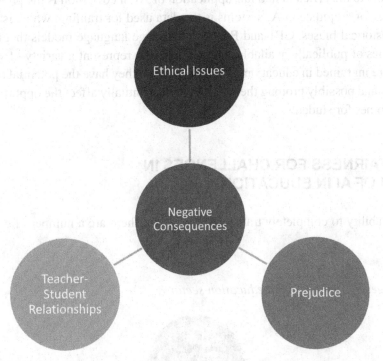

The Figure 3 gives a view that everything which shines is not gold and same applies for the introduction of AI in the education sector and what can be the negative consequences are explained in detail as follows.

1. **Ethical issues:**

AI systems demand enormous amounts of data, including private information on employees and pupils, raising severe privacy concerns. The ethical implications of using AI tools include protecting student privacy and autonomy, using student data responsibly, and ensuring that algorithms and decision-making processes are transparent.

2. **Teacher-Student Relationships:**

The introduction of artificial intelligence (AI) into education has the potential to drastically alter the relationships between teachers and students. While AI technology introduces new difficulties to the dynamics of the conventional educational connection, but over-reliance on technology can lead to a loss of interpersonal relationships and have a potential influence on the development of socio-emotional skills and a shared sense of classroom community.

3.   **Prejudice:**

A major obstacle to the efficient and fair application of AI in education is the problem of prejudice. The primary source of prejudice in AI systems is the data used for training, which is typically affected by societal and historical biases. GPT and Bard are two large language models that have been trained using vast quantities of publically available internet data that represent a variety of viewpoints. When these prejudices are ingrained in educational AI applications, they have the potential to worsen already-existing inequities and possibly prolong them, which will eventually affect the opportunities, resources, and learning outcomes for students.

8. BIAS AND FAIRNESS FOR CHALLENGES IN APPLICATION OF AI IN EDUCATION

While AI has the ability to completely transform education; there are a number of concerns about the potential hazards.

Figure 4. Challenges of applying AI in education sector

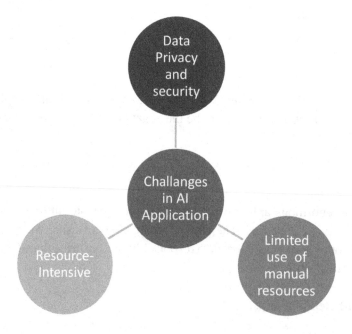

The Figure 4 is identifying the reasons why applying AI in education sector is a challenging task and the details are explained as follows.

1. **Data Privacy and security:**

Almost all technologies are impacted and worried about data security and privacy. Government surveillance and hacking are possible with regards to user location information, communications, and personal data. These worries extend to AI applications in the field of education. Artificial intelligence (AI) tools are permeating educational institutions and gathering and analysing enormous amounts of sensitive data, such as behavioural patterns, academic records, and personal information about individual students. Therefore, there are a lot of hazards for stakeholders if this data are misused or improperly accessed.

2. **Limited use of manual resources:**

AI is emerging to reduce the cost of one to one tutoring, as a result of this teaching assistants, faculty members, student counsellors, and administrative staff to worry that they may be replaced by the AI-powered Intelligent Tutor System. Moreover it will generate a sense of job insecurity between human resources that will reduce their motivation and freed from heavy knowledge transfer.

3. **Resource-Intensive:**

AI is very costly in comparison to the cost of installation, upkeep, and repair. It is frequently necessary to make large expenditures in infrastructure, technology, and ongoing professional development in order to implement personalised learning. Certain institutions can lack the necessary resources to completely implement personalised learning. Only well-funded educational institutions are able to afford such cutting-edge technologies.

9. RESULTS AND FINDINGS

From the above mentioned figures and all the detailed research and explorations made it can be analysed that AI can have very huge impact on the education sector but then there are many challenges to be faced to make AI fully executed for the education sector. Following are the few results and findings from the detailed analysis.

1. From figure 1 it can be analysed that there are many sectors which can evolve significantly if AI is introduced in the education sector as with the introduction of AI in the education sector will directly or indirectly have its effect on all the sectors. So AI can evolve the economy as whole if only and only education sector is highly and positively impacted by the use of AI

2. From figure 2 it has been made cleared that if AI is used cautiously and with the proper control then AI really has many positive outcomes and it can easily become a lifelong learning source helping the students and teachers in various manner

3. The figure 1 and figure 2 are that much exploratory and descriptive that it has helped to easily achieve the first objective of the chapter that to examine the role of artificial intelligence (AI) in management and promotion of education.

4. The figure 3 gives an analysis that what are the negative consequences if the AI is introduced to the education sector and thus makes us understand that what all consequences we should understand before executing AI in the education sector

5. The figure 4 gives an exploratory view that what are the possible challenges the education sector can face while executing the AI and why the education sector has to face all those challenges.

6. Finally from figure 3 and figure 4 it can analysed that objective -2 has been achieved which states that to examine the potential consequences and challenges of artificial intelligence in education and both the figures the negative consequences and challenges have been discussed respectively.

Hence it can be said with the complete justification that all the objectives have been achieved with making an exploratory and descriptive analysis of the available literature on the said chapter title.

10. CONCLUSION

The integration of artificial intelligence (AI) into educational settings holds immense potential to transform teaching and learning practices. As we have explored in this chapter, AI can play a multifaceted role in enhancing various aspects of education, from personalized learning experiences to administrative tasks and educational research.

One of the most promising applications of AI in education is the development of intelligent tutoring systems and adaptive learning platforms. These systems can tailor content delivery and learning paths to individual students' strengths, weaknesses, and preferences, providing a more engaging and effective learning experience. Additionally, AI-powered virtual assistants and chatbots can offer real-time support, answering students' questions and providing guidance when needed.

Beyond the classroom, AI can streamline administrative processes, such as grading assignments, managing student records, and optimizing resource allocation. Predictive analytics driven by AI can also help identify potential issues early on, allowing educators to intervene and provide the necessary support to struggling students.

Furthermore, AI has the capability to revolutionize educational research by analyzing vast amounts of data, identifying patterns, and generating insights that can inform evidence-based instructional strategies and curriculum development.

However, it is crucial to acknowledge and address the ethical considerations and potential risks associated with the widespread adoption of AI in education. Issues such as data privacy, algorithmic bias, and the need for human oversight must be carefully navigated to ensure that AI enhances rather than undermines the educational experience.

As we move forward, a collaborative effort among educators, researchers, policymakers, and technology developers is essential to harness the full potential of AI in education while mitigating its challenges. By striking the right balance, we can create a future where AI acts as a powerful ally in nurturing lifelong learners and fostering a more equitable and inclusive educational landscape.

REFERENCES

Abd Rahim, T. N. T., Abd Aziz, Z., Ab Rauf, R. H., & Shamsudin, N. (2017, November). Automated exam question generator using genetic algorithm. In *2017 IEEE Conference on e-Learning, e-Management and e-Services (IC3e)* (pp. 12-17). IEEE.

An, R., & Xi, T. (2020). Research on the Service Design of Smart Campus Based on Sustainable Strategy – Taking Smart Canteen as an Example. Lecture Notes in Computer Science (including subseries Lecture Notes in Artificial Intelligence and Lecture Notes in Bioinformatics) (Vol. 12202 LNCS, pp. 20–30). Springer.

Borowiec, S. (2016). AlphaGo seals 4-1 victory over Go grandmaster Lee Sedol. *The Guardian, 15*(6).

Catlin, D., & Blamires, M. (2019). Designing robots for special needs education. *Technology, Knowledge and Learning, 24*(2), 291-313.

Chevalier, M., Riedo, F., & Mondada, F. (2016). Pedagogical uses of thymio II: How do teachers perceive educational robots in formal education? *IEEE Robotics & Automation Magazine, 23*(2), 16–23.

Chiba, Y., Nose, T., Kase, T., Yamanaka, M., & Ito, A. (2018, July). An analysis of the effect of emotional speech synthesis on non-task-oriented dialogue system. In *Proceedings of the 19th Annual SIGdial Meeting on Discourse and Dialogue* (pp. 371-375). Academic Press.

Colchester, K., Hagras, H., Alghazzawi, D., & Aldabbagh, G. (2017). A Survey of Artificial Intelligence Techniques Employed for Adaptive Educational Systems within E-Learning Platforms. *Journal of Artificial Intelligence and Soft Computing Research, 7*(1), 47–64.

Cui, L., & Li, J. (2019). Study on Data Fields Grading Category Labeling for ERP Practical Skills Intelligent Assessment System. *DEStech Transactions on Computer Science and Engineering.*

Cui, W., Xue, Z., & Thai, K. P. (2018, November). Performance comparison of an AI-based adaptive learning system in China. In *2018 Chinese automation congress (CAC)* (pp. 3170-3175). IEEE.

Delić, V., Perić, Z., Sečujski, M., Jakovljević, N., Nikolić, J., Mišković, D., Simić, N., & ... . (2019). Speech Technology Progress Based on New Machine Learning Paradigm. *Computational Intelligence and Neuroscience, 2019*, 1–19.

Dishon, G. (2017). New data, old tensions: Big data, personalized learning, and the challenges of progressive education. *Theory and Research in Education, 15*(3), 272–289.

Dong, Z., Zhang, Y., Yip, C., Swift, S., & Beswick, K. (2020). Smart campus: Definition, framework, technologies, and services. *IET Smart Cities, 2*(1), 43–54.

Encalada, W. L., & Sequera, J. L. C. (2017). Model to implement virtual computing labs via cloud computing services. *Symmetry, 9*(7), 117.

Goel, A. K., & Polepeddi, L. (2018). Jill Watson: A virtual teaching assistant for online education. In Learning engineering for online education (pp. 120-143). Academic Press.

Grams, D. (2018). *A quantitative study of the use of DreamBox learning and its effectiveness in improving math achievement of elementary students with math difficulties* [Doctoral dissertation]. Northcentral University.

Grau, A., Indri, M., Bello, L. L., & Sauter, T. (2017, October). Industrial robotics in factory automation: From the early stage to the Internet of Things. In *IECON 2017-43rd annual conference of the IEEE industrial electronics society* (pp. 6159-6164). IEEE.

Holstein, K., McLaren, B. M., & Aleven, V. (2017, March). Intelligent tutors as teachers' aides: exploring teacher needs for real-time analytics in blended classrooms. In *Proceedings of the seventh international learning analytics & knowledge conference* (pp. 257-266). Academic Press.

Ip, H. H. S., Li, C., Leoni, S., Chen, Y., Ma, K. F., Wong, C. H. T., & Li, Q. (2018). Design and evaluate immersive learning experience for massive open online courses (MOOCs). *IEEE Transactions on Learning Technologies, 12*(4), 503–515.

Khandelwal, P., Zhang, S., Sinapov, J., Leonetti, M., Thomason, J., Yang, F., Gori, I., & ... . (2017). BWIBots: A platform for bridging the gap between AI and human–robot interaction research. *The International Journal of Robotics Research, 36*(5–7), 635–659.

Krumm, J. (Ed.). (2018). *Ubiquitous computing fundamentals*. CRC Press.

Kuo, T. H. (2020). The current situation of AI foreign language education and its influence on college Japanese teaching. *Cross-Cultural Design. Applications in Health, Learning, Communication, and Creativity: 12th International Conference, CCD 2020, Held as Part of the 22nd HCI International Conference, HCII 2020, Copenhagen, Denmark, July 19–24, 2020 Proceedings, 22*(Part II), 315–324.

Lakhal, S., Bateman, D., & Bédard, J. (2017). Blended Synchronous Delivery Modes in Graduate Programs: A Literature Review and How it is Implemented in the Master Teacher Program. *Collected Essays on Learning and Teaching, 10,* 47–60.

Li, L., Lin, Y. L., Zheng, N. N., Wang, F. Y., Liu, Y., Cao, D., ... Huang, W. L. (2018). Artificial intelligence test: A case study of intelligent vehicles. *Artificial Intelligence Review, 50,* 441–465.

Li, Q., Cao, H., & Lu, Y. (2017, November). Connecting Paper to Digitization: a Homework Data Processing System with Data Labeling and Visualization. In *Proceedings of the 14th EAI International Conference on Mobile and Ubiquitous Systems: Computing, Networking and Services* (pp. 504-510). Academic Press.

Liu, M., Ma, J., & Jin, L. (2018, August). Analysis of military academy smart campus based on big data. In *2018 10th International Conference on Intelligent Human-Machine Systems and Cybernetics (IHMSC)* (Vol. 1, pp. 105-108). Academic Press.

Miller, D. P., Nourbakhsh, I. R., & Siegwart, R. (2008). *Robots for Education*. Springer Handbook of Robotics.

Paglen, T. (2019). Invisible images: Your pictures are looking at you. *Architectural Design, 89*(1), 22–27.

Russo-Spena, T., Mele, C., & Marzullo, M. (2019). Practising value innovation through artificial intelligence: The IBM Watson case. *Journal of Creating Value, 5*(1), 11–24.

Sarma, G. P., & Hay, N. J. (2017). Robust Computer Algebra, Theorem Proving, and Oracle AI. *arXiv preprint arXiv:1708.02553.*

Sharma, D., & Bhardwaj, K. (2023). Effective Teaching Strategies for Overcoming the Challenges of E-Learning. In Social Capital in the Age of Online Networking: Genesis, Manifestations, and Implications (pp. 99-112). IGI Global.

Tripathy, S., & Devarapalli, S. (2021). Emerging trend set by a start-ups on Indian online education system: A case of Byju's. *Journal of Public Affairs, 21*(1), e2128.

van der Vorst, T., & Jelicic, N. (2019). *Artificial Intelligence in Education: Can AI bring the full potential of personalized learning to education?* Academic Press.

Villegas-Ch, W., Molina-Enriquez, J., Chicaiza-Tamayo, C., Ortiz-Garcés, I., & Luján-Mora, S. (2019). Application of a big data framework for data monitoring on a smart campus. *Sustainability, 11*(20), 5552.

Williamson, B. (2018). The hidden architecture of higher education: Building a big data infrastructure for the 'smarter university'. *International Journal of Educational Technology in Higher Education, 15*, 1–26.

Yang, J., & Zhang, B. (2019). Artificial Intelligence in Intelligent Tutoring Robots: A Systematic Review and Design Guidelines. *Applied Sciences (Basel, Switzerland), 9*(10), 2078.

Yufei, L., Saleh, S., Jiahui, H., & Abdullah, S. M. S. (2020). Review of the application of artificial intelligence in education. *International Journal of Innovation. Creativity and Change, 12*(8), 548–562.

Zhou, X. (2020). Application research of face recognition technology in smart campus. *Journal of Physics: Conference Series, 1437*(1), 012130.

Chapter 8
Comprehensive Survey of Adaptive and Intelligent Education System Using Reinforcement Learning

Mehdy Roayaei

https://orcid.org/0000-0001-9843-5886

Tarbiat Modares University, Iran

ABSTRACT

Adaptive and intelligent educational systems (AIES) have the potential to revolutionize learning by personalizing the educational experience for each student. This chapter presents a comprehensive survey of the application of reinforcement learning in AIES. The authors discuss the use of reinforcement learning to formulate personalized learning plans and pedagogical policies. The chapter also explores the integration of reinforcement learning to build intelligent environments that provide personalized learning recommendations based on students' cognitive attributes and learning styles. By reviewing contemporary work and historical contexts, this survey aims to provide a thorough understanding of the role of reinforcement learning in shaping the future of AIES.

INTRODUCTION

Traditional educational systems provide a structured framework for transferring knowledge and skills to learners. Rooted in established pedagogical methods and practices, these systems typically follow a *one-size-fits-all* approach, where instruction is delivered uniformly to all students regardless of their individual abilities, interests, or learning styles. While traditional educational systems have undoubtedly played a vital role in disseminating knowledge and fostering learning, they often fail to adequately address the diverse needs and preferences of modern learners (Muniasamy et al., 2014).

DOI: 10.4018/979-8-3693-2728-9.ch008

One significant limitation lies in their inability to accommodate the unique learning profiles of individual students. In a traditional classroom setting, students with varying levels of proficiency, interests, and cognitive abilities are often taught using standardized curricula and instructional methods, leading to gaps in understanding and engagement. Additionally, the lack of timely and personalized feedback can slow down students' progress and motivation, limiting their ability to reach their full potential.

Recognizing the shortcomings of traditional educational systems and the growing demand for more personalized and adaptive learning experiences, educators and researchers have turned to adaptive and intelligent educational systems (AIES) as a promising solution. AIES leverage advances in artificial intelligence, machine learning, and data analytics to dynamically customize learning content, progress, sequence, and assessment to the unique needs of each learner. By taking advantages of the power of AI, AIES offer a transformative approach to education, providing personalized learning pathways, real-time feedback, and adaptive support mechanisms that empower learners to achieve their learning goals more effectively (Shute & Zapata-Rivera, 2012).

The reason why personalized learning or *one-to-one learning* are more effective and more satisfying than small group learning is that one-to-one learning allow for personalized teaching strategies, but because of the high financial cost of one-to-one lessons, it is impossible to extend this approach to all groups of students. Based on this situation, the AIES was designed to allow students to develop their own personalized teaching strategies if they have access to a computer, thus allowing them to benefit from a one-to-one teaching model at a relatively low cost and allowing each student to have their own virtual teacher (Dong et al., 2022).

The need for AIES arises from the desire to provide personalized learning experiences that capture to the unique needs and abilities of individual learners. AIES uses data-driven instruction to adjust and customize learning pathways, effective feedback, and supplemental resources to each student's specific response, progress, engagement, and performance. By tracking and analyzing student data, AIES can provide personalized learning experiences that are more engaging, effective, and efficient than traditional one-size-fits-all approaches. There are evidences that supports the importance of adapting content to students to improve learning:

- **Differences in Incoming Knowledge, Skills, and Abilities**: The research shows that these differences make substantial impact on student learning and, the traditional way of teaching in current educational system is not effectively meeting the needs of the diverse student population in schools nowadays (Valerie J. Shute, 2017).
- **Differences in Demographic and Sociocultural Variables**: The research shows differences in demographics and sociocultural backgrounds among students can influence learning results and, in the end, academic accomplishments (Gilberto Q. Conchas, 2006).
- **Differences in Affective Variables**: Research shows that apart from variations in cognitive, physical, and sociocultural aspects, students also experience changes in their emotional states (like frustration, boredom, motivation, and confidence, may impact the learning process), which can differ both among individuals and within the same person over time, can substantially affect on student learning (William Lewis Johnson & Lei Qu, 2005).

Two important issues which should be addressed in any adaptive educational systems are *what* to adapt and *how* to adapt. (1) the factors to consider during the implementation of an adaptive learning system, addressing what elements should be adapted, and (2) the optimal technologies and methodologies to achieve adaptive objectives, addressing how adaptations should be carried out (Shute & Zapata-Rivera, 2012).

To address the first issue of what to adapt, AIES typically adjusts both the content and the delivery method of instructional materials for learners. The content of instruction is determined by selecting specific chapters from textbooks and deciding on formats or layouts for delivery. The delivery method informs the development of teaching strategies, which in turn dictate how the content will be presented to learners.

Addressing the second issue, how to adapt, in adaptive educational systems involves employing AI, especially reinforcement learning techniques, to adapts the content and presentation layouts based on learners' state and characteristics including the cognitive and learning styles of individual students. Reinforcement learning algorithms facilitate the dynamic adjustment of instructional content and strategies based on feedback obtained from student interactions. By continuously assessing the effectiveness of various approaches, these systems optimize the learning experience to better align with each student's needs and preferences. By considering factors such as preferred learning modalities and problem-solving strategies, adaptive systems can customize instructional approaches to maximize engagement and retention. This integration of reinforcement learning and personalized adaptation based on cognitive and learning styles enables adaptive educational systems to provide more effective and tailored learning experiences for individual students. Figure 1 illustrates the different between traditional teaching systems and AIES.

Figure 1. Traditional teaching systems vs. AIES

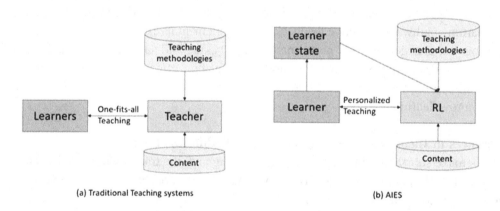

(a) Traditional Teaching systems   (b) AIES

Early AIESs emerged as researchers explored ways to adapt teaching strategies to individual student needs. The vision extended beyond mere programming; seeing AI as a tool for enhancing pedagogy and personalized learning. These systems aimed to create dynamic learning experiences, customized content delivery based on student progress and preferences. As technology advanced, so did the integration of AI into educational contexts, leading to innovative approaches that continue to shape modern education (Doroudi, 2023).

RL has become a pivotal technique within AIESs. RLATES (Reinforcement Learning-Based Adaptive and Intelligent Educational System) leverages RL algorithms to enhance teaching strategies. By observing student behavior, selecting appropriate actions, and receiving rewards or penalties, RLATES dynamically adjusts content delivery. This personalized approach optimizes learning outcomes, adapting to each student's pace, and learning style (Dong et al., 2022).

Shawky et al. (Shawky & Badawi, 2018) presented a comprehensive examination of the impact of reinforcement learning on learning outcomes in simple decision tasks. They study the framework of the proposed system, emphasizing the use of reinforcement learning to create an adaptive learning environment. By leveraging RL techniques, the system aims to dynamically adjust the difficulty level of learning tasks based on student performance, thereby enhancing the learning experience.

Liu et al. introduced a Cognitive Structure Enhanced framework for Adaptive Learning (CSEAL), which aims to enhance learning path recommendation by sequentially identifying the most suitable learning items for individual learners. The framework leverages a Markov Decision Process and applies an actor-critic algorithm to achieve this goal. By fully exploiting the multifaceted cognitive structure, including the knowledge levels of learners and the knowledge structure of learning items, CSEAL offers a comprehensive approach to adaptive learning (Liu et al., 2019).

Tang et al. presents a novel approach to personalized learning recommendation systems by formulating the problem within the Markov decision framework and proposing a reinforcement learning approach to address it. The paper emphasizes the importance of adaptive, personalized learning and the challenges associated with building a powerful recommendation engine that balances making optimal recommendations based on current knowledge and exploring new learning trajectories. By leveraging reinforcement learning, the proposed approach seeks to drive real-time personalized decisions and maximize long-term rewards (Tang et al., 2019).

Dong et al. provide a comprehensive review of adaptive and intelligent web-based educational systems, focusing on the application of artificial intelligence (AI) in the field of education. It discusses the development paradigms of adaptive and intelligent educational systems, the integration of AI technologies, and the potential of AI-enabled learning systems to support sustainable education. The paper also addresses the diverse support offered to students and teachers in web-based educational systems, the use of AI in adaptive learning, and the potential of AI to provide personalized and inclusive learning environments. Furthermore, it highlights the evolution of intelligent tutoring systems and their ability to model students' psychological states, monitor their progress, and provide personalized feedback and support (Dong et al., 2022).

Li et al. formulates the adaptive learning problem as a Markov decision process and applies a model-free deep reinforcement learning algorithm, specifically the deep Q-learning algorithm, to effectively find the optimal learning policy from data on learners' learning process without knowing the actual transition model of the learners' continuous latent traits. The proposed approach aims to efficiently discover the optimal learning policy for a learner by utilizing a transition model estimator that emulates the learner's learning process using neural networks. The paper's numerical simulation studies demonstrate the efficiency of the proposed algorithm in finding a good learning policy, particularly with the aid of a transition model estimator, enabling the discovery of the optimal learning policy after training using a small number of learners (Li et al., 2023).

Fahad Mon et al. provide a comprehensive overview of the application of reinforcement learning (RL) in educational settings. It addresses key research questions, such as the effectiveness of RL in enhancing educational outcomes, its applications in the education field, and the considerations, challenges, and future directions of RL in education. The manuscript discusses various RL techniques in the educational domain, including Markov Decision Process, Partially Observable Markov Decision Process, Deep RL

Framework, and Markov Chain. It also identifies best practices for incorporating RL into educational settings to achieve effective and rewarding outcomes (Fahad Mon et al., 2023).

As previously mentioned, numerous comprehensive reviews exist on adaptive and intelligent educational systems. This chapter specifically delves into the application of RL in AIES, where learners' states are defined by their learning and cognitive styles. Furthermore, we elaborate on the concept of AIES as RL problems, detailing each component extensively.

ADAPTIVE AND INTELLIGENT EDUCATIONAL SYSTEMS

The aim of AIES is to recommend integrating new technologies into the educational system, enabling the system to independently learn the most effective teaching strategies for students. This would enable the system to enhance its pedagogical approach, sequencing the system's content accurately based solely on the student's performance, lesson objectives, and the interrelationships among course modules (Shute & Zapata-Rivera, 2012).

The objective is to simulate human teaching behavior in a one-on-one classroom setting and to explore the application of AI techniques in automatically constructing or maintaining modules within intelligent tutoring systems. Unlike traditional learning environments, such as classroom courses, which deliver the same material to all learners, adaptive learning seeks to offer personalized learning materials and paths customized to individual learners.

In this section, we conceptualize AIES as an adaptive system and introduce its main components. Additionally, we discuss some of the challenges and main benefits associated with such systems.

Conceptual Framework

Different researches have proposed different framework for AIES and for RLAIES (Shute & Zapata-Rivera, 2012), (Iglesias et al., 2009). In the following, we present a conceptual framework for RLAIES, which presents main components and their relationships, and describe their responsibilities. The conceptual formwork is shown in Figure 2.

Content Module

The Content module is responsible for providing the educational materials and resources used in the learning process. This includes textbooks, lecture notes, videos, interactive simulations, and other instructional materials. Concepts, difficulty levels, and pedagogical strategies are carefully tagged and organized, forming a vast library of knowledge waiting to be explored. Content module is used to extract contents from raw materials and generate chunks of information for composing personalized learning materials based on the presentation layout.

This module should be augmented with different data and metadata including ID, title, abstract, icon, text components, example component, figure component, exercises; and supplementary component.

Figure 2. Conceptual framework for RLAIES

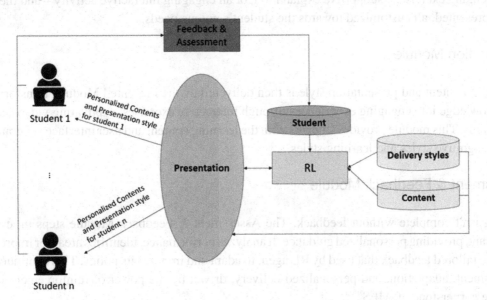

Student Module

The student module oversees the ongoing status of learners, encompassing their current knowledge level at any given moment during interaction with the AIES, as well as their individual learning and cognitive styles, which are pivotal characteristics for modeling learners (Iglesias et al., 2009). Any traditional student modeling technique capable of representing this information could be employed within the AIES framework.

Student Module, constantly crafting a dynamic portrait of each student. It carefully gathers data on cognitive traits, learning styles, and even emotional responses, building a unique profile that informs every interaction.

Delivery Styles Module

The Delivery Styles module encompasses all information pertaining to various layout strategies, teaching methodologies, instructional strategies, and everything related to how selected content is delivered to students. This module serves as a comprehensive repository detailing diverse approaches to presenting educational materials, including visual aids, interactive exercises, multimedia elements, and pedagogical techniques tailored to different learning preferences and needs.

RL Module

Reinforcement Learning Agent, the mastermind behind personalized learning experiences. Equipped with the student's profile and a deep understanding of available contents, and delivery styles, this AI continuously learns and adapts. It acts as a wise instructor, carefully selecting the next learning step – be it a challenging exercise, a supportive explanation, or an engaging interactive activity – and the way the content presented, all customized towards the student's unique needs.

Presentation Module

The chosen content and presentation style is then delivered by the Presented Module, transforming abstract knowledge into engaging experiences through interactive exercises, captivating videos, and clear explanations. This module provides students with the learning content and user interface generated based on their cognitive styles and learning styles.

Assessment & Feedback Module

Learning isn't complete without feedback. The Assessment & Feedback Module steps in, evaluating progress and providing personalized guidance. It analyzes performance, identifies areas for improvement, and offers tailored feedback that used by RL agent to adapt and improve its policy. This continuous cycle of assessment, adaptation, and personalized delivery, driven by the power of reinforcement learning, forms the cornerstone of AIES.

Challenges

Effectively achieving personalized adaptive learning mainly relies on accurately recognizing the attributes of an individual learner or a group of learners. These attributes encompass elements such as the nature and level of knowledge, skills, personality traits, and emotional states. Subsequently, the next step entails determining how to leverage this data to enrich student learning experiences. The implementation of AIES presents various challenges, including (Dieterle et al., 2022; Fahad Mon et al., 2023; Rodway & Schepman, 2023):

- **Accurate Identification of Learner Characteristics**: Precisely identifying diverse learner characteristics, such as knowledge levels, skills, personality traits, and emotional states, is a challenge. The effectiveness of adaptive systems depends on accurate data about the learners.
- **Data Privacy and Security**: Collecting and managing sensitive learner data raise concerns about privacy and security. Ensuring the protection of personal information is crucial to maintain trust and comply with regulations.
- **Personalization for Diverse Learner Profiles**: Designing adaptive systems that cater to a wide range of learner profiles, including different abilities, disabilities, interests, and backgrounds, requires careful consideration and customization.
- **Content Adaptation**: Developing adaptive content that aligns with varying learner needs and preferences while maintaining instructional quality can be challenging. It involves creating flexible materials that suit diverse learning styles.
- **Technological Infrastructure**: Implementing adaptive systems requires a robust technological infrastructure. Ensuring compatibility with existing educational technologies and overcoming technical limitations are essential for successful integration.

- **Continuous System Improvement**: Adaptive systems need to continuously evolve based on learner feedback and changing educational trends. Maintaining and updating these systems to remain relevant and effective pose ongoing challenges.
- **Cost and Resource Allocation**: The initial cost of implementing adaptive educational systems and the ongoing need for resources, including technical support and content development, can be significant challenges for educational institutions.
- **Heterogeneity of the students:** The heterogeneity of the students interacting with the system is one of the main problems in adaptive educational systems, because the system has to adapt to each student at each interaction step.
- **Training Phase Required**: ATES is not immediately available for direct teaching from the outset. Initially, its model must undergo training by being exposed to training data, enabling the system to learn which teaching strategy or presentation layout to employ when encountering students with diverse characteristics.

Benefits

Using AIES in education offers several benefits including (Dieterle et al., 2022; Fahad Mon et al., 2023; Rodway & Schepman, 2023):

- **Personalized Learning**: AIES can personalize educational experiences to the individual needs, preferences, and learning styles of each student. By adapting content, pacing, and instructional methods, these systems provide personalized learning pathways, optimizing comprehension and retention.
- **Enhanced Engagement**: AIES incorporate interactive elements, multimedia resources, and gamification techniques to increase student engagement. By making learning more interactive and enjoyable, these systems motivate students to actively participate in their educational journey.
- **Immediate Feedback**: AIES provide instant feedback on student performance, allowing learners to track their progress in real-time. This timely feedback enables students to identify areas for improvement and adjust their learning strategies accordingly, fostering a deeper understanding of the material.
- **Accessibility and Inclusivity**: AIES can accommodate diverse learning needs and preferences, including those of students with disabilities or special educational requirements. By offering customizable learning experiences and support tools, these systems promote inclusivity and accessibility for all learners.
- **Data-Driven Insights**: AIES collect and analyze vast amounts of data on student interactions, performance, and learning outcomes. Educators can use these insights to identify trends, assess the effectiveness of instructional strategies, and make informed decisions to optimize teaching and learning processes.
- **Flexibility and Adaptability**: AIES can adapt to changes in student progress, preferences, and learning goals in real-time. This flexibility allows educators to customize learning experiences, adjust instructional content, and provide targeted interventions to meet the evolving needs of students.

- **Ethical Considerations**: AIES can contribute to the development of ethical AI in education by promoting fairness, accountability, transparency, and equity in learning. It has the potential to address structural disparities and enhance diversity, equity, and inclusion in education

REINFORCEMENT LEARNING IN EDUCATION

The section begins by defining reinforcement learning, introducing its basic concepts, and its significance in personalized learning. It then presents advantages of RL in education and also review its main applications in educational systems. The section also discusses the role of RL in building intelligent environments that provide personalized learning recommendations based on students' learning styles and cognitive attributes.

Reinforcement Learning

In recent years, RL has applied in various applications including UAV networks (Arefeh Esmaili & Mehdy Roayaei, 2024), recommender systems (Rezaei Gazik & Roayaei, 2023), NLP (Uc-Cetina et al., 2023), healthcare (Coronato et al., 2020), and educational systems (Dong et al., 2022).

RL is a machine-learning technique that allows one or more agents to learn how to maximize the total reward they get from interacting with their environment over time. Agents must discover the best actions by themselves, without being instructed what to do. RL enables agents to learn and make decisions autonomously, without needing supervision or complete models of the environment (Sutton & Barto, 2018).

At time period t, the agent observes a *state* denoted as s_t, belonging to the set of possible states known as state space $\mathcal{S}$. The agent then selects an *action*, a_t, from the set of valid actions, $\mathcal{A}(s_t)$, corresponding to the observed state s_t, and then transfers to the new state $s_{t+1} \in \mathcal{S}$. This chosen action is executed on the *environment*, resulting in a *reward*, denoted by $r(s_t, a_t, s_{t+1}) \in \mathbb{R}$ (Figure 3). This process continues for a duration of T time-steps, culminating in the end of an episode.

Markov Decision Process (MDP) is employed to model and analyze this problem, if the agent possesses complete knowledge of the current state. In an MDP, the goal of the agent is to find a policy, denoted as $\pi : \mathcal{S} \to \mathcal{A}$, which maps states from the state space $\mathcal{S}$ to corresponding actions from the action space $\mathcal{A}$. The goal of this policy is to maximize the overall cumulative rewards over the long term, considering a discount factor γ for future rewards as stated in Eq. (1):

$$argmax_i : r(\pi_i) = \sum_{t=0}^{T} \gamma^t r\left(s_t, a_t, s_{t+1}\right) \tag{1}$$

ep Reinforcement Learning (DRL) is a general paradigm which combines RL and deep learning. DRL uses neural network modeling in traditional RL algorithms (as depicted in Figure 4). It uses deep neural networks to approximate the optimal policy in complex and high-dimensional environments. DRL is typically employed when traditional RL methods face challenges or limitations due to the large state space or action space (Wang et al., 2020).

Figure 3. Agent interaction with environment in reinforcement learning

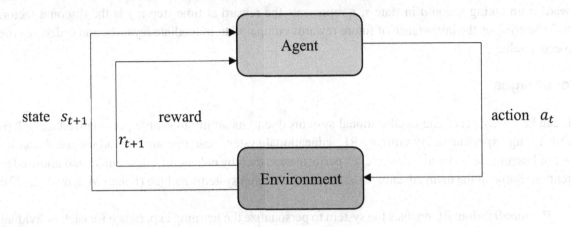

Figure 4. Neural network in deep reinforcement learning

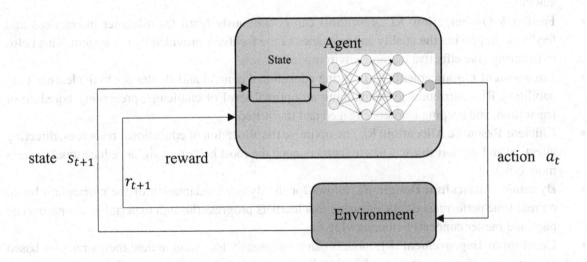

The value function represents the expected total reward an agent can achieve by following a particular strategy or policy in a given environment. It quantifies the desirability of being in a specific state or taking a certain action, considering future rewards. The value function can be denoted as $V(s)$ for state values or $Q(s,a)$. for action values, where s represents the state and a represents the action. The value functions defined as in Eq. (2) and Eq. (3).

$$V(s) = \mathbb{E}[r_{t+1} + \gamma.r_{t+2} + \gamma^2.r_{t+3} + \ldots | s_t = s] \tag{2}$$

$$Q(s,a) = \mathbb{E}[r_{t+1} + \gamma.r_{t+2} + \gamma^2.r_{t+3} + \ldots | s_t = s, a_t = a] \tag{3}$$

Where $V(s)$ represents the expected total reward from state s, $Q(s,a)$ represents the expected total reward from taking action a in state s, r_t represents the reward at time step t, γ is the discount factor, which determines the importance of future rewards compared to immediate rewards, and $\mathbb{E}$ denotes the expected value.

Advantages

RL can be highly beneficial in educational systems due to its ability to enable personalized and adaptive learning experiences. By utilizing RL, educational systems can dynamically adjust the difficulty level of learning tasks based on a student's performance, thereby enhancing engagement and knowledge retention. Some of the main advantages of RL in educational systems include (Fahad Mon et al., 2023):

- **Personalization**: RL enables the system to personalize the learning experience for each individual by adapting content and stregies based on the learner's progress, preferences, and needs.
- **Adaptability**: RL models can dynamically adjust the difficulty level of tasks, pacing of content delivery, and overall instructional approach in real-time, optimizing the learning process for each student.
- **Feedback Optimization**: RL algorithms can continuously learn from learner interactions and feedback, improving the quality and relevance of the feedback provided by the system. This helps in fostering aore effective learning environment.
- **Engagement Enhancement**: By tailoring educational content and challenges to the learner's capabilities, RL contributes to maintaining an optimal level of challenge, preventing boredom or frustration, and keeping learners engaged and motivated.
- **Efficient Resource Allocation**: RL can optimize the allocation of educational resources, directing attention and support to areas where learners need the most help, making the educational process more efficient.
- **Dynamic Curriculum Design**: RL allows for the dynamic adaptation of the curriculum based on real-time performance data, ensuring that learners progress through material at an appropriate pace and master concepts before moving on.
- **Continuous Improvement**: RL models can continuously learn and update their strategies based on new data, allowing adaptive educational systems to improve over time and stay relevant in the face of evolving learning needs.

Applications

The potential applications of RL in educational systems are diverse and impactful. RL can be utilized to create adaptive and intelligent learning environments, offering personalized learning experiences and optimized content delivery. Some of the main applications of RL in educational systems include: RL has diverse applications in education, including (Fahad Mon et al., 2023):

- **Teacher–Student Framework**: The teacher-student framework has been implemented to enhance sample efficiency through the use of an advising mechanism (Anand et al., 2021).
- **RL Techniques to Provide Hints and Quizzing**: It involves training policies to offer hints and quizzes as feedback within a task, especially in challenging subjects (Williams et al., 2016).

- **Adaptive Experimentation in Educational Platforms**: Lately, there has been a growing utilization of RL techniques for evaluating education on online platforms (Rafferty et al., 2018).
- **Instructional Sequencing in Education:** It adaptively arranges various educational activities to facilitate the student learning process (Bassen et al., 2020).
- **Modeling Students**: It simulates the behaviour of the student against the teacher. This method employs the RL agent as the student, with the teacher serving as the environment (X. Yang et al., n.d.).
- **Generating Educational Content**: RL methods can be employed for creating educational materials like videos, quizzes, and exercises (Gisslen et al., 2021).
- **Personalized Education through E-Learning**: It involves recognizing and understanding the unique needs and capabilities of each student. It then employs the most suitable teaching methods and multimedia content to address and bridge the knowledge gaps that may exist (Tang et al., 2019).
- **Personalizing a Curriculum**: One of the extensively studied applications of RL in education involves developing an educational strategy capable of training an instructional policy to deliver personalized learning materials to students (Slim et al., 2021).

INTEGRATING REINFORCEMENT LEARNING WITH COGNITIVE SCIENCE AND LEARNING STYLE FOR ADAPTIVE EDUCATIONAL SYSTEMS

The primary feature of AIES is its capability for adaptability in response to the learners' state. But, how the state of a learner can be characterized? This section studies the integration of RL with cognitive science and learning style considerations in the realm of adaptive educational systems.

As technology continues to advance, there is a growing recognition of the importance of leveraging interdisciplinary approaches to enhance the effectiveness and personalization of educational experiences. In this context, the synergy between reinforcement learning, cognitive science principles, and an understanding of individual learning and cognitive styles holds immense promise for the development of adaptive educational systems that can cater to the diverse needs and preferences of learners.

Learning styles which represent the way individuals perceive and process information have been recognized as being an important factor related to the presentation of learning materials (T. C. Yang, Hwang, et al., 2013). On the other hand, cognitive styles have been recognized as being an essential characteristic of individuals' cognitive process (Liu et al., 2019).

This section explores the foundational principles of cognitive and learning styles in educational settings, and explain how RL algorithms can be integrated to optimize adaptive learning experiences.

Learning Style

Learning styles can be defined as an individual's preferred method of understanding and retaining new information. These styles are often categorized into distinct modalities, including visual, auditory, tactile, and kinesthetic. Visual learners prefer to process information through images and spatial understanding, while auditory learners benefit from listening and discussing. Tactile learners, on the other hand, learn best through touch and movement, and kinesthetic learners prefer using their whole body in the learning process. Understanding these learning styles can help tailor educational approaches to better suit individual needs and preferences, ultimately enhancing the learning experience for students.

Recognition of learning styles has been acknowledged as a crucial element in enhancing comprehension of learning models and understanding the preferences and dispositions of students toward learning (Filippidis & Tsoukalas, 2009). Several previous studies have demonstrated the use of learning styles as one of the parameters for providing personalized learning guidance or contents (El-Sabagh, 2021; Truong, 2015, 2016; T. C. Yang, Hwang, et al., 2013).

Many researchers have acknowledged the Felder–Silverman Learning Style Model (FSLSM) as a highly appropriate framework for the development of adaptive learning systems, among various learning styles (Felder & Soloman, 1997). For example, Kuljis et al. conducted a comparative analysis of various learning style models, concluding that the FSLSM is the most suitable model for application in e-learning systems. (Kuljis & Fang Liu, 2005).

The Felder-Silverman Learning Style Model defines four dimensions of learning style, which are as follows (Figure 5) (Felder & Soloman, 1997):

- **Perception**: This dimension refers to how individuals prefer to take in information. It distinguishes between sensing (S) and intuitive (N) learners. Sensing learners prefer concrete facts and details, while intuitive learners prefer abstract concepts and theories.
- **Input**: Input refers to how individuals prefer to receive information. It distinguishes between visual (V) and verbal (V) learners. Visual learners prefer visual aids such as diagrams, graphs, and videos, while verbal learners prefer written and spoken explanations.
- **Processing**: This dimension pertains to how individuals prefer to process information. It distinguishes between active (A) and reflective (R) learners. Active learners prefer hands-on activities and group discussions, while reflective learners prefer to think and analyze information independently.
- **Understanding**: Understanding refers to how individuals prefer to understand concepts. It distinguishes between sequential (S) and global (G) learners. Sequential learners prefer to learn in a step-by-step manner, focusing on details before grasping the big picture, while global learners prefer to see the big picture first and then fill in the details.

There are two main approaches for detecting learning styles of students according two FLSLM including:

- **Self-assessment tools**: Students can provide initial insights through self-assessment tools based on FSLSM dimensions, indicating their preferred learning methods (sensing-intuiting, visual-verbal, active-reflective, sequential-global). This data readily integrates into online platforms for early personalization (Ortigosa et al., 2010).
- **Indirect assessment through interactions**: This approach involves automatically inferring students' learning styles based on their interactions and behaviors within the adaptive learning system. By tracking various user interactions, such as preferences for certain types of content, engagement levels, learning pace, and problem-solving approaches, the system can infer patterns indicative of specific learning styles aligned with the FSLSM. Machine learning algorithms and data analytics techniques can be employed to analyze these interaction data and infer students' learning styles without the need for explicit assessments (Essa et al., 2023).

Figure 5. Felder-Silverman learning style model (Felder & Soloman, 1997)

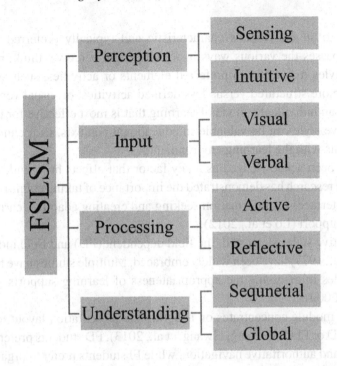

Delivery Styles Module (in Figure 2) is related to content adjustment for students of different learning styles. Different students with different FSLSM styles should receive contents differently based on their styles. Table 1 outlines the eight dimensions of FSLSM learning style model, which served as a basis for developing the personalized presentation module in the adaptive learning system described AIES (T. C. Yang, Hwang, et al., 2013).

Table 1. Delivery adjustment according to FLSLM learning styles

Learning Style	Content Adjusting Principles
Active	• more examples • illustrative examples
Reflective	• review on previously learned contents • possible questions or applications • short summaries or notes based on what they have learned in their own words
Sensing	• specific examples of concepts and procedures • applications of the concepts to practical applications
Intuitive	• interpretations or theories related to the course content • providing illustrative examples to address some easy-to-confuse concepts
Visual	• more visual materials, such as diagrams, sketches, schematics, photographs, or flow charts.
Text	• more text materials.
Sequential	• learning materials in a logical order.
Global	• Enable students to browse through the entire chapter to get an overview before learning

Cognitive Style

Cognitive style refers to an individual's characteristic and typically preferred mode of processing information. It encompasses the various ways in which people perceive, think, remember, and solve problems. Cognitive styles may differ in preferred elements or activities, such as group work versus working individually, more structured versus less defined activities, or visual versus verbal encoding. They can also relate to an individual's mode of learning that is most effective for them. Understanding an individual's cognitive style can be valuable in educational contexts, as it can inform instructional methods and interactions with the learning environment.

Cognitive style has been acknowledged as a key factor that affects how students seek and process information. Numerous research has demonstrated the importance of taking cognitive styles into account when designing user interfaces for information seeking and creating adaptive learning systems to offer personalized learning support (Lo et al., 2012).

Among many cognitive styles suggested, the field dependent (FD) and field independent (FI) styles outlined by (Witkin et al., 1977) have been widely embraced. Multiple studies have highlighted the value of FI/FD cognitive styles in assessing the appropriateness of learning supports and learning system designs (Gerjets et al., 2009).

The Delivery styles module concentrates on adapting the presentation layout to suit each student's cognitive style, either FD or FI (T. C. Yang, Hwang, et al., 2013). FD students prefer structured information, direct promotion, and authoritative navigation, while FI students prefer to organize the information themselves. In terms of course lesson navigation, the user interface for FD students is designed to display less information at a time to prevent distractions, referred to as a "Simpler interface" in this study. In contrast, the interface for FI students provides more information to facilitate a comprehensive review of the learning content, referred to as a "more complex interface," as detailed in Table 1 (T. C. Yang, Hwang, et al., 2013).

Table 2. Delivery adjustment according to FI/DI styles (T. C. Yang, Hwang, et al., 2013)

Field Dependent (FD)	Field Independent
Simpler interface	More complex interface
Less information presented at the same time	More information presented at the same time
Providing only frequently used functions and links to the information related to the current learning content	Providing links to show the full functions of the system and the schema of the entire learning content

RL Formulation

In the context of AIES, the formulation of RL involves the development of algorithms and models that enable the system to make data-driven decisions to optimize the learning experience for individual students. RL formulation in this context encompasses the design of reward structures, state representations, and action policies that align with cognitive science principles and learning style preferences. By integrating insights from cognitive science and learning style models, RL algorithms can be tailored to adaptively sequence instructional content, provide personalized feedback, and optimize the delivery of educational material.

This integration allows AIES to dynamically adjust its strategies based on students' cognitive processes and learning style, ultimately enhancing the effectiveness and personalization of the learning experience. To adaptively update the teaching strategy using RL algorithms, the problem should be formulated as an RL problem. The details of RL formulation can be stated as follows:

- **Agent**: the agent refers to the RL module of the proposed framework. RL module interacts with student through AIES, present some content using current delivery strategy, receive feedbacks from students, and updates its policy according the state of the student and the feedback it has received.
- **Environment**: All other components, including student, content, delivery strategy, are considered as environment.
- **State (S)**: A state is defined as the description of the current student's state. It should contain all information that can assist the RL module in personalizing the teaching experience for the current student, including:
  - Student learning style
  - Student cognitive style
  - Student knowledge level
  - Age & Sex
  - Personal preferences and learning habits
  - Learning process
  - Learning target
  - Content difficulty level
  - Performance history
- **Action (A):**
- Actions can be devised as a variety of personalized strategies that the RL module can employ to improve learning results, considering the student's current state. Here are some examples of actions in RL for AIES:
  - adapting presentation layouts
  - selecting appropriate learning content for individuals
  - adapting content difficulty
  - providing feedback
  - modifying instructional strategy
  - adapting pace of learning
- **Reward**: This function defines the reinforcement signals provided by the environment. This reinforcement function supplies a maximum value to meet the goals of AIES; that is to say, when the student learns the totality of the contents of the AIES. Recall that the objective of the adaptive learning system is to minimize the learning steps it takes before a learner's latent traits reach the maximum.

Based on this MDP formulation, the adaptive learning problem is essentially to find an optimal learning policy, denoted by π^* S→A, that determines the action (delivery style and content selection) based on the state (student state), such that the expected cumulative discounted reward is maximized.

ANALYZING ADAPTIVE AND INTELLIGENT EDUCATIONAL SYSTEM

Analyzing an AIES involves assessing various aspects of its functionality, effectiveness, and impact on learning outcomes. Below are some key considerations and methodologies for analyzing an AIES:

- **Performance Evaluation**:
  - Measure learning outcomes: Assess the effectiveness of the AIES in improving student performance, such as test scores, grades, and mastery of learning objectives.
  - **Evaluate adaptability**: Analyze how well the AIES adjusts its strategies and interventions based on individual student needs and feedback.
  - **Compare with benchmarks**: Benchmark the AIES against traditional teaching methods or other adaptive learning systems to gauge its relative performance.
- **User Experience Assessment**:
  - **Solicit feedback from users**: Gather input from students, teachers, and administrators regarding their experiences with the AIES, including usability, engagement, and satisfaction.
  - **Conduct surveys and interviews**: Use qualitative methods to explore user perceptions, preferences, and suggestions for improvement.
  - **Analyze interaction logs**: Examine log data to understand how students interact with the system and identify areas for enhancement in user experience.
- **Adaptation Analysis:**
  - **Trace learning trajectories**: Track individual students' progress over time to observe how the AIES adapts its interventions and content delivery based on their evolving needs and performance.
  - **Investigate policy dynamics**: Explore how the RL model learns and updates its policies in response to feedback from the environment, analyzing convergence, stability, and exploration-exploitation trade-offs.
  - **Assess policy generalization**: Evaluate the generalization capability of learned policies across diverse student populations, subject domains, and educational contexts.
- **Effectiveness of Personalization:**
  - **Assess individualization**: Determine the extent to which the AIES tailors learning experiences to individual student characteristics, preferences, and learning styles.
  - **Analyze resource allocation**: Investigate how the AIES allocates resources, such as learning materials, exercises, and feedback, to maximize learning gains for each student.
  - **Explore cognitive load management**: Examine how the AIES manages cognitive load by presenting information at an appropriate level of complexity and providing scaffolding support as needed.
- **Ethical and Social Implications:**
  - **Consider ethical considerations:** Reflect on the ethical implications of using AI in education, such as privacy, fairness, and transparency, and analyze how the AIES addresses these concerns.
  - **Explore social dynamics:** Investigate the impact of the AIES on social interactions, collaboration, and equity in the classroom, considering factors such as student motivation, peer learning, and teacher-student relationships.

Also, several metrics can be used to analyze AIES including:

- **Completion Rates**: Measure the percentage of students who complete the learning activities or courses within the AIES.
- **Time Spent**: Evaluate the amount of time students engage with the learning materials and activities, providing insights into their level of involvement.
- **Mastery Levels**: Assess the degree to which students have mastered the learning objectives and content within the AIES.
- **Feedback Scores**: Capture the quality and effectiveness of the feedback provided to students within the AIES.
- **Learning Progress**: Monitor students' advancement through the program, considering indicators such as completion rates, time spent, mastery levels, and feedback scores.
- **Learning Outcomes**: Measure the impact of the AIES on students' performance, productivity, or behavior, typically assessed through test scores, grades, certifications, or ratings.

CONCLUSION AND FUTURE DIRECTIONS

In this chapter, we conducted a comprehensive survey of Adaptive and Intelligent Education Systems utilizing Reinforcement Learning, exploring their development, functionality, and impact on educational outcomes. We began by introducing the concept of AIES and highlighting the importance of personalized learning experiences in modern education. Subsequently, we studied the role of RL in shaping adaptive educational systems, discussing its underlying principles and methodologies.

Our exploration of integrating RL with cognitive science and learning styles underscored the significance of leveraging multidisciplinary approaches to enhance the adaptability and effectiveness of AIES. By incorporating insights from cognitive psychology and individualized learning preferences, AIES can better customized instructional strategies and content delivery to meet the diverse needs of learners.

The analysis of AIES provided valuable insights into their performance, user experience, adaptation dynamics, and effectiveness of personalization. Through empirical studies and user feedback, we gained a deeper understanding of how RL-driven AIES adapt to student needs, optimize learning trajectories, and foster engagement and mastery.

In conclusion, our survey highlights the potential of RL-driven AIES to revolutionize educational practices by providing personalized, adaptive, and effective learning experiences. However, several avenues for future research and development remain to be explored. Future work in this area could focus on:

- **Advancing RL algorithms**: Developing novel RL algorithms tailored to the unique challenges and requirements of educational environments, such as handling sparse rewards, incorporating domain knowledge, and facilitating exploration in complex state spaces.
- **Enhancing user interaction**: Designing intuitive user interfaces and interactive learning environments that facilitate seamless interaction between students, educators, and AIES, promoting engagement and collaboration.
- **Scaling implementation:** Scaling up the deployment of RL-driven AIES in diverse educational settings, considering factors such as infrastructure requirements, teacher training, and cost-effectiveness.

- **Deep RL**: In the realm of AIES, many researchers continue to utilize the classical Q-learning algorithm. This preference is largely attributed to the algorithm's characteristics: it is model-free and policy-free, making it well-suited for implementation in intelligent teaching systems. However, despite its widespread adoption, Q-learning has its limitations. Particularly, it tends to exhibit sluggish processing speed, and the system's response time can increase significantly when dealing with excessively large Q-tables. Deep RL can serve as a viable alternative to the classical Q-learning algorithm.

REFERENCES

Anand, D., Gupta, V., Paruchuri, P., & Ravindran, B. (2021). An Enhanced Advising Model in Teacher-Student Framework using State Categorization. *Proceedings of the AAAI Conference on Artificial Intelligence*, *35*(8), 6653–6660. doi:10.1609/aaai.v35i8.16823

Bassen, J., Balaji, B., Schaarschmidt, M., Thille, C., Painter, J., Zimmaro, D., Games, A., Fast, E., & Mitchell, J. C. (2020). Reinforcement Learning for the Adaptive Scheduling of Educational Activities. *Proceedings of the 2020 CHI Conference on Human Factors in Computing Systems*, 1–12. 10.1145/3313831.3376518

Conchas, G. Q. (2006). *The Color of Success Race and High-Achieving Urban Youth*. Teachers College Press.

Coronato, A., Naeem, M., De Pietro, G., & Paragliola, G. (2020). Reinforcement learning for intelligent healthcare applications: A survey. *Artificial Intelligence in Medicine*, *109*, 101964. doi:10.1016/j.artmed.2020.101964 PMID:34756216

Dieterle, E., Dede, C., & Walker, M. (2022). The cyclical ethical effects of using artificial intelligence in education. *AI & Society*. Advance online publication. doi:10.1007/s00146-022-01497-w PMID:36185064

Dong, J., Mohd Rum, S. N., Kasmiran, K. A., Mohd Aris, T. N., & Mohamed, R. (2022). Artificial Intelligence in Adaptive and Intelligent Educational System: A Review. In Future Internet (Vol. 14, Issue 9). MDPI. doi:10.3390/fi14090245

Doroudi, S. (2023). The Intertwined Histories of Artificial Intelligence and Education. *International Journal of Artificial Intelligence in Education*, *33*(4), 885–928. doi:10.1007/s40593-022-00313-2

El-Sabagh, H. A. (2021). Adaptive e-learning environment based on learning styles and its impact on development students' engagement. *International Journal of Educational Technology in Higher Education*, *18*(1), 53. Advance online publication. doi:10.1186/s41239-021-00289-4

Esmaili, A., & Roayaei, M. (2024). UAV-Based Warehouse Management Using Multi-Agent RL: Applications, Challenges, and Solutions. In Applications of Machine Learning in UAV Networks (pp. 263–306). IGI Global.

Essa, S. G., Celik, T., & Human-Hendricks, N. E. (2023). Personalized Adaptive Learning Technologies Based on Machine Learning Techniques to Identify Learning Styles: A Systematic Literature Review. *IEEE Access : Practical Innovations, Open Solutions*, *11*, 48392–48409. doi:10.1109/ACCESS.2023.3276439

Fahad Mon, B., Wasfi, A., Hayajneh, M., Slim, A., & Abu Ali, N. (2023). Reinforcement Learning in Education: A Literature Review. *Informatics (MDPI)*, *10*(3), 74. doi:10.3390/informatics10030074

Felder, R. M., & Soloman, B. A. (1997). *Index of learning style questionnaire*. https://www.engr.ncsu.edu/learningstyles/ilsweb.html

Filippidis, S. K., & Tsoukalas, I. A. (2009). On the use of adaptive instructional images based on the sequential–global dimension of the Felder–Silverman learning style theory. *Interactive Learning Environments*, *17*(2), 135–150. doi:10.1080/10494820701869524

Gerjets, P., Scheiter, K., Opfermann, M., Hesse, F. W., & Eysink, T. H. S. (2009). Learning with hypermedia: The influence of representational formats and different levels of learner control on performance and learning behavior. *Computers in Human Behavior*, *25*(2), 360–370. doi:10.1016/j.chb.2008.12.015

Gisslen, L., Eakins, A., Gordillo, C., Bergdahl, J., & Tollmar, K. (2021). Adversarial Reinforcement Learning for Procedural Content Generation. *2021 IEEE Conference on Games (CoG)*, 1–8. 10.1109/CoG52621.2021.9619053

Iglesias, A., Martínez, P., Aler, R., & Fernández, F. (2009). Learning teaching strategies in an Adaptive and Intelligent Educational System through Reinforcement Learning. *Applied Intelligence*, *31*(1), 89–106. doi:10.1007/s10489-008-0115-1

Johnson, W. L., & Qu, L. (2005). Detecting the Learner's Motivational States in An Interactive Learning Environment. *Proceedings of the 2005 Conference on Artificial Intelligence in Education: Supporting Learning through Intelligent and Socially Informed Technology*.

Kuljis, J., & Fang Liu. (2005). A Comparison of Learning Style Theories on the Suitability for elearning. *Web Technologies, Applications, and Services*, 191–197.

Li, X., Xu, H., Zhang, J., & Chang, H. (2023). Deep Reinforcement Learning for Adaptive Learning Systems. *Journal of Educational and Behavioral Statistics*, *48*(2), 220–243. doi:10.3102/10769986221129847

Liu, Q., Tong, S., Liu, C., Zhao, H., Chen, E., Ma, H., & Wang, S. (2019). Exploiting cognitive structure for adaptive learning. *Proceedings of the ACM SIGKDD International Conference on Knowledge Discovery and Data Mining*, 627–635. 10.1145/3292500.3330922

Lo, J.-J., Chan, Y.-C., & Yeh, S.-W. (2012). Designing an adaptive web-based learning system based on students' cognitive styles identified online. *Computers & Education*, *58*(1), 209–222. doi:10.1016/j.compedu.2011.08.018

Muniasamy, V., Ejalani, D. I. M., & Anandhavalli, D. M. (2014). Moving towards Virtual Learning Clouds from Traditional Learning: Higher Educational Systems in India. *International Journal of Emerging Technologies in Learning*, *9*(9), 70. doi:10.3991/ijet.v9i9.4183

Ortigosa, A., Paredes, P., & Rodriguez, P. (2010). AH-questionnaire: An adaptive hierarchical questionnaire for learning styles. *Computers & Education*, *54*(4), 999–1005. doi:10.1016/j.compedu.2009.10.003

Rafferty, A. N., Ying, H., & Williams, J. J. (2018). Bandit Assignment for Educational Experiments: Benefits to Students Versus Statistical Power. doi:10.1007/978-3-319-93846-2_53

Rezaei Gazik, M. A., & Roayaei, M. (2023). Batch (Offline) Reinforcement Learning for Recommender System. *2023 31st International Conference on Electrical Engineering (ICEE)*, 245–250. 10.1109/ICEE59167.2023.10334722

Rodway, P., & Schepman, A. (2023). The impact of adopting AI educational technologies on projected course satisfaction in university students. *Computers and Education: Artificial Intelligence*, 5, 100150. doi:10.1016/j.caeai.2023.100150

Shawky, D., & Badawi, A. (2018). *A Reinforcement Learning-Based Adaptive Learning System.* doi:10.1007/978-3-319-74690-6_22

Shute, V. J. (2017). *The Future of Assessment* (C. A. Dwyer, Ed.). Routledge. doi:10.4324/9781315086545

Shute, V. J., & Zapata-Rivera, D. (2012). Adaptive educational systems. In *Adaptive Technologies for Training and Education* (pp. 7–27). Cambridge University Press. doi:10.1017/CBO9781139049580.004

Slim, A., Al Yusuf, H., Abbas, N., Abdallah, C. T., Heileman, G. L., & Slim, A. (2021). A Markov Decision Processes Modeling for Curricular Analytics. *2021 20th IEEE International Conference on Machine Learning and Applications (ICMLA)*, 415–421. 10.1109/ICMLA52953.2021.00071

Sutton, R. S., & Barto, A. G. (2018). *Reinforcement Leaning.* MIT Press.

Tang, X., Chen, Y., Li, X., Liu, J., & Ying, Z. (2019). A reinforcement learning approach to personalized learning recommendation systems. *British Journal of Mathematical & Statistical Psychology*, 72(1), 108–135. doi:10.1111/bmsp.12144 PMID:30277574

Truong, H. M. (2015). *Integrating Learning Styles into Adaptive E-Learning System.* International Educational Data Mining Society.

Truong, H. M. (2016). Integrating learning styles and adaptive e-learning system: Current developments, problems and opportunities. *Computers in Human Behavior*, 55, 1185–1193. doi:10.1016/j.chb.2015.02.014

Uc-Cetina, V., Navarro-Guerrero, N., Martin-Gonzalez, A., Weber, C., & Wermter, S. (2023). Survey on reinforcement learning for language processing. *Artificial Intelligence Review*, 56(2), 1543–1575. doi:10.1007/s10462-022-10205-5

Wang, H., Liu, N., Zhang, Y., Feng, D., Huang, F., Li, D., & Zhang, Y. (2020). Deep reinforcement learning: A survey. *Frontiers of Information Technology & Electronic Engineering*, 21(12), 1726–1744. doi:10.1631/FITEE.1900533

Williams, J. J., Kim, J., Rafferty, A., Maldonado, S., Gajos, K. Z., Lasecki, W. S., & Heffernan, N. (2016). AXIS: Generating Explanations at Scale with Learnersourcing and Machine Learning. *Proceedings of the Third (2016) ACM Conference on Learning @ Scale*, 379–388. 10.1145/2876034.2876042

Witkin, H. A., Moore, C. A., Goodenough, D., & Cox, P. W. (1977). Field-Dependent and Field-Independent Cognitive Styles and Their Educational Implications. *Review of Educational Research*, 47(1), 1–64. doi:10.3102/00346543047001001

Yang, T. C., Hwang, G. J., & Yang, S. J. H. (2013). *Development of an Adaptive Learning System with Multiple Perspectives based on Students' Learning Styles and Cognitive Styles.* https://www.researchgate.net/publication/279764849

Yang, X., Zhou, G., Taub, M., Azevedo, R., & Chi, M. (n.d.). *Student Subtyping via EM-Inverse Reinforcement Learning.* Academic Press.

Chapter 9
Enhancing Literacy Education in Higher Institutions With AI Opportunities and Challenges

Tarun Kumar Vashishth

 https://orcid.org/0000-0001-9916-9575
IIMT University, India

Vikas Sharma

 https://orcid.org/0000-0001-8173-4548
IIMT University, India

Kewal Krishan Sharma

 https://orcid.org/0009-0001-2504-9607
IIMT University, India

Bhupendra Kumar

 https://orcid.org/0000-0001-9281-3655
IIMT University, India

ABSTRACT

Enhancing literacy education in higher institutions through the integration of artificial intelligence (AI) presents significant opportunities and challenges. This chapter explores the role of AI in literacy education, showcasing its potential to revolutionize teaching methodologies, personalized learning, and student outcomes. AI-powered tools, such as natural language processing (NLP), chatbots, and adaptive learning platforms, offer unique opportunities to engage students, improve language proficiency, and address individual learning needs effectively. The chapter delves into the various opportunities AI presents in higher education literacy, emphasizing the benefits of AI-driven content recommendation systems, personalized feedback, and early intervention for struggling students. However, along with the opportunities come several challenges, including ethical considerations surrounding data privacy, faculty readiness, and the potential displacement of traditional teaching approaches.

DOI: 10.4018/979-8-3693-2728-9.ch009

1. INTRODUCTION

The intersection of Artificial Intelligence (AI) and education has given rise to transformative possibilities within higher institutions. This chapter explores the dynamic realm of literacy education in higher institutions and the integration of AI, shedding light on the profound opportunities and formidable challenges that this fusion presents. (Bhatnagar, 2020) explores the current state of AI in Indian higher education and its potential to transform the learning experience for students. As we delve into this exploration, it becomes evident that the potential of AI in literacy education transcends the conventional paradigms, offering a glimpse into a future where teaching and learning are reshaped fundamentally.

1.1 Definition and Significance

In the landscape of education, the integration of Artificial Intelligence (AI) presents a transformative paradigm shift, with profound implications for literacy education in higher institutions. Before we delve into the opportunities and challenges presented by AI in this context, it's essential to clarify its definition and understand its significance.

Defining Artificial Intelligence in Literacy Education

AI refers to the development of computer systems that have the capacity to perform tasks that typically require human intelligence. In the realm of literacy education, AI encompasses a broad spectrum of applications, from Natural Language Processing (NLP), which enables machines to understand, interpret, and generate human language, to chatbots and adaptive learning platforms that cater to individual learning needs effectively. These AI-driven tools are designed to assist both educators and students in various aspects of literacy education.

The Significance of AI in Literacy Education

The significance of AI in literacy education is underscored by several key factors:

a. Personalization of Learning: AI facilitates personalized learning experiences. Through data analysis, AI can identify the strengths and weaknesses of individual students, enabling the customization of learning paths. This adaptability is especially crucial in literacy education, where students often have varying language proficiency levels.

b. Improved Language Proficiency: AI-driven language learning platforms can enhance language proficiency by offering interactive and engaging language exercises. Such platforms can provide real-time feedback, further accelerating the learning process.

c. Efficient Resource Utilization: AI optimizes resource allocation. Instructors can focus their efforts on areas where human intervention is indispensable, while routine tasks, such as grading and data analysis, are automated, allowing educators to invest more time in providing personalized support to students.

d. Early Intervention: AI can identify struggling students early in their educational journey. By tracking performance and behavior patterns, AI systems can flag students who may require additional support, enabling timely intervention.

e. Enriched Educational Content: Content recommendation systems powered by AI can suggest supplementary reading materials, research papers, or language exercises that align with students' interests and needs. This enriches the educational experience and fosters a love for reading and language learning.

1.2 The Role of AI in Higher Education

Artificial Intelligence (AI) is rapidly reshaping the landscape of higher education. Its role is evolving to encompass a multitude of applications that are designed to enhance teaching, learning, administrative processes, and overall educational experiences. (Al Braiki et al., 2020) begin with an introduction to AI and its applications in education and course assessment. They then address prevalent issues in education addressed by AI and machine learning and explore future research prospects.

In this section, we will delve into the expanding role of AI in higher education, which extends far beyond traditional classroom settings.

a. Personalized Learning:

AI plays a pivotal role in personalizing the learning experience for students. AI-driven systems can assess individual students' learning styles, strengths, and weaknesses. This data is then used to tailor educational content and methods to suit the unique needs of each student. Personalization has been particularly beneficial in literacy education, where language proficiency can vary widely among students.

b. Intelligent Content Creation:

AI can generate educational content such as quizzes, tests, and even lesson plans. For literacy education, AI can create language exercises, reading materials, and writing prompts. These intelligently generated resources are designed to meet specific learning objectives, allowing educators to focus more on teaching and providing support to students.

c. Chatbots and Virtual Assistants:

Chatbots and virtual assistants equipped with natural language processing capabilities are increasingly being used in higher education. They offer students a 24/7 resource for information and support, including help with coursework, administrative inquiries, and even counseling services. These tools are invaluable in literacy education, offering language learners opportunities for real-time conversation and language practice.

d. Adaptive Learning Platforms:

AI-powered adaptive learning platforms continually analyze students' performance and behavior to adjust the difficulty and pace of learning materials. This adaptability is particularly relevant in literacy education, where language learning often involves mastering foundational skills before progressing to more advanced content.

e.   Early Warning Systems:

In higher education, early warning systems use AI to identify students who may be at risk of dropping out or underperforming. These systems monitor students' attendance, coursework, and engagement to provide timely interventions. In literacy education, early warning systems can pinpoint students who are struggling with language proficiency.

The integration of AI technologies with the learning procedure is depicted in Figure 1.

Figure 1. AI with learning procedure

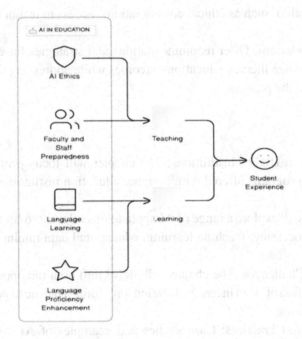

The role of AI in higher education is multifaceted, expanding opportunities for students and educators. However, the responsible integration of AI, including its ethical use and the preparedness of faculty and staff to leverage these technologies, is crucial to maximizing the benefits of AI while addressing its challenges. In the context of literacy education, AI's role is particularly significant due to its ability to cater to individual language learning needs and enhance language proficiency effectively. As we explore the integration of AI in literacy education, these roles will become more pronounced, with significant implications for teaching, learning, and the overall student experience. (Chen, Xie and Hwang 2020) provide educators and scholars with valuable insights into the status and progression of grants and publications in the field of AIEd.

1.3 Objectives and Scope of the Chapter

Objectives:

1. Explore AI Integration: Investigate the integration of artificial intelligence (AI) technologies in literacy education within higher institutions to understand its potential impact on teaching and learning processes.
2. Identify Opportunities: Identify and assess the opportunities presented by AI in enhancing literacy education, including personalized learning, adaptive assessment, and data-driven instruction methods.
3. Address Challenges: Analyze the challenges and barriers associated with the implementation of AI in literacy education, such as ethical considerations, access to technology, and faculty training needs.
4. Provide Recommendations: Offer recommendations and strategies for effectively harnessing AI technologies to optimize literacy education outcomes while addressing the challenges and limitations encountered in the process.

Scope:

1. Literacy Education in Higher Institutions: The chapter will focus primarily on literacy education initiatives and programs offered within higher education institutions, including colleges and universities.
2. AI Applications: It will explore a range of AI applications relevant to literacy education, including natural language processing, machine learning, educational data mining, and intelligent tutoring systems.
3. Opportunities and Challenges: The chapter will delve into both the opportunities and challenges posed by the integration of AI in literacy education, providing a balanced perspective on its potential benefits and limitations.
4. Case Studies and Best Practices: Case studies and examples of AI implementation in literacy education will be examined to illustrate successful initiatives and best practices adopted by higher institutions.
5. Future Directions: Lastly, the chapter will discuss future trends and directions in AI-enhanced literacy education, considering emerging technologies, pedagogical approaches, and areas for further research and innovation.

2. OPPORTUNITIES IN AI-ENHANCED LITERACY EDUCATION

Artificial intelligence (AI) offers numerous opportunities to revolutionize literacy education by enhancing teaching and learning experiences, improving student outcomes, and fostering lifelong literacy skills development. (Cantú-Ortiz et al., 2020) offers a state-of-the-art review of AI in education, supplemented by a case study demonstrating how students can be prepared with the competencies and skills essential for the ongoing digital transformation in Industry 4.0. One significant opportunity lies in personalized learning, where AI technologies can analyze individual student data, including learning preferences, strengths, and areas for improvement, to deliver tailored instruction and adaptive learning pathways.

Through personalized learning platforms and intelligent tutoring systems, students can receive targeted support, practice, and feedback that cater to their unique needs, promoting deeper engagement and understanding of literacy concepts. (Vashishth et al., 2023) explore the evolution of AI and its impact on computing, and how it is linked with literacy education. Additionally, AI-powered assessment tools enable educators to conduct adaptive assessments that adjust difficulty levels and content based on student performance, providing more accurate and timely feedback on students' literacy skills and comprehension. Furthermore, AI-enhanced literacy education promotes accessibility by leveraging text-to-speech and speech recognition technologies to accommodate students with disabilities or language barriers, ensuring equitable access to educational materials and resources. Automated feedback systems powered by AI streamline the grading process for educators, allowing them to provide instant feedback on writing assignments, spelling, grammar, and comprehension exercises, thereby facilitating continuous improvement in students' literacy skills. Moreover, AI analytics tools enable data-driven decision-making by analyzing large datasets of student performance and engagement to identify trends, patterns, and areas for improvement. Educators can use these insights to inform instructional strategies, interventions, and curriculum adjustments, optimizing the effectiveness of literacy education initiatives. (Ocaña-Fernández, Valenzuela-Fernández & Garro-Aburto, 2019) highlight the potential of AI-based approaches to significantly enhance education across various levels. This involves achieving a unique qualitative improvement, delivering precise personalization of learning according to individual requirements while seamlessly integrating diverse forms of human interaction and information and communication technologies.

Additionally, AI technologies can gamify literacy instruction by incorporating elements of competition, rewards, and interactive challenges into educational activities, increasing student motivation, engagement, and retention of literacy skills. Lifelong learning opportunities are also facilitated through AI-enhanced literacy education, as online platforms powered by AI offer accessible and flexible learning experiences that cater to diverse learners' needs and preferences. (Schiff, 2022) provides recommendations for AIED scholars on effective engagement with the policymaking process. The article emphasizes the importance of ethics and policy-oriented AIED research to influence policy discussions in the public's interest. Overall, AI presents a transformative opportunity to create more personalized, engaging, and effective literacy instruction that empowers learners to thrive in the digital age and beyond. (Laupichler et al., 2022) emphasizes the importance of introducing AI concepts to children and promoting AI literacy among adults in higher education and beyond to facilitate effective interactions with this technology.

3. CHALLENGES IN AI-ENHANCED LITERACY EDUCATION

While artificial intelligence (AI) holds immense potential to transform literacy education, its adoption also presents several challenges that must be addressed to ensure its effective implementation and impact. One significant challenge is the potential for algorithmic bias and discrimination in AI-driven literacy instruction. AI algorithms may inadvertently perpetuate or amplify existing biases present in educational data, leading to unequal treatment or opportunities for certain student groups. Educators and developers must be vigilant in identifying and mitigating bias in AI models and datasets to ensure fair and equitable learning experiences for all students. Additionally, the integration of AI technologies into literacy education requires substantial investments in infrastructure, training, and support services. Educational institutions may face financial constraints and resource limitations that hinder their ability to acquire and implement AI tools effectively. Moreover, educators may lack the necessary knowledge, skills, and competencies to leverage AI technologies in their teaching practices, highlighting the need for comprehensive training and professional development initiatives. Furthermore, concerns about data privacy and security pose significant challenges to the adoption of AI in literacy education. AI-driven platforms and tools rely on vast amounts of student data, including personal information and learning analytics, raising concerns about data breaches, unauthorized access, and misuse of sensitive information. Educational institutions must implement robust privacy safeguards and data protection measures to ensure compliance with relevant regulations and safeguard students' privacy rights. (Popenici & Kerr, 2017) investigate the emergence of artificial intelligence in higher education. They delve into the educational implications of these evolving technologies on both student learning and institutional teaching approaches. Additionally, ethical considerations surrounding the use of AI in literacy education require careful attention. Educators must navigate complex ethical dilemmas related to student consent, transparency, accountability, and the responsible use of AI technologies. Finally, the digital divide poses a significant barrier to equitable access to AI-enhanced literacy education. Students from underserved communities may lack access to reliable internet connectivity, digital devices, and technology infrastructure, limiting their ability to benefit from AI-driven learning opportunities. Addressing these challenges requires a multi-faceted approach that prioritizes equity, inclusion, transparency, and ethical considerations in the design, implementation, and evaluation of AI-enhanced literacy education initiatives. By addressing these challenges proactively, stakeholders can harness the full potential of AI to create more equitable, engaging, and effective literacy learning environments for all students. (Tanveer, Hassan & Bhaumik, 2020) analyze the integration of AI with existing educational systems to enhance learning probabilities and boost educational quality and capital in developing nations, providing practical examples for illustration.

4. REAL-WORLD EXAMPLES AND CASE STUDIES

4.1 AI-Powered Language Learning Platforms

- Duolingo: Duolingo is a widely recognized language learning platform that utilizes AI to offer personalized language courses. It adapts to the learner's proficiency level and provides real-time feedback on pronunciation and grammar. Duolingo's AI-driven approach has made language learning accessible to millions of users globally.
- Rosetta Stone: Rosetta Stone, a language learning pioneer, has integrated AI to enhance its language courses. The platform uses AI to assess learners' progress, adapt lessons to individual needs, and provide immediate feedback. This approach empowers learners to develop language skills at their own pace.
- Babbel: Babbel employs AI and natural language processing (NLP) to create personalized language courses. It focuses on real-life conversation skills and uses AI to tailor lessons according to learners' native language, goals, and progress. The platform's success lies in its ability to provide practical language skills.
- Lingvist: Lingvist is an AI-powered language learning platform that uses machine learning to optimize vocabulary learning. It adjusts to users' strengths and weaknesses, helping them memorize words more effectively. Lingvist's data-driven approach has been instrumental in improving vocabulary retention.

- Memrise: Memrise uses AI to create engaging and mnemonic-based language courses. The platform employs spaced repetition algorithms to reinforce vocabulary and grammar. AI helps Memrise ensure that learners remember what they've studied over the long term.

The Figure 2 illustrates the concept of AI integrated learning platforms.

Figure 2. AI integrated learning platforms

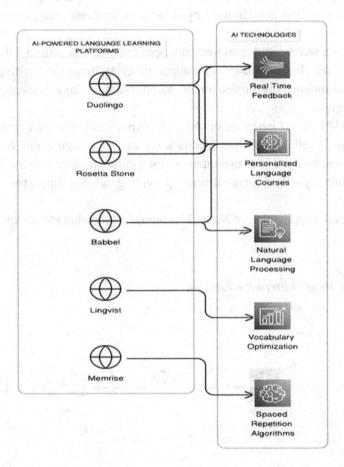

These real-world examples of AI-powered language learning platforms demonstrate how AI can revolutionize language education by providing personalized, effective, and accessible language learning experiences. They showcase the potential of AI in improving language proficiency and meeting the diverse needs of language learners.

4.2 NLP and Chatbots in Literacy Education

- Grammarly: Grammarly is a widely used writing assistant tool that incorporates Natural Language Processing (NLP) to help users improve their writing. It analyzes text for grammar, punctuation, and style errors, offering real-time suggestions. This tool has become invaluable for students, professionals, and writers seeking to enhance their writing skills.

- Microsoft Word Editor: Microsoft Word's Editor feature employs NLP to assist users in improving their writing. It provides suggestions for grammar, punctuation, and style, making it a practical tool for students and professionals. Microsoft's integration of NLP in Word aims to enhance the quality of written content.

- QuillBot: QuillBot is an AI-powered writing tool that uses NLP to paraphrase, summarize, and reword text. It is particularly helpful for learners who want to develop paraphrasing and language generation skills. QuillBot is often used by students to rephrase sentences while maintaining the original context.

- Ginger: Ginger is a writing and grammar enhancement tool that utilizes NLP to analyze and correct text in real-time. It assists users in composing clear, error-free writing. Ginger serves as a valuable resource for students, professionals, and non-native English speakers aiming to improve their language skills.

- ChatGPT: ChatGPT, an AI language model, is incorporated into educational chatbots and virtual writing assistants. It offers real-time feedback on writing assignments, helps students improve their compositions, and provides explanations for grammatical and stylistic choices. ChatGPT's applications in literacy education are diverse, providing tailored support for learners.

Figure 3 showcases the application of Natural Language Processing (NLP) and Chatbots in Literacy Education.

Figure 3. NLP and chatbots in literacy education

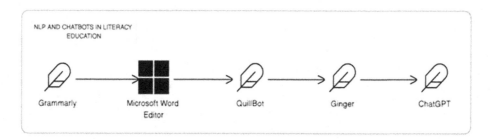

These real-world examples and case studies of NLP and chatbots in literacy education illustrate how AI-powered tools can enhance writing and language skills. They showcase the potential of NLP and chatbots to provide immediate feedback, assist with language improvement, and support students in their writing endeavors.

4.3 Adaptive Learning Systems in Action

- Khan Academy: Khan Academy is a prominent example of an adaptive learning platform. It offers a wide range of educational content and adapts to individual learners' progress and needs. Students receive personalized recommendations, practice exercises, and assessments based on their performance. Khan Academy's adaptive system helps students master various subjects at their own pace.

- Duolingo: Duolingo, a language learning platform, employs adaptive algorithms to tailor language lessons to each learner's proficiency. It adjusts the difficulty of exercises and provides instant feedback, enabling users to improve their language skills efficiently. Duolingo's gamified approach makes language learning engaging and effective.
- DreamBox: DreamBox is an adaptive math learning platform for elementary and middle school students. It adapts to students' skill levels and learning preferences, offering interactive lessons and exercises that target individual math concepts. The platform's adaptive design fosters math proficiency and confidence in young learners.
- ALEKS (Assessment and Learning in Knowledge Spaces): ALEKS is an adaptive math program used in higher education. It assesses students' math knowledge and tailors learning paths accordingly. ALEKS focuses on areas where students need improvement, helping them build a strong mathematical foundation.
- ScribeSense: ScribeSense is an AI-powered literacy tool that offers adaptive support in writing. It provides students with immediate feedback on their writing assignments, identifies areas for improvement, and guides them in enhancing their writing skills. ScribeSense's adaptability aids students in becoming proficient writers.

Figure 4 demonstrates the Adaptive Learning System.

These real-world examples and case studies of adaptive learning systems demonstrate the practical applications of AI in education. They showcase how adaptive systems cater to individual students' needs, supporting their learning journeys by offering personalized content, feedback, and assessments. Adaptive learning platforms like Khan Academy, Duolingo, and DreamBox have significantly impacted education, making learning more effective and engaging.

4.4 Impact on Student Outcomes and Success Stories

- e-Literate: e-Literate is an organization that focuses on researching and evaluating the impact of educational technology, including AI-driven solutions, on student outcomes. Their case studies and reports have highlighted success stories where institutions successfully improved student retention, performance, and engagement through AI-enhanced literacy education.
- Georgia State University: Georgia State University implemented an AI-driven chatbot system to provide academic advising and support to students. This system helped identify at-risk students, leading to an 11.3% increase in graduation rates and a significant reduction in the achievement gap among students of different demographics.
- Carnegie Mellon University's Open Learning Initiative (OLI): Carnegie Mellon's OLI uses AI to personalize learning for students. They have reported notable success in courses like statistics and economics, where students using OLI performed as well as or better than those in traditional classes, with substantial improvements in retention and mastery.
- Pearson's Aida: Pearson's AI-driven tutor, Aida, provides personalized support to students. Institutions using Aida have reported increased student engagement and better learning outcomes, with students being more likely to pass their courses.

Figure 4. Adaptive learning system

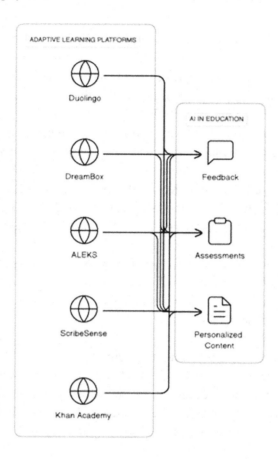

Figure 5. Impacts of AI on students and management

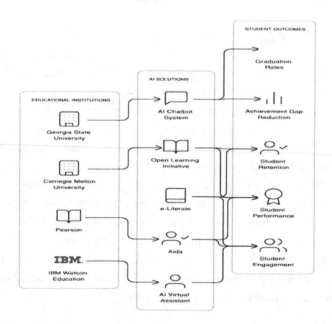

- IBM Watson Education: IBM Watson Education offers various AI-powered solutions for educational institutions. Success stories highlight improved learning experiences, increased student success rates, and more efficient administrative operations. For instance, Broward College in Florida employed IBM Watson to develop an AI virtual assistant, which resulted in higher student engagement and satisfaction.

These real-world examples and success stories illustrate the positive impact of AI-enhanced literacy education on student outcomes. Figure 5 outlines the Impacts of AI on Students & Management. From improved graduation rates to enhanced engagement and personalized support, these cases demonstrate the potential of AI to empower both students and educators in higher education.

5. ETHICAL AND PRIVACY CONSIDERATIONS

Ethical and Privacy Considerations in AI Adoption in Literacy Education

As educational institutions embrace AI technologies to enhance literacy education, it is imperative to address ethical and privacy considerations to ensure responsible and equitable implementation. One of the primary ethical concerns revolves around the potential for algorithmic bias and discrimination in AI-driven interventions. AI algorithms may inadvertently perpetuate or amplify existing biases present in educational data, leading to unequal treatment or opportunities for certain student groups. To mitigate this risk, educators and developers must prioritize fairness, transparency, and accountability in AI model development and deployment. This entails employing rigorous data validation techniques, regularly auditing AI systems for bias, and implementing mechanisms for algorithmic transparency and explainability. Moreover, educators should be vigilant in monitoring AI-generated recommendations and decisions to identify and rectify instances of bias or discrimination. (Gellai, 2022) utilizes network ethnography and discourse analysis to investigate the circulation of AI-powered technology ideas in higher education policy networks within the United Kingdom. Another ethical consideration in AI adoption in literacy education is the protection of student privacy and data security. AI-driven systems often rely on vast amounts of sensitive student data, including personal information, learning preferences, and behavioral patterns, to generate personalized learning experiences. Consequently, educational institutions must implement robust privacy safeguards and data protection measures to safeguard student privacy rights and comply with relevant data protection regulations, such as the Family Educational Rights and Privacy Act (FERPA) and the General Data Protection Regulation (GDPR). This involves obtaining informed consent from students and their guardians for data collection and processing, ensuring data anonymization and encryption practices, and limiting access to student data to authorized personnel only. Additionally, educational institutions should establish clear data retention and deletion policies to minimize the risk of data breaches and unauthorized access to student information.

Furthermore, ethical considerations extend to the responsible use of AI technologies in educational assessment and decision-making processes. AI-powered assessment tools and predictive analytics systems have the potential to enhance educators' ability to assess student performance, identify learning gaps, and provide targeted interventions. However, there is a risk of over-reliance on AI-generated insights and automated decision-making, which may undermine the role of educators and diminish the human aspect of teaching and learning. To address this concern, educators should approach AI-driven assessments as complementary tools rather than replacements for human judgment, maintaining a critical and reflective stance towards AI-generated recommendations. Additionally, transparent communication and collaboration between educators, students, and AI developers are essential to ensure that AI technologies are used ethically and responsibly to support, rather than replace, human-centered pedagogical practices in literacy education. (Wang et al., 2021) scrutinizes recent AI education policies in their country, shedding light on the clear trajectory of AI education development.

6. RECOMMENDATIONS FOR AI ADOPTION IN LITERACY EDUCATION

Recommendations for AI Adoption in Literacy Education

1. **Invest in Comprehensive Infrastructure:** The successful integration of AI in literacy education necessitates substantial investments in comprehensive infrastructure. Educational institutions should prioritize allocating resources for acquiring state-of-the-art AI technologies, including software, hardware, and digital learning platforms. Additionally, ensuring robust internet connectivity and technical support services is essential for facilitating seamless integration and utilization of AI tools by both educators and students. Adequate funding should be allocated for the ongoing maintenance, updates, and upgrades of AI infrastructure to ensure optimal functionality and longevity.

2. **Provide Extensive Educator Training:** Educator training and professional development are critical components of effective AI adoption in literacy education. Institutions must offer comprehensive training programs that equip educators with the necessary knowledge, skills, and competencies to leverage AI technologies effectively in their teaching practices. Training initiatives should cover various aspects, including AI fundamentals, data analysis techniques, pedagogical strategies, and ethical considerations. Additionally, ongoing support and mentorship should be provided to educators to facilitate their continuous growth and adaptation to evolving AI technologies and practices.

3. **Foster Collaborative Learning Communities:** Creating collaborative learning communities that foster interdisciplinary collaboration and knowledge sharing is essential for maximizing the benefits of AI adoption in literacy education. Institutions should encourage educators, researchers, and students from diverse disciplines to collaborate on AI-related projects and initiatives. Collaborative endeavors can lead to the development of innovative AI-driven solutions, instructional materials, and learning resources tailored to the unique needs and preferences of literacy learners. Moreover, fostering a culture of collaboration promotes knowledge exchange, creativity, and collective problem-solving among stakeholders.

4. **Ensure Equitable Access and Inclusion:** Equity and inclusion should be central considerations in the adoption of AI in literacy education to ensure that all learners have equitable access to AI-enabled learning opportunities. Educational institutions must prioritize efforts to address digital divides and eliminate barriers to access for students from marginalized or underserved communities. This includes providing equitable access to AI technologies, resources, and learning materials, as well as ensuring culturally responsive and inclusive pedagogical approaches. Moreover, AI-driven interventions should be designed with a focus on accessibility, considering the diverse needs and abilities of learners to promote inclusivity and diversity in literacy education.

5. **Promote Ethical AI Practices:** Ethical considerations should guide the adoption and implementation of AI technologies in literacy education to ensure responsible and ethical use. Institutions must

establish clear guidelines, policies, and protocols for the ethical development, deployment, and evaluation of AI-driven interventions. Educators and students should be educated about the ethical implications of AI adoption and empowered to critically evaluate AI-enabled learning experiences. Additionally, fostering a culture of ethical awareness and accountability among stakeholders promotes trust, transparency, and integrity in AI adoption initiatives.

7. THE FUTURE OF AI IN HIGHER EDUCATION

The future of AI in higher education holds significant promise and potential for transforming the learning landscape. Here are some key aspects that will shape the future of AI in higher education:

7.1 Potential for Empowering Students

The future of artificial intelligence (AI) in higher education holds immense potential for empowering students and revolutionizing the learning experience. AI technologies have the capability to personalize learning pathways, adapt instruction to individual student needs, and facilitate deeper engagement with course content. By harnessing the power of AI-driven adaptive learning platforms and intelligent tutoring systems, higher education institutions can offer tailored learning experiences that cater to students' diverse learning styles, preferences, and abilities. (Vashishth et al., 2024) discusses how traditional design methods can be used to enhance AI-driven decision making, specifically in the context of literacy education. Moreover, AI-powered educational tools can provide real-time feedback and support, enabling students to track their progress, identify areas for improvement, and receive targeted interventions to enhance their academic performance. Additionally, AI holds promise for democratizing access to education by breaking down traditional barriers to learning, such as geographical distance, financial constraints, and disability-related challenges. (Bholat & Susskind, 2021) offer an introductory overview of AI's expanding role in the financial industry, analyzing its effects on consumers, competition, regulators, and exploring the potential future of advanced AI. Online learning platforms powered by AI technologies can offer flexible, asynchronous learning opportunities that accommodate the diverse needs and circumstances of learners worldwide. (Roy et al., 2022) aims to evaluate the intention of educators to adopt AI-based robots in universities. Furthermore, AI-driven analytics and predictive modeling tools can help higher education institutions optimize student success initiatives, retention efforts, and graduation rates by identifying at-risk students early, providing timely interventions, and tailoring support services to address their individual needs. Overall, the future of AI in higher education is characterized by its potential to empower students as active participants in their learning journey, enabling them to access personalized, engaging, and effective educational experiences that prepare them for success in an increasingly complex and dynamic global workforce. (Chan, 2023) focuses on creating an AI education policy for higher education. The study investigates the perceptions and implications of text generative AI technologies.

7.2 Transforming the Role of Educators

The future of artificial intelligence (AI) in higher education is poised to transform the role of educators, heralding a paradigm shift towards more dynamic and student-centered teaching practices. AI technologies have the potential to augment educators' capabilities, enabling them to personalize instruction, facilitate deeper learning, and engage students in innovative ways. AI-driven adaptive learning platforms and intelligent tutoring systems can assist educators in tailoring learning experiences to meet the unique needs, preferences, and abilities of individual students. By harnessing the power of AI-generated insights and analytics, educators can gain deeper insights into student progress, learning patterns, and areas for improvement, allowing them to deliver targeted interventions and support services. Moreover, AI-powered educational tools can automate routine administrative tasks, such as grading, course planning, and content delivery, freeing up educators' time to focus on more meaningful interactions with students. Additionally, AI-driven virtual teaching assistants and chatbots can provide on-demand assistance and support to students, supplementing educators' efforts and enhancing the overall learning experience. (Adiguzel, Kaya & Cansu, 2023) provide a comprehensive examination of AI technologies, their educational prospects, and the associated challenges. The study delves into chatbots and their algorithms, which mimic human interactions and generate human-like text from natural language input. Furthermore, AI technologies have the potential to democratize access to high-quality education by expanding the reach of educational resources and opportunities beyond traditional classroom settings. However, as AI continues to evolve and become more integrated into higher education, educators must adapt to new roles and responsibilities, embracing a learner-centered approach that emphasizes collaboration, creativity, critical thinking, and lifelong learning. By embracing AI as a transformative force in higher education, educators can harness its potential to create more engaging, inclusive, and effective learning environments that empower students to succeed in the digital age. (Luan et al., 2020) focuses on how technology, particularly the surge in big data and AI, can present both new opportunities and challenges that can be effectively harnessed for pedagogical practices and learning.

7.3 Enriching the Learning Experience

The future of artificial intelligence (AI) in higher education promises to enrich the learning experience by leveraging advanced technologies to personalize instruction, promote active engagement, and foster deeper understanding. AI-driven adaptive learning platforms and intelligent tutoring systems have the potential to revolutionize the way students interact with course content, offering personalized learning pathways tailored to their individual needs, preferences, and learning styles. By analyzing vast amounts of data on student performance, behavior, and preferences, AI technologies can provide real-time feedback, identify areas for improvement, and recommend customized learning resources and activities. Additionally, AI-powered virtual reality (VR) and augmented reality (AR) applications can create immersive learning environments that simulate real-world experiences, allowing students to explore complex concepts, conduct experiments, and solve problems in interactive and engaging ways. Moreover, AI-driven chatbots and virtual teaching assistants can provide on-demand support and assistance to students, answering questions, clarifying concepts, and guiding them through the learning process. (Southworth et al., 2023) improve AI literacy among students and prepare them for the future job market, ultimately transforming the higher education landscape. Furthermore, AI-enabled collaborative learning platforms and social learning networks can facilitate peer-to-peer interaction, knowledge sharing, and collaborative problem-solving among students, fostering a sense of community and collaboration in online and blended learning environments. As AI continues to evolve and become more integrated into higher education, it has the potential to enhance the overall learning experience by providing students with personalized, engaging, and interactive learning opportunities that cater to their individual needs and preferences, ultimately empowering them to achieve their academic and professional goals.

8. CONCLUSION

In conclusion, the chapter highlights the transformative potential of artificial intelligence (AI) in revolutionizing literacy education, while also addressing the associated opportunities and challenges. AI technologies offer promising opportunities to personalize learning experiences, adapt instruction to individual student needs, and foster deeper engagement with course content. By leveraging AI-driven adaptive learning platforms, intelligent tutoring systems, and virtual teaching assistants, higher education institutions can enhance the effectiveness and accessibility of literacy education for diverse student populations. However, the integration of AI in literacy education also presents several challenges, including ethical considerations, privacy concerns, and the need for extensive educator training and support. To maximize the benefits of AI adoption in literacy education, institutions must prioritize investments in infrastructure, educator training, and collaborative learning communities, while also ensuring equitable access, inclusivity, and responsible AI use. Additionally, ongoing research and evaluation efforts are essential to monitor the impact of AI adoption on student learning outcomes, engagement, and satisfaction. Overall, while AI offers tremendous potential to enrich the learning experience and empower students in literacy education, its successful integration requires careful consideration of the opportunities and challenges inherent in leveraging AI technologies to support teaching and learning in higher education settings. By addressing these challenges and embracing AI as a transformative force in literacy education, higher institutions can create more inclusive, engaging, and effective learning environments that prepare students for success in the digital age.

REFERENCES

Adiguzel, T., Kaya, M. H., & Cansu, F. K. (2023). Revolutionizing education with AI: Exploring the transformative potential of ChatGPT. *Contemporary Educational Technology*, *15*(3), ep429. doi:10.30935/cedtech/13152

Al Braiki, B., Harous, S., Zaki, N., & Alnajjar, F. (2020). Artificial intelligence in education and assessment methods. *Bulletin of Electrical Engineering and Informatics*, *9*(5), 1998–2007. doi:10.11591/eei.v9i5.1984

Bhatnagar, H. (2020). Artificial intelligence-a new horizon in Indian higher education. *Journal of Learning and Teaching in Digital Age*, *5*(2), 30–34.

Bholat, D., & Susskind, D. (2021). The assessment: Artificial intelligence and financial services. *Oxford Review of Economic Policy*, *37*(3), 417–434. doi:10.1093/oxrep/grab015

Cantú-Ortiz, F. J., Galeano Sánchez, N., Garrido, L., Terashima-Marin, H., & Brena, R. F. (2020). An artificial intelligence educational strategy for the digital transformation. *International Journal on Interactive Design and Manufacturing*, *14*(4), 1195–1209. doi:10.1007/s12008-020-00702-8

Chan, C. K. Y. (2023). A comprehensive AI policy education framework for university teaching and learning. *International Journal of Educational Technology in Higher Education*, *20*(1), 1–25. doi:10.1186/s41239-023-00408-3

Chen, X., Xie, H., & Hwang, G. J. (2020). A multi-perspective study on artificial intelligence in education: Grants, conferences, journals, software tools, institutions, and researchers. *Computers and Education: Artificial Intelligence, 1*, 100005. doi:10.1016/j.caeai.2020.100005

Gellai, D. B. (2022). Enterprising Academics: Heterarchical Policy Networks for Artificial Intelligence in British Higher Education. *ECNU Review of Education*. Advance online publication. doi:10.1177/20965311221143798

Laupichler, M. C., Aster, A., Schirch, J., & Raupach, T. (2022). Artificial intelligence literacy in higher and adult education: A scoping literature review. *Computers and Education: Artificial Intelligence, 100101*, 100101. Advance online publication. doi:10.1016/j.caeai.2022.100101

Luan, H., Geczy, P., Lai, H., Gobert, J., Yang, S. J., Ogata, H., Baltes, J., Guerra, R., Li, P., & Tsai, C. C. (2020). Challenges and future directions of big data and artificial intelligence in education. *Frontiers in Psychology, 11*, 580820. doi:10.3389/fpsyg.2020.580820 PMID:33192896

Ocaña-Fernández, Y., Valenzuela-Fernández, L. A., & Garro-Aburto, L. L. (2019). Artificial Intelligence and Its Implications in Higher Education. *Journal of Educational Psychology-Propositos y Representaciones, 7*(2), 553–568.

Popenici, S. A., & Kerr, S. (2017). Exploring the impact of artificial intelligence on teaching and learning in higher education. *Research and Practice in Technology Enhanced Learning, 12*(1), 1–13. doi:10.1186/s41039-017-0062-8 PMID:30595727

Roy, R., Babakerkhell, M. D., Mukherjee, S., Pal, D., & Funilkul, S. (2022). Evaluating the intention for the adoption of artificial intelligence-based robots in the university to educate the students. *IEEE Access : Practical Innovations, Open Solutions, 10*, 125666–125678. doi:10.1109/ACCESS.2022.3225555

Schiff, D. (2022). Education for AI, not AI for education: The role of education and ethics in national AI policy strategies. *International Journal of Artificial Intelligence in Education, 32*(3), 527–563. doi:10.1007/s40593-021-00270-2

Southworth, J., Migliaccio, K., Glover, J., Reed, D., McCarty, C., Brendemuhl, J., & Thomas, A. (2023). Developing a model for AI Across the curriculum: Transforming the higher education landscape via innovation in AI literacy. *Computers and Education: Artificial Intelligence, 4*, 100127. doi:10.1016/j.caeai.2023.100127

Tanveer, M., Hassan, S., & Bhaumik, A. (2020). Academic policy regarding sustainability and artificial intelligence (AI). *Sustainability (Basel), 12*(22), 9435. doi:10.3390/su12229435

Vashishth, T. K., Kumar, B., Sharma, V., Chaudhary, S., Kumar, S., & Sharma, K. K. (2023). The Evolution of AI and Its Transformative Effects on Computing: A Comparative Analysis. In B. Mishra (Ed.), *Intelligent Engineering Applications and Applied Sciences for Sustainability* (pp. 425–442). IGI Global. doi:10.4018/979-8-3693-0044-2.ch022

Vashishth, T. K., Sharma, V., Sharma, K. K., Kumar, B., Panwar, R., & Chaudhary, S. (2024). AI-Driven Learning Analytics for Personalized Feedback and Assessment in Higher Education. In Using Traditional Design Methods to Enhance AI-Driven Decision Making (pp. 206-230). IGI Global.

Wang, S., Wang, G., Chen, X., Wang, W., & Ding, X. (2021). A Review of Content Analysis on China Artificial Intelligence (AI) Education Policies. *Artificial Intelligence in Education and Teaching Assessment,* 1-8. doi:10.1007/978-981-16-6502-8_1

KEY TERMS AND DEFINITIONS

Artificial Intelligence (AI): Refers to the development of computer systems that can perform tasks that typically require human intelligence, such as learning, problem-solving, decision-making, and natural language understanding.

Augmented Reality (AR): Is a technology that overlays computer-generated content, such as images, videos, or information, onto the real-world environment, enhancing the user's perception of their surroundings by blending digital and physical elements.

Natural Language Processing (NLP): Natural Language Processing (NLP) is a branch of artificial intelligence that focuses on enabling computers to understand, interpret, and interact with human language in a natural and meaningful way. NLP involves the development of algorithms and models that allow computers to process, analyze, and generate human language.

Virtual Reality (VR): Is a technology that creates a computer-generated immersive environment, allowing users to interact with and experience a three-dimensional digital world as if it were real.

Chapter 10
Evaluating the Potential of Artificial Intelligence in Islamic Religious Education:
A SWOT Analysis Overview

Mussa Saidi Abubakari
 https://orcid.org/0000-0003-3782-281X
Sultan Hassanal Bolkiah Institute of Education, Universiti Brunei Darussalam, Brunei

Wasswa Shafik
 https://orcid.org/0000-0002-9320-3186
School of Digital Science, Universiti Brunei Darussalam, Brunei & Dig Connectivity Research Laboratory (DCRLab), Kampala, Uganda

Ahmad Fathan Hidayatullah
 https://orcid.org/0000-0002-3755-2648
Department of Informatics, Universitas Islam Indonesia, Indonesia

ABSTRACT

Artificial intelligence (AI) has become enormously prominent in various industries in recent years, completely changing the way humans accomplish their daily activities, especially the educational process. While integrating AI technologies in educational settings might present new potential, there are drawbacks and challenges as well, particularly in the Islamic religious educational context. Therefore, the purpose of this chapter is to assess the viability of incorporating AI into Islamic religious educational settings by doing a thorough SWOT (strengths, weaknesses, opportunities, and threats) analysis. The chapter explores the benefits, drawbacks, opportunities, and risks of implementing AI in the context of Islamic education. Thus, the factors, both internal and external, that may have an impact on the effective integration of AI in Islamic educational environments are evaluated. Policymakers, educators, and other educational stakeholders may make well-informed judgments on the utilization of AI technologies in Islamic religious education by recognizing these analytical aspects.

DOI: 10.4018/979-8-3693-2728-9.ch010

INTRODUCTION

Artificial intelligence (AI) and other digital technologies (DT) are transforming several life aspects and changing how people learn, work, and interact. AI platforms have especially impacted the way we live and operate in several aspects of humanity because of their powerful and influential approaches, and they have generated much eagerness for their potential applications in the education sector (Shafik, 2024). Within the domain of Islamic Religious Education (IRE), which is firmly grounded in spiritual and ethical aspects, the use of AI calls for critical transparency, elucidation, and unbiasedness for both improving conventional teaching approaches and tackling persistent obstacles (Kausar et al., 2024). The rapid advancement of AI technology is leading to the convergence of analyzing the acceptability and effectiveness of a chatbot based on a large language model for Arabic learners, which is opening new opportunities for innovative learning methods and the spread of information (Zaimah et al., 2024).

AI-enabled virtual assistants, armed with advanced natural language processing skills, play a critical function in facilitating students' investigation of Islamic teachings. These virtual assistants like Google Assistant, Alexa, and Apple Siri possess the ability to respond to inquiries, participate in dialogues, and imitate debates over religious topics, providing a valuable complement to conventional classroom inter-actions and showing the possibilities of how these AI react to humanity (Thottoli et al., 2024). Virtual assistants Duolingo, Dr. Ivy, or Winston.ai are some of the tools that are having a profound impact on how students and parents interact with education, fundamentally changing the way learning takes place (Mesiono et al., 2024). Figure 1 demonstrates some of the AI applications in educational spaces.

Figure 1. Roles of AI in educational spaces (authors' creation)

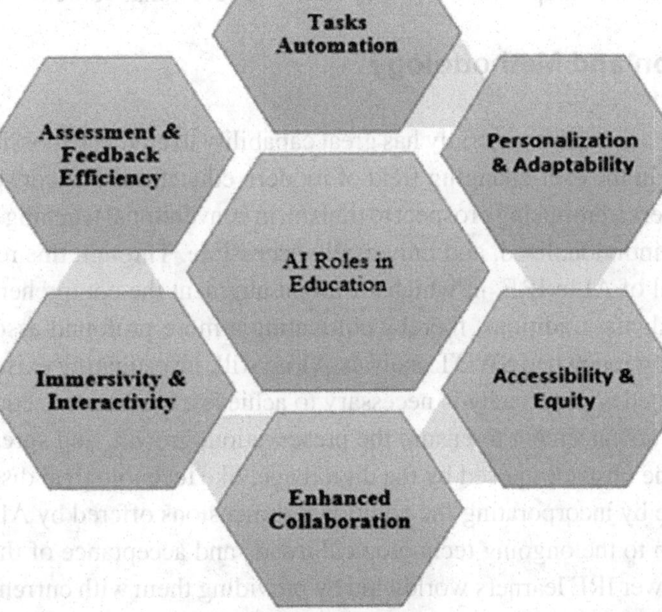

217

A nuanced approach is required to navigate the junction of tradition and innovation in Islamic education. Effective collaboration among educators, legislators, and religious academics is decisive in negotiating this intersection successfully, keeping laws at play (Strzelecki & ElArabawy, 2024). It is, therefore, crucial to value the advantages of AI while also ensuring the preservation of the genuine and human connection that is inherent in the instruction of Islamic concepts. Achieving a harmonious equilibrium between conventional practices and groundbreaking advancements guarantees that AI enriches the educational journey without compromising the fundamental principles of IRE, as was demonstrated in its application in the Holy Qur'an (Muttaqin, 2023).

Amongst the significance of AI, AI-driven technologies are automating administrative operations, enabling educators to dedicate additional time to innovative and interactive teaching methodologies (Nikmatullah et al., 2023). During the recent global Coronavirus disease (COVID-19) pandemic, virtual classrooms through various DT platforms were extensively used since personal-to-person interaction could spread the virus (Utunen et al., 2022; World Health Organization, 2020), and chatbots and instructional technologies that can understand and respond to human language enhance the quality of learning by making it more interesting and participatory (Alrumiah & Al-Shargabi, 2023). In addition, AI aids in the creation of adaptive educational resources, offering immediate feedback and personalized instruction to pupils, thereby promoting a more profound comprehension of intricate topics.

The use of AI in educational environments serves as a crucial facilitator for students to obtain new abilities, maintain their relevance in their respective fields, and negotiate the intricacies of a swiftly evolving labor market (Tubagus et al., 2023). The importance of AI in educational environments is diverse, encompassing tailored learning experiences, improved teaching methods, worldwide accessibility, and data-driven decision-making (Muttaqin, 2023). Nevertheless, trending concerns, such as restricted access to high-quality Islamic education and hardship in adjusting to novel pedagogical approaches, have necessitated Muslim reformers to reassess the conventional pedagogical methods. Thus, by utilizing the SWOT (Strengths, Weaknesses, Opportunities, and Threats) analytical tool, this chapter examines these aspects connected with the incorporation of AI in Islamic educational contexts.

Chapter Motivation and Methodology

The utilization of AI in academics generally has great capability to eradicate possible educational bottlenecks and magnitudes in the ever-changing field of modern education. The convergence of technology and religion studies offers a promising prospect to transform conventional teaching approaches, rendering them more adaptable, individualized, and universally accessible. Through this review, our objective is to explore the potential of AI in IRE, in which AI might augment the comprehension of Quranic principles, Hadiths, and Islamic traditions, thereby cultivating a more profound association with spiritual and ethical aspects using renowned SWOT analysis. More still, investigating existing challenges to help the research be conducted appropriately is necessary to achieve a harmonious equilibrium between tradition and AI-enabled advancement to ensure the preservation, growth, and spread of IRE. The aim is to aid in overcoming the obstacles posed by the digital age, like technological distrust, and enhance the educational experience by incorporating the additional dimensions offered by AI. This research makes a valuable contribution to the ongoing technological trends and acceptance of the future of education. Lastly, it aims to empower IRE learners worldwide by providing them with current domain trends while still safeguarding the fundamental values of Islamic teachings.

To achieve the chapter objectives, the study implemented a comprehensive review of related literature based on the topics covered, including Islamic education, AI and education, and SWOT literature. Thus, different academic databases such as Scopus, Google Scholar, ScienceDirect, Springer, and Web of Science were systematically used to search the related works, encompassing journal articles, conference proceedings, official reports, and book chapters. The literature studies resulting from search results were closely analyzed and synthesized, and the results are organized into various sections.

Chapter Organization

After introducing the chapter topic on AI and its applications, the next section discusses the background of IRE. The third section provides a succinct description of the SWOT analytical framework and how it relates to educational strategic planning. The next four sections delve into the SWOT aspects of AI in IRE, respectively. Section eight looks into the AI case studies and lessons taken from them. Section nine delves into the prospects of AI in IRE and provides suggestions on how to implement AI in this unique educational setting. Finally, the last section provides the concluding remarks of the whole chapter and future research directions.

BACKGROUND OF ISLAMIC EDUCATION

History of Islamic Religious Education

Islam's history of education and learning stems from the Qur'ān and the Prophet Muhammad's sunnah (way of his life), which is studied via the Prophet's hadith (Baiza, 2018). Hadith, concisely, is the Prophet's sayings and actions reported in authentic and validated narrations. For Muslim communities, the Qur'ān and the hadith serve as the two main sources of knowledge and education (Baiza, 2018). In Islam, pursuing and seeking knowledge or education is compulsory and a religious duty, as it is an essential component of believing in the Islamic faith. Muslims hold the belief that the Qur'an addresses the concepts of knowledge and education, encompassing pedagogical activities such as teaching, reading, and writing (Baiza, 2018). This belief is grounded in the earliest verses revealed to Prophet Muhammad. The Prophet, in turn, conveyed divine guidance on knowledge and education through both his words and deeds (Arjmand, 2018; Baiza, 2018). He actively promoted the quest for knowledge, expressing his value for teaching and learning through his sayings (hadith) and the example set by his way of life (sunnah) (Baiza, 2018). The enthusiasm for knowledge and education, rooted in the Qur'anic concepts, and the Prophet's pivotal role as the initial teacher and guide of the Muslim community laid the foundation for a profound love for learning (Baiza, 2018). As Muslims embraced and expanded upon this spirit, they established numerous centers of civilization and made advancements in various fields of knowledge (Daun & Arjmand, 2018). Nevertheless, in the current age, IRE is facing various challenges stemming from digital technological innovations and the globalization process.

Islamic Educational Values and Principles

IRE has a significant impact on the lives and perceptions of millions of Muslims worldwide. Islamic education aims to create decent individuals who will experience both this world and the hereafter's ultimate bliss. When all people become genuine servants and vicegerents of Allah, this ultimate bliss is inevitable (Hashim, 2005). In order to purify their spirits and improve their character, sincere servants must engage in acts of worship, or 'ibadah, in the fullest sense for their well-being. As His vicegerents, they have a responsibility to protect and maintain nature and the universe (Hashim, 2005; Rafiabadi, 2017), which are there for their benefit and sustenance, but much more so to propagate the teachings of Islam—peace—by promoting social justice (Hashim, 2005). IRE is always essential for Muslims' spiritual and moral growth, instilling believers in Islamic ethics, values, and ideals. Furthermore, it provides individuals with the skills they need to face the issues and challenges of modern life while being rooted in their religion. It is also vital in promoting Muslim solidarity and a feeling of community. The collective understanding of Islamic teachings and values forges ties amongst believers that cut over geographical boundaries and cultural divides and foster a sense of sisterhood and brotherhood.

Challenges in Islamic Educational Institutions

In the current digital age, as digital technologies become increasingly ingrained in daily life, concerns are raised regarding the place of artificial intelligence, among other DTs, in IRE, particularly in relation to the potential replacement of scholars who study the Qur'an and Hadith. Islamic religious sciences, particularly in relation to the Al-Qur'an and Hadith, are crucial in producing Muslims who possess a thorough knowledge and comprehension of Islamic values and ideals (Yulianto & Haya, 2023). Recent literature (Abubakari, Zakaria, & Musa, 2023; Abubakari & Priyanto, 2021; Qazi et al., 2021) points to the need for more focus and attention on digital-based pedagogical strategies for teaching and learning Islamic sciences through educational research practices. Consistent empirical research is necessary to fully comprehend the implications of digital technology usage and practices, particularly in the context of Islamic education (Abubakari, Zakaria, Priyanto, et al., 2023; Abubakari & Zakaria, 2023; Qazi et al., 2021). Empirical research can showcase how Muslim individuals adopt DT, such as AI tools, in Islamic education. Furthermore, digital competence is another challenging aspect that needs close examination in educational settings (Abubakari, Zakaria, Musa, et al., 2023a, 2023b), as this skill is necessary for students in Islamic education to interact with AI effectively. Thus, the trend in AI in education advancements needs a deep analysis for effective adoption in Islamic education. Therefore, this chapter, using a SWOT analytical tool, aims to evaluate this situation.

SWOT ANALYTICAL FRAMEWORK OVERVIEW

Introducing the SWOT Analysis Framework

One of the most traditional and extensively used strategic planning instruments globally is the SWOT analytical tool. SWOT analysis first appeared as a strategic planning method in the business corporate world in the middle of the 20th century (Leigh, 2009; Puyt et al., 2023; Valentin, 2001). For some decades, SWOT analysis has been dominant in two domains: business strategy and market research (Leigh, 2009). The most common application of SWOT analysis is as a technique for examining the external strengths and weaknesses and internal opportunities and threats of an institution. The initial emphasis was on business organizations with the goal of creating a systematic framework for evaluating the internal and external elements that affect an organization's performance (Benzaghta et al., 2021). With time, SWOT analysis's usefulness spread outside of the business world- and its application extended to various industries, including educational institutions (Alabool, 2023; Angelova et al., 2021; Denecke et al., 2023; Humble & Mozelius, 2022). However, the adoption of the SWOT technique is not equally implemented across different educational systems, such as Islamic education versus general educational systems, as proved by limited SWOT literature on the former system.

SWOT Analysis in Islamic Educational Strategic Planning

Among the major contributions of SWOT's historical significance is in the field of strategic planning. Scholars advocate that individuals in organizational management in modern times should properly and effectively apply the original SWOT technique, as the evolving concept of strategy is the result of an effective SWOT tool to organizational operations (Puyt et al., 2023). Thus, implementing the SWOT process as a foundational element in the institutional strategy is still relevant and helpful today; when done correctly, the process offers a number of advantages to any modern institution (Puyt et al., 2023). Therefore, Islamic education institutions can also benefit from implementing the SWOT technique for AI integration in teaching-leaning systems.

The SWOT analysis offers a systematic approach to collating data from several sources (Benzaghta et al., 2021; Farrokhnia et al., 2023). It presents a synopsis of the internal and external elements that may impact the adoption of novel technology in the educational process. Scholars view strength as a capability or resource that is internal to the specific system that enables the new technology to fulfill its stated objectives (Farrokhnia et al., 2023). Opportunity refers to external technology-related features that raise demand for the benefits that technology may offer its consumers. Weakness is a feature or restriction of the system that prevents it from moving closer to its intended objectives. Lastly, a threat is any unfavorable feature of the technology that undermines its strategy by posing a hurdle or restriction and, therefore, restricts the accomplishment of objectives, thus considered as a danger (Farrokhnia et al., 2023). Therefore, to ensure a thorough grasp of the situation, the SWOT analytical tool will operate as a guide in evaluating the viability and impact of incorporating AI tools into IRE. Figure 2 depicts some of the SWOT aspects of AI in Islamic education, followed by an explanation of each aspect in the following sections.

Figure 2. SWOT aspects of AI in Islamic education (authors' creation).

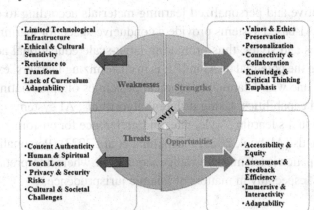

STRENGTHS IN ISLAMIC EDUCATION FOR INTEGRATING AI

The following are some of the strengths within IRE associated with successfully implementing AI in the Islamic educational system.

Emphasis on Knowledge and Critical Thinking

Seeking knowledge is highly valued and is mandatory in the Islamic faith, as the Qur'an encourages Muslims to think, reflect, gain insight, and make confirmation on matters. This dedication to learning is in perfect harmony with the goals of integrating AI into education. The Islamic educational system fosters a profound grasp of numerous fields. It places a strong emphasis on developing critical thinking abilities, reflection, and verification (For example, see Qur'an 7:179, 8:22, 10:100-101, 11:24, 39:18, 17:36, 5:105, 49:6, 12:26-27). Thus, because God created reason and perception as a source of guidance, spiritual guidance in Islam illuminates these faculties to enable them to work correctly and encourages us to use them to get a greater understanding of reality (Abdel-Maguid & Abdel-Halim, 2015). Therefore, these IRE characteristics produce an atmosphere that is open to the integration of AI technology. AI enhances knowledge acquisition by offering sophisticated tools for assessment, predictions, and problem-solving.

Preservation of Islamic Values and Ethics

The focus placed on moral conduct and ethical standards in Islamic education is one of its defining characteristics. This emphasis is in line with the trending concern about the ethical application of AI in Islamic contexts (Agil & Alkhiri, 2022; Raquib et al., 2022). The ethical framework provided by Islamic teachings ensures that individuals utilize AI ethically and for the benefit of humankind (Agil & Alkhiri, 2022; Elmahjub, 2023). This foundation provides a roadmap for integrating AI into the Islamic educational system. The moral and ethical principles inculcated in the Islamic educational system offer guidelines for dealing with moral problems arising from AI utilization.

Learning Personalization and Adaptability

In the Islamic tradition based on the Sunnah and Qur'anic teachings, IRE recognizes the importance of considering the diversity of learning needs. This IRE feature provides a venue for AI technologies to be integrated to create adaptive and personalized learning materials according to diverse learners' capabilities and preferences. AI-based systems provide a conducive space for learning adaptation that suits different learning abilities and styles, thus promoting large-scale educational accessibility for diverse populations. Thus, among the potential of AI in IRE is in customizing learners' experiences (Farrokhnia et al., 2023), which is in line with Islamic pedagogical principles of appreciating and developing each individual's qualities and capabilities. Using different algorithms, AI systems can provide assessment capability for each individual's learning style, rate, and preference for customizing educational materials suiting specific demands (Alabool, 2023; Farrokhnia et al., 2023). Personalized learning improves understanding and participation in Islamic knowledge acquisition, where interpretation and understanding differ on some occasions, especially in matters of Islamic jurisprudence.

Global Connectivity and Collaboration

Among the Islamic ideals are community solidarity and collaboration between diverse communities and a sense of unity globally. Using AI-enhanced digital platforms improves global connectedness and makes it possible for scholars and learners to collaborate on different projects, share information, and have cross-cultural conversations (Alabool, 2023). AI-powered collaborative research platforms, online discussion boards, and virtual classrooms can expand the reach and influence of Islamic education worldwide. Further, by exposing learners to diverse viewpoints and ideas, this connection improves the educational experience (Alabool, 2023) and is consistent with the Islamic goal of a global society. AI-powered platforms make it easier to collaborate globally and have access to a wealth of knowledge (Ahmad et al., 2022; Dwivedi et al., 2023). By connecting learners and academics from across the globe with AI-powered platforms, the Islamic educational system can promote diverse and collaborative educational environments.

WEAKNESSES IN IRE CHALLENGING AI INTEGRATION

Limited Technological Infrastructure

Many Islamic educational institutions from different regions of the globe lack the adequate technological infrastructures required for smooth AI integration. Among the significant limitations are restricted computer access and internet connection issues, on top of limited access to other digital resources. These technological limitations prevent the implementation of AI-based solutions intended to improve the educational process in IRE. Besides that, the lack of digitally trained personnel in most IRE institutions is prevalent, in addition to the absence of strategic plans needed to utilize AI-based platforms effectively. Thus, it is crucial to close these digital divides for IRE to attain the full potential benefits of AI.

Traditional Pedagogical Approaches

Among the most significant weaknesses is the conventional pedagogical methodologies used in Islamic religious education. Relying on rote memorization of religious texts may impede the implementation of novel teaching approaches enabled by AI. The strict adherence to existing teaching approaches may make it difficult for instructors to adopt AI-powered solutions that provide individualized and adaptable learning experiences. Traditionally, instructors who teach the Qur'an and Hadith serve as a bridge between learners who want to delve deeply into religious teachings and values and apply authentic Islamic knowledge in society (Yulianto & Haya, 2023). This conventional Islamic pedagogy has faced numerous challenges due to diverse cultural interactions and technological advancements. This situation inspired many Islamic scholars to call for Islamic pedagogical reforms in various parts of the Muslim world.

Ethical and Cultural Sensitivity

Among the priorities in IRE are ethical and moral aspects. These aspects are sensitive in IRE, as Islam emphasizes human morals and ethics. Thus, cultural and ethical considerations are inevitable for smooth AI implementation in IRE to deal with societal concerns. AI-based systems can unintentionally reinforce prejudices or misunderstand cultural peculiarities, which might result in false information. This situation implies that it is vital to ensure that AI-based systems are morally and culturally customized to prevent unintended misinterpretation of Islamic teachings or potential backlash.

Lack of Curriculum Adaptability and Standardization

The IRE system frequently adheres to a set curriculum that can be difficult to adjust, considering the rapid advances in AI technologies. Flexibility and ongoing updates are necessary for integrating AI into the curriculum, which may conflict with the existing frameworks of religious education. One major barrier to the adoption of AI solutions is the inability to adjust quickly to changing educational demands. Further, in many Muslim societies, there are no quality controls or standard measures in the IRE system. The curriculum used by various institutions may differ, and there can be significant disparities in the quality of education. Therefore, through quality control, AI integration calls for a certain uniformity and standardization to guarantee that DTs are successfully implemented and monitored across various IRE institutions.

Limited Understanding and Resistance to Transform

Resistance to adapt preceded by limited understanding is among the significant barriers impeding the potential promises of AI for transformational avenues when integrated into IRE. Teachers, students, and parents may get worried because Islamic education incorporates deeply ingrained cultural and traditional practices. Many educational systems face the challenge of resistance to change, and the IRE system is not exempt. The incorporation of AI may encounter resistance and mistrust due to the conservative stance of certain religious individuals. The exploration of AI-based technologies may suffer impediments due to a fear of departing from traditional beliefs and practices, which inhibit educators from fully utilizing these tools. Lack of knowledge of AI in the context of IRE is another major barrier. Many people involved in this educational system are likely unaware of AI's potential advantages. Misconceptions regarding AI's benefits in educational settings can breed resistance and distrust. Islamic educators could also feel unprepared or lack the expertise needed to incorporate AI tools into their lesson plans successfully. Thus, initiating and implementing comprehensive training programs that empower educators and assist them in viewing AI as a complementary tool rather than a threat is necessary to address these obstacles.

OPPORTUNITIES FOR AI IN ISLAMIC EDUCATIONAL SETTINGS

Learning Accessibility and Equity

AI applications and remote learning platforms can improve accessibility by expanding the audience and getting over geographical limitations. AI can help spread IRE throughout the world. AI-powered online platforms can transcend national borders, providing a larger audience with access to richer educational information. AI-powered platforms enable the development and distribution of vast digital resources in the field of Islamic education. Online platforms and apps offer students simple access to genuine Islamic literature, lectures, and interactive resources, promoting the development of a worldwide community of learners with an emphasis on spiritual and emotional intelligence (Sofa et al., 2024). This accessibility surpasses limitations imposed by geography, allowing a wide variety of individuals to interact with Islamic teachings effectively. Thus, AI-powered learning platforms have the potential to enhance the global community of learners by promoting collaboration and understanding across cultural boundaries. Another significant impact of AI is its potential to address educational disparity (Holstein & Doroudi, 2021). It holds the promise of democratizing education by ensuring equitable access to high-quality resources among students from diverse socioeconomic backgrounds.

Assessment and Feedback Efficiency

In AI-driven educational settings, assessment involves the use of AI tools to evaluate students' performance and understanding. AI algorithms can automatically grade student assignments and provide instant feedback (Chen et al., 2020; Cope et al., 2021). Automated grading innovation not only accelerates the grading process but also ensures consistency and objectivity in the evaluation. Moreover, the capability of AI systems to provide immediate feedback to students enables them to understand their mistakes and learn more effectively (Zipitria et al., 2013). In addition, these AI tools identify specific areas where students struggle. AI can pinpoint concepts that require more attention by analyzing patterns in student responses and performance. This not only streamlines the grading process but also offers detailed insights into student learning patterns, enabling educators to adjust teaching strategies accordingly.

Immersive Learning with Virtual Reality

Artificial Intelligence has the potential to produce engaging and interactive educational resources, such as augmented reality apps and virtual simulations, which can enhance the learning experience for students. With the help of AI, Islamic educators can build lively, immersive virtual spaces that provide students with a more realistic and captivating learning experience (Salleh et al., 2021). It is possible to create virtual simulations that can enable students to engage in collaborative instructional activities, visit historical Islamic locations, and communicate with virtual academics. Immersive learning experiences portray AI's adaptability in meeting varied learning demands while upholding the essential ideals of Islamic education.

Adaptive and Interactive Learning

Adaptive learning is one of the notable implementations of AI in the field of Islamic education. AI systems carefully examine students' learning preferences, progress, and styles, customizing educational content to suit individual needs. Adaptive learning platforms demonstrate an automatic modification of the difficulty level of Quranic studies or Arabic language classes according to the individual competency of each student, guaranteeing a customized and efficient learning experience (Mesiono et al., 2024). Gamified platforms enhance the learning process by making it interactive and pleasurable, thus stimulating students to engage more deeply with their field of study. Interactive environments in AI education involve engaging with AI-powered platforms that stimulate active learning.

THREATS OF IMPLEMENTING AI IN ISLAMIC EDUCATION

Cultural and Societal Challenges

The use of AI in IRE may be a huge issue for conservative groups in Islamic societies who worry about the loss of cultural values and customs. Concerns about the possible effects of AI on interpersonal relationships (Thottoli et al., 2024) within the religious community may also exist. Since traditional Islamic education promotes a sense of belonging and shared ideals, some may be concerned that AI might help isolate learners from the larger religious community and impede their ability to develop fully within the confines of Islam. Moreover, another set of challenges in integrating AI into IRE within the Islamic world are its cultural nuances and geographical variances. The varied interpretations, customs, and practices seen in various regions with Muslim populations necessitate a sophisticated approach to the creation and application of AI systems. Failing to consider these cultural nuances, certain populations may become alienated, or a uniform educational strategy that is incompatible with local cultures may be imposed.

Content Authenticity Concerns

Content generated by AI may unintentionally convey false or misleading information, raising severe questions about the content's theological correctness. AI chatbots like ChatGPT lack the contextual knowledge required to decipher and reliably communicate the complex meanings found in Islamic scriptures, leading to content authenticity issues (Muttaqin, 2023). This fact may result in misunderstandings that mislead teachers and students alike. There is a high probability that AI models do not encompass the nuances and sensitivities included in Islamic teachings in mind. This situation might lead to information that is inappropriate for various Islamic groups and lacks cultural context. Further, content produced by AI is easy to manipulate, alter, or misuse, which might result in the spread of false information or skewed viewpoints. In the context of IRE, where truthfulness and objectivity are critical, this is especially a grave concern.

Loss of Human and Spiritual Touch

Spiritual and interpersonal interactions are among the main threats to the incorporation of AI into the IRE system. The foundational principles of traditional IRE include interpersonal relationships, mentorship, and direct student-teacher engagement. The loss of the human touch as perceived by learners- which is crucial in imparting knowledge (Alabool, 2023), especially religious knowledge- can raise the issue of critical interpersonal interactions within religious educational environments. The use of AI may be seen as a threat to the revered practice of imparting knowledge, casting doubt on the sincerity and profundity of the spirituality of AI-driven learning environments. Scholars and religious leaders can be concerned about how this transformation to IRE might weaken the profoundly ingrained spiritual connection the traditional approach fosters.

Privacy and Cybersecurity Risks

AI in Islam's religious education comes with ethical issues such as responsible technology usage, security, and data privacy. The integrity of IRE might suffer serious threats when irresponsible persons utilize AI tools improperly to spread extremist beliefs or misconceptions of religious teachings. Thus, among the obstacles to AI integration include data security and privacy issues. Concerns regarding the gathering and usage of individuals' data by AI platforms may exist in society (Alabool, 2023). Therefore, robust data privacy standards and personal information protection safeguards should be established to overcome these challenges.

AI CASE STUDIES AND BEST PRACTICES

AI Implementations in Educational Settings

The successful implementation of AI in educational settings has shown promising results worldwide. Implementing AI in education provides an effective solution to improve the learning experience and educational outcomes. Table 1 presents several examples of AI implementation for educational purposes.

Table 1. AI apps for education

Application	Website	Domain
Duolingo	www.duolingo.com	Language learning
DreamBox Learning	www.dreambox.com	Mathematics
Codeacademy	www.codecademy.com	Programming
Labster	www.labster.com	Science, technology, engineering, and mathematics
Tarteel	www.tarteel.ai	Quranic learning

An example of a successful AI application in education is Duolingo, a platform for language learning experiences. Duolingo is one of the most popular mobile-assisted language learning (MALL) methods, and it uses a gamification approach for language learning (Govender & Arnedo-Moreno, 2020). Duolingo adapts lessons to each user's learning style and progress, thereby rendering language acquisition more accessible and efficient (Loewen et al., 2019). Duolingo distinguishes itself with interactive exercises and adaptive repetition algorithms, fortifying both retention and engagement. Its gamified approach and personalized feedback have made language learning not only effective but also enjoyable (Jiang et al., 2020, 2021).

Another learning platform is DreamBox. DreamBox Learning extends the personalized learning approach to mathematics education for K-8 students through AI. It utilizes virtual manipulatives, verbal explanations, and visual aids to engage students in mathematical reasoning and skill development (Foster, 2024). This platform ingeniously adapts in real-time to individual student responses, customizing math problems and lessons to match their skill level. This approach fosters differentiated instruction, enabling students to grasp concepts at their own pace, whereby the platform's capacity to adjust content based on real-time feedback further cements its role as an effective tool for personalized learning (Foster, 2024). Similarly, Codecademy employs AI to tailor the learning experience in programming. As a component of its educational approach, Codecademy offers various educational resources, including instructor training, classroom materials, and tracking tools for the classroom (Sharp, 2019). The platform seamlessly adapts lessons and challenges to align with the learner's progress, benefiting users at all proficiency levels, from beginners to advanced learners. With its interactive coding environment that provides real-time feedback, learners find it easier to comprehend and rectify coding errors.

In the science, technology, engineering, and mathematics (STEM) domains, Labster enhances learning through AI-powered virtual laboratory simulations. These simulations cover a wide range of scientific subjects, providing an immersive learning experience. Labster offers a vast collection of over 250 virtual laboratory simulations encompassing various disciplines, including chemistry, biology, physics, anatomy, physiology, engineering, earth science, biotechnology, ecology, and nursing (Tsirulnikov et al., 2023). These simulations have been demonstrated to significantly improve students' understanding of complex scientific concepts and theories, solidifying Labster's position as a valuable tool for science education. Moreover, the use of virtual lab simulations, such as Labster, serves as a valuable complement to traditional teaching methods in the education of lab technicians (de Vries & May, 2019).

In the case of Islamic education, there is a tool called Tarteel.ai, an AI-powered application designed for Quranic learning. The primary functions of Tarteel.ai include recitation, habit formation, retrieval, learning acquisition, and the attainment of improved Quran reading proficiency (Haryono et al., 2023). In addition, it offers unique features, such as AI-driven error detection in Quran recitation and real-time feedback to users. Its advantages include facilitating self-paced Quran learning and ensuring accessibility for users worldwide.

Lessons From Successful AI Implementations in Education

The following part discusses lessons from three different perspectives: key insights from AI implementation, specific challenges addressed, and implications for different educational levels.

Key Insights From AI Implementations

The first lesson derived from the perspective of key insights in AI implementation lies in personalized learning. AI has reshaped education by moving away from traditional, one-size-fits-all approaches toward a more tailored and individualized experience (Foster, 2024). For instance, tools such as DreamBox Learning employed in mathematics education serve as prime examples. They dynamically adapt to the unique learning styles and pace of each student, significantly enhancing the engagement and comprehension of intricate concepts.

Furthermore, AI has a substantial impact on student engagement (Almusaed et al., 2023). The incorporation of AI-driven gamification and interactive platforms has breathed new life into the learning process. Platforms such as Duolingo harness AI to create more interactive and enjoyable language-learning experiences. The integration of gamified elements is pivotal to sustaining student motivation and bolstering retention rates. In addition to benefiting students, AI also plays a crucial role in supporting educators. Tools such as automated grading systems have alleviated the burden of routine tasks for teachers, enabling them to focus more on the interactive and creative aspects of teaching (Erickson et al., 2020; Tisha et al., 2022). This shift has not only increased the efficiency of educational processes but also elevated the overall quality of education provided.

Specific Challenges Addressed

Effective AI implementation has addressed several challenges in education. One key challenge is customizing the learning styles. AI systems need to effectively cater to individual student needs, a task that can be complex given the variability in learning styles and pace (Pliakos et al., 2019). DreamBox Learning, for instance, has addressed this by using AI to analyze student performance data, tailoring math problems and lessons accordingly. This approach ensures that each student receives learning experiences that are specifically adapted to their level, thereby improving comprehension and engagement. Another significant challenge is providing real-time feedback and assistance. Timely feedback is critical for helping students understand and correct their mistakes (Zipitria et al., 2013). Existing educational platforms utilizing AI offer immediate feedback on quizzes and assignments. This immediate response mechanism allows for a more dynamic learning process, enabling students to grasp and rectify their errors quickly.

Implications for Different Educational Levels

The implications of AI in education vary significantly across different educational levels, each offering unique opportunities and challenges. In primary education, AI's impact is particularly noticeable in creating fun and engaging learning environments. At this crucial formative stage, the focus is on foundational learning, wherein AI can play a key role in making education more enjoyable and interactive. AI-powered educational game tools are excellent examples of this. Game-based learning fosters effective, engaging education through immersive problem-solving (McLaren et al., 2017; Wouters et al., 2013). These tools can transform basic concept learning, such as arithmetic or language skills, into interactive and playful experiences. For young learners, this not only aids in better concept retention but also encourages love for learning. AI systems can also assist in identifying learning disabilities or challenges at an early stage (Standen et al., 2020), allowing for timely intervention that can significantly alter a child's learning journey.

In higher education, AI's role has become more sophisticated, addressing more complex educational needs. AI is used in higher education to provide advanced research tools, create personalized learning pathways, and facilitate firsthand experiences through virtual laboratories. These applications are particularly beneficial in fields that require an elevated level of skill and understanding, such as engineering, medicine, and scientific research. For example, AI-driven virtual laboratories allow students to perform experiments and explore scenarios that might be too costly or dangerous to conduct in a physical setting (Potkonjak et al., 2016). This not only enhances their understanding of complex scientific concepts but also prepares them for real-world challenges. Furthermore, AI in higher education can tailor learning experiences to match individual students' career goals and learning preferences, thus making education more relevant and effective.

AI Integration Best Practices for Islamic Education

Integrating AI into Islamic educational settings requires a nuanced approach that respects cultural and religious values while enhancing the learning experience. This integration is not just about implementing technology but adapting it to fit the unique context of Islamic education. At the core of this integration is the need to align AI technologies with cultural sensitivities and religious norms (Gabriel, 2020). This involves close collaboration with Islamic scholars and educators in developing AI tools to ensure they are in harmony with Islamic teachings and values. For instance, AI applications for teaching the Quran or Islamic history should accurately and respectfully interpret Islamic texts and historical events. This alignment ensures that the technology supports traditional learning methods, enriching the educational experience without overshadowing the essence of Islamic teachings.

The strategy for effectively integrating AI in Islamic education involves a phased and collaborative approach. Initially, it is crucial to identify specific educational needs, followed by a gradual introduction of AI tools tailored to these needs. Training educators to use these tools effectively ensures that AI complements rather than replaces traditional teaching methods. For example, AI-driven tools for learning Arabic can supplement traditional teaching, offering additional practice and personalized feedback. This strategy aligns with the educational and cultural context of Islamic teachings.

Focusing on Islamic studies, AI can significantly support teaching through tailored learning modules. These modules, utilizing natural language processing, can engage students in interactive learning, especially in language courses like Arabic. Platforms like Tarteel.ai, which offer feedback on Quranic recitation, exemplify how AI can be specifically adapted to the needs of Islamic education, providing unique and culturally relevant learning experiences. The use of virtual AI, particularly in teaching subjects like the Hajj and Islamic history, offers immersive learning experiences. Technologies like virtual reality can simulate historical events or the experience of Hajj (Salleh et al., 2021), providing students with a deeper, more engaging understanding of these critical aspects of Islam. This technology not only makes learning more engaging but also memorable, bringing historical and religious studies to life.

Gamification in AI-powered educational tools can also play a significant role in Islamic education. By incorporating Islamic history and principles into interactive games, learning can become more enjoyable and effective, particularly for younger students. This approach is especially useful for memorization and understanding religious texts, making education more engaging and interactive. AI can also promote inclusivity in Islamic educational settings by providing materials that cater to a diverse range of learning needs. Adaptive learning systems, which adjust the difficulty level of tasks based on individual performance, make education more accessible to students with varying abilities. This inclusivity is crucial in Islamic education, ensuring that all students, regardless of their learning abilities, have equal opportunities to gain experience and grow.

Lastly, it is important to tailor AI tools to different age groups and educational levels within the Islamic educational system. For younger students, AI can focus on basic concepts and interactive learning, while for older students, it can provide more complex analysis and critical thinking exercises. This ensures that the content and approach are age-appropriate and effective for each stage of learning.

FUTURE PROSPECTS AND RECOMMENDATIONS

AI utilization in Islamic education has vast potential benefits for exploring many things. The following are some examples of AI-based platforms and aspects that people in Islamic educational spaces can utilize to enhance their academic tasks.

AI-driven Chatbots and Content Creation

AI-driven chatbots offer time flexibility to students when answering questions related to Islam. These platforms can also be used for non-Arabic speakers to learn the Arabic language, which is essential for studying Islamic literature. Through the apps, learners can get some guidance regarding how to pronounce words, memorize vocabulary, and make real-time translations. Moreover, AI tools can assist scholars and educators in creating content for Islamic courses, textbooks, and other online resources. Using AI can save time in developing Islamic content and ensure the consistency of the materials. Furthermore, the generated content by AI can then be reviewed and refined by experts to align with Islamic principles.

AI-powered Virtual Reality

The utilization of AI-powered virtual reality (VR) can be considered an alternative to learning Islamic materials. For example, creating virtual Islamic history tours can change the way learners learn Islamic history by bringing them to historical Islamic sites and events. In addition, learners can visit Islamic buildings worldwide through VR to learn their histories and obtain new knowledge about Islam. Another example is that learners can experience themselves before performing Umrah or Hajj using VR platforms. Using AI-powered VR, learners can feel as though they are doing real Umrah or Hajj.

Islamic Ethics in AI

As AI development continues to advance, Islamic ethics must be a compulsory element in AI-powered educational applications. Ethical considerations of Islamic values should be a priority to ensure that AI tools do not go against Islamic principles. For example, when developing AI-powered VR for Islamic history education, developers should ensure accuracy and authenticity when illustrating historical events. In addition, cultural sensitivity should be a vital part of avoiding stereotypes and biases. Furthermore, developers should also consider several aspects, such as respect for other beliefs, values, and privacy rights of users, to ensure that apps adhere to Islamic rules.

Islamic Texts Summarization

Text summarization tools can be one of the prospects in Islamic education. It can be used to simplify and provide a concise summary of texts related to Islam. Moreover, these AI-powered text summarization tools can help teachers and learners easily grasp and analyze lengthy texts from Islamic literature.

AI-enhanced Islamic Counseling

As Muslims, mental and spiritual support based on Islamic principles is essential. Therefore, AI-enhanced Islamic counseling can be leveraged as a solution for Muslims to assist them in maintaining their mental and spiritual health. AI counselors can guide individuals facing personal or spiritual issues. Moreover, they can offer advice based on Islamic teachings and refer them to human counselors for more intensive assistance.

Ethical Guidelines for AI Utilization in Islamic Education

Avoiding Text Misinterpretation

When interpreting Islamic texts, people must interpret them carefully and correctly to avoid misinterpretation. Misinterpretation of Islamic texts can mislead people and are harmful because they involve sharia. Regarding the integration of AI into Islamic education, ensuring that Islamic teachings and texts are correctly interpreted is essential. Therefore, collaboration between developers and Islamic scholars with a deep understanding of Islam should be conducted intensively. Scholars can validate and provide insights for developers during the development of AI systems.

Preservation of Human Interaction

Although AI can be a powerful tool for enhancing learning, it must not replace the crucial role of human teachers and mentors in Islamic education. Human involvement in Islamic education is still needed and cannot be separated. The connection between teachers and students in Islamic education plays an essential role in their moral and spiritual development. Thus, AI should complement human guidance in Islamic education rather than replace it. Additionally, Islamic educators must strive to balance leveraging AI during the education process to maintain the essential human elements that contribute to the holistic growth of learners.

Respect for Privacy

Privacy is among the crucial aspects that must be considered in the integration of AI in Islamic education. This is because religious discussions and personal reflections are sensitive. Collecting unnecessary personal information and sharing sensitive discussions should be avoided. Therefore, the implementation of AI systems in Islamic education must adhere to and respect privacy standards.

Transparency and Accountability

For individuals to adhere to responsible usage of AI in Islamic religious education, transparency is among the core requirements. Educators, learners, and developers should be transparent about the incorporation of AI into the learning process. Students and their families should be informed about when and how AI is employed in their educational journey. This transparency builds trust and allows individuals to make informed choices about their participation in AI-enhanced educational programs. Moreover, there should be a well-defined mechanism to hold AI systems and their developers accountable for any ethical violations or errors in content. This accountability ensures that ethical standards are upheld and that any deviations are addressed promptly. It may involve the establishment of regulatory bodies or independent audits to assess the ethical compliance of AI systems used in Islamic education.

Recommendations for Ethical AI Integration in IRE

Training and Collaboration

To effectively integrate AI into Islamic education while maintaining ethical standards, educators should undergo training on how to incorporate AI into their teaching methods. Collaboration between technology experts and Islamic scholars should be actively encouraged. This collaboration ensures that AI systems are developed and utilized in ways that align with Islamic values. It also allows educators to harness AI's capabilities to enhance the learning experience while adhering to ethical principles.

Adaptive Curriculum Design

Curriculum designers should play a pivotal role in creating AI-friendly content that aligns seamlessly with Islamic values and principles. This entails developing educational materials that not only leverage AI's capabilities but also ensure that the content respects and reinforces the ethical foundations of Islamic education. Curriculum designers should collaborate closely with Islamic scholars to ensure content accuracy and adherence to Islamic teachings.

Regulation and Oversight

Policymakers have a crucial role to play in establishing regulations and oversight bodies dedicated to monitoring the use of AI in Islamic education. These regulatory frameworks should be designed to ensure that AI applications comply with ethical guidelines and uphold the integrity of Islamic education. Oversight bodies can conduct regular assessments, audits, and evaluations to maintain transparency and accountability.

Public Awareness

It is crucial to raise awareness among Islamic society members, such as students, parents, and other common citizens, about the benefits and ethical considerations of AI in Islamic education. This approach will foster informed decision-making and encourage active engagement in ethical discussions surrounding AI integration. Public awareness campaigns can serve to simplify the concept behind AI technological usage, remove doubts and misconceptions, and underscore the hopeful impacts AI platforms can have when implemented responsibly in Islamic education.

CONCLUSION AND FUTURE DIRECTIONS

To conclude the chapter on evaluating AI's potentiality in IRE, the analysis of the literature indicates that integrating AI-driven systems comprises opportunities, difficulties, and transformational possibilities. The uncovered aspects, like improved accessibility and customized learning experiences, demonstrate the beneficial impacts that AI-based platforms can have on acquiring Islamic knowledge among diverse individuals. Besides that, the threats and challenges, ranging from resistance to transformation to ethical worries, emphasize the necessity for heedful and nuanced approaches when it comes to the adoption of AI-based platforms in Islamic religious educational contexts.

The best practices described in the case studies explored in this chapter offer directions for successful AI implementations. They demonstrate that when used responsibly and effectively, AI-enhanced systems can improve the quality of Islamic education on a worldwide scale. These examples are not only inspiring but also practical for Islamic educators and administrators looking to use DTs to improve IRE. The emphasis on adaptive learning platforms, online tools, and immersive experiences demonstrates AI's adaptability in meeting varied learning demands while upholding the essential principles of Islamic education.

Besides that, the future avenues and suggestions provided in this chapter serve as the platform for further study and development. Emerging AI technologies, such as natural language processing and virtual reality, suggest intriguing opportunities for further improving learning experiences. Policymakers, educators, and religious leaders are encouraged to collaborate to create ethical principles for appropriate AI practices in Islamic education. Furthermore, continued study into resolving concerns about the legitimacy of AI-generated content, cybersecurity issues, and cultural sensitivity is required to enable a more resilient and long-term incorporation of AI in religious educational contexts.

For the future trajectory of scientific studies on this intriguing topic, it is vital to dig deeper into the impacts of AIs on the spiritual level and ethical components of IRE. Priority should be on investigating how AI might help with moral thinking and reasoning, character development, and a better grasp of Islamic teachings. Furthermore, longitudinal studies that follow up on the success of AI-driven solutions over time can provide beneficial insights into the long-term effects of these DTs on learners' academic and spiritual development. As the subject evolves, cross-disciplinary collaboration among theologians, ethicists, technologists, and Islamic educators will be critical to ensuring that AI integration is consistent with Islamic education's ideals and purpose.

REFERENCES

Abdel-Maguid, T., & Abdel-Halim, R. (2015). The Qur'ān and the development of rational thinking. *Urology Annals*, 7(2), 135–140. doi:10.4103/0974-7796.152926 PMID:25837451

Abubakari, M. S. (2021). Information and Communication Technology Acceptance in Madrasa Education: Religious' Perspective in Tanzania. *International Journal of Social Sciences & Educational Studies*, 8(3), 129–148. doi:10.23918/ijsses.v8i3p129

Abubakari, M. S., & Zakaria, G. A. N. (2023). Technology Acceptance Model in Islamic Education (TAMISE) for Digital Learning: Conceptual Framework Proposal. *Canadian Journal of Educational and Social Studies*, 3(4), 25–42. doi:10.53103/cjess.v3i4.153

Abubakari, M. S., Zakaria, G. A. N., & Musa, J. (2023). Digital Learning Acceptance in Islamic Education: Validity and Reliability Testing of the Modified Technology Acceptance Model. *Canadian Journal of Educational and Social Studies*, 3(6), 27–42. doi:10.53103/cjess.v6i1.185

Abubakari, M. S., Zakaria, G. A. N., Musa, J., & Kalinaki, K. (2023a). Assessing Digital Competence in Higher Education: A Gender Analysis of DigComp 2.1 Framework in Uganda. *SAGA: Journal of Technology and Information System*, 1(4), 114–120. doi:10.58905/saga.v1i4.210

Abubakari, M. S., Zakaria, G. A. N., Musa, J., & Kalinaki, K. (2023b). Validating the Digital Competence (Dig-Comp 2.1) Framework in Higher Education Using Confirmatory Factor Analysis: Non-Western Perspective. *Canadian Journal of Educational and Social Studies, 3*(6), 15–26. doi:10.53103/cjess.v6i1.184

Abubakari, M. S., Zakaria, G. A. N., Priyanto, P., & Triantini, D. T. (2023). Analysing Technology Acceptance for Digital Learning in Islamic Education: The Role of Religious Perspective on ICT. *Journal of Computing Research and Innovation, 8*(1), 1–16. doi:10.24191/jcrinn.v8i1.344

Agil, T., & Alkhiri, A. (2022). Islamic Ethical Foundations of AI and Its Modern Applications. *International Journal of Computer Science and Network Security, 22*(5), 741–746. doi:10.22937/IJCSNS.2022.22.5.101

Ahmad, I., Sharma, S., Singh, R., Gehlot, A., Priyadarshi, N., & Twala, B. (2022). MOOC 5.0: A Roadmap to the Future of Learning. *Sustainability (Basel), 14*(18), 11199. doi:10.3390/su141811199

Alabool, H. M. (2023). ChatGPT in Education: SWOT analysis approach. *2023 International Conference on Information Technology (ICIT), September*, 184–189. 10.1109/ICIT58056.2023.10225801

Almusaed, A., Almssad, A., Yitmen, I., & Homod, R. Z. (2023). Enhancing Student Engagement: Harnessing "AIED"'s Power in Hybrid Education—A Review Analysis. *Education Sciences, 13*(7), 632. doi:10.3390/educsci13070632

Alrumiah, S. S., & Al-Shargabi, A. A. (2023). Intelligent Quran Recitation Recognition and Verification: Research Trends and Open Issues. *Arabian Journal for Science and Engineering, 48*(8), 9859–9885. doi:10.1007/s13369-022-07273-8

Angelova, G., Nisheva-Pavlova, M., Eskenazi, A., & Ivanova, K. (2021, April). Role of Education and Research for Artificial Intelligence Development in Bulgaria Until 2030. *Mathematics and Education in Mathematics, 50*, 71–82.

Arjmand, R. (2018). Introduction to Part I: Islamic Education: Historical Perspective, Origin, and Foundation. In Handbook of Islamic Education (pp. 3–31). doi:10.1007/978-3-319-64683-1_3

Baiza, Y. (2018). Islamic Education and Development of Educational Traditions and Institutions. In *Handbook of Islamic Education* (pp. 77–97). Springer. doi:10.1007/978-3-319-64683-1_7

Benzaghta, M. A., Elwalda, A., Mousa, M., Erkan, I., & Rahman, M. (2021). SWOT analysis applications: An integrative literature review. *Journal of Global Business Insights, 6*(1), 55–73. doi:10.5038/2640-6489.6.1.1148

Chen, L., Chen, P., & Lin, Z. (2020). Artificial Intelligence in Education: A Review. *IEEE Access : Practical Innovations, Open Solutions, 8*, 75264–75278. doi:10.1109/ACCESS.2020.2988510

Cope, B., Kalantzis, M., & Searsmith, D. (2021). Artificial intelligence for education: Knowledge and its assessment in AI-enabled learning ecologies. *Educational Philosophy and Theory, 53*(12), 1229–1245. doi:10.1080/00131857.2020.1728732

Daun, H., & Arjmand, R. (2018). *Handbook of Islamic Education* (Vol. 7). Springer International Publishing. doi:10.1007/978-3-319-64683-1 de Vries, L. E., & May, M. (2019). Virtual laboratory simulation in the education of laboratory technicians–motivation and study intensity. *Biochemistry and Molecular Biology Education*, *47*(3), 257–262. doi:10.1002/bmb.21221 PMID:30748084

Denecke, K., Glauser, R., & Reichenpfader, D. (2023). Assessing the Potential and Risks of AI-Based Tools in Higher Education: Results from an eSurvey and SWOT Analysis. *Trends in Higher Education*, *2*(4), 667–688. doi:10.3390/higheredu2040039

Dwivedi, Y. K., Kshetri, N., Hughes, L., Slade, E. L., Jeyaraj, A., Kar, A. K., Baabdullah, A. M., Koohang, A., Raghavan, V., Ahuja, M., Albanna, H., Albashrawi, M. A., Al-Busaidi, A. S., Balakrishnan, J., Barlette, Y., Basu, S., Bose, I., Brooks, L., Buhalis, D., ... Wright, R. (2023). Opinion Paper: "So what if ChatGPT wrote it?" Multidisciplinary perspectives on opportunities, challenges and implications of generative conversational AI for research, practice and policy. *International Journal of Information Management*, *71*(March), 102642. doi:10.1016/j.ijinfomgt.2023.102642

Elmahjub, E. (2023). Artificial Intelligence (AI) in Islamic Ethics: Towards Pluralist Ethical Benchmarking for AI. *Philosophy & Technology*, *36*(4), 73. doi:10.1007/s13347-023-00668-x

Erickson, J. A., Botelho, A. F., McAteer, S., Varatharaj, A., & Heffernan, N. T. (2020). The automated grading of student open responses in mathematics. *Proceedings of the Tenth International Conference on Learning Analytics & Knowledge*, 615–624. 10.1145/3375462.3375523

Farrokhnia, M., Banihashem, S. K., Noroozi, O., & Wals, A. (2023). A SWOT analysis of ChatGPT: Implications for educational practice and research. *Innovations in Education and Teaching International*, *00*(00), 1–15. doi:10.1080/14703297.2023.2195846

Foster, M. E. (2024). Evaluating the Impact of Supplemental Computer-Assisted Math Instruction in Elementary School: A Conceptual Replication. *Journal of Research on Educational Effectiveness*, *17*(1), 94–118. doi:10.1080/19345747.2023.2174919

Gabriel, I. (2020). Artificial Intelligence, Values, and Alignment. *Minds and Machines*, *30*(3), 411–437. doi:10.1007/s11023-020-09539-2

Govender, T., & Arnedo-Moreno, J. (2020). A Survey on Gamification Elements in Mobile Language-Learning Applications. *Eighth International Conference on Technological Ecosystems for Enhancing Multiculturality*, 669–676. 10.1145/3434780.3436597

Haryono, K., Rajagede, R. A., & Negara, M. U. A. S. (2023). Quran Memorization Technologies and Methods: Literature Review. *IJID*, *11*(1), 192–201. doi:10.14421/ijid.2022.3746

Hashim, R. (2005). Rethinking Islamic Education in Facing the Challenges of the Twenty-first Century. *American Journal of Islam and Society*, *22*(4), 133–147. doi:10.35632/ajis.v22i4.1676

Holstein, K., & Doroudi, S. (2021). *Equity and Artificial Intelligence in Education: Will "AIEd" Amplify or Alleviate Inequities in Education?* (Issue 3). https://doi.org//arXiv.2104.12920 doi:10.48550

Humble, N., & Mozelius, P. (2022). The threat, hype, and promise of artificial intelligence in education. *Discover Artificial Intelligence*, *2*(1), 22. doi:10.1007/s44163-022-00039-z

Jiang, X., Rollinson, J., Plonsky, L., Gustafson, E., & Pajak, B. (2021). Evaluating the reading and listening outcomes of beginning-level Duolingo courses. *Foreign Language Annals, 54*(4), 974–1002. doi:10.1111/flan.12600

Jiang, X., Rollinson, J., Plonsky, L., & Pajak, B. (2020). Duolingo efficacy study: Beginning-level courses equivalent to four university semesters. *Duolingo Research Report, 2020*, 1–11. https://www.duolingo.com/efficacy

Kausar, S., Leghari, A. R., & Soomro, A. S. (2024). Analysis of the Islamic Law and its Compatibility with Artificial Intelligence as a Emerging Challenge of the Modern World. *Annals of Human and Social Sciences, 5*(1), 99–114. doi:10.35484/ahss.2024(5-I)10

Leigh, D. (2009). SWOT Analysis. In *Handbook of Improving Performance in the Workplace* (Vol. 1-3, pp. 115–140). Wiley. doi:10.1002/9780470592663.ch24

Loewen, S., Crowther, D., Isbell, D. R., Kim, K. M., Maloney, J., Miller, Z. F., & Rawal, H. (2019). Mobile-assisted language learning: A Duolingo case study. *ReCALL, 31*(3), 293–311. doi:10.1017/S0958344019000065

McLaren, B. M., Adams, D. M., Mayer, R. E., & Forlizzi, J. (2017). A Computer-Based Game that Promotes Mathematics Learning More than a Conventional Approach. *International Journal of Game-Based Learning, 7*(1), 36–56. doi:10.4018/IJGBL.2017010103

Mesiono, M., Fahada, N., Irwansyah, I., Diana, D., & Siregar, A. S. (2024). SWOT Analysis of ChatGPT: Implications for Educational Practice and Research. *JMKSP (Jurnal Manajemen, Kepemimpinan, Dan Supervisi Pendidikan), 9*(1), 181–196. https://doi.org/ doi:10.31851/jmksp.v9i1.14137

Muttaqin, Z. (2023). Implementation of Islamic Education Learning with Artificial Intelligence (CHAT-GPT). *The 6th ICIS (2023): Islamic Thought and the Digital Challenge: Exploring the Future of Education, Business, Law, and Society*, 1–9.

Nikmatullah, C., Wahyudin, W., Tarihoran, N., & Fauzi, A. (2023). Digital Pesantren: Revitalization of the Islamic Education System in the Disruptive Era. *Al-Izzah: Jurnal Hasil-Hasil Penelitian, 1*, 1. Advance online publication. doi:10.31332/ai.v0i0.5880

Pliakos, K., Joo, S.-H., Park, J. Y., Cornillie, F., Vens, C., & Van den Noortgate, W. (2019). Integrating machine learning into item response theory for addressing the cold start problem in adaptive learning systems. *Computers & Education, 137*, 91–103. doi:10.1016/j.compedu.2019.04.009

Potkonjak, V., Gardner, M., Callaghan, V., Mattila, P., Guetl, C., Petrović, V. M., & Jovanović, K. (2016). Virtual laboratories for education in science, technology, and engineering: A review. *Computers & Education, 95*, 309–327. doi:10.1016/j.compedu.2016.02.002

Puyt, R. W., Lie, F. B., & Wilderom, C. P. M. (2023). The origins of SWOT analysis. *Long Range Planning, 56*(3), 102304. doi:10.1016/j.lrp.2023.102304

Qazi, A., Hardaker, G., Ahmad, I. S., Darwich, M., Maitama, J. Z., & Dayani, A. (2021). The Role of Information & Communication Technology in Elearning Environments: A Systematic Review. *IEEE Access : Practical Innovations, Open Solutions, 9*, 45539–45551. doi:10.1109/ACCESS.2021.3067042

Rafiabadi, H. N. (2017). Contribution of Islamic Civilisation to Science Education and Technology: Some Fresh Insights. *Indonesian Journal of Interdisciplinary Islamic Studies*, *1*(1), 49–75. doi:10.20885/ijiis.vol1.iss1.art3

Raquib, A., Channa, B., Zubair, T., & Qadir, J. (2022). Islamic virtue-based ethics for artificial intelligence. *Discover Artificial Intelligence*, *2*(1), 11. doi:10.1007/s44163-022-00028-2

Salleh, S. M., Hasan, A. S. M., Salleh, N. M., Sapiai, N. S., Ghazali, S. A. M., Rusok, N. H. M., & Zawawi, M. Z. M. (2021). Virtual Reality Technology of Hajj Practice: An Innovation of The Future. *Jurnal Islam Dan Masyarakat Kontemporari*, *22*(2), 56–63. doi:10.37231/jimk.2021.22.2.577

Shafik, W. (2024). Introduction to ChatGPT. In A. J. Obaid, B. Bhushan, M. S., & S. S. Rajest (Eds.), *Advanced Applications of Generative AI and Natural Language Processing Models* (pp. 1–25). IGI Global. doi:10.4018/979-8-3693-0502-7.ch001

Sharp, J. H. (2019). Using Codecademy Interactive Lessons as an Instructional Supplement in a Python Programming Course. *Information Systems Education Journal*, *17*(3), 20–28.

Sofa, A. R., Mundir, H., & Ubaidillah, H. (2024). Learning Islamic Religious Education Based on Spiritual and Emotional Intelligence to Build the Morals of Zainul Hasan Genggong Islamic University Students. *International Journal of Educational Narratives*, *2*(1), 42–47. doi:10.55849/ijen.v2i1.609

Standen, P. J., Brown, D. J., Taheri, M., Galvez Trigo, M. J., Boulton, H., Burton, A., Hallewell, M. J., Lathe, J. G., Shopland, N., Blanco Gonzalez, M. A., Kwiatkowska, G. M., Milli, E., Cobello, S., Mazzucato, A., Traversi, M., & Hortal, E. (2020). An evaluation of an adaptive learning system based on multimodal affect recognition for learners with intellectual disabilities. *British Journal of Educational Technology*, *51*(5), 1748–1765. doi:10.1111/bjet.13010

Strzelecki, A., & ElArabawy, S. (2024). Investigation of the moderation effect of gender and study level on the acceptance and use of generative AI by higher education students: Comparative evidence from Poland and Egypt. *British Journal of Educational Technology*, *00*(3), 1–22. doi:10.1111/bjet.13425

Thottoli, M. M., Alruqaishi, B. H., & Soosaimanickam, A. (2024). Robo academic advisor: Can chatbots and artificial intelligence replace human interaction? *Contemporary Educational Technology*, *16*(1), ep485. doi:10.30935/cedtech/13948

Tisha, S. M., Oregon, R. A., Baumgartner, G., Alegre, F., & Moreno, J. (2022). An automatic grading system for a high school-level computational thinking course. *Proceedings of the 4th International Workshop on Software Engineering Education for the Next Generation*, 20–27. 10.1145/3528231.3528357

Tsirulnikov, D., Suart, C., Abdullah, R., Vulcu, F., & Mullarkey, C. E. (2023). Game on: Immersive virtual laboratory simulation improves student learning outcomes & motivation. *FEBS Open Bio*, *13*(3), 396–407. doi:10.1002/2211-5463.13567 PMID:36723273

Tubagus, M., Haerudin, Fathurohman, A., Adiyono, & Slan. (2023). The Impact of Technology on Islamic Pesantren Education and the Learning Outcomes of Santri: New trends and possibilities. *Indonesian Journal of Education*, *3*(3), 443–450.

Utunen, H., Attias, M., George, R., O'Connell, G., & Tokar, A. (2022). Learning multiplier effect of OpenWHO.org: use of online learning materials beyond the platform. In *WHO Weekly epidemiological record* (Vol. 97, pp. 1–7). World Health Organization. https://www.who.int/publications/i/item/WER9701-02-1-7

Valentin, E. K. (2001). Swot Analysis from a Resource-Based View. *Journal of Marketing Theory and Practice*, 9(2), 54–69. doi:10.1080/10696679.2001.11501891

World Health Organization. (2020). Digital technology for COVID-19 response. *World Health Organization*. https://www.who.int/news-room/detail/03-04-2020-digital-technology-for-covid-19-response

Wouters, P., van Nimwegen, C., van Oostendorp, H., & van der Spek, E. D. (2013). A meta-analysis of the cognitive and motivational effects of serious games. *Journal of Educational Psychology*, 105(2), 249–265. doi:10.1037/a0031311

Yulianto, S. F., & Haya, F. (2023). Study of AI and Technology as a Substitute for the Presence of a Teacher Learning the Qur'an Hadith in Bond of Knowledge Perspective. *International Conference on Education, 1*, 433–442.

Zaimah, N. R., Hartanto, E. B., & Zahro, F. (2024). Acceptability and Effectiveness Analysis of Large Language Model-Based Artificial Intelligence Chatbot Among Arabic Learners. *Mantiqu Tayr: Journal of Arabic Language*, 4(1), 1–20. doi:10.25217/mantiqutayr.v4i1.3951

Zipitria, I., Arruarte, A., & Elorriaga, J. (2013). Discourse measures for Basque summary grading. *Interactive Learning Environments*, 21(6), 528–547. doi:10.1080/10494820.2011.606503

Chapter 11
Navigating AI Integration:
Case Studies and Best Practices in Educational Transformation

Shahinaz Abdelrahman Osman
(iD) https://orcid.org/0000-0002-0822-5576
City University Ajman, UAE

Zeinab E. Ahmed
(iD) https://orcid.org/0000-0002-6144-8533
Department of Computer Engineering, University of Gezira, Sudan & Department of Electrical and Computer Engineering, International Islamic University Malaysia, Malaysia

ABSTRACT

This chapter explores the practical applications and effective methods of integrating artificial intelligence (AI) into various educational settings. It examines how educational institutions, ranging from K-12 to higher education, have successfully utilized AI to enhance teaching methods, strategies, and learning outcomes through the presentation of compelling case studies. In addition to theoretical frameworks, the chapter offers practical insights into the challenges faced, strategies employed, and lessons learned during the implementation of AI-enhanced teaching approaches. The adoption of AI in education can facilitate personalized learning journeys by tailoring instruction, materials, pacing, and resources to individual learners' needs and preferences. It also enables adaptive assessments and feedback systems that provide real-time feedback, identify areas for improvement, and contribute to more nuanced grading systems. The chapter highlights examples of AI-powered platforms, such as adaptive learning platforms, intelligent tutoring systems, smart content recommendation systems, and gamified learning paths, illustrating their effectiveness in meeting the unique requirements of students and promoting engagement and mastery. Furthermore, it discusses the importance of immediate and targeted feedback and individualized content structuring in adaptive learning environments. The chapter also explores AI-assessment tools, real-time feedback systems, learning analytics dashboards, and peer learning facilitation platforms as valuable resources for educators. By leveraging AI technologies, educational institutions can transform teaching and learning practices, promote personalized and adaptive learning, and ensure the alignment of AI-based systems with human values.

DOI: 10.4018/979-8-3693-2728-9.ch011

1. INTRODUCTION

Artificial Intelligence (AI) technology has revolutionized various aspects of our lives, and education is no exception. With its ability to analyze data, recognize patterns, and make intelligent decisions, AI has emerged as a powerful tool in the field of education. It has the potential to enhance the learning experience, personalize instruction, and foster independent learning among students. However, the integration of AI into educational institutions comes with its own set of challenges, including privacy concerns and the need to align AI systems with human values. The goal of this chapter is to offer a thorough analysis of practical applications and efficient methods for incorporating artificial intelligence (AI) into diverse educational contexts. The chapter will explore how educational institutions, from K–12 to higher education, have successfully used AI to improve teaching methods, strategies, and learning results by providing several interesting case examples. Beyond theoretical frameworks, the chapter will provide practical insights into the obstacles faced, the tactics used, and the lessons discovered throughout the adoption of AI-enhanced teaching approaches.

Navigating and Adopting AI

AI technology has been a breakthrough in education as it can help students learn more easily and become more independent. This does not necessarily entail the overly dominant role of the teacher but allows the teacher to move to an enlightening level with important keywords. More importantly, teachers must return to the essence of teaching, which is moral education. Navigating AI in education involves implementing various practices to effectively integrate artificial intelligence technologies into educational settings. There are two ways to use AI in education:

- First, the transfer of teacher responsibility to the AI system, which serves as a tutor for all students. Smart tutor systems, which use smart technology to tailor content for each student, have been widely used in many classrooms (Moleenar, 2021).
- An alternative function of artificial intelligence involves enhancing human intelligence and aiding individuals in learning activities. AI has the capability to elevate the standards of teaching and learning through personalized feedback, recognition of data patterns, and facilitation of collaborative learning. Nevertheless, integrating AI into educational institutions presents challenges, including the need to address privacy and ethical concerns and ensure that AI-based systems align with human values (Renz & Vladova, 2021).

2. PERSONALIZED LEARNING JOURNEYS

In order to meet specific needs and learning objectives, it includes customizing aspects including instruction pace, materials, the sequencing process, technological adoption, quality of material, instructional methods, and learning resources. Personalized learning is an instructional strategy that tailors the learning process, content, pace, and objectives to the individual learner's needs, preferences, and goals, and it's a way to encourage learners to take responsibility for their own learning, develop abilities to self-regulate, and promote lifelong learning behaviors, its a way of enhancing learning outcomes by providing learners with personalized feedback, instructions, and assistance, as well as opportunities for options, collaboration, and a vision for transforming education by leveraging AI technologies. (Yu Lu, 2021)

Learner models must be updated and modified in response to fresh data regarding the learner's behavior, affective states, and knowledge in order to deliver dynamic tailored learning. Artificial intelligence and educational data mining offer cutting-edge technologies that can be used for fine-grained learner modeling to achieve this. Initially, artificial intelligence in education has mostly supported the development of intelligent tutoring systems. Second, educational data mining is indispensable for providing information about the learning process and learner behavior. (Vandewaetere, 2014)

Several examples highlight how well AI-powered personalized learning systems work, showing how well they can adjust to the unique demands of each student, track their development, and provide focused interventions. We will examine particular instances to clarify these accomplishments depending on its functionality:

- Adaptive Learning Platforms:

Knewton and DreamBox use AI algorithms to adapt content based on individual student progress.

With an emphasis on higher education, Knewton released Knewton Alta, a new platform aiming to provide individualized learning experiences within a variety of educational contexts. The application creates a tailored learning path that considers the strengths and weaknesses of every student by using advanced algorithms to customize information to meet their specific needs. This helps students gain a greater understanding and mastery of the course materials by giving them access to focused tools and feedback. Moreover, DreamBox, a flexible math program for pupils in kindergarten through eighth grade, uses artificial intelligence algorithms that automatically adjust to the unique learning preferences and speeds of each student. As seen in the DreamBox platform accompanying figure, the program has had favorable results, including increased engagement, improved math competency, and improved teacher-student interactions.

Figure 1. Personalize learning in Knewton platform

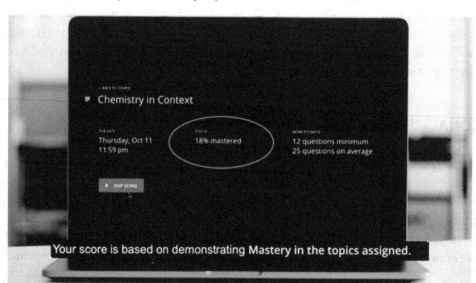

- Intelligent Tutoring Systems:

Carnegie Learning's Carnegie Learning's Cognitive Tutor evaluates student reactions to problems, recognizes misunderstandings, and provides personalized feedback across a spectrum of subjects, spanning from mathematics, literacy, and English Language Arts (ELA) to world languages and applied sciences. Carnegie offers tutoring services and professional learning, aiming to provide extensive and inventive educational solutions for students. Carnegie Learning's focus is to promote lifelong learning, and they achieve this with dynamic classroom exercises and their ongoing research. Their services allow students to build conceptual understanding that helps in solving mathematical problems, developing language skills, amongst other benefits.

- Smart Content Recommendation:

Learning management systems (LMS) integrated with AI, like Canvas by Instructure, analyze students' past activities and suggest relevant learning materials, videos, or quizzes to reinforce concepts.

Figure 2. Canvas quiz attempt

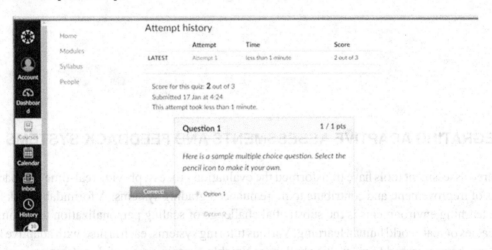

- Gamified Learning Paths: Duolingo, a language learning app, uses AI to adapt lessons based on a user's proficiency and learning style.

Duolingo's gamification strategy, deeply rooted in the Octalysis framework, artfully dissects the driving forces of resonation, culminating in captivating and gratifying user experiences.

Duolingo employs a gamification strategy centered around three core elements: points, levels, and rewards. The accumulation of points holds significance as learners adeptly navigate lessons and exercises, offering a tangible gauge of their progress and fostering a friendly sense of competition among users. Proficiency levels in language serve as significant milestones, inspiring learners to pursue mastery in their language learning pursuits. A captivating variety of rewards, extending from virtual badges to tangible prizes, functions as a powerful motivator, urging learners to complete tasks and achieve noteworthy milestones in their journey of learning a language.

The excitement of competition thrives as users compete for top positions on leaderboards, highlighting their proficiency in points and levels. The enticing idea of streaks encourages learners to sustain their commitment by rewarding consecutive days of practice, instilling a gratifying daily learning routine. Furthermore, setting daily goals establishes tangible targets, nurturing a sense of achievement with each unlocked milestone (Ogamify, 2023).

Figure 3. Duolingo gamification

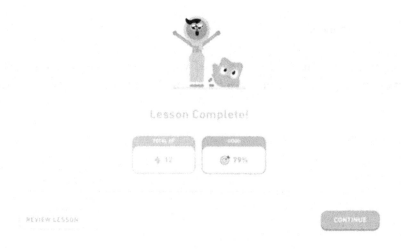

3. INTEGRATING ADAPTIVE ASSESSMENTS AND FEEDBACK SYSTEMS

AI-powered assessment tools have transformed the evaluation process, provide real-time feedback, identify areas of improvement, and contribute to more nuanced grading systems. A formidable task faced by adaptive learning environments is the substantial challenge of scaling personalization to accommodate the intricacies of real-world human learning. Various tutoring systems, each armed with adaptive learning instructions, have emerged to meet this challenge. Notably, certain successful systems are serving tens or even hundreds of thousands of students annually, and their usage continues to expand. (Baker, 2016). It has been proved that adaptive learning is much more efficient than a traditional learning environment like classroom learning (Desmarais & d Baker, 2012; Romero & Ventura, 2020). For an adaptive learning environment to flourish, proficiency in two key forms of adaptation is imperative:

1.   Immediate and Targeted Feedback:

A critical aspect involves providing prompt, specific, and effective feedback during problem-solving exercises. This real-time guidance enhances the learning process, offering learners the insights needed for continuous improvement.

2. Individualized Content Structuring:

Equally important is the ability to structure adaptive learning content according to the unique skill proficiency of each student. Customizing the learning path ensures that individuals receive content tailored to their current capabilities, optimizing the educational experience for diverse learners.

Some Examples of AI-assessment tools:

- AI-powered assessment tools, like Smart Sparrow, create dynamic assessments that adjust difficulty in real-time. This ensures students are appropriately challenged and receive feedback tailored to their level of understanding.

Figure 4. Smart sparrow AI assessment and personal feedback

- Real-Time Feedback Systems: Example: Khan Academy's AI-driven system provides immediate feedback on quizzes and assignments. It analyzes each student's responses, identifies areas of struggle, and offers targeted suggestions for improvement.

Khan Academy meticulously assesses individual student responses, pinpointing areas of difficulty and providing specific suggestions for improvement. Through its practice challenges, instructional videos, and personalized learning dashboard, Khan Academy offers students the opportunity to learn at their own pace in and out outside the classroom. The site provides information from K–14 education and preparation for exams for an extensive variety of subjects, including math, science, computing, history, art history, economics, and more.

- Learning Analytics Dashboards: for example Brightspace by D2L, utilizes learning analytics to offer dashboards for instructors. These dashboards indicate the growth of each learner, patterns in their participation, and areas that could benefit from more help uses learning analytics to create dashboards for educators.

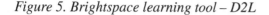

Figure 5. Brightspace learning tool – D2L

- Peer Learning Facilitation: Example: AI algorithms in discussion forums, such as Piazza, The D2L peer learning enhancement tool in Figure 5 is an example of how artificial intelligence (AI) algorithms in forums for discussion, like Piazza, may detect students who are excellent in a subject and motivate them to help struggling peers, thereby encouraging collaborative learning.

Through the power of community engagement, the Piazza platform offers a simple and engaging Q&A environment that attempts to save time and improve student learning. The platform enables seamless interaction in a single area using a format similar to Wikipedia. Major features incorporate a LaTeX editor, syntax highlighting, and code blocking to improve readability in technical discussions. Questions and comments requiring quick responses are guaranteed to be noticed owing to the Piazza system. The ability of instructors to give their approval of responses contributes to the class's overall coherence and focus. Every student is allowed to participate actively by providing the option to post anonymously. The platform additionally offers simple integration with all major Learning Management Systems (LMS) and flexible online polls.

Integrating Automated Grading Systems

Utilize AI-powered grading tools such as Gradescope or Turnitin Feedback Studio to automate the grading process for assignments and assessments. This ensures quicker feedback, allowing students to track their progress in real-time.

This guarantees swift feedback, enabling students to monitor their progress in real-time. The popular AI-powered grading platforms, Gradescope and Turnitin Feedback Studio, offer an extensive selection of features and services that have entirely altered how grades are handed out in educational institutions. Gradescope is a program that combines multiple-choice questions and open-ended responses to evaluate assignments in a variety of formats using artificial intelligence and machine learning. By taking advantage of the platform's collaborative grading feature, different teachers can assess assignments simultaneously and maintain rating standardization. Furthermore, Gradescope offers teachers an array of data that sheds light on student performance and points up areas that could need more focus.

However, Turnitin Feedback Studio is well-known for its capacity to detect occurrences of plagiarism. It finds possible copyright infringement by thoroughly scanning assignments using advanced algorithms and cross-referencing them with a large academic content database. Turnitin Feedback Studio provides wide-ranging feedback options that allow teachers to provide detailed comments on students' work in addition to its plagiarism detecting features. The platform stresses the significance of academic integrity and enables teachers to cultivate a culture of innovation.

The ease of use of both systems' interfaces enables educators to quickly navigate through assignments, view analytical reports, and modify grading criteria. Furthermore, they frequently integrate with popular learning management systems, improving student performance.

Figure 6. Gradescope grading platform

4. VIRTUAL CLASSROOMS AND REMOTE LEARNING

Examine best practices in the implementation of AI-driven virtual classrooms. These virtual assistants are capable of answering basic inquiries, allowing teachers to participate in more customized discussions.

- Intelligent Virtual Assistants: Implement AI-driven virtual assistants like IBM Watson Assistant or Google's Dialogflow to provide instant responses to common student queries. Using chatbots to offer student assistance on online learning systems is an additional application. Institutions may enhance the entire educational process by integrating AI chatbots to provide students with immediate assistance with technical issues, general inquiries, or course navigation.

Through the utilization of natural language, chatbots are software programs that simulate human communication and improve virtual service interactions. Chatbots are software applications designed to replicate human conversation, simplifying interactions with online services through natural language. They play a crucial role in automating tasks across diverse business functions, including customer support, marketing, and sales. Numerous tools, such as Dialogflow CX and IBM Watson, are accessible in the market for the development of chatbots.

Ashok K. Goel orchestrated a notable prank in the annals of artificial intelligence. In an online course, Mr. Goel, a computer science professor at the Georgia Institute of Technology, enlisted the support of nine teaching assistants, including one named Jill Watson, to address inquiries from the 300 students. Towards the conclusion of the term, Mr. Goel disclosed to the students that Jill was, in reality, a computerized assistant driven by IBM's Watson technology, specifically designed for answering questions. (Ben Gose, 2016)

Figure 7. Ashok Goel, a computer-science professor at Georgia Tech, is surrounded by his teaching assistants, including "Jill Watson" (on the screen)

Dialogflow empowers educators to build next-level bots and voice applications: craft delightful chatbots that handle student's inquiries, guide students, and offer personalized experiences; design voice interfaces for smart speakers and effortlessly turn text into conversations; or seamlessly integrate educators bots with external systems for powerful automation – all while leveraging Dialogflow's intuitive platform and robust capabilities.

- AI-Powered Content Creation: Leverage tools like OpenAI's ChatGPT, Google Bard Gemeni and Microsoft's Bing to assist educators in creating engaging and diverse learning materials. AI can help generate quiz questions, design interactive content, and even produce virtual simulations for complex subjects.

An enhanced language model created on the GPT-3.5 architecture is called ChatGPT, built by OpenAI. With its capacity to translate as well as generate natural language, this cutting-edge machine can have meaningful discussions with humans that are suitable for the situation. Drawing upon a vast amount of diverse internet text for training, ChatGPT is capable of comprehending complex queries, providing informative responses, and even generating creative content. Its adaptability includes an array of applications including providing support, creating text, establishing interactive conversations, and responding to queries. Although it has its disadvantages, ChatGPT is a major advancement in natural language processing and demonstrates how large-scale language models can improve communication between humans and computers in a wide range of contexts (AI Business,2021)

Bard is powered by the cutting-edge Gemini language model; Bard is like a wordsmith with superpowers. Imagine a vast library digitized and distilled into an AI capable of weaving stories, translating languages, composing code, and answering your questions in a flash. Gemini unlocks new depths of comprehension, allowing Bard to grasp your intent, navigate complex topics, and even generate creative text formats, from poems to musical pieces. With each interaction, Bard learns and evolves, making it not just a tool, but a companion on your journey through the ever-expanding universe of knowledge and imagination.

Microsoft Bing is an AI-enhanced web search experience search engine experience. It utilizes the use of various cutting-edge technologies from OpenAI and Microsoft, such as DALL-E, a deep learning model, and GPT-4, an innovative large language model (LLM) that creates digital photos from natural language descriptions. Additionally, Microsoft has unveiled "Make Every feature Binary" (MEB), a new large-scale sparse model that is meant to be employed in combination with Transformer-based deep learning algorithms including Google's Switch Transformer, OpenAI's GPT-3, and Microsoft's Turing NLG.

Microsoft Copilot: Microsoft Copilot: To support individuals in their professional lives, Microsoft developed Copilot, a chatbot that makes utilizes a large language model (LLM). It was released in February 2023 and can be accessed through Microsoft 365 applications, including Teams, Word, Excel, and PowerPoint. Copilot is more than an ordinary chatbot; it's an advanced coordination processing engine that links the organization's data in Microsoft Graph, the power of LLMs (including GPT-4), and the Microsoft 365 applications. With its processing of natural language capabilities, it is meant to assist users in discovering new growth prospects, increase efficiency, and work more productively.

Figure 8. Microsoft Bing AI model chat

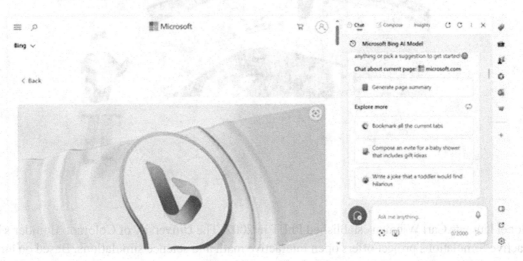

Adaptive Learning Platforms: Integrate adaptive learning platforms, such as Smart Sparrow or DreamBox, to tailor content delivery based on individual student Needs. This tailoring personalization enhances participation and supports wide range of learning paces.

Virtual Labs and Simulations

Integrate AI-driven virtual labs and simulations, such as Labster, or Phet for subjects that require hands-on experience. These tools offer a rich learning experience, allowing students to conduct experiments in a virtual environment.

Labster's Virtual Lab provides an unparalleled immersive science learning experience with over 300 high-quality virtual labs. These simulations offer students realistic 3D environments where they engage in experiments aligned with specific missions. The platform combines scientific theory with compelling storylines, supplemented by animations and other interactive elements. Accessible via a basic internet connection, Labster's 24/7 science campus in the cloud supports on-campus, remote, and hybrid learning programs. Integration with Learning Management Systems (LMS) is seamless, and the Labster app extends accessibility across various devices. The platform is designed with multilingual and accessibility support, ensuring inclusivity. Embedded throughout the simulations are automatically graded quizzes, providing ongoing assessment for students. Educators can monitor progress and assess results through the Labster Dashboard, which includes features such as automated grading, progress tracking, customizable quizzes, lab report templates, and outcome-based reporting.

Figure 9. Labster virtual lab

Nobel laureate Carl Wieman established PhET in 2002. The University of Colorado Boulder's PhET Interactive Simulations project offers open interactive math and science simulations. Based on an array of educational research, PhET simulations attract students to participate by providing a simple to utilize, gaming-like environment in which they are able to discover new things. It provides fun, free, interactive, research-based science and mathematics simulations. The simulations are written in HTML5 (with some legacy simulations in Java or Flash) and can be processed online or downloaded on personal computers. All simulations are open source.

PhET uses several tools in the simulations to provide an interactive experience such as: click and drag to interact with simulation features, use sliders to increase and decrease parameters, choose between options with radio buttons, make measurements in your experiments with various instruments – rulers, stop-watches, voltmeters, and thermometers.

As users interact with these tools, they get immediate feedback about the effect of the changes they made. That allows them to investigate the simulation to uncover answers to scientific issues while looking into cause-and-effect linkages.

- AI-Based Proctoring Solutions: Implement AI-driven proctoring tools such as Proctorio or ExamSoft to maintain exam integrity during remote assessments. These tools use facial recognition and behavior analysis to deter cheating.

Proctoring is software that works based on artificial intelligence (AI). The student'scomputer gets connected to this software during this system test. A camera is mounted on a computer or laptop monitor. Due to artificial intelligence, there is complete monitoring of the movement of the student's eyes and hands. Consider, for instance, the utilization of a mobile device or a book during an examination. The system tracks the fingerprint's proximity to the keyboard while ensuring the absence of any other individuals in the room. Simultaneously, it monitors all software activities through the camera's "third eye." Alerts are triggered if a student turns or moves excessively, signaling potential misconduct. Following two warnings, a third violation results in the student being disqualified from the exam. Technological advancements have spurred numerous transformations in higher education, with fair proctoring being a notable development. The growing landscape of online instruction has further emphasized the necessity for online proctoring. As illustrated in Figure 1, online exams offer various advantages. The surge in online proctoring is particularly evident amid the global pandemic, accompanied by concerns arising within the home environment where students undertake exams under the vigilant gaze of third-party proctoring systems. (Aurelia et al, 2023)

Figure 10. Features offered by Proctorio platform to secure exams

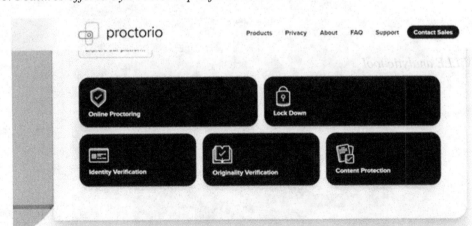

5. NAVIGATING TEACHER AD STUDENTS SUPPORT AND PROFESSIONAL DEVELOPMENT USING AI

AI has been utilized to support teachers in their roles. for lesson planning, automated grading, and personalized professional development.

- Personalized Professional Development Plans: AI tools analyze a teacher's strengths, such as proficiency in technology integration, and areas for improvement, like student engagement strategies. Based on this analysis, a personalized plan is generated, recommending workshops, courses, or resources aligned with the teacher's needs.

Enhanced by artificial intelligence, learning analytics solutions have emerged to reinforce and augment various teaching methodologies, particularly within the realm of mathematics. Several tools have been created to assist educators in this endeavor. The Eduten platform, for instance, furnishes teachers with weekly plans and streamlines the assessment process through automation. Similarly, the ViLLE platform is specifically crafted to aid teachers in generating or choosing digital content that fosters computational thinking skills. Moreover, the system is adept at facilitating teachers in the automated assessment of student performance. (Celik et al., 2022)

Figure 11. Edute platform analysis to personalize learning

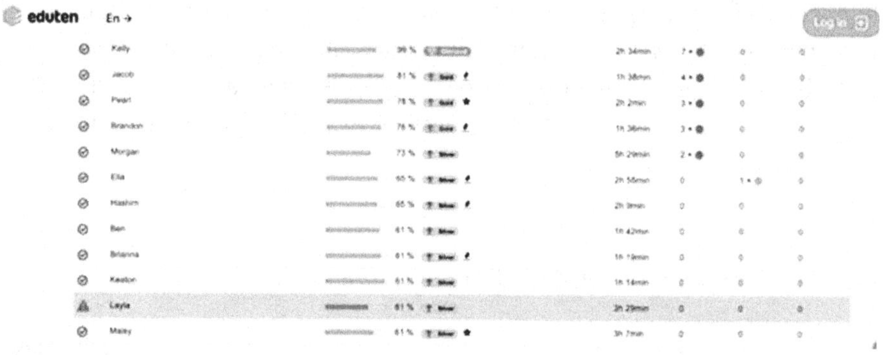

Figure 12. ViLLE analytic tool

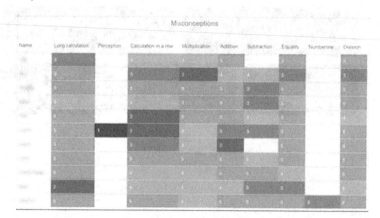

- AI-Powered Learning Management Systems (LMS): An AI-enhanced LMS tracks a teacher's and student's interactions within the system, noting preferences for certain types of content and learning formats. Based on the teacher's student options, the system then suggests appropriate educational courses, exercises, webinars, and conferences.
- A learning management system incorporating artificial intelligence (AI) elements allows teachers and students to streamline and organize their online learning environment. This type of system is also referred to as machine learning or AI-powered LMS. These functions involve tracking grades, assessing student progress, and optimizing content management.

In the following some of the AI-powered Learning Management Systems and their features:

Canvas by Instructure

- Adaptive Learning: Based on performance of learners, Canvas utilizes AI to personalize learning paths and update content.
- Analytics: By detecting students who are at risk, predictive analytics enables immediate action.

Blackboard Learn

- Virtual tutoring: Blackboard may also be incorporated with IBM Watson along with other virtual tutoring platforms to offer students AI-driven guidance.
- Natural Language Processing (NLP) Chatbots: Chatbots that respond to questions from students and offer guidance are powered by natural language processing.

Edmodo

- Automated Assessments: Edmodo employs AI for automated grading and provides instant feedback to students.
- Content Curation: AI algorithms recommend educational resources tailored to individual learning preferences.

Knewton

- Adaptive Learning Engine: To customize the method of delivery of content, Knewton's adaptive learning engine analyzes student data.
- Continuous Learning: Recommended additional assignments to continually enhance skills and knowledge.

Coursera

- Predictive Analytics: Coursera utilizes AI to predict learner success and recommends study strategies accordingly.
- Security Measures: AI is employed to monitor and detect unusual patterns during online assessments to prevent fraud.

D2L Brightspace

- Virtual Mentoring: Students can establish objectives while receiving specific suggestions with the support of D2L's Intelligent Agent tool.
- Continuous Improvement: AI analytics provides data on how effective courses are in addition to recommendations for improvements.

McGraw-Hill Connect

- Adaptive Learning Modules: McGraw-Hill Connect makes use of artificial intelligence (AI) to adjust the complexity of questions depending on the student's performance.
- Customized Study Plans: AI creates personalized study schedules to assist students in focusing on their areas of weakness.

Squirrel AI

- AI Tutors: Squirrel AI offers tutoring services driven by AI that adjust to the personal learning preferences and speed of the learner.
- Big Data Analytics: Improves and enhances its adaptive learning algorithms by analyzing massive amounts of student data.

Figure 13. SquairAi platform

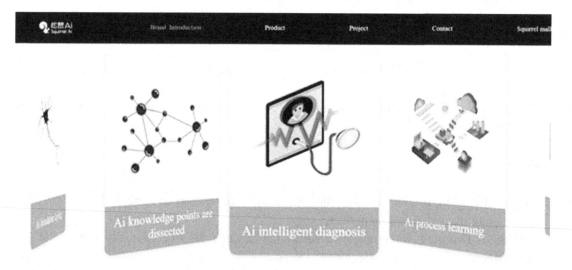

These examples showcase how AI is integrated into Learning Management Systems to enhance personalization, adaptability, and overall effectiveness in education. Each system employs AI technologies to address specific educational challenges and provide a more tailored learning experience.

- Automated Lesson Plan Evaluation: AI algorithms evaluate lesson plans against predefined criteria, providing instant feedback on elements such as learning objectives, assessment strategies, and alignment with curriculum standards. This ensures that lesson plans meet quality standards.

Automated Lesson Plan Evaluation involves using technology and algorithms to assess the effectiveness, alignment, and quality of educational lesson plans the evaluation can assess the content Relevance to ensure alignment with educational standards and curriculum objectives, assess the differentiation and inclusion by checking for the incorporation of differentiated instruction and inclusive practices to accommodate students with various abilities and backgrounds, assess the learning objectives Alignment to evaluates whether the stated learning objectives in the lesson plan align with the overall course objectives, assess the strategies it assesses whether the chosen methods effectively measure the attainment of learning objectives and provide a comprehensive view of student understanding, assess the engagement and Interactivity Evaluation, assess the technology Integration, assess the alignment with learning styles, assess the language and clarity.

Lesson Plans AI: This platform uses AI to generate lesson plans based on your input and then provides feedback on their alignment with learning objectives, engagement potential, and differentiation for various learning styles, AiLessonPlan: This tool helps teachers create custom lesson plans and also offers an AI-powered "Smart Review" feature that analyzes the plan for alignment with standards, engagement factors, and potential differentiation strategies, and automated lesson plan evaluation streamlines the process for educators, providing quick feedback on the quality of their instructional materials and helping enhance the overall teaching and learning experience.

AI algorithms can curate lesson plans, videos, and other instructional materials based on the individual teacher's needs and preferences. Teachers can ask specific questions, and the system provides targeted resources, and it provides AI-powered video coaching platform designed to support teachers' professional development, Such as: TeacherAdvisor from IBM, Edthena, Cognii, Microsoft Education Insights and Squirrel AI

Figure 14. AiLessonPlan features

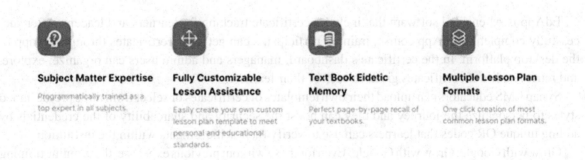

Subject Matter Expertise
Programmatically trained as a top expert in all subjects.

Fully Customizable Lesson Assistance
Easily create your own custom lesson plan template to meet personal and educational standards.

Text Book Eidetic Memory
Perfect page-by-page recall of your textbooks.

Multiple Lesson Plan Formats
One click creation of most common lesson plan formats.

- Virtual Coaching Assistants: Virtual coaching assistants use natural language processing to analyze teacher-student interactions during online classes. They offer immediate suggestions for improving engagement, fostering a positive learning environment, and addressing potential challenges Here are some examples to consider: Coach.me: Utilizes AI to recommend coaching activities and resources based on your needs and goals it features include goal setting, progress tracking, and feedback management, Grow with Google: Leverages Google's AI expertise to offer personalized insights and recommendations for educators. Focuses on professional development, classroom management, and student engagement.

Degreed uses AI to automate tasks like data entry, credential verification, and expiration tracking. It also uses machine learning to recommend relevant training and development opportunities to employees.

- Collaborative Professional Learning Networks: An AI-driven platform identifies teachers with shared interests or expertise in specific subjects. It facilitates connections and collaborations, enabling teachers to share best practices, exchange lesson plans, and engage in joint projects.

Microsoft Teams for Education employs AI features to facilitate the formation of collaborative learning networks among teachers, BloomBoard uses AI to match educators based on their teaching styles, subject expertise, and professional development needs.

Some educational institutions create custom Professional Learning Communities with AI integration. These platforms analyze teachers' expertise, preferences, and collaborative activities to identify peers with shared interests.

Through AI algorithms in specific events, it's possible to analyze attendees' profiles and match them based on shared interests or professional backgrounds LinkedIn, and Facebook using this algorithm to connect likeminded members, it can analyze vast amounts of attendee data, identifying trends and patterns that might go unnoticed by human analysis.

- Automated Certification Tracking: AI tools manage and track teachers' professional certifications. They provide timely notifications about upcoming certification renewals, suggest relevant professional development courses, and ensure compliance with ongoing requirements.

EdApp is AI enabled software that includes certificate tracking for learners and leaders. After successfully completing EdApp course, training participants can get their certificates through the app or the desktop platform. In the certificate's dashboard, managers and admin users can organize, explore, and retrieve a list of certificates given to each of their learners.

Synap LMS educators can upload their own templates of certificates or select from three pre-designed styles to personalize the journey and they can boost the security and shareability of the credentials by adding unique QR codes that learners can use to verify their achievements within the institution.

Grow with Google: Grow with Google: Even for those without previous expertise, these online training courses give learners highly-desired skills in rapidly growing industries like IT support, data analytics, and user experience design. compared to conventional certificates, Google's curriculum stresses application in real life and real-world assignments rather than just academic understanding. Upon completion, participants earn a certificate recognized by industry leaders, and are connected with potential employers

Figure 15. EdApp features and services

through Google's network. Moreover, Google doesn't require separate tracking of certificates; completion data is seamlessly integrated with your Google account, making verification and sharing effortless.

6. INCLUSIVE EDUCATION WITH AI

In typical classrooms, all students participate in learning activities at a uniform pace. However, learners with learning difficulties (LD), often characterized by a perceived lower efficiency in processing information, may encounter challenges in keeping up with the rest of the class, this may cause depression, poor academic performance, and low self-esteem. (Toyokawaet al., 2023)

The Jomtien, Thailand (1990) declaration, known as the World Declaration on Education for All, articulates a comprehensive vision: ensuring access to education for every child, youth, and adult globally while emphasizing equity. The commitment involves taking proactive measures to recognize and address the obstacles that hinder many individuals from accessing educational opportunities. Furthermore, it entails identifying the necessary resources to overcome these barriers and promote inclusivity in education. (UNESCO, 2009)

The literature in inclusive education concerning the application of AI and new technologies in inclusive education for minority students specifically, machine learning is an emerging technology gaining prominence in the education sector. There is a prevailing belief that AI and ML algorithms have the potential to customize learning experiences based on individual student needs. (Popenici & Kerr, 2017, Knox,2019, Yi, 2018)

Incorporating artificial intelligence (AI) into inclusive education apps has the potential to enrich the learning experiences of all students, catering to diverse needs. For instance:

- DreamBox utilizes AI algorithms to craft personalized learning paths, adjusting content based on individual performance.
- Microsoft Learning Tools integrates AI to offer features like speech-to-text and text-to-speech, aiding students facing challenges in reading and writing.
- zSpace employs augmented reality (AR) to design immersive, interactive learning experiences, offering particular advantages for students with varied learning styles and preferences.

- In the case of Flipgrid, it promotes collaborative learning through features enhanced by artificial intelligence (AI). This platform enables students to participate in video discussions, thereby nurturing communication and collaboration within diverse learner groups.
- Book Creator, an inclusive app, empowers students to create multimedia-rich content, utilizing AI features to generate accessible material suitable for various learning needs.
- Rethink Ed utilizes AI for social-emotional learning support, analyzing student behavior and providing resources to address emotional challenges, fostering a positive learning environment.
- Additionally, Google Translate, powered by AI, assists English language learners and speakers of other languages. These examples represent just a fraction of the diverse AI applications in inclusive education.

Figure 16. The home page of Flipgrid

Create a group and invite students   Post a topic   Watch the magic

7. AI FOR TEACHERS AND STUDENTS' WELLBEING AND BURNOUT

Predictive analytics algorithms analyze factors such as workload, student behavior data, and teacher feedback. Early warning signs of burnout are identified, allowing administrators to intervene with targeted support and resources. In addition to mitigating burnout, AI holds the promise of bolstering teachers and students' well-being through the enhancement of work-life balance. By automating time-intensive responsibilities, educators can regain valuable hours beyond the classroom, affording them more time for personal and family pursuits. This refined equilibrium not only contributes to overall well-being but also serves as a preventative measure against teacher exhaustion, ultimately fostering positive outcomes for both educators and students (TeachFlow, 2023).

Various AI applications are advancing well-being support, with examples like Woebot an AI chatbot providing mental health support through engaging conversations; Affectiva, an AI platform using facial and vocal emotion recognition technology; Headspace and other meditation apps that utilize AI to provide individuals with customized experiences; wearable technology that uses healthcare artificial intelligence (AI) to track stress, sleeping patterns, and exercise routines, such as Fitbit and Apple Watch; Wysa, is an AI-powered mental health software that offers a virtual therapy; Spring Health is a platform that evaluates the risk of mental health problems and burnout using statistical analysis. These applications, which range from virtual therapy to recognizing emotions and proactive burnout prevention, highlight the various roles that AI performs in supporting mental health and overall wellness.

Figure 17. Waysa app features

8. SMART IN-CAMPUS SOLUTIONS

The effectiveness of Smart Campus monitoring is boosted by the widespread use of sensors and actuators integrated to bolster geospatial IoT awareness. More precisely, predictions of geospatial location and estimations of arrival time are achievable thanks to stochastic processes reliant on IoT networks. Within these systems, a publish-subscribe utility can be employed to allocate sensors' activity to specific geospatial data sources containing observed measurements utilized for surveillance objectives (Anagnostopoulos et al., 2021).

In the contemporary fast-paced landscape, technology, particularly Artificial Intelligence (AI), has seamlessly woven itself into the fabric of our daily lives, exerting a profound impact on educational settings. Institutions of higher learning, such as colleges and universities, are swiftly embracing AI to cultivate 'Smart Campuses'— technologically enriched environments that bring about substantial enhancements in the student experience, operational efficiency, and educational achievements.

The smart campus is meticulously designed to offer personalized services, tailoring all functions to meet the specific needs of teachers and students in their daily lives, learning endeavors, and professional work. Essential technologies supporting the smart campus encompass learning scenario recognition, environmental perception technology, connected mobile campus technology, and social network analysis technology. Among these, context-awareness technology stands out as the foundational element. Within the smart campus, comprehensive perception involves two key aspects. Firstly, sensors are deployed to continuously capture and transmit information about individuals, devices, and resources from any location at any time. Secondly, there is a focus on recognizing, capturing, and delivering information about learners' characteristics, including learning preferences, cognitive traits, attention status, and learning styles, as well as details about learning scenarios such as time, location, space, learning partners, and activities (Yu Yu Lu, 2021).

The Integration of AI and Advanced Technologies In-Campus

A smart campus transcends the aggregation of disparate applications or technologies within the academic domain. It integrates advanced technologies, such as artificial intelligence, machine learning in:

Facial recognition, the foundational AI platform delivers a sophisticated and user-friendly experience within the campus environment. Users can engage with the AI system through various interfaces, including video, voice, gesture, and touch. This AI platform is intricately designed to cater to the specific needs of the campus community, facilitating seamless interactions and optimizing operational processes, TechU showcases a comprehensive integration of AI technologies across various interfaces, contributing to a technologically advanced and user-friendly campus environment. Remember, this is a fictional example, and the implementation of such technologies depends on the policies, regulations, and decisions of each specific institution.

Smart sensors strategically, and enabling functions like automated attendance tracking, Within the smart campus framework, significant documents and items are equipped with QR codes and GPS labels, allowing the system to effectively perceive and monitor their locations. This system serves the dual purpose of facilitating the positioning and monitoring of vehicles entering and exiting the campus, thereby ensuring orderly traffic management. An essential security measure involves the strategic placement of intelligent sensors in crucial campus areas and essential facilities. These sensors play a pivotal role in alerting the management center to any suspicious circumstances and conducting a thorough analysis of the incident. The incorporation of Radio-Frequency Identification (RFID) technology into the identification cards of teachers and students, as well as into books, instruments, elevators, lamps, and various other items, offers a comprehensive solution for personnel management (Yu Lu, 2021). This includes access to buildings, intelligent attendance tracking in classrooms and conferences, self-service borrowing and returning of resources, anti-theft measures, positioning of valuable equipment, laboratory control, and the management of lighting, air conditioning, and ventilation systems.

Venue analytics, leveraging artificial intelligence (AI) for venue analytics entails utilizing advanced technologies to analyze data gathered within venues like stadiums, conference centers, or entertainment venues. The primary objective is to boost operational efficiency, enhance visitor experiences, and optimize venue management. Key applications include crowd management, predictive maintenance, analysis of visitor behavior, personalized experiences, security and threat detection, heatmaps and foot traffic analysis, as well as sentiment analysis. These AI-driven applications collectively contribute to a comprehensive approach for improving the overall functionality and appeal of diverse event venues.

Process automation, incorporating artificial intelligence (AI) into process automation entails harnessing AI technologies to optimize and streamline diverse business processes. Workflow optimization, cognitive automation, robotic process automation (RPA), natural language processing (NLP), intelligent document processing, predictive analytics, and machine learning in decision-making are some of the significant uses and advantages of integrating AI into process automation. This integration enhances thinking skills, promotes productivity, while rendering informed decisions easier throughout a range of organizational functions.

Some Best Practices of Using AI In-Campus Solutions

Several procedures center on using AI to intelligent solutions on campus, such as:

The football field at Arizona State University's football stadium has recently undergone a $300 million restoration which involved the installation of smart sensors and cameras to improve its efficiency in operation. For example, these sensors are designed to send data regarding water usage, concession sales, and even noise levels in the surrounding area. has received a $300 million refurbishment that includes intelligent sensors and cameras aimed at enhancing operational efficiencies. These sensors, for instance, are designed to transmit data on various aspects such as water consumption, concession sales, and even ambient noise levels.

The Oizom intelligent algorithms communicate data by presenting suggestive actions for citizens, empowering them to make healthcare decisions based on data. Additionally, this solution provides the maintenance crew and real estate management with a comprehensive overview of environmental conditions within their premises (Oizom, 2020).

Figure 18. Oizom smart campus

Cisco's Smart Building Solution is a transformative initiative embedded in various living labs, aiming to establish intuitive and intelligent facilities that contribute to public health, productivity, sustainability, and energy efficiency. Positioned as the fourth utility, the network is integral to the smart building concept. Comprising five key building blocks, including Cisco Catalyst Series switches, collaboration devices, case studies, a smart campus of the future, and Cisco Spaces, the solution integrates cutting-edge technologies. Notably, it leverages Cisco Catalyst access points for sustainability benefits, such as adjusting thermostats based on occupancy. The use of advanced networks facilitates real-time insights, behavior optimization, and deep analytics to create smarter workplaces. The incorporation of Software-Defined Access, aligned with intent-based networking principles, brings policy-based automation, end-to-end segmentation, and improved operational effectiveness to the forefront. Cisco's Smart Building Solution extends its impact to hybrid learning, sustainability, and smart zero initiatives, showcasing a comprehensive and forward-looking approach to building intelligence (Cisco, 2023).

Figure 19. SMP security robot

By presenting a rich tapestry of case studies and best practices, this chapter provides a nuanced understanding of the transformative impact of AI in diverse educational contexts. Each case study will offer valuable insights into the practical implementation of AI-enhanced teaching methods and contribute to a collective understanding of successful strategies for educational transformation, with clear links to the AI example in specific implementation and will show case some countries, institutions and big companies' best practices and highlight some successful examples.

9. CHALLENGES AND CONSIDERATIONS

- **Ethical and Social Implications:**

The incorporation of AI into teacher education brings forth notable ethical and social considerations. One primary concern revolves around the potential biases embedded within AI algorithms, which could exacerbate existing societal disparities. Additionally, apprehensions arise regarding data privacy and security, given the substantial volumes of information gathered by AI systems on both students and educators. Traditionally, humanities departments evaluate students based on their essays, and the conferment of doctorates often hinges on the quality of thesis compositions. However, there are apprehensions regarding the ramifications of automating the essay-writing process on originality and ethical standards. Several researchers argue that the advent of generative AI may fuel ethical dilemmas, as students might exploit AI capabilities to attain academic accolades (Thurzo et al., 2023; Qadir, 2022).

- **Technical Hurdles:**

Incorporating AI into teacher education also entails various technical obstacles. One such challenge is the substantial computational resources demanded by AI systems, which may not be universally accessible across educational environments. Additionally, designing and developing AI systems pose their own set of challenges, including the imperative to guarantee accuracy, reliability, and validity. (Afiya, 2023)

- **Cultural Barriers:**

Incorporating AI into teacher education may encounter cultural resistance. Some teachers and educators may perceive AI as a threat to their professional autonomy, leading to reluctance in its adoption. Moreover, AI technologies engage with diverse global societies and cultures, each with its own unique values and interpretive norms, potentially leading to cultural discrepancies. It is imperative to address these cultural incongruences. (Prabhakaran et al., 2022)

- **Addressing Research Plagiarism:**

While open AI chatbot platforms such as ChatGPT aid in text generation, failure to cite sources properly or obtain consent from copyright holders can result in legal disputes if a researcher utilizes AI-generated text without appropriate acknowledgment. (Thurzo et al., 2023)

While the challenges mentioned above highlight significant hurdles in the integration of AI into teacher education, it's important to recognize that they represent only a portion of the complexities involved. Beyond technical, ethical, and cultural challenges, there are additional factors to consider. These may include issues related to accessibility, funding constraints, scalability, and the need for ongoing professional development. Moreover, the rapid pace of technological advancements introduces new challenges and considerations that educators and policymakers must continually address. Therefore, while acknowledging the identified challenges is crucial, it's equally essential to remain vigilant and adaptive in navigating the evolving landscape of AI in education.

10. CONCLUSION

Artificial Intelligence (AI) has profoundly transformed education, reshaping the learning experience for students in two keyways: by delegating teacher responsibilities to AI systems and enhancing human intelligence through personalized feedback and collaborative learning. Personalized learning journeys, a potent instructional strategy, tailor the learning process to individual needs, preferences, and goals. AI-driven adaptive learning platforms like Knewton and DreamBox provide customized content, fostering increased engagement, improved competency, and enriched teacher-student interactions. In the realm of assessments and feedback systems, AI-powered tools have revolutionized the evaluation process. Adaptive assessments and feedback systems, utilizing AI algorithms, deliver real-time feedback, identify areas for improvement, and contribute to nuanced grading. Platforms such as Smart Sparrow and Khan Academy's AI-driven system offer dynamic assessments and immediate feedback, ensuring appropriate challenges and personalized guidance for students. AI has also facilitated collaborative learning through platforms like Piazza, where algorithms identify proficient students to assist struggling peers, fostering knowledge sharing. Automated grading systems like Gradescope and Turnitin Feedback Studio streamline the grading process, providing quicker feedback and enabling real-time progress tracking for students. However, integrating AI into education poses challenges, including the need to address privacy and ethical concerns and ensure alignment with human values. Striking a balance between leveraging AI for its benefits, considering ethical implications, and maintaining human interactions is crucial. Overall, AI has the potential to revolutionize education by personalizing learning experiences, offering adaptive assessments, and enhancing teaching and learning effectiveness. Its integration can create a more inclusive and engaging learning environment, empowering students as independent learners and cultivating a culture of lifelong learning.

REFERENCES

D2L. (n.d.). *Brightspace*. Retrieved from https://www.d2l.com/brightspace/

Affectiva. (n.d.). Retrieved from https://www.affectiva.com/

AILessonPlan. (n.d.). Retrieved from https://ailessonplan.com/

Anagnostopoulos, T., Kostakos, P., Zaslavsky, A., Kantzavelou, I., Tsotsolas, N., Salmon, I., . . . Harle, R. (2021). Challenges and solutions of surveillance systems in IoT-enabled smart campus: a survey. *IEEE Access, 9*, 131926-131954.https://ieeexplore.ieee.org/abstract/document/9543662

Aurelia, S., Thanuja, R., Chowdhury, S., & Hu, Y. C. (2023). AI-based online proctoring: A review of the state-of-the-art techniques and open challenges. *Multimedia Tools and Applications*, *83*(11), 1–23. doi:10.1007/s11042-023-16714-x

Baker, R. S. (2016). Stupid tutoring systems, intelligent humans. *International Journal of Artificial Intelligence in Education*, *26*(2), 600–614. doi:10.1007/s40593-016-0105-0

Blackboard. (n.d.). *Log in to Learn.* Retrieved from https://help.blackboard.com/Learn/Student/Ultra/Getting_Started/Log_in_to_Learn

Bloomboard. (n.d.). Retrieved from https://bloomboard.com/

Business, A. I. (2021, August). *Microsoft uses new machine learning model to enhance Bing searches.* https://aibusiness.com/ml/microsoft-uses-new-machine-learning-model-to-enhance-bing-searches

Celik, I., Dindar, M., Muukkonen, H., & Järvelä, S. (2022). The promises and challenges of artificial intelligence for teachers: A systematic review of research. *TechTrends*, *66*(4), 616–630. doi:10.1007/s11528-022-00715-y

Cisco. (n.d.). *Smart Campus Living Lab*. https://www.cisco.com/c/dam/global/en_au/solutions/industries/government/smart-campus-living-lab.pdf

Cloud, G. (n.d.). *Dialogflow*. Retrieved from https://cloud.google.com/dialogflow

Coach.me. (n.d.). Retrieved from https://www.coach.me/

Coursera. (n.d.). Retrieved from https://www.coursera.org/

Creator, B. (n.d.). *Book Creator*. Retrieved from https://bookcreator.com/

Degreed. (n.d.). Retrieved from https://degreed.com/

Department of Defense Education Activity. (n.d.). *English Language Arts Curriculum*. Retrieved from https://www.dodea.edu/curriculum/english-language-arts-ela

Desmarais, M. C., & Baker, R. S. D. (2012). A review of recent advances in learner and skill modeling in intelligent learning environments. *User Modeling and User-Adapted Interaction*, 22(1-2), 9–38. doi:10.1007/s11257-011-9106-8

DreamBox. (n.d.). Retrieved from https://www.dreambox.com/

EdApp. (n.d.). Retrieved from https://www.edapp.com/

Edmodo. (n.d.). Retrieved from https://edmodo.online

Edshelf. (n.d.). *Education Technology Dictionary*. Edshelf. https://edshelf.com/education-technology-dictionary/

Flip. (n.d.). *Flip Learning*. Retrieved from https://info.flip.com/en-us.html

Google. (n.d.-a). *Google Certificates*. Retrieved from https://grow.google/intl/en_ph/certificates/

Google. (n.d.-b). *Google Digital Skills*. Retrieved from https://grow.google/intl/mena/

Gose, B. (2016). When the teaching assistant is a robot. *The Chronicle of Higher Education*.

IBM. (n.d.). *Chatbots*. IBM. https://www.ibm.com/topics/chatbots

Instructure. (n.d.). *Canvas*. Retrieved from https://www.instructure.com/canvas

Jamal, A. (2023). The Role Of Artificial Intelligence (AI) In Teacher Education: Opportunities & Challenges. *International Journal of Research and Analytical Reviews, 10*(1). Retrieved 31 March 2024 from: https://www.researchgate.net/profile/Afiya-Jamal/publication/369384184_The_Role_of_Artificial_Intelligence_AI_in_Teacher_Education_Opportunities_Challenges/links/64197dd792cfd54f8418b429/The-Role-of-Artificial-Intelligence-AI-in-Teacher-Education-Opportunities-Challenges.pdf

Khan Academy. (n.d.). *About*. Retrieved from https://www.khanacademy.org/about

Knewton. (n.d.). Retrieved from https://www.knewton.com/

Knox, J., Yu, W., & Gallagher, M. (2019). *Artificial intelligence and inclusive education*. Springer Singapore. doi:10.1007/978-981-13-8161-4

Labster. (n.d.). *Platform Overview*. Retrieved from https://www.labster.com/platform-overview

LessonPlans.ai. (n.d.). Retrieved from https://www.lessonplans.ai/

McGraw Hill. (n.d.). *McGraw Hill Education*. Retrieved from https://accounts.mheducation.com/login

Microsoft. (n.d.-a). *Copilot in Bing: Our approach to responsible AI*. Microsoft Support. https://support.microsoft.com/en-us/topic/copilot-in-bing-our-approach-to-responsible-ai-45b5eae8-7466-43e1-ae98-b48f8ff8fd44

Microsoft. (n.d.-b). *Microsoft Copilot.* Retrieved from https://www.microsoft.com/en-us/microsoft-copilot

Molenaar, I. (2021). Personalisation of learning: Towards hybrid human-AI learning technologies. *Blockchain, and Robots*, 57-77. https://ogamify.com/gamification/duolingo-case-study/

Oizom. (n.d.). *Smart Campus Monitoring.* Retrieved from https://oizom.com/wp-content/uploads/2020/12/Oizom_Smart_Campus_Monitoring_V4-1.pdf

OpenA. I. (n.d.). *ChatGPT.* Retrieved from https://chat.openai.com/

Popenici, S. A., & Kerr, S. (2017). Exploring the impact of artificial intelligence on teaching and learning in higher education. *Research and Practice in Technology Enhanced Learning*, *12*(1), 1–13. doi:10.1186/s41039-017-0062-8 PMID:30595727

Prabhakaran, V., Qadri, R., & Hutchinson, B. (2022). *Cultural Incongruencies in Artificial Intelligence, Computer Science, Computers and Society.* Cornel University. https://doi.org//arXiv.2211.13069 doi:10.48550

QadirJ. (2022). Engineering Education in the Era of ChatGPT: Promise and Pitfalls of Generative AI for Education. TechRxiv. doi:10.36227/techrxiv.21789434.v1

Rethink, E. D. (n.d.). *RethinkED.* Retrieved from https://www.rethinked.com/

Rezaei, A. (2009). *LMS Field Guide.* California State University. https://home.csulb.edu/~arezaei/ETEC551/web/LMS_fieldguide_20091.pdf

Romero, C., & Ventura, S. (2020). Educational data mining and learning analytics: An updated survey. *Wiley Interdisciplinary Reviews. Data Mining and Knowledge Discovery*, *10*(3), e1355. doi:10.1002/widm.1355

SquirrelA. I. (n.d.). *Squirrel AI.* Retrieved from https://squirrelai.com/#

Synap. (n.d.). Synap. Retrieved from https://synap.ac/

TeachFlow. (2023). *The impact of AI on teachers wellbeing and burnout.* Author.

Thurzo, A., Strunga, M., Urban, R., Surovkova, J., & Afrashtehfar, K. I. (2023). Impact of Artificial Intelligence on Dental Education: A Review and Guide for Curriculum Update. *Education Sciences*, *13*(2), 150. doi:10.3390/educsci13020150

Toyokawa, Y., Horikoshi, I., Majumdar, R., & Ogata, H. (2023). Challenges and opportunities of AI in inclusive education: A case study of data-enhanced active reading in Japan. *Smart Learning Environments*, *10*(1), 67. doi:10.1186/s40561-023-00286-2

UNESCO. (2009). *Policy guidelines on inclusion in education.* UNESCO.

UNESCO. (n.d.). *Artificial Intelligence in Education.* UNESCO. https://ar.unesco.org/themes/ict-education/action/ai-in-education

University of Colorado Boulder. (n.d.). *PhET Interactive Simulations.* Retrieved from https://phet.colorado.edu/en/about

US Department of Education. (2016). *Future ready learning: Reimagining the role of technology in education*. Office of Educational Technology.

Vandewaetere, M., & Clarebout, G. (2014). Advanced technologies for personalized learning, instruction, and performance. Handbook of research on educational communications and technology, 425-437.

VentureBeat. (2021, August). *Microsoft details AI model designed to improve Bing search*. https://venturebeat.com/business/microsoft-details-ai-model-designed-to-improve-bing-search/

Woebot Health. (n.d.). Retrieved from https://woebothealth.com/

Wysa. (n.d.). Retrieved from https://www.wysa.com/

Xi, S. M. (2013). Application of natural language processing for information retrieval. *Applied Mechanics and Materials*, *380*, 2614–2618. doi:10.4028/www.scientific.net/AMM.380-384.2614

Yi, H. (2019). Robotics and kinetic design for underrepresented minority (URM) students in building education: Challenges and opportunities. *Computer Applications in Engineering Education*, *27*(2), 351–370. doi:10.1002/cae.22080

Yu, S., & Lu, Y. (2021). *An introduction to artificial intelligence in education*. Springer.

KEY TERMS AND DEFINITIONS

Chatbots: A chatbot is a computer program that simulates human conversation with an end user. Though not all chatbots are equipped with artificial intelligence (AI), modern chatbots increasingly use conversational AI techniques like natural language processing (NLP) to understand the user's questions and automate responses to them (IBM, 2023).

Chapter 12
Navigating the AI Landscape:
Student and Teacher Perceptions of AI in Assessments in High School and College Settings

Leesha Nicole Roberts
https://orcid.org/0000-0001-7881-0087
The University of Trinidad and Tobago, Trinidad and Tobago

Fanta N. Solomon
Bishop's Centenary College, Trinidad and Tobago

Reccia Cummings
The University of Trinidad and Tobago, Trinidad and Tobago

ABSTRACT

This chapter examines AI's role in Caribbean high school and college assessments, analyzing teacher and student perspectives. A quantitative study surveyed 160 students and 102 teachers via Google Forms in September 2023, investigating AI tool usage, its effects on grading and feedback, fairness, and ethical concerns. Key findings include students' prevalent use of Grammarly and ChatGPT and plagiarism software by teachers, with significant AI encounters at the high school level. Positive correlations emerged between teachers' views on AI's grading efficiency, optimism for its future, and students' appreciation for AI's timely feedback. Concerns about AI-induced discrimination showed no significant differences across countries or educational levels, highlighting ethics and transparency as crucial. The need for targeted AI integration training is emphasized, suggesting future research should address AI biases and explore new tools for enhancing Caribbean educational outcomes.

DOI: 10.4018/979-8-3693-2728-9.ch012

INTRODUCTION

Education in the Caribbean has undergone significant evolution shaped by a complex interplay of cultural, socioeconomic, and political factors across its diverse islands (Brissett, 2018). Historically, education in the Caribbean was driven by colonial interests, with European powers primarily establishing educational systems to serve their needs rather than the local populations (Campbell, 2003; Sherlock, 1950). Fast forward to the post-colonial era, many Caribbean countries sought to decolonize their education systems by incorporating local languages, history, and cultural traditions into the curriculum, but it has been a challenging transition (Brissett, 2021; Jules, 2008). Despite the challenges of the decolonization of educational systems, such as limited resources, inadequate infrastructure, and socioeconomic factors, the Caribbean has made significant academic strides in recent decades. Many countries have implemented initiatives to improve literacy rates, expand secondary and tertiary education access, and enhance vocational training opportunities (Ahmad, 2020; Brissett, 2021; Louisy, 2004).

Additionally, regional organizations such as the Caribbean Community (CARICOM) have promoted cooperation and collaboration in education, facilitating the exchange of ideas, resources, and best practices among member states. Furthermore, alignment with UNESCO's EFA goals has continued to move Caribbean education systems forward in a way that embraces 21st-century teaching and learning. Continued investment in education and a commitment to addressing systemic issues are essential for the region's future development and prosperity (UNESCO, 2023).

Caribbean nations have demonstrated notable progress in incorporating Information and Communication Technology (ICT) within educational frameworks in the past decade, enriching 21st-century learning methodologies (Mayne, 2014). This advancement aligns with the objectives of UNESCO's Education for All (EFA) initiative. Commenced in 2000, the EFA goals seek to guarantee inclusive and fair access to quality education for all, emphasizing the core tenets of accessibility, equity, and educational quality (Bowe, 2015).

However, Caribbean countries face challenges in ICT in education due to many socioeconomic and political factors. These challenges hinder the effective adoption of digital technologies in education. Additionally, the rapid emergence of Artificial Intelligence (AI) in education adds complexity to this issue, requiring careful policy consideration and strategic planning. This chapter examines AI's role in Caribbean high school and college assessments from the perspectives of teachers and students.

Education policymakers within the Caribbean stress the significance of tackling education-related challenges by implementing initiatives advocated by the Caribbean Community (CARICOM). CARICOM has sanctioned the use of UNESCO's guidance documents for the modernization and alignment of 21st-century skills, which includes guiding documents such as the ICT Competency Framework for Teachers, AI, and Education: A Guidance for Policymakers and the latest Guidance for Generative AI in Education and Research. These frameworks provide helpful direction for policymakers and educators to effectively integrate AI and digital technologies in education worldwide, accommodating the Caribbean's socioeconomic and political issues. Specifically, AI's increasing role in education for societal transformation is now an integral part of global discussions (Holmes & Miao, 2023; Mayne, 2014; Miao et al., 2021). Notably, AI is gaining traction in the Caribbean in education due to the sharp growth of ICTs in education and assessment practices.

CURRENT STATE OF ASSESSMENT PRACTICES AND CHALLENGES

In the Caribbean, assessment practices vary across countries and educational institutions, but there are some commonalities in the approaches used. Traditional methods such as entrance and exit examinations in the form of objective and constructed response tests to and from secondary schools remain remnants of colonial education practices. However, the emphasis on rote learning in the Caribbean has limitations, such as prioritizing memorizing facts over critical thinking and applying knowledge. While memorization can be imperative to the learning process, rote memorization hinders higher-order thinking and stifles student creativity and innovation (Ivie, 1998; Miedijensky et al., 2021). Additionally, standardized tests, such as the Caribbean Secondary Education Certificate (CSEC) examinations, pressure students and educators to perform well (De Lisle et al., 2017). Another commonality among Caribbean countries is the issue of large class sizes. Classrooms are often overcrowded, with large student-to-teacher ratios. As a result of overcrowding, students are disconnected from their lessons, teacher feedback becomes unmanageable, learning outcomes and overall educational experience are negatively impacted, and innovative and authentic assessment strategies are often never attempted (Chan, 2023). For example, the emerging trend of performance-based assessments requires students to demonstrate their skills in real-world contexts (Gao et al., 2024). Also, there is a need for more formative assessment practices that provide ongoing feedback to students to support their learning (McCallum & Milner, 2021).

The utilization of AI technologies has the potential to address various challenges and revolutionize assessment practices in the Caribbean at all school levels (i.e., early childhood, middle school, high school, and tertiary). The use of AI in assessments can be beneficial for primary school students in the Caribbean who are preparing for their transition to secondary schools and taking exams such as the Secondary Entrance Examination (SEA) in Trinidad, Primary Exit Profile (PEP) in Jamaica, and similar transitional exams throughout the region. AI can help revolutionize the learning experience for these students by offering personalized assessments that cater to their individual learning needs, making them better prepared for these critical exams. Teachers can benefit from AI's ability to automate grading and provide detailed insights into student performance, enabling targeted instruction. Parents can also benefit from AI-driven assessments by receiving real-time feedback on their child's progress, promoting a collaborative approach to education, and ensuring that students are well-prepared for these important exams.

Furthermore, these tools can analyze student data and identify patterns and trends to inform instructional strategies and curriculum development (VanLehn, 2011). Automated grading systems that utilize AI algorithms are already in use in the Caribbean to assess student work and provide immediate feedback to students, saving teachers time. Additionally, intelligent tutoring systems provide tailored instruction to students based on their specific learning needs and styles (Castaño-Muñoz et al., 2018). Additionally, AI in assessments can significantly enhance the learning experience for students with special needs by providing personalized and adaptive testing. For instance, AI can adjust the difficulty level of questions in real time based on a student's responses, ensuring that the assessment is neither too challenging nor too simplistic. This adaptability can help create a more equitable testing environment for special needs students.

Additionally, AI-powered tools can offer instant feedback, highlighting areas of improvement and success. This immediate feedback is crucial for special needs students, as it allows for timely intervention and support. Moreover, AI can assist in making assessments more accessible, with features like text-to-speech for students with reading difficulties or visual aids for those with visual impairments (Mouti & Rihawi, 2023). In fact, the use of AI in assessments can provide a more inclusive and supportive environment for special needs students, enabling them to demonstrate their knowledge and skills effectively and create that inclusive educational context as outlined in the EFA Goals.

Purposefully, applying AI technologies in assessment practices can potentially revolutionize the Caribbean education system. However, from an operational standpoint, if teachers and students utilize this emerging technology in their assessments, it is imperative to address critical ethical considerations. A significant challenge is to ensure that AI algorithms are designed and monitored to prevent biases and not disadvantage certain student groups (Baker & Hawn, 2021; Reeves & Lin, 2020). Furthermore, privacy and security concerns arise as these systems require access to large amounts of student data (Huang, 2023). It is essential to gather input from educators and students regarding their current assessment practices and the potential benefits or challenges of personalized feedback and informed instructional strategies when using AI in assessments. It is also crucial to weigh ethical considerations carefully to ensure these technologies are utilized reasonably and beneficially to promote the continued development of Caribbean information societies.

EMERGING AI TECHNOLOGIES IN CARIBBEAN EDUCATION

Overview of AI in Caribbean Education

In 2001, UNESCO created the Information for All Programme (IFAP) to guide the emerging global information society on the ethical, legal, and societal consequences of ICT developments for the organization's member states. Since numerous Caribbean countries are members of UNESCO, they have been guided by the support UNESCO provides for "…formulating information policies aimed at building inclusive, equitable and sustainable knowledge societies, including harnessing the opportunities offered by information and communication technologies (ICTs)" (UNESCO, 2023, p. 4). Through these efforts, the Caribbean continues to make strides in using ICTs in education, including AI among educational systems.

The definition of AI has been an ongoing discussion among education stakeholders, and several definitions have been proposed across various fields. UNICEF (2021, p. 16) explains that AI can be seen as computer-based systems that predict, recommend, or make decisions that impact real or virtual environments based on human-defined objectives. These systems interact with learners and affect their surroundings directly or indirectly. AI systems often operate autonomously and can adapt their behaviour by learning from their context by following rules, learning from examples (supervised or unsupervised), or through trial and error (reinforcement learning). Many AI applications, such as recommendation systems and intelligent robots, rely heavily on machine learning techniques for pattern recognition. By detecting patterns in data, computers can process text, voice, images, or videos and make informed plans and decisions accordingly.

Additionally, Holmes and Tuomi (2022) refer to the term "AI for Education (AIED) and have suggested that various learning theories can be associated with AI use in the teaching and learning environment. However, Fengchun and Wayne (2023), in their UNESCO eBook, specifically focused on Generative AI technology that produces content in response to prompts. These authors state that although AI can produce impressive output, it cannot generate new ideas or comprehend real-world objects or social relations. The AI responses are not always trustworthy, which creates implications for use within the educational context. The statement above highlights that AI technology can be an effective ICT instructional tool for teachers and students. It is utilized efficiently to attain favorable learning outcomes, enhancing the overall quality of assessment practices from a Caribbean context.

AI is increasingly revolutionizing education worldwide, including in the Caribbean region (UNESCO, 2023; UNICEF, 2021). In the Caribbean, AI is being embraced as a tool to enhance the quality and efficiency of education. One key area of AI integration is assessment practices. AI-powered assessment tools offer several advantages over traditional methods. They can provide real-time feedback to students and teachers, allowing immediate intervention and support. Additionally, AI can analyze vast amounts of data to identify patterns and trends in student performance, which can inform instructional strategies (Qin et al., 2020; Salas-Pilco & Yang, 2022).

One type of AI technology being adopted in Caribbean classrooms is automated grading systems. These systems use AI algorithms to assess student work, such as objective and constructed response tests, providing immediate feedback to students. AI feedback saves teachers time and allows students to learn from their mistakes more quickly. Automated grading systems can also help standardize assessment practices across schools and ensure consistency in grading. Another AI technology gaining popularity in the Caribbean is intelligent tutoring systems (ITS). ITS are computer programs that provide personalized instruction to students based on their learning needs and styles. These systems can adapt to each student's pace and level of understanding, providing additional support and challenges as needed. ITS can be particularly beneficial in math and science, where students may require extra practice or explanation. However, most of these AI systems originated from Western countries and do not entirely align with the Caribbean curriculum regarding the cultural context in which Caribbean education systems are trying to decolonize. However, during the COVID-19 lockdown periods, these ITS systems benefited many Caribbean learning contexts. In addition to assessment tools, AI is used in Caribbean classrooms to enhance the learning experience. For example, AI-powered chatbots can give students instant answers to their questions, helping them stay engaged and motivated. Virtual Reality (VR) and Augmented Reality (AR) are also being used to create immersive learning experiences, allowing students to explore complex concepts more interactively (Qin et al., 2020; Reeves & Lin, 2020; Salas-Pilco & Yang, 2022; UNICEF, 2021).

Although AI has made significant strides in Caribbean education, there are still challenges to its widespread adoption. One major obstacle is the limited infrastructure and resources available in certain Caribbean countries, which can hinder access to AI technologies. Additionally, ethical concerns such as data privacy and algorithm bias have been raised around the use of AI in education (Miao et al., 2021; Qin et al., 2020; UNESCO, 2023). Despite this, AI assessment technologies can be increasingly vital in Caribbean education. By embracing AI assessment, Caribbean educators can enhance their students' learning experiences and improve educational outcomes. However, it is crucial to address the challenges and ensure that AI technologies are implemented responsibly and ethically, particularly from the perspectives of teachers and students. Policymakers can incorporate their feedback when designing policies for the rapidly emerging area of assessment practices that AI is currently being embedded into within the Caribbean.

Implications for Fair Evaluations

Integrating AI technologies into assessment practices offers several potential benefits, including increased efficiency, personalized feedback, and standardized evaluation processes (Gardner et al., 2021; Holstein et al., 2018). AI-powered systems can analyze student responses in real time, identifying areas of strength and weakness and providing immediate feedback to students (Gardner et al., 2021). This feedback can help students improve their learning outcomes by allowing them to focus on areas where they need the most help (Castaño-Muñoz et al., 2018). Additionally, AI can help educators track student progress more effectively, enabling them to tailor instruction to meet individual needs (VanLehn, 2011).

Another potential benefit of AI in assessment is its ability to standardize evaluation processes (Hooda et al., 2022). AI algorithms can be trained to evaluate student work against predefined criteria, ensuring consistency in grading across different evaluators and institutions (Gao et al., 2024; Gardner et al., 2021). Standardizing assessments can help reduce bias and ensure students are evaluated based on their performance (Fang et al., 2023).

Despite these benefits, several challenges and ethical considerations are associated with using AI in assessment. One of the main challenges is ensuring the accuracy and reliability of AI algorithms (Baker & Hawn, 2021). AI systems are only as good as the data they are trained on, and if the data is biased or incomplete, it can lead to inaccurate assessments (Fengchun & Wayne, 2023). Additionally, there is a risk that AI algorithms could perpetuate or even amplify existing biases in assessments, mainly if they are not carefully designed and monitored (Hooda et al., 2022).

Another challenge is ensuring the security and privacy of student data (Baker & Hawn, 2021). AI systems require access to large amounts of student data to function effectively, raising concerns about data protection and privacy (UNICEF, 2021). Caribbean educators and policymakers must ensure that appropriate safeguards are in place to protect student data and that students are informed about how their data will be used (Miao et al., 2021; UNESCO, 2023; UNICEF, 2021).

Ethical considerations are also fundamental when using AI in assessment (Lim et al., 2023). Caribbean educators must ensure that assessments are fair and equitable for all students, regardless of their background or circumstances (Castaño-Muñoz et al., 2018). This requires careful consideration of the design and implementation of AI algorithms to minimize bias and ensure that assessments are culturally sensitive and inclusive (O'Reilly-Shah et al., 2020).

In educational settings, it is crucial to solicit feedback from teachers and students on integrating Artificial Intelligence (AI) in assessment practices. As critical stakeholders in the educational process, their perspectives provide valuable insights into the effectiveness and impact of AI tools in assessment. Understanding their viewpoints is essential, given the widespread use of AI tools for assignments and grading in secondary and college-level education. While students commonly utilize AI tools like Grammarly and ChatGPT, teachers often rely on AI for grading efficiency, highlighting the importance of understanding their experiences and perceptions regarding these tools. Despite the significance of their perspectives, research often overlooks them, focusing instead on the technical aspects of AI assessments or the impact AI assessments have on learning outcomes. This gap in research underscores the necessity for studies that explore teachers' and students' views on AI in assessments. Engaging teachers and students in research will yield valuable insights that can inform the development and implementation of AI technologies in assessments, ensuring their efficacy and alignment with educational objectives that consider all stakeholders at the operational level of education.

THE STUDY

This study focused on Caribbean teachers' and students' perspectives regarding integrating AI in high school and college educational assessments. The objectives of the study were to understand the frequency and nature of AI-based assessments encountered by students, explore teacher experiences with AI tools and their perceptions of their impact on grading efficiency and feedback, investigate student perceptions of AI's fairness, objectivity, and overall impact on their learning experience; and identify concerns and potential areas of improvement related to using AI in assessments from a Caribbean educational perspective.

The study used a quantitative approach and was restricted to secondary and tertiary levels of education in the Caribbean, where there is a higher likelihood of AI use. The researchers used the snowballing non-probability sampling method to collect data from teachers and students across the Caribbean who taught various subject areas in high schools and colleges over three weeks during the September 2023 school term. The researchers used this sampling method because of its flexibility and adaptability, where the researchers asked participants to assist researchers in identifying other potential participants. The strategy allowed teachers to share the student survey with their class and the teacher survey with colleagues in their school environment. Students were also able to recommend that their peers take the survey. Data was collected from both students and teachers using the Google Forms application. The researchers administered two surveys: one for students and another for teachers. Although the questionnaires had similar questions, the student survey had 30 questions, while the teacher survey had 36 questions. The researchers used these surveys to compare the perspectives of students and teachers on the use of AI in assessment. The survey questions covered various themes such as demographic information, experiences of students/teachers with the use of AI in assessments, educational policies about the use of AI in classrooms, and ethical considerations when using AI in assessments. These themes were based on the following research questions:

1. What is the frequency of AI-based tools used in assessments by high school and college students?
2. How do high school and college teachers rate the impact of AI tools on grading efficiency and feedback?
3. To what extent do high school and college students perceive AI-based assessments as fair and objective?
4. What are students' and teachers' most common concerns regarding using AI in educational assessments?

The data cleaning preceded the analysis, involving consistency checks and addressing missing responses. SPSS was used to identify out-of-range values with absent responses indicated by the "99" code. Univariate analysis focused on frequency analysis, and non-metric analysis was done on all survey items. The analysis determined the presence and stability of relationships between variables at the multivariate level, employing statistical tests such as mean, standard deviation, chi-square, Cramer's V, Spearman's correlation, and Kruskal-Wallis tests.

Cronbach's alpha measured the reliability of the two quantitative instruments, with internal consistencies of 0.767 for student survey questions, 0.91 for teacher questions, and 0.83 for combined questions. Bonett and Wright (2015) consider Cronbach's alpha ≥ 0.7 acceptable for internal consistency.

This section presents the results of the descriptive analysis of the teachers and students who participated in the survey. The teacher and student surveys were meant to find out about the frequency of AI-based tools students used for assessments, the impact of AI tools on grading efficiency and feedback among teachers, the perceptions of students that regard assessments as fair and objective, and the most common concerns expressed by both populations regarding the use of AI in educational assessments.

Demographic Insights

Researchers analyzed participant demographics to provide context for the study and identify potential variations in perspectives based on age, gender, education level, and teaching experience.

The population of this study was high school and college teachers in various subject areas with a range of qualifications. The intended sample was 160 participants in both surveys. The response rate for the student survey was 99.3%, and the teachers' survey was 63.75%. The analysis will look at the student and then the teacher demographics.

Student Demographics

There were 159 student participants in the study, with 86.2% identifying as female and 12.6% as male. The average age of participants was 31.8 years, with a relatively high standard deviation of 16.9 years. This substantial variance suggests a broad age range among participants, indicating that the sample includes younger and older individuals (18 to over 30 years). Participants resided in various countries, with the majority originating from Trinidad and Tobago (39.6%), followed by St Vincent and the Grenadines (23.9%), St Eustatius (13.8%), Grenada (6.3%), and Dominica (3.8%). The remaining countries each contributed between 1.3% and 2.5% of the participants. Regarding educational levels, 5% held an Associate Degree, 24.5% had a High School education, 0.6% were Technical College graduates, 5.7% were University Graduates, and 64.2% were University Undergraduates. This distribution indicates that most student participants were undergraduates, followed by high school students.

Teacher Demographics

In the study, 102 teachers participated, with 77.5% identifying as female and 22.5% as male. The age range of teachers spanned from 25 to over 55 years, with the highest percentage falling within the 35 to 44 age group (40.2%), followed by the 25–34 age group (21.6%), and then the 45–54 age group (20.6%). In examining the age distribution of the study participants, the mean age was found to be 20.4 years, with a notably high standard deviation of 14.3 years. This substantial variation indicates a wide age range among participants, highlighting the diverse nature of the sample. The breadth of this range suggests that the findings may be applicable across various age demographics, from adolescence to older adulthood. Regarding country of residence, the majority of teachers were from Trinidad and Tobago (77.5%), while the remaining participants hailed from countries such as St. Eustatius, St. Vincent and the Grenadines, Jamaica, Barbados, and others, comprising the remaining 22.5%. Teachers' areas of study varied from natural sciences to social sciences, reflecting the diverse subjects they taught. The data showed that most teachers (33.3%) had 11–20 years of teaching experience, followed by 30.4% with more than 20 years, 20.6% with 1–5 years, and 14.7% with 6–10 years of teaching experience.

Teachers' Experiences With AI

This section is related to the research question, "How do high school and college teachers rate the impact of AI tools on grading efficiency and feedback." The data explored teachers' encounters with AI-based assessment tools, including the impact on grading efficiency and feedback. The data revealed that most of the teachers encountered the use of AI in their High School classes (31.4%) and College Classes (22.5%).

The data reported here supports the assumption that since 65.2% of students' educational levels were undergraduates and 24.5% were high school students, teachers at the high school level seem to encounter the use of AI more frequently. Furthermore, a part of the data that stands out is that 19.6% of the teachers indicated, "I have not encountered AI-based assessments." According to (Kaplan-Rakowski et al., 2023), the more frequently teachers use AI, the more positive their perspectives on the technology tool will evolve. However, this result is reasonable given Caribbean teachers' various challenges regarding ICT integration and assessment practices.

Additionally, the data shows that when teachers were asked about the kinds of AI tools they have used or are aware of in their teaching context, the majority of teachers indicated that they used plagiarism detection software (44.1%), Automated grading systems (27.5%), and AI-generated quizzes/exams (17.6%). The remaining 5.9% used AI-driven personalized learning platforms, AI-driven writing tools, and ChatGPT. Nonetheless, 4.9% of the teachers said they never used AI tools in teaching and learning.

The researchers used a Spearman's correlation test to find out whether there was a correlation between teachers' perception of AI's impact on grading efficiency and their optimism about the future of AI in education, and the results indicated a moderate positive correlation between teachers' perception of AI's impact on grading efficiency and their optimism about the future of AI in education $r_s (100) = 0.455$, p $= 1.57$. These results suggest that teachers who perceive AI as improving grading efficiency tend to be more optimistic about the future of AI in education.

Equally important is the relationship between teachers' views on the fairness of AI assessments and their agreement with the need for strict ethical guidelines and oversight. The Spearman's correlation results indicated a moderate positive correlation between teachers' views on the fairness of AI assessments and their agreement with the need for strict ethical guidelines and oversight $r_s (100) = 0.492$, p $= 1.55$. These results suggest that teachers who view AI assessments as fair are also more likely to agree with the need for strict ethical guidelines and oversight. These findings provide valuable insights into teachers' attitudes towards AI in education, highlighting the interconnections between perceptions of AI's efficacy, fairness, and the importance of ethical considerations.

Furthermore, a Chi-Square Test of Independence assessed the association between gender and the learning context in which participants have encountered AI-based assessments. The learning contexts included various educational settings where AI assessments might be encountered. The results indicated no significant association between the learning context and gender, $\chi^1 = 1.33$, p $= .970$. To quantify the strength of this non-significant association, Cramér's V was calculated, yielding a value of 0.11. This value suggests a very weak association between the two variables. Given the high p-value and the low Cramér's V, the null hypothesis that there is no significant association between the learning context for AI-based assessments and gender cannot be rejected. These findings suggest that gender does not significantly influence the type of learning context in which individuals encounter AI-based assessments.

Additionally, A Chi-square test of independence was conducted to examine the relationship between the types of AI tools used and the educational level of respondents. The results indicated that there was no significant association between the types of AI tools used and the educational level of respondents, $\chi^1 = 15.07$, p $= 0.989$. Cramér's V was calculated as 0.17, suggesting a weak association between the variables. These results suggest that the types of AI tools used do not vary significantly based on the educational level of the respondents. The weak association between the variables indicates that while there may be some relationship, it is not strong enough to be considered significant. Finally, the association between the initial set of AI tools and participants' country of residence was analyzed using the Chi-square test of independence, and the results indicated no significant association, $\chi^{36} = 38.26$, p $=$

.367. This finding suggests that the country of residence does not significantly influence the selection of these AI tools. Moreover, the measure of association strength, Cramér's V, was calculated to be 0.25, denoting a weak association between country of residence and the use of these AI tools.

Students' Encounters With AI

This section is related to two research questions: "What is the frequency of AI-based tools used in assessments by high school and college students?" and "To what extent do high school and college students perceive AI-based assessments as fair and objective?" Specifically, the data examined students' experiences with AI-based assessments, focusing on the frequency of encounters, perceived fairness, and the impact on their learning experiences. The data revealed that students used Grammarly frequently when completing their graded assessments, ChatGPT, Google Bard (now called Gemini), and Bing Chat (now called Copilot). It should be noted that 17% of the students indicated they never used AI tools for assessments (see Table 1).

Table 1. Students use AI to complete school assignments

Students	Responses	Percent
Bing Chat	9	5.7%
ChatGPT	37	23.3%
Google Bard	17	10.7%
Grammarly	65	40.9%
Never Used AI Tools for Assessments	27	17.0%
OTHER: Cite fast	1	.6%
OTHER: Magic school. Ai	1	.6%
OTHER: Quill Bot	1	.6%
OTHER: Snapchat AI	1	.6%
Total	159	100.0%

Source:(Roberts, Solomon, and Cummings, 2024)

A Spearman's correlation test investigated the relationship between students' perceptions of artificial intelligence (AI) being used negatively in assessments and their comfort with AI systems analyzing and assessing their academic work. The results indicated a weak, negative correlation between the two variables, r_s (198) = -0.148, p = 0.062. This suggests that as students' perceptions of the negative use of AI in assessments increase, their comfort with AI analyzing and assessing their academic work slightly decreases. However, this correlation was not statistically significant at the conventional p < .05 level, failing to reject the null hypothesis of no significant relationship between the variables. Overall, the data reveals when students think AI is used negatively in assessments, they are a bit less comfortable with AI grading their work. However, this link is weak and is not strong enough to say it is definitely true. So, we cannot know for sure that how students feel about AI in tests affects how comfortable they are with AI grading their work.

A Spearman's correlation analysis was conducted to examine the relationship between students' comfort with artificial intelligence (AI) systems analyzing and assessing their academic work and their perception that AI assessments can provide more timely and valuable feedback compared to traditional methods. The analysis revealed a moderate, positive correlation $r_s(198) = -0.387$, p = 0.001, indicating that students comfortable with AI assessing their work are likelier to perceive AI assessments as providing timely and valuable feedback. Given the statistically significant p-value, the null hypothesis of no significant relationship between the variables was rejected, supporting the alternative hypothesis of a significant relationship.

A Chi-square test of independence was also conducted to examine the relationship between the types of AI tools used and students' age. The results indicated that there was no significant association, $\chi^{24} = 17.29$, p = 0.836. Cramér's V was calculated as 0.21, implying a weak association between the variables. Also, the relationship between the AI tools used and the participants' country of residence was examined using the Chi-square test of independence. The results indicated no significant association, $\chi^{36} = 38.26$, p = .367. This finding suggests that the country of residence does not significantly influence the selection of these AI tools. Moreover, the measure of association strength, Cramér's V, was calculated to be 0.25, denoting a weak association between country of residence and the use of these AI tools.

The Kruskal-Wallis H Test was conducted to analyze the differences in concern about potential discrimination in AI assessments across various countries of residence. The results revealed no statistically significant differences in the levels of concern about possible discrimination in AI assessments across different countries within the dataset $\chi^2 = 13.6164$, p = 0.3259. The p-value obtained from the Kruskal-Wallis H Test was greater than the common alpha levels (e.g., 0.05), indicating insufficient evidence to reject the Null Hypothesis (H_0). This suggests that perceptions of potential discrimination in AI assessments do not significantly vary by country of residence among the participants in this study.

A Kruskal-Wallis H test was performed to examine whether schools should prioritize ethics and transparency when addressing concerns related to AI in assessments across various countries of residence. The findings did not indicate a statistically significant difference in the emphasis on ethics and transparency in AI assessments among participants from different countries $\chi^2 (12) = 19.36$, p =.080. This outcome suggests that the valuation of ethics and transparency in the context of AI assessments does not significantly vary by country of residence among the survey participants,

Perceptions and Concerns

This section is related to "What are students' and teachers' most common concerns regarding using AI in educational assessments?" and will analyze responses to gauge the overall perceptions of students and teachers. Special attention was given to concerns about bias, privacy, and the potential for complementing traditional assessment methods.

A Spearman's rank-order correlation was conducted to assess the relationship between participants' perceptions of AI assessments' timeliness and usefulness compared to traditional methods and their preference for using AI assessments as a complement to traditional assessment methods. Results indicated a moderate, positive correlation between the two variables, $r_s(259) = 0.41$, p = .001, suggesting that participants who perceive AI assessments as providing more timely and valuable feedback are more likely to prefer using AI assessments to complement traditional assessment methods. This finding underscores the importance of addressing both the practical benefits and the complementary role of AI in education to enhance its acceptance among teachers and students.

In exploring the students' and teachers' perspectives on AI in education, a significant and moderate positive correlation was found between the belief in the importance of personalized AI assessments and the belief in AI's potential to enhance educational quality r_s (259) = 0.45, p = .001. This suggests a strong link between valuing personalized learning experiences facilitated by AI and recognizing the broader benefits of AI in improving educational outcomes. Such findings highlight the potential of AI to cater to individual learning needs while contributing to the overall improvement of education.

The data also revealed students' and teachers' perspectives on ethical considerations of AI in education. This study uncovered a significant and strong positive correlation between the advocacy for involving students, educators, and stakeholders in addressing AI-related ethical concerns and the belief in the necessity of prioritizing ethics and transparency in AI assessments r_s (259) = 0.59, p = .001. This correlation underscores a holistic view of ethical AI implementation among students and teachers in educational settings. It reflects a shared belief in the importance of both engaging a broad range of voices in ethical discussions and ensuring that clear ethical standards and transparency govern AI applications in assessments.

Additionally, in examining the interplay between ethical considerations in AI-assisted education among teachers and students, the data revealed no significant correlation between the belief that AI assessments respect and protect privacy and data security and concerns regarding potential discrimination in AI assessments r_s (259) = 0.03, p = .615. This outcome suggests that perceptions of AI's capability to safeguard privacy and data security are not closely related to apprehensions about discrimination through AI use in educational assessments. These findings highlight the complexity of ethical concerns surrounding AI in education, indicating that teachers and students may differentiate between various ethical dimensions, such as privacy and fairness when assessing AI technologies.

DISCUSSION

These results indicate that students generally perceive the efficiency and assistance provided by AI tools in completing assessments, with a significant majority finding these tools helpful. A considerable portion of students are either neutral or uncertain about the potential negative aspects of AI in assessments, including privacy, discrimination, and ethical issues. However, a considerable number of students also acknowledge these concerns, with more students agreeing or strongly agreeing than disagreeing or strongly disagreeing about the issues raised. These findings offer valuable insights into students' perceptions of AI in educational assessments, highlighting areas where more transparency, ethical considerations, and efforts to address privacy and fairness could improve acceptance and trust in AI-driven educational tools.

Equally important is the data on teacher perceptions about AI-based assessments. From the results presented, a significant number of teachers perceive AI-based assessments as improving the efficiency of grading and feedback, with a notable preference for timely and helpful feedback provided by AI over traditional methods. Additionally, there is a strong consensus that institutions should implement mechanisms for providing feedback on experiences with AI assessments. The results also indicated that while there is some neutrality and disagreement, a substantial portion of teachers perceive AI-based assessments as potentially fair and objective, especially when implemented with fairness and transparency. There is strong agreement in the belief that AI assessments can be valuable when they are fair and transparent, which highlights the importance of ethical considerations in AI implementation in education. The data also highlighted a consensus among teachers for a responsible, ethical, and inclusive approach to integrating AI into educational assessments. They underscore the importance of regulatory frameworks, ethical guidelines, stakeholder involvement, and awareness programs to address potential ethical issues and ensure AI technologies' fair, secure, and effective use in education.

When the teacher and student data were combined, the findings suggest that while there is interest in the potential benefits of AI in assessments, significant attention needs to be paid to addressing ethical concerns, reducing bias, and ensuring the privacy and security of assessment data.

FUTURE RESEARCH DIRECTIONS

Future research directions could address the identified concerns and challenges related to using AI in educational assessments. For example, researchers could investigate ways to mitigate bias in AI algorithms and ensure the privacy and security of student data. Additionally, studies could explore innovative AI tools and approaches that enhance the assessment process and improve learning outcomes for students in the Caribbean. Overall, the dynamic intersection of AI and educational assessments in the Caribbean presents opportunities and challenges that warrant further exploration and research.

CONCLUSION

In summary, the study provides valuable insights into the perspectives of teachers and students regarding the integration of AI in educational assessments in the Caribbean. While the results cannot be generalized, the findings suggest that while there is a growing recognition of the potential benefits of AI, such as improved grading efficiency and personalized feedback, there are also concerns about bias, privacy, and the need for ethical considerations.

For educational practice, the study highlights the importance of providing training and support to teachers and students to integrate AI tools into assessments effectively. Teachers should be encouraged to use various AI tools, such as plagiarism detection software and automated grading systems, to enhance their grading efficiency and provide timely feedback to students. Additionally, educators should prioritize ethics and transparency when using AI in assessments, ensuring that assessments are fair and objective for all students.

REFERENCES

Ahmad, T. (2020). Student perceptions on using cell phones as learning tools: Implications for mobile technology usage in Caribbean higher education institutions. *PSU Research Review*, *4*(1), 25–43. doi:10.1108/PRR-03-2018-0007

Baker, R. S., & Hawn, A. (2021). Algorithmic bias in education. *International Journal of Artificial Intelligence in Education*, 1–41.

Bonett, D. G., & Wright, T. A. (2015). Cronbach's alpha reliability: Interval estimation, hypothesis testing, and sample size planning. *Journal of Organizational Behavior*, *36*(1), 3–15. doi:10.1002/job.1960

Bowe, A. G. (2015). The development of education indicators for measuring quality in the English-speaking Caribbean: How far have we come? *Evaluation and Program Planning, 48*, 31–46. doi:10.1016/j.evalprogplan.2014.08.008 PMID:25299825

Brissett, N. (2021). A Critical Appraisal of Education in the Caribbean and Its Evolution From Colonial Origins to Twenty-First Century Responses. In Oxford Research Encyclopedia of Education. doi:10.1093/acrefore/9780190264093.013.1650

Brissett, N. O. (2018). Education for social transformation (EST) in the Caribbean: A post-colonial perspective. *Education Sciences, 8*(4), 197. doi:10.3390/educsci8040197

Campbell, C. (2003). *Education in the Caribbean, 1930–90. General History of the Caribbean* (Vol. 5). The Caribbean in the Twentieth Century.

Castaño-Muñoz, J., Kalz, M., Kreijns, K., & Punie, Y. (2018). Who is taking MOOCs for teachers' professional development on the use of ICT? A cross-sectional study from Spain. *Technology, Pedagogy and Education, 27*(5), 607–624. doi:10.1080/1475939X.2018.1528997

Chan, C. K. Y. (2023). A comprehensive AI policy education framework for university teaching and learning. *International Journal of Educational Technology in Higher Education, 20*(1), 38. doi:10.1186/s41239-023-00408-3

De Lisle, J., Laptiste-Francis, N., McMillan-Solomon, S., & Bowrin-Williams, C. (2017). Student assessment systems in the Caribbean as an obstacle to inclusive education. *Caribbean discourse in inclusive education: Historical and contemporary issues,* 87.

Fang, Y., Roscoe, R. D., & McNamara, D. S. (2023). Artificial intelligence-based assessment in education. In *Handbook of artificial intelligence in education* (pp. 485–504). Edward Elgar Publishing. doi:10.4337/9781800375413.00033

Fengchun, M., & Wayne, H. (2023). *Guidance for generative AI*. Academic Press.

Gao, R., Merzdorf, H. E., Anwar, S., Hipwell, M. C., & Srinivasa, A. R. (2024). Automatic assessment of text-based responses in post-secondary education: A systematic review. *Computers and Education: Artificial Intelligence, 6*, 100206. https://doi.org/https://doi.org/10.1016/j.caeai.2024.100206

Gardner, J., O'Leary, M., & Yuan, L. (2021). Artificial intelligence in educational assessment: 'Breakthrough? Or buncombe and ballyhoo?'. *Journal of Computer Assisted Learning, 37*(5), 1207–1216. doi:10.1111/jcal.12577

Holmes, W., & Miao, F. (2023). *Guidance for generative AI in education and research*. UNESCO Publishing.

Holmes, W., & Tuomi, I. (2022). State of the art and practice in AI in education. *European Journal of Education, 57*(4), 542–570. doi:10.1111/ejed.12533

Holstein, K., McLaren, B. M., & Aleven, V. (2018). Student learning benefits of a mixed-reality teacher awareness tool in AI-enhanced classrooms. *Artificial Intelligence in Education: 19th International Conference, AIED 2018,* London, UK, June 27–30, 2018, *Proceedings, Part I 19.*

Huang, L. (2023). Ethics of artificial intelligence in education: Student privacy and data protection. *Science Insights Education Frontiers*, *16*(2), 2577–2587. doi:10.15354/sief.23.re202

Ivie, S. D. (1998). Ausubel's learning theory: An approach to teaching higher order thinking skills. *High School Journal*, *82*(1), 35–42.

Jules, D. (2008). Rethinking education for the Caribbean: A radical approach. *Comparative Education*, *44*(2), 203–214. doi:10.1080/03050060802041142

Kaplan-Rakowski, R., Grotewold, K., Hartwick, P., & Papin, K. (2023). Generative AI and teachers' perspectives on its implementation in education. *Journal of Interactive Learning Research*, *34*(2), 313–338.

Lim, T., Gottipati, S., & Cheong, M. L. (2023). Ethical Considerations for Artificial Intelligence in Educational Assessments. In Creative AI Tools and Ethical Implications in Teaching and Learning (pp. 32-79). IGI Global. doi:10.4018/979-8-3693-0205-7.ch003

Louisy, D. P. (2004). Whose context for what quality? Informing education strategies for the Caribbean. *Compare: A Journal of Comparative Education*, *34*(3), 285–292. doi:10.1080/0305792042000257121

Mayne, H. (2014). The Social Reconstructionist Approach to Teacher Education: A necessary component to achieving excellence and quality education for all. *Research in Comparative and International Education*, *9*(1), 48–55. doi:10.2304/rcie.2014.9.1.48

McCallum, S., & Milner, M. M. (2021). The effectiveness of formative assessment: Student views and staff reflections. *Assessment & Evaluation in Higher Education*, *46*(1), 1–16. doi:10.1080/02602938.2020.1754761

Miao, F., Holmes, W., Huang, R., & Zhang, H. (2021). *AI and education: A guidance for policymakers*. UNESCO Publishing.

Miedijensky, S., Sasson, I., & Yehuda, I. (2021). Teachers' Learning Communities for Developing High Order Thinking Skills—A Case Study of a School Pedagogical Change. *Interchange*, *52*(4), 1–22. doi:10.1007/s10780-021-09423-7

Mouti, S. & Rihawi, S. (2023). Special Needs Classroom Assessment Using a Sign Language Communicator (CASC) Based on Artificial Intelligence (AI) Techniques. *International Journal of e-Collaboration (IJeC)*, *19*(1), 1-15. doi:10.4018/IJeC.313960

O'Reilly-Shah, V. N., Gentry, K. R., Walters, A. M., Zivot, J., Anderson, C. T., & Tighe, P. J. (2020). Bias and ethical considerations in machine learning and the automation of perioperative risk assessment. *British Journal of Anaesthesia*, *125*(6), 843–846. doi:10.1016/j.bja.2020.07.040 PMID:32838979

Qin, F., Li, K., & Yan, J. (2020). Understanding user trust in artificial intelligence-based educational systems: Evidence from China. *British Journal of Educational Technology*, *51*(5), 1693–1710. doi:10.1111/bjet.12994

Reeves, T. C., & Lin, L. (2020). The research we have is not the research we need. *Educational Technology Research and Development*, *68*(4), 1991–2001. doi:10.1007/s11423-020-09811-3 PMID:32837123

Salas-Pilco, S. Z., & Yang, Y. (2022). Artificial intelligence applications in Latin American higher education: A systematic review. *International Journal of Educational Technology in Higher Education*, *19*(1), 21. doi:10.1186/s41239-022-00326-w

Sherlock, P. M. (1950). Education in the Caribbean area. *Caribbean Quarterly*, *1*(3), 9–18. doi:10.1080/00086495.1950.11829194

UNESCO. (2023). *Information for All (IFAP) strategic plan, 2023-2029* [programme and meeting document]. UNESCO. https://unesdoc.unesco.org/ark:/48223/pf0000386173

UNICEF. (2021). *Policy guidance on AI for children: 2.0 November 2021*. https://www.unicef.org/globalinsight/media/2356/file/UNICEF-Global-Insight-policy-guidance-AI-children-2.0-2021.pdf.pdf

VanLehn, K. (2011). The Relative Effectiveness of Human Tutoring, Intelligent Tutoring Systems, and Other Tutoring Systems. *Educational Psychologist*, *46*(4), 197–221. doi:10.1080/00461520.2011.611369

ADDITIONAL READING

Ivie, S. D. (1998). Ausubel's learning theory: An approach to teaching higher order thinking skills. *High School Journal*, *82*(1), 35–42.

Mehta, P., Chillarge, G. R., Sapkal, S. D., Shinde, G. R., & Kshirsagar, P. S. (2023). Inclusion of Children With Special Needs in the Educational System, Artificial Intelligence (AI). In A. Kumar, A. Nayyar, R. Sachan, & R. Jain (Eds.), *AI-Assisted Special Education for Students With Exceptional Needs* (pp. 156–185). IGI Global. doi:10.4018/979-8-3693-0378-8.ch007

Meshram, V. A., Kumar, S., Meshram, V. V., Patil, V., Patil, K., Bewoor, L., & Gawande, P. (2023). Methodology and Framework for AI-Based Solutions for Special Education. In A. Kumar, A. Nayyar, R. Sachan, & R. Jain (Eds.), *AI-Assisted Special Education for Students With Exceptional Needs* (pp. 23–46). IGI Global. doi:10.4018/979-8-3693-0378-8.ch002

Miedijensky, S., Sasson, I., & Yehuda, I. (2021). Teachers' Learning Communities for Developing High Order Thinking Skills—A Case Study of a School Pedagogical Change. *Interchange*, *52*(4), 1–22. doi:10.1007/s10780-021-09423-7

Minn, S. (2022). AI-assisted knowledge assessment techniques for adaptive learning environments. *Computers and Education: Artificial Intelligence*, *3*, 100050.

Tlili, A., Huang, R., Mustafa, M. Y., Zhao, J., Bozkurt, A., Xu, L., Wang, H., Salha, S., Altinay, F., & Affouneh, S. (2023). Speaking of transparency: Are all Artificial Intelligence (AI) literature reviews in education transparent? *Journal of Applied Learning and Teaching*, *6*(2).

UNICEF. (2022). *Education in Latin America and the Caribbean at a crossroads: Regional monitoring report SDG4-Education 2030*. UNESCO Publishing.

Zhai, X., Chu, X., Chai, C. S., Jong, M. S. Y., Istenic, A., Spector, M., Liu, J.-B., Yuan, J., & Li, Y. (2021). A Review of Artificial Intelligence (AI) in Education from 2010 to 2020. *Complexity*, *2021*, 1–18. doi:10.1155/2021/8812542

KEY TERMS AND DEFINITIONS

21st-Century Learning: This is a concept of learning that emphasizes critical thinking, creativity, collaboration, communication, and technology integration to prepare students for a rapidly changing global landscape.

Adaptive Learning: A method of education that uses AI algorithms to adapt learning content and activities to the individual learner's abilities and preferences.

AI-Assisted Education: Artificial intelligence-assisted education involves using artificial intelligence technologies to enhance teaching and learning processes. It includes personalized learning, intelligent tutoring systems, automated grading, and data-driven insights to improve student outcomes. AI helps tailor educational experiences to individual needs, making learning more efficient, engaging, and accessible.

AI-Driven: The use of artificial intelligence technologies to support, enhance, and optimize existing processes within educational institutions.

AI-Efficacy: This refers to the effectiveness of AI technologies when used within educational settings. It involves using AI tools or applications to increase efficiency, improve teacher productivity, and enhance educational performance.

Chatbots: AI-powered conversational agents that can interact with students in natural language, providing assistance, answering questions, and facilitating learning.

Digital Technologies: The use of hardware, software, and online tools that create personalized learning experiences, enrich educational practices, and transform the traditional learning environment.

Educational Data Mining (EDM): The process of analyzing educational data to improve learning outcomes. EDM can use AI techniques to identify patterns and provide insights into student learning behaviors.

Educational Digital Transformation: The integration of digital technology into all aspects of the school system, fundamentally changing its operations and value delivery from top down to bottom up. It involves rethinking operational models, teaching and learning models, embracing new approaches, and increasing agility to respond to educational changes. Specifically, from a school operational level, it includes adopting digital tools, using data analytics, and personalizing learning experiences.

Educational Predictive Analytics: This form of educational analysis uses a combination of student data, statistical algorithms, and machine learning techniques to identify various teaching and learning issues, such as identifying students needing additional learning support in literacy and numeracy.

Formative Assessment Tools: Digital tools and platforms that support ongoing assessment and feedback during the learning process, helping students monitor their progress and identify areas for improvement.

Learning Analytics: The measurement, collection, analysis, and reporting of data about learners and their contexts. AI can enhance learning analytics to provide real-time feedback and personalized learning paths.

Performance-Based Assessment: An individualized learning approach that focuses on the development of critical thinking and problem-solving skills through real-world projects rather than relying on traditional measures of testing such as written examinations. Performance-based assessments help students gain practical experience and develop meaningful strategies that prepare them for challenges beyond the classroom.

Quality of Education: Quality education is a concept that refers to the provision of education that is not only accessible and equitable but also relevant and effective in equipping learners with the knowledge, skills, and values they need to lead successful and fulfilling lives. It encompasses various dimensions, including well-trained teachers, adequate resources, safe and inclusive learning environments, and curricula that promote critical thinking, creativity, and lifelong learning.

Chapter 13
Preparing Students for an AI–Enhanced Future

Rawya Elmahi Gobara Elmahi Gobara
 https://orcid.org/0009-0006-0460-4946
Sudan University of Science and Technology, Sudan

Zeinab E. Ahmed
 https://orcid.org/0000-0002-6144-8533
Department of Computer Engineering, University of Gezira, Sudan & Department of Electrical and Computer Engineering, International Islamic University Malaysia, Malaysia

ABSTRACT

In this regard, the purpose of this study is to examine artificial intelligence and its impact on technology, the future of students, and education. It can be said that education is one of the most important areas that will be affected sooner or later by the development of technology, especially artificial intelligence techniques. This impact naturally has both positive and negative aspects, so how can we benefit from it? This chapter discusses the most important potential applications of artificial intelligence that can be used in the educational process. It explains to them the positive and negative impact of technology on education, clarifies the strengths and weaknesses, and shows how to benefit from these points. It also helps them develop critical thinking skills, enhances creativity and development, and encourages them to experiment with tools.

1. INTRODUCTION

In recent years, there has been great development in all fields of knowledge, to the point that the current era has been given many names, including the information age and the era of the scientific and cognitive revolution. Artificial intelligence is what the general public expresses as the ability of machines or computers to think and act like humans, which represents efforts towards computerized systems to imitate the human mind and its actions (Artman and Combs, 2018). In this regard, the basic definition of artificial intelligence can be expressed as the skill of imitating human behavior or the human mind through

DOI: 10.4018/979-8-3693-2728-9.ch013

tools or software (Muhammad and Watson, 2019). According to Times (2016), it may be an illusion of the current architecture to believe that AI will come within the computational format used at home. It can enter our lives in different forms and functions. Ng (2017) claims that AI is the new electricity of this era. Artificial intelligence is expected to be the cornerstone of the Fifth Industrial Revolution by presenting itself as a powerful factor in ensuring economic development with its potential (see Gulick, 2019). Karsenty (2019) points out that these new forms of technology will fill our lives and interest our youth in the future. Schools may have no choice but to make way for them with AI technology. The term intelligence comes from the Latin language and means the ability to understand. Over the years, the term has been used to refer to a variety of fields, from military strategy to economics. Currently, its general-purpose use is mostly associated with reasoning, good grades, and problem-solving skills (Cohen et al., 2009) from a cognitive perspective. Artificial intelligence has witnessed tremendous development in recent years and has become a technology that will revolutionize lifestyles. This technology has been introduced into higher education (Hinojo-Lucena et al., 2019). Artificial intelligence connects the fields of learning. The neural network classifies, distinguishes, and explains, representing a paradigm shift in knowledge construction (Jena, 2018). Khair, Stuart, and Khair (2018 indicate that artificial intelligence has a positive impact on students' outcomes and futures. Zidane (2018) explained that one of the most prominent strengths of this chapter is that the use of artificial intelligence in teaching contributes to developing the skills of students and trainees, and artificial intelligence also contributes to improving the leadership level of students through self-education according to the interactive method and educational stages. From the scientific material. Training on the test and knowing the correct answer lead to self-evaluation and knowledge of the individual's level, in addition to increasing the student's creative abilities and imagination through the use of graphic and pictorial programs to highlight the scientific material. Strengths contribute to the classroom, providing the opportunity to share strengths and share resources and experiences. humanity, embracing different viewpoints and diversity, and benefiting from the analysis of past experiences. Despite the great progress achieved by research in the field of artificial intelligence in giving computers some of the characteristics of artificial intelligence, it is still too early to say that there are programs capable of relating to the human mind in the way of thinking and creativity. Artificial intelligence programs are merely a development in specific software, specialized in specific applied fields, where the machine takes into account the result of human experience in a specific field, so the person decides to act based on his feelings, knowledge, and experience, intentionally or unintentionally. Artificial intelligence is only a means to facilitate education and should not It must be relied upon, especially in the absence of controls. This is considered one of the weak points (Yoshika, Sage, 2007). From the above, it is clear that artificial intelligence is one of the sciences that relies primarily on the computer and its programs. It collects, classifies, distinguishes, and explains learning domains in a neural network. It is a qualitative leap in acquiring knowledge that has a positive impact on the student's success and future.

2. THE FOCUS OF THE ARTICLE

The study conducted by Manyika et al. (2017) points out that there will still be good teachers whose teaching focuses on developing students' emotional intelligence, creativity, and communication. According to these authors, the development of artificial intelligence and automation "will make people more human." Referring to educational research on AI, Hasisky (2019) succinctly presents the findings of this study as follows: Using AI in education will make learning more individualized and enable learning experiences. Through active learning, students can discover their talents. Develop your creative abilities and reduce the burden on teachers. However, there are also contradictory concepts. In AI research, transferring the role of teacher to the computer is seen as a threat (Humble and Mozelius, 2019). To prepare for this future, states and nations must profile teachers participating in these support structures (Wogu, Misra, Olu-Owolabi, Assibong, & Udoh, 2018). As the use of artificial intelligence in education increases, we can expect significant changes in educational systems and processes. Based on the study results, Cekiroğlu, Demmiller, and Tuncal (2019) concluded that AI can help teachers improve their students' personalized learning. AI can provide access to advanced AI-related learning opportunities for marginalized individuals and communities, people with disabilities, refugees, out-of-school students, and people living in isolated communities (Pedro, Subosa, Rivas, & Valverde, 2019). . Research shows how effective and personalized approaches can be delivered with the support of AI technologies and smart learning environments (Mohammed and Watson, 2019).

There are several ways to prepare students for the future of artificial intelligence, including teaching students the basics of artificial intelligence. To teach them the basics, it is necessary to introduce students to artificial intelligence, how it works, and some of the potential applications, and to help them understand how technology affects their lives and the world around them. Understanding these basics gives students a better foundation on which to build more privacy in the future.

' Artificial intelligence uses various techniques, such as machine learning, natural language processing, and image recognition. Data is at the heart of these technologies and forms the foundational level of artificial intelligence. This level mainly focuses on preparing data for AI applications. With the advancement of technology, artificial intelligence (AI) has become one of the fastest breakthroughs. The idea of a machine that learns and makes independent decisions may seem very interesting. Artificial intelligence is a set of algorithms and programs designed to process data and learn from the results. These algorithms are used to support and make decisions. Algorithms have been exploited to develop many useful applications, such as big data analytics, improving industrial efficiency, improving healthcare, politics, agriculture, and Earth and space observation and exploration. Travel and logistics. Assessing the social impact of new technologies. AI can bridge this gap by supporting students to understand the fundamentals of AI and essential 21st century skills. Therefore, this is an important item on the agenda. Decision-makers must deepen their understanding of the next generation of AI skills and equip them with all the elements needed to meet the needs of industry and society in the future. Despite its enormous advantages, artificial intelligence still faces many limitations and challenges, including its ability to make ethically complex and intelligent decisions. AI can process more information than humans, but this does not include our ability to think in a similar way. This way of thinking is the greatest strength of human intelligence. While humans can find solutions to new problems by drawing on relationships with familiar situations, artificial intelligence is practically unable to do so. This is the conclusion of Claire Stevenson, a researcher interested in intelligence and normative thinking in artificial intelligence, the intelligence of children, and how they can learn from each other. Introduction to some potential applications of artificial intelligence. In recent years, the world has witnessed a revolution in the field of artificial intelligence, the effects of which have appeared in most areas of life. There is hardly any field that is devoid of employing applications of this artificial intelligence, in medicine, engineering, armaments, manufacturing, investment, space sciences, and communications. The most prominent potential applications of artificial intelligence that can be employed in the educational process for students can be explained, including:

1. Chabot: Chabot is a typical example of an artificial intelligence system, and one of the most basic and widely used examples of intelligent human-machine interaction is Chabot. One of the most widely used AI technologies to support teaching and learning activities is Chabot. (Okonkwo and Ade-Ibejola, 2020). Chabot: Chabot is a typical example of an artificial intelligence system, and one of the most basic and widely used examples of intelligent human-machine interaction is Chabot. One of the most widely used AI technologies to support teaching and learning activities is Chabot. (Okonku and Adi Ibigola, 2020). Chabot is an intelligent agent that can interact with others, for example, by answering a series of questions and providing the appropriate answer. Clarizia.,2018) Chabot, as a dialogue system, must be able to understand the content of the dialogue and recognize needs. The social and emotional impact of the user's conversation partner during a conversation simulates and interprets human communication, allowing people to use digital devices as if they were talking to a real person (Ciechanowski, 2019). Moreover, the performance of a chatbot depends on its size and accuracy. database, which means that a larger database size leads to better performance (Aleedy et al., 2022). These applications can take different forms, such as messaging applications, websites, and applications on smart devices or phones. Students can interact with them by asking questions about their field, and the robot then plays an active role by answering the questions posed to it. And solutions, support, tips, and tricks, depending on what users need help with.

2. Augmented Reality (a simultaneous interactive technology that adds a layer of information (text, image, audio, video, etc. in multi-dimensional forms) to the displayed reality); Turns seemingly static text, images, or shapes into reality by simply pointing at them with your smartphone using the screen camera (thanks to the augmented reality app).

3. Virtual Reality: An interactive computer simulation of real reality that gives the student the opportunity to interact with it, immerse themselves in it, control it, and move around in it, for example, by conducting dangerous experiments in a laboratory or participating in field visits to sit in a different place. environment. Like a home or classroom that moves and interacts with it. This requires the use of special equipment such as helmets, gloves, and goggles equipped with location and motion sensors.

4. Audio production: a digital program that processes written text out loud. Depending on the default language you choose, you can use it on websites, mobile apps, and books. Materials and documentation for online learning. (2018) Chabot, as a dialogue system, must be able to understand the content of dialogue and recognize the social and emotional needs of the user during the conversation. It simulates and interprets human communication, allowing people to use digital devices as if they were talking to a real person (Ciechanowski, 2019). Moreover, the performance of the chabot depends on its size and accuracy. database, which means that a larger database size leads to better performance (Aleedy et al., 2022).

These applications can take different forms, such as messaging applications, websites, and applications on smart devices or phones. Students can interact with them by asking questions about their field, and the robot then plays an active role by answering the questions posed to it. And solutions, support, tips, and tricks, depending on what users need help with.

5. Augmented Reality (simultaneous interactive technology that adds a layer of information (text, image, audio, video, etc. in multi-dimensional forms) to the displayed reality); Turns seemingly

      static texts, images, or shapes into reality by simply pointing at them with your smartphone using the screen camera (thanks to the augmented reality app).

6. Virtual Reality: An interactive computer simulation of real reality that gives the student the opportunity to interact with it, immerse themselves in it, control it, and move around in it, for example, by conducting dangerous experiments in a laboratory or participating in field visits by sitting in a different place. environment. Like a home or classroom that moves and interacts with it. This requires the use of special equipment such as helmets, gloves, and goggles equipped with location and motion sensors.

7. Audio Production: digital software that processes written text out loud. Depending on the default language you choose, you can use it on websites, mobile apps, and books. Materials and documentation for online learning.

    Expert systems are complex computer systems that collect specific information from one area of human knowledge and prepare it in a form that allows the computer to apply that information in relevant situations. Expert systems are the basis for artificial intelligence-based learning systems. The expert system can act as an intelligent teacher. There may no longer be a need for teachers and students to gather in the same classroom. These processes require teaching to become dynamic, as Hussein and Maryam (2012) said. The main goal of expert systems is to support and assist students in their thinking processes, not to provide them with information. Expert systems rely on their databases to make decisions and perform tasks. In addition to being easy to use, these systems allow students to practice their skills in interactive learning environments, respond to their wishes and questions, provide individual advice and guidance, and find solutions to learning problems, as well as being easy to use and supporting scientific communication. It also helps spread the human experience; use it to make sound decisions, save time and effort, and provide the appropriate method for detecting and correcting errors. You will also learn what distinguishes specialized systems and helps the student focus, excel, learn quickly, and be creative in implementing learning activities by recording students' behavior as they interact with the learning environment.

9. Educational robot: Robots are electromechanical machines that can perform their tasks by following a series of instructions stored in the device's electronic memory. These controls are developed using special computer programs and connected to the robot's parts. Robot roles can be classified as those of a learning agent or the equivalent of a teacher or student creating a robot during a learning activity, where learning occurs on the robot, with the robot, and from the robot.

10. Intelligent adaptive learning: It involves the use of artificial intelligence methods to meet the different educational needs of each student, so that computer algorithms derived from the student's answers to questions can be used to customize the presentation of educational materials, provide customized resources, and learn activities that best meet cognitive needs and provide feedback. Targeted and immediate for the student without the need for a teacher.

11. Smart educational games: games programmed by the computer to achieve a specific educational goal. They are characterized by excitement, challenge, imagination, and competition and aim to stimulate mental activity, increase concentration, and improve the performance of logical decisions. And solve problems quickly. Strengthening social relationships and ties.

12. Intelligent assessment: Computer programs can assess higher-order thinking skills, automatically grade complex assignments and tests, review a variety of data, analyze student performance, high-

light students' strengths and weaknesses, and provide them with the support they need in a timely manner.

13. Character recognition and reading: These are computer programs that convert printed images or handwritten text into editable text files, analyze the document, and compare it with the letters stored in a database or with the typical characteristics of the letters. These programs also use the spell checker to guess unknown words. (Rospigliosi, 2023).

14. Text summarization: computer programs capable of summarizing long texts in a very accurate and easy-to-read manner, fixing errors in the code, or creating new codes. (Iki, 2023) [28] Users can understand the summary and extract the most important information from the original texts in record time, whether they are articles or not. Or social media posts.

In traditional schools, the disadvantages of artificial intelligence in education are the following: limiting students' ability to engage in adaptive learning. The use of individual teaching and learning materials adapted to students' needs can reduce their ability to adapt to adaptive learning, that is, adapting to unexpected learning situations, because they are always... The availability of ready-made materials and templates, high costs, limited creativity, increased unemployment, ethical dilemmas, complete dependence on machines, privacy concerns, and lack of transparency, dependency, and reliability are all among the disadvantages of artificial intelligence. Through artificial intelligence, artificial intelligence is relied upon for many educational tasks. Improving the quality of learning: Artificial intelligence will help improve the learning process by providing students and teachers with accurate and immediate feedback on student performance and identifying weak areas that need improvement. Artificial intelligence can provide very important information based on collecting a large amount of data in real time, including, for example, the effect of the physical learning environment (ventilation, heat, noise) and reading some signals that monitor children's activity. kidding. Students in class at a certain point in a lesson, for example, B. Body language and more.

In this chapter, it is possible to take advantage of the weak points in human habits and exploit them to influence human decision-making mechanisms.

There is a UNESCO (Beijing Consensus) report on AI and education for 2019.Representatives of Member States, international organizations, academia, civil society, and the private sector unanimously adopted the Beijing Consensus on AI and Education at the International Conference on AI and Education. Briefing from May 16 to 18, 2019 in Beijing. The first is a one-year document that provides guidelines and recommendations on how Member States can best respond to the opportunities and challenges of AI to accelerate progress towards SDG 4 (Quality Education). The Beijing Consensus emphasizes a humanistic approach to implementing AI technologies in education to improve human intelligence, protect human rights, and promote sustainable development through effective human-machine cooperation in living, learning, and working. The consensus describes some policy mechanisms for AI in education in five areas:

Artificial intelligence in education management and implementation; artificial intelligence enhances teaching and teachers; artificial intelligence for learning and teaching assessment; shaping the values and skills needed to live and work in the age of artificial intelligence; Artificial intelligence will provide lifelong learning opportunities for everyone. (UNESCO, Beijing Consensus, 2019).

2.1 Applications of Artificial Intelligence in Education

Artificial intelligence technology has a long, evolving, and ever-increasing history. Artificial intelligence is an interdisciplinary subject that includes computer science, logic, perception and reasoning, systems science, and biology (Hons, 2019). The science has been in computers, pattern recognition, machine learning, natural language processing, game theory, machine and automated programming, and expert systems. Knowledge bases, intelligent robots, etc. The fields achieved practical results (Jackson, 2019). Technology has radically changed the culture of the educational system for students. With the development of artificial intelligence technology, modern education will be combined with more technologies, such as speech semantic recognition, image recognition, augmented reality, virtual reality, machine learning, brain neuroscience, etc. These technologies are collectively referred to as smart technologies and are being continuously and rapidly integrated into education. The intelligent modernization of the education industry is well underway. Nowadays, more and more AI education products have been applied to school education (Yan, 2017). Typical scenarios of AI education applications include: teacher-assisted intelligent personal teaching and learning; intelligent assistants such as educational robots; children's partners at home; and assessment. Intelligent intelligence mining, educational data analysis, learning and learning analysis, digital images, etc. Literature studies show that AI technology has been used in education in several aspects: automatic grading systems, interval reminders, teacher feedback systems, virtual teachers, personalized learning, adaptive learning (augmented reality, virtual reality), close reading, smart campuses, and distance learning. Automatic Grading System: An automated scoring system is Artificial Intelligence, a professional computer program that simulates a teacher's behavior on a task "working in learning environments. Assessing students' knowledge and curriculum, analyzing their responses, providing feedback, and developing customized training programs. Many applications use artificial intelligence in this program.

During the test, the system automatically gives the student a grade. This method can help teachers better understand the educational status of their students on the platform, and on the other hand, children become more aware of their academic success and cognitive levels. Competition. An example of an automated grading system used in educational applications is the Israeli music education app (Shang, 2019). This app focuses more on classroom teaching hours and provides teaching and assessment tools for teachers and students. It uses modern, advanced technologies to transform every aspect of music education, from teaching to learning to practice. Wolf's automatic grading system helps music teachers and students correct errors in exercises and provides teachers and students with a completely different way of musical transmission and educational interaction.

Interval reminder: When someone is about to forget what he knows, repetition of the knowledge process is an effective technical solution to improve understanding and memory, thanks to repeated memories at a specific time. Polish inventor Piotr Woźniak proposes educational applications based on time-lapse effects (Nazemi, Breyer, Burkhardt, Stab, & Kohlhammer, 2014). This app keeps track of what people have learned and when. Using these artifacts, the app can identify when someone is likely to forget something and suggest they change it. Just a few reminders to be on the safe side: bits of information have been stored in the human brain for years. Teacher feedback is the student's evaluation of the teacher and is an existing method of feedback. He has been working in the education sector for a while. Despite the shift from paper surveys to online surveys, there have been few or no follow-up surveys. None have made any progress at all in the field of feedback (Holstein, McLaren, & Aleven, 2019). Of course, student evaluations of teaching are often the most valuable source of information. It must be increased. New technologies, such as chatbots based on artificial intelligence, machine learning, and natural language processing, offer exciting possibilities for improving the quality of feedback (Peters, 2019). For example, Chabot can collect opinions through a conversational interface like a real interlocutor but does not. It only requires a small amount, which others use. The conversation can be tailored to the students' answers and personalities. Virtual Tutor: In recent years, there has been a focus on developing artificial intelligence, and some entrepreneurs have begun offering online students a "virtual tutor" that uses artificial intelligence to help children learn (Goel and Bulibidi, 2016). At Georgia Tech, students quickly became enamored with teaching assistant Jill Watson, who responded meticulously to the students' wishes. But the students did not know that Mr. Watson's true identity is actually a computer running an artificial intelligence system from IBM. There is also a company in London called Whiz Education (Whizz Education, 2014). Online educational program The company has developed a program of extracurricular activities in line with study time. Students can ask questions at any time during the learning process. The virtual teacher will answer students' questions step by step and will modify your answer according to the students' feedback until the student masters what he has learned. At the same time, the system also provides parents with real-time reports so they can monitor their children. Track your child's learning progress and better understand if they can keep up. Although artificial intelligence has made great progress in education, there are still obstacles to its widespread use. The scarcity of resources in some countries is a major barrier that can hinder the adoption of AI technologies. Moreover, the application of AI in education has raised ethical questions about algorithmic bias and data privacy (Miao et al., 2021; Chen et al., 2020; UNESCO, 2023). However, AI assessment methods may become increasingly important in education. Educators can improve the educational outcomes and learning experiences of their students by implementing AI assessments. However, considering the perspectives of teachers and students in particular, it is necessary to address the issues and ensure that AI techniques are applied correctly and ethically.

The future of the education system is practically determined by the development of technology, and although some teachers and experts reject the trend of using online learning tools and applications in all aspects of the education system, it is right to consider technology as a resource for the student. The integration of distraction technology guides students to a better understanding of all concepts. According to the latest information on how modern students prefer technology and the impact of technology use on their learning, it has been found that students' use of modern devices, technologies, and tools for learning and interaction is increasing. You will also find that it is more interactive and full of interesting areas when it is supported by technology. Knowledge transfer becomes very simple, practical, and effective. This means that our minds these days tend to work faster when we support them with modern technology, whether this applies to all areas of life or not. In this chapter, we talk about education. The reliability and adoption of such innovations that make life easy and comfortable are now quite inevitable, even in schools, universities, and colleges. Currently, students can use technology in the following ways: Being online and connected throughout the day In the past decade, the importance of the Internet has increased many times. Its importance in the world of education can no longer be questioned. Despite the risks and drawbacks of fraud, using the Internet is a boon for students. Nowadays, the Internet is in almost everything we use. From televisions to gaming consoles to our phones, the Internet is literally everywhere. The importance of technology in teaching: The role of technology in education has four aspects: integrating it into the curriculum, as an educational system, as a means to support teaching, and as a tool to improve the overall learning process. Thanks to technology, education has evolved from passive and interactive education to interactive and aggressive education. Education is essential in business and academic environments. In the first case, additional training or education aims to help employees do things differently than before. Finally, the goal of education is to stimulate students' curiosity. Either way, using technology can help students understand and remember concepts better.

There are factors influencing the use of technology in education. I. Jung talks about the enormous challenge that teachers face in our society due to the rapid development of knowledge. New technologies require teachers to learn how to use these technologies in their classrooms. These new technologies, therefore, increase the training needs of teachers. Grissard and Lloyd (1985) state that teachers' attitudes towards computers are a key factor in the successful implementation of ICT in education. They noted that teachers do not always have a positive attitude toward computers and that their poor attitudes can lead to failure. Of computer projects. Frequently mentioned obstacles are:

1. Lack of time.
2. Lack of access.
3. Lack of resources.
4. Lack of experience.
5. Lack of support

Another obstacle mentioned by Butler and Selbom (2002) and Chismar and Williams (2001) is reliability. Reliability includes hardware failures, incompatible software between home and school, a poor or slow internet connection, and outdated software often available at school while students or teachers have newer software at home. Impact of ICT on Education In the educational context, ICT can improve access to education and improve its relevance and quality. Tinio (2002) stated that ICT has a tremendous impact on education in the acquisition and assimilation of knowledge by teachers and students by promoting active learning. ICT tools that help in calculating and analyzing exam information as well as student performance reports are computerized and available for easy review. Unlike learning by rote or rote learning, ICT encourages the participation of students who decide what they want to learn at their own pace and work to solve problems that arise in real-world situations.2. Collaborative and cooperative learning: ICT enhances interaction and cooperation between students and teachers, regardless of the distance between them. It also gives students the opportunity to work with people from different cultures and professions. In groups, which helps students improve their communication skills and general awareness. Researchers have found that the use of ICT generally leads to more collaboration between students inside and outside of school, as well as a more interactive relationship between students and teachers (Gregoire et al., 1996).

3. HELPING STUDENTS DEVELOP CRITICAL THINKING SKILLS

The role of the teacher in developing critical thinking skills is very important, as he plays an important role in building the personalities of his students and instilling various skills. Preparing students to think critically in the classroom is crucial to creating a classroom full of motivated students who are eager to learn. The importance of critical thinking for students: Critical thinking is one of the higher skills that students need to learn. Critical thinking skills are essential for learning in times of change. Logical thinking skills are related to accessing, analyzing, and synthesizing information, which makes this possible and must be taught and mastered. To understand the learning process, students need to develop deep, high-level thinking skills. Understanding Science Students need to develop deep and advanced thinking skills. Critical thinking is essential in real life, especially in the education sector. Understanding critical thinking in education is the thinking process upon which decisions are made with different fundamentals such as tests, methods, standards, context, perception, and relevant sources of information. As a respected student or future teacher, you will therefore be able to easily identify various problems related to education. Identify and analyze the cause and severity of the problem, and prepare reports on a specific issue.Solutions can be formulated and evaluated in the form of information on whether national examination tasks are necessary or not. This form of critical thinking in the world of education is very important because it improves students' skills and recognition in training activities. A student with critical thinking skills will gain many of the benefits of these skills in the classroom (learning in the world of work or in social life; et al. (2008) describe critical thinking as useful for improving the ability to understand, construct, and make decisions, freeing a person from the doctrine of bias).

4. ENCOURAGING STUDENTS TO BE CREATIVE

Creativity has become an essential skill for success in all areas of business. Creativity can be developed by teaching students to think outside the box and solve problems creatively. The creative process begins when the gap between "who we are and what we do" narrows (Kane, 2004). This is Rousseau's principle: I am myself as much as I am creative. Therefore, the teacher's primary task in developing creativity is to encourage students to discover their identity by identifying their specific interests and talents. So, if you want to encourage creativity in the education system, the first step may be to help students find what they truly love and help them immerse themselves in the field, be it poetry, physics, engineering, or dance. When young people engage in what they love, the foundation of creativity is created (Csikszentmihalyi, 2006, pp. xix–xx). Once students have identified their areas of interest, they can be encouraged to explore more specific topics, projects, and specializations. And the professional fields that interest them. Kane (2004) argues that in the twenty-first century, play has replaced work as the dominant means of generating meaning. In higher education, students can be encouraged to play with ideas and connections between concepts by asking themselves the following questions: Are we giving students enough freedom to play? 2. As teachers, are we enthusiastic about and enjoying our subjects? How can we encourage students to combine creative thinking, critical thinking, and brainstorming? reasoning, judgement, exploration, and precision in a way that enhances their creativity? How can we encourage students to ask questions they want to pursue rather than simply impart knowledge? By engaging in dialogue around these topics, we can find concrete ways to encourage students to connect things in creative and fun ways that they may not have done before. Fostering Student Creativity: If creativity is so important, how can we encourage it? In-depth and comprehensive reviews of the vast literature base in creativity, teaching, and learning have been conducted by Stein (1988) and Fryer (2003), among others. However, there is a lack of critical examination of the introduction of creativity into the higher education system. In fact, Gardner (1982) points out that previous research on learning and development has largely neglected creativity. This gap has been recently addressed by Jackson, Oliver, Shaw, and Wisdom (2006), who focus on the role of creativity in higher education. Csikszentmihalyi (2006) believes that the foundation for creativity is laid when young people engage in what they want. love. This means that teachers themselves must model the joy of learning and be able to inspire it in their students. Students. Similarly, teaching methods should aim to stimulate students' imagination and engagement. Since the late 1990s, several studies have identified common themes in student and faculty statements about how best to enhance student creativity in higher education. For example, Cropley (2001) points out that research has shown that teachers, at least in theory, overwhelmingly support creativity as something that should be encouraged in the classroom. In addition, teachers who actively encourage creativity are more likely to encourage creativity. Independent learning, taking student questions seriously, promoting self-esteem, rewarding courage and rigor, and following a collaborative and socially responsible teaching style. Oliver et al. (2006), on students' experiences of creativity in different disciplines, highlighted specific teaching techniques that students consider creative. These include role plays, debates, and posters for classroom presentations. Some traditional forms of teaching are also considered creative teaching, especially dialogic teaching, which involves discussions focused on students' understanding or existing beliefs. Individual tutorials are especially useful for students because they provide suggestions, examples, or comments. Teachers must remember that the key to success lies in the way we use these technologies, not just in integrating them into our technology repertoire.

5. HOW TO USE ARTIFICIAL INTELLIGENCE ETHICALLY

Creativity has become an essential skill for success in all areas of business. Creativity can be developed by teaching students to think outside the box and solve problems creatively. The creative process begins when the gap between "who we are and what we do" narrows (Kane, 2004). This is Rousseau's principle: I am myself as much as I am creative. Therefore, the teacher's primary task in developing creativity is to encourage students to discover their identity by identifying their specific interests and talents. So, if you want to encourage creativity in the education system, the first step may be to help students find what they truly love and help them immerse themselves in the field, be it poetry, physics, engineering, or dance. When young people engage in what they love, the foundation of creativity is created (Csikszentmihalyi, 2006, pp. xix–xx). Once students have identified their areas of interest, they can be encouraged to explore more specific topics, projects, and specializations. And the professional fields that interest them. Kane (2004) argues that in the twenty-first century, play has replaced work as the dominant means of generating meaning. In higher education, students can be encouraged to play with ideas and connections between concepts by asking themselves the following questions: Are we giving students enough freedom to play? 2. As teachers, are we enthusiastic about and enjoying our subjects? How can we encourage students to combine creative thinking, critical thinking, and brainstorming? reasoning, judgement, exploration, and precision in a way that enhances their creativity? How can we encourage students to ask questions they want to pursue rather than simply impart knowledge? By engaging in dialogue around these topics, we can find concrete ways to encourage students to connect things in creative and fun ways that they may not have done before. Fostering Student Creativity: If creativity is so important, how can we encourage it? In-depth and comprehensive reviews of the vast literature base in creativity, teaching, and learning have been conducted by Stein (1988) and Fryer (2003), among others. However, there is a lack of critical examination of the introduction of creativity into the higher education system. In fact, Gardner (1982) points out that previous research on learning and development has largely neglected creativity. This gap has been recently addressed by Jackson, Oliver, Shaw, and Wisdom (2006), who focus on the role of creativity in higher education. Csikszentmihalyi (2006) believes that the foundation for creativity is laid when young people engage in what they want. love. This means that teachers themselves must model the joy of learning and be able to inspire it in their students. Students. Similarly, teaching methods should aim to stimulate students' imagination and engagement. Since the late 1990s, several studies have identified common themes in student and faculty statements about how best to enhance student creativity in higher education. For example, Cropley (2001) points out that research has shown that teachers, at least in theory, overwhelmingly support creativity as something that should be encouraged in the classroom. In addition, teachers who actively encourage creativity are more likely to encourage creativity. Independent learning, taking student questions seriously, promoting self-esteem, rewarding courage and rigor, and following a collaborative and socially responsible teaching style. Oliver et al. (2006), on students' experiences of creativity in different disciplines, highlighted specific teaching techniques that students consider creative. These include role plays, debates, and posters for classroom presentations. Some traditional forms of teaching are also considered creative teaching, especially dialogic teaching, which involves discussions focused on students' understanding or existing beliefs. Individual tutorials are especially useful for students because they provide suggestions, examples, or comments. Teachers must remember that the key to success lies in the way we use these technologies, not just in integrating them into our technology repertoire.

6. HOW TO USE ARTIFICIAL INTELLIGENCE ETHICALLY

Artificial intelligence (AI) is a key technology within national governments and has attracted significant interest and support in countries around the world (Rolle and Willie 2016). In the past five years, the Chinese and Finnish governments have launched policy programs to promote the development of artificial intelligence. Therefore, artificial intelligence is not just a technological or engineering problem but is closely linked to ethics. AI-based learning requires ethical foundations: the latest effective and advanced technologies in computer programming have opened new doors for AI-based teaching and learning (Niemi, 2021), and AI is increasingly being used in education. It was discussed how AI can increase student engagement, leading to better educational outcomes. Integrated technologies include interaction, dialogue, automatic question generation, and learning analytics (Bozkurt et al., 2021). We have a lot to promise. For example, evidence from previous research demonstrates that AI already exists and is used to predict students' academic success, identify at-risk students, conduct formative assessment, provide descriptive information about teaching, and contribute to teacher development by creating. Effective learning tools and implementation of adaptive learning environments (e.g., Mohammadi et al., 2017; Paneres et al., 2019; Paradog and Pal, 2011; Kay, 2012; Vinuesa et al., 2020) In a review study by Goksel and Bozkurt (2019), three general themes of AI learning were identified: Adaptive learning, personalization, and modeling learning; specialized systems and intelligent teaching systems; and artificial intelligence as a fundamental building block for the future of educational processes. Systematic examination of AI-based learning offers huge potential when artificial intelligence is an integral part of the educational process and openness increases questions. To be answered are, for example, ethical guidelines for the use of AI learning tools.There are national guidelines for AI-based learning within and outside the education sector, including:Inclusion and privatization, justice and security, transparency and accountability, autonomy, and sustainable development.

Encourages students to experiment with AI tools As AI continues to develop and evolve, it has become necessary to train students on how to use AI tools. Here are some reasons why it is important to train and encourage them to use AI tools. Since AI is already being used in many situations, it makes sense to continue doing so. By seeking training in using these tools, you will be better prepared for the jobs of tomorrow, will be more competitive in the job market, and will have greater opportunities. Problem solving: AI tools can help students analyze large amounts of data quickly and accurately, improving their decision-making and problem-solving skills. It also increases productivity: AI tools can increase students' efficiency and help them focus on more creative tasks. And complex ones that require human brains.

7. TEACHING STUDENTS TO USE ARTIFICIAL INTELLIGENCE TOOLS

Artificial intelligence in education (AIEd) refers to the application of artificial intelligence technologies and tools such as chatbots, automatic assessment systems, intelligent tutoring systems, and student performance prediction platforms that support and improve education (Chiu et al., 2023). The majority of AIEd research has focused on developing AI tools and systems that cover the effectiveness of learning algorithms as well as AI ethics and the fundamental rights of AI students (Berendt et al., 2020; Chiu et al., 2022; Al, 2020; McStay, 2020; Lukin and Cukurova, 2019). An AIEd systematic review indicates that AI technologies have been integrated into four major educational areas: teaching, learning, assessment, and management (Chiu et al., 2023). For example, intelligent teaching systems can recommend subject content, assignments, and teaching strategies; chatbots can provide feedback to support students' self-regulation of learning and answer their administrative questions; Automated evaluation systems can enable more efficient evaluation. Studies have highlighted that current AIEd research reflects a weak relationship with pedagogical perspectives or approaches and ignores the complexity and multifaceted challenges and risks associated with learning and teaching using AI (Guilherme, 2019; Holmes et al., 2019, Article 165; Williamsona et Inuna, 2020; Chatbots and Student Experiences). Chatbots are AI-powered applications designed to mimic human interactions and hold spontaneous conversations with people in real time, and their role in classroom learning, especially language teaching, is contingent (Fryer et al., 2019; Shah et al., 2016; Yin et al., 2021). Previous related research has focused on how to understand human conversations and motivate students to learn. Using AI tools Research conducted on the capabilities (i.e., understanding) of chatbots has shown that their ability to have "real" conversations can be limited. The generation has been developed. Chatbots first emerged as language learning tools in the 2000s, and interacting with them can be frustrating for students. For example, students had to type prompts correctly (Kuniam, 2008). In addition, chatbots were not always able to accurately answer students' questions to continue the conversation (Fryer et al., 2019; Yin et al., 2021).

Inspire students with stories of people using AI for good.AI is the reason behind many important advances. There are several real-life examples of AI doing good. According to the Harvard Business Review, the Associated Press produced 12 times more stories by training its AI software to write short articles about revenue. These efforts allowed the agency's journalists to write more in-depth articles. Deep Patient, an artificial intelligence tool developed by the Icahn School of Medicine at Mount Sinai, allows doctors to identify at-risk patients before diagnosing the disease. According to InsideBIGDATA, the tool analyzes a patient's medical history to predict approximately 80 diseases annually. "Artificial intelligence has radically changed people's lives," said Gerard Quinn, Special Rapporteur on the Rights of Persons with Disabilities. These new technologies can bring enormous benefits to people with disabilities and accelerate the pursuit of global equality in many areas, such as work, education, and independent living. However, there are some known effects of discrimination. Quinn made these statements when presenting his report to the Human Rights Council. In his report, Quinn defines AI as machines created to "behave like or resemble humans, but faster, better, more reliably, and without human bias." People with disabilities represent people with disabilities. helpless. These include the right to privacy, independence, education, work, health, independent living, and participation. Artificial intelligence-based systems have a positive impact on the lives of people with disabilities. "Obstacles that we thought were insurmountable suddenly became scalable," Quinn noted, including technology to help blind people improve their mobility. Adaptive learning platforms also provide personalized learning experiences tailored to the specific needs of students with disabilities. In addition, robots and other AI-based tools provide home care and other assistance, enabling people with disabilities to live independently. "Past human decisions and value judgments can be wrong for many reasons," Quinn continued. The report concludes that AI tools can lead to human bias and the exclusion of people with disabilities. One example is recruitment, where processes increasingly rely on algorithms to select candidates and weed out undesirables. "Reasonable accommodations" that enable them to perform the essential functions of the job. In his report, Quinn proposed new steps to realize the practical benefits that artificial intelligence can bring to people with disabilities and put their human rights at the center of the debate about these new benefits. In other recommendations, it called on countries to integrate a disability perspective into their AI strategies, to insist on commitments to "reasonable accommodation," and to explicitly consider disability in the development and procurement of AI products and services. AI applications and technologies have also been used to facilitate the Hajj and Umrah pilgrimages for pilgrims to perform. Their rituals. During the Hajj season last year, the government of the Kingdom of Saudi Arabia attached great importance to the safety, health, and security of pilgrims and placed the protection of human life at the top of its priorities while providing all necessary facilities that would facilitate the Hajj. Assisting pilgrims in performing Hajj and enabling them to reach the holy sites easily. To facilitate the Hajj, the smart barley card has been introduced. This is a step towards improving digital services for God's guests and linking operations and services on an integrated electronic platform that works using short-distance communication technology. NFC technology allows cards to be read using Masher's self-service terminals. It offers many features and functions, such as storing personal information and information related to their residence for pilgrims, guiding them to their places of residence in the holy sites, controlling access to various facilities, and reducing irregular Hajj cases. A systematic review conducted by AIEd shows that AI technologies have been integrated into four major educational areas: teaching, learning, assessment, and management (Chiu et al., 2023). It operates with an automatic control system based on a pre-programmed map. At a level that works to improve environmental safety, health, and the atmosphere, intelligently analyzes sterilization requirements, and operates for 5 to 8 hours without human intervention within the framework of disseminating technical services during this year's Hajj season, and taking into account precautionary measures, the "Automated Fatwa" service was launched in the mosques of the holy shrines and places. Local, which allows remote visual communication between the mufti's interlocutors, who can be reached around the clock, and guarantees him the attention and guidance he needs throughout the season thanks to the automatic control system based on programmed paths and sensitive motion sensors.

8. FUTURE RESEARCH DIRECTIONS

Specific issues and difficulties surrounding the application of AI in educational assessments may be the focus of future areas of research. For example, scientists could consider measures to protect the privacy and security of student data and reduce bias in AI algorithms. In addition, research could investigate cutting-edge AI techniques and tools that increase overall student learning outcomes and improve the assessment process.

9. CONCLUSION

This study provides the goals of artificial intelligence, its applications, its impact on technology, and the future of students and their education. It must be emphasized that applications of artificial intelligence are ultimately no different from being one of the important educational tools for training future students who depend on activating the roles of teachers in using them, especially the future challenges that will be imposed on them. The study underscores how important it is to give teachers and students the guidance and assistance they need to use technology and artificial intelligence (AI) tools in the classroom. It is recommended that teachers make use of artificial intelligence (AI) resources, such as plagiarism detection software and automated grading systems, in order to improve grading efficiency and provide timely feedback to students. In order to ensure that assessments are impartial and fair for every student, teachers must also give top priority to ethics and openness while using AI in assessments.

REFERENCES

Alberta Education. (2013). *Learning and technology policy framework 2013*. Retrieved from http://www.education.alberta.ca/media/7792655/learning-and-technology-policy-framework-web.pdf

Aleedy, M., Atwell, E., & Meshoul, S. (2022). Using AI Chatbots in Education: Recent Advances Challenges and Use Case. In Artificial Intelligence and Sustainable Computing. *Proceedings of ICSISCET, 2021*, 661–675. doi:10.1007/978-981-19-1653-3_50

Eze, Iwu, & Dubihlela. (2022). Students' views regarding the barriers to learning critical thinking. *International Journal of Research in Business and Social Science, 11*(4), 355–364. . doi:10.20525/ijrbs.v11i4.1797

Anirudh, K., Bishwajeet, P., Kushagra, V., Kartik, K., & Bhale, P. (2015). Das Teerath. A Study of Today's A.I. through Chatbots and Rediscovery of Machine Intelligence. *International Journal of u- and e-Service Science and Technology, 8*(7), 277–284.

Arifuddin, M., Thalib, S. B., & Ali, M. S. (2022). The Development of Modeling Physics Learning to Improve Critical Thinking Ability of Student. *Asian Journal of Applied Sciences, 10*(1). Advance online publication. doi:10.24203/ajas.v10i1.6842

Bailey, L. W. (2019). New Technology for the Classroom: Mobile Devices, Artificial Intelligence, Tutoring Systems, and Robotics. In Educational Technology and the New World of Persistent Learning (pp. 1-11). IGI Global.

Bansal, H., & Khan, R. (2018). A review paper on human computer interaction. *International Journal of Advanced Research in Computer Science and Software Engineering, 8*(4), 53. doi:10.23956/ijarcsse.v8i4.630

Bergdahl, N., Nouri, J., & Fors, U. (2020). Disengagement, engagement and digital skills in technology-enhanced learning. *Education and Information Technologies*, 25(2), 957–983. doi:10.1007/s10639-019-09998-w

Beringer, V. (2009, October 20). *For kids, pen's mightier than keyboard*. futurity.org. Retrieved February 25th 2013 from http://www.futurity.org/society-culture/for-kids-pens-mightier-than-keyboard/#more-4909

Bozkurt, A., Karadeniz, A., Baneres, D., Guerrero-Roldán, A. E., & Rodríguez, M. E. (2021). Artificial intelligence and reflections fromeducational landscape: A review of AI Studies in half a century. *Sustainability*, 13(2), 1–16. doi:10.3390/su13020800 PMID:34123411

Ceylan, Ö. (2022). The effect of the waste management themed summer program on gifted students' environmental attitude, creative thinking skills and critical thinking dispositions. *Journal of Adventure Education and Outdoor Learning*, 22(1), 53–65. doi:10.1080/14729679.2020.1859393

Chiu, T. K. F., Xia, Q., Zhou, X., Chai, C. S., & Cheng, M. (2023). Systematic literature review on opportunities, challenges, and future research recommendations of artificial intelligence in education. *Computers and Education: Artificial Intelligence*, 100118. Advance online publication. doi:10.1016/j.caeai.2022.100118

Chusni, M. M., Saputro, S., Suranto, S., & Rahardjo, S. B. (2022). High School Students through Discovery-Based Multiple Representations Learning Model. *International Journal of Instruction*, 15(1), 927–945. doi:10.29333/iji.2022.15153a

Clarizia, F., Colace, F., Lombardi, M., Pascale, F., & Santaniello, D. (2018). Chatbot: An education support system for student. *International symposium on cyberspace safety and security*. Springer. https://doi.org/10.1007/978-3-030-01689-0_23.13

Cohen, R. J., Swerdlik, M. E., & Sturman, E. D. (2009). *Psychological Testing and Assessment: An Introduction to Tests and Measurement* (7th ed.). McGraw-Hill.

Cropley, A. J. (2001). *Creativity in Education and Learning: A Guide for Teachers and Educators*. Kogan Page.

Csikszentmihalyi, M. (2006). Foreword: developing creativity. In N. Jackson, M. Oliver, M. Shaw, & J. Wisdom (Eds.), *Developing Creativity in Higher Education* (pp. xviii–xx). Routledge.

Djavanshir, G. R., Lee, M. R., & Liew, J. K.-S. (2020). Spotlight on AI!—Whyeveryone should pay attention now! *IT Professional*, 22(4), 18–20. doi:10.1109/MITP.2020.3006945

Duan, Y., Edwards, J. S., & Dwivedi, Y. K. (2019). Artificial intelligence fordecision making in the era of big data – evolution, challenges and research agenda. *International Journal of Information Management*, 48, 63–71. doi:10.1016/j.ijinfomgt.2019.01.021

Eke, O. D. (2023). ChatGPT and the rise of generative AI: Threat to academic integrity? *Journal of Responsible Technology*, 13, 100060. doi:10.1016/j.jrt.2023.100060

Farmer, E. C., Catalano, A. J., & Halpern, A. J. (2019). Exploring Student Preference between Textbook Chapters and Adaptive Learning Lessons in an Introductory Environmental Geology Course. *TechTrends*, 1–8.

Fryer, L. K., Nakao, K., & Thompson, A. (2019). Chatbot learning partners: Connecting learning experiences, interest and competence. *Computers in Human Behavior, 93*, 279–289. doi:10.1016/j.chb.2018.12.023

Fryer, M. (2003). *Creativity across the Curriculum: A Review and Analysis of Programmes Designed to Develop Creativity.* Qualifications and Curriculum Authority.

Gardner, H. (1982). *Art, Mind, Brain: A Cognitive Approach to Creativity.* Basic Books.

Goel, A. K., & Polepeddi, L. (2016). *Jill Watson: A virtual teaching assistant for online education.* Georgia Institute of Technology.

Goksel, N., & Bozkurt, A. (2019). Artificial intelligence in education: Current insights and future perspectives. In S. Sisman-Ugur & G. Kurubacak (Eds.), *Handbook of research on learning in the age of transhumanis m* (pp. 224–236). IGI Global. doi:10.4018/978-1-5225-8431-5.ch014

Guilherme, A. (2019). AI and education: The importance of teacher and student relations. *AI & Society, 34*(1), 47–54. doi:10.1007/s00146-017-0693-8

Golic, Z. (2019). Finance and artificial intelligence: The fifth industrial revolution and its impact on the financial sector. *Zbornik radova Ekonomskog fakulteta u Istočnom Sarajevu*, (19), 67–81.

Haseski, H. I. (2019). What do Turkish pre-service teachers think about artificial intelligence? *International Journal of Computer Science Education in Schools, 3*(2), 3–23. Advance online publication. doi:10.21585/ijcses.v3i2.55

Hossein, M.G. & Maryam, R. (2012). An Adaptive and Intelligent Tutor by Expert Systems for Mobile Devices. *International Journal of Managing Public.*

Humble, N., & Mozelius, P. (2019, October). *Artificial Intelligence in Education-a Promise, a Threat or Hype?* Academic Press.

Hinojo-Lucena, F.-J., Aznar-Díaz, I., Cáceres-Reche, M.-P., & Romero-Rodríguez, J.-M. (2019). Artificial Intelligence in Higher Education: A Bibliometric Study on Its Impact in the Scientific Literature. *Education Sciences, 9*(1), 51. doi:10.3390/educsci9010051

Holotescu, C., & Grosseck, G. (2018). Towards a MOOC-related Strategy in Romania. BRAIN. *Broad Research in Artificial Intelligence and Neuroscience, 9*, 99–109.

Holstein, K., McLaren, B. M., & Aleven, V. (2019, June). Designing for Complementarity:Teacher and Student Needs for Orchestration Support in AI-Enhanced Classrooms. In *International Conference on Artificial Intelligence in Education* (pp. 157-171).Springer.

Huttar, C. M., & BrintzenhofeSzoc, K. (2019). Virtual Reality and Computer Simulation in Social Work Education. *Systematic Reviews.*

Jackson, P. C. (2019). *Introduction to artificial intelligence.* Courier Dover Publications.

Karsenti, T. (2019). Artificial intelligence in education: the urgent need to prepare teachers for tomorrow's schools. *Formation et profession, 27*(1), 112–116. . doi:10.18162/fp.2019.a166

Kose, U. (Ed.). (2014). *Artificial Intelligence applications in distance education.* IGI Global.

Kose, U., Mohammed, P. S., & Watson, E. N. (2019). Towards inclusive education in the age of artificial intelligence: perspectives, challenges, and opportunities. In J. Knox, Y. Wang, & M. Gallagher (Eds.), *Artificial Intelligence and Inclusive Education. Perspectives on Rethinking and Reforming Education.* Springer. doi:10.1007/978-981-13-8161-4_2

Manyika, J., Chui, M., Miremadi, M., Bughin, J., George, K., Willmott, P., & Dewhurst, M. (2017). *A future that works: Automation, employment, and productivity.* McKinsey Global Institute.

Martin, J., Bohuslava, J., & Igor, H. (2018, September). Augmented Reality in Education 4.0. In *2018 IEEE 13th International Scientific and Technical Conference on Computer Sciences and Information Technologies (CSIT)* (Vol. 1, pp. 231-236). IEEE.

Martinez, C. (2022). Developing 21st century teaching skills: A case study of teaching and learning through project-based curriculum. *Cogent Education, 9*(1), 2024936. doi:10.1080/2331186X.2021.2024936

Miao, F., Holmes, W., Huang, R., & Zhang, H. (2021). *AI and education: A guidance for policymakers.* UNESCO Publishing.

Mohammed, P. S., & Watson, E. N. (2019). Towards inclusive education in the age of artificial intelligence: perspectives, challenges, and opportunities. In J. Knox, Y. Wang, & M. Gallagher (Eds.), *Artificial Intelligence and Inclusive Education. Perspectives on Rethinking and Reforming Education.* Springer. doi:10.1007/978-981-13-8161-4_2

Nazemi, K., Breyer, M., Burkhardt, D., Stab, C., & Kohlhammer, J. (2014). SemaVis: A new approach for visualizing semantic information. In *Towards the Internet of Services: The THESEUS Research Program* (pp. 191–202). Springer. doi:10.1007/978-3-319-06755-1_15

Niemi, H. (2021). AI in learning: Preparing grounds for future learning. *Journal of Pacific Rim Psychology, 15*, 1–12. doi:10.1177/18344909211038105

Okonkwo, C. W., & Ade-Ibijola, A. (2020). Python-bot: A chatbot for teaching python programming. *Engineering Letters, 29*(1), 25–35.

Oliver, M., Shah, B., McGoldrick, C., & Edwards, M. (2006). 'Students' experiences of creativity. In N. J. Jackson (Ed.), *Developing Creativity in Higher Education: an Imaginative Curriculum.* Routledge-Falmer.

Opfer, A., Kilgore, W., & Crosslin, M. (2018). Bot-teachers in hybrid massive open online courses (MOOCs): A post-humanist experience. *Australasian Journal of Educational Technology, 34*(3).

Opfer, V. D., Kaufman, J. H., & Thompson, L. E. (2016). *Implementation of K–12 state standards for mathematics and English language arts and literacy.* RAND Corporation.

Pollarolo, E., Størksen, I., Skarstein, T. H., & Kucirkova, N. (2022). Children's critical thinking skills: Perceptions of Norwegian early childhood educators. *European Early Childhood Education Research Journal*, 1–13. doi:10.1080/1350293X.2022.2081349

Roll, I., & Wylie, R. (2016). Evolution and revolution in artificial intelligence in education. *International Journal of Artificial Intelligence in Education, 26*(2), 582–599. doi:10.1007/s40593-016-0110-3

Rospigliosi, P. A. (2023). Artificial intelligence in teaching and learning: What questions should we ask of ChatGPT? *Interactive Learning Environments*, *31*(1), 1–3. doi:10.1080/10494820.2023.2180191

Sekeroglu, B., Dimililer, K., & Tuncal, K. (2019). Artificial intelligence in education: application in student performance evaluation. Dilemas Contemporáneos: Educación. *Política y Valores*, *7*(1), 1–21.

Shang, M. (2019, August). The Application of Artificial Intelligence in Music Education. In *International Conference on Intelligent Computing* (pp. 662-668). Springer. 10.1007/978-3-030-26969-2_62

Stein, M. I. (1988). Creativity: The process and its stimulation. In F. Flach (Ed.), *The creative mind* (pp. 50–75). Bearly Limited.

Touretzky, D., Gardner-McCune, C., Martin, F., & Seehorn, D. (2019). Envisioning ai for k-12: What should every child know about AI? Proceedings of the AAAI conference on artificial intelligence, 33(1), 9795–9799. doi:10.1609/aaai.v33i01.33019795

Wartman, S. A., & Combs, C. D. (2018). Medical education must move from the information age to the age of artificial intelligence. *Academic Medicine*, *93*(8), 1107–1109. doi:10.1097/ACM.0000000000002044 PMID:29095704

Whizz Education. (2014). *Math whizz*. Author.

Wisdom, J. (2006). Developing higher education teachers to teach creatively. In N. Jackson, M. Oliver, M. Shaw, & J. Wisdom (Eds.), *Developing Creativity in Higher Education* (pp. 183–197). Routledge.

Wogu, I. A. P., Misra, S., Olu-Owolabi, E. F., Assibong, P. A., & Udoh, O. D. (2018). Artificial intelligence, artificial teachers and the fate of learners in the 21st century education sector: Implications for theory and practice. *International Journal of Pure and Applied Mathematics*, *119*(16), 2245–2259.

Zhou, X., Van Brummelen, J., & Lin, P. (2020). *Designing AI learning experiences for k-12: emerging works, future opportunities and a design framework*. https://doi.org//arXiv.2009.10228. doi:10.48550

Chapter 14
The Impact and Future of AI–Enhanced Teaching Methods in the Use of Business Simulations

Hélder Fanha Martins

(iD) https://orcid.org/0000-0003-3544-0703

Polytechnic University of Lisbon, Portugal

ABSTRACT

This chapter examines the transformative role of AI-enhanced teaching methods in business simulation studies. With a focus on the integration of AI in education, it highlights a paradigm shift towards more dynamic, personalized, and effective learning environments. The chapter delves into the implications of AI in enhancing decision-making knowledge, student engagement, and learning outcomes, aligning educational practices with future business leadership and management needs. It underscores AI's role in fostering a practice-oriented approach, enhancing teaching processes and creating personalized learning experiences. Furthermore, the chapter explores the impact of AI on teaching and learning in business education, emphasizing the need for educators to adapt and leverage AI tools to augment pedagogical approaches and improve student outcomes. As AI reshapes the educational landscape, the chapter calls for a collaborative approach among technology developers, educators, and policymakers to integrate AI tools effectively and ethically into educational frameworks.

INTRODUCTION

The integration of Artificial Intelligence (AI) in education, particularly in business simulation studies, represents a transformative shift in teaching methodologies. AI technology has enabled the construction of complex business models featuring both human and software-agent participation, which significantly enhances decision-making knowledge and game balance in educational simulations (Kobayashi et al., 2003). This integration signifies a broader shift in educational paradigms, necessitating a redesign of education systems to prepare future generations for a rapidly evolving technological landscape (Alkashri et al., 2020).

DOI: 10.4018/979-8-3693-2728-9.ch014

In an era where technology and education increasingly intersect, AI stands at the forefront of transformative educational methodologies. The introduction of AI into teaching and learning environments heralds a new dawn for personalized education, offering unprecedented opportunities for student engagement, adaptive learning, and data-driven insights into learning processes. By harnessing AI's capabilities, educators can tailor their teaching strategies to meet the diverse needs of students, creating immersive and interactive learning experiences that transcend traditional boundaries. This chapter illuminates the pivotal role AI plays in redefining educational paradigms, particularly through the lens of business simulations, where its impact on decision-making, problem-solving, and strategic thinking skills is profound and far-reaching.

Recent advancements in AI, such as knowledge representation and frame-based simulation, have found practical applications in both education and business simulation studies, enabling more dynamic and contextually rich learning environments. These technological enhancements not only improve the educational experience but also significantly contribute to the development of essential skills, such as entrepreneurial attitude and decision-making, in business simulation games (Jia et al., 2022). Moreover, AI's role in education extends to reducing instructors' burdens, improving students' contextualized learning experiences, and advancing sophisticated tutoring systems (Ojha et al., 2023). These applications highlight AI's capability to create personalized teaching-learning environments characterized by features such as pattern recognition, decision-making, and problem-solving (Kumar et al., 2019). The amalgamation of AI in business simulation studies not only caters to the current educational needs but also aligns with the future trajectory of business leadership and management, addressing global sustainability challenges and transforming traditional educational frameworks (Goralski et al., 2020).

In the rapidly evolving digital age, the integration of AI into educational practices presents an unparalleled opportunity to redefine pedagogical methodologies and enhance learning experiences. This study is motivated by the urgent need to understand and harness the potential of AI-enhanced teaching methods, particularly in the field of business simulations. As traditional educational approaches struggle to keep pace with the dynamic demands of the global business environment, AI offers a transformative solution. It promises to not only augment educational outcomes but also to personalize learning, thereby preparing students more effectively for the complexities of the modern workforce. By investigating the impact and future implications of AI in business simulation-based education, this research seeks to illuminate pathways towards more engaging, efficient, and adaptive educational models, ultimately contributing to the discourse on the future of learning in an increasingly digital world.

This chapter aims to delve into the nuances of AI-enhanced teaching methods in business simulation studies, examining their impact on learning outcomes, student engagement, and the broader educational landscape. The importance of integrating AI into teaching methodologies, especially post-2021, is underscored by its potential to revolutionize the learning landscape. AI enables a practice-oriented approach to learning, encouraging students to cultivate AI-related skills and improve human-machine collaboration (Xie et al. 2021). This integration is not merely a technological upgrade but a paradigm shift in how teaching and learning are designed and delivered, tailoring educational services to individual student needs and interests (Lameras, 2022).

The radical changes brought by AI extend educational settings beyond the traditional classroom, offering novel and flexible learning environments (Niemi et al., 2021). In addition to enhancing teaching processes, AI and learning analytics focus on improving teachers' behaviors, perceptions, and digital competencies, thereby enriching the overall educational experience (Salas-Pilco et al., 2022). Furthermore, AI's potential to revolutionize the integration of human and artificial intelligence impacts both learning and teaching, redefining the collaboration between humans and machines in an educational context (Ifenthaler et al., 2023). AI in education can focus on individualized, self-adaptive learning for students, assist teaching for educators, and improve school management efficiency, thereby addressing diverse educational needs and objectives (Xu, 2020).

By integrating AI into teaching methodologies, educators can create a more satisfactory and effective learning environment, methods, and outcomes, promoting the development of intelligent teaching systems across various disciplines (Jia et al., 2021; Huang et al., 2021). This integration is essential in adapting to the dynamic needs of contemporary education, where AI not only enhances teaching levels and students' learning quality but also promotes education reform and innovation.

After the introduction, which establishes the transformative role of AI in education, the chapter gives an overview of AI-enhanced teaching methods, illustrating their growing importance in business education. The chapter then explores the impact on learning outcomes, demonstrating how AI applications in simulations improve various educational metrics. It proceeds to discuss the technological and pedagogical integration of AI, showcasing its contribution to personalized learning environments and instructional design. The chapter addresses challenges and future directions, identifying areas for further research and potential obstacles in integrating AI into business education. Finally, it concludes by summarizing the profound and multifaceted effects of AI-enhanced teaching methods on business simulations, emphasizing improved learning experiences, personalization, and administrative efficiency. This study employs a comprehensive literature review methodology to explore the impact and future of AI-enhanced teaching methods in the use of business simulations. By systematically analyzing existing research, publications, and case analyses within the domain, this approach allows for an extensive synthesis of current knowledge and emerging trends in AI applications in education. The literature review spans a wide array of sources, including peer-reviewed journals, conference proceedings, industry reports, and educational technology frameworks, ensuring a robust and diverse collection of insights. This methodological approach facilitates a deep dive into the nuances of AI's role in educational innovation, highlighting its benefits, challenges, and potential pathways for integration into business education.

Drawing conclusions from the literature, the chapter synthesizes findings to identify patterns, gaps, and opportunities for future research and practical application. This involves critically evaluating the effectiveness of AI-enhanced teaching methods, assessing their impact on learning outcomes and student engagement, and considering the implications for curriculum development and instructional design. Through this analysis, the chapter aims to contribute to the broader discourse on educational technology by offering evidence-based recommendations for integrating AI into business simulations. The conclusions drawn are grounded in the comprehensive review of literature, providing a well-rounded perspective on the state of AI in education and its prospects for enhancing teaching and learning in the business domain.

AN OVERVIEW OF AI-ENHANCED TEACHING METHODS

In recent years, the integration of AI into business education has become increasingly important, as evidenced by various studies from 2021 to 2023. Business schools are recognizing the crucial role it plays in education, particularly in incorporating relevant AI competencies into their curricula. This approach is essential in meeting the growing demand for AI-trained professionals in the business sector, thereby aligning educational outcomes with industry needs.

The impact of AI on teaching and learning within business education is notable. It has been shown to improve teaching levels and enhance the quality of student learning, addressing the future challenges and evolving demands of the educational landscape (Huang et al., 2021). Moreover, AI is transforming teaching and learning processes in significant ways, necessitating changes in expertise and prompting future innovations in the field (Niemi et al., 2021). The awareness and adoption of AI among educators in business schools vary, with some educators more willing to embrace AI in their teaching methodologies than others. Understanding and addressing the factors that guide future AI-based management education efforts is crucial for the effective integration of AI in business education (Walia et al., 2022). Furthermore, the mutual enhancement of AI and human intelligence in education, especially in business studies, is a key area of development. AI's ability to analyze large datasets and assist in intelligent decision-making complements the human aspect of teaching, making it particularly relevant in business education, where data-driven decisions are increasingly important (Ifenthaler et al., 2023).

AI-enhanced teaching methods in business education represent a significant stride forward. They not only align with the modern business world's technological trends but also enrich the educational process, equipping students with essential skills and knowledge for thriving in AI-influenced business environments.

The integration of Artificial Intelligence (AI) in education has led to a transformative shift in the role of teachers, as highlighted by recent studies. This transformation is multi-faceted, impacting various aspects of the educational landscape. Firstly, AI integration has resulted in a reformation of the teaching system, transforming both the curriculum and teaching paradigms. Teachers and students are increasingly recognizing the importance of AI technology in education, leading to reshaped instructional methods. This recognition is paving the way for new experiences in teaching roles, with an emphasis on leveraging AI tools to enhance lesson delivery and effectiveness (Jia et al., 2021). Moreover, AI helps teachers integrate various science content more effectively, enabling them to follow courses and validate lesson plan products efficiently. This integration leads to novel experiences in their roles, with AI tools facilitating enhanced lesson delivery and effectiveness.

A significant shift from a teacher-directed approach to a more student-centered approach is also evident, aligning with modern educational paradigms that prioritize student engagement and personalized learning experiences. This shift is a direct consequence of integrating AI into the educational process (Oliver et al., 1994). In addition to enhancing traditional courses, the integration of AI and information and communication technology in education makes e-learning a viable and effective alternative to face-to-face courses. This expansion of the teacher's role beyond the conventional classroom setting is a crucial development in the education sector (Assar et al., 2011). Furthermore, AI has the potential to act as an assistant to teachers, making them more effective and competent in their teaching practices. By handling routine tasks, AI allows teachers to focus on more complex aspects of teaching and personalized student engagement (Shirin, 2022).

Lastly, the integration of AI and learning analytics into teacher education enhance teaching practices and improves the digital competence of both pre-and in-service teachers. This enhancement enables teachers to effectively use technology in their teaching methodologies, preparing them for the evolving demands of the educational sector (Salas-Pilco et al., 2022). In conclusion, the integration of AI in education is reshaping the role of teachers by reforming teaching systems, enhancing content integration, shifting teaching approaches, and improving digital competencies. This transformation is vital for adapting to the changing demands of the educational sector and for preparing students for a future influenced by technological advancements.

IMPACT ON LEARNING OUTCOMES

The integration of AI in business simulations has significantly influenced learning outcomes, particularly enhancing self-efficacy and cultural responsiveness in teaching. Recent studies illustrate these impacts in various educational contexts. AI-based algorithms in simulated teaching environments have been shown to increase self-efficacy related to culturally responsive teaching significantly. These environments provide teachers with practical, hands-on experiences that improve their instructional self-efficacy, particularly in classroom settings where cultural diversity is prevalent (Christensen et al., 2022). This advancement is crucial in equipping teachers with the confidence and skills necessary to address the diverse needs of their students.

Additionally, business simulation games have been found to positively impact students' perceptions of competence, autonomy, and relatedness, leading to enhanced self-efficacy. These games promote cognitive, emotional, and behavioral engagement, which are key components in effective learning and teaching. The immersive and interactive nature of these simulations plays a vital role in fostering an environment where students can develop a sense of mastery and control, thereby enhancing their overall learning experience (Buil et al., 2020).

Furthermore, simulations in different contexts, such as robotics and game design, have led to higher gains in culturally responsive teaching self-efficacy. These tools provide teachers with innovative ways to integrate computational thinking and culturally responsive practices into their teaching, further enhancing their ability to engage students from diverse backgrounds (Leonard et al., 2018). In essence, the integration of AI in business education, especially through simulations, has a profound impact on learning outcomes. It not only enhances teachers' self-efficacy in culturally responsive teaching but also fosters an environment where students can develop key competencies in a manner that is both engaging and effective. This progression in educational methods underscores the importance of AI in addressing the dynamic and diverse needs of contemporary classrooms.

Recent advancements in machine learning have significantly contributed to the improvement of decision knowledge and game balance in business simulations. These advancements encompass various aspects of machine learning and its application in educational contexts. Machine learning agents equipped with classifier systems (LCSs) are enhancing decision knowledge and game balance in business simulations, particularly in marketing domains. These systems simulate complex business environments, providing realistic scenarios that improve decision-making skills and understanding of business dynamics (Kobayashi et al., 2003).

Recent developments in reinforcement learning, such as multi-agent reinforcement learning (MARL), have successfully solved sequential decision-making problems. This technology is applicable in machine learning games like Go and Poker, and its principles can be translated to business simulations, enhancing decision-making processes and strategic thinking (Zhang et al., 2019). Knowledge-based computer game simulation using software agents assists decision-making across supply chains, improving understanding of operational management. This application is particularly relevant in business simulations, where understanding the supply chain dynamics is crucial (Pal et al., 2020). The progress of machine learning, driven by new learning algorithms and theory, leads to more evidence-based decision-making in various fields, including education. This progress impacts how business simulations are designed and executed, making them more effective in teaching decision-making skills (Jordan & Mitchell, 2015). An agent-based framework in business simulations allows learners to make decisions and provides decision support. Agents learn how the model works through reinforcement learning techniques, enhancing the effectiveness of business simulations as educational tools (Remondino, 2008). Recent deep learning advances in video game playing have unique requirements for different game genres. This research can be applied to business simulations, dealing with large decision spaces and sparse rewards, thus improving the learning experience for students (Justesen et al., 2017).

In summary, the integration of advanced machine learning techniques in business simulations has greatly enhanced both decision knowledge and game balance. These advancements foster a more effective and equitable learning environment, equipping students with essential skills for strategic decision-making in business contexts.

Recent advancements in AI have greatly influenced the cultivation of practical problem-solving abilities in business education. Business schools have been identified as playing a crucial role in meeting the growing organizational demand for AI competencies. By incorporating these competencies into their curricula, business schools are preparing students with the necessary skills to solve real-world problems using AI. Some educational programs have focused on imparting practical skills and competencies in AI models and methods (Eremeev et al., 2022). These programs enable students to implement prototypes of modern AI systems for various purposes, thereby enhancing their problem-solving capabilities.

Also, a study by Jiao et al. (2020) highlighted the importance of integrating AI with innovation and entrepreneurship education in universities. This integration is essential for cultivating innovative talents capable of solving practical problems in the AI field. The study recognizes the growing demand for AI professionals and the talent gap in the field, emphasizing the importance of integrating innovation and entrepreneurship education into AI talent training programs. The authors propose a curriculum practice framework that incorporates open-source AI platforms, promoting the use of deep learning, model libraries, and end-to-end development tools. This framework aims to lower the entry barriers to AI technology and encourage students to innovate and develop high-quality AI applications by studying, renovating, and reusing open-source projects. They also suggest designing innovative practice projects that combine basic AI concepts, development history, and classical algorithms with real-world problem-solving. Examples include projects based on the MNIST dataset for handwritten numeral recognition and the CIFAR-10 dataset for image classification using deep learning. Furthermore, the authors advocate for a teaching model that integrates AI education with other disciplines, such as computer control, mathematics, statistics, and physics. They propose a rotating laboratory internship system for undergraduates in interdisciplinary disciplines to foster academic interest, research skills, and innovative thinking. The study concludes that universities can meet the demand for AI professionals by cultivating innovative and entrepreneurial AI talents. It calls for continuous improvement in the construction of innovative and entrepreneurial education courses, faculty teaching models, and practical links in the field of AI.

The AIGO platform, for example, aims to cultivate AI talents and enable them to tackle real-world industrial problems through competition, learning, and community. This approach is geared towards equipping students with the necessary tools and knowledge to apply AI in practical scenarios (Tseng et al., 2019). The platform's effectiveness is underscored by its tangible results. AIGO has successfully curated a wide array of real-world problems from various industrial sectors, particularly in information service activities. The outcomes from the competitions are noteworthy, with a significant number of AI-powered proposals and awarded solutions. Moreover, the competition serves as a learning conduit, where winning solutions are meticulously documented and shared for future reference, promoting a culture of continuous learning and improvement. AIGO stands out as an innovative and effective platform for cultivating AI talent. Its success is evident in the growing number of participants and the breadth of industrial problems it addresses. The synergy among its three core components, Competition, Learning, and Community, creates a dynamic and nurturing environment that not only equips AI practitioners with the necessary skills but also fosters a self-sustaining ecosystem of continuous learning and innovation. Additionally, students improve their scientific cognitive skills of problem-solving by applying cross-disciplinary problem-based learning and AI new knowledge. This method demonstrates the effectiveness of integrating AI into problem-solving learning processes.

In summary, the integration of AI into business education in recent years has significantly enhanced the cultivation of practical problem-solving abilities. This integration not only prepares students for the current demands of the business world but also equips them with skills that are essential for future challenges and innovations.

On the other hand, recent studies have highlighted the significant role of AI and business simulations in improving skills acquisition and knowledge retention and encouraging entrepreneurship. Business simulations are recognized for their effectiveness in simulating real-world enterprise environments. These simulations enhance skills acquisition, knowledge retention, and entrepreneurship by offering students practical, hands-on experiences that mirror real business scenarios (Alves et al., 2018). Immersive learning simulations, including AI and business simulations, have been shown to improve skills acquisition and knowledge retention significantly. They provide an engaging and interactive learning environment that encourages students to develop entrepreneurial skills and attitudes (Vastag & Yerushalmy, 2009).

Simulation games are effective in developing students' entrepreneurial skills, encouraging entrepreneurial activities, and improving analytical skills and business knowledge. By participating in these simulations, students can apply theoretical knowledge in practical settings, enhancing their problem-solving and decision-making skills (Thanasi-Boçe, 2020).

Combining AI with business simulation games has been shown to improve entrepreneurial attitude by simulating real-world competitors, providing targeted feedback for failures, and improving the overall game experience. This approach not only enhances students' business skills but also fosters an entrepreneurial mindset, which is essential in the current business landscape (Chen et al., 2022).

In summary, AI and business simulations play a crucial role in the modern educational landscape by enhancing skill acquisition and knowledge retention and fostering entrepreneurship. These tools provide students with realistic and interactive learning experiences, preparing them for the challenges of the contemporary business world.

TECHNOLOGICAL AND PEDAGOGICAL INTEGRATION

Artificial intelligence contributes significantly to personalized teaching-learning environments, enhancing various features like recognition, pattern matching, decision-making, reasoning, and problem-solving, thereby contributing to personalized teaching-learning environments. These skills are particularly useful in mechatronics and robotics education, demonstrating AI's broad applicability in various educational fields (Kalazhokov et al., 2021).

Intelligent teaching-learning systems use AI techniques like case-based reasoning and fuzzy pattern recognition to adapt to individual learning needs dynamically. These systems can evaluate a student's performance and customize the learning experience accordingly, enhancing the effectiveness of the educational process (Martínez et al., 2007). AI can also optimize blended teaching methods by breaking traditional physical spaces, promoting personalized thinking, and optimizing evaluation methods. This approach facilitates a more adaptable and individualized learning experience, catering to diverse student needs (Zheng, 2020). In the field of intelligent tutor systems, AI is the backbone, helping to develop qualities such as self-reflection, answering deep questions, resolving conflict statements, generating creative questions, and choice-making skills. These systems provide a more interactive and engaging learning environment (Malik, 2018).

These systems excel in simulating real-world business scenarios, prompting learners to reflect on their decisions, analyze complex business dilemmas, and navigate through conflicting information. By generating creative questions, these AI tutors encourage innovative thinking and strategic decision-making, essential in the business world. Furthermore, they facilitate the development of choice-making abilities, preparing students to tackle the multifaceted challenges of today's dynamic business environment. This AI-driven approach not only makes the learning process more interactive and engaging but also closely aligns with the practical needs and fast-paced nature of the business sector. It mirrors the dynamic decision-making and problem-solving processes found in real-world business environments, offering students a hands-on experience that prepares them for the complexities of modern business challenges. Through this enhanced interactivity, learners are better equipped to understand and apply business concepts, strategies, and practices, ensuring they are ready to innovate and lead in a competitive market landscape.

AI technology in education can improve efficiency in teaching, optimize course design, and engage students in deep learning, leading to personalized and in-depth learning experiences. This technology can tailor content and teaching methods to individual students, thereby enhancing learning outcomes (Liu et al., 2022). In their 2022 study, Liu et al. explored the significant impact of artificial intelligence on education, emphasizing its role in enhancing both teaching and learning processes. The research highlighted how AI technology can greatly improve the efficiency of teaching. This includes automating routine tasks such as grading, providing personalized feedback to students, and allowing teachers to concentrate on more complex and creative teaching aspects. Moreover, the study shed light on AI's capability to optimize course design. By analyzing extensive datasets, AI can identify the most effective teaching methods and materials, leading to course structures that are more engaging and tailored to the diverse needs and learning styles of students. This optimization is crucial for creating educational experiences that are both effective and captivating. Another key area where AI contributes is in deepening student engagement in the learning process. AI-driven tools can offer interactive and immersive learning experiences, which not only enhance students' understanding of complex concepts but also promote critical thinking and problem-solving skills. This aspect of AI in business education is particularly important for developing higher-order cognitive skills among learners.

Additionally, the study by Liu et al. (2022) underscored the role of AI in personalizing learning experiences. AI technologies can analyze student performance and learning habits to customize educational content and adjust pacing according to individual student needs. This personalization ensures that each student receives an education that is best suited to their unique learning trajectory, thus maximizing learning outcomes. Apart from classroom applications, AI also shows immense potential in administrative aspects of education. AI can streamline processes such as admission, student record management, and resource allocation within educational institutions. This administrative efficiency allows educational institutions to manage their resources better and focus more on educational quality and student support. Overall, Liu et al.'s study (2022) presents AI as a transformative force in the field of education, highlighting its capacity to enhance teaching efficiency, optimize course design, deepen learning engagement, personalize learning experiences, and improve administrative efficiency. This research underscores the growing significance of AI in reshaping the educational landscape to meet contemporary educational challenges.

In summary, AI contributes to personalized teaching-learning environments by providing tailored educational experiences that cater to the unique needs of individual students. This technology enhances key educational features such as recognition, pattern matching, decision-making, reasoning, and problem-solving, thereby improving the overall quality and effectiveness of education.

As far as instructional design is concerned, AI technology plays a crucial role in enhancing the effectiveness of various instructional design features in simulation-based education. Recent research has delved into how AI contributes to creating more efficient, adaptive, and effective educational models. The AI-assisted integrated teaching-learning framework (AL-ITLF) in higher education exemplifies this contribution. It creates a more efficient educational model with high accuracy, improved performance, lower processing costs, and a high prediction rate with low error (Chang et al., 2022). This framework demonstrates how AI can be used to tailor education to individual student needs while maintaining high quality and efficiency. In their 2022 study, Chang et al. explored the transformative potential of artificial intelligence (AI) in enhancing higher education through the AI-assisted integrated teaching-learning framework (AL-ITLF). This framework is designed to improve the efficiency of educational models significantly. By incorporating AI technologies, it processes educational data with high accuracy and efficiency, resulting in enhanced performance while reducing processing costs compared to traditional educational models.

A key feature of the AL-ITLF is its adaptability, allowing it to cater to the diverse learning needs and styles prevalent in higher education. This flexibility is essential in addressing the varied backgrounds, abilities, and preferences of students. The framework's effectiveness surpasses traditional schooling methods thanks to its precision in operations. This ensures that educational content and assessments are precisely tailored to individual student needs, thus enhancing learning outcomes. Moreover, the high performance of the AL-ITLF, backed by AI technologies, enables it to handle complex educational tasks effectively. It delivers content in a manner that is engaging and pedagogically sound, ensuring that students are not only absorbing information but are also actively engaged in the learning process. Another significant advantage of the AL-ITLF is the reduction in processing costs. Leveraging AI technologies minimizes the need for extensive physical resources and human intervention in routine educational tasks. This efficiency allows for the reallocation of resources to more critical areas of education.

What's more, the framework is characterized by its high prediction accuracy in student performance and learning outcomes, coupled with a low error rate. This precision is crucial for creating personalized learning paths and providing accurate, timely feedback to students, thereby optimizing the educational experience. Overall, Chang et al.'s study underscores the importance of integrating AI into higher education, highlighting its role in creating more efficient, adaptable, and effective teaching and learning environments. This research points to the growing necessity of AI in reshaping the educational landscape to better meet the needs of students and educators in the modern era. The study by Chang et al. (2022) on the integration of artificial intelligence (AI) in higher education, particularly through the AI-assisted integrated teaching-learning framework (AL-ITLF), offers profound insights that can be effectively linked to business education and business simulation.

In business education, the implementation of the AL-ITLF can revolutionize the way business concepts are taught and learned. The framework's emphasis on efficiency, adaptability, and effectiveness aligns seamlessly with the dynamic and fast-paced nature of business education. By integrating AI into business curricula, educators can provide students with a more personalized and interactive learning experience. This is especially relevant in areas like market analysis, financial decision-making, and strategic planning, where real-time data analysis and adaptive learning play crucial roles. Moreover, the application of AI in business simulations can greatly enhance the educational value of these simulations. Business simulations are designed to mimic real-world business scenarios, and the integration of AI can make these simulations more realistic and responsive. AI can analyze student decisions and provide immediate, personalized feedback, thus improving learning outcomes. Additionally, AI can simulate complex market dynamics, enabling students to experience and respond to realistic business challenges and opportunities.

The high prediction accuracy and low error rate of the AL-ITLF, as highlighted by Chang et al. (2022), are particularly beneficial in business simulations. They ensure that the simulated environment accurately reflects the consequences of students' strategic decisions, thereby providing a rich learning experience that prepares students for real-world business challenges.

In conclusion, the ideas presented regarding the integration of AI in higher education have significant implications for business education and business simulations. The AI-assisted framework the authors propose can enhance the effectiveness of business education by providing more personalized, realistic, and interactive learning experiences. This integration not only aligns with the needs of modern business education but also equips students with the essential skills and knowledge needed to succeed in today's dynamic business environment.

Augmented intelligence and Knowledge-Based System (KBS) technology have also been developed to support curriculum and administrative tasks in distance learning applications. These technologies enhance the effectiveness of instructional design features in simulation-based education by offering more personalized and engaging learning experiences (Crowe et al., 2017). On the other hand, pedagogical agents simulated through AI technology have been found to improve learning and motivation in simulation-based education effectively. These agents provide adaptive guidance and instruction that can evaluate learners and classify or cluster them, contributing to personalized educational systems that are more effective in meeting individual student needs (Kim & Baylor, 2016). Moreover, AI technologies like WASTON and WASTON2 have shown promise in improving efficiency in teaching, optimizing course design, and engaging students in deep learning. This leads to enhanced teaching and learning processes that are more aligned with the demands of contemporary education (Liu et al., 2022).

The importance of ongoing professional development for educators, particularly in the context of rapidly evolving technologies like AI, cannot be overstated. As AI continues to reshape the educational landscape, the need for educators to remain current with these changes is critical. This necessity transcends mere familiarity with new tools; it involves a deep understanding of how AI can transform teaching methodologies, curriculum design, and student engagement. Professional development programs offer educators the opportunity to explore innovative AI applications within education, learn best practices for integrating technology into their classrooms, and develop strategies to enhance learning outcomes through personalized and adaptive teaching methods.

Moreover, ongoing professional development supports educators in navigating the ethical considerations and challenges associated with AI, such as data privacy, bias in AI algorithms, and ensuring equitable access to technology-enhanced learning. By engaging in continuous learning, educators can lead by example, fostering a culture of curiosity and lifelong learning among their students. Institutions play a pivotal role in facilitating this development, offering resources, time, and support for educators to participate in workshops, conferences, and courses. Ultimately, investing in professional development is essential for empowering educators to leverage AI technologies effectively, ensuring they can deliver a relevant, engaging, and high-quality education that prepares students for the future.

CHALLENGES

Implementing AI-enhanced teaching methods in business education and business simulations presents several challenges and opens up avenues for future directions. Recent studies have identified a range of issues that need to be addressed for the successful integration of AI in these areas.

One of the primary challenges lies in the development of AI courses in business schools. It is essential to strike a balance between teaching the fundamentals of AI and keeping abreast of the latest developments in the field. Creating a curriculum that effectively encompasses both aspects can be challenging but is crucial for providing students with a comprehensive understanding of AI in a business context (Xu et al., 2021). Another significant challenge is the lack of data sovereignty, uncertainty, and understanding of data, which are critical for effectively implementing AI-enhanced teaching methods and business simulations. (Renz et al., 2020). These limitations can impede the ability to leverage AI technologies in educational settings fully.

Business simulations face challenges in integrating these technologies into traditional postgraduate business education programs. Despite their potential to deliver meaningful learning outcomes, incorporating these simulations into existing curricula and ensuring they align with educational objectives can be a complex process (Clarke, 2009). A key challenge in traditional teaching methods is translating abstract knowledge into efficient practice. Business simulations can help bridge this gap by providing a realistic environment for students to apply theoretical knowledge. However, integrating these simulations into the curriculum requires careful consideration of their design and execution (Töyli et al., 2006). Looking toward the future, addressing these challenges will require a concerted effort to enhance AI integration in business education. This involves developing curricula that are responsive to the latest AI trends, ensuring data sovereignty and understanding, and designing business simulations that effectively complement traditional teaching methods. As AI continues to evolve, its role in business education and simulations will likely become more pronounced, offering innovative ways to enrich learning experiences and prepare students for the dynamic business world.

However, integrating these simulations into the curriculum requires careful consideration of their design and execution. Beyond this, the integration of AI into business simulations introduces several challenges. Firstly, there is the technical complexity and resource requirement, which may be prohibitive for institutions lacking the necessary infrastructure or expertise. Ensuring the AI components are up-to-date and capable of simulating realistic business scenarios demands continuous investment and development. Secondly, there is the challenge of data privacy and ethical considerations, as AI systems often require access to vast amounts of data, raising concerns about student privacy and the ethical use of educational data. Additionally, there's the need for faculty and students to acquire new skills to effectively engage with these advanced technologies, which can be a significant hurdle in terms of training and adaptation. Addressing these challenges necessitates a multifaceted approach, including investment in technology, professional development for educators, and a commitment to ethical standards in AI use, to fully leverage the potential of AI in enhancing business education.

Addressing scalability and accessibility in the context of AI-enhanced business simulations involves navigating a complex landscape of challenges. Technological constraints and financial resources present significant hurdles, especially for institutions with limited access to cutting-edge tools and infrastructure. The variability in technological advancement across different regions exacerbates these challenges, creating disparities in access and quality of education. To mitigate these obstacles, a concerted effort toward developing scalable AI solutions that are resource-efficient and adaptable to diverse educational settings is crucial. This includes leveraging cloud-based technologies to facilitate easier access and reduce the need for extensive local infrastructure.

The digital divide underscores the importance of making AI-enhanced simulations accessible to a broader audience. Overcoming this divide requires not just technological solutions but also initiatives aimed at reducing costs, enhancing digital literacy, and providing support for educators and learners to adapt to these new tools. Collaborative partnerships between educational institutions, tech companies, and government entities can play a pivotal role in bridging this gap. By focusing on inclusive design and widespread availability, we can ensure that the benefits of AI-enhanced business simulations reach all corners of the educational landscape, preparing a more diverse workforce for the challenges of the global business environment.

FUTURE DIRECTIONS

Exploring potential future developments and research areas in AI-enhanced business education and business simulations reveals a landscape ripe with opportunities for innovation and growth. The integration of AI in these domains promises to transform how business concepts are taught and understood, paving the way for a more dynamic and interactive learning environment.

One area of future development is the creation of simulation-based learning environments that integrate AI and multimedia technologies. Such environments could include role-playing simulators, providing students with realistic and practical experiences in their field of study. This approach not only enhances the learning experience but also prepares students for real-world applications in their respective careers. Another promising area is the use of AI-based simulations in audit education. These simulations could potentially enhance students' moral sensitivity and help them develop situation-adequate moral sensitivity, which is crucial in the business world. Such advancements would not only improve technical skills but also foster ethical decision-making in future business leaders (Bhavani, 2020). Moreover, future research in AI in business education is likely to focus on topics such as robots, IoT, law, and ethics. These areas represent new challenges and opportunities for business education, necessitating a rethinking of traditional business curricula to include these emerging technologies (Loureiro et al., 2021). Additionally, AI-enhanced teaching and learning in business education must navigate both the bright and dark sides of AI, addressing current limitations and trends while exploring new avenues for development. This exploration will likely encompass issues related to ethical concerns, instructor roles, and student support in an increasingly AI-driven educational landscape (Devedžić, 2021).

In summary, the future of AI-enhanced business education and business simulations is marked by the potential for significant advancements in creating more engaging, ethical, and practical learning experiences. These developments will require ongoing research and innovation to fully realize the benefits of AI in business education, preparing students for the challenges and opportunities of the modern business environment.

CONCLUSION

In conclusion, the impact of AI-enhanced teaching methods on business simulation studies has been profound and multifaceted. These advanced methods have transformed traditional business education by integrating cutting-edge technology to create more dynamic, interactive, and effective learning experiences. AI technologies in business simulations have notably enhanced the realism and practicality of these educational tools. They provide students with immersive environments that closely mimic real-world business scenarios, allowing for the practical application of theoretical knowledge. This has led to improved decision-making skills, better understanding of complex business dynamics, and enhanced problem-solving abilities.

Furthermore, AI-enhanced teaching methods have facilitated personalized learning experiences. AI's ability to analyze individual student performance and tailor educational content accordingly has resulted in more effective and efficient learning outcomes. This personalization ensures that each student's learning journey is optimized to their unique needs and learning styles. The integration of AI in business education has also broadened the scope of what can be taught and learned. By simulating various business environments and scenarios, AI has enabled the exploration of areas that were previously difficult to teach in traditional classroom settings. This includes complex data analysis, market trend predictions, and strategic planning under varying market conditions. Moreover, AI's contribution to business simulations extends to administrative aspects of education, such as grading, feedback, and course design. This has not only enhanced the educational experience for students but also reduced the workload for educators, allowing them to focus more on teaching and less on administrative tasks. In essence, AI-enhanced teaching methods have revolutionized business simulation studies, making them more relevant, effective, and aligned with the needs of the modern business world. As these technologies continue to evolve, they promise to enhance further and expand the possibilities of business education.

Reflecting on the future of AI in business education reveals a landscape rich with potential and marked by transformative implications for both educators and students. For educators, the continued evolution of AI in business education represents an opportunity to augment their teaching methodologies. AI technologies offer tools for creating more engaging and interactive classroom experiences, reducing administrative burdens, and providing richer, data-driven insights into student performance and learning needs. Educators can leverage these tools to enhance their pedagogical approaches, making learning more adaptive and personalized. However, this also implies a need for educators to adapt and upskill, staying abreast of technological advancements to integrate AI into their teaching strategies effectively.

For students, the future of AI in business education promises a more tailored educational journey. AI's ability to personalize learning experiences based on individual performance and preferences means that students can expect a more supportive and efficient learning environment. This will likely lead to improved outcomes, including better knowledge retention, enhanced critical thinking skills, and greater preparedness for real-world business challenges. Additionally, exposure to AI-driven learning tools will equip students with essential digital literacy skills, preparing them for a workplace increasingly characterized by technological integration.

The implications of AI in business education also extend to the broader educational system. As AI continues to develop, it will likely prompt educational institutions to rethink curriculum design, pedagogical approaches, and assessment methods. This will necessitate ongoing collaboration between technology developers, educators, and policymakers to ensure that AI tools are effectively and ethically integrated into educational frameworks.

The future of AI in business education is poised to bring about significant changes for educators and students alike. These changes, while challenging, offer exciting opportunities for enhancing the quality and relevance of business education. As AI reshapes the educational landscape, it will be crucial for all stakeholders to engage proactively with these technologies to harness their full potential for advancing business education.

REFERENCES

Alkashri, Siyam, & Alqaryouti. (2020). *A detailed survey of Artificial Intelligence and Software Engineering: Emergent Issues.* . doi:10.1109/ICISC47916.2020.9171118

Alves, J. M. A., Soares, R. D. B., Moutinho, N. F. L., & Pereira, J. P. R. (2018). SimEmp: A game simulation in management teaching. In *2018 13th Iberian Conference on Information Systems and Technologies (CISTI)* (pp. 1-6). IEEE. 10.23919/CISTI.2018.8399166

Assar, S., Boughzala, I., & Isckia, T. (2011). eGovernment Trends in the Web 2.0 Era and the Open Innovation Perspective: An Exploratory Field Study. In Electronic Government. EGOV 2011. Lecture Notes in Computer Science, vol 6846. Springer. doi:10.1007/978-3-642-22878-0_18

Bhavani, G. (2020). Artificial Intelligence: Simulations in Audit Education. In *2020 11th International Conference on Computing, Communication and Networking Technologies (ICCCNT)* (pp. 1-5). IEEE.

Buil, I., Catalán, S., & Martínez, E. (2020). Engagement in business simulation games: A self-system model of motivational development. *British Journal of Educational Technology*, *51*(1), 297–311. doi:10.1111/bjet.12762

Chang, Q., Pan, X., Manikandan, N., & Ramesh, S. (2022). Artificial Intelligence Technologies for Teaching and Learning in Higher Education. *International Journal of Reliability Quality and Safety Engineering*, *29*(05), 2240006. doi:10.1142/S021853932240006X

Chen, Tang, Tian, Ou, Wang, & Quan. (2022). The effect of mobile business simulation games in entrepreneurship education: a quasi-experiment. *Library Hi Tech., 41.* doi:10.1108/LHT-12-2021-0509

Christensen, R., & Knezek, G. (2022). Using Digital Simulation to Address Implicit Bias in Teaching. In E. Langran (Ed.), *Proceedings of Society for Information Technology & Teacher Education International Conference* (pp. 477-483). San Diego, CA, United States: Association for the Advancement of Computing in Education (AACE).

Clarke, E. (2009). Learning outcomes from business simulation exercises: Challenges for the implementation of learning technologies. *Education + Training*, *51*(5/6), 448–459. doi:10.1108/00400910910987246

Crowe, D., LaPierre, M., & Kebritchi, M. (2017). Knowledge based artificial augmentation intelligence technology: Next step in academic instructional tools for distance learning. *TechTrends*, *61*(5), 494–506. doi:10.1007/s11528-017-0210-4

Devedžić, V. (2021). Quo Vadis, AI? Management. *Journal of Sustainable Business and Management Solutions in Emerging Economies*, *26*(1), 1–12.

Eremeev, A. P., Paniavin, N. A., & Marenkov, M. A. (2022). An Object-Oriented Approach to Ontology Modelling in Specialists Education of Methods and Technologies of Artificial Intelligence. In *2022 VI International Conference on Information Technologies in Engineering Education (Inforino)* (pp. 1-4). IEEE. 10.1109/Inforino53888.2022.9782954

Goralski, M. A., & Tan, T. K. (2020). Artificial intelligence and sustainable development. *International Journal of Management Education, 18*(1), 100330. doi:10.1016/j.ijme.2019.100330

Huang, R., Miao, F., Holmes, W., & Zhang, H. (2021). *AI and education: A guidance for policymakers.* UNESCO Publishing.

Ifenthaler, D., & Schumacher, C. (2023). Reciprocal issues of artificial and human intelligence in education. *Journal of Research on Technology in Education, 55*(1), 1–6. doi:10.1080/15391523.2022.2154511

Jia, G., Xu, G., Shi, L., & Zhang, Z. (2021). Personalized course recommendation system fusing with knowledge graph and collaborative filtering. *Computational Intelligence and Neuroscience, 2021*, 1–8. doi:10.1155/2021/6686826 PMID:34616447

Jiao, G., Li, L., Deng, H., Zheng, G., Zou, Y., & Zhao, J. (2020). Exploration on cultivation of practical ability of artificial intelligence talents in universities in the context of innovation and entrepreneurship education. In *2020 IEEE 2nd International Conference on Computer Science and Educational Informatization (CSEI)* (pp. 186-189). IEEE. 10.1109/CSEI50228.2020.9142488

Jordan, M. I., & Mitchell, T. M. (2015). Machine learning: Trends, perspectives, and prospects. *Science, 349*(6245), 255–260. doi:10.1126/science.aaa8415 PMID:26185243

Justesen, N., Bontrager, P., Togelius, J., & Risi, S. (2019). Deep learning for video game playing. *IEEE Transactions on Games, 12*(1), 1–20. doi:10.1109/TG.2019.2896986

Kalazhokov, Z. K., Senov, K. M., Shogenov, B. V., & Yakhutlov, M. M. (2021). The Unique Challenges of Teaching Artificial Intelligence Systems to Mechatronics and Robotics Students. In *2021 International Conference on Quality Management, Transport and Information Security, Information Technologies (IT&QM&IS)* (pp. 653-655). IEEE. 10.1109/ITQMIS53292.2021.9642750

Kim, Y., & Baylor, A. L. (2016). Evidence-based design of pedagogical agent roles: A review, progress, and recommendations. *International Journal of Artificial Intelligence in Education, 26*(1), 160–169. doi:10.1007/s40593-015-0055-y

Kobayashi, M., & Terano, T. (2003). Learning agents in a business simulator. *Proc. IEEE Int. Symp. Computational Intelligence in Robotics and Automation, 3*, 1323-1327.

Kumar, D. N. (2019). Implementation of artificial intelligence in imparting education and evaluating student performance. *Journal of Artificial Intelligence and Capsule Networks, 1*(1), 1–9. doi:10.36548/jaicn.2019.1.001

Lameras, P. (2022). A Vision of Teaching and Learning with AI. In *2022 IEEE Global Engineering Education Conference (EDUCON)* (pp. 1796-1803). IEEE. 10.1109/EDUCON52537.2022.9766718

Leonard, J., Mitchell, M., Barnes-Johnson, J., Unertl, A., Outka-Hill, J., Robinson, R., & Hester-Croff, C. (2018). Preparing Teachers to Engage Rural Students in Computational Thinking Through Robotics, Game Design, and Culturally Responsive Teaching. *Journal of Teacher Education*, *69*(4), 386–407. doi:10.1177/0022487117732317

Liu, C., Chen, X., Zou, D., Xie, H., & Cheng, G. (2022). Two decades of artificial intelligence in education. *Journal of Educational Technology & Society*, *25*(1), 28–47.

Loureiro, S. M. C., Guerreiro, J., & Tussyadiah, I. (2021). Artificial intelligence in business: State of the art and future research agenda. *Journal of Business Research*, *129*, 911–926. doi:10.1016/j.jbusres.2020.11.001

Malik, M. (2018). Meta-analysis and review of the use of Artificial Intelligence and Learning Analytics within Engineering Education at University level. *Time for Change*, 38.

Martinez, N., León, M., Medina, D., & García, Z. (2007). Two approaches to generate intelligent teaching-learning systems using artificial intelligence techniques. In *2007 Sixth Mexican International Conference on Artificial Intelligence, Special Session (MICAI)* (pp. 333-341). IEEE.

Niemi, H., & Liu, J. (2021). AI in learning: Intelligent digital tools and environments for education. *Journal of Pacific Rim Psychology*, *15*. doi:10.1177/18344909211038110

Ojha, S., Narendra, A., Mohapatra, S., & Misra, I. (2023). *From Robots to Books: An Introduction to Smart Applications of AI in Education (AIEd)*. arXiv preprint arXiv:2301.10026.

Oliver, R. (1994). Information technology courses in teacher education: The need for integration. *Journal of Information Technology for Teacher Education*, *3*(2), 135–146. doi:10.1080/0962029940030202

Pal, K., & Karakostas, B. (2020). A Game-Based Approach for Simulation and Design of Supply Chains. *Supply Chain and Logistics Management: Concepts, Methodologies, Tools, and Applications*, 527-549.

Remondino, M. (2008). A web based business game built on system dynamics using cognitive agents as virtual tutors. In *Tenth International Conference on Computer Modeling and Simulation (uksim 2008)* (pp. 568-572). IEEE. 10.1109/UKSIM.2008.84

Renz, A., & Hilbig, R. (2020). Prerequisites for artificial intelligence in further education: Identification of drivers, barriers, and business models of educational technology companies. *International Journal of Educational Technology in Higher Education*, *17*(1), 1–21. doi:10.1186/s41239-020-00193-3

Salas-Pilco, S. Z., Xiao, K., & Hu, X. (2022). Artificial intelligence and learning analytics in teacher education: A systematic review. *Education Sciences*, *12*(8), 569. doi:10.3390/educsci12080569

ShirinA. (2022). Artificial Intelligence Technology on Teaching Learning: Exploring Bangladeshi Teachers' Perceptions. Embedded Selforganising Systems. 9. doi:10.14464/ess.v9i4.553

Thanasi-Boçe, M. (2020). Enhancing students' entrepreneurial capacity through marketing simulation games. *Education + Training*, *62*(9), 999–1013. doi:10.1108/ET-06-2019-0109

Töyli, J., Hansén, S. O., & Smeds, R. (2006). Plan for profit and achieve profit: Lessons learnt from a business management simulation. *Production Planning and Control*, *17*(6), 584–595. doi:10.1080/09537280600866686

Tseng, H. C., Kuo, C. W., Yang, H. L., Liao, H. C., Hu, S. H., Yeh, C. H., & Tsai, I. C. (2019). AIGO: A comprehensive platform for cultivating AI talent using real-world industrial problems. In *2019 IEEE International Conference on Engineering, Technology and Education (TALE)* (pp. 1-5). IEEE.

Vastag, G., & Yerushalmy, M. (2009). Automating Serious Games. Springer Handbook of Automation, 1299-1311. doi:10.1007/978-3-540-78831-7_73

Walia, J. S., & Kumar, P. (2022). Tech transition: An exploratory study on educators' AI awareness. *International Journal of Virtual and Personal Learning Environments*, *12*(1), 1–17. doi:10.4018/IJVPLE.295310

Xie, T., Liu, R., Chen, Y., & Liu, G. (2021). MOCA: A motivational online conversational agent for improving student engagement in collaborative learning. *IEEE Transactions on Learning Technologies*, *14*(5), 653–664. doi:10.1109/TLT.2021.3129800

Xu, J. J., & Babaian, T. (2021). Artificial intelligence in business curriculum: The pedagogy and learning outcomes. *International Journal of Management Education*, *19*(3), 100550. doi:10.1016/j.ijme.2021.100550

Xu, L. (2020). The dilemma and countermeasures of AI in educational application. In *Proceedings of the 2020 4th International Conference on Computer Science and Artificial Intelligence* (pp. 289-294). 10.1145/3445815.3445863

Zhang, K., Yang, Z., & Başar, T. (2021). Decentralized multi-agent reinforcement learning with networked agents: Recent advances. *Frontiers of Information Technology & Electronic Engineering*, *22*(6), 802–814. doi:10.1631/FITEE.1900661

Zheng, Y., & Chen, Y. (2020). Construction and implementation of blended teaching ecology based on cloud class. In *2020 IEEE 2nd International Conference on Computer Science and Educational Informatization (CSEI)* (pp. 292-295). IEEE. 10.1109/CSEI50228.2020.9142492

Chapter 15
Transforming Classroom Dynamics:
The Social Impact of AI in Teaching and Learning

Tarun Kumar Vashishth
🆔 https://orcid.org/0000-0001-9916-9575
IIMT University, India

Bhupendra Kumar
🆔 https://orcid.org/0000-0001-9281-3655
IIMT University, India

Vikas Sharma
🆔 https://orcid.org/0000-0001-8173-4548
IIMT University, India

Sachin Chaudhary
🆔 https://orcid.org/0000-0002-8415-0043
IIMT University, India

Kewal Krishan Sharma
🆔 https://orcid.org/0009-0001-2504-9607
IIMT University, India

Rajneesh Panwar
🆔 https://orcid.org/0009-0000-5974-191X
IIMT University, India

ABSTRACT

The integration of artificial intelligence (AI) in education is reshaping classroom dynamics and fostering a social impact on teaching and learning. This chapter explores the historical evolution of classroom dynamics, from traditional settings to 21st-century learning environments, highlighting the pivotal role of AI in this transformative journey. Understanding AI in education involves delving into its historical overview and current landscape. The research investigates AI's influence on teacher support and development, encompassing AI-assisted lesson planning, teacher training, and enhanced classroom management. The conclusion reflects on the future directions and trends, emphasizing the global potential of AI to democratize education, address language barriers, and provide inclusive learning experiences. The study envisions a future where AI optimally contributes to creating a more equitable, interconnected, and culturally sensitive educational landscape globally.

DOI: 10.4018/979-8-3693-2728-9.ch015

1. INTRODUCTION

The modern classroom is undergoing a profound transformation, driven by the inexorable rise of artificial intelligence (AI). The impact of AI on teaching and learning is nothing short of revolutionary, altering the dynamics of education in ways we are only beginning to comprehend. Education has always been a cornerstone of society, a cornerstone now being reshaped by AI. Ungerer and Slade (2022) emphasize the imperative to view AI and AI in education through a lens that recognizes their entanglement with ideological, political, social, economic, and technological factors, dispelling the notion of neutrality. The classroom, once a realm of textbooks and chalkboards, is evolving into a dynamic space where AI-driven tools assist educators, customize learning experiences, and engage students in unprecedented ways. This transformation challenges the traditional roles of teachers and learners, blurring the lines between instruction and exploration. In this chapter, we set the stage for our exploration of AI's impact on education. We begin by defining the scope and significance of AI in teaching and learning. We delve into the historical context of AI in education, tracing its roots and highlighting key milestones. From early computer-assisted instruction to today's advanced AI-driven platforms, the journey of AI in education has been marked by innovation and potential. We also examine the current landscape of AI in education, showcasing notable developments and trends that are shaping classrooms worldwide. AI-powered personalization, adaptive learning systems, and virtual learning environments are becoming integral components of the modern educational experience. Bozkurt et al. (2021) employ a systematic review approach spanning half a century (1970–2020) to investigate AI studies in education, incorporating social network analysis and text-mining methods for comprehensive insights.

However, our focus goes beyond the technological aspects. We emphasize the social impact of AI in education. What does it mean for teachers, students, and society as a whole when AI becomes a partner in the learning journey? How does AI impact access to education, address disparities, and redefine the skills needed for the future? As we embark on this exploration, we recognize that AI in education is not a mere trend but a transformative force that demands our attention. It is a force that raises questions about the role of educators, the ethics of data-driven decision-making, and the nature of knowledge itself.

1.1 The Role of AI in Education

The role of Artificial Intelligence (AI) in education is rapidly evolving and expanding, with the potential to transform the way students learn and teachers instruct. AI is making significant inroads into various aspects of education, from personalized learning experiences to administrative tasks. Here are some key roles that AI plays in education:

- Personalized Learning: AI-driven educational platforms can adapt to the individual needs of students. By analyzing a student's performance, preferences, and learning style, AI can provide tailored content and exercises. This ensures that each student can learn at their own pace and grasp concepts more effectively.
- Assessment and Feedback: AI can automate the grading process for multiple-choice questions and even essays. This not only saves teachers time but also allows for more immediate and detailed feedback to students. AI algorithms can identify areas where a student may be struggling and offer additional resources for improvement.

- Virtual Tutors and Assistants: AI-powered virtual tutors can provide additional support to students outside of regular class hours. They can answer questions, explain complex concepts, and offer practice problems. These virtual assistants are available 24/7, making learning more accessible.
- Administrative Efficiency: AI can streamline administrative tasks within educational institutions. Chatbots can handle inquiries from students, parents, and staff. AI algorithms can help with class scheduling, resource allocation, and even predictive maintenance for school equipment.
- Data-Driven Insights: AI can analyze vast amounts of data generated in educational settings to provide valuable insights. Schools and institutions can use these insights to make informed decisions about curriculum, resource allocation, and policies. It can also help identify at-risk students who may need additional support.
- Language Learning: AI-powered language learning platforms use natural language processing to teach languages more effectively. They can provide real-time pronunciation feedback, language exercises, and even hold conversations to practice language skills.
- Accessibility: AI can make education more accessible to individuals with disabilities. For example, AI-powered screen readers can provide audio descriptions of text and images for visually impaired students.
- Early Intervention: AI algorithms can identify early signs of learning disabilities or behavioral issues in students. This allows educators to intervene promptly and provide appropriate support.
- Content Creation: AI can assist educators in creating educational content. For example, it can generate quizzes, worksheets, and even educational videos based on specific learning objectives.
- Global Access: AI-powered online platforms provide access to education for individuals around the world. This is especially important for remote or underserved communities where traditional education infrastructure may be lacking.

While AI has immense potential in education, it also raises important ethical considerations, such as data privacy, bias in algorithms, and the role of human teachers. Striking the right balance between the capabilities of AI and the expertise of educators is a critical challenge as the role of AI in education continues to evolve. Escotet (2023) discusses the rapid evolution of Artificial Intelligence, emphasizing its vast potential in education and higher education. The article takes an optimistic stance on the future of higher education with AI.

1.2 The Evolution of Classroom Dynamics

The evolution of classroom dynamics is a reflection of how teaching and learning paradigms have transformed over time. Classroom dynamics encompass the interactions, relationships, and learning environments within a classroom. These dynamics have evolved significantly, influenced by societal changes, technological advancements, and educational philosophies. Here's an overview of the evolution of classroom dynamics:

1.2.1 Traditional Classroom (Pre-Industrial Revolution)

In the pre-Industrial Revolution era, the traditional classroom was characterized by a rigid structure and limited access to educational resources. Education was primarily localized, with students gathering in physical spaces to receive instruction from a single teacher. The teaching methods were heavily reliant on oral communication, textbooks were scarce, and the curriculum was often tailored to meet the needs of specific communities or societal elites. The teacher held a central role as the primary source of knowledge, and students were passive recipients of information. Classroom dynamics were deeply influenced by the scarcity of educational resources, making the learning environment less interactive and dynamic. Students had limited opportunities for individual exploration or critical thinking, and the pace of learning was often dictated by the teacher. The lack of technological advancements restricted access to a diverse range of learning materials, limiting the scope of education.

Moreover, the traditional classroom of this era reflected societal structures, with education often serving to reinforce existing hierarchies. Access to education was unevenly distributed, with only a select few enjoying the privilege of formal learning. The dynamics were shaped by social norms, and the emphasis was more on rote memorization than on fostering creativity and critical inquiry.

The traditional classroom before the Industrial Revolution was characterized by a constrained and hierarchical structure. Limited resources, oral communication, and a centralized role for the teacher defined the dynamics, reflecting the societal norms and restrictions of the time. As we delve into subsequent eras, we will witness the transformative impact of technological advancements, including the integration of AI, on reshaping these dynamics and unlocking new possibilities for teaching and learning.

1.2.2 Progressive Education (Late 19th to Early 20th Century):

The late 19th to early 20th century witnessed a significant shift in educational philosophy with the advent of progressive education. This era marked a departure from the rigid structures of the traditional classroom and embraced a more child-centered approach. Pioneered by educators such as John Dewey, progressive education aimed to foster a holistic development of students, emphasizing experiential learning, critical thinking, and collaboration. In the progressive classroom, the dynamics evolved to be more interactive and student-focused. Teachers played the role of facilitators, guiding students through hands-on activities and real-world experiences. The emphasis shifted from rote memorization to understanding concepts through exploration and experimentation. Classrooms became dynamic spaces where students actively engaged with the learning process, promoting a deeper understanding of subjects. Moreover, the progressive education movement sought to address societal inequities in access to education. It advocated for inclusivity and recognized the diverse learning needs of students. This period saw the emergence of schools that aimed to provide education to a broader segment of the population, challenging the elitist nature of traditional education.

The introduction of new pedagogical methods and a more inclusive approach marked a transformative phase in classroom dynamics. Progressive education laid the foundation for fostering creativity, critical thinking, and adaptability—attributes that are increasingly recognized as essential in the 21st-century context. As we delve further into the evolution of classroom dynamics, the integration of artificial intelligence promises to build upon these principles, offering innovative solutions to enhance personalized and inclusive learning experiences.

1.2.3 Post-World War II (Mid-20th Century)

In the mid-20th century, post-World War II, the landscape of education underwent a transformative shift influenced by social, technological, and economic changes. The aftermath of the war brought about a heightened awareness of the importance of education in rebuilding societies and fostering global progress. This period witnessed the emergence of a more standardized and structured approach to education, shaped by the need for skilled workers in a rapidly industrializing world. Classroom dynamics during this era were characterized by a focus on efficiency, uniformity, and mass education. The implementation of standardized curricula and testing aimed to ensure that education could meet the demands of a rapidly changing workforce. Teachers played a central role in delivering information to large groups of students, and rote learning became a prevalent method to achieve uniform academic outcomes.

Technological advancements, such as the introduction of audio-visual aids and later, television, began to influence teaching methods. These tools were seen as a means to enhance the dissemination of information and engage students in new ways. However, the overall dynamics still maintained a teacher-centric structure, with technology serving as a supplementary rather than a transformative force. Post-World War II education was also marked by efforts to address issues of accessibility and equity. Initiatives such as the expansion of higher education and the push for desegregation aimed to make education more inclusive. Despite these strides, challenges related to inequality persisted, reflecting broader social issues.

As we reflect on the evolution of classroom dynamics, this mid-20th century period set the stage for subsequent educational reforms. The advent of artificial intelligence in teaching and learning holds the promise of redefining classroom dynamics once again, offering personalized and adaptive approaches that can cater to diverse learning needs in the 21st century.

1.2.4 Digital Age (Late 20th Century to Present)

Entering the Digital Age marked a revolutionary shift in classroom dynamics, transforming the landscape of education and learning methodologies. The late 20th century saw the integration of technology, particularly computers and the internet, into educational practices, ushering in an era of unprecedented connectivity and access to information. The advent of personal computers and the internet brought forth a paradigmatic change in how educators approached teaching and students engaged with learning. The traditional classroom setup evolved into a more dynamic and interactive environment, with the ability to access a wealth of information at one's fingertips. The role of teachers expanded beyond being information providers to becoming facilitators of knowledge exploration.

This era witnessed the rise of e-learning platforms, online resources, and collaborative tools that fostered a more student-centric approach. Learning became personalized, allowing students to progress at their own pace and explore subjects in-depth. The boundaries of the traditional classroom extended to virtual spaces, enabling remote learning and global collaboration. The Digital Age not only changed the tools of education but also influenced pedagogical strategies. Project-based learning, interactive simulations, and multimedia presentations became integral components of the modern classroom. Teachers leveraged technology to create engaging and immersive learning experiences that catered to diverse learning styles.

As we navigate the present, the impact of artificial intelligence (AI) in teaching and learning is becoming increasingly pronounced. AI-driven educational technologies offer adaptive learning experiences, personalized assessments, and intelligent tutoring systems. This integration of AI has the potential to further revolutionize classroom dynamics by providing tailored support to individual students, addressing learning gaps, and preparing learners for the challenges of the 21st-century workforce.

The Digital Age has not only reshaped the physical and virtual spaces where education occurs but has also set the stage for the transformative potential of AI in shaping the future of classroom dynamics. The ongoing evolution reflects a continuous effort to align educational practices with the rapidly changing needs of learners in an interconnected and technologically driven world.

1.2.5 21st Century Learning (Present and Beyond)

In the current era of 21st-century learning, the evolution of classroom dynamics continues to be profoundly influenced by technological advancements and societal shifts. The traditional concept of a classroom has expanded beyond physical boundaries, embracing a more holistic and interconnected approach to education. The advent of the internet, mobile devices, and sophisticated educational technologies has ushered in an era of unprecedented connectivity and accessibility. Students today have instant access to a vast array of information, enabling self-directed learning and exploration. The classroom is no longer confined to a specific location; rather, it exists in the digital realm, fostering global collaboration and diverse perspectives.

21st-century learning emphasizes skills such as critical thinking, creativity, collaboration, and communication—collectively known as the "Four Cs." These skills are considered essential for preparing students to thrive in a rapidly evolving, technology-driven world. The role of educators has evolved into that of facilitators and mentors, guiding students in developing these skills and applying them to real-world challenges. Moreover, the integration of artificial intelligence (AI) has emerged as a transformative force in teaching and learning. AI-powered tools offer personalized learning experiences, adaptive assessments, and intelligent feedback. Virtual assistants and chatbots provide additional support, enhancing the overall learning journey. As AI continues to evolve, its role in education is expected to expand, further individualizing learning experiences and addressing the unique needs of each student. Beyond technology, the 21st-century classroom recognizes the importance of social and emotional learning (SEL). Educators focus on nurturing students' emotional intelligence, resilience, and interpersonal skills to prepare them for the complexities of the modern world. Collaborative projects, experiential learning, and an emphasis on empathy contribute to a more holistic educational experience. Renzé, Krishnaraja and Gronau (2020) offer a concise overview of the current landscape of Learning Analytics and Artificial Intelligence in education in the initial section of their paper.

Looking forward, the future of classroom dynamics holds the promise of even more innovation and adaptation. Virtual and augmented reality, immersive simulations, and continued advancements in AI are poised to reshape educational experiences. As we navigate this dynamic landscape, the key will be to strike a balance between leveraging technology for enhanced learning outcomes and preserving the essential human elements of education.

In conclusion, 21st-century learning represents a paradigm shift in classroom dynamics, blending technology, interpersonal skills, and adaptability to prepare students for a future characterized by constant change and innovation. The evolution continues, driven by a commitment to providing students with the skills and knowledge needed to thrive in an ever-evolving global society.

The evolution of classroom dynamics continues as educators adapt to an ever-changing landscape influenced by technological innovations, educational research, and evolving societal needs. The integration of AI, augmented reality, and other emerging technologies is expected to further transform classroom dynamics in the future, offering new possibilities for personalized, collaborative, and engaging learning experiences.

1.3 Organization of the Chapter

The rest of the chapter is organized as: Section 2 elaborates Understanding AI in Education. Section 3 presents a AI-Powered Personalized Learning. Section 4 delves the AI in Teacher Support and Development. Section 5 outlines the Social Impacts of AI in Education. Section 6 presents the Enhancing Student Engagement. Section 7 outline the Transforming Assessment and Evaluation. Section 8 presents a Case Studies. Section 9 delves the Challenges and Limitations. Section 10 outlines the Future of AI in Education. Section 11 provides a Concluding Remarks.

2. UNDERSTANDING AI IN EDUCATION

Understanding AI in Education involves a multifaceted exploration of what artificial intelligence means in the context of learning and teaching. To grasp the significance and potential of AI in education, one must examine its definition, historical development, and the current educational landscape it shapes.

Figure 1: AI in Teaching & Learning depicts the integration of artificial intelligence (AI) technologies in educational practices, demonstrating how AI-driven tools and algorithms are revolutionizing teaching methodologies and learning experiences in various educational settings.

Figure 1. AI in teaching and learning

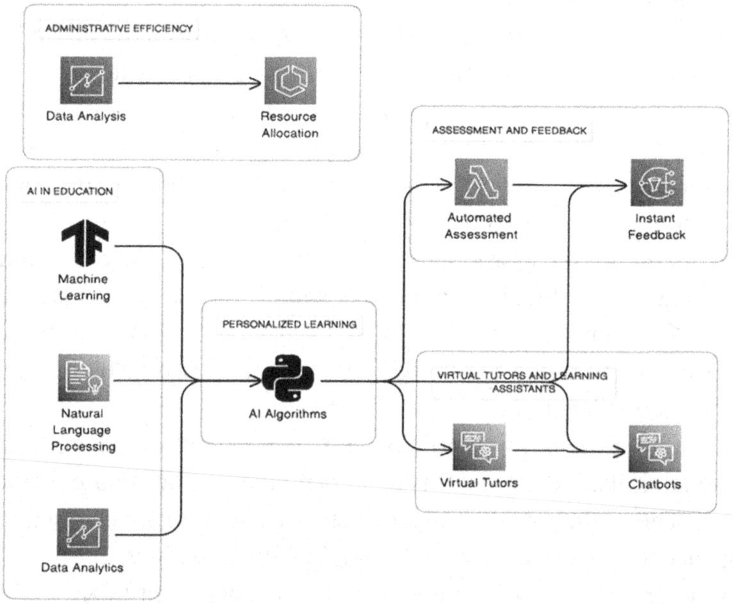

2.1 Defining Artificial Intelligence in the Educational Context

Artificial Intelligence (AI) in the realm of education represents a transformative force that is reshaping the landscape of teaching and learning. In the context of education, AI refers to the development of computer systems capable of performing tasks that typically require human intelligence. These tasks encompass a range of activities, from basic data analysis to more complex functions like natural language processing, problem-solving, and decision-making.

In the educational context, AI serves as a powerful tool to enhance various aspects of the learning experience. One fundamental application is personalized learning, where AI algorithms analyze individual student performance data to tailor educational content based on their unique strengths, weaknesses, and learning preferences. This adaptability allows students to progress at their own pace, fostering a more customized and effective learning journey. Additionally, AI facilitates intelligent tutoring systems that provide real-time feedback and guidance to students. These systems can identify areas where a student may be struggling, offer targeted support, and track progress over time. As a result, educators can optimize their instructional strategies, focusing on areas that require additional attention while acknowledging and reinforcing areas of proficiency. Natural language processing capabilities of AI also contribute to language learning applications, enabling interactive and contextually relevant language instruction. AI-powered chatbots and virtual assistants engage with students, providing language practice, answering queries, and offering language immersion experiences. Rienties, Simonsen, and Herodotou (2020) deliver a succinct review encompassing four distinct research domains: Artificial Intelligence and EDucation (AIED), Computer-Supported Collaborative Learning (CSCL), Educational Data Mining (EDM), and Learning Analytics (LA).

Moreover, AI contributes to the automation of administrative tasks, freeing up valuable time for educators to focus on instructional design and student engagement. Intelligent grading systems, for instance, can efficiently evaluate assessments, providing prompt feedback to students and streamlining the grading process. However, the integration of AI in education is not without challenges. Concerns related to data privacy, ethical considerations, and the potential for reinforcing biases in algorithms demand careful attention. Striking the right balance between leveraging AI for educational benefits and addressing these ethical and privacy concerns is crucial for the responsible deployment of AI in the educational domain.

Defining AI in the educational context reveals its potential to revolutionize teaching and learning. By providing personalized learning experiences, intelligent tutoring, language instruction, and administrative support, AI becomes a catalyst for transforming classroom dynamics and enhancing the overall social impact of education. The continued exploration and ethical implementation of AI in education hold the promise of fostering a more inclusive, adaptive, and effective educational environment.

2.2 Historical Overview of AI in Education

The integration of Artificial Intelligence (AI) in education has a fascinating historical trajectory, marked by evolving technological capabilities and a growing recognition of the potential impact on teaching and learning. While the contemporary AI applications in education are cutting-edge, the roots of using technology for educational purposes can be traced back several decades. In the early stages, computer-assisted instruction (CAI) emerged as a precursor to AI in education. During the 1960s and 1970s, mainframe computers were utilized to deliver programmed instruction, allowing students to interact with instructional content and receive immediate feedback. This represented a foundational step toward personalized learning experiences facilitated by technology. The advent of intelligent tutoring systems in the 1980s marked a significant leap in AI's role in education. These systems employed AI algorithms to adaptively guide students through coursework, providing customized feedback based on individual performance. Early attempts at AI-driven tutoring paved the way for more sophisticated applications in subsequent decades. Vashishth et al. (2024) delves into the potential of AI-driven learning analytics to provide personalized feedback and assessment in higher education. This not only has the potential to enhance traditional teaching methods but also has a significant social impact on the classroom dynamics.

The late 20th century witnessed a surge in educational software and multimedia applications, with AI making strides in areas like speech recognition and natural language processing. These technologies contributed to the development of interactive learning environments, laying the groundwork for the AI-driven educational tools prevalent today. In the 21st century, the intersection of big data, machine learning, and advanced analytics has fueled the rapid evolution of AI applications in education. Berendt, Littlejohn and Blakemore (2020) examine the possibilities of AI and 'Big Data' in enhancing real-time monitoring of the education system while deliberating on their implications for the fundamental rights and freedoms of educators and learners alike. Learning analytics, powered by AI, enables educators to harness vast amounts of data to gain insights into student performance, engagement patterns, and learning preferences. This data-driven approach enhances decision-making and instructional strategies. Moreover, the rise of Massive Open Online Courses (MOOCs) and virtual learning platforms has leveraged AI for adaptive learning experiences, automated assessments, and intelligent content recommendations. AI-driven educational technology continues to evolve, with ongoing developments in natural language understanding, virtual reality, and augmented reality promising even more immersive and interactive learning environments. Vashishth et al. (2023) explore the potential to transform classroom dynamics and have a significant social impact on teaching and learning.

As we navigate the historical landscape of AI in education, it is evident that the journey has been characterized by continuous innovation, experimentation, and adaptation. The historical overview highlights the progression from rudimentary computer-assisted instruction to today's sophisticated AI applications that revolutionize classroom dynamics and contribute to the broader social impact of AI in teaching and learning. Understanding this historical context is crucial for appreciating the transformative potential of AI in shaping the future of education.

2.3 The Current Landscape of AI in Education

In the contemporary educational landscape, Artificial Intelligence (AI) has become a transformative force, revolutionizing teaching and learning experiences. AI applications in education are multifaceted, encompassing adaptive learning platforms, intelligent tutoring systems, and data analytics tools that contribute to a personalized and efficient learning environment. Adaptive learning platforms, driven by AI algorithms, are designed to cater to individual student needs. These platforms analyze students' strengths and weaknesses, adapting the content and pace of instruction accordingly. This personalized approach fosters a more engaging and effective learning experience, allowing students to progress at their own pace. Intelligent tutoring systems, a more sophisticated evolution of early AI-driven educational tools, leverage machine learning to provide dynamic and responsive guidance. These systems can understand students' learning styles, track their progress, and offer targeted feedback, creating a supportive learning environment that mirrors the benefits of one-on-one tutoring. Learning analytics, another facet of AI in education, involves the collection and analysis of vast amounts of data generated by students' interactions with digital platforms. This data-driven approach allows educators to gain insights into students' performance patterns, identify potential challenges, and tailor instructional strategies to meet individual needs. Wang et al. (2023) investigate a range of AI applications, including personalized learning, adaptive testing, predictive analytics, and chatbots in the context of international student education. This research offers insights into how AI can enhance learning efficiency and provide tailored educational support.

Furthermore, natural language processing (NLP) has empowered AI to enhance language learning experiences. NLP-driven applications can assess language proficiency, provide contextualized language exercises, and even facilitate language translation, breaking down barriers in global education. In higher education, AI is increasingly playing a role in automating administrative tasks, such as grading assessments and managing course logistics. This allows educators to focus more on personalized interactions with students, fostering a deeper understanding of the subject matter. The current landscape of AI in education is marked by a commitment to inclusivity and accessibility. AI-driven tools aim to address diverse learning styles, accommodate individual needs, and bridge educational gaps. However, challenges such as data privacy, ethical considerations, and ensuring equity in access to AI-driven education tools remain focal points for ongoing discussions and developments. Tight (2020) reports on a systematic review of research pertaining to student retention and student engagement in higher education (HE).

As AI continues to evolve, its role in education is poised to expand, offering new possibilities for immersive and interactive learning experiences. The current educational landscape reflects a dynamic interplay between technology and pedagogy, with AI at the forefront of innovations that are transforming classroom dynamics and shaping the social impact of education.

3. AI-POWERED PERSONALIZED LEARNING

AI-powered personalized learning is revolutionizing education by tailoring instructional methods and content to the unique needs, abilities, and learning styles of individual students. Vashishth et al. (2023) provides a comprehensive analysis of how AI has evolved and its impact on computing and also delve into the social impact of AI in teaching and learning, and how it has transformed classroom dynamics. This approach recognizes that one-size-fits-all instruction may not be the most effective way to educate diverse groups of learners.

Figure 2: AI-Powered Personalized Learning System illustrates the implementation of artificial intelligence (AI) technologies in educational environments, highlighting the development and utilization of personalized learning systems that adapt to individual student needs and preferences.

3.1 Personalization in Education

- Customized Learning Paths: AI algorithms analyze each student's performance, learning pace, and preferences to create customized learning paths. This ensures that students receive content that is challenging enough to promote growth but not so difficult as to cause frustration.
- Differentiated Instruction: AI can adapt instructional methods to match students' strengths and weaknesses. For instance, if a student excels in mathematics but struggles with reading, AI can provide additional support in reading while offering advanced math content.
- Continuous Assessment: Personalized learning platforms use continuous assessment to gauge a student's understanding of concepts in real-time. This allows for immediate intervention when a student is struggling.

Figure 2. AI-powered personalized learning system

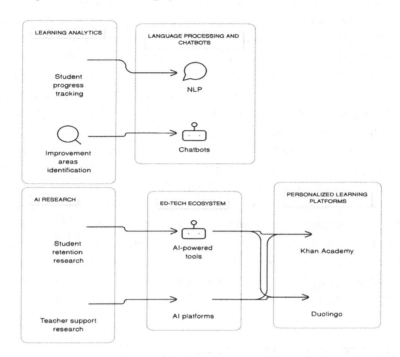

- Self-Paced Learning: AI-powered systems enable self-paced learning, allowing students to progress through material at their own speed. Advanced students can move quickly, while those needing extra help can take their time.

3.2 Adaptive Learning Systems

- Data-Driven Adaptation: Adaptive learning systems use data analytics to track student progress. They adjust the difficulty and content of lessons based on a student's performance and preferences.
- Recommendations: These systems recommend additional resources, exercises, or activities to reinforce learning or address areas of weakness.
- Engagement: Adaptive systems are designed to keep students engaged by providing challenges that are neither too easy nor too difficult.

3.3 Case Studies: Personalized Learning Success Stories

- **Khan Academy:** Khan Academy is a widely recognized personalized learning platform. It provides a range of instructional videos, practice exercises, and assessments that adapt to students' abilities. Khan Academy's success lies in its ability to provide students with immediate feedback and a personalized learning journey.
- **Duolingo:** Duolingo, a language learning app, uses AI to adapt lessons based on individual progress and strengths. It provides targeted exercises to improve areas where a learner is struggling and offers a gamified experience to keep learners engaged.

- **DreamBox:** DreamBox is an adaptive math program for elementary students. It uses AI to provide students with math lessons that adapt to their skill level. DreamBox's success is evidenced by improved math proficiency in participating schools.
- **ScribeSense:** ScribeSense is an AI-powered platform that provides personalized feedback on handwritten assignments, enabling teachers to focus on individual learning needs.

These case studies illustrate the impact of AI-powered personalized learning in diverse educational contexts. By catering to individual learning needs and preferences, AI is making education more effective, engaging, and accessible to students of all backgrounds and abilities.

4. AI IN TEACHER SUPPORT AND DEVELOPMENT

In this chapter, we delve into how Artificial Intelligence (AI) is revolutionizing teacher support and professional development. AI is not just transforming the way students learn; it's also enhancing the capabilities of educators, helping them plan lessons, develop their skills, and manage classrooms more effectively.

4.1 AI-Assisted Lesson Planning

- Personalized Lesson Plans: AI algorithms analyze student performance data to suggest customized lesson plans. Teachers can tailor their instruction to meet the specific needs and abilities of their students.
- Content Recommendations: AI can recommend instructional materials, including videos, articles, and interactive exercises, to enrich lesson plans and engage students.
- Time Optimization: AI tools help teachers optimize their time by automating routine tasks like scheduling, grading, and administrative work, allowing educators to focus on teaching.

Figure 3: Artificial Intelligence (AI) is revolutionizing teacher support and professional development and Lesson Planning demonstrates the transformative impact of artificial intelligence (AI) on teacher support, professional development, and lesson planning processes within the educational landscape.

4.2 Teacher Training and Professional Development

Artificial Intelligence (AI) is playing a transformative role in teacher training and professional development, reshaping the landscape of education by offering innovative approaches to enhance educators' skills and knowledge. Through AI-driven platforms, teachers can access personalized training modules, resources, and real-time feedback tailored to their individual needs. AI algorithms analyze educators' performance data, including classroom interactions, assessment results, and teaching methodologies, to identify areas for improvement and suggest targeted professional development opportunities. This personalized approach ensures that teachers receive training that aligns with their specific strengths and challenges, fostering continuous growth and refinement of their teaching practices. Moreover, AI facilitates collaborative learning communities, enabling teachers to connect with peers, share best practices, and engage in discussions around effective teaching strategies. This collaborative aspect enhances the social impact of AI in teaching and learning by creating a supportive network where educators can

Figure 3. Artificial intelligence (AI) is revolutionizing teacher support and professional development and lesson planning

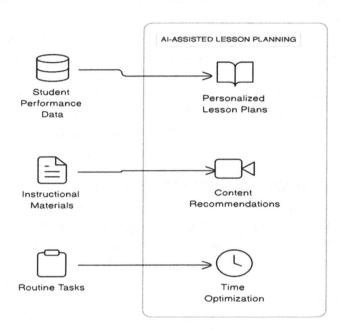

learn from each other and collectively address challenges. AI also offers immersive experiences through virtual reality (VR) and augmented reality (AR) simulations, allowing teachers to practice and refine their skills in a risk-free environment. These simulations provide realistic scenarios, such as classroom management challenges or student interactions, allowing teachers to hone their abilities in a safe and controlled setting. Zhang, Wu and Ouyang (2023) propose a teaching and learning analytics (TLA) tool that integrates multiple data sources from the instructor and students during the educational process. They leverage various analytic methods to visualize results and offer supportive feedback, with the goal of providing data-driven evidence for educational improvement.

Despite these advancements, ethical considerations and the human touch in education remain paramount. Striking a balance between AI-driven insights and the nuanced, empathetic qualities of effective teaching is a critical aspect of integrating AI into teacher support and development. Ensuring that AI enhances, rather than replaces, the human connection between educators and students is essential for the continued success of AI in education. Ciolacu et al. (2018) introduce an innovative approach to promoting AI in Education 4.0.

In essence, AI in teacher training and professional development is empowering educators to embrace lifelong learning, adapt to evolving pedagogical approaches, and contribute to the broader transformation of classroom dynamics. Through personalized training, collaborative communities, and immersive experiences, AI is fostering a more dynamic and impactful educational ecosystem.

4.3 AI-Enhanced Classroom Management

Artificial Intelligence (AI) is revolutionizing classroom management practices by providing educators with innovative tools and insights to create more effective and engaging learning environments.

AI-enhanced classroom management goes beyond traditional methods, offering real-time monitoring and adaptive strategies to address the unique needs of each student. AI algorithms analyze various data points, including student behavior, engagement levels, and academic performance, to identify patterns and trends. This information allows teachers to tailor their classroom management strategies to optimize student participation and foster a positive learning atmosphere. For instance, AI can provide suggestions for differentiated instruction, helping educators cater to diverse learning styles within a single classroom. Moreover, AI contributes to proactive behavior intervention by identifying potential challenges before they escalate. By detecting early signs of disengagement or frustration, AI-equipped systems can prompt teachers to intervene with targeted support, preventing disruptions and ensuring a more inclusive learning environment. Liu, Subbareddy and Raghavendra (2022) introduce the Artificial Intelligence Based Inquiry Evaluation Student Learning System (AI-IESLS), designed to enhance interactive learning in a non-linear setting. The system employs concept mapping within a chatbot to enhance students' understanding of specific subjects, ultimately improving their learning outcomes.

The integration of AI in classroom management also enables personalized feedback for students, offering insights into their progress, strengths, and areas that need improvement. This personalized feedback loop promotes a collaborative relationship between teachers and students, empowering learners to take an active role in their educational journey.

While AI offers significant benefits in classroom management, ethical considerations and responsible use are crucial. Striking the right balance between technology-driven insights and human judgment is essential to maintain a student-centered and empathetic approach to education. Teachers remain central to the learning experience, and AI serves as a valuable tool to enhance their capabilities and contribute to the positive transformation of classroom dynamics.

5. THE SOCIAL IMPACTS OF AI IN EDUCATION

AI's integration into education has far-reaching social implications that go beyond the classroom. This section explores how AI in education affects equity, accessibility, privacy, ethics, and society as a whole.

5.1 Equity and Accessibility

- Reducing Educational Disparities: AI can help level the educational playing field by providing personalized support to students with diverse needs, including those with learning disabilities or from disadvantaged backgrounds.
- Global Access: Online learning platforms powered by AI can extend education to remote or underserved areas, bridging geographic gaps in access to quality education.
- Economic Disparities: There's a risk that AI-powered education may deepen economic disparities if access to technology and AI-driven resources is not equitable.

5.2 Privacy and Ethical Considerations

- Data Privacy: The collection and analysis of student data raise concerns about privacy. Schools and ed-tech companies must ensure data protection and compliance with privacy laws.

- Algorithmic Bias: AI algorithms may inadvertently perpetuate bias in education, favoring certain groups or learning styles over others. Mitigating bias in AI is an ongoing challenge.
- Transparency and Accountability: The opacity of AI algorithms can raise ethical concerns. Educational institutions and developers should be transparent about AI's role and decision-making processes.
- Informed Consent: Students and parents should have a clear understanding of how AI is used in education and should provide informed consent for data collection and analysis.

5.3 Societal Implications of AI in Education

- Workforce Readiness: AI's impact on education extends to workforce preparation. It raises questions about what skills students need in an AI-driven world.
- Educational Transformation: AI challenges traditional educational models, potentially altering the role of teachers and the structure of curricula.
- Evolving Teaching Methods: The integration of AI encourages educators to adopt new teaching methods and adapt to changing educational technologies.
- Digital Citizenship: AI in education necessitates digital literacy and responsible use of technology, preparing students to navigate a digitally driven society.

6. ENHANCING STUDENT ENGAGEMENT

Student engagement is a pivotal factor in effective learning. This section explores how Artificial Intelligence (AI) enhances student engagement through gamification, virtual reality (VR) and augmented reality (AR) experiences, and collaborative learning.

6.1 Gamification and AI

- Gamification Elements: AI-powered educational platforms incorporate game-like elements such as rewards, badges, and leader boards to motivate and engage students.
- Adaptive Challenges: AI can create adaptive challenges that align with a student's skill level, ensuring that they are neither too easy nor too difficult, maintaining interest.
- Instant Feedback: AI provides instant feedback on performance, reinforcing positive behavior and enabling learners to make immediate corrections.
- Personalized Learning Paths: Gamification powered by AI can provide customized learning paths, allowing students to choose their own adventures in the learning process.

Figure 4: Integration of Artificial Intelligence (AI) & Gamification illustrates the synergy between artificial intelligence (AI) and gamification techniques in educational contexts, showcasing how AI-powered gamified learning platforms enhance engagement, motivation, and learning outcomes for students.

Figure 4. Integration of artificial intelligence (AI) and gamification

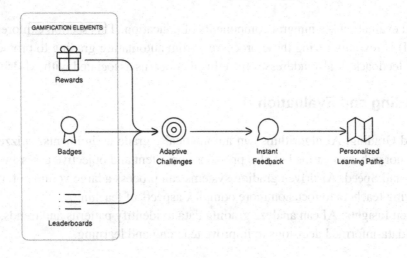

6.2 Virtual Reality and Augmented Reality in Education

- Immersive Learning: VR and AR create immersive educational experiences that transport students to virtual environments or enhance the real world with digital information.
- Complex Concepts: These technologies make it easier to visualize complex concepts, such as molecular structures in chemistry or historical events in social studies.
- Hands-On Learning: VR and AR enable hands-on learning experiences that promote active engagement and deeper understanding.
- Collaborative VR/AR: AI can facilitate collaborative VR/AR experiences, allowing students to interact and learn together in shared virtual spaces.

6.3 AI-Enhanced Collaborative Learning

- Collaborative Tools: AI can enhance collaboration among students by providing tools for communication, content sharing, and group project management.
- Group Formation: AI algorithms can form student groups based on complementary skills and learning objectives, fostering productive teamwork.
- Peer Assessment: AI can facilitate peer assessment, allowing students to provide feedback and evaluations on each other's work.
- Real-Time Collaboration: AI-powered collaborative platforms enable real-time interaction and information sharing, promoting active participation.

7. TRANSFORMING ASSESSMENT AND EVALUATION

Assessment and evaluation are integral components of education. This section explores how Artificial Intelligence (AI) is revolutionizing these processes, from automating grading to providing continuous assessment and feedback. It also addresses the ethical concerns associated with AI-driven assessment.

7.1 AI in Grading and Evaluation

- Automated Grading: AI algorithms can automatically grade assignments, quizzes, and even essays. This not only saves time but also provides consistent and objective assessments.
- Efficiency and Speed: AI-driven grading systems can process a large volume of assignments rapidly, allowing teachers to focus on more complex aspects of teaching.
- Data-Driven Insights: AI can analyze grading data to identify patterns and trends, helping educators make data-informed decisions to improve teaching and learning.

7.2 Continuous Assessment and Feedback

- Real-Time Feedback: AI-powered educational platforms offer real-time feedback to students on their performance, allowing them to track their progress and make immediate improvements.
- Adaptive Assessment: AI can adapt assessments to a student's skill level, providing questions and challenges tailored to their abilities.
- Formative Assessment: AI enables formative assessment, which focuses on identifying areas for improvement rather than assigning grades.

7.3 Ethical Concerns in AI-Driven Assessment

- Bias and Fairness: AI algorithms can inadvertently introduce bias in assessment, favoring certain demographics or learning styles. Ensuring fairness and equity is a crucial ethical consideration.
- Privacy and Data Security: Collecting and analyzing student data for assessment purposes must adhere to strict privacy and data security standards. Protecting sensitive information is paramount.
- Transparency and Accountability: The opacity of AI algorithms used in assessment raises questions about transparency and accountability. Students, educators, and institutions should have a clear understanding of how assessments are conducted.

8. CASE STUDIES: AI IN REAL-WORLD CLASSROOMS

This section delves into real-world case studies of AI implementations across different educational levels. It showcases success stories, highlights challenges overcome, and offers valuable lessons learned from these experiences.

8.1 Elementary School

Case Study: AI-Powered Math Tutoring for Elementary Students

- Implementation: An AI-powered math tutoring platform was introduced in an elementary school to support students in math.
- Successes: The platform provided personalized lessons, helping struggling students improve their math skills. Teachers noted increased engagement and enthusiasm among students.
- Lessons Learned: Effective implementation required teacher training, careful monitoring of student progress and ongoing support for students who needed additional assistance.

8.2 High School

Case Study: AI-Enhanced Language Learning in High School

- Implementation: A high school integrated an AI-driven language learning platform into its foreign language curriculum.
- Successes: Students reported improved language proficiency and higher test scores. Teachers were able to track individual progress more efficiently.
- Lessons Learned: Effective AI integration required a clear alignment with curriculum goals and continuous communication between teachers and developers.

8.3 Higher Education

Case Study: AI-Enhanced Lecture Engagement in Higher Education

- Implementation: A university incorporated AI-driven tools to enhance student engagement during lectures.
- Successes: Students reported higher levels of engagement and better understanding of course material. Attendance rates improved.
- Lessons Learned: Training faculty to effectively use AI tools was crucial. The university had to address privacy concerns and ensure the ethical use of data.

8.4 Online Learning

Case Study: AI-Powered Online Course Personalization

- Implementation: An online learning platform utilized AI to personalize course content and assessments.
- Successes: Students praised the tailored learning experience. Completion rates increased, and dropout rates decreased.
- Lessons Learned: Ensuring data privacy was a top priority. Regularly updating and improving the AI algorithms was essential to maintain engagement.

8.5 Special Education

Case Study: AI-Assisted Special Education Support

- Implementation: A school district introduced AI-driven tools to support students with special needs.
- Successes: Special education teachers found that AI tools helped individualize instruction, making learning more accessible for students with diverse needs.
- Lessons Learned: Customization and adaptability were critical. AI tools had to be flexible to accommodate varying disabilities and learning styles.

These case studies highlight the versatility and potential impact of AI across different educational levels. While success stories demonstrate the benefits of AI integration, the lessons learned underscore the importance of careful planning, training, and ethical considerations in AI implementations in real-world classrooms.

9. CHALLENGES AND LIMITATIONS

While Artificial Intelligence (AI) holds great promise in education, its adoption and implementation are not without challenges and limitations. This section explores some of the key obstacles in integrating AI into educational settings.

9.1 Technical Challenges

- Infrastructure and Connectivity: Many educational institutions, especially in underserved areas, lack the necessary technological infrastructure and high-speed internet access required for AI-powered education.
- Data Integration: Integrating AI systems with existing educational data and management systems can be technically complex and may require significant customization.
- Resource Requirements: Implementing AI in education often demands substantial financial and technical resources, which not all institutions can afford.
- Compatibility: Ensuring that AI-powered educational tools are compatible with various devices, operating systems, and software can be challenging.

9.2 Teacher and Student Resistance

- Lack of Familiarity: Teachers and students may resist AI adoption due to a lack of familiarity with these technologies or a fear of job displacement.
- Privacy Concerns: Concerns about student data privacy and the potential misuse of AI in monitoring and assessment may lead to resistance.
- Pedagogical Concerns: Some educators may worry that AI-driven teaching methods may not align with their pedagogical philosophies or may depersonalize the learning experience.

- Training Needs: Teachers often require training and professional development to effectively use AI tools in their classrooms.

9.3 Integration and Implementation Challenges

- Curriculum Alignment: Integrating AI into existing curricula may require adjustments to ensure that AI-enhanced content aligns with educational goals and standards.
- Change Management: Implementing AI can disrupt established teaching practices, requiring effective change management strategies and support.
- Scaling Issues: Successfully implementing AI in one classroom or school does not guarantee scalability across an entire educational system. Scaling up can pose significant challenges.
- Ethical Considerations: The integration of AI must consider ethical concerns, including bias, fairness, and transparency, which can complicate the implementation process.

10. FUTURE DIRECTIONS AND TRENDS

The future of AI in education holds tremendous potential for transforming how we teach and learn. In this chapter, we explore the evolving landscape of AI in education, emerging technologies and innovations, and the global impact of AI on education.

10.1 The Future of AI in Education

The future of AI in education promises to be dynamic and transformative, shaping the landscape of learning in unprecedented ways. As we delve into the next frontier of educational technology, several key directions and trends are poised to influence the future of AI in education. One notable direction is the continued refinement and expansion of AI-powered adaptive learning systems. These systems, driven by machine learning algorithms, will become increasingly adept at tailoring educational content to individual student needs, preferences, and learning styles. This personalized approach holds the potential to enhance student engagement and achievement by providing targeted support and challenges. Additionally, the integration of AI in assessments is expected to evolve, moving beyond traditional testing methods. AI-driven assessment tools can offer real-time feedback, assess a broader range of skills, and adapt to the evolving needs of learners. This shift towards more dynamic and holistic assessment practices aligns with the broader goal of fostering comprehensive skill development.

Furthermore, the collaborative nature of AI and human educators is likely to strengthen. Rather than replacing teachers, AI will continue to serve as a valuable support system, offering insights, automating administrative tasks, and enabling educators to focus more on personalized instruction and mentorship. As the educational landscape becomes increasingly globalized, AI is anticipated to play a crucial role in breaking down language barriers and facilitating inclusive learning environments. Translation services, language learning apps, and AI-driven content creation tools will contribute to a more interconnected and accessible educational experience for students worldwide. Ethical considerations, data privacy, and responsible AI use will be central to the future development of AI in education. Striking a balance between innovations and safeguarding student well-being will require ongoing collaboration between educators, policymakers, and technology developers.

In conclusion, the future of AI in education holds the promise of a more adaptive, personalized, and globally inclusive learning experience. Embracing these future directions and trends ensures that AI continues to contribute positively to the transformation of classroom dynamics, preparing students for the challenges and opportunities of the evolving digital era.

10.2 Emerging Technologies and Innovations

- Natural Language Processing (NLP): NLP will enhance AI-driven chatbots, virtual tutors, and language learning platforms, making communication and language acquisition more effective.
- Immersive Learning: Virtual Reality (VR) and Augmented Reality (AR) will become more integrated into education, offering immersive and interactive learning experiences.
- Emotion Recognition: AI will incorporate emotion recognition to gauge student engagement and well-being, allowing educators to provide timely support.
- Blockchain in Credentialing: Blockchain technology may play a role in verifying and securely storing educational credentials and achievements.

Figure 5: Future of AI in education provides insights into the anticipated advancements and potential applications of artificial intelligence (AI) in shaping the future of education, highlighting emerging trends, innovations, and opportunities for leveraging AI technologies to enhance teaching, learning, and educational outcomes.

10.3 The Potential for Global Impact

The potential for global impact through the integration of AI in education represents a significant trend that is poised to shape the future of classroom dynamics. As AI technologies continue to advance, their ability to transcend geographical boundaries and address educational challenges on a global scale becomes increasingly evident. One key aspect of this potential impact is the democratization of education. AI-powered educational tools have the capacity to bring quality learning resources to underserved regions, providing students with access to high-quality content and personalized learning experiences irrespective of their geographical location. This has the potential to narrow educational disparities and foster a more inclusive global learning community. Moreover, AI can play a pivotal role in addressing language barriers, enabling multilingual support and translation services. This enhances communication and ensures that educational content is accessible to students in their native languages, fostering a more diverse and culturally sensitive learning environment. Zawacki-Richter (2019) provides an overview of research on AI applications in higher education through a systematic review.

In regions with limited access to experienced educators, AI-driven platforms can act as force multipliers, providing intelligent tutoring, personalized feedback, and mentorship. This can contribute to the development of a skilled global workforce by empowering students with resources that align with the demands of the modern job market. Collaborative efforts among educational institutions, governments, and technology developers are crucial to harnessing the full potential of AI in education on a global scale. Considerations of ethical use, data privacy, and cultural sensitivity must be prioritized to ensure that the benefits of AI in education are realized without exacerbating existing disparities.

Figure 5. Future of AI in education

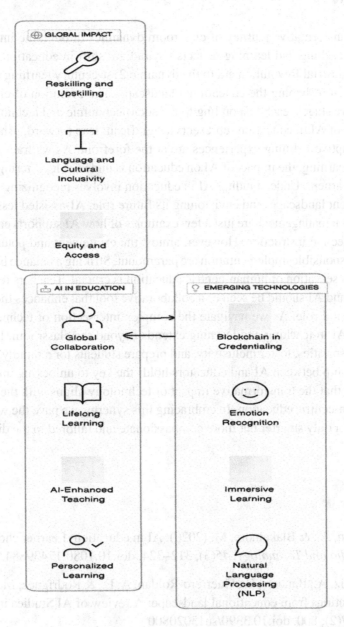

The potential for global impact through the incorporation of AI in education holds promise for creating a more equitable and interconnected world of learning. By leveraging the transformative capabilities of AI, education can transcend borders, offering students worldwide access to a quality, personalized, and culturally relevant learning experience.

11. CONCLUSION

In conclusion, the transformative journey of classroom dynamics through the integration of Artificial Intelligence (AI) in teaching and learning reflects a paradigm shift in education. From the traditional settings of the pre-Industrial Revolution era to the dynamic 21st-century learning environments, AI has played a pivotal role in reshaping the educational landscape. The evolution of classroom dynamics is marked by progressive stages, each responding to the socio-economic and technological changes of its time. The emergence of AI in education represents a significant leap forward, ushering in an era where personalized and adaptive learning experiences are at the forefront. As we transition from the Digital Age to 21st-century learning, the impact of AI on education is undeniable, offering new possibilities for both educators and learners. Understanding AI in education involves recognizing its historical context, appreciating the current landscape, and envisioning its future role. AI-assisted lesson planning, teacher training, and classroom management are just a few examples of how AI supports educators in delivering more tailored and effective instruction. However, amidst the excitement and potential benefits, ethical considerations and responsible implementation are paramount. Striking a balance between technological innovation and the preservation of human-centric education is crucial. Teachers remain the heart of the educational process, and AI should be seen as a collaborative tool that enhances their capabilities rather than replacing their vital role. As we navigate the complex intersection of technology and education, the social impact of AI in teaching and learning extends beyond the classroom. It has the potential to bridge educational disparities, foster inclusivity, and prepare students for a rapidly changing world. The collaborative partnership between AI and educators holds the key to unlocking innovative pedagogical approaches, ensuring that the transformative impact of technology aligns with the values of equity, accessibility, and human-centric education. In embracing this synergy, we pave the way for a future where education becomes not only smarter but more compassionate and tailored to the diverse needs of every learner.

REFERENCES

Berendt, B., Littlejohn, A., & Blakemore, M. (2020). AI in education: Learner choice and fundamental rights. *Learning, Media and Technology*, *45*(3), 312–324. doi:10.1080/17439884.2020.1786399

Bozkurt, A., Karadeniz, A., Baneres, D., Guerrero-Roldán, A. E., & Rodríguez, M. E. (2021). Artificial intelligence and reflections from educational landscape: A review of AI Studies in half a century. *Sustainability (Basel)*, *13*(2), 800. doi:10.3390/su13020800

Ciolacu, M., Tehrani, A. F., Binder, L., & Svasta, P. M. (2018, October). Education 4.0-Artificial Intelligence assisted higher education: early recognition system with machine learning to support students' success. In *2018 IEEE 24th International Symposium for Design and Technology in Electronic Packaging (SIITME)* (pp. 23-30). IEEE. DOI: 10.1109/SIITME.2018.8599203

Escotet, M. Á. (2023). The optimistic future of Artificial Intelligence in higher education. *Prospects*, 1–10. doi:10.1007/s11125-023-09642-z

Liu, L., Subbareddy, R., & Raghavendra, C. G. (2022). AI Intelligence Chatbot to Improve Students Learning in the Higher Education Platform. *Journal of Interconnection Networks*, *22*(Supp02). doi:10.1142/S0219265921430325

Renz, A., Krishnaraja, S., & Gronau, E. (2020). Demystification of Artificial Intelligence in Education–How much AI is really in the Educational Technology? *International Journal of Learning Analytics and Artificial Intelligence for Education*, *2*(1), 14. doi:10.3991/ijai.v2i1.12675

Rienties, B., Køhler Simonsen, H., & Herodotou, C. (2020, July). Defining the boundaries between artificial intelligence in education, computer-supported collaborative learning, educational data mining, and learning analytics: A need for coherence. In *Frontiers in Education* (Vol. 5, p. 128). Frontiers Media SA. doi:10.3389/feduc.2020.00128

Tight, M. (2020). Student retention and engagement in higher education. *Journal of Further and Higher Education*, *44*(5), 689–704. doi:10.1080/0309877X.2019.1576860

Ungerer, L., & Slade, S. (2022). Ethical considerations of artificial intelligence in learning analytics in distance education contexts. In Learning Analytics in Open and Distributed Learning: Potential and Challenges (pp. 105-120). Singapore: Springer Nature Singapore. doi:10.1007/978-981-19-0786-9_8

Vashishth, T. K., Kumar, B., Sharma, V., Chaudhary, S., Kumar, S., & Sharma, K. K. (2023). The Evolution of AI and Its Transformative Effects on Computing: A Comparative Analysis. In *Intelligent Engineering Applications and Applied Sciences for Sustainability* (pp. 425–442). IGI Global. doi:10.4018/979-8-3693-0044-2.ch022

Vashishth, T. K., Sharma, V., Chaudhary, S., Panwar, R., Sharma, S., & Kumar, P. (2023). Advanced Technologies and AI-Enabled IoT Applications in High-Tech Agriculture. In Handbook of Research on AI-Equipped IoT Applications in High-Tech Agriculture (pp. 155-166). IGI Global. doi:10.4018/978-1-6684-9231-4.ch008

Vashishth, T. K., Sharma, V., Sharma, K. K., Kumar, B., Panwar, R., & Chaudhary, S. (2024). AI-Driven Learning Analytics for Personalized Feedback and Assessment in Higher Education. In Using Traditional Design Methods to Enhance AI-Driven Decision Making (pp. 206-230). IGI Global.

Wang, T., Lund, B. D., Marengo, A., Pagano, A., Mannuru, N. R., Teel, Z. A., & Pange, J. (2023). Exploring the Potential Impact of Artificial Intelligence (AI) on International Students in Higher Education: Generative AI, Chatbots, Analytics, and International Student Success. *Applied Sciences (Basel, Switzerland)*, *13*(11), 6716. doi:10.3390/app13116716

Zawacki-Richter, O., Marín, V. I., Bond, M., & Gouverneur, F. (2019). Systematic review of research on artificial intelligence applications in higher education–where are the educators? *International Journal of Educational Technology in Higher Education*, *16*(1), 1–27. doi:10.1186/s41239-019-0171-0

Zhang, L., Wu, M., & Ouyang, F. (2023). The design and implementation of a teaching and learning analytics tool in a face-to-face, small-sized course in China's higher education. *Education and Information Technologies*, 1–24. doi:10.1007/s10639-023-11940-0

KEY TERMS AND DEFINITIONS

Artificial Intelligence (AI): Refers to the development of computer systems that can perform tasks that typically require human intelligence, such as learning, problem-solving, decision-making, and natural language understanding.

Augmented Reality (AR): Is a technology that overlays computer-generated content, such as images, videos, or information, onto the real-world environment, enhancing the user's perception of their surroundings by blending digital and physical elements.

Intelligent Tutoring Systems (ITS): Are computer-based educational systems that use artificial intelligence to provide personalized and adaptive instruction to learners. These systems mimic the role of a human tutor by assessing a student's progress and tailoring lessons to their individual needs.

Natural Language Processing (NLP): Is a field of artificial intelligence that focuses on enabling computers to understand, interpret, and generate human language in a way that is both meaningful and contextually relevant.

Virtual Reality (VR): Is a technology that creates a computer-generated immersive environment, allowing users to interact with and experience a three-dimensional digital world as if it were real.

Compilation of References

Abd Rahim, T. N. T., Abd Aziz, Z., Ab Rauf, R. H., & Shamsudin, N. (2017, November). Automated exam question generator using genetic algorithm. In *2017 IEEE Conference on e-Learning, e-Management and e-Services (IC3e)* (pp. 12-17). IEEE.

Abdalgane, M., & Othman, K. A. J. (2023). Utilizing Artificial Intelligence Technologies in Saudi EFL Tertiary Level Classrooms. *Journal of Intercultural Communication*, 23(1), 92–99. Advance online publication. doi:10.36923/jicc. v23i1.124

Abdalla, R. S., Mahbub, S. A., Mokhtar, R. A., Ali, E. S., & Saeed, R. A. (2020). IoE Design Principles and Architecture; Book: Internet of Energy for Smart Cities: Machine Learning Models and Techniques. *Internet of Energy for Smart Cities: Machine Learning Models and Techniques*.

Abdel-Maguid, T., & Abdel-Halim, R. (2015). The Qur'ān and the development of rational thinking. *Urology Annals*, 7(2), 135–140. doi:10.4103/0974-7796.152926 PMID:25837451

Abrenilla, E. M., Redido, C., Abendan, C. F., & Kilag, O. K. (2023). The Next Chapter of ELT: Embracing AI-Infused Pedagogies and Evolving Educational Strategies in the Post-Pandemic Landscape. *Excellencia: International Multidisciplinary Journal of Education, 1*(5), 124-135.

Abu Owda, M. F., Abu Mousa, A. H., Shakfa, M. D., & Al-Hidabi, D. A. (2023). *The Impact of Teaching Artificial Intelligence Concepts and Tools in Improving Creative Thinking Skills Among Talented Students Technological Sustainability and Business Competitive Advantage*. Springer.

Abubakari, M. S. (2021). Information and Communication Technology Acceptance in Madrasa Education: Religious' Perspective in Tanzania. *International Journal of Social Sciences & Educational Studies*, 8(3), 129–148. doi:10.23918/ijsses.v8i3p129

Abubakari, M. S., & Zakaria, G. A. N. (2023). Technology Acceptance Model in Islamic Education (TAMISE) for Digital Learning: Conceptual Framework Proposal. *Canadian Journal of Educational and Social Studies*, 3(4), 25–42. doi:10.53103/cjess.v3i4.153

Abubakari, M. S., Zakaria, G. A. N., & Musa, J. (2023). Digital Learning Acceptance in Islamic Education: Validity and Reliability Testing of the Modified Technology Acceptance Model. *Canadian Journal of Educational and Social Studies*, 3(6), 27–42. doi:10.53103/cjess.v6i1.185

Abubakari, M. S., Zakaria, G. A. N., Musa, J., & Kalinaki, K. (2023a). Assessing Digital Competence in Higher Education: A Gender Analysis of DigComp 2.1 Framework in Uganda. *SAGA: Journal of Technology and Information System*, 1(4), 114–120. doi:10.58905/saga.v1i4.210

Abubakari, M. S., Zakaria, G. A. N., Musa, J., & Kalinaki, K. (2023b). Validating the Digital Competence (Dig-Comp 2.1) Framework in Higher Education Using Confirmatory Factor Analysis: Non-Western Perspective. *Canadian Journal of Educational and Social Studies*, *3*(6), 15–26. doi:10.53103/cjess.v6i1.184

Abubakari, M. S., Zakaria, G. A. N., Priyanto, P., & Triantini, D. T. (2023). Analysing Technology Acceptance for Digital Learning in Islamic Education: The Role of Religious Perspective on ICT. *Journal of Computing Research and Innovation*, *8*(1), 1–16. doi:10.24191/jcrinn.v8i1.344

Abu-Ghuwaleh, M., & Saffaf, R. (2023). *Integrating AI and NLP with Project-Based Learning in STREAM Education*. Academic Press.

Adiguzel, T., Kaya, M. H., & Cansu, F. K. (2023). Revolutionizing education with AI: Exploring the transformative potential of ChatGPT. *Contemporary Educational Technology*, *15*(3), ep429. doi:10.30935/cedtech/13152

Affectiva. (n.d.). Retrieved from https://www.affectiva.com/

Aggarwal, D. (2023). Integration of innovative technological developments and AI with education for an adaptive learning pedagogy. *China Petroleum Processing and Petrochemical Technology*, *23*(2).

Agil, T., & Alkhiri, A. (2022). Islamic Ethical Foundations of AI and Its Modern Applications. *International Journal of Computer Science and Network Security*, *22*(5), 741–746. doi:10.22937/IJCSNS.2022.22.5.101

Ahmad, I., Sharma, S., Singh, R., Gehlot, A., Priyadarshi, N., & Twala, B. (2022). MOOC 5.0: A Roadmap to the Future of Learning. *Sustainability (Basel)*, *14*(18), 11199. doi:10.3390/su141811199

Ahmad, K., Iqbal, W., El-Hassan, A., Qadir, J., Benhaddou, D., Ayyash, M., & Al-Fuqaha, A. (2023). Data-driven artificial intelligence in education: A comprehensive review. *IEEE Transactions on Learning Technologies*.

Ahmad, S., Alam, M. M., Rahmat, M. K., Mubarik, M., & Hyder, S. (2022). Academic and administrative role of artificial intelligence in education. *Sustainability (Basel)*, *14*(3), 1101. doi:10.3390/su14031101

Ahmad, T. (2020). Student perceptions on using cell phones as learning tools: Implications for mobile technology usage in Caribbean higher education institutions. *PSU Research Review*, *4*(1), 25–43. doi:10.1108/PRR-03-2018-0007

Ahmed, Z. E., Hashim, A. A., Saeed, R. A., & Saeed, M. M. (2023). Mobility management enhancement in smart cities using software-defined networks. *Scientific African*, *22*, e01932. doi:10.1016/j.sciaf.2023.e01932

Aibar-Almazán, A., Castellote-Caballero, Y., Carcelén-Fraile, M. D. C., Rivas-Campo, Y., & González-Martín, A. M. (2024). Gamification in the classroom: Kahoot! As a tool for university teaching innovation. *Frontiers in Psychology*, *15*, 1370084. doi:10.3389/fpsyg.2024.1370084

AILessonPlan. (n.d.). Retrieved from https://ailessonplan.com/

Akgun, S., & Greenhow, C. (2022). Artificial intelligence in education: Addressing ethical challenges in K-12 settings. *AI and Ethics*, *2*(3), 431–440. doi:10.1007/s43681-021-00096-7 PMID:34790956

Akram, B., Yoder, S., Tatar, C., Boorugu, S., Aderemi, I., & Jiang, S. (2022). Towards an AI-Infused Interdisciplinary Curriculum for Middle-Grade Classrooms. *Proceedings of the AAAI Conference on Artificial Intelligence*. 10.1609/aaai.v36i11.21544

Al Braiki, B., Harous, S., Zaki, N., & Alnajjar, F. (2020). Artificial intelligence in education and assessment methods. *Bulletin of Electrical Engineering and Informatics*, *9*(5), 1998–2007. doi:10.11591/eei.v9i5.1984

Alabool, H. M. (2023). ChatGPT in Education: SWOT analysis approach. *2023 International Conference on Information Technology (ICIT), September*, 184–189. 10.1109/ICIT58056.2023.10225801

Alam, A. (2021a, November). Possibilities and apprehensions in the landscape of artificial intelligence in education. In *2021 International Conference on Computational Intelligence and Computing Applications (ICCICA)* (pp. 1-8). IEEE.10.1109/ICCICA52458.2021.9697272

Alam, A. (2021b, December). Should robots replace teachers? Mobilisation of AI and learning analytics in education. In *2021 International Conference on Advances in Computing, Communication, and Control (ICAC3)* (pp. 1-12). IEEE.10.1109/ICAC353642.2021.9697300

Alam, A. (2022). Employing adaptive learning and intelligent tutoring robots for virtual classrooms and smart campuses: Reforming education in the age of artificial intelligence. *Advanced Computing and Intelligent Technologies Proceedings of ICACIT, 2022*, 395–406.

Alam, A. (2023). Developing a Curriculum for Ethical and Responsible AI: A University Course on Safety, Fairness, Privacy, and Ethics to Prepare Next Generation of AI Professionals. In *Intelligent Communication Technologies and Virtual Mobile Networks* (pp. 879–894). Springer Nature Singapore. doi:10.1007/978-981-99-1767-9_64

Al-Ansi, A. M., Jaboob, M., Garad, A., & Al-Ansi, A. (2023). Analyzing augmented reality (AR) and virtual reality (VR) recent development in education. *Social Sciences & Humanities Open*, 8(1), 100532. doi:10.1016/j.ssaho.2023.100532

Alaziz, S. N., Albayati, B., El-Bagoury, A. A., & Shafik, W. (2023). Clustering of COVID-19 Multi-Time Series-Based K-Means and PCA With Forecasting. *International Journal of Data Warehousing and Mining*, 19(3), 1–25. doi:10.4018/IJDWM.317374

Albacete, P., Jordan, P., Katz, S., Chounta, I.-A., & Mclaren, B. M. (2019). *The impact of student model updates on contingent scaffolding in a natural-language tutoring system*. Academic Press.

Alberta Education. (2013). *Learning and technology policy framework 2013*. Retrieved from http://www.education.alberta.ca/media/7792655/learning-and-technology-policy-framework-web.pdf

Aleedy, M., Atwell, E., & Meshoul, S. (2022). Using AI Chatbots in Education: Recent Advances Challenges and Use Case. In Artificial Intelligence and Sustainable Computing. *Proceedings of ICSISCET, 2021*, 661–675. doi:10.1007/978-981-19-1653-3_50

Aleven, V., McLaren, B., Sewall, J., & Koedinger, K. R. (2009). *Example-tracing tutors: A new paradigm for intelligent tutoring systems*. Academic Press.

AlFarsi, G., Tawafak, R. M., ElDow, A., Malik, S. I., Jabbar, J., & Al Sideiri, A. (2021). *Smart classroom technology in artificial intelligence: A review paper*. Paper presented at the International Conference on Culture Heritage, Education, Sustainable Tourism, and Innovation Technologies.

Ali, A. (2023). Exploring the Transformative Potential of Technology in Overcoming Educational Disparities. *International Journal of Multidisciplinary Sciences and Arts*, 2(1). Advance online publication. doi:10.47709/ijmdsa.v2i1.2559

Ali, E. S., Hasan, M. K., Hassan, R., Saeed, R. A., Hassan, M. B., Islam, S., Nafi, N. S., & Bevinakoppa, S. (2021). Machine learning technologies for secure vehicular communication in internet of vehicles: Recent advances and applications. *Security and Communication Networks, 2021*, 1–23. doi:10.1155/2021/8868355

Ali, F., Choy, D., Divaharan, S., Tay, H., & Chen, W. (2023). Supporting self-directed learning and self-assessment using teachergaia, a generative ai chatbot appli-cation: Learning approaches and prompt engineering. Learning. *Research and Practice*, 9(2), 135–147.

Alkashri, Siyam, & Alqaryouti. (2020). *A detailed survey of Artificial Intelligence and Software Engineering: Emergent Issues.* . doi:10.1109/ICISC47916.2020.9171118

Almusaed, A., Almssad, A., Yitmen, I., & Homod, R. Z. (2023). Enhancing Student Engagement: Harnessing "AIED"'s Power in Hybrid Education—A Review Analysis. *Education Sciences*, *13*(7), 632. doi:10.3390/educsci13070632

Alqahtani, T., Badreldin, H. A., Alrashed, M., Alshaya, A. I., Alghamdi, S. S., bin Saleh, K., Alowais, S. A., Alshaya, O. A., Rahman, I., Al Yami, M. S., & Albekairy, A. M. (2023). The emergent role of artificial intelligence, natural learning processing, and large language models in higher education and research. *Research in Social & Administrative Pharmacy*, *19*(8), 1236–1242. doi:10.1016/j.sapharm.2023.05.016 PMID:37321925

Alqurashi, F. A., Alsolami, F., Abdel-Khalek, S., Sayed Ali, E., & Saeed, R. A. (2022). Machine learning techniques in internet of UAVs for smart cities applications. *Journal of Intelligent & Fuzzy Systems*, *42*(4), 3203–3226. doi:10.3233/JIFS-211009

Alrakhawi, H. A., Jamiat, N., & Abu-Naser, S. S. (2023). Intelligent Tutoring Systems in Education: A Systematic Review of Usage, Tools, Effects and Evaluation. *Journal of Theoretical and Applied Information Technology*, *101*(4), 1205–1226.

Alrumiah, S. S., & Al-Shargabi, A. A. (2023). Intelligent Quran Recitation Recognition and Verification: Research Trends and Open Issues. *Arabian Journal for Science and Engineering*, *48*(8), 9859–9885. doi:10.1007/s13369-022-07273-8

Alsobhi, H. A., Alakhtar, R. A., Ubaid, A., Hussain, O. K., & Hussain, F. K. (2023). Blockchain-based micro-credentialing system in higher education institutions: Systematic literature review. *Knowledge-Based Systems*, *265*, 110238. doi:10.1016/j.knosys.2022.110238

Altememy, H. A., Neamah, N. R., Mazhair, R., Naser, N. S., & Fahad, A. A., Abdulghffar Al-Sammarraie, N., . . . Al-Muttar, M. Y. O. (2023). AI Tools' Impact on Student Performance: Focusing on Student Motivation & Engagement in Iraq. *Social Space*, *23*(2), 143–165.

Alter, S. (2022). Understanding artificial intelligence in the context of usage: Contributions and smartness of algorithmic capabilities in work systems. *International Journal of Information Management*, *67*, 102392. doi:10.1016/j.ijinfomgt.2021.102392

Alves, J. M. A., Soares, R. D. B., Moutinho, N. F. L., & Pereira, J. P. R. (2018). SimEmp: A game simulation in management teaching. In *2018 13th Iberian Conference on Information Systems and Technologies (CISTI)* (pp. 1-6). IEEE. 10.23919/CISTI.2018.8399166

Alwarthan, S., Aslam, N., & Khan, I. U. (2022). An Explainable Model for Identifying At-Risk Student at Higher Education. *IEEE Access : Practical Innovations, Open Solutions*, *10*, 107649–107668. doi:10.1109/ACCESS.2022.3211070

An, K. (2022). Exploration of Intelligent Teaching Methods for Ideological and Political Education in Colleges and Universities under the Background of "Mass Entrepreneurship and Innovation." In International Journal of Antennas and Propagation (Vol. 2022). doi:10.1155/2022/2294908

An, R., & Xi, T. (2020). Research on the Service Design of Smart Campus Based on Sustainable Strategy – Taking Smart Canteen as an Example. Lecture Notes in Computer Science (including subseries Lecture Notes in Artificial Intelligence and Lecture Notes in Bioinformatics) (Vol. 12202 LNCS, pp. 20–30). Springer.

Anagnostopoulos, T., Kostakos, P., Zaslavsky, A., Kantzavelou, I., Tsotsolas, N., Salmon, I., . . . Harle, R. (2021). Challenges and solutions of surveillance systems in IoT-enabled smart campus: a survey. *IEEE Access, 9*, 131926-131954. https://ieeexplore.ieee.org/abstract/document/9543662

Anand, D., Gupta, V., Paruchuri, P., & Ravindran, B. (2021). An Enhanced Advising Model in Teacher-Student Framework using State Categorization. *Proceedings of the AAAI Conference on Artificial Intelligence*, *35*(8), 6653–6660. doi:10.1609/aaai.v35i8.16823

Angelova, G., Nisheva-Pavlova, M., Eskenazi, A., & Ivanova, K. (2021, April). Role of Education and Research for Artificial Intelligence Development in Bulgaria Until 2030. *Mathematics and Education in Mathematics*, *50*, 71–82.

Anirudh, K., Bishwajeet, P., Kushagra, V., Kartik, K., & Bhale, P. (2015). Das Teerath. A Study of Today's A.I. through Chatbots and Rediscovery of Machine Intelligence. *International Journal of u- and e-Service Science and Technology*, *8*(7), 277–284.

Ansari, A., Ahmad, S., & Bhutta, S. (2023). Mapping the global evidence around the use of chatgpt in higher education: A systematic scoping review. *Education and Information Technologies*. Advance online publication. doi:10.1007/s10639-023-12223-4

Arifuddin, M., Thalib, S. B., & Ali, M. S. (2022). The Development of Modeling Physics Learning to Improve Critical Thinking Ability of Student. *Asian Journal of Applied Sciences*, *10*(1). Advance online publication. doi:10.24203/ajas.v10i1.6842

Arjmand, R. (2018). Introduction to Part I: Islamic Education: Historical Perspective, Origin, and Foundation. In Handbook of Islamic Education (pp. 3–31). doi:10.1007/978-3-319-64683-1_3

Arthars, N., Dollinger, M., Vigentini, L., Liu, D. Y.-T., Kondo, E., & King, D. M. (2019). Empowering Teachers to Personalize Learning Support: Case Studies of Teachers' Experiences Adopting a Student-and Teacher-Centered Learning Analytics Platform at Three Australian Universities. *Utilizing learning analytics to support study success*, 223-248.

Asiah, M., Zulkarnaen, K. N., Safaai, D., Hafzan, M. Y. N. N., Saberi, M. M., & Syuhaida, S. S. (2019). A review on predictive modeling technique for student academic performance monitoring. In *MATEC Web of Conferences* (Vol. 255, p. 03004). EDP Sciences.10.1051/matecconf/201925503004

Assar, S., Boughzala, I., & Isckia, T. (2011). eGovernment Trends in the Web 2.0 Era and the Open Innovation Perspective: An Exploratory Field Study. In Electronic Government. EGOV 2011. Lecture Notes in Computer Science, vol 6846. Springer. doi:10.1007/978-3-642-22878-0_18

Aswathy, R. H., Suresh, P., Sikkandar, M. Y., Abdel-Khalek, S., Alhumyani, H., Saeed, R. A., & Mansour, R. F. (2022). Optimized tuned deep learning model for chronic kidney disease classification. *Computers, Materials & Continua*, *70*, 2097–2111. doi:10.32604/cmc.2022.019790

AuCoin, A., Porter, G. L., & Baker-Korotkov, K. (2020). New Brunswick's journey to inclusive education. *Prospects*, *49*(3-4), 313–328. doi:10.1007/s11125-020-09508-8

Aurelia, S., Thanuja, R., Chowdhury, S., & Hu, Y. C. (2023). AI-based online proctoring: A review of the state-of-the-art techniques and open challenges. *Multimedia Tools and Applications*, *83*(11), 1–23. doi:10.1007/s11042-023-16714-x

Azhari, E. L. (2023). K., Hilal, I., Daoudi, N., Ajhoun, R.: Smart chatbots in the e-learning domain: A systematic literature review. *International Journal of Interactive Mobile Technologies*, *17*(15), 4–37. doi:10.3991/ijim.v17i15.40315

Bachiri, Y. A., Mouncif, H., & Bouikhalene, B. (2023). Artificial intelligence empowers gamification: Optimizing student engagement and learning outcomes in e-learning and moocs. *International Journal of Engineering Pedagogy*, *13*(8), 4–19. doi:10.3991/ijep.v13i8.40853

Badal, Y. T., & Sungkur, R. K. (2023). Predictive modelling and analytics of students' grades using machine learning algorithms. *Education and Information Technologies*, *28*(3), 3027–3057. doi:10.1007/s10639-022-11299-8 PMID:36097545

Bahroun, Z., Anane, C., Ahmed, V., & Zacca, A. (2023). Transforming education: A com-prehensive review of generative artificial intelligence in educational settings through bibliometric and content analysis. *Sustainability (Basel)*, *15*(17), 12983. doi:10.3390/su151712983

Baidoo-Anu, D., & Ansah, L. O. (2023). Education in the era of generative artificial intelligence (AI): Understanding the potential benefits of ChatGPT in promoting teaching and learning. *Journal of AI*, *7*(1), 52–62. doi:10.61969/jai.1337500

Bailey, L. W. (2019). New Technology for the Classroom: Mobile Devices, Artificial Intelligence, Tutoring Systems, and Robotics. In Educational Technology and the New World of Persistent Learning (pp. 1-11). IGI Global.

Baiza, Y. (2018). Islamic Education and Development of Educational Traditions and Institutions. In *Handbook of Islamic Education* (pp. 77–97). Springer. doi:10.1007/978-3-319-64683-1_7

Bajaj, R., & Sharma, V. (2018). Smart Education with artificial intelligence based determination of learning styles. *Procedia Computer Science*, *132*, 834–842. doi:10.1016/j.procs.2018.05.095

Baker, R. S. (2016). Stupid tutoring systems, intelligent humans. *International Journal of Artificial Intelligence in Education*, *26*(2), 600–614. doi:10.1007/s40593-016-0105-0

Baker, R. S., Gašević, D., & Karumbaiah, S. (2021). Four paradigms in learning analytics: Why paradigm convergence matters. *Computers and Education: Artificial Intelligence*, *2*, 100021. Advance online publication. doi:10.1016/j.caeai.2021.100021

Baker, R., & Hawn, A. (2021). Algorithmic bias in education. *International Journal of Artificial Intelligence in Education*, *32*(4), 1052–1092. doi:10.1007/s40593-021-00285-9

Balaji, K., Selvam, M., & Rajeswari, R. (2022). Impact of Artificial Intelligence (AI), Internet of Things (IoT) & STEM Social Enterprise Learning Based Applications in the Teaching and Learning Process of Engineering Education. In *ICDSMLA 2020: Proceedings of the 2nd International Conference on Data Science, Machine Learning and Applications* (pp. 1217-1226). Springer Singapore. 10.1007/978-981-16-3690-5_116

Balfaqih, M. (2023). A Hybrid Movies Recommendation System Based on Demographics and Facial Expression Analysis using Machine Learning. *International Journal of Advanced Computer Science and Applications*, *14*(11). Advance online publication. doi:10.14569/IJACSA.2023.0141177

Balfaqih, M., & Alharbi, S. A. (2022). Associated Information and Communication Technologies Challenges of Smart City Development. *Sustainability (Basel)*, *14*(23), 16240. doi:10.3390/su142316240

Bansal, H., & Khan, R. (2018). A review paper on human computer interaction. *International Journal of Advanced Research in Computer Science and Software Engineering*, *8*(4), 53. doi:10.23956/ijarcsse.v8i4.630

Baş, İ., Alp, D., Ergenç, L. C., Koçak, A. E., & Yalçın, S. (2023). DancÆR: Efficient and Accurate Dance Choreography Learning by Feedback Through Pose Classification. doi:10.1007/978-3-031-36336-8_115

Basham, J. D., Hall, T. E., Carter, R. A. Jr, & Stahl, W. M. (2016). An operationalized understanding of personalized learning. *Journal of Special Education Technology*, *31*(3), 126–136. doi:10.1177/0162643416660835

Baskara, F. R. (2023). Personalised learning with ai: implications for Ignatian pedagogy. *International Journal of Educational Best Practices*, *7*(1), 1–16. doi:10.31258/ijebp.v7n1.p1-16

Bassen, J., Balaji, B., Schaarschmidt, M., Thille, C., Painter, J., Zimmaro, D., Games, A., Fast, E., & Mitchell, J. C. (2020). Reinforcement Learning for the Adaptive Scheduling of Educational Activities. *Proceedings of the 2020 CHI Conference on Human Factors in Computing Systems*, 1–12. 10.1145/3313831.3376518

Batzos, Z., Saoulidis, T., Margounakis, D., Fountoukidis, E., Grigoriou, E., Moukoulis, A., . . . Bibi, S. (2023). *Gamification and Serious Games for Cybersecurity Awareness and First Responders Training: An overview*. Academic Press.

Bennani, S., Maalel, A., & Ben Ghezala, H. (2022). Adaptive gamification in E-learning: A literature review and future challenges. *Computer Applications in Engineering Education*, *30*(2), 628–642. doi:10.1002/cae.22477

Benzaghta, M. A., Elwalda, A., Mousa, M., Erkan, I., & Rahman, M. (2021). SWOT analysis applications: An integrative literature review. *Journal of Global Business Insights*, *6*(1), 55–73. doi:10.5038/2640-6489.6.1.1148

Berendt, B., Littlejohn, A., & Blakemore, M. (2020). AI in education: Learner choice and fundamental rights. *Learning, Media and Technology*, *45*(3), 312–324. doi:10.1080/17439884.2020.1786399

Bergdahl, N., Nouri, J., & Fors, U. (2020). Disengagement, engagement and digital skills in technology-enhanced learning. *Education and Information Technologies*, *25*(2), 957–983. doi:10.1007/s10639-019-09998-w

Beringer, V. (2009, October 20). *For kids, pen's mightier than keyboard*. futurity.org. Retrieved February 25th 2013 from http://www.futurity.org/society-culture/for-kids-pens-mightier-than-keyboard/#more-4909

Berondo, R. (2023a). *From holograms to virtual classrooms: An investigation into the future of remote education*. https://doi.org/ doi:10.48047/ecb/2023.12.10.0882023.30/06/2023

Berondo, R. (2023b). *Harnessing the power of artificial intelligence for personalized learning in education*. https://doi.org/ doi:10.48047/ecb/2023.12.10.0892023.30/06/2023

Berondo, R. (2023c). Revolutionizing education: Exploring the impact of augmented reality in the classroom. *European Chemical Bulletin*, *12*(10), 1221–1228. doi:10.48047/ecb/2023.12.10.0872023.30/06/2023

Bezzina, S., & Dingli, A. (2023). *Rethinking gamification through artificial intelligence*. Paper presented at the International Conference on Human-Computer Interaction.

Bhatnagar, H. (2020). Artificial intelligence-a new horizon in Indian higher education. *Journal of Learning and Teaching in Digital Age*, *5*(2), 30–34.

Bhavani, G. (2020). Artificial Intelligence: Simulations in Audit Education. In *2020 11th International Conference on Computing, Communication and Networking Technologies (ICCCNT)* (pp. 1-5). IEEE.

Bholat, D., & Susskind, D. (2021). The assessment: Artificial intelligence and financial services. *Oxford Review of Economic Policy*, *37*(3), 417–434. doi:10.1093/oxrep/grab015

Bienkowski, M., Feng, M., & Means, B. (2012). *Enhancing Teaching and Learning through Educational Data Mining and Learning Analytics: An Issue Brief*. Office of Educational Technology, US Department of Education.

Bilgic, E., Gorgy, A., Yang, A., Cwintal, M., Ranjbar, H., Kahla, K., Reddy, D., Li, K., Ozturk, H., Zimmermann, E., Quaiattini, A., Abbasgholizadeh-Rahimi, S., Poenaru, D., & Harley, J. M. (2022). Exploring the roles of artificial intelligence in surgical education: A scoping review. In American Journal of Surgery (Vol. 224, Issue 1). doi:10.1016/j.amjsurg.2021.11.023

Blackboard. (n.d.). *Log in to Learn*. Retrieved from https://help.blackboard.com/Learn/Student/Ultra/Getting_Started/Log_in_to_Learn

Bloomboard. (n.d.). Retrieved from https://bloomboard.com/

Böckle, M., Novak, J., & Bick, M. (2017). *Towards adaptive gamification: a synthesis of current developments*. Academic Press.

Bonett, D. G., & Wright, T. A. (2015). Cronbach's alpha reliability: Interval estimation, hypothesis testing, and sample size planning. *Journal of Organizational Behavior*, *36*(1), 3–15. doi:10.1002/job.1960

Borowiec, S. (2016). AlphaGo seals 4-1 victory over Go grandmaster Lee Sedol. *The Guardian, 15*(6).

Boubker, O. (2024). From chatting to self-educating: Can ai tools boost student learning outcomes? *Expert Systems with Applications, 238*, 238. doi:10.1016/j.eswa.2023.121820

Bowe, A. G. (2015). The development of education indicators for measuring quality in the English-speaking Caribbean: How far have we come? *Evaluation and Program Planning, 48*, 31–46. doi:10.1016/j.evalprogplan.2014.08.008 PMID:25299825

Bozkurt, A., Karadeniz, A., Baneres, D., Guerrero-Roldán, A. E., & Rodríguez, M. E. (2021). Artificial intelligence and reflections fromeducational landscape: A review of AI Studies in half a century. *Sustainability, 13*(2), 1–16. doi:10.3390/su13020800 PMID:34123411

Brissett, N. (2021). A Critical Appraisal of Education in the Caribbean and Its Evolution From Colonial Origins to Twenty-First Century Responses. In Oxford Research Encyclopedia of Education. doi:10.1093/acrefore/9780190264093.013.1650

Brissett, N. O. (2018). Education for social transformation (EST) in the Caribbean: A post-colonial perspective. *Education Sciences, 8*(4), 197. doi:10.3390/educsci8040197

Brusilovsky, P. (2023). AI in Education, Learner Control, and Human-AI Collaboration. *International Journal of Artificial Intelligence in Education*, 1–14.

Brynjolfsson, E., & McAfee, A. (2014). *The second machine age: Work, progress, and prosperity in a time of brilliant technologies*. WW Norton & Company.

Bucea-Manea-țoniș, R., Kuleto, V., Gudei, S. C. D., Lianu, C., Lianu, C., Ilić, M. P., & Păun, D. (2022). Artificial Intelligence Potential in Higher Education Institutions Enhanced Learning Environment in Romania and Serbia. *Sustainability (Basel), 14*(10), 5842. Advance online publication. doi:10.3390/su14105842

Buil, I., Catalán, S., & Martínez, E. (2020). Engagement in business simulation games: A self-system model of motivational development. *British Journal of Educational Technology, 51*(1), 297–311. doi:10.1111/bjet.12762

Bulger, M. (2016). Personalized learning: The conversations we're not having. *Data and Society, 22*(1), 1–29.

Burton, R. R. (2013). The environment module of intelligent tutoring systems. In *Foundations of intelligent tutoring systems* (pp. 109–142). Psychology Press.

Busch, F., Adams, L. C., & Bressem, K. K. (2023). Biomedical Ethical Aspects Towards the Implementation of Artificial Intelligence in Medical Education. *Medical Science Educator, 33*(4), 1–6. doi:10.1007/s40670-023-01815-x PMID:37546190

Business, A. I. (2021, August). *Microsoft uses new machine learning model to enhance Bing searches*. https://aibusiness.com/ml/microsoft-uses-new-machine-learning-model-to-enhance-bing-searches

Campbell, C. (2003). *Education in the Caribbean, 1930–90. General History of the Caribbean* (Vol. 5). The Caribbean in the Twentieth Century.

Cantú-Ortiz, F. J., Galeano Sánchez, N., Garrido, L., Terashima-Marin, H., & Brena, R. F. (2020). An artificial intelligence educational strategy for the digital transformation. *International Journal on Interactive Design and Manufacturing, 14*(4), 1195–1209. doi:10.1007/s12008-020-00702-8

Carr, N. (2010). *The shallows: How the internet is changing the way we think, read and remember*. Atlantic Books Ltd.

Carvalho, L., Martinez-Maldonado, R., Tsai, Y.-S., Markauskaite, L., & De Laat, M. (2022). How can we design for learning in an AI world? *Computers and Education: Artificial Intelligence, 3*, 100053. doi:10.1016/j.caeai.2022.100053

Castaño-Muñoz, J., Kalz, M., Kreijns, K., & Punie, Y. (2018). Who is taking MOOCs for teachers' professional development on the use of ICT? A cross-sectional study from Spain. *Technology, Pedagogy and Education*, 27(5), 607–624. doi:10.1080/1475939X.2018.1528997

Catlin, D., & Blamires, M. (2019). Designing robots for special needs education. *Technology, Knowledge and Learning*, 24(2), 291-313.

Cavus, N., Ibrahim, I., Okonkwo, M. O., Ayansina, N. B., & Modupeola, T. (2023). The Effects of Gamification in Education: A Systematic Literature Review. BRAIN. *Broad Research in Artificial Intelligence and Neuroscience*, 14(2), 211–241. doi:10.18662/brain/14.2/452

Celik, I., Dindar, M., Muukkonen, H., & Järvelä, S. (2022). The promises and challenges of artificial intelligence for teachers: A systematic review of research. *TechTrends*, 66(4), 616–630. doi:10.1007/s11528-022-00715-y

Ceylan, Ö. (2022). The effect of the waste management themed summer program on gifted students' environmental attitude, creative thinking skills and critical thinking dispositions. *Journal of Adventure Education and Outdoor Learning*, 22(1), 53–65. doi:10.1080/14729679.2020.1859393

Chaka, C. (2023). Fourth industrial revolution—A review of applications, prospects, and challenges for artificial intelligence, robotics and blockchain in higher education. *Research and Practice in Technology Enhanced Learning, 18*.

Chalong, P., & Sripicharn, P. (2023). The Effects of Data-Driven Learning Approach in a Content and Language Integration Learning Classroom: A Study of Economics Subject in a Thai High School. *English Language Teaching*, 16(7), 1–59. doi:10.5539/elt.v16n7p59

Chan, C., & Lee, K. (2023). The ai generation gap: Are gen z students more interested in adopting generative ai such as chatgpt in teaching and learning than their gen x and millennial generation teachers? *Smart Learning Environments, 10*(1).

Chan, C. K. Y. (2023). A comprehensive AI policy education framework for university teaching and learning. *International Journal of Educational Technology in Higher Education*, 20(1), 38. Advance online publication. doi:10.1186/s41239-023-00408-3

Chang, C.-c. (2023). Enhancing EFL University Students' Readiness for Learning Academic Content in English: The Effectiveness of Combining MOOCs with Data-Driven Learning Activities in an English Language Classroom. *English Teaching & Learning*, 1-26.

Chang, Q., Pan, X., Manikandan, N., & Ramesh, S. (2022). Artificial Intelligence Technologies for Teaching and Learning in Higher Education. *International Journal of Reliability Quality and Safety Engineering*, 29(05), 2240006. doi:10.1142/S021853932240006X

Chapman, C., & Ward, S. (2003). *Project risk management processes, techniques, and insights*. John Wiley & Sons Ltd.

Chassignol, M., Khoroshavin, A., Klimova, A., & Bilyatdinova, A. (2018). Artificial Intelligence trends in education: A narrative overview. *Procedia Computer Science*, 136, 16–24. Advance online publication. doi:10.1016/j.procs.2018.08.233

Chatti, M. A., Lukarov, V., Thüs, H., Muslim, A., Yousef, A. M. F., Wahid, U., . . . Schroeder, U. (2014). Learning analytics: Challenges and future research directions. *eleed, 10*(1).

Chen, H. (2024). The ethical challenges of educational artificial intelligence and coping measures: A discussion in the context of the 2024 World Digital Education Conference. *Science Insights Education Frontiers, 20*(2), 3263-3281.

Chen, Tang, Tian, Ou, Wang, & Quan. (2022). The effect of mobile business simulation games in entrepreneurship education: a quasi-experiment. *Library Hi Tech., 41*. doi:10.1108/LHT-12-2021-0509

Chen, C. M., Wang, J. Y., & Hsu, L. C. (2021). An interactive test dashboard with diagnosis and feedback mechanisms to facilitate learning performance. *Computers and Education: Artificial Intelligence, 2*, 100015. Advance online publication. doi:10.1016/j.caeai.2021.100015

Chen, L., Chen, P., & Lin, Z. (2020). Artificial intelligence in education: A review. *IEEE Access : Practical Innovations, Open Solutions, 8*, 75264–75278. doi:10.1109/ACCESS.2020.2988510

Chen, L., Wang, P., Dong, H., Shi, F., Han, J., Guo, Y., Childs, P. R. N., Xiao, J., & Wu, C. (2019). An artificial intelligence based data-driven approach for design ideation. *Journal of Visual Communication and Image Representation, 61*, 10–22. doi:10.1016/j.jvcir.2019.02.009

Chen, X., Xie, H., & Hwang, G. J. (2020). A multi-perspective study on artificial intelligence in education: Grants, conferences, journals, software tools, institutions, and researchers. *Computers and Education: Artificial Intelligence, 1*, 100005. doi:10.1016/j.caeai.2020.100005

Chen, Y., Jensen, S., Albert, L., Gupta, S., & Lee, T. (2023). Artificial intelligence (ai) student assistants in the classroom: Designing chatbots to support student success. *Information Systems Frontiers, 25*(1), 161–182. doi:10.1007/s10796-022-10291-4

Chen, Z., Wu, M., Chan, A., Li, X., & Ong, Y. S. (2023). Survey on AI Sustainability: Emerging Trends on Learning Algorithms and Research Challenges. *IEEE Computational Intelligence Magazine, 18*(2), 60–77. doi:10.1109/MCI.2023.3245733

Cheung, S. K., Kwok, L. F., Phusavat, K., & Yang, H. H. (2021). Shaping the future learning environments with smart elements: Challenges and opportunities. *International Journal of Educational Technology in Higher Education, 18*(1), 1–9. doi:10.1186/s41239-021-00254-1 PMID:34778521

Chevalier, M., Riedo, F., & Mondada, F. (2016). Pedagogical uses of thymio II: How do teachers perceive educational robots in formal education? *IEEE Robotics & Automation Magazine, 23*(2), 16–23.

Chiba, Y., Nose, T., Kase, T., Yamanaka, M., & Ito, A. (2018, July). An analysis of the effect of emotional speech synthesis on non-task-oriented dialogue system. In *Proceedings of the 19th Annual SIGdial Meeting on Discourse and Dialogue* (pp. 371-375). Academic Press.

Chiu, T. (2024). Future research recommendations for transforming higher education with generative ai. *Computers and Education: Artificial Intelligence, 6.*

Chiu, T. K. F., Xia, Q., Zhou, X., Chai, C. S., & Cheng, M. (2023). Systematic literature review on opportunities, challenges, and future research recommendations of artificial intelligence in education. In Computers and Education: Artificial Intelligence (Vol. 4). Elsevier B.V. doi:10.1016/j.caeai.2022.100118

Chiu, T. K., Meng, H., Chai, C. S., King, I., Wong, S., & Yam, Y. (2021). Creation and evaluation of a pretertiary artificial intelligence (AI) curriculum. *IEEE Transactions on Education, 65*(1), 30–39. doi:10.1109/TE.2021.3085878

Chiu, T., Moorhouse, B., Chai, C., & Ismailov, M. (2023). Teacher support and student motivation to learn with artificial intelligence (ai) based chatbot. *Interactive Learning Environments*, 1–17. doi:10.1080/10494820.2023.2172044

Choi, S. W., Lee, E. B., & Kim, J. H. (2021). The engineering machine-learning automation platform (emap): A big-data-driven ai tool for contractors' sustainable management solutions for plant projects. *Sustainability (Basel), 13*(18), 10384. doi:10.3390/su131810384

Chomsky, N. (1980). Rules and representations. *Behavioral and Brain Sciences, 3*(1), 1–15. doi:10.1017/S0140525X00001515

Christensen, R., & Knezek, G. (2022). Using Digital Simulation to Address Implicit Bias in Teaching. In E. Langran (Ed.), *Proceedings of Society for Information Technology & Teacher Education International Conference* (pp. 477-483). San Diego, CA, United States: Association for the Advancement of Computing in Education (AACE).

Chusni, M. M., Saputro, S., Suranto, S., & Rahardjo, S. B. (2022). High School Students through Discovery-Based Multiple Representations Learning Model. *International Journal of Instruction*, *15*(1), 927–945. doi:10.29333/iji.2022.15153a

Chu, W., Wuniri, Q., Du, X., Xiong, Q., Huang, T., & Li, K. (2021). Cloud control system architectures, technologies and applications on intelligent and connected vehicles: A review. *Chinese Journal of Mechanical Engineering*, *34*(1), 1–23. doi:10.1186/s10033-021-00638-4

Ciampa, K. (2014). Learning in a mobile age: An investigation of student motivation. *Journal of Computer Assisted Learning*, *30*(1), 82–96. doi:10.1111/jcal.12036

Ciolacu, M., Svasta, P. M., Berg, W., & Popp, H. (2017a). Education 4.0 for tall thin engineer in a data driven society. In *2017 IEEE 23rd International Symposium for Design and Technology in Electronic Packaging (SIITME)* (pp. 432-437). IEEE.

Ciolacu, M., Tehrani, A. F., Beer, R., & Popp, H. (2017b). Education 4.0—Fostering student's performance with machine learning methods. In *2017 IEEE 23rd international symposium for design and technology in electronic packaging (SIITME)* (pp. 438-443). IEEE.

Ciolacu, M., Tehrani, A. F., Binder, L., & Svasta, P. M. (2018, October). Education 4.0-Artificial Intelligence assisted higher education: early recognition system with machine learning to support students' success. In *2018 IEEE 24th International Symposium for Design and Technology in Electronic Packaging (SIITME)* (pp. 23-30). IEEE. DOI: 10.1109/SIITME.2018.8599203

Cisco. (n.d.). *Smart Campus Living Lab*. https://www.cisco.com/c/dam/global/en_au/solutions/industries/government/smart-campus-living-lab.pdf

Clarizia, F., Colace, F., Lombardi, M., Pascale, F., & Santaniello, D. (2018). Chatbot: An education support system for student. *International symposium on cyberspace safety and security*. Springer. https://doi.org/10.1007/978-3-030-01689-0_23.13

Clarke, E. (2009). Learning outcomes from business simulation exercises: Challenges for the implementation of learning technologies. *Education + Training*, *51*(5/6), 448–459. doi:10.1108/00400910910987246

Clark, T. (2023). Investigating the use of an artificial intelligence chatbot with general chemistry exam questions. *Journal of Chemical Education*, *100*(5), 1905–1916. doi:10.1021/acs.jchemed.3c00027

Cloud, G. (n.d.). *Dialogflow*. Retrieved from https://cloud.google.com/dialogflow

Coach.me. (n.d.). Retrieved from https://www.coach.me/

Cohen, R. J., Swerdlik, M. E., & Sturman, E. D. (2009). *Psychological Testing and Assessment: An Introduction to Tests and Measurement* (7th ed.). McGraw-Hill.

Colchester, K., Hagras, H., Alghazzawi, D., & Aldabbagh, G. (2017). A Survey of Artificial Intelligence Techniques Employed for Adaptive Educational Systems within E-Learning Platforms. *Journal of Artificial Intelligence and Soft Computing Research*, *7*(1), 47–64.

Conchas, G. Q. (2006). *The Color of Success Race and High-Achieving Urban Youth*. Teachers College Press.

Cope, B., Kalantzis, M., & Searsmith, D. (2021). Artificial intelligence for education: Knowledge and its assessment in AI-enabled learning ecologies. *Educational Philosophy and Theory*, 53(12), 1229–1245. doi:10.1080/00131857.2020.1728732

Coronato, A., Naeem, M., De Pietro, G., & Paragliola, G. (2020). Reinforcement learning for intelligent healthcare applications: A survey. *Artificial Intelligence in Medicine*, 109, 101964. doi:10.1016/j.artmed.2020.101964 PMID:34756216

Coursera. (n.d.). Retrieved from https://www.coursera.org/

Creator, B. (n.d.). *Book Creator*. Retrieved from https://bookcreator.com/

Criollo-C, S., Abad-Vásquez, D., Martic-Nieto, M., Velásquez-G, F. A., Pérez-Medina, J. L., & Luján-Mora, S. (2021). Towards a new learning experience through a mobile application with augmented reality in engineering education. *Applied Sciences (Basel, Switzerland)*, 11(11), 4921. doi:10.3390/app11114921

Cropley, A. J. (2001). *Creativity in Education and Learning: A Guide for Teachers and Educators*. Kogan Page.

Crosthwaite, C. (2021). Engineering futures 2035 engineering education programs, priorities & pedagogies. *Australian Council of Engineering Deans, Report*.

Crowe, D., LaPierre, M., & Kebritchi, M. (2017). Knowledge based artificial augmentation intelligence technology: Next step in academic instructional tools for distance learning. *TechTrends*, 61(5), 494–506. doi:10.1007/s11528-017-0210-4

Cruz, M. L., Saunders-Smits, G. N., & Groen, P. (2020). Evaluation of competency methods in engineering education: A systematic review. *European Journal of Engineering Education*, 45(5), 729–757. doi:10.1080/03043797.2019.1671810

Csikszentmihalyi, M. (2006). Foreword: developing creativity. In N. Jackson, M. Oliver, M. Shaw, & J. Wisdom (Eds.), *Developing Creativity in Higher Education* (pp. xviii–xx). Routledge.

Cui, L., & Li, J. (2019). Study on Data Fields Grading Category Labeling for ERP Practical Skills Intelligent Assessment System. *DEStech Transactions on Computer Science and Engineering*.

Cui, W., Xue, Z., & Thai, K. P. (2018, November). Performance comparison of an AI-based adaptive learning system in China. In *2018 Chinese automation congress (CAC)* (pp. 3170-3175). IEEE.

Cui, Y., Ma, Z., Wang, L., Yang, A., Liu, Q., Kong, S., & Wang, H. (2023). A survey on big data-enabled innovative online education systems during the COVID-19 pandemic. *Journal of Innovation & Knowledge*, 8(1), 100295. doi:10.1016/j.jik.2022.100295

D2L. (n.d.). *Brightspace*. Retrieved from https://www.d2l.com/brightspace/

Dahalan, F., Alias, N., & Shaharom, M. S. N. (2023). Gamification and game based learning for vocational education and training: A systematic literature review. *Education and Information Technologies*, 1–39. PMID:36688221

Dakakni, D., & Safa, N. (2023). Artificial intelligence in the L2 classroom: Implications and challenges on ethics and equity in higher education: A 21st century Pandora's box. *Computers and Education: Artificial Intelligence*, 100179.

Damasevicius, R. (2014). Towards empirical modelling of knowledge transfer in teach-ing/learning process. *Communications in Computer and Information Science*, 465, 359–372. doi:10.1007/978-3-319-11958-8_29

Damasevicius, R. (2023). *The rise of chatgpt and the demise of bloom's taxonomy of learning stages*. Creative AI Tools and Ethical Implications in Teaching and Learning.

Darmawansah, D., Hwang, G.-J., Chen, M.-R. A., & Liang, J.-C. (2023). Trends and research foci of robotics-based STEM education: A systematic review from diverse angles based on the technology-based learning model. *International Journal of STEM Education*, *10*(1), 1–24. doi:10.1186/s40594-023-00400-3

Daun, H., & Arjmand, R. (2018). *Handbook of Islamic Education* (Vol. 7). Springer International Publishing. doi:10.1007/978-3-319-64683-1

Davis, R. O., & Lee, Y. J. (2024). Prompt: Chatgpt, create my course, please! *Education Sciences*, *14*(1), 24. doi:10.3390/educsci14010024

De Lisle, J., Laptiste-Francis, N., McMillan-Solomon, S., & Bowrin-Williams, C. (2017). Student assessment systems in the Caribbean as an obstacle to inclusive education. *Caribbean discourse in inclusive education: Historical and contemporary issues,* 87.

de Vries, L. E., & May, M. (2019). Virtual laboratory simulation in the education of laboratory technicians–motivation and study intensity. *Biochemistry and Molecular Biology Education*, *47*(3), 257–262. doi:10.1002/bmb.21221 PMID:30748084

de Winter, J. C. F., Dodou, D., & Stienen, A. H. A. (2023). Chatgpt in education: Empow-ering educators through methods for recognition and assessment. *Informatics (MDPI)*, *10*(4), 87. doi:10.3390/informatics10040087

Deeva, G., Bogdanova, D., Serral, E., Snoeck, M., & De Weerdt, J. (2021). A review of automated feedback systems for learners: Classification framework, challenges and opportunities. *Computers & Education*, *162*, 104094. doi:10.1016/j.compedu.2020.104094

Degreed. (n.d.). Retrieved from https://degreed.com/

Delić, V., Perić, Z., Sečujski, M., Jakovljević, N., Nikolić, J., Mišković, D., Simić, N., & … . (2019). Speech Technology Progress Based on New Machine Learning Paradigm. *Computational Intelligence and Neuroscience*, *2019*, 1–19.

Demertzi, V., & Demertzis, K. (2023). A Hybrid Ontology Matching Mechanism for Adaptive Educational eLearning Environments. *International Journal of Information Technology & Decision Making*, *22*(6), 1813–1841. Advance online publication. doi:10.1142/S0219622022500936

Denecke, K., Glauser, R., & Reichenpfader, D. (2023). Assessing the Potential and Risks of AI-Based Tools in Higher Education: Results from an eSurvey and SWOT Analysis. *Trends in Higher Education*, *2*(4), 667–688. doi:10.3390/higheredu2040039

Department of Defense Education Activity. (n.d.). *English Language Arts Curriculum*. Retrieved from https://www.dodea.edu/curriculum/english-language-arts-ela

Desmarais, M. C., & Baker, R. S. D. (2012). A review of recent advances in learner and skill modeling in intelligent learning environments. *User Modeling and User-Adapted Interaction*, *22*(1-2), 9–38. doi:10.1007/s11257-011-9106-8

Devedžić, V. (2021). Quo Vadis, AI? Management. *Journal of Sustainable Business and Management Solutions in Emerging Economies*, *26*(1), 1–12.

Dieterle, E., Dede, C., & Walker, M. (2022). The cyclical ethical effects of using artificial intelligence in education. *AI & Society*. Advance online publication. doi:10.1007/s00146-022-01497-w PMID:36185064

Dignum, V. (2021). The role and challenges of education for responsible ai. *London Review of Education*, *19*(1). Advance online publication. doi:10.14324/LRE.19.1.01

Dimitriadou, E., & Lanitis, A. (2023). A critical evaluation, challenges, and future perspectives of using artificial intelligence and emerging technologies in smart classrooms. *Smart Learning Environments, 10*(1), 1–26. doi:10.1186/s40561-023-00231-3

Dirar, R. O., Saeed, R. A., Hasan, M. K., & Mahmud, M. (2017). Persistent overload control for backlogged machine to machine communications in long term evolution advanced networks. *Journal of Telecommunication, Electronic and Computer Engineering, 9*(3-10), 109-113.

Dishon, G. (2017). New data, old tensions: Big data, personalized learning, and the challenges of progressive education. *Theory and Research in Education, 15*(3), 272–289.

Dixit, A., Quaglietta, J., & Gaulton, C. (2021). *Preparing for the future: How organizations can prepare boards, leaders, and risk managers for artificial intelligence.* Paper presented at the Healthcare Management Forum. 10.1177/08404704211037995

Djavanshir, G. R., Lee, M. R., & Liew, J. K.-S. (2020). Spotlight on AI!—Whyeveryone should pay attention now! *IT Professional, 22*(4), 18–20. doi:10.1109/MITP.2020.3006945

Dolence, M. G., & Norris, D. M. (1995). *Transforming higher education.* Society for College and University Planning.

Dong, J., Mohd Rum, S. N., Kasmiran, K. A., Mohd Aris, T. N., & Mohamed, R. (2022). Artificial Intelligence in Adaptive and Intelligent Educational System: A Review. In Future Internet (Vol. 14, Issue 9). MDPI. doi:10.3390/fi14090245

Dong, Z., Zhang, Y., Yip, C., Swift, S., & Beswick, K. (2020). Smart campus: Definition, framework, technologies, and services. *IET Smart Cities, 2*(1), 43–54.

Doroudi, S. (2023). The Intertwined Histories of Artificial Intelligence and Education. *International Journal of Artificial Intelligence in Education, 33*(4), 885–928. doi:10.1007/s40593-022-00313-2

DreamBox. (n.d.). Retrieved from https://www.dreambox.com/

Dsouza, K., Zhu, L., Varma-Nelson, P., Fang, S., & Mukhopadhyay, S. (2023, May). AI-Augmented Peer Led Team Learning for STEM Education. In *2023 IEEE 17th International Symposium on Applied Computational Intelligence and Informatics (SACI)* (pp. 000581-000586). IEEE.

Du Boulay, B. (2016). Artificial intelligence as an effective classroom assistant. *IEEE Intelligent Systems, 31*(6), 76–81. doi:10.1109/MIS.2016.93

Duan, Y., Edwards, J. S., & Dwivedi, Y. K. (2019). Artificial intelligence fordecision making in the era of big data – evolution, challenges and research agenda. *International Journal of Information Management, 48*, 63–71. doi:10.1016/j.ijinfomgt.2019.01.021

Dumont, H., & Ready, D. D. (2023). On the promise of personalized learning for educational equity. *NPJ Science of Learning, 8*(1), 26. doi:10.1038/s41539-023-00174-x PMID:37542046

Dunn, K. E., Airola, D. T., Lo, W.-J., & Garrison, M. (2013). Becoming data driven: The influence of teachers' sense of efficacy on concerns related to data-driven decision making. *Journal of Experimental Education, 81*(2), 222–241. doi:10.1080/00220973.2012.699899

Dwivedi, Y. K., Kshetri, N., Hughes, L., Slade, E. L., Jeyaraj, A., Kar, A. K., Baabdullah, A. M., Koohang, A., Raghavan, V., Ahuja, M., Albanna, H., Albashrawi, M. A., Al-Busaidi, A. S., Balakrishnan, J., Barlette, Y., Basu, S., Bose, I., Brooks, L., Buhalis, D., ... Wright, R. (2023). Opinion Paper: "So what if ChatGPT wrote it?" Multidisciplinary perspectives on opportunities, challenges and implications of generative conversational AI for research, practice and policy. *International Journal of Information Management, 71*(March), 102642. doi:10.1016/j.ijinfomgt.2023.102642

Eager, B., & Brunton, R. (2023). Prompting higher education towards AI-augmented teaching and learning practice. *Journal of University Teaching & Learning Practice, 20*(5), 02.

EdApp. (n.d.). Retrieved from https://www.edapp.com/

Edmodo. (n.d.). Retrieved from https://edmodo.online

Edshelf. (n.d.). *Education Technology Dictionary*. Edshelf. https://edshelf.com/education-technology-dictionary/

Einarsson, H., Lund, S. H., & Jónsdóttir, A. H. (2024). Application of ChatGPT for automated problem reframing across academic domains. *Computers and Education: Artificial Intelligence, 6*, 100194. Advance online publication. doi:10.1016/j.caeai.2023.100194

Eke, O. D. (2023). ChatGPT and the rise of generative AI: Threat to academic integrity? *Journal of Responsible Technology, 13*, 100060. doi:10.1016/j.jrt.2023.100060

El Koshiry, A., Eliwa, E., Abd El-Hafeez, T., & Shams, M. Y. (2023). Unlocking the power of blockchain in education: An overview of innovations and outcomes. Blockchain: Research and Applications, 100165.

Elfatih, N. M., Hasan, M. K., Kamal, Z., Gupta, D., Saeed, R. A., Ali, E. S., & Hosain, M. S. (2022). Internet of vehicle's resource management in 5G networks using AI technologies: Current status and trends. *IET Communications, 16*(5), 400–420. doi:10.1049/cmu2.12315

Elliott, D., & Soifer, E. (2022). Ai technologies, privacy, and security. *Frontiers in Artificial Intelligence, 5*. PMID:35493613

Elmahjub, E. (2023). Artificial Intelligence (AI) in Islamic Ethics: Towards Pluralist Ethical Benchmarking for AI. *Philosophy & Technology, 36*(4), 73. doi:10.1007/s13347-023-00668-x

Elmoiz Alatabani, L., Sayed Ali, E., Mokhtar, R. A., Saeed, R. A., Alhumyani, H., & Kamrul Hasan, M. (2022). Deep and reinforcement learning technologies on internet of vehicle (IoV) applications: Current issues and future trends. *Journal of Advanced Transportation, 2022*, 2022. doi:10.1155/2022/1947886

El-Sabagh, H. A. (2021). Adaptive e-learning environment based on learning styles and its impact on development students' engagement. *International Journal of Educational Technology in Higher Education, 18*(1), 53. Advance online publication. doi:10.1186/s41239-021-00289-4

Encalada, W. L., & Sequera, J. L. C. (2017). Model to implement virtual computing labs via cloud computing services. *Symmetry, 9*(7), 117.

Eremeev, A. P., Paniavin, N. A., & Marenkov, M. A. (2022). An Object-Oriented Approach to Ontology Modelling in Specialists Education of Methods and Technologies of Artificial Intelligence. In *2022 VI International Conference on Information Technologies in Engineering Education (Inforino)* (pp. 1-4). IEEE. 10.1109/Inforino53888.2022.9782954

Erickson, J. A., Botelho, A. F., McAteer, S., Varatharaj, A., & Heffernan, N. T. (2020). The automated grading of student open responses in mathematics. *Proceedings of the Tenth International Conference on Learning Analytics & Knowledge*, 615–624. 10.1145/3375462.3375523

Es, T. M. S., Rodrigues, J. J., & de la Torre, I. (2011). Personal Learning Environment Box (PLEBOX): A New Approach to E-Learning Platforms. *Education, 5*, 6.

Escotet, M. Á. (2023). The optimistic future of Artificial Intelligence in higher education. *Prospects*, 1–10. doi:10.1007/s11125-023-09642-z

Eslit, E. R. (2023). *Revitalizing English Language Teaching (ELT)*. Unveiling Evolving Pedagogies and AI-Driven Dynamics in the Post-Pandemic Era.

Esmaili, A., & Roayaei, M. (2024). UAV-Based Warehouse Management Using Multi-Agent RL: Applications, Challenges, and Solutions. In Applications of Machine Learning in UAV Networks (pp. 263–306). IGI Global.

Essa, S. G., Celik, T., & Human-Hendricks, N. E. (2023). Personalized Adaptive Learning Technologies Based on Machine Learning Techniques to Identify Learning Styles: A Systematic Literature Review. *IEEE Access : Practical Innovations, Open Solutions, 11*, 48392–48409. doi:10.1109/ACCESS.2023.3276439

Eze, Iwu, & Dubihlela. (2022). Students' views regarding the barriers to learning critical thinking. *International Journal of Research in Business and Social Science, 11*(4), 355–364. . doi:10.20525/ijrbs.v11i4.1797

Fahad Mon, B., Wasfi, A., Hayajneh, M., Slim, A., & Abu Ali, N. (2023). Reinforcement Learning in Education: A Literature Review. *Informatics (MDPI), 10*(3), 74. doi:10.3390/informatics10030074

Fang, C., & Tse, A. W. C. (2023). Case Study: Postgraduate Students' Class Engagement in Various Online Learning Contexts When Taking Privacy Issues to Incorporate with Artificial Intelligence Applications. *International Journal of Learning and Teaching, 9*(2). Advance online publication. doi:10.18178/ijlt.9.2.90-95

Fang, Y., Roscoe, R. D., & McNamara, D. S. (2023). Artificial intelligence-based assessment in education. In *Handbook of artificial intelligence in education* (pp. 485–504). Edward Elgar Publishing. doi:10.4337/9781800375413.00033

Fan, X., & Zhong, X. (2022). Artificial intelligence-based creative thinking skill analysis model using human–computer interaction in art design teaching. *Computers & Electrical Engineering, 100*, 107957. Advance online publication. doi:10.1016/j.compeleceng.2022.107957

Farmer, E. C., Catalano, A. J., & Halpern, A. J. (2019). Exploring Student Preference between Textbook Chapters and Adaptive Learning Lessons in an Introductory Environmental Geology Course. *TechTrends*, 1–8.

Farran, D. C., Meador, D., Christopher, C., Nesbitt, K. T., & Bilbrey, L. E. (2017). Data-driven improvement in prekindergarten classrooms: Report from a partnership in an urban district. *Child Development, 88*(5), 1466–1479. doi:10.1111/cdev.12906 PMID:28752921

Farrokhnia, M., Banihashem, S. K., Noroozi, O., & Wals, A. (2023). A SWOT analysis of ChatGPT: Implications for educational practice and research. *Innovations in Education and Teaching International, 00*(00), 1–15. doi:10.1080/14703297.2023.2195846

Fei, Q. (2022). Innovative Research on Ideological and Political Education in Colleges and Universities Based on Intelligent Wireless Network Environment. *Wireless Communications and Mobile Computing, 2022*, 1–10. Advance online publication. doi:10.1155/2022/1960520

Felder, R. M., & Soloman, B. A. (1997). *Index of learning style questionnaire*. https://www.engr.ncsu.edu/learningstyles/ilsweb.html

Feng, M., Huang, C., & Collins, K. (2023, June). Promising Long Term Effects of ASSISTments Online Math Homework Support. In *International Conference on Artificial Intelligence in Education* (pp. 212-217). Cham: Springer Nature Switzerland. 10.1007/978-3-031-36336-8_32

Fengchun, M., & Wayne, H. (2023). *Guidance for generative AI*. Academic Press.

Filippidis, S. K., & Tsoukalas, I. A. (2009). On the use of adaptive instructional images based on the sequential–global dimension of the Felder–Silverman learning style theory. *Interactive Learning Environments, 17*(2), 135–150. doi:10.1080/10494820701869524

Fitria, T. N. (2023). Augmented Reality (AR) and Virtual Reality (VR) Technology in Education: Media of Teaching and Learning: A Review. *International Journal of Computer and Information System, 4*(1), 14–25.

Flip. (n.d.). *Flip Learning*. Retrieved from https://info.flip.com/en-us.html

Foster, M. E. (2024). Evaluating the Impact of Supplemental Computer-Assisted Math Instruction in Elementary School: A Conceptual Replication. *Journal of Research on Educational Effectiveness, 17*(1), 94–118. doi:10.1080/19345747.2023.2174919

Fryer, L. K., Nakao, K., & Thompson, A. (2019). Chatbot learning partners: Connecting learning experiences, interest and competence. *Computers in Human Behavior, 93*, 279–289. doi:10.1016/j.chb.2018.12.023

Fryer, M. (2003). *Creativity across the Curriculum: A Review and Analysis of Programmes Designed to Develop Creativity*. Qualifications and Curriculum Authority.

Furube, T., Takeuchi, M., Kawakubo, H., Matsuda, S., Fukuda, K., Nakamura, R., & Kitagawa, Y. (2023). Automated phase recognition for esophageal endoscopic submucosal dissection using artificial intelligence. *Gastrointestinal Endoscopy, 97*(6), AB763. Advance online publication. doi:10.1016/j.gie.2023.04.1248 PMID:38185182

Gabriel, I. (2020). Artificial Intelligence, Values, and Alignment. *Minds and Machines, 30*(3), 411–437. doi:10.1007/s11023-020-09539-2

Gambo, Y., & Shakir, M. Z. (2023). Evaluating students' experiences in self-regulated smart learning environment. *Education and Information Technologies, 28*(1), 547–580. doi:10.1007/s10639-022-11126-0 PMID:35814807

Gao, R., Merzdorf, H. E., Anwar, S., Hipwell, M. C., & Srinivasa, A. R. (2024). Automatic assessment of text-based responses in post-secondary education: A systematic review. *Computers and Education: Artificial Intelligence, 6*, 100206. https://doi.org/https://doi.org/10.1016/j.caeai.2024.100206

Gao, R., Merzdorf, H. E., Anwar, S., Hipwell, M. C., & Srinivasa, A. R. (2024). Automatic assessment of text-based responses in post-secondary education: A systematic review. *Computers and Education: Artificial Intelligence, 6*, 24. doi:10.1016/j.caeai.2024.100206

Gardner, H. (1982). *Art, Mind, Brain: A Cognitive Approach to Creativity*. Basic Books.

Gardner, J., O'Leary, M., & Yuan, L. (2021). Artificial intelligence in educational assessment: 'Breakthrough? Or buncombe and ballyhoo?'. *Journal of Computer Assisted Learning, 37*(5), 1207–1216. doi:10.1111/jcal.12577

Garg, S., & Sharma, S. (2020). Impact of artificial intelligence in special need education to promote inclusive pedagogy. *International Journal of Information and Education Technology (IJIET), 10*(7), 523–527. doi:10.18178/ijiet.2020.10.7.1418

Gartner, S., & Krašna, M. (2023, June). Artificial intelligence in education-ethical framework. In *2023 12th Mediterranean Conference on Embedded Computing (MECO)* (pp. 1-7). IEEE. 10.1109/MECO58584.2023.10155012

Gellai, D. B. (2022). Enterprising Academics: Heterarchical Policy Networks for Artificial Intelligence in British Higher Education. *ECNU Review of Education*. Advance online publication. doi:10.1177/20965311221143798

George, B., & Wooden, O. (2023). Managing the strategic transformation of higher education through artificial intelligence. *Administrative Sciences, 13*(9), 196. doi:10.3390/admsci13090196

Gerjets, P., Scheiter, K., Opfermann, M., Hesse, F. W., & Eysink, T. H. S. (2009). Learning with hypermedia: The influence of representational formats and different levels of learner control on performance and learning behavior. *Computers in Human Behavior, 25*(2), 360–370. doi:10.1016/j.chb.2008.12.015

Getman, Y., Phan, N., Al-Ghezi, R., Voskoboinik, E., Singh, M., Grosz, T., Kurimo, M., Salvi, G., Svendsen, T., Strombergsson, S., Smolander, A., & Ylinen, S. (2023). Developing an AI-Assisted Low-Resource Spoken Language Learning App for Children. *IEEE Access : Practical Innovations, Open Solutions, 11*, 86025–86037. doi:10.1109/ACCESS.2023.3304274

Gilbert, I. (2014). *Why do I need a teacher when I've got google?: The Essential Guide to the big issues for every teacher.* Routledge. doi:10.4324/9781315767628

Gisslen, L., Eakins, A., Gordillo, C., Bergdahl, J., & Tollmar, K. (2021). Adversarial Reinforcement Learning for Procedural Content Generation. *2021 IEEE Conference on Games (CoG)*, 1–8. 10.1109/CoG52621.2021.9619053

Giuffra Palomino, C. E., Azambuja Silveira, R., & Nakayama, M. K. (2014). An intelligent LMS model based on intelligent tutoring systems. *Intelligent Tutoring Systems: 12th International Conference, ITS 2014, Honolulu, HI, USA, June 5-9, 2014 Proceedings, 12*, 567–574.

Glaser, N. (2023). Exploring the potential of chatgpt as an educational technology: An emerging technology report. Technology. *Knowledge and Learning, 28*(4), 1945–1952. doi:10.1007/s10758-023-09684-4

Gligorea, I., Cioca, M., Oancea, R., Gorski, A.-T., Gorski, H., & Tudorache, P. (2023). Adaptive Learning Using Artificial Intelligence in e-Learning: A Literature Review. *Education Sciences, 13*(12), 1216. doi:10.3390/educsci13121216

Goel, A. K., & Polepeddi, L. (2018). Jill Watson: A virtual teaching assistant for online education. In Learning engineering for online education (pp. 120-143). Academic Press.

Goel, A. K., & Polepeddi, L. (2016). *Jill Watson: A virtual teaching assistant for online education.* Georgia Institute of Technology.

Goksel, N., & Bozkurt, A. (2019). Artificial intelligence in education: Current insights and future perspectives. In S. Sisman-Ugur & G. Kurubacak (Eds.), *Handbook of research on learning in the age of transhumanis m* (pp. 224–236). IGI Global. doi:10.4018/978-1-5225-8431-5.ch014

Golic, Z. (2019). Finance and artificial intelligence: The fifth industrial revolution and its impact on the financial sector. *Zbornik radova Ekonomskog fakulteta u Istočnom Sarajevu*, (19), 67–81.

Gomede, E., de Barros, R. M., & Mendes, L. de S. (2021). Deep auto encoders to adaptive E-learning recommender system. *Computers and Education: Artificial Intelligence, 2*, 100009. Advance online publication. doi:10.1016/j.caeai.2021.100009

González-Calatayud, V., Prendes-Espinosa, P., & Roig-Vila, R. (2021). Artificial intelligence for student assessment: A systematic review. *Applied Sciences (Basel, Switzerland), 11*(12), 5467. doi:10.3390/app11125467

Gonzalez, L. A., Neyem, A., Contreras-McKay, I., & Molina, D. (2022). Improving learning experiences in software engineering capstone courses using artificial intelligence virtual assistants. *Computer Applications in Engineering Education, 30*(5), 1370–1389. doi:10.1002/cae.22526

Google. (n.d.-a). *Google Certificates.* Retrieved from https://grow.google/intl/en_ph/certificates/

Google. (n.d.-b). *Google Digital Skills.* Retrieved from https://grow.google/intl/mena/

Goralski, M. A., & Tan, T. K. (2020). Artificial intelligence and sustainable development. *International Journal of Management Education, 18*(1), 100330. doi:10.1016/j.ijme.2019.100330

Gose, B. (2016). When the teaching assistant is a robot. *The Chronicle of Higher Education.*

Govender, T., & Arnedo-Moreno, J. (2020). A Survey on Gamification Elements in Mobile Language-Learning Applications. *Eighth International Conference on Technological Ecosystems for Enhancing Multiculturality*, 669–676. 10.1145/3434780.3436597

Graesser, A. C., Hu, X., Nye, B. D., VanLehn, K., Kumar, R., Heffernan, C., Heffernan, N., Woolf, B., Olney, A. M., Rus, V., Andrasik, F., Pavlik, P., Cai, Z., Wetzel, J., Morgan, B., Hampton, A. J., Lippert, A. M., Wang, L., Cheng, Q., ... Baer, W. (2018). ElectronixTutor: An intelligent tutoring system with multiple learning resources for electronics. *International Journal of STEM Education*, *5*(1), 1–21. doi:10.1186/s40594-018-0110-y PMID:30631705

Grájeda, A., Burgos, J., Córdova, P., & Sanjinés, A. (2024). Assessing student-perceived impact of using artificial intelligence tools: Construction of a synthetic index of application in higher education. *Cogent Education*, *11*(1), 2287917. Advance online publication. doi:10.1080/2331186X.2023.2287917

Grams, D. (2018). *A quantitative study of the use of DreamBox learning and its effectiveness in improving math achievement of elementary students with math difficulties* [Doctoral dissertation]. Northcentral University.

Grassini, S. (2023). Shaping the future of education: Exploring the potential and con-sequences of ai and chatgpt in educational settings. *Education Sciences*, *13*(7), 692. doi:10.3390/educsci13070692

Grau, A., Indri, M., Bello, L. L., & Sauter, T. (2017, October). Industrial robotics in factory automation: From the early stage to the Internet of Things. In *IECON 2017-43rd annual conference of the IEEE industrial electronics society* (pp. 6159-6164). IEEE.

Grubaugh, S., Levitt, G., & Deever, D. (2023). Harnessing AI to Power Constructivist Learning: An Evolution in Educational Methodologies. *EIKI Journal of Effective Teaching Methods*, *1*(3). Advance online publication. doi:10.59652/jetm.v1i3.43

Guan, C., Mou, J., & Jiang, Z. (2020). Artificial intelligence innovation in education: A twenty-year data-driven historical analysis. *International Journal of Innovation Studies*, *4*(4), 134–147. doi:10.1016/j.ijis.2020.09.001

Guerreiro-Santalla, S., Crompton, H., & Bellas, F. (2023). *RoboboITS: A Simulation-Based Tutoring System to Support AI Education Through Robotics*. doi:10.1007/978-3-031-36336-8_62

Guilherme, A. (2019). AI and education: The importance of teacher and student relations. *AI & Society*, *34*(1), 47–54. doi:10.1007/s00146-017-0693-8

Guterman, J. T. (2014). *Mastering the art of solution-focused counseling*. John Wiley & Sons.

Han, S., Jung, J., Ji, H., Lee, U., & Liu, M. (2023). *The Role of Social Presence in MOOC Students' Behavioral Intentions and Sentiments Toward the Usage of a Learning Assistant Chatbot: A Diversity*. Equity, and Inclusion Perspective Examination. doi:10.1007/978-3-031-36336-8_36

Harry, A. (2023). *Role of ai in education. Interdisciplinary Journal and Humanity*.

Haryono, K., Rajagede, R. A., & Negara, M. U. A. S. (2023). Quran Memorization Technologies and Methods: Literature Review. *IJID*, *11*(1), 192–201. doi:10.14421/ijid.2022.3746

Haseski, H. I. (2019). What do Turkish pre-service teachers think about artificial intelligence? *International Journal of Computer Science Education in Schools*, *3*(2), 3–23. Advance online publication. doi:10.21585/ijcses.v3i2.55

Hashem, R., Ali, N., Zein, F., Fidalgo, P., & Khurma, O. (2024). Ai to the rescue: Explor-ing the potential of chatgpt as a teacher ally for workload relief and burnout prevention. *Research and Practice in Technology Enhanced Learning*, 19.

Hashim, R. (2005). Rethinking Islamic Education in Facing the Challenges of the Twenty-first Century. *American Journal of Islam and Society*, *22*(4), 133–147. doi:10.35632/ajis.v22i4.1676

Hasibuan, R., Parta, I. B. M. W., Sholihah, H. I. a., Damayanto, A., & Farihatun, F. (2023). Transformation of Indonesian language learning with artificial intelligence applications: The era of the independent curriculum for learning in universities in Indonesia. *Indonesian Journal of Education*, *3*(2), 341–363.

Hassan, M. B., Ali, E. S., Nurelmadina, N., & Saeed, R. A. (2021). Artificial intelligence in IoT and its applications. In *Intelligent Wireless Communications* (pp. 33-58). Institution of Engineering and Technology. doi:10.1049/PBTE094E_ch2

Heck, T., & Meurers, D. (2023). *Exercise Generation Supporting Adaptivity in Intelligent Tutoring Systems*. doi:10.1007/978-3-031-36336-8_102

Hilbert, S., Coors, S., Kraus, E., Bischl, B., Lindl, A., Frei, M., Wild, J., Krauss, S., Goretzko, D., & Stachl, C. (2021). Machine learning for the educational sciences. *Review of Education*, *9*(3), e3310. doi:10.1002/rev3.3310

Hinojo-Lucena, F.-J., Aznar-Díaz, I., Cáceres-Reche, M.-P., & Romero-Rodríguez, J.-M. (2019). Artificial Intelligence in Higher Education: A Bibliometric Study on Its Impact in the Scientific Literature. *Education Sciences*, *9*(1), 51. doi:10.3390/educsci9010051

Hogg, H. D. J., Brittain, K., Teare, D., Talks, J., Balaskas, K., Keane, P., & Maniatopoulos, G. (2023). Safety and efficacy of an artificial intelligence-enabled decision tool for treatment decisions in neovascular age-related macular degeneration and an exploration of clinical pathway integration and implementation: Protocol for a multi-methods validation study. *BMJ Open*, *13*(2), e069443. Advance online publication. doi:10.1136/bmjopen-2022-069443 PMID:36725098

Holmes, W., & Miao, F. (2023). *Guidance for generative AI in education and research*. UNESCO Publishing.

Holmes, W., Porayska-Pomsta, K., Holstein, K., Sutherland, E., Baker, T., Shum, S. B., ... Koedinger, K. R. (2021). Ethics of AI in education: Towards a community-wide framework. *International Journal of Artificial Intelligence in Education*, 1–23.

Holmes, W., & Tuomi, I. (2022). State of the art and practice in AI in education. *European Journal of Education*, *57*(4), 542–570. doi:10.1111/ejed.12533

Holotescu, C., & Grosseck, G. (2018). Towards a MOOC-related Strategy in Romania. BRAIN. *Broad Research in Artificial Intelligence and Neuroscience*, *9*, 99–109.

Holstein, K. (2018). Towards teacher-ai hybrid systems. *Companion Proceedings of the Eighth International Conference on Learning Analytics & Knowledge*.

Holstein, K., & Doroudi, S. (2021). *Equity and Artificial Intelligence in Education: Will "AIEd" Amplify or Alleviate Inequities in Education?* (Issue 3). https://doi.org//arXiv.2104.12920 doi:10.48550

Holstein, K., & Doroudi, S. (2021). Equity and Artificial Intelligence in Education: Will "AIEd" Amplify or Alleviate Inequities in Education? *arXiv preprint arXiv:2104.12920*.

Holstein, K., McLaren, B. M., & Aleven, V. (2017, March). Intelligent tutors as teachers' aides: exploring teacher needs for real-time analytics in blended classrooms. In *Proceedings of the seventh international learning analytics & knowledge conference* (pp. 257-266). Academic Press.

Holstein, K., McLaren, B. M., & Aleven, V. (2018). Student learning benefits of a mixed-reality teacher awareness tool in AI-enhanced classrooms. *Artificial Intelligence in Education: 19th International Conference, AIED 2018,* London, UK, June 27–30, 2018, *Proceedings, Part I 19*.

Holstein, K., McLaren, B. M., & Aleven, V. (2019, June). Designing for Complementarity:Teacher and Student Needs for Orchestration Support in AI-Enhanced Classrooms. In *International Conference on Artificial Intelligence in Education* (pp. 157-171).Springer.

Hong, Y., Nguyen, A., Dang, B., & Nguyen, B. P. T. (2022, July). Data Ethics Framework for Artificial Intelligence in Education (AIED). In *2022 International Conference on Advanced Learning Technologies (ICALT)* (pp. 297-301). IEEE. 10.1109/ICALT55010.2022.00095

Hooda, M., Rana, C., Dahiya, O., Rizwan, A., & Hossain, M. S. (2022). Artificial intelligence for assessment and feedback to enhance student success in higher education. *Mathematical Problems in Engineering, 2022,* 2022. doi:10.1155/2022/5215722

Hossein, M.G. & Maryam, R. (2012). An Adaptive and Intelligent Tutor by Expert Systems for Mobile Devices. *International Journal of Managing Public.*

Howitz, W. J., Thane, T. A., Frey, T. L., Wang, X. S., Gonzales, J. C., Tretbar, C. A., Seith, D. D., Saluga, S. J., Lam, S., Nguyen, M. M., Tieu, P., Link, R. D., & Edwards, K. D. (2020). Online in no time: Design and implementation of a remote learning first quarter general chemistry laboratory and second quarter organic chemistry laboratory. *Journal of Chemical Education, 97*(9), 2624–2634. doi:10.1021/acs.jchemed.0c00895

Hsieh, Y. Z., Lin, S. S., Luo, Y. C., Jeng, Y. L., Tan, S. W., Chen, C. R., & Chiang, P. Y. (2020). ARCS-assisted teaching robots based on anticipatory computing and emotional Big Data for improving sustainable learning efficiency and motivation. *Sustainability (Basel), 12*(14), 5605. Advance online publication. doi:10.3390/su12145605

Huang, L. (2023). Ethics of artificial intelligence in education: Student privacy and data protection. *Science Insights Education Frontiers, 16*(2), 2577–2587. doi:10.15354/sief.23.re202

Huang, L. (2023). *Ethics of artificial intelligence in education: Student privacy and data protection.* Science Insights Education Frontiers.

Huang, X., Zou, D., Cheng, G., Chen, X., & Xie, H. (2023). Trends, research issues and applications of artificial intelligence in language education. *Journal of Educational Technology & Society, 26*(1), 112–131.

Humble, N., & Mozelius, P. (2019, October). *Artificial Intelligence in Education-a Promise, a Threat or Hype?* Academic Press.

Humble, N., & Mozelius, P. (2022). The threat, hype, and promise of artificial intelligence in education. *Discover Artificial Intelligence, 2*(1), 22. doi:10.1007/s44163-022-00039-z

Hutchins, N., & Biswas, G. (2023). Co-designing teacher support technology for problem-based learning in middle school science. *British Journal of Educational Technology.*

Huttar, C. M., & BrintzenhofeSzoc, K. (2019). Virtual Reality and Computer Simulation in Social Work Education. *Systematic Reviews.*

Hu, W. (2023). The Application of Artificial Intelligence and Big Data Technology in Basketball Sports Training. *EAI Endorsed Transactions on Scalable Information Systems, 10*(4), e2. Advance online publication. doi:10.4108/eetsis.v10i3.3046

Hu, X., Goh, Y. M., & Lin, A. (2021). Educational impact of an Augmented Reality (AR) application for teaching structural systems to non-engineering students. *Advanced Engineering Informatics, 50,* 101436. doi:10.1016/j.aei.2021.101436

Hu, Y.-H. (2022). Effects and acceptance of precision education in an AI-supported smart learning environment. *Education and Information Technologies, 27*(2), 2013–2037. doi:10.1007/s10639-021-10664-3

Hwang, G. J., Xie, H., Wah, B. W., & Gašević, D. (2020). Vision, challenges, roles and research issues of Artificial Intelligence in Education. *Computers and Education: Artificial Intelligence*, *1*, 100001. doi:10.1016/j.caeai.2020.100001

Iacucci, M., Cannatelli, R., Parigi, T. L., Buda, A., Labarile, N., Nardone, O. M., Tontini, G. E., Rimondi, A., Bazarova, A., Bhandari, P., Bisschops, R., De Hertogh, G., Del Amor, R., Ferraz, J. G., Goetz, M., Gui, S. X., Hayee, B., Kiesslich, R., Lazarev, M., ... Grisan, E. (2022). A virtual chromoendoscopy artificial intelligence system to detect endoscopic and histologic remission in ulcerative colitis. *Gastrointestinal Endoscopy*, *95*(6), AB229–AB230. Advance online publication. doi:10.1016/j.gie.2022.04.585 PMID:36228649

IBM. (n.d.). *Chatbots.* IBM. https://www.ibm.com/topics/chatbots

Ifenthaler, D., Mah, D.-K., & Yau, J. Y.-K. (2019). Utilising Learning Analytics for Study Success: Reflections on Current Empirical Findings. In Utilizing Learning Analytics to Support Study Success (pp. 27–36). Springer International Publishing. doi:10.1007/978-3-319-64792-0_2

Ifenthaler, D., & Gibson, D. (Eds.). (2020). *Adoption of data analytics in higher education learning and teaching.* Springer. doi:10.1007/978-3-030-47392-1

Ifenthaler, D., & Schumacher, C. (2023). Reciprocal issues of artificial and human intelligence in education. *Journal of Research on Technology in Education*, *55*(1), 1–6. doi:10.1080/15391523.2022.2154511

Iglesias, A., Martínez, P., Aler, R., & Fernández, F. (2009). Learning teaching strategies in an Adaptive and Intelligent Educational System through Reinforcement Learning. *Applied Intelligence*, *31*(1), 89–106. doi:10.1007/s10489-008-0115-1

Imran, M., & Almusharraf, N. (2023). Analyzing the role of chatgpt as a writing assistant at higher education level: A systematic review of the literature. *Contemporary Educational Technology*, *15*(4), ep464. doi:10.30935/cedtech/13605

Ingavelez-Guerra, P., Robles-Bykbaev, V. E., Perez-Munoz, A., Hilera-Gonzalez, J., & Oton-Tortosa, S. (2022). Automatic Adaptation of Open Educational Resources: An Approach From a Multilevel Methodology Based on Students' Preferences, Educational Special Needs, Artificial Intelligence and Accessibility Metadata. *IEEE Access : Practical Innovations, Open Solutions*, *10*, 9703–9716. doi:10.1109/ACCESS.2021.3139537

Instructure. (n.d.). *Canvas.* Retrieved from https://www.instructure.com/canvas

Ip, H. H. S., Li, C., Leoni, S., Chen, Y., Ma, K. F., Wong, C. H. T., & Li, Q. (2018). Design and evaluate immersive learning experience for massive open online courses (MOOCs). *IEEE Transactions on Learning Technologies*, *12*(4), 503–515.

Irfan, M., Aldulaylan, F., & Alqahtani, Y. (2023). Ethics and Privacy in Irish Higher Education: A Comprehensive Study of Artificial Intelligence (AI) Tools Implementation at University of Limerick. *Global Social Sciences Review*, *8*(2), 201–210. doi:10.31703/gssr.2023(VIII-II).19

Ivie, S. D. (1998). Ausubel's learning theory: An approach to teaching higher order thinking skills. *High School Journal*, *82*(1), 35–42.

Jackson, P. C. (2019). *Introduction to artificial intelligence.* Courier Dover Publications.

Jamal, A. (2023). The Role Of Artificial Intelligence (AI) In Teacher Education: Opportunities & Challenges. *International Journal of Research and Analytical Reviews, 10*(1). Retrieved 31 March 2024 from: https://www.researchgate.net/profile/Afiya-Jamal/publication/369384184_The_Role_of_Artificial_Intelligence_AI_in_Teacher_Education_Opportunities_Challenges/links/64197dd792cfd54f8418b429/The-Role-of-Artificial-Intelligence-AI-in-Teacher-Education-Opportunities-Challenges.pdf

Jeon, J., & Lee, S. (2023). Large language models in education: A focus on the comple-mentary relationship between human teachers and chatgpt. *Education and Information Technologies*, *28*(12), 15873–15892. doi:10.1007/s10639-023-11834-1

Jia, G., Xu, G., Shi, L., & Zhang, Z. (2021). Personalized course recommendation system fusing with knowledge graph and collaborative filtering. *Computational Intelligence and Neuroscience, 2021*, 1–8. doi:10.1155/2021/6686826 PMID:34616447

Jiang, X., Rollinson, J., Plonsky, L., & Pajak, B. (2020). Duolingo efficacy study: Beginning-level courses equivalent to four university semesters. *Duolingo Research Report, 2020*, 1–11. https://www.duolingo.com/efficacy

Jiang, X., Rollinson, J., Plonsky, L., Gustafson, E., & Pajak, B. (2021). Evaluating the reading and listening outcomes of beginning-level Duolingo courses. *Foreign Language Annals, 54*(4), 974–1002. doi:10.1111/flan.12600

Jian, M. J. K. O. (2023). *Personalized learning through ai.* Advances in Engineering In-novation. doi:10.54254/2977-3903/5/2023039

Jiao, G., Li, L., Deng, H., Zheng, G., Zou, Y., & Zhao, J. (2020). Exploration on cultivation of practical ability of artificial intelligence talents in universities in the context of innovation and entrepreneurship education. In *2020 IEEE 2nd International Conference on Computer Science and Educational Informatization (CSEI)* (pp. 186-189). IEEE. 10.1109/CSEI50228.2020.9142488

Johnson, W. L., & Qu, L. (2005). Detecting the Learner's Motivational States in An Interactive Learning Environment. *Proceedings of the 2005 Conference on Artificial Intelligence in Education: Supporting Learning through Intelligent and Socially Informed Technology.*

Joksimović, S., Kovanović, V., & Dawson, S. (2019). The journey of learning analytics. *HERDSA Review of Higher Education, 6*, 27–63.

Jordan, M. I., & Mitchell, T. M. (2015). Machine learning: Trends, perspectives, and prospects. *Science, 349*(6245), 255–260. doi:10.1126/science.aaa8415 PMID:26185243

Jules, D. (2008). Rethinking education for the Caribbean: A radical approach. *Comparative Education, 44*(2), 203–214. doi:10.1080/03050060802041142

Justesen, N., Bontrager, P., Togelius, J., & Risi, S. (2019). Deep learning for video game playing. *IEEE Transactions on Games, 12*(1), 1–20. doi:10.1109/TG.2019.2896986

Kabudi, T., Pappas, I., & Olsen, D. H. (2021). AI-enabled adaptive learning systems: A systematic mapping of the literature. *Computers and Education: Artificial Intelligence, 2*, 100017. doi:10.1016/j.caeai.2021.100017

Kakish, K., Robertson, C., & Pollacia, L. (2022). Advancing Adaptive Learning via Artificial Intelligence. *Intelligent Systems and Applications: Proceedings of the 2021 Intelligent Systems Conference (IntelliSys), 3.*

Kalazhokov, Z. K., Senov, K. M., Shogenov, B. V., & Yakhutlov, M. M. (2021). The Unique Challenges of Teaching Artificial Intelligence Systems to Mechatronics and Robotics Students. In *2021 International Conference on Quality Management, Transport and Information Security, Information Technologies (IT&QM&IS)* (pp. 653-655). IEEE. 10.1109/ITQMIS53292.2021.9642750

Kamalov, F., Santandreu Calonge, D., & Gurrib, I. (2023). New era of artificial intelligence in education: Towards a sustainable multifaceted revolution. *Sustainability (Basel), 15*(16), 12451. doi:10.3390/su151612451

Kao, C. L., Chien, L. C., Wang, M. C., Tang, J. S., Huang, P. C., Chuang, C. C., & Shih, C. L. (2023). The development of new remote technologies in disaster medicine education: A scoping review. In Frontiers in Public Health (Vol. 11). doi:10.3389/fpubh.2023.1029558

Kaplan-Rakowski, R., Grotewold, K., Hartwick, P., & Papin, K. (2023). Generative AI and teachers' perspectives on its implementation in education. *Journal of Interactive Learning Research, 34*(2), 313–338.

Karsenti, T. (2019). Artificial intelligence in education: the urgent need to prepare teachers for tomorrow's schools. *Formation et profession, 27*(1), 112–116. . doi:10.18162/fp.2019.a166

Kataria, K. (2023). Ai-powered learning: The future of education. *International Journal of Advanced Research, 11*(9), 199–203. doi:10.21474/IJAR01/17520

Kausar, S., Leghari, A. R., & Soomro, A. S. (2024). Analysis of the Islamic Law and its Compatibility with Artificial Intelligence as a Emerging Challenge of the Modern World. *Annals of Human and Social Sciences, 5*(1), 99–114. doi:10.35484/ahss.2024(5-I)10

Kay, A. E., Hardy, J., & Galloway, R. K. (2020). Student use of PeerWise: A multi-institutional, multidisciplinary evaluation. *British Journal of Educational Technology, 51*(1), 23–35. doi:10.1111/bjet.12754

Kay, J. (2012). Ai and education: Grand challenges. *IEEE Intelligent Systems, 27*(5), 66–69. doi:10.1109/MIS.2012.92

Kent, M., & Bennett, R. (2017). What was all that about? Peak MOOC hype and post-MOOC legacies. *Massive open online courses and higher education: What went right, what went wrong and where to next*, 1-8.

Kerimbayev, N., Nurym, N., Akramova, A., & Abdykarimova, S. (2023). Educational Robotics: Development of computational thinking in collaborative online learning. *Education and Information Technologies, 28*(11), 1–23. doi:10.1007/s10639-023-11806-5 PMID:37361771

Khan Academy. (n.d.). *About*. Retrieved from https://www.khanacademy.org/about

Khan, S., Blessing, L., & Ndiaye, Y. (2023, January). Artificial intelligence for competency assessment in design education: a review of literature. In *International Conference on Research into Design* (pp. 1047-1058). Singapore: Springer Nature Singapore.10.1007/978-981-99-0428-0_85

Khan, A., Li, J. P., Hasan, M. K., Varish, N., Mansor, Z., Islam, S., Saeed, R. A., Alshammari, M., & Alhumyani, H. (2022). PackerRobo: Model-based robot vision self supervised learning in CART. *Alexandria Engineering Journal, 61*(12), 12549–12566. doi:10.1016/j.aej.2022.05.043

Khandelwal, P., Zhang, S., Sinapov, J., Leonetti, M., Thomason, J., Yang, F., Gori, I., & … . (2017). BWIBots: A platform for bridging the gap between AI and human–robot interaction research. *The International Journal of Robotics Research, 36*(5–7), 635–659.

Khensous, G., Labed, K., & Labed, Z. (2023). Exploring the evolution and applications of natural language processing in education. *Romanian Journal of Information Technology and Automatic Control, 33*(2), 61–74.

Khoshkangini, R., Valetto, G., Marconi, A., & Pistore, M. (2021). Automatic generation and recommendation of personalized challenges for gamification. *User Modeling and User-Adapted Interaction, 31*(1), 1–34. doi:10.1007/s11257-019-09255-2

Kim, J. (2023). Leading teachers' perspective on teacher-ai collaboration in education. *Education and Information Technologies*. Advance online publication. doi:10.1007/s10639-023-12109-5

Kim, M., & Adlof, L. (2023). Adapting to the future: Chatgpt as a means for supporting constructivist learning environments. *TechTrends*.

Kim, Y., & Baylor, A. L. (2016). Evidence-based design of pedagogical agent roles: A review, progress, and recommendations. *International Journal of Artificial Intelligence in Education, 26*(1), 160–169. doi:10.1007/s40593-015-0055-y

Kleimola, R., & Leppisaari, I. (2022). Learning analytics to develop future competences in higher education: A case study. *International Journal of Educational Technology in Higher Education, 19*(1), 1–25. doi:10.1186/s41239-022-00318-w PMID:35013716

Knewton. (n.d.). Retrieved from https://www.knewton.com/

Knox, J. (2020). Artificial intelligence and education in China. *Learning, Media and Technology*, *45*(3), 298–311. doi: 10.1080/17439884.2020.1754236

Knox, J., Yu, W., & Gallagher, M. (2019). *Artificial intelligence and inclusive education*. Springer Singapore. doi:10.1007/978-981-13-8161-4

Kobayashi, M., & Terano, T. (2003). Learning agents in a business simulator. *Proc. IEEE Int. Symp. Computational Intelligence in Robotics and Automation*, 3, 1323-1327.

Kokku, R., Sundararajan, S., Dey, P., Sindhgatta, R., Nitta, S., & Sengupta, B. (2018, April). Augmenting classrooms with AI for personalized education. In 2018 IEEE international conference on acoustics, speech and signal processing (ICASSP) (pp. 6976-6980). IEEE. doi:10.1109/ICASSP.2018.8461812

Kose, U. (Ed.). (2014). *Artificial Intelligence applications in distance education*. IGI Global.

Kose, U., Mohammed, P. S., & Watson, E. N. (2019). Towards inclusive education in the age of artificial intelligence: perspectives, challenges, and opportunities. In J. Knox, Y. Wang, & M. Gallagher (Eds.), *Artificial Intelligence and Inclusive Education. Perspectives on Rethinking and Reforming Education*. Springer. doi:10.1007/978-981-13-8161-4_2

Krishnamoorthy, C. S., & Rajeev, S. (2018). *Artificial intelligence and expert systems for engineers*. CRC press.

Krumm, J. (Ed.). (2018). *Ubiquitous computing fundamentals*. CRC Press.

Kuljis, J., & Fang Liu. (2005). A Comparison of Learning Style Theories on the Suitability for elearning. *Web Technologies, Applications, and Services*, 191–197.

Kumar, D. N. (2019). Implementation of artificial intelligence in imparting education and evaluating student performance. *Journal of Artificial Intelligence and Capsule Networks*, *1*(1), 1–9. doi:10.36548/jaicn.2019.1.001

Kuo, T. H. (2020). The current situation of AI foreign language education and its influence on college Japanese teaching. *Cross-Cultural Design. Applications in Health, Learning, Communication, and Creativity: 12th International Conference, CCD 2020, Held as Part of the 22nd HCI International Conference, HCII 2020, Copenhagen, Denmark, July 19–24, 2020 Proceedings*, *22*(Part II), 315–324.

Kuppusamy, P. (2020). Emerging technologies to smart education. *International Journal of Computer Trends and Technology*, *68*(2), 5–16. doi:10.14445/22312803/IJCTT-V68I2P102

Laato, S., Farooq, A., Tenhunen, H., Pitkamaki, T., Hakkala, A., & Airola, A. (2020, July). Ai in cybersecurity education-a systematic literature review of studies on cybersecurity moocs. In *2020 IEEE 20th International Conference on Advanced Learning Technologies (ICALT)* (pp. 6-10). IEEE. 10.1109/ICALT49669.2020.00009

Labadze, L., Grigolia, M., & Machaidze, L. (2023). Role of ai chatbots in education: Sys-tematic literature review. *International Journal of Educational Technology in Higher Education*, *20*(1), 56. doi:10.1186/s41239-023-00426-1

Labster. (n.d.). *Platform Overview*. Retrieved from https://www.labster.com/platform-overview

Lakhal, S., Bateman, D., & Bédard, J. (2017). Blended Synchronous Delivery Modes in Graduate Programs: A Literature Review and How it is Implemented in the Master Teacher Program. *Collected Essays on Learning and Teaching*, *10*, 47–60.

Lameras, P. (2022). A Vision of Teaching and Learning with AI. In *2022 IEEE Global Engineering Education Conference (EDUCON)* (pp. 1796-1803). IEEE. 10.1109/EDUCON52537.2022.9766718

Lane, H. C., & D'Mello, S. K. (2019). Uses of physiological monitoring in intelligent learning environments: A review of research, evidence, and technologies. *Mind, Brain and Technology: Learning in the Age of Emerging Technologies*, 67-86.

Laupichler, M. C., Aster, A., Schirch, J., & Raupach, T. (2022). Artificial intelligence literacy in higher and adult education: A scoping literature review. *Computers and Education: Artificial Intelligence*, *100101*, 100101. Advance online publication. doi:10.1016/j.caeai.2022.100101

Lee, S., Mott, B., Ottenbreit-Leftwich, A., Scribner, A., Taylor, S., Park, K., ... Lester, J. (2021). AI-infused collaborative inquiry in upper elementary school: A game-based learning approach. *Proceedings of the AAAI conference on artificial intelligence*. 10.1609/aaai.v35i17.17836

Lee, S., Mott, B., Ottenbriet-Leftwich, A., Scribner, A., Taylor, S., Glazewski, K., ... Lester, J. (2020). Designing a collaborative game-based learning environment for AI-infused inquiry learning in elementary school classrooms. *Proceedings of the 2020 ACM conference on innovation and technology in computer science education*. 10.1145/3341525.3393981

Leigh, D. (2009). SWOT Analysis. In *Handbook of Improving Performance in the Workplace* (Vol. 1-3, pp. 115–140). Wiley. doi:10.1002/9780470592663.ch24

Leite, A., & Blanco, S. A. (2020). Effects of human vs. automatic feedback on students' understanding of AI concepts and programming style. *Proceedings of the 51st ACM Technical Symposium on Computer Science Education*. 10.1145/3328778.3366921

Leonard, J., Mitchell, M., Barnes-Johnson, J., Unertl, A., Outka-Hill, J., Robinson, R., & Hester-Croff, C. (2018). Preparing Teachers to Engage Rural Students in Computational Thinking Through Robotics, Game Design, and Culturally Responsive Teaching. *Journal of Teacher Education*, *69*(4), 386–407. doi:10.1177/0022487117732317

LessonPlans.ai. (n.d.). Retrieved from https://www.lessonplans.ai/

Li, Q., Cao, H., & Lu, Y. (2017, November). Connecting Paper to Digitization: a Homework Data Processing System with Data Labeling and Visualization. In *Proceedings of the 14th EAI International Conference on Mobile and Ubiquitous Systems: Computing, Networking and Services* (pp. 504-510). Academic Press.

Liang, J.-C., Hwang, G.-J., Chen, M.-R. A., & Darmawansah, D. (2023). Roles and research foci of artificial intelligence in language education: An integrated bibliographic analysis and systematic review approach. *Interactive Learning Environments*, *31*(7), 4270–4296. doi:10.1080/10494820.2021.1958348

Li, L., Lin, Y. L., Zheng, N. N., Wang, F. Y., Liu, Y., Cao, D., ... Huang, W. L. (2018). Artificial intelligence test: A case study of intelligent vehicles. *Artificial Intelligence Review*, *50*, 441–465.

Lim, T., Gottipati, S., & Cheong, M. L. (2023). Ethical Considerations for Artificial Intelligence in Educational Assessments. In Creative AI Tools and Ethical Implications in Teaching and Learning (pp. 32-79). IGI Global. doi:10.4018/979-8-3693-0205-7.ch003

Limna, P., Kraiwanit, T., Jangjarat, K., Klayklung, P., & Chocksathaporn, P. (2023). The use of chatgpt in the digital era: Perspectives on chatbot implementation. *Journal of Applied Learning and Teaching*, *6*(1), 64–74.

Lin, C.C., Huang, A., & Lu, O. (2023). Artificial intelligence in intelligent tutoring systems toward sustainable education: a systematic review. *Smart Learning Environments, 10*(1).

Lin, C. J., & Mubarok, H. (2021). Learning analytics for investigating the mind map-guided AI chatbot approach in an EFL flipped speaking classroom. *Journal of Educational Technology & Society*, *24*(4), 16–35.

Lin, C.-C., Huang, A. Y., & Lu, O. H. (2023). Artificial intelligence in intelligent tutoring systems toward sustainable education: A systematic review. *Smart Learning Environments*, *10*(1), 41. doi:10.1186/s40561-023-00260-y

Lindegger, D. J., Wawrzynski, J., & Saleh, G. M. (2022). Evolution and Applications of Artificial Intelligence to Cataract Surgery. *Ophthalmology Science*, *2*(3), 100164. Advance online publication. doi:10.1016/j.xops.2022.100164 PMID:36245750

Lin, F., & Chan, C. K. (2018). Examining the role of computer-supported knowledge-building discourse in epistemic and conceptual understanding. *Journal of Computer Assisted Learning*, *34*(5), 567–579. doi:10.1111/jcal.12261

Linsey, J., Hammond, T., Douglas, K., Viswanathan, V., Krishnamurthy, V., Merzdorf, H., Jaison, D., Ray, S., Weaver, M., & Li, W. (2022, August), *Sketchtivity, an Intelligent Tutoring Software: Broadening Applications and Impact* Paper presented at 2022 ASEE Annual Conference & Exposition, Minneapolis, MN. 10.18260/1-2--42014

Litman, D. (2016). Natural language processing for enhancing teaching and learning. *Proceedings of the AAAI conference on artificial intelligence*. 10.1609/aaai.v30i1.9879

Liu, M., Ma, J., & Jin, L. (2018, August). Analysis of military academy smart campus based on big data. In *2018 10th International Conference on Intelligent Human-Machine Systems and Cybernetics (IHMSC)* (Vol. 1, pp. 105-108). Academic Press.

Liu, C., Chen, X., Zou, D., Xie, H., & Cheng, G. (2022). Two decades of artificial intelligence in education. *Journal of Educational Technology & Society*, *25*(1), 28–47.

Liu, L. T., Wang, S., Britton, T., & Abebe, R. (2023). Reimagining the machine learning life cycle to improve educational outcomes of students. *Proceedings of the National Academy of Sciences of the United States of America*, *120*(9), e2204781120. doi:10.1073/pnas.2204781120 PMID:36827260

Liu, L., Subbareddy, R., & Raghavendra, C. G. (2022). AI Intelligence Chatbot to Improve Students Learning in the Higher Education Platform. *Journal of Interconnection Networks*, *22*(Supp02). doi:10.1142/S0219265921430325

Liu, M., Zhang, L. J., & Biebricher, C. (2024). Investigating students' cognitive processes in generative AI-assisted digital multimodal composing and traditional writing. *Computers & Education*, *211*, 104977. doi:10.1016/j.compedu.2023.104977

Liu, Q., Tong, S., Liu, C., Zhao, H., Chen, E., Ma, H., & Wang, S. (2019). Exploiting cognitive structure for adaptive learning. *Proceedings of the ACM SIGKDD International Conference on Knowledge Discovery and Data Mining*, 627–635. 10.1145/3292500.3330922

Liu, X., Gao, F., & Jiao, Q. (2021). Massive open online course fast adaptable computer engineering education model. *Complexity*, *2021*, 1–11. doi:10.1155/2021/7428927

Liu, X., Han, X., Lin, X., & Yang, J. H. (2022). National Ballad Creation Education Under Artificial Intelligence and Big Data. *Frontiers in Psychology*, *13*, 883096. Advance online publication. doi:10.3389/fpsyg.2022.883096 PMID:35800943

Liu, Z. (2023). Construction and Application of Smart Learning Space in Local Universities in China. *International Journal of Education and Humanities*, *7*(1), 70–73. doi:10.54097/ijeh.v7i1.5064

Liu, Z., Vobolevich, A., & Oparin, A. (2023). The influence of ai chatgpt on improving teachers' creative thinking. International Journal of Learning. *Teaching and Educational Research*, *22*(12), 124–139.

Li, X., Xu, H., Zhang, J., & Chang, H. (2023). Deep Reinforcement Learning for Adaptive Learning Systems. *Journal of Educational and Behavioral Statistics*, *48*(2), 220–243. doi:10.3102/10769986221129847

Li, Z. (2023). Application of artificial intelligence and internet of things in medical imaging teaching. *Journal of Biotech Research*, 15.

Loewen, S., Crowther, D., Isbell, D. R., Kim, K. M., Maloney, J., Miller, Z. F., & Rawal, H. (2019). Mobile-assisted language learning: A Duolingo case study. *ReCALL*, *31*(3), 293–311. doi:10.1017/S0958344019000065

Lo, J.-J., Chan, Y.-C., & Yeh, S.-W. (2012). Designing an adaptive web-based learning system based on students' cognitive styles identified online. *Computers & Education*, *58*(1), 209–222. doi:10.1016/j.compedu.2011.08.018

Lokey-Vega, A., & Stephens, S. (2019). A batch of one: A conceptual framework for the personalized learning movement. *Journal of Online Learning Research*, *5*(3), 311–330.

López-Fernández, D., Ezquerro, J. M., Rodríguez, J., Porter, J., & Lapuerta, V. (2019). Motivational impact of active learning methods in aerospace engineering students. *Acta Astronautica*, *165*, 344–354. doi:10.1016/j.actaastro.2019.09.026

Louisy, D. P. (2004). Whose context for what quality? Informing education strategies for the Caribbean. *Compare: A Journal of Comparative Education*, *34*(3), 285–292. doi:10.1080/0305792042000257121

Loureiro, S. M. C., Guerreiro, J., & Tussyadiah, I. (2021). Artificial intelligence in business: State of the art and future research agenda. *Journal of Business Research*, *129*, 911–926. doi:10.1016/j.jbusres.2020.11.001

Luan, H., Geczy, P., Lai, H., Gobert, J., Yang, S. J., Ogata, H., Baltes, J., Guerra, R., Li, P., & Tsai, C. C. (2020). Challenges and future directions of big data and artificial intelligence in education. *Frontiers in Psychology*, *11*, 580820. doi:10.3389/fpsyg.2020.580820 PMID:33192896

Madaev, S., Turluev, R., & Batchaeva, Z. (2023). *Robotics and Automation in Education*. Paper presented at the SHS Web of Conferences.

Maghsudi, S., Lan, A.S., Xu, J., & Schaar, M. (2021). *Personalized education in the ai era: What to expect next?* ArXiv abs/2101.10074.

Malik, H., Srivastava, S., Sood, Y. R., & Ahmad, A. (2018). Applications of artificial intelligence techniques in engineering. *Sigma, 1*.

Malik, M. (2018). Meta-analysis and review of the use of Artificial Intelligence and Learning Analytics within Engineering Education at University level. *Time for Change*, 38.

Mander, J. (1978). *Four arguments for the elimination of television*. Quill.

Mandhala, V. N., Bhattacharyya, D., & Midhunchakkaravarthy, D. (2022). Need of miti-gating bias in the datasets using machine learning algorithms. *2022 International Conference on Advances in Computing, Communication and Applied Informatics (ACCAI)*. 10.1109/ACCAI53970.2022.9752643

Mangina, E., Psyrra, G., Screpanti, L., & Scaradozzi, D. (2023). Robotics in the Context of Primary and Pre-School Education: A Scoping Review. *IEEE Transactions on Learning Technologies*.

Manyika, J., Chui, M., Miremadi, M., Bughin, J., George, K., Willmott, P., & Dewhurst, M. (2017). *A future that works: Automation, employment, and productivity*. McKinsey Global Institute.

Martin, J., Bohuslava, J., & Igor, H. (2018, September). Augmented Reality in Education 4.0. In *2018 IEEE 13th International Scientific and Technical Conference on Computer Sciences and Information Technologies (CSIT)* (Vol. 1, pp. 231-236). IEEE.

Martinez, C. (2022). Developing 21st century teaching skills: A case study of teaching and learning through project-based curriculum. *Cogent Education*, *9*(1), 2024936. doi:10.1080/2331186X.2021.2024936

Martínez-Comesaña, M., Rigueira-Díaz, X., Larrañaga-Janeiro, A., Martínez-Torres, J., Ocarranza-Prado, I., & Kreibel, D. (2023). Impact of artificial intelligence on assessment methods in primary and secondary education: systematic literature review. *Revista de Psicodidáctica (English ed.).* doi:10.1016/j.psicoe.2023.06.002

Martinez, N., León, M., Medina, D., & García, Z. (2007). Two approaches to generate intelligent teaching-learning systems using artificial intelligence techniques. In *2007 Sixth Mexican International Conference on Artificial Intelligence, Special Session (MICAI)* (pp. 333-341). IEEE.

Martonosi, S. E., & Williams, T. D. (2016). A survey of statistical capstone projects. *Journal of Statistics Education : An International Journal on the Teaching and Learning of Statistics, 24*(3), 127–135. doi:10.1080/10691898.2016.1257927

Masood, A., Hashmi, A., Masood, A., & Hashmi, A. (2019). AIOps: predictive analytics & machine learning in operations. *Cognitive Computing Recipes: Artificial Intelligence Solutions Using Microsoft Cognitive Services and TensorFlow,* 359-382.

Mayne, H. (2014). The Social Reconstructionist Approach to Teacher Education: A necessary component to achieving excellence and quality education for all. *Research in Comparative and International Education, 9*(1), 48–55. doi:10.2304/rcie.2014.9.1.48

McCallum, S., & Milner, M. M. (2021). The effectiveness of formative assessment: Student views and staff reflections. *Assessment & Evaluation in Higher Education, 46*(1), 1–16. doi:10.1080/02602938.2020.1754761

McCardle, J. R. (2002). The challenge of integrating ai & smart technology in design education. *International Journal of Technology and Design Education, 12*(1), 59–76. doi:10.1023/A:1013089404168

McGraw Hill. (n.d.). *McGraw Hill Education.* Retrieved from https://accounts.mheducation.com/login

McLaren, B. M., Adams, D. M., Mayer, R. E., & Forlizzi, J. (2017). A Computer-Based Game that Promotes Mathematics Learning More than a Conventional Approach. *International Journal of Game-Based Learning, 7*(1), 36–56. doi:10.4018/IJGBL.2017010103

Meepung, T., Kannikar, P., Chaiyarak, S., & Meepueng, S. (2023). Digital Learning on Smart Space to Promote High Performance Digital University. *International Journal of Educational Communications and Technology, 3*(2), 64–73.

Mesiono, M., Fahada, N., Irwansyah, I., Diana, D., & Siregar, A. S. (2024). SWOT Analysis of ChatGPT: Implications for Educational Practice and Research. *JMKSP (Jurnal Manajemen, Kepemimpinan, Dan Supervisi Pendidikan), 9*(1), 181–196. https://doi.org/ doi:10.31851/jmksp.v9i1.14137

Metsämuuronen, J., & Lehikko, A. (2023). Challenges and possibilities of educational equity and equality in the post-COVID-19 realm in the Nordic countries. *Scandinavian Journal of Educational Research, 67*(7), 1100–1121. doi:10.1080/00313831.2022.2115549

Mhlanga, D. (2023). Open AI in education, the responsible and ethical use of ChatGPT towards lifelong learning. In *FinTech and Artificial Intelligence for Sustainable Development: The Role of Smart Technologies in Achieving Development Goals* (pp. 387–409). Springer Nature Switzerland. doi:10.1007/978-3-031-37776-1_17

Miao, X., Brooker, R., & Monroe, S. (2024). Where Generative AI Fits Within and in Addition to Existing AI K12 Education Interactions: Industry and Research Perspectives. *Machine Learning in Educational Sciences: Approaches, Applications and Advances,* 359-384.

Miao, F., Holmes, W., Huang, R., & Zhang, H. (2021). *AI and education: A guidance for policymakers.* UNESCO Publishing.

Michael, J. (1984). Verbal behavior. *Journal of the Experimental Analysis of Behavior, 42*(3), 363–376. doi:10.1901/jeab.1984.42-363 PMID:16812395

Microsoft. (n.d.-a). *Copilot in Bing: Our approach to responsible AI*. Microsoft Support. https://support.microsoft.com/en-us/topic/copilot-in-bing-our-approach-to-responsible-ai-45b5eae8-7466-43e1-ae98-b48f8ff8fd44

Microsoft. (n.d.-b). *Microsoft Copilot*. Retrieved from https://www.microsoft.com/en-us/microsoft-copilot

Miedijensky, S., Sasson, I., & Yehuda, I. (2021). Teachers' Learning Communities for Developing High Order Thinking Skills—A Case Study of a School Pedagogical Change. *Interchange, 52*(4), 1–22. doi:10.1007/s10780-021-09423-7

Miller, D. P., Nourbakhsh, I. R., & Siegwart, R. (2008). *Robots for Education*. Springer Handbook of Robotics.

Minn, S. (2022). AI-assisted knowledge assessment techniques for adaptive learning environments. *Computers and Education: Artificial Intelligence, 3*, 100050.

Mitchell, M. (2019). Artificial intelligence: A guide for thinking humans. Academic Press.

Mittal, A., Ramachandran, K. K., Lakshmi, K. K., Hasbullah, N. N., Ravichand, M., & Lourens, M. (2023, May). Human-cantered Artificial Intelligence in Education, present and future opportunities. In *2023 3rd International Conference on Advance Computing and Innovative Technologies in Engineering (ICACITE)* (pp. 1003-1008). IEEE. 10.1109/ICACITE57410.2023.10182647

Mnguni, L. (2023). A critical reflection on the affordances of web 3.0 and artificial intelligence in life sciences education. *Journal of Pedagogical Sociology and Psychology*. doi:10.33902/jpsp.202322298

Molenaar, I. (2021). Personalisation of learning: Towards hybrid human-AI learning technologies. *Blockchain, and Robots*, 57-77. https://ogamify.com/gamification/duolingo-case-study/

Montebello, M. (2018). *AI injected e-learning*. Cham: Springer International Publishing.

Montebello, M. (2021). *Personalized learning environments. 2021 International Sympo-sium on Educational Technology*. ISET.

Mora-Salinas, R. J., Perez-Rojas, D., & De La Trinidad-Rendon, J. S. (2022, September). Real-Time Sensory Adaptive Learning for Engineering Students. In *International Conference on Interactive Collaborative Learning* (pp. 820-831). Cham: Springer International Publishing.

Mounsey, R., Vandehey, M., & Diekhoff, G. (2013). Working and non-working university students: Anxiety, depression, and grade point average. *College Student Journal, 47*(2), 379–389.

Mouti, S. & Rihawi, S. (2023). Special Needs Classroom Assessment Using a Sign Language Communicator (CASC) Based on Artificial Intelligence (AI) Techniques. *International Journal of e-Collaboration (IJeC), 19*(1), 1-15. doi:10.4018/IJeC.313960

Mpu, Y. (2023). *Bridging the Knowledge Gap on Special Needs Learner Support: The Use of Artificial Intelligence (AI) to Combat Digital Divide Post-COVID-19 Pandemic and beyond–A Comprehensive Literature Review*. Academic Press.

Muniasamy, V., Ejalani, D. I. M., & Anandhavalli, D. M. (2014). Moving towards Virtual Learning Clouds from Traditional Learning: Higher Educational Systems in India. *International Journal of Emerging Technologies in Learning, 9*(9), 70. doi:10.3991/ijet.v9i9.4183

Murtaza, M., Ahmed, Y., Shamsi, J. A., Sherwani, F., & Usman, M. (2022). AI-Based Personalized E-Learning Systems: Issues, Challenges, and Solutions. In IEEE Access (Vol. 10, pp. 81323–81342). Institute of Electrical and Electronics Engineers Inc. doi:10.1109/ACCESS.2022.3193938

Mutizwa, M. R., Ozdamli, F., & Karagozlu, D. (2023). Smart Learning Environments during Pandemic. *Trends in Higher Education*, 2(1), 16–28. doi:10.3390/higheredu2010002

Muttaqin, Z. (2023). Implementation of Islamic Education Learning with Artificial Intelligence (CHATGPT). *The 6th ICIS (2023): Islamic Thought and the Digital Challenge: Exploring the Future of Education, Business, Law, and Society*, 1–9.

Nazaretsky, T., Ariely, M., Cukurova, M., & Alexandron, G. (2022). Teachers' trust in AI-powered educational technology and a professional development program to improve it. *British Journal of Educational Technology*, 53(4), 914–931. doi:10.1111/bjet.13232

Nazemi, K., Breyer, M., Burkhardt, D., Stab, C., & Kohlhammer, J. (2014). SemaVis: A new approach for visualizing semantic information. In *Towards the Internet of Services: The THESEUS Research Program* (pp. 191–202). Springer. doi:10.1007/978-3-319-06755-1_15

Ngoc, T. N., Tran, Q. N., Tang, A., Nguyen, B., Nguyen, T., & Pham, T. (2023). AI-assisted Learning for Electronic Engineering Courses in High Education. *arXiv preprint arXiv:2311.01048*.

Ng, P. K., Koo, V. C., Ng, Y. J., & Yeow, J. A. (2023). Blending a sweet pill to swallow with TRIZ and industry talks for enhanced learning during the COVID-19 pandemic. *Human Systems Management*, 42(2), 163–178. Advance online publication. doi:10.3233/HSM-220080

Nguwi, Y. Y. (2023). Technologies for Education: From Gamification to AI-enabled Learning. *International Journal of Multidisciplinary Perspectives in Higher Education*, 8(1).

Nguyen, A., Järvelä, S., Rosé, C., Järvenoja, H., & Malmberg, J. (2023). Examining socially shared regulation and shared physiological arousal events with multimodal learning analytics. *British Journal of Educational Technology*, 54(1), 293–312. doi:10.1111/bjet.13280

Nguyen, N. D. (2023). Exploring the role of AI in education. *London Journal of Social Sciences*, (6), 84–95. doi:10.31039/ljss.2023.6.108

Ni, A., & Cheung, A. (2023). Understanding secondary students' continuance intention to adopt AI-powered intelligent tutoring system for English learning. *Education and Information Technologies*, 28(3), 3191–3216. doi:10.1007/s10639-022-11305-z PMID:36119127

Niedbał, R., Sokołowski, A., & Wrzalik, A. (2023). Students' Use of the Artificial Intelligence Language Model in their Learning Process. *Procedia Computer Science*, 225, 3059–3066. doi:10.1016/j.procs.2023.10.299

Niemi, H. (2021). AI in learning: Preparing grounds for future learning. *Journal of Pacific Rim Psychology*, 15, 18344909211038105. doi:10.1177/18344909211038105

Niemi, H., & Liu, J. (2021). AI in learning: Intelligent digital tools and environments for education. *Journal of Pacific Rim Psychology*, 15. doi:10.1177/18344909211038110

Niemi, H., Pea, R. D., & Lu, Y. (2022). AI in Learning: Designing the Future. In *AI in Learning: Designing the Future*. Springer International Publishing. doi:10.1007/978-3-031-09687-7

Nikmatullah, C., Wahyudin, W., Tarihoran, N., & Fauzi, A. (2023). Digital Pesantren: Revitalization of the Islamic Education System in the Disruptive Era. *Al-Izzah: Jurnal Hasil-Hasil Penelitian*, 1, 1. Advance online publication. doi:10.31332/ai.v0i0.5880

Niyozov, N., Saburov, S., Ganiyev, S., & Olimov, S. (2023). AI-powered learning: revolutionizing technical higher education institutions through advanced power supply fundamentals. In *E3S Web of Conferences* (Vol. 461, p. 01092). EDP Sciences. doi:10.1051/e3sconf/202346101092

Ntoutsi, E., Fafalios, P., Gadiraju, U., Iosifidis, V., Nejdl, W., Vidal, M. E., Ruggieri, S., Turini, F., Papadopoulos, S., Krasanakis, E., Kompatsiaris, I., Kinder-Kurlanda, K., Wagner, C., Karimi, F., Fern'andez, M., Alani, H., Berendt, B., Kruegel, T., Heinze, C., ... Staab, S. (2020). Bias in data-driven artificial intelligence systems—An introduc-tory survey. *Wiley Interdisciplinary Reviews. Data Mining and Knowledge Discovery*, 10.

O'Reilly-Shah, V. N., Gentry, K. R., Walters, A. M., Zivot, J., Anderson, C. T., & Tighe, P. J. (2020). Bias and ethical considerations in machine learning and the automation of perioperative risk assessment. *British Journal of Anaesthesia*, *125*(6), 843–846. doi:10.1016/j.bja.2020.07.040 PMID:32838979

Ocaña-Fernández, Y., Valenzuela-Fernández, L. A., & Garro-Aburto, L. L. (2019). Artificial Intelligence and Its Implica-tions in Higher Education. *Journal of Educational Psychology-Propositos y Representaciones*, *7*(2), 553–568.

Ofori, F., Maina, E., & Gitonga, R. (2020). Using machine learning algorithms to predict students' performance and improve learning outcome: A literature based review. *Journal of Information Technology*, *4*(1), 33–55.

Oizom. (n.d.). *Smart Campus Monitoring*. Retrieved from https://oizom.com/wp-content/uploads/2020/12/Oizom_Smart_Campus_Monitoring_V4-1.pdf

Ojha, S., Narendra, A., Mohapatra, S., & Misra, I. (2023). *From Robots to Books: An Introduction to Smart Applications of AI in Education (AIEd)*. arXiv preprint arXiv:2301.10026.

Okello, H. T. I. (2023). *Analyzing the impacts of artificial intelligence on education*. IAA Journal of Education. doi:10.59298/IAAJE/2023/2.10.1000

Okewu, E., Adewole, P., Misra, S., Maskeliunas, R., & Damasevicius, R. (2021). Artificial neural networks for educa-tional data mining in higher education: A systematic literature review. *Applied Artificial Intelligence*, *35*(13), 983–1021. doi:10.1080/08839514.2021.1922847

Okonkwo, C. W., & Ade-Ibijola, A. (2020). Python-bot: A chatbot for teaching python programming. *Engineering Let-ters*, *29*(1), 25–35.

Oliveira, W., & Bittencourt, I. I. (2019). *Tailored gamification to educational technologies* (Vol. 10). Springer Singapore. doi:10.1007/978-981-32-9812-5

Oliver, M., Shah, B., McGoldrick, C., & Edwards, M. (2006). 'Students' experiences of creativity. In N. J. Jackson (Ed.), *Developing Creativity in Higher Education: an Imaginative Curriculum*. Routledge-Falmer.

Oliver, R. (1994). Information technology courses in teacher education: The need for integration. *Journal of Information Technology for Teacher Education*, *3*(2), 135–146. doi:10.1080/0962029940030202

Omirzak, I., Alzhanov, A., Kartashova, O., & Ananishnev, V. (2022). Integrating Mobile Technologies in a Smart Classroom to Improve the Quality of the Educational Process: Synergy of Technological and Pedagogical Tools. *World Journal on Educational Technology: Current Issues*, *14*(3), 560–578. doi:10.18844/wjet.v14i3.7194

OpenA. I. (n.d.). *ChatGPT*. Retrieved from https://chat.openai.com/

Opfer, A., Kilgore, W., & Crosslin, M. (2018). Bot-teachers in hybrid massive open online courses (MOOCs): A post-humanist experience. *Australasian Journal of Educational Technology*, *34*(3).

Opfer, V. D., Kaufman, J. H., & Thompson, L. E. (2016). *Implementation of K–12 state standards for mathematics and English language arts and literacy*. RAND Corporation.

Ortigosa, A., Paredes, P., & Rodriguez, P. (2010). AH-questionnaire: An adaptive hierarchical questionnaire for learning styles. *Computers & Education*, *54*(4), 999–1005. doi:10.1016/j.compedu.2009.10.003

Otero-Cano, P. A., & Pedraza-Alarcón, E. C. (2021). Recommendation systems in education: A review of recommendation mechanisms in e-learning environments. *Revista Ingenierías Universidad De Medellín, 20*(38), 147–158. doi:10.22395/rium.v20n38a9

Ouyang, F., Dinh, T. A., & Xu, W. (2023). A systematic review of AI-driven educational assessment in STEM education. *Journal for STEM Education Research, 6*(3), 408–426. doi:10.1007/s41979-023-00112-x

Ouyang, F., & Jiao, P. (2021). Artificial intelligence in education: The three paradigms. *Computers and Education: Artificial Intelligence, 2*, 100020. doi:10.1016/j.caeai.2021.100020

Ouyang, F., Wu, M., Zheng, L., Zhang, L., & Jiao, P. (2023). Integration of artificial intelligence performance prediction and learning analytics to improve student learning in online engineering course. *International Journal of Educational Technology in Higher Education, 20*(1), 1–23. doi:10.1186/s41239-022-00372-4 PMID:36683653

Ouyang, F., Zheng, L., & Jiao, P. (2022). Artificial intelligence in online higher education: A systematic review of empirical research from 2011 to 2020. *Education and Information Technologies, 27*(6), 7893–7925. doi:10.1007/s10639-022-10925-9

Owoc, M. L., Sawicka, A., & Weichbroth, P. (2021). *Artificial Intelligence Technologies in Education: Benefits.* Challenges and Strategies of Implementation. doi:10.1007/978-3-030-85001-2_4

Pˇavˇaloaia, V. D., & Necula, S. C. (2023). Artificial intelligence as a disruptive technol-ogy—A systematic literature review. *Electronics (Basel), 12*(5), 1102. doi:10.3390/electronics12051102

Pacheco-Mendoza, S., Guevara, C., Mayorga-Alb'an, A., & Fern'andez-Escobar, J. (2023). Artificial intelligence in higher education: A predictive model for academic performance. *Education Sciences, 13*(10), 990. doi:10.3390/educsci13100990

Paek, S., & Kim, N. (2021). Analysis of worldwide research trends on the impact of artificial intelligence in education. *Sustainability (Basel), 13*(14), 7941. doi:10.3390/su13147941

Paglen, T. (2019). Invisible images: Your pictures are looking at you. *Architectural Design, 89*(1), 22–27.

Pal, K., & Karakostas, B. (2020). A Game-Based Approach for Simulation and Design of Supply Chains. *Supply Chain and Logistics Management: Concepts, Methodologies, Tools, and Applications,* 527-549.

Papaioannou, G., Volakaki, M.-G., Kokolakis, S., & Vouyioukas, D. (2023). Learning Spaces in Higher Education: A State-of-the-Art Review. *Trends in Higher Education, 2*(3), 526–545. doi:10.3390/higheredu2030032

Pappano, L. (2012). The Year of the MOOC. *The New York Times, 2*(12).

Pardamean, B., Suparyanto, T., Cenggoro, T. W., Sudigyo, D., & Anugrahana, A. (2022). AI-Based Learning Style Prediction in Online Learning for Primary Education. *IEEE Access : Practical Innovations, Open Solutions, 10*, 35725–35735. doi:10.1109/ACCESS.2022.3160177

Pavlik, J. V. (2023). Collaborating with ChatGPT: Considering the implications of generative artificial intelligence for journalism and media education. *Journalism & Mass Communication Educator, 78*(1), 84–93. doi:10.1177/10776958221149577

Pedro, F., Subosa, M., Rivas, A., & Valverde, P. (2019). *Artificial intelligence in education: Challenges and opportunities for sustainable development.* Academic Press.

Pedro, F., Subosa, M., Rivas, A., & Valverde, P. (2019). *Artificial intelligence in education: Challenges and opportunities for sustainable development.* Academic Press.

Pheng, H. S., Chin, T. A., Lai, L. Y., & Choon, T. L. (2022). E-Learning as a Supplementary Tool for Enhanced Students' Satisfaction. *AIP Conference Proceedings, 2433*, 030005. Advance online publication. doi:10.1063/5.0072901

Piaget, J. (2005). *The psychology of intelligence*. Routledge. doi:10.4324/9780203981528

Pinnell, J., Sabine, A., & Caroll-Meehan, C. (2021). *Engaging Children Online at The Study Buddy Club: A Novel Case Study*. Academic Press.

Pliakos, K., Joo, S.-H., Park, J. Y., Cornillie, F., Vens, C., & Van den Noortgate, W. (2019). Integrating machine learning into item response theory for addressing the cold start problem in adaptive learning systems. *Computers & Education*, *137*, 91–103. doi:10.1016/j.compedu.2019.04.009

Pogorskiy, E., & Beckmann, J. F. (2023). From procrastination to engagement? An experimental exploration of the effects of an adaptive virtual assistant on self-regulation in online learning. *Computers and Education: Artificial Intelligence*, *4*, 100111. Advance online publication. doi:10.1016/j.caeai.2022.100111

Pokrivcakova, S. (2019). Preparing teachers for the application of AI-powered technologies in foreign language education. *Journal of Language and Cultural Education*, *7*(3), 135–153. doi:10.2478/jolace-2019-0025

Pollarolo, E., Størksen, I., Skarstein, T. H., & Kucirkova, N. (2022). Children's critical thinking skills: Perceptions of Norwegian early childhood educators. *European Early Childhood Education Research Journal*, 1–13. doi:10.1080/13 50293X.2022.2081349

Popenici, S. A., & Kerr, S. (2017). Exploring the impact of artificial intelligence on teaching and learning in higher education. *Research and Practice in Technology Enhanced Learning*, *12*(1), 1–13. doi:10.1186/s41039-017-0062-8 PMID:30595727

Potkonjak, V., Gardner, M., Callaghan, V., Mattila, P., Guetl, C., Petrović, V. M., & Jovanović, K. (2016). Virtual laboratories for education in science, technology, and engineering: A review. *Computers & Education*, *95*, 309–327. doi:10.1016/j.compedu.2016.02.002

Prasad, V. S., Padala, V. K., & Kishore, C. (n.d.). *A Novel Machine Learning Approach for Tracking and Predicting Student Performance in Degree Programs*. Academic Press.

Pratama, M. P., Sampelolo, R., & Lura, H. (2023). Revolutionizing education: Harnessing the power of artificial intelligence for personalized learning. *Klasikal: Journal of Education, Language Teaching And Science*, *5*(2), 350–357. doi:10.52208/klasikal.v5i2.877

Psoinos, D. I. (2021). *Adapting Approaches and Methods to Teaching English Online: Theory and Practice*. Springer Nature. doi:10.1007/978-3-030-79919-9

Puyt, R. W., Lie, F. B., & Wilderom, C. P. M. (2023). The origins of SWOT analysis. *Long Range Planning*, *56*(3), 102304. doi:10.1016/j.lrp.2023.102304

QadirJ. (2022). Engineering Education in the Era of ChatGPT: Promise and Pitfalls of Generative AI for Education. TechRxiv. doi:10.36227/techrxiv.21789434.v1

Qadir, J. (2023, May). Engineering education in the era of ChatGPT: Promise and pitfalls of generative AI for education. In *2023 IEEE Global Engineering Education Conference (EDUCON)* (pp. 1-9). IEEE. 10.1109/EDU-CON54358.2023.10125121

Qazi, A., Hardaker, G., Ahmad, I. S., Darwich, M., Maitama, J. Z., & Dayani, A. (2021). The Role of Information & Communication Technology in Elearning Environments: A Systematic Review. *IEEE Access : Practical Innovations, Open Solutions*, *9*, 45539–45551. doi:10.1109/ACCESS.2021.3067042

Qian, K., Shea, R., Li, Y., Fryer, L. K., & Yu, Z. (2023). *User Adaptive Language Learning Chatbots with a Curriculum*. doi:10.1007/978-3-031-36336-8_48

Qin, F., Li, K., & Yan, J. (2020). Understanding user trust in artificial intelligence-based educational systems: Evidence from China. *British Journal of Educational Technology*, *51*(5), 1693–1710. doi:10.1111/bjet.12994

Qi, S., Liu, L., Kumar, B. S., & Prathik, A. (2022). An English teaching quality evaluation model based on Gaussian process machine learning. *Expert Systems: International Journal of Knowledge Engineering and Neural Networks*, *39*(6), e12861. Advance online publication. doi:10.1111/exsy.12861

Rachha, A., & Seyam, M. (2023). Explainable AI In Education: Current Trends, Challenges, And Opportunities. *SoutheastCon*, 232–239. doi:10.1109/SoutheastCon51012.2023.10115140

Rafferty, A. N., Ying, H., & Williams, J. J. (2018). Bandit Assignment for Educational Experiments: Benefits to Students Versus Statistical Power. doi:10.1007/978-3-319-93846-2_53

Rafiabadi, H. N. (2017). Contribution of Islamic Civilisation to Science Education and Technology: Some Fresh Insights. *Indonesian Journal of Interdisciplinary Islamic Studies*, *1*(1), 49–75. doi:10.20885/ijiis.vol1.iss1.art3

Rahem, A. A. T., Ismail, M., Najm, I. A., & Balfaqih, M. (2017). Topology sense and graph-based TSG: Efficient wireless ad hoc routing protocol for WANET. *Telecommunication Systems*, *65*(4), 739–754. doi:10.1007/s11235-016-0242-7

Rahman, M. M., Arshi, A. S., Hasan, M. M., Mishu, S. F., Shahriar, H., & Wu, F. (2023, June). Security Risk and Attacks in AI: A Survey of Security and Privacy. In *2023 IEEE 47th Annual Computers, Software, and Applications Conference (COMPSAC)* (pp. 1834-1839). IEEE. 10.1109/COMPSAC57700.2023.00284

Rahman, M., & Watanobe, Y. (2023). Chatgpt for education and research: Opportunities, threats, and strategies. *Applied Sciences (Basel, Switzerland)*, *13*(9), 5783. doi:10.3390/app13095783

Raj, A., Sharma, V., Rani, S., Balusamy, B., Shanu, A. K., & Alkhayyat, A. (2023, February). Revealing AI-Based Ed-Tech Tools Using Big Data. In *2023 3rd International Conference on Innovative Practices in Technology and Management (ICIPTM)* (pp. 1-6). IEEE. 10.1109/ICIPTM57143.2023.10118162

Raj, R. K., Parrish, A., Impagliazzo, J., Romanowski, C. J., Aly, S. G., Bennett, C. C., ... Sundin, L. (2019). An empirical approach to understanding data science and engineering education. In *Proceedings of the working group reports on innovation and technology in computer science education* (pp. 73-87). 10.1145/3344429.3372503

Ramandanis, D., & Xinogalos, S. (2023). Investigating the support provided by chatbots to educational institutions and their students: A systematic literature review. *Multimodal Technologies and Interaction*, *7*(11), 103. doi:10.3390/mti7110103

Rane, N. (2023). ChatGPT and Similar Generative Artificial Intelligence (AI) for Smart Industry: Role, Challenges and Opportunities for Industry 4.0, Industry 5.0 and Society 5.0. *Challenges and Opportunities for Industry, 4*.

Raquib, A., Channa, B., Zubair, T., & Qadir, J. (2022). Islamic virtue-based ethics for artificial intelligence. *Discover Artificial Intelligence*, *2*(1), 11. doi:10.1007/s44163-022-00028-2

Rasul, T., Nair, S., Kalendra, D., Robin, M., Santini, F., Ladeira, W., Sun, M., Day, I., Rather, R., & Heathcote, L. (2023). The role of chatgpt in higher education: Benefits, challenges, and future research directions. *Journal of Applied Learning and Teaching*, *6*(1), 41–56.

Rayhan, R., & Rayhan, S. (2023). *AI and Human Rights: Balancing Innovation and Privacy in the Digital Age*. Academic Press.

Redondo, A. C., de Pablo Lerchundi, I., Martí-Blanc, G., Martín, J. L., & Núñez, J. A. S. (2018). Training profile of faculty in applied sciences. *International Journal of Engineering Education*, *34*(5), 1504–1515.

Reeves, T. C., & Lin, L. (2020). The research we have is not the research we need. *Educational Technology Research and Development*, *68*(4), 1991–2001. doi:10.1007/s11423-020-09811-3 PMID:32837123

Remondino, M. (2008). A web based business game built on system dynamics using cognitive agents as virtual tutors. In *Tenth International Conference on Computer Modeling and Simulation (uksim 2008)* (pp. 568-572). IEEE. 10.1109/UKSIM.2008.84

Renz, A., & Hilbig, R. (2020). Prerequisites for artificial intelligence in further education: Identification of drivers, barriers, and business models of educational technology companies. *International Journal of Educational Technology in Higher Education*, *17*(1), 1–21. doi:10.1186/s41239-020-00193-3

Renz, A., Krishnaraja, S., & Gronau, E. (2020). Demystification of Artificial Intelligence in Education–How much AI is really in the Educational Technology? *International Journal of Learning Analytics and Artificial Intelligence for Education*, *2*(1), 14. doi:10.3991/ijai.v2i1.12675

Rethink, E. D. (n.d.). *RethinkED*. Retrieved from https://www.rethinked.com/

Rezaei Gazik, M. A., & Roayaei, M. (2023). Batch (Offline) Reinforcement Learning for Recommender System. *2023 31st International Conference on Electrical Engineering (ICEE)*, 245–250. 10.1109/ICEE59167.2023.10334722

Rezaei, A. (2009). *LMS Field Guide*. California State University. https://home.csulb.edu/~arezaei/ETEC551/web/LMS_fieldguide_20091.pdf

Richter, F. (2021, October). Ethics of AI as practical ethics. In *2021 IEEE International Symposium on Technology and Society (ISTAS)* (pp. 1-1). IEEE.

Rienties, B., Køhler Simonsen, H., & Herodotou, C. (2020, July). Defining the boundaries between artificial intelligence in education, computer-supported collaborative learning, educational data mining, and learning analytics: A need for coherence. In *Frontiers in Education* (Vol. 5, p. 128). Frontiers Media SA. doi:10.3389/feduc.2020.00128

Rismanchian, S., & Doroudi, S. (2023). *Four Interactions Between AI and Education: Broadening Our Perspective on What AI Can Offer Education*. Academic Press.

Rodway, P., & Schepman, A. (2023). The impact of adopting AI educational technologies on projected course satisfaction in university students. *Computers and Education: Artificial Intelligence*, *5*, 100150. doi:10.1016/j.caeai.2023.100150

Roll, I., & Wylie, R. (2016). Evolution and revolution in artificial intelligence in education. *International Journal of Artificial Intelligence in Education*, *26*(2), 582–599. doi:10.1007/s40593-016-0110-3

Romero, C., & Ventura, S. (2020). Educational data mining and learning analytics: An updated survey. *Wiley Interdisciplinary Reviews. Data Mining and Knowledge Discovery*, *10*(3), e1355. doi:10.1002/widm.1355

Roschelle, J., Lester, J., & Fusco, J. (2020). *AI and the Future of Learning: Expert Panel Report*. Digital Promise. doi:10.51388/20.500.12265/106

Roscoe, R. D., Salehi, S., Nixon, N., Worsley, M., Piech, C., & Luckin, R. (2022). *Inclusion and equity as a paradigm shift for artificial intelligence in education Artificial intelligence in STEM education: The paradigmatic shifts in research, education, and technology*. CRC Press.

Roshanaei, M. (2024). Towards best practices for mitigating artificial intelligence implicit bias in shaping diversity, inclusion and equity in higher education. *Education and Information Technologies*, 1–26. doi:10.1007/s10639-024-12605-2

Roshanaei, M., Olivares, H., & Lopez, R. R. (2023). Harnessing AI to Foster Equity in Education: Opportunities, Challenges, and Emerging Strategies. *Journal of Intelligent Learning Systems and Applications*, *15*(04), 123–143. doi:10.4236/jilsa.2023.154009

Rospigliosi, P. A. (2023). Artificial intelligence in teaching and learning: What questions should we ask of ChatGPT? *Interactive Learning Environments*, *31*(1), 1–3. doi:10.1080/10494820.2023.2180191

Roy, R., Babakerkhell, M. D., Mukherjee, S., Pal, D., & Funilkul, S. (2022). Evaluating the intention for the adoption of artificial intelligence-based robots in the university to educate the students. *IEEE Access : Practical Innovations, Open Solutions*, *10*, 125666–125678. doi:10.1109/ACCESS.2022.3225555

Ruiz-Rojas, L. I., Acosta-Vargas, P., De-Moreta-Llovet, J., & Gonzalez-Rodriguez, M. (2023). Empowering Education with Generative Artificial Intelligence Tools: Approach with an Instructional Design Matrix. *Sustainability (Basel)*, *15*(15), 11524. doi:10.3390/su151511524

Russell, R. G., Lovett Novak, L., Patel, M., Garvey, K. V., Craig, K. J. T., Jackson, G. P., Moore, D., & Miller, B. M. (2023). Competencies for the Use of Artificial Intelligence-Based Tools by Health Care Professionals. *Academic Medicine*, *98*(3), 348–356. Advance online publication. doi:10.1097/ACM.0000000000004963 PMID:36731054

Russo-Spena, T., Mele, C., & Marzullo, M. (2019). Practising value innovation through artificial intelligence: The IBM Watson case. *Journal of Creating Value*, *5*(1), 11–24.

S'anchez-Ruiz, L. M., Moll-L'opez, S., Nu~nez-P'erez, A., Mora~no-Fern'andez, J. A., & Vega-Fleitas, E. (2023). Chatgpt challenges blended learning methodologies in en-gineering education: A case study in mathematics. *Applied Sciences (Basel, Switzerland)*, *13*(10).

Saaida, M. B. (n.d.). *AI-Driven transformations in higher education: Opportunities and challenges*. Academic Press.

Saeed, M. M., Ali, E. S., & Saeed, R. A. (2023). Data-Driven Techniques and Security Issues in Wireless Networks. *Data-Driven Intelligence in Wireless Networks: Concepts, Solutions, and Applications*, 107.

Saeed, M. M., Mohammed, H. N. R., Gazem, O. A. H., Saeed, R. A., Morei, H. M. A., Eidah, A. E. T., . . . Al-Madhagi, M. G. Q. (2023, October). Machine Learning Techniques for Detecting DDOS Attacks. In *2023 3rd International Conference on Emerging Smart Technologies and Applications (eSmarTA)* (pp. 1-6). IEEE.10.1109/eSmarTA59349.2023.10293366

Saeed, M. M., Saeed, R. A., Azim, M. A., Ali, E. S., Mokhtar, R. A., & Khalifa, O. (2022, May). Green Machine Learning Approach for QoS Improvement in Cellular Communications. In *2022 IEEE 2nd International Maghreb Meeting of the Conference on Sciences and Techniques of Automatic Control and Computer Engineering (MI-STA)* (pp. 523-528). IEEE.10.1109/MI-STA54861.2022.9837585

Saeed, M. M., Saeed, R. A., Gaid, A. S., Mokhtar, R. A., Khalifa, O. O., & Ahmed, Z. E. (2023, August). Attacks Detection in 6G Wireless Networks using Machine Learning. In *2023 9th International Conference on Computer and Communication Engineering (ICCCE)* (pp. 6-11). IEEE.

Saeed, M. M., Saeed, R. A., Mokhtar, R. A., Khalifa, O. O., Ahmed, Z. E., Barakat, M., & Elnaim, A. A. (2023, August). Task Reverse Offloading with Deep Reinforcement Learning in Multi-Access Edge Computing. In *2023 9th International Conference on Computer and Communication Engineering (ICCCE)* (pp. 322-327). IEEE.10.1109/ICCCE58854.2023.10246081

Saeed, M. M. A., Ahmed, E. S. A., Saeed, R. A., & Azim, M. A. Green machine learning protocols for cellular communication. In *Green Machine Learning Protocols for Future Communication Networks* (pp. 15–62). CRC Press.

Saeed, M. M., Hasan, M. K., Obaid, A. J., Saeed, R. A., Mokhtar, R. A., Ali, E. S., Akhtaruzzaman, M., Amanlou, S., & Hossain, A. Z. (2022). A comprehensive review on the users' identity privacy for 5G networks. *IET Communications*, *16*(5), 384–399. doi:10.1049/cmu2.12327

Saeed, M. M., Kamrul Hasan, M., Hassan, R., Mokhtar, R., Saeed, R. A., Saeid, E., & Gupta, M. (2022). Preserving Privacy of User Identity Based on Pseudonym Variable in 5G. *Computers, Materials & Continua*, *70*(3). Advance online publication. doi:10.32604/cmc.2022.017338

Saeed, M. M., Saeed, R. A., Abdelhaq, M., Alsaqour, R., Hasan, M. K., & Mokhtar, R. A. (2023). Anomaly Detection in 6G Networks Using Machine Learning Methods. *Electronics (Basel)*, *12*(15), 3300. doi:10.3390/electronics12153300

Saeed, M. M., Saeed, R. A., Mokhtar, R. A., Alhumyani, H., & Ali, E. S. (2022). A novel variable pseudonym scheme for preserving privacy user location in 5G networks. *Security and Communication Networks*, *2022*, 2022. doi:10.1155/2022/7487600

Saeed, M. M., Saeed, R. A., & Saeid, E. (2019, December). Preserving privacy of paging procedure in 5 th G using identity-division multiplexing. In *2019 First International Conference of Intelligent Computing and Engineering (ICOICE)* (pp. 1-6). IEEE.

Saeed, M. M., Saeed, R. A., & Saeid, E. (2021, March). Identity division multiplexing based location preserve in 5G. In *2021 International Conference of Technology, Science and Administration (ICTSA)* (pp. 1-6). IEEE.10.1109/ICTSA52017.2021.9406554

Saeed, R. A., Omri, M., Abdel-Khalek, S., Ali, E. S., & Alotaibi, M. F. (2022). Optimal path planning for drones based on swarm intelligence algorithm. *Neural Computing & Applications*, *34*(12), 10133–10155. doi:10.1007/s00521-022-06998-9

Saeed, R. A., Saeed, M. M., Mokhtar, R. A., Alhumyani, H., & Abdel-Khalek, S. (2021). Pseudonym Mutable Based Privacy for 5G User Identity. *Computer Systems Science and Engineering*, *39*(1). Advance online publication. doi:10.32604/csse.2021.015593

Sajja, R., Sermet, Y., Cwiertny, D., & Demir, I. (2023). Platform-independent and curriculum-oriented intelligent assistant for higher education. *International Journal of Educational Technology in Higher Education*, *20*(1), 42. doi:10.1186/s41239-023-00412-7

Salas-Pilco, S. Z., Xiao, K., & Hu, X. (2022). Artificial intelligence and learning analytics in teacher education: A systematic review. *Education Sciences*, *12*(8), 569. doi:10.3390/educsci12080569

Salas-Pilco, S. Z., & Yang, Y. (2022). Artificial intelligence applications in Latin American higher education: A systematic review. *International Journal of Educational Technology in Higher Education*, *19*(1), 21. doi:10.1186/s41239-022-00326-w

Saleem, A. N., Noori, N. M., & Ozdamli, F. (2022). Gamification applications in E-learning: A literature review. Technology. *Knowledge and Learning*, *27*(1), 139–159. doi:10.1007/s10758-020-09487-x

Salleh, S. M., Hasan, A. S. M., Salleh, N. M., Sapiai, N. S., Ghazali, S. A. M., Rusok, N. H. M., & Zawawi, M. Z. M. (2021). Virtual Reality Technology of Hajj Practice: An Innovation of The Future. *Jurnal Islam Dan Masyarakat Kontemporari*, *22*(2), 56–63. doi:10.37231/jimk.2021.22.2.577

Samsul, S. A., Yahaya, N., & Abuhassna, H. (2023). Education big data and learning analytics: A bibliometric analysis. *Humanities & Social Sciences Communications*, *10*(1), 1–11. doi:10.1057/s41599-023-02176-x

Santamaría-Bonfil, G., Ibáñez, M. B., Pérez-Ramírez, M., Arroyo-Figueroa, G., & Martínez-Álvarez, F. (2020). Learning analytics for student modeling in virtual reality training systems: Lineworkers case. *Computers & Education*, *151*, 103871. doi:10.1016/j.compedu.2020.103871

Sanusi, I. T., & Olaleye, S. A. (2022). An Insight into Cultural Competence and Ethics in K-12 Artificial Intelligence Education. *IEEE Global Engineering Education Conference, EDUCON, 2022-March*, 790–794. 10.1109/EDU-CON52537.2022.9766818

Sanusi, I. T., Olaleye, S. A., Oyelere, S. S., & Dixon, R. A. (2022). Investigating learners' competencies for artificial intelligence education in an African K-12 setting. *Computers and Education Open, 3*, 100083. doi:10.1016/j.caeo.2022.100083

Sanusi, I. T., Oyelere, S. S., Vartiainen, H., Suhonen, J., & Tukiainen, M. (2023). A systematic review of teaching and learning machine learning in K-12 education. *Education and Information Technologies, 28*(5), 5967–5997. doi:10.1007/s10639-022-11416-7

Saputra, I., Astuti, M., Sayuti, M., & Kusumastuti, D. (2023). Integration of Artificial Intelligence in Education: Opportunities, Challenges, Threats and Obstacles. A Literature Review. *Indonesian Journal of Computer Science, 12*(4). Advance online publication. doi:10.33022/ijcs.v12i4.3266

Saranya, V., Devi, T., & Deepa, N. (2023). Text Normalization by Bi-LSTM Model with Enhanced Features to Improve Tribal English Knowledge. *Proceedings of the 7th International Conference on Intelligent Computing and Control Systems, ICICCS 2023*. 10.1109/ICICCS56967.2023.10142508

Šarić, I., Grubišić, A., Šerić, L., & Robinson, T. J. (2019). *Data-driven student clusters based on online learning behavior in a flipped classroom with an intelligent tutoring system*. Paper presented at the Intelligent Tutoring Systems: 15th International Conference, ITS 2019, Kingston, Jamaica.

Sarma, G. P., & Hay, N. J. (2017). Robust Computer Algebra, Theorem Proving, and Oracle AI. *arXiv preprint arXiv:1708.02553*.

Saunders, F. C., Gale, A. W., & Sherry, A. H. (2015). Conceptualising uncertainty in safety-critical projects: A practitioner perspective. *International Journal of Project Management, 33*(2), 467–478. doi:10.1016/j.ijproman.2014.09.002

Saxena, S., Sethi, S., & Singh, M. (2023). Transforming Decision Making in Higher Education: The Impact of Artificial Intelligence Interventions. *Themes/Subthemes for the Special Issues of University News, 61*, 12.

Schiff, D. (2022). Education for AI, not AI for education: The role of education and ethics in national AI policy strategies. *International Journal of Artificial Intelligence in Education, 32*(3), 527–563. doi:10.1007/s40593-021-00270-2

Schifter, C., Natarajan, U., Ketelhut, D. J., & Kirchgessner, A. (2014). Data-driven decision-making: Facilitating teacher use of student data to inform classroom instruction. *Contemporary Issues in Technology & Teacher Education, 14*(4), 419–432.

Seeroo, O., & Bekaroo, G. (2021, December). Enhancing Student Support via the Application of a Voice User Interface System: Insights on User Experience. In *Proceedings of the International Conference on Artificial Intelligence and its Applications* (pp. 1-6). 10.1145/3487923.3487936

Sein-Echaluce, M. L., Fidalgo-Blanco, A., & García-Peñalvo, F. J. (Eds.). (2019). *Innovative trends in flipped teaching and adaptive learning*. IGI Global. doi:10.4018/978-1-5225-8142-0

Sekeroglu, B., Dimililer, K., & Tuncal, K. (2019). Artificial intelligence in education: application in student performance evaluation. Dilemas Contemporáneos: Educación. *Política y Valores, 7*(1), 1–21.

Sghir, N., Adadi, A., & Lahmer, M. (2023). Recent advances in Predictive Learning Analytics: A decade systematic review (2012–2022). *Education and Information Technologies, 28*(7), 8299–8333. doi:10.1007/s10639-022-11536-0 PMID:36571084

Shafik, W. (2023). *Artificial intelligence and Blockchain technology enabling cybersecurity in telehealth systems. In Artificial Intelligence and Blockchain Technology in Modern Telehealth Systems.* IET. doi:10.1049/PBHE061E_ch11

Shafik, W. (2024a). *Navigating Emerging Challenges in Robotics and Artificial Intelligence in Africa. Examining the Rapid Advance of Digital Technology in Africa* (Vol. 1). IGI Global. doi:10.4018/978-1-6684-9962-7.ch007

Shafik, W. (2024b). *Toward a More Ethical Future of Artificial Intelligence and Data Science. In The Ethical Frontier of AI and Data Analysis.* IGI Global. doi:10.4018/979-8-3693-2964-1.ch022

Shafik, W. (2024c). *Introduction to ChatGPT. Advanced Applications of Generative AI and Natural Language Processing Models* (Vol. 1). IGI Global. doi:10.4018/979-8-3693-0502-7.ch001

Shafique, R., Aljedaani, W., Rustam, F., Lee, E., Mehmood, A., & Choi, G. S. (2023). Role of Artificial Intelligence in Online Education: A Systematic Mapping Study. *IEEE Access : Practical Innovations, Open Solutions, 11*, 52570–52584. doi:10.1109/ACCESS.2023.3278590

Shah, P. (2023). *AI and the Future of Education: Teaching in the Age of Artificial Intelligence.* Jossey-Bass, An Imprint of Wiley.

Shaheen, N. L., & Watulak, S. L. (2019). Bringing disability into the discussion: Examining technology accessibility as an equity concern in the field of instructional technology. *Journal of Research on Technology in Education, 51*(2), 187–201. doi:10.1080/15391523.2019.1566037

Shaik, T., Tao, X., Li, Y., Dann, C., McDonald, J., Redmond, P., & Galligan, L. (2022). A review of the trends and challenges in adopting natural language processing methods for education feedback analysis. *IEEE Access : Practical Innovations, Open Solutions, 10*, 56720–56739. doi:10.1109/ACCESS.2022.3177752

Shang, M. (2019, August). The Application of Artificial Intelligence in Music Education. In *International Conference on Intelligent Computing* (pp. 662-668). Springer. 10.1007/978-3-030-26969-2_62

Sharma, D., & Bhardwaj, K. (2023). Effective Teaching Strategies for Overcoming the Challenges of E-Learning. In Social Capital in the Age of Online Networking: Genesis, Manifestations, and Implications (pp. 99-112). IGI Global.

Sharp, J. H. (2019). Using Codecademy Interactive Lessons as an Instructional Supplement in a Python Programming Course. *Information Systems Education Journal, 17*(3), 20–28.

Shawky, D., & Badawi, A. (2019). Towards a personalized learning experience using reinforcement learning. *Machine learning paradigms: Theory and application*, 169-187.

Shawky, D., & Badawi, A. (2018). *A Reinforcement Learning-Based Adaptive Learning System.* doi:10.1007/978-3-319-74690-6_22

Shen, Y., Yu, P., Lu, H., Zhang, X., & Zeng, H. (2021). An AI-based virtual simulation experimental teaching system in space engineering education. *Computer Applications in Engineering Education, 29*(2), 329–338. doi:10.1002/cae.22221

Sherlock, P. M. (1950). Education in the Caribbean area. *Caribbean Quarterly, 1*(3), 9–18. doi:10.1080/00086495.1950.11829194

ShirinA. (2022). Artificial Intelligence Technology on Teaching Learning: Exploring Bangladeshi Teachers' Perceptions. Embedded Selforganising Systems. 9. doi:10.14464/ess.v9i4.553

Shute, V. J. (2017). *The Future of Assessment* (C. A. Dwyer, Ed.). Routledge. doi:10.4324/9781315086545

Shute, V. J., & Zapata-Rivera, D. (2012). Adaptive educational systems. In *Adaptive Technologies for Training and Education* (pp. 7–27). Cambridge University Press. doi:10.1017/CBO9781139049580.004

Shvetsova, I. (2023). *The Use of Artificial intelligence in education as an effective tool for developing foreign language communicative competency*. Academy of Silesi.

Sidekerskiene, T., & Damasevicius, R. (2023). Out-of-the-box learning: Digital escape rooms as a metaphor for breaking down barriers in stem education. *Sustainability (Basel)*, *15*(9), 7393. doi:10.3390/su15097393

Singer, C. G. (2023). *Educational Data Mining: An Application of a Predictive Model of Online Student Enrollment Decisions*. Arizona State University.

Skrabut, S. (2023). *80 Ways to Use ChatGPT in the Classroom: Using AI to Enhance Teaching and Learning*. Academic Press.

Slim, A., Al Yusuf, H., Abbas, N., Abdallah, C. T., Heileman, G. L., & Slim, A. (2021). A Markov Decision Processes Modeling for Curricular Analytics. *2021 20th IEEE International Conference on Machine Learning and Applications (ICMLA)*, 415–421. 10.1109/ICMLA52953.2021.00071

Slimi, Z., & Carballido, B. V. (2023). Navigating the Ethical Challenges of Artificial Intelligence in Higher Education: An Analysis of Seven Global AI Ethics Policies. *TEM Journal, 12*(2).

Soelistiono, S., & Wahidin. (2023). Educational Technology Innovation: AI-Integrated Learning System Design in AILS-Based Education. *Influence: International Journal of Science Review*, *5*(2), 470–480. doi:10.54783/influencejournal.v5i2.175

Sofa, A. R., Mundir, H., & Ubaidillah, H. (2024). Learning Islamic Religious Education Based on Spiritual and Emotional Intelligence to Build the Morals of Zainul Hasan Genggong Islamic University Students. *International Journal of Educational Narratives*, *2*(1), 42–47. doi:10.55849/ijen.v2i1.609

Somasundaram, M., Junaid, K. M., & Mangadu, S. (2020). Artificial intelligence (AI) enabled intelligent quality management system (IQMS) for personalized learning path. *Procedia Computer Science*, *172*, 438–442. doi:10.1016/j.procs.2020.05.096

Southworth, J., Migliaccio, K., Glover, J., Reed, D., McCarty, C., Brendemuhl, J., & Thomas, A. (2023). Developing a model for AI Across the curriculum: Transforming the higher education landscape via innovation in AI literacy. *Computers and Education: Artificial Intelligence*, *4*, 100127. doi:10.1016/j.caeai.2023.100127

SquirrelA. I. (n.d.). *Squirrel AI*. Retrieved from https://squirrelai.com/#

Srinivasa, K. G., Kurni, M., & Saritha, K. (2022). *Harnessing the Power of AI to Education*. doi:10.1007/978-981-19-6734-4_13

Srinivasan, V. (2022). AI & learning: A preferred future. *Computers and Education: Artificial Intelligence*, *3*, 100062. Advance online publication. doi:10.1016/j.caeai.2022.100062

Sriram, R. D. (2012). *Intelligent systems for engineering: a knowledge-based approach*. Springer Science & Business Media.

Standen, P. J., Brown, D. J., Taheri, M., Galvez Trigo, M. J., Boulton, H., Burton, A., Hallewell, M. J., Lathe, J. G., Shopland, N., Blanco Gonzalez, M. A., Kwiatkowska, G. M., Milli, E., Cobello, S., Mazzucato, A., Traversi, M., & Hortal, E. (2020). An evaluation of an adaptive learning system based on multimodal affect recognition for learners with intellectual disabilities. *British Journal of Educational Technology*, *51*(5), 1748–1765. doi:10.1111/bjet.13010

Stein, M. I. (1988). Creativity: The process and its stimulation. In F. Flach (Ed.), *The creative mind* (pp. 50–75). Bearly Limited.

Strzelecki, A., & ElArabawy, S. (2024). Investigation of the moderation effect of gender and study level on the acceptance and use of generative AI by higher education students: Comparative evidence from Poland and Egypt. *British Journal of Educational Technology, 00*(3), 1–22. doi:10.1111/bjet.13425

Stuikys, V., & Burbaite, R. (2018). *Smart STEM-Driven Computer Science Education: Theory.* Methodology and Robot-based Practices. doi:10.1007/978-3-319-78485-4

Su, J., & Yang, W. (2023). Unlocking the power of ChatGPT: A framework for applying generative AI in education. *ECNU Review of Education.*

Su, J., Ng, D. T. K., & Chu, S. K. W. (2023). Artificial Intelligence (AI) Literacy in Early Childhood Education: The Challenges and Opportunities. In Computers and Education: Artificial Intelligence (Vol. 4). Elsevier B.V. doi:10.1016/j.caeai.2023.100124

Subkhan, E. (2012). *Paradigm shifts on educational technology and its possibilities for transformative action.* Paper presented at the First International Conference on Current Issues in Education (ICCIE) held by Yogyakarta State University and National University of Malaysia, Yogyakarta.

Sutton, R. S., & Barto, A. G. (2018). *Reinforcement Leaning.* MIT Press.

Synap. (n.d.). Synap. Retrieved from https://synap.ac/

Tahir, A., & Tahir, A. (2023). *AI-driven Advancements in ESL Learner Autonomy: Investigating Student Attitudes Towards Virtual Assistant Usability.* Paper presented at the Linguistic Forum-A Journal of Linguistics.

Tambuskar, S. (2022). Challenges and Benefits of 7 Ways Artificial Intelligence in Education Sector. *Review of Artificial Intelligence in Education, 3*(00), e03. Advance online publication. doi:10.37497/rev.artif.intell.education.v3i00.3

Tan, E., Lerouge, E., Du Caju, J., & Du Seuil, D. (2023). Verification of Education Credentials on European Blockchain Services Infrastructure (EBSI): Action Research in a Cross-Border Use Case between Belgium and Italy. *Big Data and Cognitive Computing, 7*(2), 79. doi:10.3390/bdcc7020079

Tanga, H., & Chen, Q. (2023). *The Opportunities, Challenges and Realization Path of Educational Equity in the age of Artificial Intelligence.* Academic Press.

Tang, X., Chen, Y., Li, X., Liu, J., & Ying, Z. (2019). A reinforcement learning approach to personalized learning recommendation systems. *British Journal of Mathematical & Statistical Psychology, 72*(1), 108–135. doi:10.1111/bmsp.12144 PMID:30277574

Tanveer, M., Hassan, S., & Bhaumik, A. (2020). Academic policy regarding sustainability and artificial intelligence (AI). *Sustainability (Basel), 12*(22), 9435. doi:10.3390/su12229435

Tarisayi, K. S. (2023). Lustre and shadows: Unveiling the gaps in South African University plagiarism policies amidst the emergence of AI-generated content. *AI and Ethics,* 1–7. doi:10.1007/s43681-023-00333-1

TeachFlow. (2023). *The impact of AI on teachers wellbeing and burnout.* Author.

Teh, Y. Y., & Baskaran, V. (2022). The Effectiveness of eAssessments to Encourage Learning Among Gen Z Students. In *Alternative Assessments in Malaysian Higher Education* (pp. 259–267). Springer Singapore. doi:10.1007/978-981-16-7228-6_26

Tew, Y., Lim, K. Y., & Joan, H. (2022). An Evaluation of Virtual Classroom Performance with Artificial Intelligence Components. *The Journal of The Institution of Engineers, Malaysia, 82*(3). Advance online publication. doi:10.54552/v82i3.116

Thanasi-Boçe, M. (2020). Enhancing students' entrepreneurial capacity through marketing simulation games. *Education + Training*, 62(9), 999–1013. doi:10.1108/ET-06-2019-0109

Thierer, A., & Castillo, A. (2016). *Preparing for the future of artificial intelligence*. Public Interest Comment.

Thottoli, M. M., Alruqaishi, B. H., & Soosaimanickam, A. (2024). Robo academic advisor: Can chatbots and artificial intelligence replace human interaction? *Contemporary Educational Technology*, 16(1), ep485. doi:10.30935/cedtech/13948

Thunstrom, A. O. (2022). We asked GPT-3 to write an academic paper about itself: Then we tried to get it published. *Scientific American*, 30.

Thurzo, A., Strunga, M., Urban, R., Surovkova, J., & Afrashtehfar, K. I. (2023). Impact of Artificial Intelligence on Dental Education: A Review and Guide for Curriculum Update. *Education Sciences*, 13(2), 150. doi:10.3390/educsci13020150

Tight, M. (2020). Student retention and engagement in higher education. *Journal of Further and Higher Education*, 44(5), 689–704. doi:10.1080/0309877X.2019.1576860

Tisha, S. M., Oregon, R. A., Baumgartner, G., Alegre, F., & Moreno, J. (2022). An automatic grading system for a high school-level computational thinking course. *Proceedings of the 4th International Workshop on Software Engineering Education for the Next Generation*, 20–27. 10.1145/3528231.3528357

Tiwari, H. P. (2023). An optimization-based artificial intelligence framework for teaching English at the college level. *LLT Journal: A Journal on Language and Language Teaching*, 26(1). doi:10.24071/llt.v26i1.5954

Tiwari, C. K., Bhaskar, P., & Pal, A. (2023). Prospects of augmented reality and virtual reality for online education: A scientometric view. *International Journal of Educational Management*, 37(5), 1042–1066. doi:10.1108/IJEM-10-2022-0407

Tlili, A., Shehata, B., Adarkwah, M. A., Bozkurt, A., Hickey, D. T., Huang, R., & Agyemang, B. (2023). What if the devil is my guardian angel: ChatGPT as a case study of using chatbots in education. *Smart Learning Environments*, 10(1), 15. doi:10.1186/s40561-023-00237-x

Tomasevic, N., Gvozdenovic, N., & Vranes, S. (2020). An overview and comparison of supervised data mining techniques for student exam performance prediction. *Computers & Education*, 143, 103676. doi:10.1016/j.compedu.2019.103676

Touretzky, D., Gardner-McCune, C., Martin, F., & Seehorn, D. (2019). Envisioning ai for k-12: What should every child know about AI? Proceedings of the AAAI conference on artificial intelligence, 33(1), 9795–9799. doi:10.1609/aaai.v33i01.33019795

Töyli, J., Hansén, S. O., & Smeds, R. (2006). Plan for profit and achieve profit: Lessons learnt from a business management simulation. *Production Planning and Control*, 17(6), 584–595. doi:10.1080/09537280600866686

Toyokawa, Y., Horikoshi, I., Majumdar, R., & Ogata, H. (2023). Challenges and opportunities of AI in inclusive education: A case study of data-enhanced active reading in Japan. *Smart Learning Environments*, 10(1), 67. doi:10.1186/s40561-023-00286-2

Tripathy, S., & Devarapalli, S. (2021). Emerging trend set by a start-ups on Indian online education system: A case of Byju's. *Journal of Public Affairs*, 21(1), e2128.

Truong, H. M. (2015). *Integrating Learning Styles into Adaptive E-Learning System*. International Educational Data Mining Society.

Truong, H. M. (2016). Integrating learning styles and adaptive e-learning system: Current developments, problems and opportunities. *Computers in Human Behavior*, 55, 1185–1193. doi:10.1016/j.chb.2015.02.014

Truong, H., Qi, D., Ryason, A., Sullivan, A. M., Cudmore, J., Alfred, S., Jones, S. B., Parra, J. M., De, S., & Jones, D. B. (2022). Does your team know how to respond safely to an operating room fire? Outcomes of a virtual reality, AI-enhanced simulation training. *Surgical Endoscopy*, *36*(5), 3059–3067. Advance online publication. doi:10.1007/s00464-021-08602-y PMID:34264400

Tseng, H. C., Kuo, C. W., Yang, H. L., Liao, H. C., Hu, S. H., Yeh, C. H., & Tsai, I. C. (2019). AIGO: A comprehensive platform for cultivating AI talent using real-world industrial problems. In *2019 IEEE International Conference on Engineering, Technology and Education (TALE)* (pp. 1-5). IEEE.

Tsirulnikov, D., Suart, C., Abdullah, R., Vulcu, F., & Mullarkey, C. E. (2023). Game on: Immersive virtual laboratory simulation improves student learning outcomes & motivation. *FEBS Open Bio*, *13*(3), 396–407. doi:10.1002/2211-5463.13567 PMID:36723273

Tubagus, M., Haerudin, Fathurohman, A., Adiyono, & Slan. (2023). The Impact of Technology on Islamic Pesantren Education and the Learning Outcomes of Santri: New trends and possibilities. *Indonesian Journal of Education*, *3*(3), 443–450.

Tuli, N., Singh, G., Mantri, A., & Sharma, S. (2022). Augmented reality learning environment to aid engineering students in performing practical laboratory experiments in electronics engineering. *Smart Learning Environments*, *9*(1), 1–20. doi:10.1186/s40561-022-00207-9

Uc-Cetina, V., Navarro-Guerrero, N., Martin-Gonzalez, A., Weber, C., & Wermter, S. (2023). Survey on reinforcement learning for language processing. *Artificial Intelligence Review*, *56*(2), 1543–1575. doi:10.1007/s10462-022-10205-5

UNESCO. (2009). *Policy guidelines on inclusion in education*. UNESCO.

UNESCO. (2023). *Information for All (IFAP) strategic plan, 2023-2029* [programme and meeting document]. UNESCO. https://unesdoc.unesco.org/ark:/48223/pf0000386173

UNESCO. (n.d.). *Artificial Intelligence in Education*. UNESCO. https://ar.unesco.org/themes/ict-education/action/ai-in-education

Ungerer, L., & Slade, S. (2022). Ethical considerations of artificial intelligence in learning analytics in distance education contexts. In Learning Analytics in Open and Distributed Learning: Potential and Challenges (pp. 105-120). Singapore: Springer Nature Singapore. doi:10.1007/978-981-19-0786-9_8

UNICEF. (2021). *Policy guidance on AI for children: 2.0 November 2021*. https://www.unicef.org/globalinsight/media/2356/file/UNICEF-Global-Insight-policy-guidance-AI-children-2.0-2021.pdf.pdf

University of Colorado Boulder. (n.d.). *PhET Interactive Simulations*. Retrieved from https://phet.colorado.edu/en/about

US Department of Education. (2016). *Future ready learning: Reimagining the role of technology in education*. Office of Educational Technology.

Utunen, H., Attias, M., George, R., O'Connell, G., & Tokar, A. (2022). Learning multiplier effect of OpenWHO.org: use of online learning materials beyond the platform. In *WHO Weekly epidemiological record* (Vol. 97, pp. 1–7). World Health Organization. https://www.who.int/publications/i/item/WER9701-02-1-7

Valentin, E. K. (2001). Swot Analysis from a Resource-Based View. *Journal of Marketing Theory and Practice*, *9*(2), 54–69. doi:10.1080/10696679.2001.11501891

van den Berg, G., & du Plessis, E. (2023). Chatgpt and generative ai: Possibilities for its contribution to lesson planning, critical thinking and openness in teacher education. *Education Sciences*, *13*(10), 998. doi:10.3390/educsci13100998 van der Vorst, T., & Jelicic, N. (2019). *Artificial Intelligence in Education: Can AI bring the full potential of personalized learning to education?* Academic Press.

Van Schoors, R., Elen, J., Raes, A., & Depaepe, F. (2023). Tinkering the teacher–technology nexus: The case of teacher- and technology-driven per-sonalisation. *Education Sciences*, 13(4), 349. doi:10.3390/educsci13040349

Vandewaetere, M., & Clarebout, G. (2014). Advanced technologies for personalized learning, instruction, and performance. Handbook of research on educational communications and technology, 425-437.

VanLehn, K. (2011). The Relative Effectiveness of Human Tutoring, Intelligent Tutoring Systems, and Other Tutoring Systems. *Educational Psychologist*, 46(4), 197–221. doi:10.1080/00461520.2011.611369

Vashishth, T. K., Sharma, V., Chaudhary, S., Panwar, R., Sharma, S., & Kumar, P. (2023). Advanced Technologies and AI-Enabled IoT Applications in High-Tech Agriculture. In Handbook of Research on AI-Equipped IoT Applications in High-Tech Agriculture (pp. 155-166). IGI Global. doi:10.4018/978-1-6684-9231-4.ch008

Vashishth, T. K., Sharma, V., Sharma, K. K., Kumar, B., Panwar, R., & Chaudhary, S. (2024). AI-Driven Learning Analytics for Personalized Feedback and Assessment in Higher Education. In Using Traditional Design Methods to Enhance AI-Driven Decision Making (pp. 206-230). IGI Global.

Vashishth, T. K., Kumar, B., Sharma, V., Chaudhary, S., Kumar, S., & Sharma, K. K. (2023). The Evolution of AI and Its Transformative Effects on Computing: A Comparative Analysis. In B. Mishra (Ed.), *Intelligent Engineering Applications and Applied Sciences for Sustainability* (pp. 425–442). IGI Global. doi:10.4018/979-8-3693-0044-2.ch022

Vastag, G., & Yerushalmy, M. (2009). Automating Serious Games. Springer Handbook of Automation, 1299-1311. doi:10.1007/978-3-540-78831-7_73

VentureBeat. (2021, August). *Microsoft details AI model designed to improve Bing search.* https://venturebeat.com/business/microsoft-details-ai-model-designed-to-improve-bing-search/

Viberg, O., Khalil, M., & Baars, M. (2020). Self-regulated learning and learning analytics in online learning environments. *Proceedings of the Tenth International Conference on Learning Analytics & Knowledge*, 524–533. 10.1145/3375462.3375483

Vigotsky, L. S. (1939). Thought and speech. *Psychiatry*, 2(1), 29–54. doi:10.1080/00332747.1939.11022225

Villegas-Ch, W., Molina-Enriquez, J., Chicaiza-Tamayo, C., Ortiz-Garcés, I., & Luján-Mora, S. (2019). Application of a big data framework for data monitoring on a smart campus. *Sustainability*, 11(20), 5552.

Vinutha, D. C., Kavyashree, S., Vijay, C. P., & Raju, G. T. (2022). Innovative Practices in Education Systems Using Artificial Intelligence for Advanced Society. *The New Advanced Society: Artificial Intelligence and Industrial Internet of Things Paradigm*, 351-372.

Walia, J. S., & Kumar, P. (2022). Tech transition: An exploratory study on educators' AI awareness. *International Journal of Virtual and Personal Learning Environments*, 12(1), 1–17. doi:10.4018/IJVPLE.295310

Wang, A. I., & Lieberoth, A. (2016). *The effect of points and audio on concentration, engagement, enjoyment, learning, motivation, and classroom dynamics using Kahoot.* Paper presented at the European conference on games based learning.

Wang, S., Wang, G., Chen, X., Wang, W., & Ding, X. (2021). A Review of Content Analysis on China Artificial Intelligence (AI) Education Policies. *Artificial Intelligence in Education and Teaching Assessment*, 1-8. doi:10.1007/978-981-16-6502-8_1

Wang, D., Tao, Y., & Chen, G. (2024). Artificial intelligence in classroom discourse: A systematic review of the past decade. *International Journal of Educational Research*, *123*, 102275. doi:10.1016/j.ijer.2023.102275

Wang, H., Liu, N., Zhang, Y., Feng, D., Huang, F., Li, D., & Zhang, Y. (2020). Deep reinforcement learning: A survey. *Frontiers of Information Technology & Electronic Engineering*, *21*(12), 1726–1744. doi:10.1631/FITEE.1900533

Wang, T., Lund, B. D., Marengo, A., Pagano, A., Mannuru, N. R., Teel, Z. A., & Pange, J. (2023). Exploring the Potential Impact of Artificial Intelligence (AI) on International Students in Higher Education: Generative AI, Chatbots, Analytics, and International Student Success. *Applied Sciences (Basel, Switzerland)*, *13*(11), 6716. doi:10.3390/app13116716

Wang, X., Li, L., Tan, S. C., Yang, L., & Lei, J. (2023). Preparing for AI-enhanced education: Conceptualizing and empirically examining teachers' AI readiness. *Computers in Human Behavior*, *146*, 107798. doi:10.1016/j.chb.2023.107798

Wang, Y. (2020). When artificial intelligence meets educational leaders' data-informed decision-making: A cautionary tale. *Studies in Educational Evaluation*.

Wartman, S. A., & Combs, C. D. (2018). Medical education must move from the information age to the age of artificial intelligence. *Academic Medicine*, *93*(8), 1107–1109. doi:10.1097/ACM.0000000000002044 PMID:29095704

Wei, J., Marimuthu, K., & Prathik, A. (2022). College music education and teaching based on AI techniques. *Computers & Electrical Engineering*, *100*, 107851. Advance online publication. doi:10.1016/j.compeleceng.2022.107851

Weng, C., Chen, C., & Ai, X. (2023). A pedagogical study on promoting students' deep learning through design-based learning. *International Journal of Technology and Design Education*, *33*(4), 1653–1674. Advance online publication. doi:10.1007/s10798-022-09789-4 PMID:36466720

Whizz Education. (2014). *Math whizz*. Author.

Wiburg, K. (2003). Technology and the new meaning of educational equity. *Computers in the Schools*, *20*(1-2), 113–128. doi:10.1300/J025v20n01_09

Wilkinson, M. D., Dumontier, M., Aalbersberg, I. J., Appleton, G., Axton, M., Baak, A., Blomberg, N., Boiten, J.-W., da Silva Santos, L. B., Bourne, P. E., Bouwman, J., Brookes, A. J., Clark, T., Crosas, M., Dillo, I., Dumon, O., Edmunds, S., Evelo, C. T., Finkers, R., ... Mons, B. (2016). The FAIR Guiding Principles for scientific data management and stewardship. *Scientific Data*, *3*(1), 1–9. doi:10.1038/sdata.2016.18 PMID:26978244

Williams, J. J., Kim, J., Rafferty, A., Maldonado, S., Gajos, K. Z., Lasecki, W. S., & Heffernan, N. (2016). AXIS: Generating Explanations at Scale with Learnersourcing and Machine Learning. *Proceedings of the Third (2016) ACM Conference on Learning @ Scale*, 379–388. 10.1145/2876034.2876042

Williamson, B. (2018). The hidden architecture of higher education: Building a big data infrastructure for the 'smarter university'. *International Journal of Educational Technology in Higher Education*, *15*, 1–26.

Williamson, B., Eynon, R., & Potter, J. (2020). Pandemic politics, pedagogies and practices: Digital technologies and distance education during the coronavirus emergency. *Learning, Media and Technology*, *45*(2), 107–114. doi:10.1080/17439884.2020.1761641

Wisdom, J. (2006). Developing higher education teachers to teach creatively. In N. Jackson, M. Oliver, M. Shaw, & J. Wisdom (Eds.), *Developing Creativity in Higher Education* (pp. 183–197). Routledge.

Witkin, H. A., Moore, C. A., Goodenough, D., & Cox, P. W. (1977). Field-Dependent and Field-Independent Cognitive Styles and Their Educational Implications. *Review of Educational Research*, *47*(1), 1–64. doi:10.3102/00346543047001001

Woebot Health. (n.d.). Retrieved from https://woebothealth.com/

Wogu, I. A. P., Misra, S., Olu-Owolabi, E. F., Assibong, P. A., & Udoh, O. D. (2018). Artificial intelligence, artificial teachers and the fate of learners in the 21st century education sector: Implications for theory and practice. *International Journal of Pure and Applied Mathematics, 119*(16), 2245–2259.

Wogu, I., Misra, S., Assibong, P., Olu-Owolabi, E. F., Maskeliunas, R., & Dama-sevicius, R. (2019). Artificial intelligence, smart classrooms and online education in the 21st century: Implications for human development. *Journal of Cases on Information Technology, 21*(3), 66–79. doi:10.4018/JCIT.2019070105

World Health Organization. (2020). Digital technology for COVID-19 response. *World Health Organization*. https://www.who.int/news-room/detail/03-04-2020-digital-technology-for-covid-19-response

Wouters, P., van Nimwegen, C., van Oostendorp, H., & van der Spek, E. D. (2013). A meta-analysis of the cognitive and motivational effects of serious games. *Journal of Educational Psychology, 105*(2), 249–265. doi:10.1037/a0031311

Wysa. (n.d.). Retrieved from https://www.wysa.com/

Xie, T., Liu, R., Chen, Y., & Liu, G. (2021). MOCA: A motivational online conversational agent for improving student engagement in collaborative learning. *IEEE Transactions on Learning Technologies, 14*(5), 653–664. doi:10.1109/TLT.2021.3129800

Xi, S. M. (2013). Application of natural language processing for information retrieval. *Applied Mechanics and Materials, 380*, 2614–2618. doi:10.4028/www.scientific.net/AMM.380-384.2614

Xue, R., & Wu, Z. (2019). A survey of application and classification on teaching-learning-based optimization algorithm. *IEEE Access : Practical Innovations, Open Solutions, 8*, 1062–1079. doi:10.1109/ACCESS.2019.2960388

Xu, J. J., & Babaian, T. (2021). Artificial intelligence in business curriculum: The pedagogy and learning outcomes. *International Journal of Management Education, 19*(3), 100550. doi:10.1016/j.ijme.2021.100550

Xu, J., Moon, K. H., & Van Der Schaar, M. (2017). A machine learning approach for tracking and predicting student performance in degree programs. *IEEE Journal of Selected Topics in Signal Processing, 11*(5), 742–753. doi:10.1109/JSTSP.2017.2692560

Xu, L. (2020). The dilemma and countermeasures of AI in educational application. In *Proceedings of the 2020 4th International Conference on Computer Science and Artificial Intelligence* (pp. 289-294). 10.1145/3445815.3445863

Xu, W., & Ouyang, F. (2022). The application of AI technologies in STEM education: A systematic review from 2011 to 2021. *International Journal of STEM Education, 9*(1), 1–20. doi:10.1186/s40594-022-00377-5

Yachen, W. (2022). Application of AI-Enhanced Analytic Hierarchy Process in the Online PHP System. *6th International Conference on I-SMAC (IoT in Social, Mobile, Analytics and Cloud), I-SMAC 2022 - Proceedings.*

Yang, T. C., Hwang, G. J., & Yang, S. J. H. (2013). *Development of an Adaptive Learning System with Multiple Perspectives based on Students' Learning Styles and Cognitive Styles*. https://www.researchgate.net/publication/279764849

Yang, X., Zhou, G., Taub, M., Azevedo, R., & Chi, M. (n.d.). *Student Subtyping via EM-Inverse Reinforcement Learning*. Academic Press.

Yang, J., & Zhang, B. (2019). Artificial Intelligence in Intelligent Tutoring Robots: A Systematic Review and Design Guidelines. *Applied Sciences (Basel, Switzerland), 9*(10), 2078.

Yang, X., Wang, Q., & Lyu, J. (2023). *Assessing chatgpt's educational capabilities and application potential*. ECNU Review of Education.

Yau, K.-L. A., Lee, H. J., Chong, Y.-W., Ling, M. H., Syed, A. R., Wu, C., & Goh, H. G. (2021). Augmented intelligence: Surveys of literature and expert opinion to understand relations between human intelligence and artificial intelligence. *IEEE Access : Practical Innovations, Open Solutions, 9*, 136744–136761. doi:10.1109/ACCESS.2021.3115494

Yi, H. (2019). Robotics and kinetic design for underrepresented minority (URM) students in building education: Challenges and opportunities. *Computer Applications in Engineering Education, 27*(2), 351–370. doi:10.1002/cae.22080

Younis, H. A., Ruhaiyem, N. I. R., Ghaban, W., Gazem, N. A., & Nasser, M. (2023). A Systematic Literature Review on the Applications of Robots and Natural Language Processing in Education. *Electronics (Basel), 12*(13), 2864. doi:10.3390/electronics12132864

Yu, H., Liu, Z., & Guo, Y. (2023, April). application Status, Problems and Future Prospects of Generative ai in education. In *2023 5th International Conference on Computer Science and Technologies in Education (CSTE)* (pp. 1-7). IEEE.

Yu, S., & Lu, Y. (2021). *An introduction to artificial intelligence in education.* Springer.

Yufei, L., Saleh, S., Jiahui, H., & Abdullah, S. M. S. (2020). Review of the application of artificial intelligence in education. *International Journal of Innovation. Creativity and Change, 12*(8), 548–562.

Yulianto, S. F., & Haya, F. (2023). Study of AI and Technology as a Substitute for the Presence of a Teacher Learning the Qur'an Hadith in Bond of Knowledge Perspective. *International Conference on Education, 1*, 433–442.

Zaimah, N. R., Hartanto, E. B., & Zahro, F. (2024). Acceptability and Effectiveness Analysis of Large Language Model-Based Artificial Intelligence Chatbot Among Arabic Learners. *Mantiqu Tayr: Journal of Arabic Language, 4*(1), 1–20. doi:10.25217/mantiqutayr.v4i1.3951

Zaman, B. U. (2023). *Transforming Education Through AI.* Benefits, Risks, and Ethical Considerations.

Zare, J., Karimpour, S., & Aqajani Delavar, K. (2023). Classroom concordancing and English academic lecture comprehension: An implication of data-driven learning. *Computer Assisted Language Learning, 36*(5-6), 885–905. doi:10.1080/09588221.2021.1953081

Zawacki-Richter, O., Marín, V. I., Bond, M., & Gouverneur, F. (2019). Systematic review of research on artificial intelligence applications in higher education–where are the educators? *International Journal of Educational Technology in Higher Education, 16*(1), 1–27. doi:10.1186/s41239-019-0171-0

Zhang, L., & Zhou, Y. (2021). *Education Informatization: An Effective Way to Promote Educational Equity.* Paper presented at the 2020 International Conference on Data Processing Techniques and Applications for Cyber-Physical Systems: DPTA 2020. 10.1007/978-981-16-1726-3_103

Zhang, K., & Aslan, A. B. (2021). AI technologies for education: Recent research & future directions. *Computers and Education: Artificial Intelligence, 2*, 100025. doi:10.1016/j.caeai.2021.100025

Zhang, K., Yang, Z., & Başar, T. (2021). Decentralized multi-agent reinforcement learning with networked agents: Recent advances. *Frontiers of Information Technology & Electronic Engineering, 22*(6), 802–814. doi:10.1631/FITEE.1900661

Zhang, L., Wu, M., & Ouyang, F. (2023). The design and implementation of a teaching and learning analytics tool in a face-to-face, small-sized course in China's higher education. *Education and Information Technologies*, 1–24. doi:10.1007/s10639-023-11940-0

Zhao, T. (2023). *AI in Educational Technology.* Academic Press.

Zhao, X., Ren, Y., & Cheah, K. S. (2023). Leading Virtual Reality (VR) and Augmented Reality (AR) in Education: Bibliometric and Content Analysis From the Web of Science (2018–2022). *SAGE Open, 13*(3). doi:10.1177/21582440231190821

Zheng, Y., & Chen, Y. (2020). Construction and implementation of blended teaching ecology based on cloud class. In *2020 IEEE 2nd International Conference on Computer Science and Educational Informatization (CSEI)* (pp. 292-295). IEEE. 10.1109/CSEI50228.2020.9142492

Zhou, J., Li, P., Zhou, Y., Wang, B., Zang, J., & Meng, L. (2018). Toward new-generation intelligent manufacturing. *Engineering (Beijing)*, *4*(1), 11–20. doi:10.1016/j.eng.2018.01.002

Zhou, X. (2020). Application research of face recognition technology in smart campus. *Journal of Physics: Conference Series*, *1437*(1), 012130.

Zipitria, I., Arruarte, A., & Elorriaga, J. (2013). Discourse measures for Basque summary grading. *Interactive Learning Environments*, *21*(6), 528–547. doi:10.1080/10494820.2011.606503

Zirar, A. (2023). Exploring the impact of language models, such as chatgpt, on student learning and assessment. *Review of Education*, *11*(3), e3433. doi:10.1002/rev3.3433

About the Contributors

Zeinab E. Ahmed received her Ph.D. in Computer Engineering and Networks from the University of Gezira, Sudan. Dr. Zeinab has been working as an assistant professor in the Department of Computer Engineering at the University of Gezira, Sudan since June 2020. Currently, she is working as a postdoc fellow at the Department of Electrical and Computer Engineering, International Islamic University Malaysia, Malaysia. Dr. Zeinab has served as Head of the Department of Computer Engineering, Faculty of Engineering Technology, and the University of Gezira, Sudan. I've been engaged in some projects related to the field of computer engineering and networks. She has published more than eight research papers and book chapters on networking in peer-reviewed academic venues. Her areas of research interest are wireless communication networks. An experienced lecturer with a demonstrated history of working in the higher education industry. She is skilled in research, e-learning, programming, and lecturing.

Aisha A. Hassan received her Ph.D in Computer Engineering (2007), M.Sc. in Computer Science (1996) and B.Sc. in Electronics Engineering (1990). She won the Best Graduating Ph.D Student Award during the IIUM Convocation ceremony in 2007. She joined IIUM in 1997 and is currently a Professor at the Department of Electrical and Computer Engineering. Professor Aisha has taught several courses related to Communication and Computer Engineering and is actively involved in curriculum development and programme accreditation. She has been a member of the Department Board of Studies for several years. She received the Best Teacher Award during IIUM Quality Day in 2007. Prof. Aisha has been appointed as external examiner/visiting professor/adjunct professor at different universities. Professor Aisha who is actively involved in research and postgraduate programmes, has published more than 200 journal/conference papers, and supervised/co-supervised more than 40 Ph.D/Master's students. She received the Promising Researcher Award in 2009 during IIUM Quality Day. She has also received many medals/awards in different national/international research exhibitions. One of her research exhibitions won the Promising Commercial Value Award (Second Runner Up) in IRIIE 2014. As a researcher, she has secured research grants from IIUM, Ministry of Higher Education (MOHE) and Ministry of Science, Technology and Innovation (MOSTI). She has actively contributed as a reviewer /technical committee member in many journals/conferences. Professor Aisha has established several teaching/ research networks between IIUM and overseas universities. She has been appointed as IIUMÂ Internationalisation Ambassador to Sudan (October 2014) and has participated in initiating several MoUs as well as encouraging the PhD Student Mobility programme between IIUM and Sudanese Universities. Professor Aisha also participates in community services. She was appointed as a Board of Studies member at the International Islamic School, Malaysia. She also served as Parent/Teacher Committee member at the school for more than 10 years.

Rashid A. Saeed obtained a Ph.D. from Universiti Putra Malaysia (UPM) in Communications Network Engineering. Currently, he holds positions as a professor in the Computer Engineering Department at Taif University and is also in the Electronics Department at the Sudan University of Science and Technology (SUST). His professional experience extends beyond academia, having served as a senior researcher in Telekom Malaysia™ Research and Development (TMRND) and MIMOS. Additionally, he has held significant administrative roles, including Deputy Director of the Scientific Research and Innovation Directorate at the Ministry of Higher Education and Scientific Research, Sudan, and Deputy Dean for Scientific Research at SUST. Prof. Rashid has made substantial contributions to research with over 200 publications, including research papers, books, and book chapters, focusing on wireless communications and networking. His research interests primarily revolve around wireless communication networks, and he holds 13 patents in related areas. Prof. Rashid has supervised more than 50 MSc and Ph.D. students. He is recognized for his professional affiliations, including Senior Membership in IEEE and memberships in IEM (I.E.M), SigmaXi, and SEC. Furthermore, Prof. Rashid plays an active role in organizing conferences and serving on editorial boards. He is the co-founder and Technical Committee Chair (TPC) of the International Conference on Computing, Electrical, and Electronics Engineering (ICCEEE) in Sudan and has served as General Chair for EAI AFRICOMM from 2022 to 2024. He also serves as an editorial board member for the Journal of Advances in Computer Sciences and as an editor for Scientific African (SCIAF) journal, in addition to his role as a guest editor for various journals.

* * *

Mussa S. Abubakari is a Ph.D. in Education candidate at Sultan Hassanal Bolkiah Institute of Education, Universiti Brunei Darussalam, and is expected to graduate in August 2025. Before this, in 2022, he used to be an instructor in the Department of Physics and Mathematics at Kondoa Islamic Secondary School, Tanzania. Mr. Mussa obtained a Master's degree of Education in Electronics and Informatics Engineering at Yogyakarta State University, Indonesia, in July 2021. Moreover, he obtained his BSc. in Telecommunications Engineering at the University of Dodoma in June 2016. His academic and research interests include educational technology, technology-enhanced learning, technology acceptance, open and distance (online) learning, and digital competence, among others. He has over 13 journal articles published in internationally indexed journals and papers presented at international conferences.

Zain Balfagih holds a PhD in Computer and Information Technology from Universiti Teknologi PETRONAS Malaysia (2013) and specializes in Service Oriented Architecture (SOA), Cloud computing, and wireless networking. His current focus includes Big data and Internet of Things (IoT), particularly in developing mechanisms for utilizing IoT for water and energy applications. Additionally, he conducts research on identifying obstacles hindering the adoption of these technologies in Middle Eastern countries and seeks solutions to address these challenges. Dr. Zain has a background as a researcher in various Malaysian universities before joining Effat University in 2012, where he currently serves as the Chair of the Computer Science Department.

Mohammed Balfaqih received the Ph.D. degree in electrical, electronics, and systems engineering from Universiti Kebangsaan Malaysia, Malaysia. He is currently an Assistant Professor with the Department of Computer and Network Engineering, University of Jeddah, Saudi Arabia. He has published several journals and conference papers and patents. His principal research interests include wireless communication, mobility management, the IoT, and artificial intelligence.

Komal Bhardwaj is currently working at Maharishi Markandeshwar Institute of Management, Maharishi Markandeshwar Univeristy as Assistant Professor of Finance. She has a rich experience of more than 8 years of teaching in the field of Management. She has a research experience in the areas of Assets Pricing, Derivatives, Option Pricing and study on stock volatility. Her research interest includes consumer behavior, investments, corporate governance, and assets liability management. She also worked as a Thesis Supervisor for a program called upgrad-LJMU MBA at upgrade education private limited.

Sachin Chaudhary completed his Graduation from MJPRU, and Post Graduation from AKTU, Moradabad, U.P. Currently Pursuing his Ph.D. in Computer Science and Engineering from Govt. Recognized University. Presently, he is working as an Assistant Professor in the Department of Computer Science and Applications, IIMT University, Meerut, U.P, India. He has been awarded as Excellence in teaching award 2019. He is the reviewer member of some reputed journals. He has published several book chapters and research papers of national and international reputed journals.

Reccia Cummings is from Trinidad and Tobago with over 15 years of experience in the field of Information and Communications Technology (ICT), embarked on a new chapter of her career in St. Eustatius in 2023. Before her relocation, she served as the Information Systems Specialist at the International School of Port of Spain, where she honed her expertise in managing and optimising educational technologies. In her current role as an ICT Teacher at the Gwendoline Van Putten Secondary School, Ms. Cummings continues to expand her impact on the field of education through direct student engagement. Ms. Cummings' profound commitment to leveraging technology in education goes beyond her professional duties, which significantly influences her work environment and helps to establish new standards for the integration of technology in teaching and learning. Her forward-thinking approach, combined with a relentless dedication to advancing her knowledge and skills, marks her as a leading figure in integrating technology in the classroom. As she continues to make strides in educational technology, Ms. Cummings' influence is evident in the enriched learning experiences of her students.

Salaheldin M. I. Edam received his PhD in engineering in communications and information systems from the Beijing University of Posts and Telecommunications (BUPT), china, the M.Sc. degrees from the Sudan University of Science & Technology (SUST), Khartoum, Sudan, & the Postgraduate Diploma in Information Technology (Advanced Networking & Telecommunications) from the International Institute of Information Technology (I2IT), Pune, India, & the B.Sc. degree in electronics engineering from the Sudan University of Science and Technology (SUST). He used to be an Engineer at Sudan Telecommunication Company (Sudatel). He is currently an Assistant Professor with the School of Electronics Engineering, SUST. He supervised many M.Sc. students in addition to co-supervisor for many Ph.D. students. He published many research papers in journals and conferences. His research interests include wireless communications, software-defined networking, the IoT, WSNs, computer network systems, and an applications of artificial intelligence in communications.

Abdul Guddoos Gaid earned his B. Eng. in Electronics Engineering from Sudan University for Science and Technology (SUST) in 2000, followed by a master's degree and PhD in Electrical, Electronics, and Systems Engineering in 2004 and 2010 respectively, both from University Kebangsaan Malaysia (UKM). He served as a lecturer at Taylor's University from Sep 2010 to Aug 2012 and joined Taiz University in Sep 2012, where he continues his work. Dr. Gaid's research focuses on microstrip antennas, wireless communications, and he also has a keen interest in Engineering Education.

Ahmad Fathan Hidayatullah is an assistant professor at the Department of Informatics, Faculty of Industrial Engineering, Universitas Islam Indonesia. He is currently pursuing his PhD in Computer Science Programme, School of Digital Science, Universiti Brunei Darussalam with The UBD Graduate Scholarship (UGS). He earned his Master's degree in computer science (M.Cs.) from Universitas Gadjah Mada, Indonesia, in 2014. Previously, he completed his Bachelor's degree (B. Eng) in Informatics in 2010 from Universitas Islam Negeri Sunan Kalijaga Yogyakarta, Indonesia. His research interests are mainly related to text mining, natural language processing, and data science. He is also actively involved in several research in Center of Data Science, Universitas Islam Indonesia.

Bhupendra Kumar completed his Graduation and Post Graduation from Chaudhary Charan Singh University, Meerut, U.P. and Ph.D. in Computer Science and Engineering from Mewar University, Hapur. Presently, he is working as a Professor in the Department of Computer Science and Applications, IIMT University, Meerut, U.P. He has been a huge teaching experience of 19 years. He is the reviewer member of some reputed journals. He has published several book chapters and research papers of national and international reputed journals.

Hélder Fanha Martins currently holds the position of Full Professor at the Lisbon Accounting and Business School, part of the Polytechnic University of Lisbon (LABS-ISCAL). Furthermore, he is an Integrated Researcher affiliated with CETAPS at NOVA University of Lisbon. With a doctoral degree conferred by Nova University (UNL), Professor Martins has dedicated his research endeavours to the fields of Business Simulation Studies, Languages for Specific Purposes, and Computer-Assisted Language Learning. He serves on the editorial boards of multiple academic journals. Within LABS-ISCAL, he is responsible for overseeing the Department of Information and Communication Sciences and spearheads the International Business Simulation course.

Rania Mokhtar (IEEE member since 2003) received the B.Sc. degree in Electronics Engineering (Computer Engineering) from the Sudan University of Science & Technology (SUST), Khartoum, Sudan, in 2001, & the Postgraduate Diploma in Information Technology (Advanced Networking & Telecommunications) from the International Institute of Information Technology (I2IT), Pune, India, in 2003, & the M.Sc. & PhD. degrees from the University Putra Malaysia (UPM), Kuala Lumpur, Malaysia, in 2005 & 2010, respectively. In May 2009, she earned the IEEE Wireless Communication Professional (IEEE WCP) certificate of the Wireless Communication Engineering Technology (WCET) Exam. Currently, she is an associate professor and Director, Electronics System Research Centre, Faculty of Engineering, Sudan University of Science and Technology, Khartoum, Sudan. She has been award Elsevier Foundation Award for women in Engineering in 2017. She published over 30 scientific papers and two books.

Shahinaz Osman is an Associate Professor of Educational Technology with 16 years of experience in higher education teaching, research, and administration. Skilled in integrating technology into education, certified as a Google trainer and Microsoft master trainer. Demonstrated leadership as the Chair of the Global Collaboration PLN at the International Society for Technology in Education (ISTE) and as a Google Educator Group leader. Committed to sustainable development goals in education and fostering digital skills. Strong background in curriculum development, instructional design, and online learning. Accomplished in mentoring students and faculty, contributing to research and innovation, and actively participating in professional networks. Adept at delivering engaging and impactful training programs.

Rajneesh Panwar graduated and post graduated in Mathematics and Computer Application from Ch. Charan Singh University, Meerut (U.P.) and received his M. Tech. in Computer Science from Shobhit University, Meerut. Presently, he is working as an Assistant Professor in the School of Computer Science and Application IIMT University, Meerut, U.P. He qualifies GATE 2021 and UGC-NET June 2020 and December 2020. He has published several book chapters and research papers of national and international repute.

Mehdy Roayaei received his B.S., M.S., and Ph.D. in Computer Engineering from Amirkabir University of Technology (AUT) in 2008, 2010, 2016. He is currently an Assistant Professor of Computer Engineering at Tarbiat Modares University. He is interested in using reinforcement learning approaches for handling complex problems in real-world environments.

Leesha Roberts is an Assistant Professor at the Center of Education Programmes at The University of Trinidad and Tobago. With twenty-two years of experience in education and computing, she currently leads as the Discipline Leader for Educational Technology and Instructional Design subjects for the University's undergraduate and postgraduate programs. Her research focuses on ICT integration in the Caribbean and Management Information Systems (MIS), where she supervises postgraduate students' research in these areas. She began her career in the public service, particularly at the Ministry of Education, from 2002 to 2006, where her responsibilities included leading projects to implement technology-based solutions. Her work involved acquiring, evaluating, and implementing ICTs in primary schools throughout Trinidad and Tobago, designing and developing the initial Ministry's website, and re-engineering the I.T. unit to align with the government's Vision 2020 Plan. She also contributed to database design and implementation, processing local examinations, and the ICT Help Desk for the Ministry of Education. She has also participated in various Ministry of Education international and regional programmes such as PIRLS, TIMSS, and Microsoft Partners in Learning. Additionally, Leesha has trained staff and lectured extensively on various ICT-related subjects at institutions like the National Energy Skill Center, COSTAATT, and The University of the West Indies Global Campus. She holds a Ph.D. in Education focused on ICT integration and instructional design. Her work aims to equip students with the necessary technology integration skills for teaching and learning while contributing to research in ICT integration at the educational level in Trinidad and Tobago and the Caribbean.

Mamoon Mohammed Ali Saeed is Deputy Dean of the College of Engineering and Information Technology, and Director of the University Branch, and a Lecturer at the Department of Communication and Electronics Engineering, UMS University, Yemen. received his Bachelor's degree in Communication and Electronics Engineering from Sana'a University, Yemen 2005, and his M.S. degree from the Department of Computer Networks and Information Security in Yemen Academy for Graduate Studies Yemen 2013. Recently, a Ph.D. in Alzaiem Alazhari University, Faculty of Engineering, Electrical Engineering Department, Khartoum, Sudan 2021. His research areas include information security, communication security, and network security.

Wasswa Shafik is a remarkable computer scientist, information technologist, and educator, hails from the vibrant capital city of Uganda, Kampala. His passion extends beyond technology, encompassing people's health, justice, and the responsible use of technological advancements, regardless of race, religion, or sex. With a strong educational background, he holds a bachelor's degree in information technology engineering with a minor in mathematics from Ndejje University, Uganda. He further pursued a master of engineering degree in information technology engineering (MIT) with a computer and communication network option from Yazd University, Iran, and a PhD in Computer Science at Universiti Brunei Darussalam, Brunei Darussalam. As a member of the IEEE, Shafik has made significant contributions in various domains such as smart agriculture, health informatics, computer vision, network science, and security and privacy. His passion for sustainable solutions and his deep understanding of the health and environmental challenges we face today have propelled him to the forefront of sustainable measures. Shafik's interest extends to Smart Cities, where he investigates the intersection of Big Data, IoT, and Artificial Intelligence. His work delves into energy management, privacy, and performance evaluation in the context of Internet of Things (IoT) applications within smart urban environments. Additionally, Shafik explores fog computing architectures, privacy, and security solutions. His work also encompasses the evaluation and analysis of fog-mobile edge performance in IoT scenarios. Wasswa's expertise extends to artificial intelligence and its application in cybersecurity and cyberdefense. He reviews the theoretical understanding of deep learning in the context of analysis of UAV biomedical engineering technologies. He has published more than 80 research articles, book sections, and conferences in many reputed journals, including Scopus Q1, Q2, and SCI in different publishers. He served as departmental support for Mathematics for Data Science, Advanced Topics in Computing, and Advanced Algorithms at the School of Digital Science, Universiti Brunei Darussalam. He served in different capacities, including a community data officer at Pace-Uganda, research associate at TechnoServe, research assistant at PSI-Uganda, research lead at Socio-economic Data Center (SEDC-Uganda), research lab head at the Dig Connectivity Research Laboratory (DCRLab), Kampala, Uganda, and ag. managing director at Asmaah Charity Organisation. Shafik's journey is one of curiosity, innovation, and a deep-rooted desire to positively impact the world through technology, education, and sustainability.

Kewal Krishan Sharma is a professor in computer sc. in IIMT University, Meerut, U.P, India. He did his Ph.D. in computer network with this he has MCA, MBA and Law degree also. He did variously certification courses also. He has an overall experience of around 33 year in academic, business and industry. He wrote a number of research papers and books.

Vikas Sharma completed his Graduation and Post Graduation from Chaudhary Charan Singh University, Meerut, U.P. Currently Pursuing his Ph.D. in Computer Science and Engineering from Govt. Recognized University. Presently, he is working as an Assistant Professor in the Department of Computer Science and Applications, IIMT University, Meerut, U.P. He has been awarded as Excellence in teaching award 2019. He is the reviewer member of some reputed journals. He has published several book chapters and research papers of national and international reputed journals.

Tatjana Sidekerskienė obtained a Bachelor of Science degree in Mathematics from the Faculty of Fundamental Sciences at Kaunas University of Technology (KTU) in Kaunas, Lithuania, in 2003. She went on to complete her Master of Science studies in 2006. She is presently employed as a Lecturer at the Department of Applied Mathematics at KTU, where she teaches mathematics courses. Her primary research interest was in the field of time series analysis. Currently, her research is focused on STEAM education. Tatjana Sidekerskienė has achieved notable success, having won the internal competition twice for her contributions to enhancing the quality of education and promoting innovative teaching practices at the Kaunas University of Technology.

Fanta Solomon from Trinidad and Tobago, holds a diverse academic background and professional experience, shaping her into a multifaceted educator and researcher in the fields of environmental science and educational technology. With a passion for both environmental sustainability and innovative learning methodologies, Ms. Solomon has dedicated her career to fostering knowledge and understanding in these critical areas. After obtaining her Bachelor's degree in Biology with minors in Chemistry and Psychology, Ms. Solomon pursued further education, earning a Master's degree in Environmental Science Management. This academic journey deepened her understanding of environmental issues and equipped her with the knowledge to develop effective strategies for environmental conservation and sustainability. Driven by a desire to integrate technology into education and enhance learning experiences for her son, Ms. Solomon pursued a second Master's degree in Education and Educational Technology. This interdisciplinary background uniquely positions her at the intersection of environmental science and education, allowing her to explore innovative approaches to teaching and learning. Ms. Solomon's career in education spans over twelve years, during which she served as both a primary and secondary school educator. Her dedication to teaching has left a lasting impact on countless students, instilling in them a passion for environmental stewardship and digital literacy. As a researcher, Ms. Solomon's interests encompass environmental management and planning, e-learning methodologies, and digital citizenship. Currently, Ms. Solomon serves as a Learning Systems Manager, where she oversees the implementation of educational technologies and digital learning platforms. In addition to her administrative role, she also teaches classes in Information and Communication Technologies (ICT) and Human Social Biology (HSB), at the secondary school level. Ms. Solomon's commitment to education, environmental sustainability, and technological innovation continues to drive her work, as she strives to create meaningful learning experiences and contribute to positive change in both the educational and environmental spheres.

Tarun Kumar Vashishth is an active academician and researcher in the field of computer science with 22 years of experience. He earned Ph.D. Mathematics degree specialized in Operations Research; served several academic positions such as HoD, Dy. Director, Academic Coordinator, Member Secretary of Department Research Committee, Assistant Center superintendent and Head Examiner in university examinations. He is involved in academic development and scholarly activities. He is member of International Association of Engineers, The Society of Digital Information and Wireless Communications, Global Professors Welfare Association, International Association of Academic plus Corporate (IAAC), Computer Science Teachers Association and Internet Society. His research interest includes Cloud Computing, Artificial Intelligence, Machine Learning and Operations Research; published more than 25 research articles with 2 books and 15 book chapters in edited books. He is contributing as member of editorial and reviewers boards in conferences and various computer journals published by CRC Press, Taylor and Francis, Springer, IGI global and other universities.

Index

21st-Century Learning 269, 284, 322, 327, 344

A

Adaptive Assessments 36, 62, 77, 102, 203, 240, 244, 263-264, 327
Adaptive Educational Systems 177-178, 187, 193
Adaptive Learning 3, 6-8, 18, 25-26, 31-32, 37, 40-41, 43-44, 48, 61-62, 66-68, 82, 89, 92-94, 97, 100-102, 108-109, 113-115, 125, 132, 136, 146, 148, 153-154, 162-163, 172, 177, 179-180, 182, 186-191, 198-200, 202, 206-208, 211-213, 225, 230, 234, 240, 244-245, 249, 263, 284, 291-292, 297, 299, 306, 313, 323, 326, 330, 332, 341, 344
Adaptive Learning Platforms 6, 61, 67-68, 101, 113, 153-154, 172, 198-200, 207, 211-213, 225, 234, 240, 249, 263, 299, 330
Adaptive Learning Systems 25, 31-32, 43, 62, 67, 89, 100, 109, 114-115, 125, 136, 146, 148, 163, 188, 190, 206-207, 230, 323, 332, 341
AI Assessments 273, 276, 278-279, 293
AI Ethics 121, 298
AI Feedback 272
AI Integration 18, 38, 46, 66, 89, 91, 108, 110, 115, 117, 132, 153, 221, 223-224, 227, 229, 233-234, 240, 256, 268, 272, 308, 315, 340
AI-Assisted Assessment and Feedback Systems 61
AI-Assisted Education 279, 284
AI-Driven 1, 3-5, 11, 15, 17, 19, 25-26, 30, 36, 41, 46-47, 65, 71-73, 88-91, 93-94, 97, 102, 109-111, 113, 115-116, 122-125, 136, 147-148, 150, 153-154, 198-200, 203-204, 209, 211-213, 218, 225-226, 228-230, 233-234, 247, 250, 260, 263, 270, 276, 279, 284, 312, 316-317, 323, 326, 328-331, 333-334, 338, 341-342
AI-Efficacy 284
AI-Powered Education 35, 152
Algorithmic Bias 16, 78, 96, 134, 172, 203, 209, 293
Artifacts 160, 292

Artificial Intelligence (AI) 1, 25-26, 28-30, 32, 35-44, 46, 48, 61, 63-67, 89, 91-93, 96-98, 100-101, 108, 125, 132, 134, 136-137, 143, 145, 147-148, 151, 160-167, 169-172, 177, 179, 198-200, 202-204, 211-213, 215-217, 220, 225, 240-242, 246, 248, 251-252, 257-260, 263, 267, 269, 273, 277-278, 284, 286-288, 291-293, 296-300, 305-306, 308, 311-313, 322-331, 333-338, 340, 342, 344, 346
Assessment Automation 43, 132, 146, 155
Augmented Reality (AR) 15, 34, 62, 80, 82-83, 96-97, 100, 109, 118, 132, 139, 149, 163, 212, 215, 225, 272, 292, 327, 330, 334, 336-337, 346

B

Bias in AI 203, 280, 299, 314
Business Education 305, 307-318
Business Leadership 305-306
Business Simulations 305-307, 309-311, 314-317

C

Chatbots 1, 3, 89, 93-95, 100, 109, 111, 132-134, 136, 144, 150, 172, 198-200, 205-206, 212, 218, 226, 230, 247-248, 267, 272, 284, 293, 298, 327, 329, 331
ChatGPT 1, 3-4, 12-16, 30, 36, 97-98, 109, 226, 248, 263, 268, 273, 276-277
Classroom Dynamics 1, 26, 35, 322, 324-327, 329-331, 334-335, 342, 344
Cognitive Style 190
Customization 41, 101, 108-110, 113, 144

D

Data Security 17, 136, 151, 171, 209, 227, 279
Data-Driven Classrooms 27, 29, 44, 48
Decision-making 15, 38-39, 44, 48, 65-66, 70, 90, 93, 101, 109-110, 112, 121-122, 124, 132-134,

138, 154, 160, 164, 169, 203, 209, 215, 218, 233, 260, 291, 298, 305-306, 308-313, 316-317, 323, 329-330, 346

Digital Learning 161, 166

Digital Technologies 18, 102, 139, 217, 220, 269, 284

Digital Technology 18, 113, 220, 284

E

Educational Data Mining (EDM) 3, 31, 33, 44, 98, 242, 284, 329

Educational Digital Transformation 284

Educational Methodologies 1, 8, 102, 306

Educational Paradigms 1, 8, 30-31, 305-306, 308

Educational Practice 280

Educational Predictive Analytics 284

Educational Transformation 240, 262

Ethical and Societal Considerations 108, 121, 125

Ethical Considerations 1, 4, 6, 17, 19, 48, 88, 96, 99, 101-102, 120, 124, 136, 151, 169, 172, 198, 204, 209, 213, 223, 231, 233, 271, 273-274, 276, 279-280, 314-315, 324, 329, 331, 334-335, 340-341, 344

Ethical Issues 62, 78, 98, 121, 226, 279-280

F

Formative Assessment Tools 284

G

Grading Efficiency 268, 273-276, 280, 300

H

Higher Education 2-3, 30, 36, 38-39, 47, 89, 98, 120-121, 161, 198-201, 203-204, 209, 211-213, 229, 240-242, 251, 287, 295-297, 313-314, 324, 326, 330-331, 339, 342

Higher Institutions 198-199, 213

I

Instruction and Learning 38, 61, 89

Intelligent Tutoring Systems (ITS) 25, 32, 40, 42-43, 61-62, 82, 89, 93-96, 100, 102, 110-111, 113, 116, 136, 145, 149, 172, 179-180, 203, 211-213, 240, 242, 270, 272, 284, 298, 326, 329-330, 346

Islamic Education 216, 218-226, 228-234

L

Learning Analytics 1, 3, 31, 33, 41-42, 44, 48, 82, 93-95, 98-99, 101, 109, 146, 150-151, 154, 162, 204, 240, 252, 284, 297, 306, 308, 327, 329-330, 334

Learning Experiences 2-4, 6, 9-10, 15, 17, 19, 25, 33, 38-39, 41, 46, 48, 64, 67-69, 79-83, 88, 90-91, 93-97, 101-102, 113-116, 118, 124-125, 135-136, 141-142, 144, 149, 151, 153, 161, 166, 172, 177-178, 181-182, 186-187, 193, 202-203, 205, 209, 211-213, 218, 223, 225, 227, 229-230, 233-234, 242, 257, 264, 272, 277, 279, 284, 288, 293, 299, 305-308, 311-312, 314-317, 322-323, 325-331, 342, 344

Learning Outcomes 8, 17, 19, 25, 27, 36, 42, 46, 67-70, 78, 83, 89, 91, 93, 96-97, 99, 101, 112, 116-117, 125, 135, 139, 154, 161-162, 167, 170, 179, 192, 213, 240-241, 270, 272-273, 280, 284, 300, 305-307, 309, 312-315, 317, 327, 335-336

Learning Recommendation 1, 14, 16, 179

Learning Styles 2, 7-10, 15, 17, 32, 38, 97, 99-101, 135, 139-141, 143-144, 146, 153, 176, 178, 181-182, 184, 187-189, 193, 200, 211-212, 228-229, 255, 260, 312, 317, 326, 330-331, 335, 341

Literacy Education 198-206, 209-211, 213

N

Natural Language Processing (NLP) 7, 15, 25, 33, 39, 43, 62-63, 70, 72, 76, 93-94, 111, 116, 132-133, 144, 162, 198-200, 206, 215, 217, 230, 234, 260, 267, 288, 292-293, 329-331, 346

P

Pedagogical Frameworks 108-109, 113-114, 116

Performance-Based Assessment 285

Personalized Feedback 8, 33, 36, 43, 89-90, 99, 110, 112-113, 116, 125, 177, 179, 191, 198, 227, 230, 242-243, 263, 271-272, 280, 312, 314, 330, 335, 342

Personalized Learning 1-2, 6-7, 10-11, 14-16, 26, 32, 36-41, 43, 48, 61-62, 67, 89-92, 94-102, 108-109, 112-117, 124, 132, 135-136, 139, 144, 148, 153, 155, 166, 172, 176-181, 184, 186, 188, 190, 193, 198, 202-203, 209, 212, 222, 227-229, 240-242, 245, 263, 276, 279, 284, 288, 292, 299, 305, 307-308, 313, 317, 323, 327-333, 342

Preparing Students 10, 286, 294, 306, 308, 310, 312, 316, 327, 342

Q

Quality of Education 19, 36, 43, 150, 224, 228, 285, 315

R

Real-Time Data Analysis 108-110, 113, 125, 313
Reinforcement Learning 70, 113, 176, 178-179, 181-182, 184-185, 187, 193, 271, 309
Revolutionizing Education 272, 331

S

Secondary Schools 97, 270
Smart Learning 27, 37, 48, 288
Social Impact 288, 322-323, 329-331, 333, 344
Student Engagement 4, 7-8, 10, 17, 19, 25, 27, 36, 66, 70, 83, 90, 92, 96-97, 100, 111-113, 125, 135-136, 140-141, 145, 152, 228, 297, 305-308, 312, 314, 328-329, 331, 336, 341
Student Perceptions 274
SWOT Analysis 216, 218, 220-221

T

Teacher Perceptions 268, 279
Teaching and Learning 1, 4, 6, 19, 25, 33, 38, 42, 47-48, 69, 112, 115, 124-125, 139-140, 143, 162, 172, 199, 202, 209, 213, 219-220, 240, 255, 264, 269, 271, 276, 284, 291-292, 297, 305-308, 312-314, 316, 322-331, 333-334, 344
Teaching Methods 1-4, 6, 9, 19, 25, 34, 39-42, 46, 78, 88-89, 96, 102, 110, 116, 132, 135-136, 139, 141, 143, 149, 218, 228, 230, 233, 240-241, 262, 295-296, 305-308, 311-312, 314-317, 324, 326, 330
Technological Revolution in Learning 30, 48
Tertiary Education 269
Transformative Impact of AI 262
Transformative Shifts 30

V

Virtual Reality (VR) 5, 15, 34, 38, 61-62, 80, 83, 99, 109-110, 139, 153, 163, 212, 215, 225, 230-231, 234, 272, 292, 330, 334, 336-337, 346

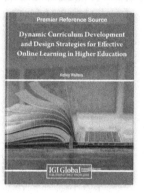
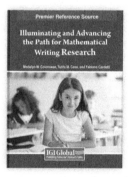

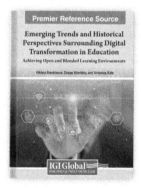

 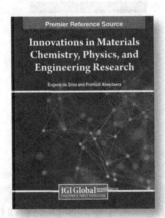 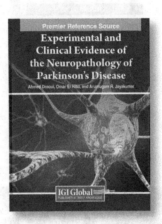 

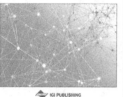